PROGRAMMING IN VISUAL BASIC .NET

Visual Basic .NET 2005 Edition

Julia Case Bradley
Mt. San Antonio College

Anita C. Millspaugh
Mt. San Antonio College

 McGraw-Hill
Irwin

Boston   Burr Ridge, IL   Dubuque, IA   Madison, WI   New York   San Francisco   St. Louis
Bangkok   Bogotá   Caracas   Kuala Lumpur   Lisbon   London   Madrid   Mexico City
Milan   Montreal   New Delhi   Santiago   Seoul   Singapore   Sydney   Taipei   Toronto

McGraw-Hill
Irwin

PROGRAMMING IN VISUAL BASIC .NET:
VISUAL BASIC .NET 2005 EDITION

Published by McGraw-Hill/Irwin, a business unit of The McGraw-Hill Companies, Inc., 1221 Avenue of the Americas, New York, NY, 10020. Copyright © 2006 by The McGraw-Hill Companies, Inc. All rights reserved. No part of this publication may be reproduced or distributed in any form or by any means, or stored in a database or retrieval system, without the prior written consent of The McGraw-Hill Companies, Inc., including, but not limited to, in any network or other electronic storage or transmission, or broadcast for distance learning.

Some ancillaries, including electronic and print components, may not be available to customers outside the United States.

This book is printed on acid-free paper.

1 2 3 4 5 6 7 8 9 0 QPD/QPD 0 9 8 7 6 5

ISBN 0-07-226215-X

Executive editor: *Paul Ducham*
Developmental editor: *Kelly L. Delso*
Marketing manager: *Sankha Basu*
Senior media producer: *Victor Chiu*
Senior project manager: *Lori Koetters*
Production supervisor: *Debra R. Sylvester*
Coordinator freelance design: *Artemio Ortiz Jr.*
Senior media project manager: *Rose M. Range*
Developer, Media technology: *Brian Nacik*
Cover design: *Brian Perveneckis*
Typeface: *11/13 Bodoni*
Compositor: *Cenveo*
Printer: *Quebecor World Dubuque Inc.*

Library of Congress Cataloging-in-Publication Data

Bradley, Julia Case.
    Programming in Visual Basic.Net / Julia Case Bradley, Anita C. Millspaugh.—Visual basic.NET 2005 ed.
        p. cm.
    ISBN 0-07-226215-X (alk. paper)
    1. Microsoft Visual BASIC. 2. BASIC (Computer program language) 3. Microsoft .NET. I. Millspaugh, A. C. (Anita C.) II. Title.
QA76.73.B3B697 2006
005.26'2—dc22
                                                                        2005041645

www.mhhe.com

PREFACE

Visual Basic (VB) has become the most popular programming language for several reasons. VB is easy to learn, which makes it an excellent tool for understanding elementary programming concepts. In addition, it has evolved into such a powerful and popular product that skilled Visual Basic programmers are in demand in the job market.

Visual Basic .NET is fully object-oriented and compatible with many other languages using the .NET Framework. This book incorporates the object-oriented concepts throughout, as well as the syntax and terminology of the language.

Visual Basic .NET is designed to allow the programmer to develop applications that run under Windows and/or in a Web browser without the complexity generally associated with programming. With very little effort, the programmer can design a screen that holds standard elements such as buttons, check boxes, radio buttons, text boxes, and list boxes. Each of these objects operates as expected, producing a "standard" Windows or Web user interface.

About This Text

This textbook is intended for use in an introductory programming course, which assumes no prior knowledge of computer programming. The later chapters are also appropriate for professional programmers who are learning a new language to upgrade their skills.

This text assumes that the student is familiar with the Windows operating environment and can use an Internet browser application.

Approach

This text incorporates the basic concepts of programming, problem solving, programming logic, as well as the design techniques of an object-oriented, event-driven language. VB .NET is a fully object-oriented language, which includes inheritance and polymorphism. Object-oriented programming (OOP) is introduced in Chapter 1 and its features appear in every chapter of the book.

Chapter topics are presented in a sequence that allows the programmer to learn how to deal with a visual interface while acquiring important programming skills such as creating projects with objects, decisions, loops, and data management.

A high priority is given to writing applications that are easy for the user to understand and to use. Students are presented with interface design guidelines throughout the text.

TEXT FEATURES

OBJECT-ORIENTED CONCEPTS
are presented throughout the text to offer students a better understanding of how to write applications.

CHAPTER 2

User Interface Design

at the completion of this chapter, you will be able to . . .

1. Use text boxes, masked text boxes, group boxes, check boxes, radio buttons, and picture boxes effectively.

2. Set the BorderStyle property to make controls appear flat or three-dimensional.

3. Select multiple controls and move them, align them, and set common properties.

4. Make your projects easy for the user to understand and operate by defining access keys, setting an accept and a cancel button, controlling the tab sequence, resetting the focus during program execution, and causing ToolTips to appear.

5. Clear the contents of text boxes and labels.

6. Change text color during program execution.

7. Code multiple statements for one control using the With and End With statements.

8. Concatenate (join) strings of text.

9. Make a control visible or invisible at run time by setting its Visible property.

Good Programming Habits

1. Always test the tab order on your forms. Fix it if necessary by changing the TabIndex properties of the controls.

2. Provide visual separation for input fields and output fields and always make it clear to the user which are which.

3. Make sure that your forms can be navigated and entered from the keyboard. Always set a default button (AcceptButton property) for every form.

4. To make a label maintain its size regardless of the value of the Text property, set AutoSize to False.

5. To make the text in a text box right justified or centered, set the TextAlign property.

6. You can use the Checked property of a check box to set other properties that must be True or False.

INTERFACE GUIDELINES
are presented to offer students a better understanding of how to design screens.

Note: Some people find the IntelliSense feature annoying rather than helpful. You can turn off the feature by selecting *Tools / Options*. In the *Options* dialog box, make sure that *Show All Settings* is selected and choose *Text Editor / Basic / General;* deselect *Auto list members* and *Parameter information.*

► **Feedback 3.2**

Write a declaration using the Dim statement for the following situations; make up an appropriate variable identifier.

1. You need variables for payroll processing to store the following:
   (a) Number of hours, which can hold a decimal value.
   (b) Employee's name.
   (c) Department number (not used in calculations).
2. You need variables for inventory control to store the following:
   (a) Integer quantity.
   (b) Description of the item.
   (c) Part number.
   (d) Cost.
   (e) Selling price.

Scope and Lifetime of Variables

A variable may exist and be visible for an entire project, for only one form, or for only one procedure. The visibility of a variable is referred to as its **scope.** Visibility really means "this variable can be used or 'seen' in this location." The scope is said to be namespace, module level, local, or block. A **namespace-level variable** may be used in all procedures of the namespace, which is generally the entire project. **Module-level variables** are accessible from all procedures of a form. A **local variable** may be used only within the procedure in which it is declared and a **block-level variable** is used only within a block of code inside a procedure.

FEEDBACK QUESTIONS
give students time to reflect on the current topic and to evaluate their understanding of details.

TIPS
in the margins help students avoid potential trouble spots in their programs and encourage them to develop good programming habits.

When you define access keys, you need to watch for several pitfalls. First, try to use the Windows-standard keys whenever possible. For example, use the x of Exit and the S of Save. Second, make sure you don't give two controls the same access key. It confuses the user and doesn't work correctly. Only the next control (from the currently active control) in the tab sequence is activated when the user presses the access key.

Note: To view the access keys on controls or menus in Windows 2000 or Windows XP, you may have to press the Alt key, depending on your system settings.

☑**TIP**

Use two ampersands when you want to make an ampersand appear in the Text property: &Health && Welfare for "Health & Welfare". ■

Setting the Accept and Cancel Buttons

Are you a keyboard user? If so, do you mind having to pick up the mouse and click a button after typing text into a text box? Once a person's fingers are on the keyboard, most people prefer to press the Enter key, rather than to click the mouse. If one of the buttons on the form is the accept button, pressing Enter is the same as clicking the button.

You can make one of your buttons the accept button by setting the **AcceptButton property** of the form to the button name. When the user presses Enter, that button is automatically selected.

You also can select a *cancel button.* The cancel button is the button that is

---

► **Feedback 4.2**

Assume that frogsInteger = 10, toadsInteger = 5, and polliwogsInteger = 6. What will be displayed for each of the following statements?

```
1. If frogsInteger > polliwogsInteger Then
       Me.frogsRadioButton.Checked = True
   Else
       Me.frogsRadioButton.Checked = False
   End If
2. If frogsInteger > toadsInteger + polliwogsInteger Then
       Me.resultTextBox.Text = "It's the frogs"
   Else
       Me.resultTextBox.Text = "It's the toads and the polliwogs"
   End If
3. If polliwogsInteger > toadsInteger And frogsInteger <> 0 _
       Or toadsInteger = 0 Then
       Me.resultTextBox.Text = "It's true"
   Else
       Me.resultTextBox.Text = "It's false"
   End If
```

4. Write the statements necessary to compare the numeric values stored in applesTextBox.Text and orangesTextBox.Text. Display in mostTextBox.Text which has more, the apples or the oranges.
5. Write the Basic statements that will test the current value of balanceDecimal. When balanceDecimal is greater than zero, the check box for Funds Available, called fundsCheckBox, should be selected, the balanceDecimal set back to zero, and countInteger incremented by one. When balanceDecimal is zero or less, fundsCheckBox should not be selected (do not change the value of balanceDecimal or increment the counter).

☑**TIP**

Indentation can help you catch errors. Visual Basic always matches an Else with the last unmatched If regardless of the indentation. ■

Using If Statements with Radio Buttons and Check Boxes

In Chapter 2 you used the CheckedChanged event for radio buttons and check boxes to carry out the desired action. Now that you have used If statements, you

TEXT FEATURES

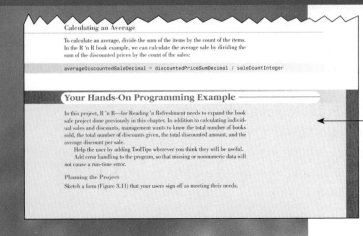

Calculating an Average

To calculate an average, divide the sum of the items by the count of the items. In the R 'n R book example, we can calculate the average sale by dividing the sum of the discounted prices by the count of the sales:

```
averageDiscountedSaleDecimal = discountedPriceSumDecimal / saleCountInteger
```

Your Hands-On Programming Example

In this project, R 'n R—for Reading 'n Refreshment needs to expand the book sale project done previously in this chapter. In addition to calculating individual sales and discounts, management wants to know the total number of books sold, the total number of discounts given, the total discounted amount, and the average discount per sale.

Help the user by adding ToolTips wherever you think they will be useful.

Add error handling to the program, so that missing or nonnumeric data will not cause a run-time error.

Planning the Project

Sketch a form (Figure 3.11) that your users sign off as meeting their needs.

YOUR HANDS-ON PROGRAMMING EXAMPLES

guide students through the process of planning, writing, and executing Visual Basic programs.

PROGRAMMING EXERCISES

test students' understanding of the specific programming skills covered in that chapter.

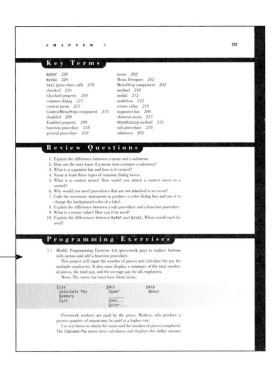

CASE STUDIES

provide continuing-theme exercises that may be used throughout the course, providing many opportunities to expand on previous projects.

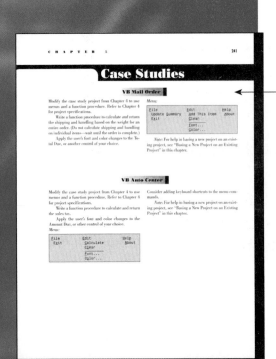

FOR THE STUDENT

STUDENT CD-ROM

packaged for free with the text offers a debugging project, database files for the programming exercises and case studies, graphics, and sound files.

Visit the **VISUAL BASIC .NET** Web site at: http://www.mhhe.com/vbnet2005/ for instructor and student resources.

INSTRUCTOR RESOURCE CD

includes: Instructor Manual with teaching hints, outlines, and a matrix of the chapter features required for each programming exercise; PowerPoint Slides; Testing Files (using EZ Test and in Word files); as well as Solutions to End-of-Chapter Exercises.

Julia Case Bradley
Anita C. Millspaugh

Programming in Visual Basic .NET

2005 Edition

Copyright © 2006 by The McGraw-Hill Companies, Inc. All rights reserved.

THIS CD-ROM CONTAINS
• Instructor's Manual
• Test Bank
• Computerized Test Bank
• PowerPoint® Presentations
• Solutions Manual

0-07-226216-8

System Requirements
Windows 98 Second Edition or better (includes ME, 2000, and XP); minimum 128 MB main memory, 256 recommended; 100 MB or better free hard disk space; Microsoft Word 2000 or better; Internet Explorer 6.0 or better; Sun Microsystems Java 1.4.2_05 or better (installer included)

Starting the Program
If the CD doesn't launch automatically:

1. Click on the **Start** button on the taskbar. Scroll down and select Run.
2. Type the letter of your CD-ROM drive followed by \Start_Here.exe For example, if your CD_ROM drive is named D, you would type D:\ Start_Here.exe
3. Click **OK** or press [Enter].

For technical assistance, call 800-331-5094 or visit http://www.mhhe.com/support

Instructor's Resource CD-ROM

featuring EZ TEST Version 5.0

McGraw-Hill Irwin

POWERPOINT PRESENTATIONS

provide instructors with complete, detailed presentations that walk students through the important concepts covered in each chapter.

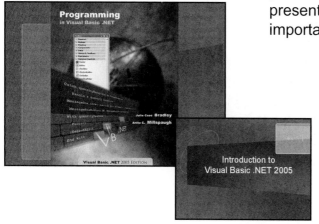

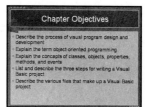

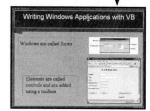

Visit the **VISUAL BASIC .NET** Web site at: http://www.mhhe.com/vbnet2005/ for instructor and student resources.

Changes in This Edition

This revision of the text is based on the beta version of Visual Basic .NET 2005. This new update to the VB language includes significant changes, including greatly simplified database programming and Web development. The text includes many of the new features of .NET, including smart tags, the Web-Browser control, MenuStrips, ToolStrips, Splash Screen and About Box templates, and the `Using` clause.

In code, references to controls and components now include the `Me` keyword, which gives easy access to Intellisense. This technique greatly reduces the typing required of students and allows them to understand that all components on the form are objects belonging to that form. Output is displayed in read-only text boxes, which allows for easier cleanup procedures using the `Clear` method of the TextBox control.

All menus use the new MenuStrip component. Although the older style menu is still available, it is destined to be eliminated from future product releases and is merely there for backward compatibility. The new controls offer much greater flexibility including drop-down boxes in addition to buttons.

The student can create database applications by using drag-and-drop techniques with absolutely no code from the programmer. Even better, the applications can use the new DataGridView or include details in text boxes with a navigation bar. An example also shows how to use combo boxes to navigate through the records rather than using the navigation bar.

We have reorganized and expanded some sections of the text. Chapter 6 now covers multiple-form applications. The templates for creating splash screens and about forms are included. Creating classes and using inheritance have been moved to Chapter 12. Students have the opportunity to learn more techniques, such as multiple forms in action, before creating multiple classes.

Visual Studio .NET 2005 includes a new Web server that avoids the complications of using IIS for Web development. Students can create Web applications on their own storage devices (floppies, Zips, flash drives, hard drives). The projects can easily be copied and run on other machines.

Web applications are created with Visual Web Developer, which Microsoft has introduced as a separate product and also included in Visual Studio .NET.

Drag-and-drop is now covered in the graphics chapter (Chapter 13). Students learn the development techniques for this familiar operation. The Sound-Player control also is introduced, to provide an easy way to play sounds in an application.

Chapter 14 includes the new WebBrowser control, which makes it easy to incorporate Web content on a Windows form. Other new features included are ToolStrips, StatusStrips, and code snippets.

The narrative, step-by-step exercises, screen captures, and appendices have all been updated to VB .NET 2005. The screen captures are all based on Windows XP.

Changes to coding conventions include the use of the `Friend` keyword. Module-level variables are declared either as `Private` or `Friend`.

Features of This Text

Each chapter begins with identifiable objectives and a brief overview. Numerous coding examples as well as hands-on projects with guidance for the planning and coding appear throughout. Thought-provoking feedback questions give students time to reflect on the current topic and to evaluate their understanding of the details. The end-of-chapter items include a chapter review, questions, programming exercises, and four case studies.

Chapter 1, "Introduction to Visual Basic .NET 2005," introduces Microsoft's Visual Studio integrated development environment (IDE). The single environment is used for multiple programming languages. A step-by-step program gets students into programming very quickly (quicker than most books). The chapter introduces the OOP concepts of objects, properties, methods, and events. The elements of debugging and using the Help system are also introduced.

Chapter 2, "User Interface Design," demonstrates techniques for good program design, including making the interface easy for users as well as guidelines for designing maintainable programs. Several controls are introduced, including text boxes, group boxes, check boxes, radio buttons, and picture boxes.

Chapter 3, "Variables, Constants, and Calculations," presents the concepts of using data and declaring the data type. Students learn to follow standards to indicate the data type and scope of variables and constants and always to use Option Strict, which forces adherence to strong data typing.

Error handling is accomplished using structured exception handling. The `Try/Catch/Finally` structure is introduced in this chapter along with calculations. The student learns to display error messages using the MessageBox class and also learns about the OOP concept of overloaded constructors.

Chapter 4, "Decisions and Conditions," introduces taking alternate actions based on conditions formed with the relational and logical operators. This chapter uses the `If` statement to validate input data. Multiple decisions are handled with both nested `If` statements and the `Select Case` structure.

The debugging features of the IDE are covered, including a step-by-step exercise covering stepping through program statements and checking intermediate values during execution.

Chapter 5, "Menus, Common Dialog Boxes, Sub Procedures, and Function Procedures," covers the concepts of writing and calling general sub procedures and function procedures. Students learn to include both menus and context menus in projects, display the Windows common dialog boxes, and use the input provided by the user.

Chapter 6, "Multiform Projects," adds splash forms and About forms to a project. Summary data are presented on a separate form. The `Friend` keyword is introduced.

Chapter 7, "Lists, Loops, and Printing," incorporates list boxes and combo boxes into projects, providing the opportunity to discuss looping procedures and printing lists of information. Printing is accomplished in .NET using a graphics object and a callback event. The printing controls also include a Print Preview, which allows students and instructors to view output without actually printing it.

Chapter 8, "Arrays," introduces arrays, which follow logically from the lists covered in Chapter 7. Students learn to use single- and multidimension arrays, table lookups, and arrays of structures.

Chapter 9, "Programming with Visual Web Developer," introduces Web applications using VB .NET Web Forms. Students learn to design and develop simple Web applications that consist of Web pages that execute in a browser application.

Chapter 10, "Accessing Database Files," introduces ADO.NET, which is Microsoft's latest technology for accessing data in a database. This chapter shows how to create binding sources, table adapters, and datasets. Programs include accessing data from both Windows Forms and Web Forms. Students learn to bind data tables to a data grid and bind individual data fields to controls such as labels and text boxes.

Chapter 11, "Saving Data in Files," presents the .NET object-oriented techniques for data file handling. Students learn to save and read small amounts of data using streams. The StreamWriter and StreamReader objects are used to store and reload the contents of a combo box.

Chapter 12, "OOP: Creating Object-Oriented Programs," explains more of the theory of object-oriented programming. Although we have been using OOP concepts since Chapter 1, in this chapter students learn the terminology and application of OOP. Inheritance is covered for visual objects (forms) and for extending existing classes. The samples are kept simple enough for an introductory class.

Chapter 13, "Graphics, Animation, Sound, and Drag-and-Drop," covers the classes and methods of GDI+. The chapter covers graphics objects, pens, and brushes for drawing shapes and lines. Animation is accomplished using the Timer control and the `SetBounds` method for moving controls. The new My.Computer.Audio.Play is used to provide sound, and drag-and-drop events are used to transfer the contents of a text box to a list box.

Chapter 14, "Additional Topics in Visual Basic," introduces some advanced VB topics. This final chapter covers validating user input using Error Providers and the Validating event of controls. Students learn to create applications using multiple document interfaces (MDI), create toolbars and status bars using the new ToolStrip and StatusStrip controls, and add Web content to a Windows form using the WebBrowser control. The new code snippet feature is introduced.

The appendices offer important additional material. Appendix A holds the answers to all Feedback questions. Appendix B covers methods and functions for math, string handling, and date manipulation. In the new OOP style, most actions that were formerly done with functions are now accomplished with methods of the Math class and String class.

Appendix C, on mastering the Visual Studio environment, is based on the .NET 2005 IDE and includes instructions for using the new snap lines for form design. Appendix D discusses security issues for both Windows and Web programming.

Acknowledgments

Many people have worked very hard to design and produce this text. We would like to thank our editors, Paul Ducham and Kelly Delso. Our thanks also to the many people who produced this text, including Lori Koetters, Betsy Blumenthal, and Artemio Ortiz.

We greatly appreciate Theresa Berry of Mt. San Antonio College and Robert Price of Antelope Valley Community College for their thorough technical reviews, constructive criticism, and many valuable suggestions. We would like to thank Brenda Nielsen of Mesa Community College for her work in creating the PowerPoint Presentations that accompany this text. And most importantly, we are grateful to Dennis and Richard for their support and understanding through the long days and busy phone lines.

The Authors

We have had fun teaching and writing about Visual Basic. We hope that this feeling is evident as you read this book and that you will enjoy learning or teaching this outstanding programming language.

Julia Case Bradley
Anita C. Millspaugh

TO THE STUDENT

The best way to learn to program in Visual Basic is to do it. If you enter and run the sample projects, you will be on your way to writing applications. Reading the examples without trying to run them is like trying to learn a foreign language or mathematics by just reading about it. Enter the projects, look up your questions in the extensive MSDN Help files, and make those projects *run*.

Installing Visual Basic

For the programs in this text, you need to install the .NET Framework, Visual Basic, and the MSDN (Microsoft Developers Network) library, which contains all of Help and many instructive articles. You do not need to install C++ or C#.

You can download the Express Edition of Visual Basic and Visual Web Developer from msdn.microsoft.com/express. Using these two products, you can complete all exercises in this text.

Format Used for Visual Basic Statements

Visual Basic statements, methods, and functions are shown in `this font`. Any values that you must supply are in *`italics`*. Optional items are in [square brackets]. Braces and a vertical bar indicate that you must choose one or the other value {`one` | other}.

Examples

```
Const Identifier [As Datatype] = Value
Do {While | Until} Condition
```

As you work your way through this textbook, note that you may see a subset of the available options for a Visual Basic statement or method. Generally, the options that are included reflect those covered in the chapter. If you want to see the complete format for any statement or all versions of a method, refer to Help.

J.C.B.
A.C.M.

About the Authors

Julia Bradley is a professor emeritus of Computer Information Systems at Mt. San Antonio College. She developed and taught computer programming courses for 25 years and then took early retirement from teaching in order to write full time. Most recently she has taught courses in introductory and advanced Visual Basic, Access programming, and Microsoft Office. She began writing BASIC textbooks in 1984 using MS-BASIC (GW-BASIC) and has authored or co-authored texts in Macintosh Basic, QuickBasic, QBasic, Visual Basic, Java, the Internet, and desktop publishing using PageMaker, Ventura Publisher, and Publish It.

Anita Millspaugh teaches programming courses in Visual Basic, C#, and Java at Mt. San Antonio College and has served as chair of the department for eight years. She received her MBA from California State Polytechnic University, with a bachelor's degree in Computer Information Systems. She has taught faculty at the National Computer Educator's Institute and also has led Great Teacher's Conferences for Mt. Sac and for California Vocational Faculty.

BRIEF CONTENTS

CONTENTS

3 Variables, Constants, and Calculations 95

4 Decisions and Conditions 145

C H A P T E R

1

Introduction to Visual Basic .NET 2005

at the completion of this chapter, you will be able to . . .

1. Describe the process of visual program design and development.

2. Explain the term *object-oriented programming*.

3. Explain the concepts of classes, objects, properties, methods, and events.

4. List and describe the three steps for writing a Visual Basic project.

5. Describe the various files that make up a Visual Basic project.

6. Identify the elements in the Visual Studio environment.

7. Define design time, run time, and debug time.

8. Write, run, save, print, and modify your first Visual Basic project.

9. Identify syntax errors, run-time errors, and logic errors.

10. Use AutoCorrect to correct syntax errors.

11. Look up Visual Basic topics in Help.

Writing Windows Applications with Visual Basic

Using this text, you will learn to write computer programs that run in the Microsoft Windows environment. Your projects will look and act like standard Windows programs. You will use the tools in Visual Basic .NET (VB) and Windows Forms to create windows with familiar elements such as labels, text boxes, buttons, radio buttons, check boxes, list boxes, menus, and scroll bars. Figure 1.1 shows some sample Windows user interfaces.

Beginning in Chapter 9, you will create programs using Web Forms and Visual Web Developer .NET. You can run Web applications in a browser such

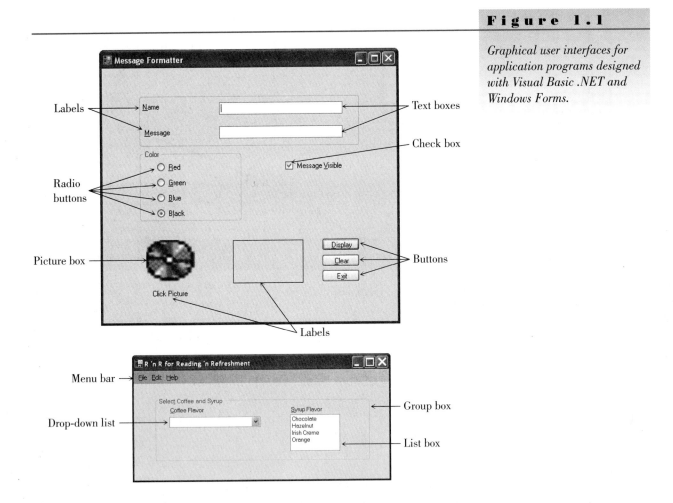

Figure   1.1

Graphical user interfaces for application programs designed with Visual Basic .NET and Windows Forms.

as Internet Explorer, on the Internet, or on a company intranet. Figure 1.2 shows a Web Form application.

The Windows Graphical User Interface

Microsoft Windows uses a **graphical user interface**, or **GUI** (pronounced "gooey"). The Windows GUI defines how the various elements look and function. As a Visual Basic programmer, you have available a toolbox of these

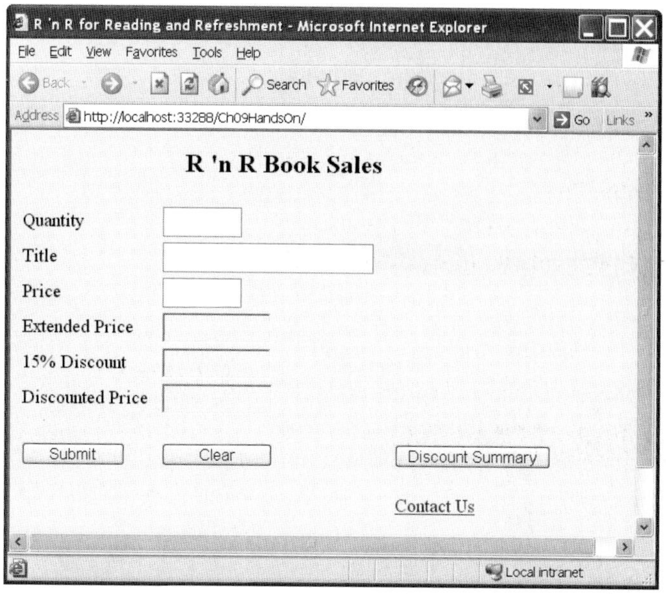

Figure 1.2

A Web Form application created with Visual Web Developer .NET, running in a browser.

elements. You will create new windows, called **forms**. Then you will use the toolbox to add the various elements, called **controls**. The projects that you will write follow a programming technique called **object-oriented programming (OOP)**.

Programming Languages—Procedural, Event Driven, and Object Oriented

There are literally hundreds of programming languages. Each was developed to solve a particular type of problem. Most traditional languages, such as BASIC, C, COBOL, FORTRAN, PL/I, and Pascal, are considered *procedural* languages. That is, the program specifies the exact sequence of all operations. Program logic determines the next instruction to execute in response to conditions and user requests.

The newer programming languages, such as Visual Basic .NET, C#, and Java, use a different approach: object-oriented programming. As a stepping stone between procedural programming and object-oriented programming, the early versions of Visual Basic provided many (but not all) elements of an object-oriented language. For that reason, Microsoft referred to Visual Basic (version 6 and earlier) as an event-driven programming language rather than an object-oriented language. But with the release of Visual Studio .NET, which includes Visual Basic .NET, C#, and J#, Microsoft has produced three programming languages that are truly object-oriented. (Another language, C++, has elements of OOP and of procedural programming, and doesn't conform fully to either paradigm.)

In the OOP model, programs are no longer procedural. They do not follow a sequential logic. You, as the programmer, do not take control and determine the sequence of execution. Instead, the user can press keys and click various buttons and boxes in a window. Each user action can cause an event to occur, which triggers a Basic procedure that you have written. For example, the user clicks on a button labeled Calculate. The clicking causes the button's Click event to occur, and the program automatically jumps to a procedure you have written to do the calculation.

The Object Model

In Visual Basic you will work with **objects**, which have **properties, methods,** and **events.** Each object is based on a **class.**

Objects

Think of an object as a thing, or a noun. Examples of objects are forms and controls. *Forms* are the windows and dialog boxes you place on the screen; *controls* are the components you place inside a form, such as text boxes, buttons, and list boxes.

Properties

Properties tell something about or control the behavior of an object, such as its name, color, size, or location. You can think of properties as adjectives that describe objects.

When you refer to a property, you first name the object, add a period, and then name the property. For example, refer to the Text property of a form called salesForm as salesForm.Text (pronounced "sales form dot text").

Methods

Actions associated with objects are called *methods*. Methods are the verbs of object-oriented programming. Some typical methods are `Close`, `Show`, and `Clear`. Each of the predefined objects has a set of methods that you can use. You will learn to write additional methods to perform actions in your programs.

You refer to methods as Object.Method ("object dot method"). For example, a `Show` method can apply to different objects: `billingForm.Show` shows the form object called billingForm; `exitButton.Show` shows the button object called exitButton.

Events

You can write procedures that execute when a particular event occurs. An event occurs when the user takes an action, such as clicking a button, pressing a key, scrolling, or closing a window. Events also can be triggered by actions of other objects, such as repainting a form or a timer reaching a preset point.

Classes

A class is a template or blueprint used to create a new object. Classes contain the definition of all available properties, methods, and events.

Each time that you create a new object, it must be based on a class. For example, you may decide to place three buttons on your form. Each button is based on the Button class and is considered one object, called an *instance* of the class. Each button (or instance) has its own set of properties, methods, and events. One button may be labeled "OK", one "Cancel", and one "Exit". When the user clicks the OK button, that button's Click event occurs; if the user

The term *members* is used to refer to both properties and methods. ∎

clicks on the Exit button, that button's Click event occurs. And, of course, you have written different program instructions for each of the buttons' Click events.

An Analogy

If the concepts of classes, objects, properties, methods, and events are still a little unclear, maybe an analogy will help. Consider an Automobile class. When we say *automobile*, we are not referring to a particular auto, but we know that an automobile has a make and model, a color, an engine, and a number of doors. These elements are the *properties* of the Automobile class.

Each individual auto is an object, or an instance of the Automobile class. Each Automobile object has its own settings for the available properties. For example, each object has a Color property, such as myAuto.Color = Blue and yourAuto.Color = Red.

The methods, or actions, of the Automobile class might be `Start`, `SpeedUp`, `SlowDown`, and `Stop`. To refer to the methods of a specific object of the class, use `myAuto.Start` and `yourAuto.Stop`.

The events of an Automobile class could be Arrive or Crash. In a VB program you write procedures that specify the actions you want to take when a particular event occurs for an object. For example, you might write a procedure for the yourAuto.Crash event.

Note: Chapters 6 and 12 present object-oriented programming in greater depth.

Microsoft's Visual Studio .NET

The latest version of Microsoft's Visual Studio, called Visual Studio .NET 2005, includes Visual Basic, Visual C++, C# (C sharp), J# (J sharp), and the .NET 2.0 Framework.

The .NET Framework

The programming languages in Visual Studio .NET run in the .NET Framework. The Framework provides for easier development of Web-based and Windows-based applications, allows objects from different languages to operate together, and standardizes how the languages refer to data and objects. Several third-party vendors have announced or have released versions of other programming languages to run in the .NET Framework, including .NET versions of APL by Dyalog, FORTRAN by Lahey Computer Systems, COBOL by Fujitsu Software Corporation, Pascal by the Queensland University of Technology (free), PERL by ActiveState, RPG by ASNA, and Java, known as IKVM.NET. See http://www.gotdotnet.com/team/lang/ for the latest details.

The .NET languages all compile to (are translated to) a common machine language, called Microsoft Intermediate Language (MSIL). The MSIL code, called *managed code*, runs in the Common Language Runtime (CLR), which is part of the .NET Framework.

Visual Basic .NET

Microsoft Visual Basic .NET comes with Visual Studio .NET. You also can purchase VB .NET by itself (without the other languages but *with* the .NET Framework). VB .NET is available in an **Express Edition**, a **Standard Edition**, a **Professional Edition**, and a **Team System Edition**. Anyone planning to do professional application development that includes the advanced features of database management should use the Professional Edition or the Team System Edition. You can find a matrix showing the features of each edition in Help. The Professional Edition is available to educational institutions through the Microsoft Academic Alliance program and is the best possible deal. When a campus department purchases the Academic Alliance, the school can install Visual Studio .NET on all classroom and lab computers and provide the software to all students and faculty at no additional charge.

This text is based on Visual Basic .NET 2005, the current version. You cannot run the projects in this text in any earlier version of VB.

Writing Visual Basic Projects

When you write a Visual Basic application, you follow a three-step process for planning the project and then repeat the process for creating the project. The three steps involve setting up the user interface, defining the properties, and then creating the code.

The Three-Step Process   *In Class Example*

Planning

1. *Design the user interface.* When you plan the **user interface**, you draw a sketch of the screens the user will see when running your project. On your sketch, show the forms and all the controls that you plan to use. Indicate the names that you plan to give the form and each of the objects on the form. Refer to Figure 1.1 for examples of user interfaces.

   Before you proceed with any more steps, consult with your user and make sure that you both agree on the look and feel of the project.

2. *Plan the properties.* For each object, write down the properties that you plan to set or change during the design of the form.

3. *Plan the Basic code.* In this step, you plan the classes and procedures that will execute when your project runs. You will determine which events require action to be taken and then make a step-by-step plan for those actions.

   Later, when you actually write the Visual Basic **code**, you must follow the language syntax rules. But during the planning stage, you will write out the actions using **pseudocode**, which is an English expression or comment that describes the action. For example, you must plan for the event that occurs when the user clicks on the Exit button. The pseudocode for the event could be *Terminate the project* or *Quit*.

Programming

After you have completed the planning steps and have approval from your user, you are ready to begin the actual construction of the project. Use the same three-step process that you used for planning.

1. *Define the user interface.* When you define the user interface, you create the forms and controls that you designed in the planning stage.

Think of this step as defining the objects you will use in your application.

2. *Set the properties.* When you set the properties of the objects, you give each object a name and define such attributes as the contents of a label, the size of the text, and the words that appear on top of a button and in the form's title bar.

You might think of this step as describing each object.

3. *Write the Basic code.* You will use Basic programming statements (called *Basic code*) to carry out the actions needed by your program. You will be surprised and pleased by how few statements you need to create a powerful Windows program.

You can think of this third step as defining the actions of your program.

Visual Basic Application Files

A Visual Basic application, called a **solution**, can consist of one or more projects. Since all of the solutions in this text have only one project, you can think of one solution = one project. Each project can contain one or more form files. In Chapters 1 through 5, all projects have only one form, so you can think of one project = one form. Starting in Chapter 6, your projects will contain multiple forms and additional files. As an example, the HelloWorld application that you will create later in this chapter creates the following files:

HelloWorld.sln	The **solution file**. A text file that holds information about the solution and the projects it contains. This is the primary file for the solution —the one that you open to work on or run your project.	*Readable*
HelloWorld.suo	Solution user options file. Stores information about the state of the IDE so that all customizations can be restored each time you open the solution.	*unreadable*
helloForm.vb	A .vb file. Holds the definition of a form, its controls, and code procedures. This is a text file that you can open in any editor. *Warning*: You should not modify this file unless you are using the editor in the Visual Studio environment.	*The Code*
helloForm.resx	A resource file for the form. This text file defines all resources used by the form, including strings of text, numbers, and any graphics.	
HelloWorld.vbproj	A **project file**. A text file that describes the project and lists the files included in the project.	*Readable*
HelloWorld.vbproj.user	The project user option file. This text file holds IDE option settings so that the next time you open the project, all customizations will be restored.	*Readable*
app.config	A configuration file for the application. In Web projects, which you create in Chapter 9, Web.config replaces app.config.	*Readable*

Note: You can display file extensions using My Computer. In the My Computer *Tools* menu, select *Folder Options* and the *View* tab. Deselect the check box for *Hide extensions for known file types*.

After you run your project, you will find several more files created by the system. These include the AssemblyInfo.vb, MyApplication.myapp, MyEvents.vb, Resourses.resx, and Resources.vb. The only file that you open directly is the .sln, or solution file.

The Visual Studio Environment

The **Visual Studio environment** is where you create and test your projects. A development environment, such as Visual Studio, is called an ***integrated development environment* (IDE)**. The IDE consists of various tools, including a form designer, which allows you to visually create a form; an editor, for entering and modifying program code; a compiler, for translating the Visual Basic statements into the intermediate machine code; a debugger, to help locate and correct program errors; an object browser, to view the available classes, objects, properties, methods, and events; and a Help facility.

In versions of Visual Studio prior to .NET, each language had its own IDE. For example, to create a VB project you would use the VB IDE and to create a C++ project you would use the C++ IDE. But in Visual Studio .NET, you use the one IDE to create projects in any of the .NET languages.

Note that this text is based on the beta version of Visual Studio. The screens may be somewhat different from those that you see.

Default Environment Settings

Visual Studio 2005 provides a new option that allows the programmer to select the default profile for the IDE. The first time you open Visual Studio, you are presented with the *Choose Default Environment Settings* dialog box (Figure 1.3), where you can choose *Visual Basic Development Settings*. Notice the instructions in the dialog box: you can make a different selection later from the *Tools* menu.

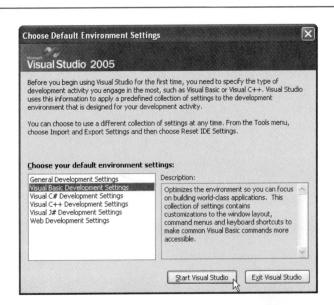

Figure 1.3

The first time you open the Visual Studio IDE, you must select the default environment settings for a Visual Basic developer.

The IDE Initial Screen

When you open the Visual Studio IDE, you generally see an empty environment with a Start Page (Figure 1.4). However, it's easy to customize the environment, so you may see a different view. In the step-by-step exercise later in this chapter, you will learn to reset the IDE layout to its default view.

Figure 1.4

The Visual Studio IDE with the Start Page open, as it first appears in Windows XP, without an open project.

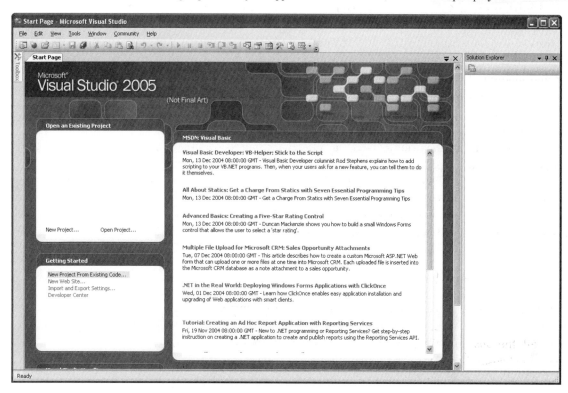

The contents of the Start Page vary, depending on whether you are connected to the Internet. Microsoft has added links that can be updated, so you may find new and interesting information on the Start page each time you open it. To display or hide the Start Page, select *View / Start Page*.

You can open an existing project or begin a new project using the Start Page or the *File* menu.

The New Project Dialog

You will create your first Visual Basic projects by selecting *File / New Project* or clicking *New Project* on the Start Page, either of which opens the *New Project* dialog (Figure 1.5). In the *New Project* dialog, select *Visual Basic* and *Windows* in the *Project Types* box and *Windows Application* in the *Templates* box. You also give the project a name on this dialog box.

The IDE Main Window

Figure 1.6 shows the Visual Studio environment's main window and its various child windows. Note that each window can be moved, resized, opened, closed,

Figure 1.5

Begin a new VB .NET Windows project using the Windows Application template.

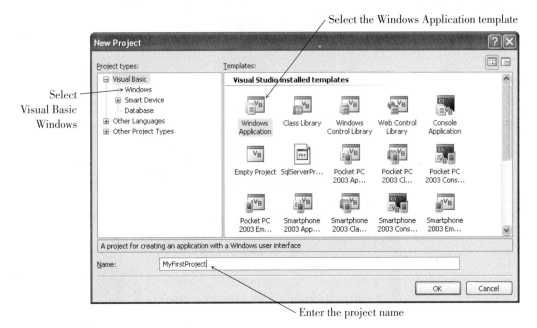

Figure 1.6

The Visual Studio environment. Each window can be moved, resized, closed, or customized.

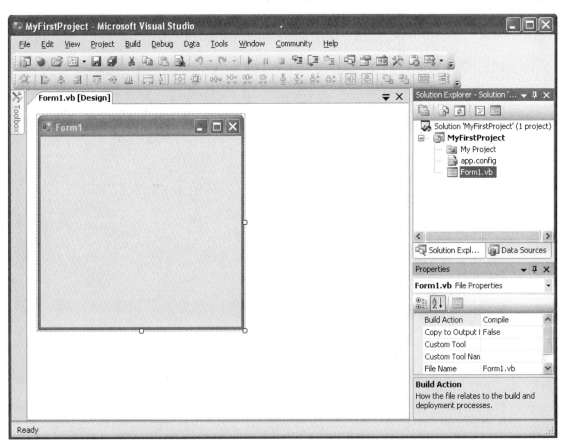

and customized. Some windows have tabs that allow you to display different contents. Your screen may not look exactly like Figure 1.6; in all likelihood you will want to customize the placement of the various windows. The windows in the IDE are considered either document windows or tool windows. The tool windows are listed under the *View* menu; document windows are generally docked together in the center of the IDE, but the locations and docking behavior are all customizable.

The IDE main window holds the Visual Studio menu bar and the toolbars.

The Toolbars

You can use the buttons on the **toolbars** as shortcuts for frequently used operations. Each button represents a command that also can be selected from a menu. Figure 1.7*a* shows the toolbar buttons on the Standard toolbar, which displays in the main window of the IDE; Figure 1.7*b* shows the Layout toolbar, which displays in the Form Designer; and Figure 1.7*c* shows the Text Editor toolbar, which appears when the Editor window is displayed. Select *View / Toolbars* to display or hide these and other toolbars.

Figure 1.7

The Visual Studio toolbars contain buttons that are shortcuts for menu commands. You can display or hide each of the toolbars: a. the Standard toolbar; b. the Layout toolbar; and c. the Text Editor toolbar.

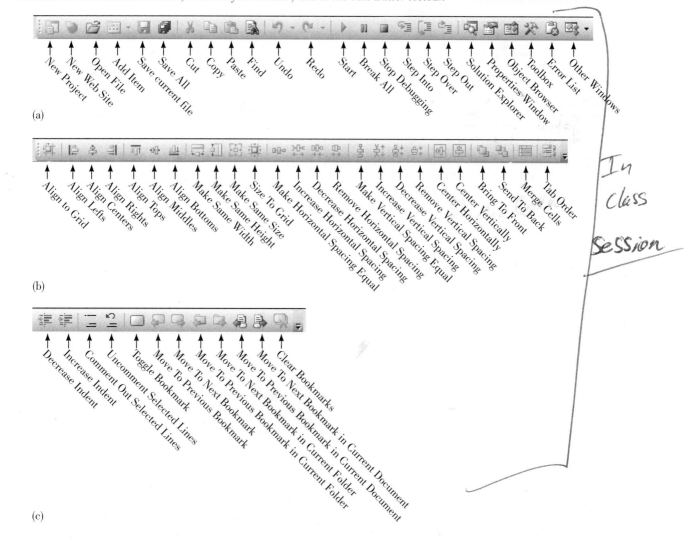

In Class Session

The Document Window

The largest window in the center of the screen is the **Document window**. Notice the tabs across the top of the window, which allow you to switch between open documents. The items that display in the Document window include the Form Designer, the Code Editor, and the Object Browser.

You can switch from one tab to another, or close any of the documents using its Close button.

TIP

Use Ctrl + Tab to cycle through the open documents in the Documents window. ■

The Form Designer

The **Form Designer** is where you design a form that makes up your user interface. In Figure 1.6, the Form Designer for Form1 is currently displaying. You can drag the form's sizing **handle** or selection border to change the size of the form.

When you begin a new Visual Basic Windows project, a new form is added to the project with the default name Form1. In the step-by-step exercise later in the chapter, you will learn to change the form's name.

The Solution Explorer Window

The **Solution Explorer window** holds the filenames for the files included in your project and a list of the classes it references. The Solution Explorer window and the Window's title bar hold the name of your solution (.sln) file, which is WindowsApplication1 by default unless you give it a new value in the *New Project* dialog box. In Figure 1.6, the name of the solution is MyFirstProject.

The Properties Window

You use the **Properties window** to set the properties for the objects in your project. See "Set Properties" later in this chapter for instructions on changing properties.

TIP

You can sort the properties in the window either *alphabetically* or *by categories*. Use the buttons on the Properties window. ■

The Toolbox

The **toolbox** holds the tools you use to place controls on a form. You may have more or different tools in your toolbox, depending on the edition of Visual Basic you are using (Express, Standard, Professional, or Team System). Figure 1.8 shows the toolbox.

Help

Visual Studio has an extensive **Help** feature that is greatly expanded for .NET. Help includes the Microsoft Developer Network library (MSDN), which contains reference materials for Visual Basic, C++, C#, J#, and Visual Studio; several books; technical articles; and the Microsoft Knowledge Base, a database of frequently asked questions and their answers.

Help includes the entire reference manual, as well as many coding examples. See the topic "Visual Studio Help" later in this chapter for help on Help.

Figure 1.8

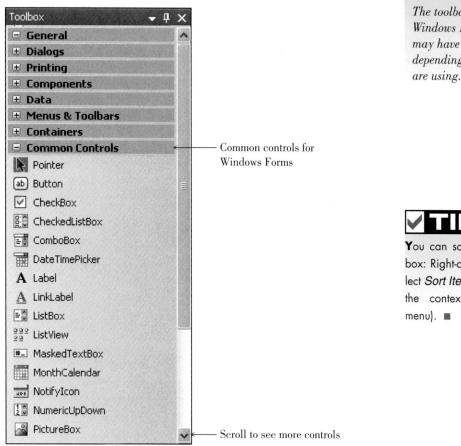

The toolbox for Visual Studio Windows Forms. Your toolbox may have more or fewer tools, depending on the edition you are using.

Common controls for Windows Forms

Scroll to see more controls

☑TIP

You can sort the tools in the toolbox: Right-click the toolbox and select *Sort Items Alphabetically* from the context menu (the shortcut menu). ■

When you make a selection from the *Help* menu, the requested item appears in a new window that floats on top of the IDE window (Figure 1.9), so you can keep both open at the same time. It's a good idea to set the *Filtered By* entry to *Visual Basic*.

Design Time, Run Time, and Debug Time

Visual Basic has three distinct modes. While you are designing the user interface and writing code, you are in **design time**. When you are testing and running your project, you are in **run time**. If you get a run-time error or pause project execution, you are in **debug time**. The IDE window title bar indicates (Running) or (Debugging) to indicate that a project is no longer in design time.

Writing Your First Visual Basic Project

For your first VB project, you will create a form with three controls (see Figure 1.10). This simple project will display the message "Hello World" in a label when the user clicks the Push Me button and will terminate when the user clicks the Exit button.

Figure 1.9

Help displays in a new window, independent of the Visual Studio IDE window.

Help Search   Help with Specific Tasks

Filter →

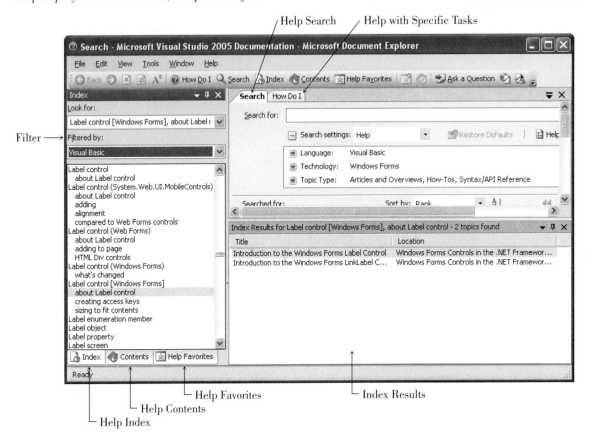

Help Index

Help Contents

Help Favorites

Index Results

Figure 1.10

The Hello World form. The "Hello World" message will appear in a label when the user clicks on the Push Me button. The label does not appear until the button is pressed.

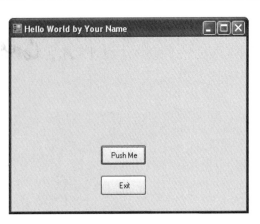

Set Up Your Workspace

Before you can begin a project, you must run the Visual Studio IDE. You also may need to customize your workspace.

Run Visual Studio

These instructions assume that Visual Studio .NET is installed in the default location. If you are running in a classroom or lab, the program may be installed in an alternate location, such as directly on the desktop.

STEP 1: Click the Windows *Start* button and move the mouse pointer to *All Programs.*

STEP 2: Locate *Microsoft Visual Studio 2005* (or *Microsoft Visual Studio 2005 Beta*).

STEP 3: In the submenu that pops up, select *Microsoft Visual Studio 2005.* Visual Studio (VS) will start and display an empty environment (refer to Figure 1.4). If this is the first time that VS has been opened on this computer, you may need to select *Visual Basic Development* from the *Choose Default Environment Setting* dialog box (refer to Figure 1.3).

Note: The VS IDE can be customized to show the Start Page when it opens.

Start a New Project

STEP 1: Select *File / New Project.* The *New Project* dialog box opens (refer to Figure 1.5). Make sure that *Visual Basic* is selected for *Project types* and *Windows Application* is selected for the template. If you are using Visual Basic Express, the dialog box differs slightly, but you can still choose a Windows Application.

STEP 2: Enter "HelloWorld" (without the quotes) for the name of the new project (Figure 1.11) and click the OK button. The new project opens (Figure 1.12). At this point, your project is stored in a temporary directory. You specify the location for the project later when you save it.

Note: Your screen may look significantly different from the figure since the environment can be customized.

Figure 1.11

Enter the name for the new project.

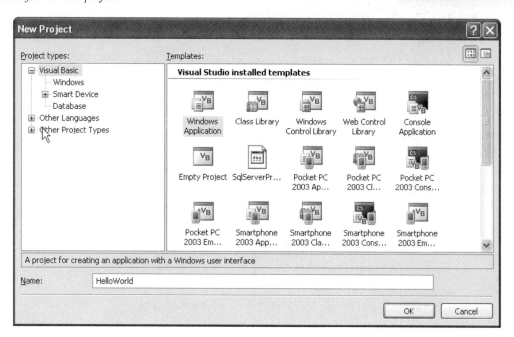

Figure 1.12

The Visual Studio IDE with the new HelloWorld project.

Toolbox →

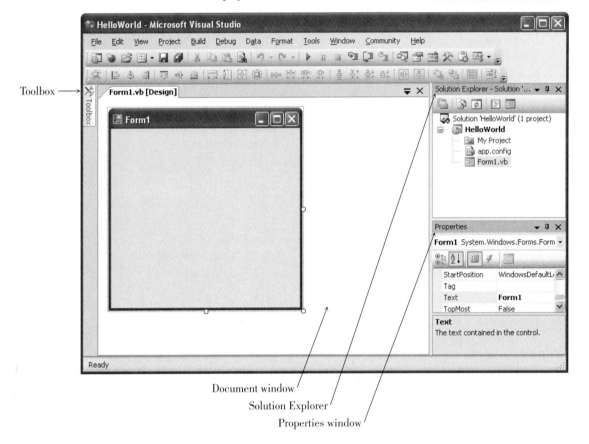

Document window

Solution Explorer

Properties window

Set Up Your Environment

In this section, you will customize the environment. For more information on customizing windows, floating and docking windows, and altering the location and contents of the various windows, see Appendix C.

STEP 1: Reset the IDE's default layout by choosing *Window / Reset Window Layout*. The IDE should now match Figure 1.12.

Note: If the Data Sources window appears on top of the Solution Explorer window, click on the Solution Explorer tab to make it appear on top.

STEP 2: Point to the icon for the toolbox at the left of the IDE window. The Toolbox window pops open. Notice the pushpin icon at the top of the window (Figure 1.13); clicking this icon makes the window remain on the screen rather than AutoHide.

STEP 3: Click the AutoHide pushpin icon for the Toolbox window; the toolbox will remain open.

Figure 1.13

The Toolbox window.

Toolbox icon →

Pushpin icon →

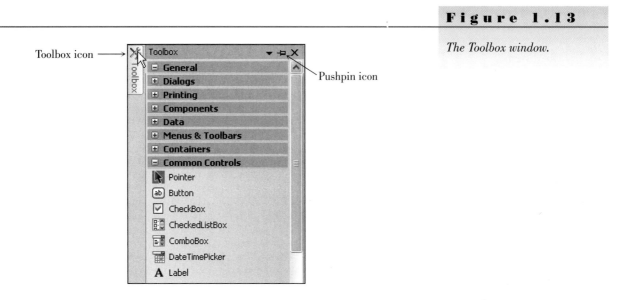

Plan the Project

The first step in planning is to design the user interface. Figure 1.14 shows a sketch of the form that includes a label and two buttons. You will refer to the sketch as you create the project.

Figure 1.14

A sketch of the HelloWorld form for planning.

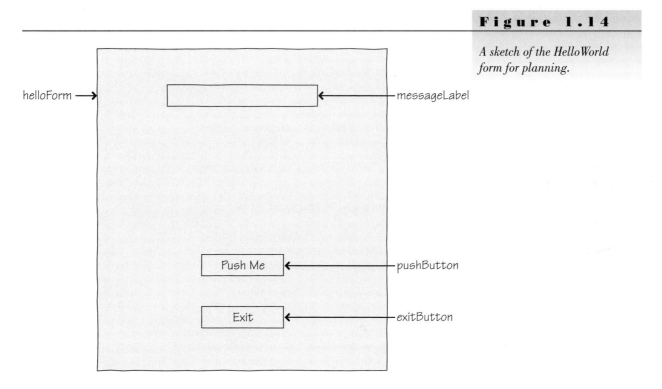

helloForm →

messageLabel

Push Me → pushButton

Exit → exitButton

The next two steps, planning the properties and the code, have already been done for this first sample project. You will be given the values in the steps that follow.

Define the User Interface

Set Up the Form

Notice that the new form in the Document window has all the standard Windows features, such as a title bar, maximize and minimize buttons, and a close button.

STEP 1: Resize the form in the Document window: Drag the handle in the lower-right corner down and to the right (Figure 1.15).

F i g u r e   1 . 1 5

Make the form larger by dragging its lower-right handle diagonally. The handles disappear as you drag the corner of the form.

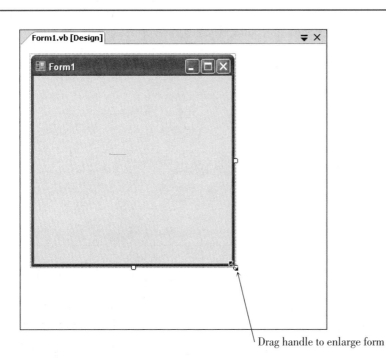

Drag handle to enlarge form

Place Controls on the Form

You are going to place three controls on the form: a **Label** and two **Buttons**.

STEP 1: Point to the Label tool in the toolbox and click. Then move the pointer over the form. Notice that the pointer becomes a crosshair with a big A and the Label tool appears selected, indicating it is the active tool (Figure 1.16).

Figure 1.16

When you click on the Label tool in the toolbox, the tool's button is activated and the mouse pointer becomes a crosshair.

Crosshair pointer

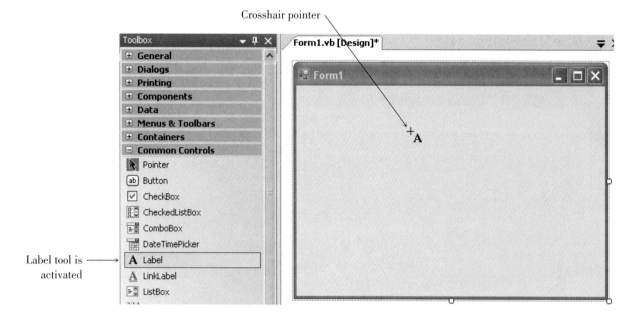

Label tool is
activated

STEP 2: Point to a spot where you want the left edge of the label and click. The
label and its default contents (Label1) will appear (Figure 1.17).

Figure 1.17

*The newly created label
appears outlined, indicating
that it is selected. Notice that
the contents of the label are set
to Label1 by default.*

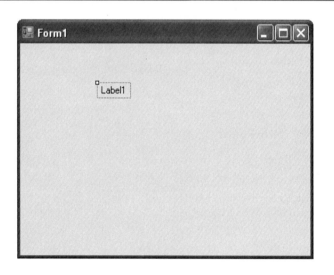

As long as the label is selected, you can press the Delete key to
delete it, or drag it to a new location.

You can tell that a label is selected; it has a black border as shown
in Figure 1.17 when the AutoSize property is True [the default] or sizing handles if you set the AutoSize property to False.

STEP 3:   Draw a button on the form: Click on the Button tool in the toolbox,
position the crosshair pointer for one corner of the button, and drag
to the diagonally opposite corner (Figure 1.18). When you release
the mouse button, the new button should appear selected and have
resizing handles. The blue lines that appear are called **snap lines**,
which can help you align your controls.

Figure 1.18

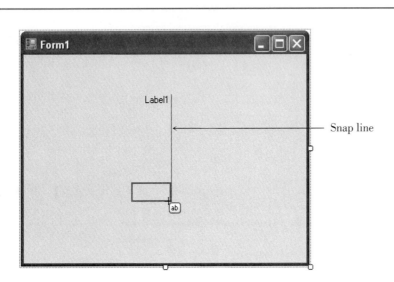

*Select the Button tool and
drag diagonally to create a
new Button control. The blue
snap lines help to align
controls.*

While a control is selected, you can delete it or move it. If it has resizing handles, you can also resize it. Refer to Table 1.1 for instructions for selecting, deleting, resizing, and moving controls. Click
outside of a control to deselect it.

Selecting, Deleting, Moving, and Resizing Controls on a Form   **Table 1.1**

Select a control	Click on the control.
Delete a control	Select the control and then press the Delete key on the keyboard.
Move a control	Select the control, point inside the control (not on a handle), press the mouse button, and drag it to a new location.
Resize a control	Make sure the control is selected and has resizing handles; then either point to one of the handles, press the mouse button, and drag the handle; or drag the form's bottom border to change the height or the side border to change the width. Note that the default format for Labels does not allow resizing.

STEP 4:   Create another button using this alternative technique: While the first
button is still selected, point to the Button tool in the toolbox and
double-click. A new button of the default size will appear on top of
the last-drawn control (Figure 1.19).

STEP 5:   Keep the new button selected, point anywhere inside the button (not on
a handle), and drag the button below your first button (Figure 1.20).

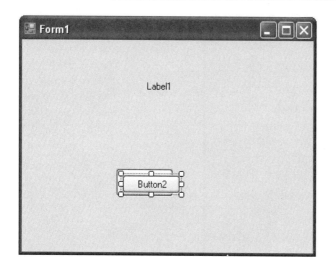

Figure 1.19

Place a new button on the form by double-clicking the Button tool in the toolbox. The new button appears on top of the previously selected control.

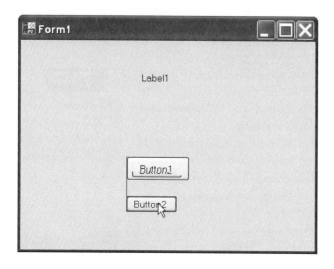

Figure 1.20

Drag the new button (Button2) below Button1.

✓TIP

If no control is selected when you double-click a tool, the new control is added to the upper left corner of the form. ■

STEP 6: Select each control and move and resize the controls as necessary. Make the two buttons the same size and line them up. Use the snap lines to help with the size and alignment. Note that you can move but not resize the label.

STEP 7: Point to one of the controls and click the right mouse button to display a **context menu**. On the context menu, select *Lock Controls* (Figure 1.21). Locking prevents you from accidentally moving the controls. When your controls are locked, a selected control has no handles, but instead has a small lock symbol in the upper-left corner.

    Note: You can unlock the controls at any time if you wish to re-design the form. Just click again on *Lock Controls* on the context menu to deselect it.

At this point you have designed the user interface and are ready to set the properties.

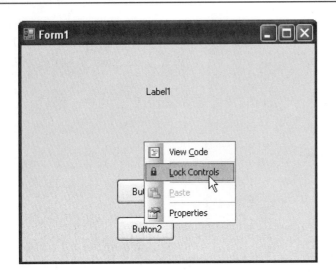

After the controls are placed into the desired location, lock them in place by selecting Lock Controls *from the context menu. Remember that context menus differ depending on the current operation and system setup.*

Set Properties

Set the Name and Text Properties for the Label

STEP 1: Click on the label you placed on the form; an outline appears around the control. Next click on the title bar of the Properties window to make it the active window (Figure 1.22). *Note*: If the Properties window is not displaying, select *View / Properties Window*.

Notice that the Object box at the top of the Properties window is showing *Label1* (the name of the object) and *System.Windows.Forms.Label* as the class of the object. The actual class is Label; System.Windows.Forms is called the **namespace**, or the hierarchy used to locate the class.

STEP 2: In the Properties window, click on the Alphabetic button to make sure the properties are sorted in alphabetic order. Then select the Name property, which appears near the top of the list. Click on *(Name)* and notice that the Settings box shows *Label1*, the default name of the label (Figure 1.23).

TIP

If the Properties window is not visible, you can choose *View / Properties Window* from the menu or press the F4 shortcut key to show it. ■

Figure 1.22

The currently selected control is shown in the Properties window.

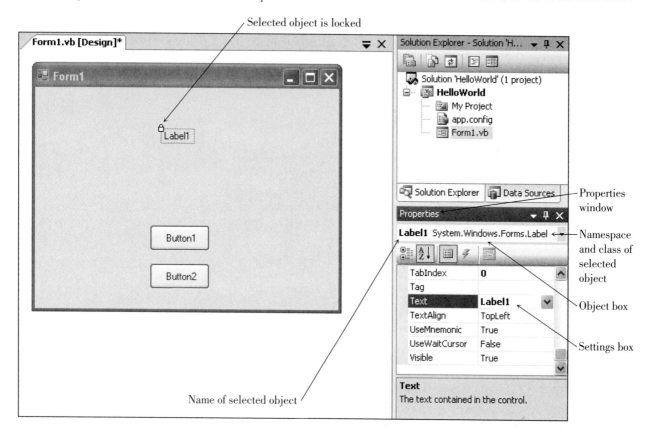

Selected object is locked

Properties window

Namespace and class of selected object

Object box

Settings box

Name of selected object

Figure 1.23

The Properties window. Click on the Name property to change the value in the Settings box.

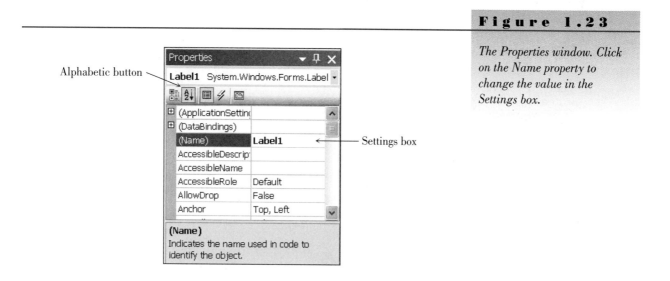

Alphabetic button

Settings box

STEP 3: Type "messageLabel" (without the quotation marks). See Figure 1.24. As a shortcut, you may wish to delete the 1 from the end of Label1, press the Home key to get to the beginning of the word, and then type "message".

After you change the name of the control and press Enter or Tab, you can see the new name in the Object box's drop-down list.

Figure   1.24

Type "messageLabel" into the Settings box for the Name property.

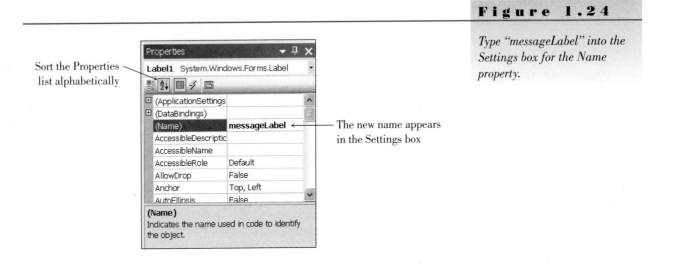

Sort the Properties list alphabetically

The new name appears in the Settings box

STEP 4: Click on the Text property to select it. (Scroll the list if necessary.)

The **Text property** of a control determines what will be displayed on the form. Because nothing should display when the program begins, you must delete the value of the Text property (as described in the next two steps).

STEP 5: Double-click on *Label1* in the Settings box; the entry should appear selected (highlighted). See Figure 1.25.

Figure   1.25

Double-click in the Settings box to select the entry.

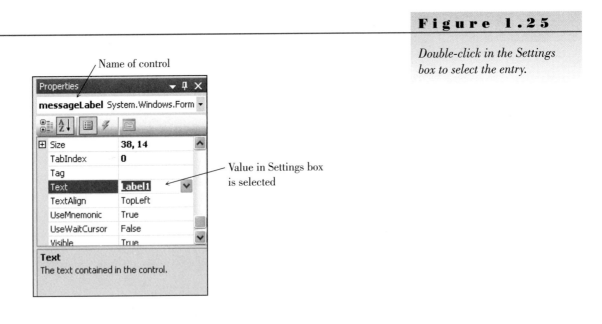

Name of control

Value in Settings box is selected

STEP 6: Press the Delete key to delete the value of the Text property. Then press Enter and notice that the label on the form seems to disappear. All you see is the lock symbol (Figure 1.26), and if you click anywhere else on the form, which deselects the label, you cannot see it at all.

Delete the value for the Text property from the Settings box; the label on the form also appears empty and the control shrinks in size because the AutoSize property is set to True.

Label is empty and selected

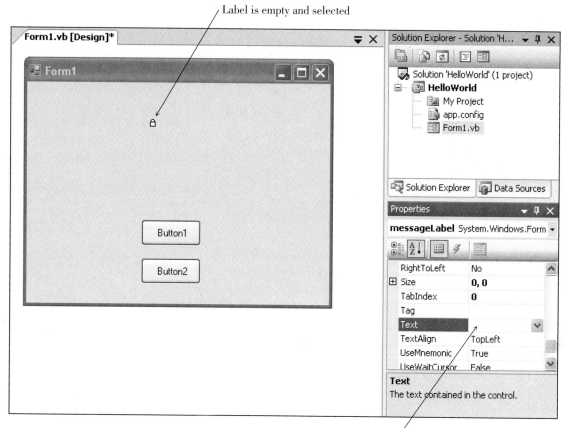

Text deleted from the Settings box

Labels have an AutoSize property, which is set to True by default. Labels shrink or grow to adjust for the Text property. You can set the AutoSize property to False if you want to specify the Label's size, in which case you can see the outline of the Label on the form.

Note that if you want text to flow to multiple lines in a label, you should set its AutoSize property to False and use the sizing handle to make the label large enough.

If you need to select the label after deselecting it, use the Properties window: Drop down the Object list at the top of the window; you can see a list of all controls on the form and can make a selection (Figure 1.27).

Figure 1.27

Drop down the Object box in the Properties window to select any control on the form.

TIP

Don't confuse the Name property with the Text property. You will use the Name property to refer to the control in your Basic code. The Text property determines what the user will see on the form. Visual Basic sets both of these properties to the same value by default, and it is easy to confuse them. ∎

Note: As an alternate technique for deleting a property, you can double-click on the property name, which automatically selects the entry in the Settings box. Then you can press the Delete key or just begin typing to change the entry.

Set the Name and Text Properties for the First Button

STEP 1: Click on the first button (Button1) to select it and then look at the Properties window. The Object box should show the name (*Button1*) and class (*System.Windows.Forms.Button*) of the button. See Figure 1.28.

Problem? If you should double-click and code appears in the Document window, simply click on the *Form1.vb [Design]* tab at the top of the window.

Figure 1.28

Change the properties of the first button.

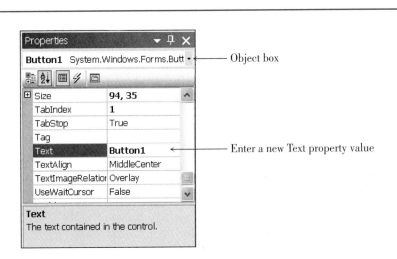

STEP 2: Change the Name property of the button to "pushButton" (without the quotation marks).

Although the project would work fine without this step, we prefer to give this button a meaningful name, rather than use Button1, its default name. The guidelines for naming controls appear later in this chapter in the section "Naming Rules and Conventions for Objects."

STEP 3: Change the Text property to "Push Me" (without the quotation marks). This step changes the words that appear on top of the button.

Set the Name and Text Properties for the Second Button

STEP 1: Select Button2 and change its Name property to "exitButton".

STEP 2: Change the Text property to "Exit".

Change Properties of the Form

STEP 1: Click anywhere on the form, except on a control. The Properties window Object box should now show the form as the selected object (*Form1* as the object's name and *System.Windows.Forms.Form* as its class).

STEP 2: Change the Text property to "Hello World by Your Name" (again, no quotation marks and use your own name).

The Text property of a form determines the text to appear in the title bar. Your screen should now look like Figure 1.29.

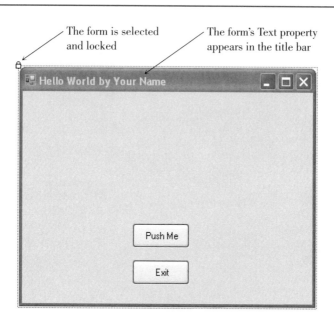

The form is selected and locked

The form's Text property appears in the title bar

Figure 1.29

Change the form's Text property to set the text that appears in the form's title bar.

STEP 3: Click on the StartPosition property and notice the arrow on the property setting, indicating a drop-down list. Drop down the list and select *CenterScreen*. This will make your form appear in the center of the screen when the program runs.

STEP 4: Change the form's Name property to "helloForm". This step changes the name of the form's class but not the name of the form's disk file, which is still Form1.

STEP 5: In the Solution Explorer, right-click on Form1.vb and choose *Rename* from the context menu. Change the filename to "helloForm.vb", making sure to retain the .vb extension. Press Enter when finished. (See Figure 1.30.)

Figure 1.30

The Properties window shows the file's properties with the new name for the file. You can change the filename in the Properties window or the Solution Explorer.

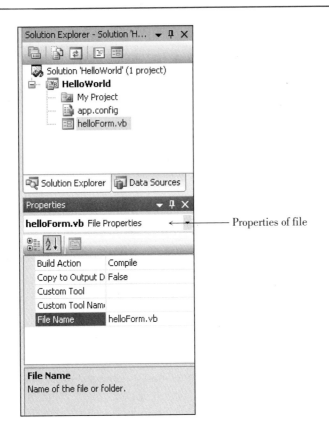

Properties of file

STEP 6: Click on the form in the Document window, anywhere except on a control. The name of the file appears on the tab at the top of the Designer window and the Properties window shows properties for the form's class, not the file. The VB designer changed the name of the form's class to match the name of the file (Figure 1.31).

> ✓ **TIP**
>
> If you change the form's filename before changing the form's class name, the IDE automatically changes the form's class name to match the filename. It does not make the change if you have changed the form's class name yourself. ■

Write Code

Visual Basic Events

While your project is running, the user can do many things, such as move the mouse around; click on either button; move, resize, or close your form's window; or jump to another application. Each action by the user causes an event to occur in your Visual Basic project. Some events (like clicking on a button) you care about, and some events (like moving the mouse and resizing the window) you do not care about. If you write Basic code for a particular event, then Visual Basic will respond to the event and automatically execute your procedure. *VB ignores events for which no procedures are written.*

Visual Basic Event Procedures

You write code in Visual Basic in **procedures**. For now, each of your procedures will be a **sub procedure**, which begins with the words `Private Sub` and ends with `End Sub`. (Later you will also learn about other types of procedures.) Note that many programmers refer to sub procedures as subprograms or

Figure 1.31

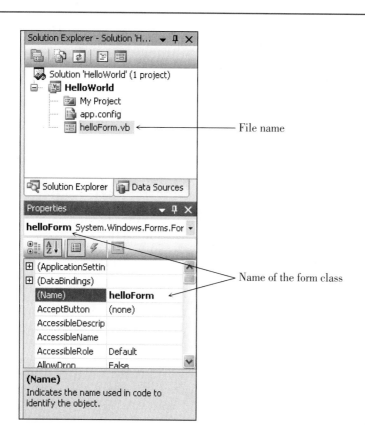

The Properties window for the form. The form's class name now matches the name of the form's file.

subroutines. Subprogram is acceptable; subroutine is not, because Basic actually has a different statement for a subroutine, which is not the same as a sub procedure.

Visual Basic automatically names your **event procedures**. The name consists of the object name, an underscore (_), and the name of the event. For example, the Click event for your button called pushButton will be pushButton_Click. For the sample project you are writing, you will have a pushButton_Click procedure and an exitButton_Click procedure.

Visual Basic Code Statements

This first project requires two Visual Basic statements: the **remark** and the **assignment statement**. You also will execute a method of an object.

The Remark Statement

Remark statements, sometimes called *comments*, are used for project documentation only. They are not considered "executable" and have no effect when the project runs. The purpose of remarks is to make the project more readable and understandable by the people who read it.

Good programming practices dictate that programmers include remarks to clarify their projects. Every procedure should begin with a remark that describes its purpose. Every project should have remarks that explain the purpose of the program and provide identifying information such as the name of the programmer and the date the program was written and/or modified. In addition, it is a good idea to place remarks within the logic of a project, especially if the purpose of any statements might be unclear.

When you try to read someone else's code, or your own after a period of time, you will appreciate the generous use of remarks.

Visual Basic remarks begin with an apostrophe. Most of the time your remarks will be on a separate line that starts with an apostrophe. You can also add an apostrophe and a remark to the right end of a line of code.

The Remark Statement—Examples

```
' This project was written by Jonathon Edwards.
' Exit the project.
Me.messageLabel.Text = "Hello World" ' Assign the message to the Text property.
```

The Me keyword

You can use the VB keyword **Me** to save time and typographical errors when you enter code. Me refers to the current object and in most cases is not required. In all statements shown in this chapter, you can omit Me and the programs will run just fine, because VB defaults to the current object (the form) if you don't include the object name. However, any time that you save by not typing Me will be more than offset by your having to type the entire control name, spelling it correctly, every time.

The controls on a form "belong to" the form; they are part of what's called a *collection*. You can easily pop up an IntelliSense list of the controls (and other selectable form elements) by using the Me keyword. When you type Me followed by a period, a list pops up showing the objects, properties, and methods for the form. As you start to type the control name, the selected position in the list changes until the unique item appears. For example, type "me.m" in your code and the first item that begins with "m" displays; when you type two more letters, "me.mes", me.messageLabel appears selected (Figure 1.32). To accept the selected term, you can press the next character (the one that follows the complete name), such as a period, the Spacebar, or the Enter key, and the editor completes the word for you. Note that you don't have to capitalize "me". As soon as you press Enter on the line, the smart editor capitalizes the text correctly.

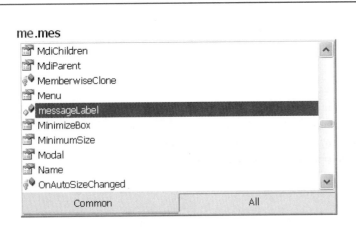

Figure 1.32

Type "me." and the start of the control name to save keystrokes. As soon as the correct name appears, type the next character (space, period, or Enter key) to accept the name and continue typing.

The Assignment Statement

The assignment statement assigns a value to a property or variable (you learn about variables in Chapter 3). Assignment statements operate from right to left; that is, the value appearing on the right side of the equal sign is assigned to the property named on the left of the equal sign. It is often helpful to read the equal sign as "is replaced by." For example, the following assignment statement would read "Me.messageLabel.Text is replaced by Hello World."

```
Me.messageLabel.Text = "Hello World"
```

The Assignment Statement—General Form

General Form

```
Object.Property = value
```

The value named on the right side of the equal sign is assigned to (or placed into) the property named on the left.

The Assignment Statement—Examples

Examples

```
Me.titleLabel.Text = "A Snazzy Program"
Me.addressLabel.Text = "1234 South North Street"
Me.messageLabel.AutoSize = True
numberInteger = 12
```

Notice that when the value to assign is some actual text (called a *literal*), it is enclosed in quotation marks. This convention allows you to type any combination of alpha and numeric characters. If the value is numeric, do not enclose it in quotation marks. And do not place quotation marks around the terms True and False, which Visual Basic recognizes as special key terms.

Ending a Program by Executing a Method

To execute a method of an object, you write

```
Object.Method()
```

Notice that methods always have parentheses. Although this might seem like a bother, it's helpful to distinguish between properties and methods: Methods always have parentheses; properties don't.

Examples

```
Me.helloButton.Hide()
Me.messageLabel.Show()
```

To execute a method of the current object (the form itself), you use the Me keyword for the object. And the method that closes the form and terminates the project execution is Close.

```
Me.Close()
```

In most cases, you will include `Me.Close()` in the sub procedure for an Exit button or an *Exit* menu choice.

Note: Remember, the keyword `Me` refers to the current object. You can omit `Me` since a method without an object reference defaults to the current object.

Code the Event Procedures for Hello World

Code the Click Event for the Push Me Button

STEP 1: Double-click the Push Me button. The Visual Studio editor opens with the first and last lines of your sub procedure already in place, with the insertion point indented inside the sub procedure (Figure 1.33).

Figure 1.33

The Editor window, showing the first and last lines of the pushButton_Click sub procedure.

The class list   The method list

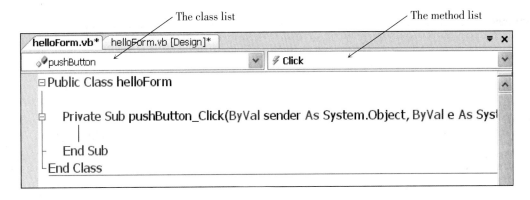

STEP 2: Type this remark statement:

```
' Display the Hello World message.
```

Notice that the editor automatically displays remarks in green (unless you or someone else has changed the color with an Environment option).

Follow good coding conventions and indent all lines between `Private Sub` and `End Sub`. The smart editor attempts to help you follow this convention. Also, always leave a blank line after the remarks at the top of a sub procedure.

STEP 3: Press Enter twice and then type this assignment statement:

```
Me.messageLabel.Text = "Hello World"
```

Note: When you type the period after messageLabel, an IntelliSense list pops up showing the properties and methods available for a Label control. Although you can type the entire word *Text*, you can allow IntelliSense to help you. As soon as you type the *T*, the list automatically scrolls to the first word that begins with *T*. Type the next letter, *e*, and the property *Text* appears highlighted. You can press the spacebar to select the word and continue typing the rest of the statement.

This assignment statement assigns the literal "Hello World" to the Text property of the control called messageLabel. Compare your screen to Figure 1.34.

Figure 1.34

Type the remark and assignment statement for the pushButton_Click event procedure.

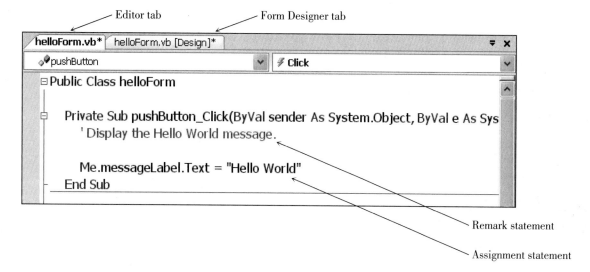

Editor tab

Form Designer tab

Remark statement

Assignment statement

STEP 4: Return to the form's design view (Figure 1.29) by clicking on the *helloForm.vb [Design]* form designer tab on the Document window (refer to Figure 1.34).

Code the Click Event for the Exit Button

STEP 1: Double-click the Exit button to open the editor for the exitButton_Click event.

STEP 2: Type this remark:

```
' Exit the project.
```

STEP 3: Press Enter twice and type this Basic statement:

```
Me.Close()
```

STEP 4: Make sure your code looks like the code shown in Figure 1.35.

Figure 1.35

Type the code for the exitButton_Click event procedure. Notice that an asterisk appears on the tab at the top of the window, indicating that there are unsaved changes in the file.

Asterisk indicates unsaved changes

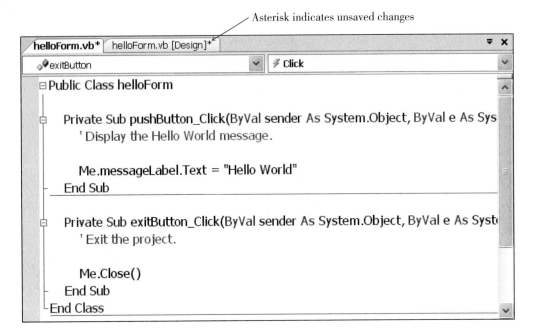

Run the Project

After you have finished writing the code, you are ready to run the project. Use one of these three techniques:

1. Open the *Debug* menu and choose *Start*.
2. Press the Start button on the toolbar.
3. Press F5, the shortcut key for the *Start* command.

Start the Project Running

STEP 1:   Choose one of the three methods previously listed to start your project running (Figure 1.36).
         Problems? See "Finding and Fixing Errors" later in this chapter. You must correct any errors and restart the program.

If all went well, the Visual Studio title bar now indicates that you are running.

Click the Push Me Button

STEP 1:   Click the Push Me button. Your "Hello World" message appears in the label (Figure 1.37).

Click the Exit Button

STEP 1:   Click the Exit button. Your project terminates, and you return to design time.

If your form disappears during run time, click its button on the Windows task bar. ■

Figure 1.36

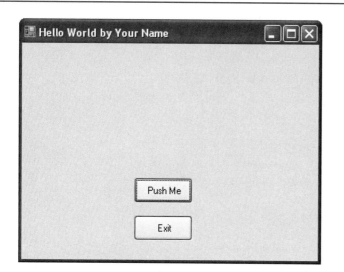

*The form of the running
application.*

Figure 1.37

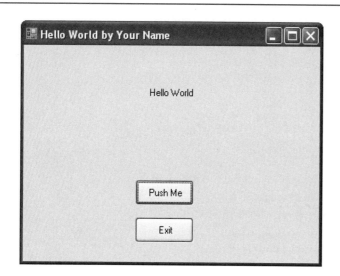

*Click the Push Me button and
"Hello World" appears in the
label.*

Save Your Work

Of course, you must always save your work often. Except for a very small project like this one, you will usually save your work as you go along. Unless you
(or someone else) has changed the setting in the IDE's *Options* dialog box, your
files are automatically saved each time you build (compile) or execute (run)
your project *after* your initial save. You also can save the files as you work.

Click the Save All toolbar button to
quickly save all of your work. ■

Save the Files

STEP 1: Open the Visual Studio *File* menu and choose *Save All*. This option saves the current form, project, and solution files. You already selected the name for the project when you first created the project. When saving the first time, you may select to discard your work or to save the project. This feature allows you to open a project to just test something simple without cluttering your system with a lot of unwanted projects. For the ones that you do want to save, make sure to set the location to the folder in which you want to store the project. Press the *Browse* button to select a location other than the one specified.

Note: Do not attempt to choose a new name for the project to save a modified version. If you want to move or rename the project, close it first. See Appendix C for help.

Close the Project

STEP 1: Open the *File* menu and choose *Close Solution*. If you haven't saved since your last change, you will be prompted to save.

Open the Project

Now is the time to test your save operation by opening the project from disk. You can choose one of two ways to open a saved project:

- Select *Open Project* from the Visual Studio *File* menu and browse to find your .sln file.

- Choose the project from the *Files / Recent Projects* menu item.

- Choose the project from the Start Page.

Open the Project File

STEP 1: Open your project by choosing one of the previously listed methods. Remember that the file to open is the solution (.sln) file.

If you do not see your form on the screen, check the Solution Explorer window—it should say *HelloWorld* for the project. Select the icon for your form: helloForm.vb. You can double-click the icon or single-click and click on the *View Designer* button at the top of the Solution Explorer (Figure 1.38); your form will appear in the Designer window. Notice that you also can click on the View Code button to display your form's code in the Editor window.

Figure 1.38

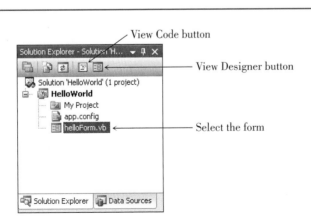

View Code button

View Designer button

Select the form

To display the form layout, select the form name and click on the View Designer button, or double-click on the form name. Click on the View Code button to display the code in the editor.

Modify the Project

Now it's time to make some changes to the project. We'll change the size of the "Hello World" message, display the message in two different languages, and display the programmer name (that's you) on the form.

Change the Size and Alignment of the Message

STEP 1: Right-click one of the form's controls to display the context menu. If your controls are currently locked, select *Lock Controls* to unlock the controls so that you can make changes.

STEP 2: Drop down the Object list at the top of the Properties window and select messageLabel, which will make the tiny label appear selected.

STEP 3: Scroll to the Font property in the Properties window. The Font property is actually a Font object that has a number of properties. To see the Font properties, click on the small plus sign on the left (Figure 1.39); the Font properties will appear showing the current values (Figure 1.40).

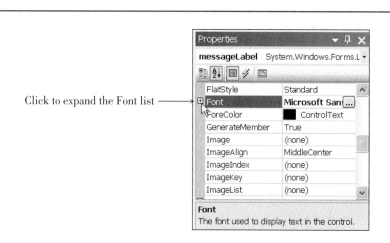

Click to expand the Font list ——▶

Figure 1.39

Click on the Font's plus sign to view the properties of the Font object.

Figure 1.40

You can change the individual properties of the Font object.

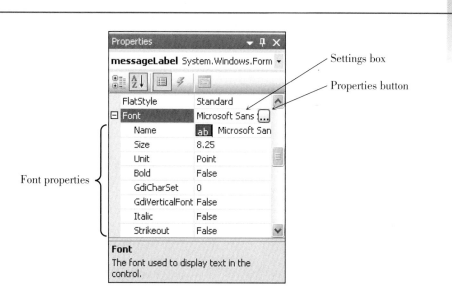

Settings box

Properties button

Font properties

You can change any of the Font properties in the Properties window, such as setting the Font's Size, Bold, or Italic properties. You also can display the *Font* dialog box and make changes there.

STEP 4: Click the Properties button for the font (the button with the ellipsis on top) to display the *Font* dialog box (Figure 1.41). Select 12 point if it is available. (If it isn't available, choose another number larger than the current setting.) Click OK to close the *Font* dialog box.

F i g u r e   1 . 4 1

Choose 12 point on the Font dialog box.

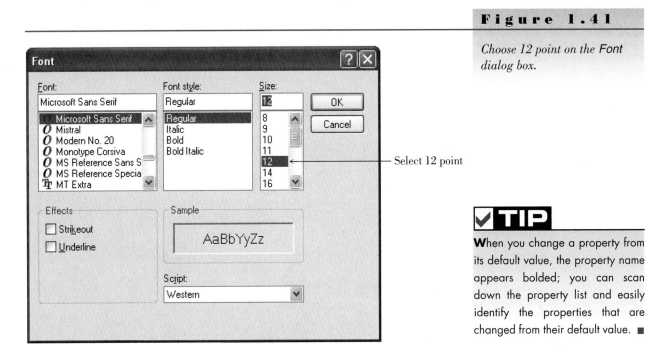

Select 12 point

✓**TIP**

When you change a property from its default value, the property name appears bolded; you can scan down the property list and easily identify the properties that are changed from their default value. ■

STEP 5: Select the TextAlign property. The Properties button that appears with the down-pointing arrow indicates a drop-down list of choices. Drop down the list (Figure 1.42) and choose the center box; the alignment property changes to *MiddleCenter*.

F i g u r e   1 . 4 2

Select the center box for the TextAlign property.

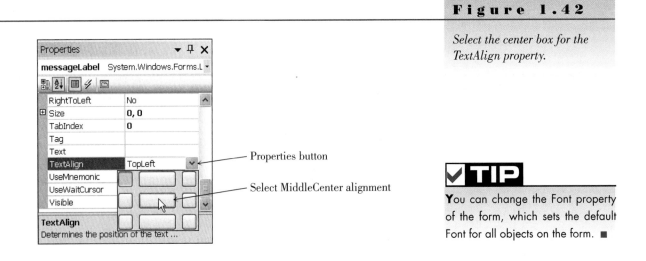

Properties button

Select MiddleCenter alignment

✓**TIP**

You can change the Font property of the form, which sets the default Font for all objects on the form. ■

Add a New Label for Your Name

STEP 1: Click on the Label tool in the toolbox and create a new label along the bottom edge of your form (Figure 1.43). (You can resize the form if necessary, but you must unlock the controls first.)

Figure 1.43

Add a new label for your name at the bottom of the form.

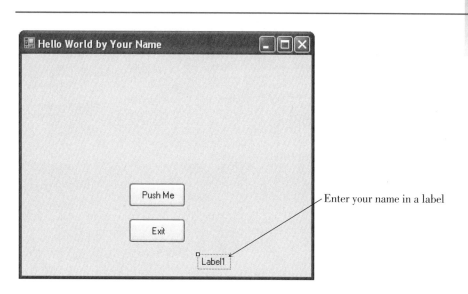

Enter your name in a label

STEP 2: Change the label's Text property to "by Your Name". (Use your name and omit the quotation marks.)

   Note: You do not need to name this label because it will never be referred to in the code.

Change the Location and Text of the Push Me Button

Because we plan to display the message in one of two languages, we'll change the text on the Push Me button to "English" and move the button to allow for a second button.

STEP 1: Select the Push Me button and change its Text property to English.

STEP 2: Move the English button to the left to make room for a Spanish button (see Figure 1.44).

   Note: If you cannot move the button, check your *Lock Controls* setting in the context menu.

Figure 1.44

Move the English button to the left and add a Spanish button.

Add a Spanish Button

STEP 1:   Add a new button. Move and resize it as necessary, referring to Figure 1.44.

STEP 2:   Change the Name property of the new button to spanishButton.

STEP 3:   Change the Text property of the new button to Spanish.

An easy way to create multiple similar controls is to copy an existing control and paste it on the form. You can paste multiple times to create multiple controls. ▪

Add an Event Procedure for the Spanish Button

STEP 1:   Double-click on the Spanish button to open the editor for spanishButton_Click.

STEP 2:   Add a remark:

```
' Display the Hello World message in Spanish.
```

STEP 3:   Press Enter twice and type the following Basic code line:

```
Me.messageLabel.Text = "Hola Mundo"
```

STEP 4:   Return to design view.

Lock the Controls

STEP 1:   When you are satisfied with the placement of the controls on the form, display the context menu and select *Lock Controls* again.

Save and Run the Project

STEP 1:   Save your project again. You can use the *File / Save All* menu command or the Save All toolbar button.

STEP 2:   Run your project again. Try clicking on the English button and the Spanish button.

Problems? See "Finding and Fixing Errors" later in this chapter.

STEP 3:   Click the Exit button to end program execution.

Add Remarks

Good documentation guidelines require some more remarks in the project. Always begin each procedure with remarks that tell the purpose of the procedure. In addition, each project file needs identifying remarks at the top.

The **Declarations section** at the top of the file is a good location for these remarks.

STEP 1:   Display the code in the editor and click in front of the first line (`Public Class helloForm`). Make sure that you have an insertion point; if the entire first line is selected, press the left arrow to set the insertion point.

STEP 2:   Press Enter to create a blank line.

Warning: If you accidentally deleted the first line, click Undo (or press Ctrl + Z) and try again.

STEP 3:   Move the insertion point up to the blank line and type the following remarks, one per line (Figure 1.45):

Press Ctrl + Home to quickly move the insertion point to the top of the file. ▪

```
' Project:        Hello World
' Programmer:     Your Name (Use your own name here.)
' Date:           (Fill in today's date.)
' Description:    This project will display a "Hello World"
'                 message in two different languages.
```

Figure 1.45

Enter remarks at the top of the form file.

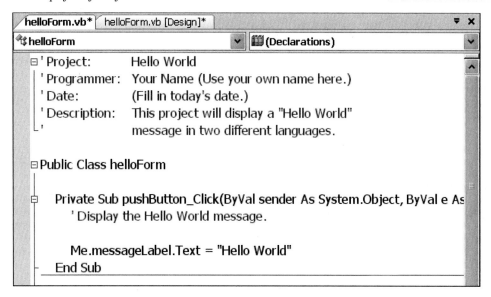

Explore the Editor Window

STEP 1: Notice the two drop-down list boxes at the top of the Editor window, called the *Class Name list* and the *Method Name list*. You can use these lists to move to any procedure in your code.

STEP 2: Click on the left down-pointing arrow to view the Class Name list. Notice that every object in your form is listed there (Figure 1.46). At the top of the list, you see the name of your form: *helloForm*.

Figure 1.46

View the list of objects in this form by dropping down the Class Name list. Select an object from the list to display the sub procedures for that object.

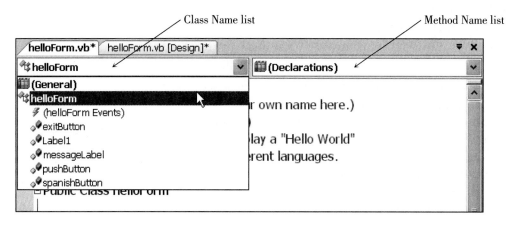

STEP 3: Select spanishButton from the Class Name list. The insertion point jumps to the first line within the spanishButton_Click event procedure.

STEP 4: Drop down the Method Name list (the right list); it shows all possible events for a Button control. Notice that the Click event is bold and the rest are not. Any event for which you have written an event procedure appears in bold.

To write code for more than one event for an object, you can use the Method Name drop-down list. When you select a new event from the Method Name list, the editor generates the `Private Sub` and `End Sub` lines for that procedure and moves the insertion point to the new procedure.

Finish Up

STEP 1: Save the project again.

Print the Code

Select the Printing Options

STEP 1: Make sure that the Editor window is open, showing your form's code. The *File / Print* command is disabled unless the code is displaying and its window selected.

STEP 2: Open the *File* menu and choose *Print*. Click OK.

A Sample Printout

This output is produced when you print the form's code. Notice the ⬐ symbol used to continue long lines on the printout. On the screen, those long lines are not split, but scroll off the right side of the screen.

```
C:\Documents and Settings\ . . . \HelloWorld\helloForm.vb                        1

'Project:           Hello World
'Programmer:        Your Name
'Date:              Today's Date
'Description:       This project will display a "Hello World"
'                   message in two different languages.

Public Class helloForm

  Private Sub pushButton_Click(ByVal sender As System.Object, ByVal e As System.EventArgs) ⬐
  Handles pushButton.Click
    ' Display the Hello World Message.

    Me.messageLabel.Text = "Hello World"
  End Sub
```

```
Private Sub exitButton_Click(ByVal sender As System.Object, ByVal e As System.EventArgs) ↙
Handles exitButton.Click
    ' Exit the project.

    Me.Close()
End Sub

Private Sub spanishButton_Click(ByVal sender As System.Object, ByVal e As System. ↙
EventArgs) Handles spanishButton.Click
    ' Display the Hello World message in Spanish.

    Me.messageLabel.Text = "Hola Mundo"
End Sub

End Class
```

Finding and Fixing Errors

You already may have seen some errors as you entered the first sample project. Programming errors come in three varieties: **syntax errors**, **run-time errors**, and **logic errors**.

Syntax Errors

When you break VB's rules for punctuation, format, or spelling, you generate a syntax error. Fortunately, the smart editor finds most syntax errors and even corrects many of them for you. The syntax errors that the editor cannot identify are found and reported by the compiler as it attempts to convert the code into intermediate machine language. A compiler-reported syntax error may be referred to as a *compile error*.

The editor can correct some syntax errors by making assumptions, and not even report the error to you. For example, a string of characters must have opening and closing quotes, such as "Hello World". But if you type the opening quote and forget the closing quote, the editor automatically adds the closing quote when you move to the next line. And if you forget the opening and closing parentheses after a method name, such as `Close()`, again the editor will add them for you when you move off the line. Of course, sometimes the editor will make a wrong assumption, but you will be watching, right?

The editor identifies syntax errors as you move off the offending line. A blue squiggly line appears under the part of the line that the editor cannot interpret. You can view the error message by pausing the mouse pointer over the error, which pops up a box that describes the error (Figure 1.47). You also can display an Error List window (*View / Error List*), which appears at the bottom of the Editor window and shows all error messages along with the line number of the statement that caused the error. You can display line numbers on the source code (Figure 1.48) with *Tools / Options*. If *Show All Settings* is selected in the *Options* dialog box, choose *Text Editor / Basic* and check *Line Numbers*; if *Show All Settings* is not checked, then choose *Text Editor / Basic / Editor* and check *Line Numbers*.

Figure 1.47

The editor identifies a syntax error with a squiggly blue line and you can point to an error to pop up the error message.

Figure 1.48

You can display the Error List window and line numbers in the source code to help locate the error lines.

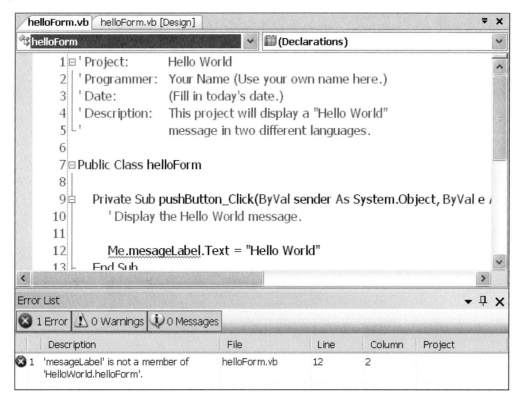

The quickest way to jump to an error line is to point to a message in the Error List window and double-click. The line in error will display in the Editor window with the error highlighted (Figure 1.49).

Figure 1.49

Quickly jump to the line in error by double-clicking on the error message in the Error List window.

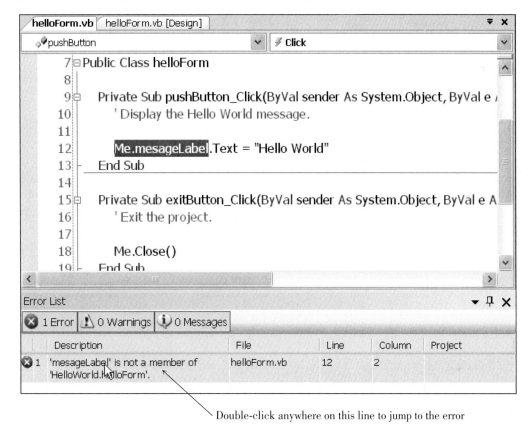

Double-click anywhere on this line to jump to the error

At times the editor can recognize errors and offer suggested solutions. This is more likely to occur in later chapters as you begin to use new keywords. In Chapter 3 you learn to declare elements that can use a data type called *Decimal*. If you accidentally mistype the word Decimal, a small red line appears at the end of the word. Point to the line and an **AutoCorrect** box appears, offering to change the word to the correct spelling. Figures 1.50 and 1.51 show AutoCorrect in action.

☑ TIP

Visual Basic 2005 has a new AutoCorrect feature that can suggest corrections for common syntax errors. ■

Figure 1.50

The AutoCorrect feature pops up a message and a box with a down arrow. Display the suggestions by clicking the down arrow or pressing Shift + Alt + F10, as suggested in the popup message.

Type 'Decmal' is not defined.

Dim amountDecimal As Decmal

Error Correction Options (Shift+Alt+F10)

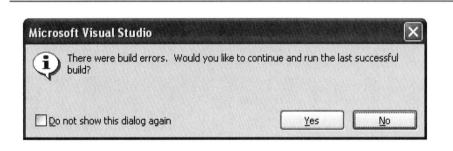

Figure 1.51

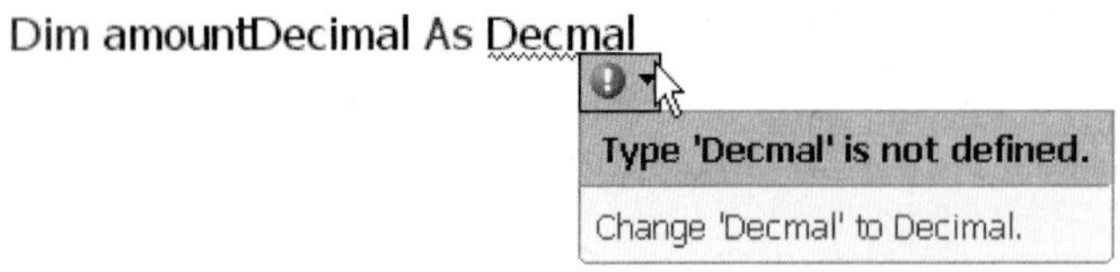

The Error Corrections Options box displays suggested corrections. You can make a selection from the list.

If a syntax error is found by the compiler, you will see the dialog box shown in Figure 1.52. Click No and return to the editor, correct your errors, and run the program again.

Figure 1.52

When the compiler identifies syntax errors, it cannot continue. Click No to return to the editor and correct the error.

Run-Time Errors

If your project halts during execution, it is called a *run-time error* or an *exception*. Visual Basic displays a dialog box and highlights the statement causing the problem.

Statements that cannot execute correctly cause run-time errors. The statements are correctly formed Basic statements that pass the syntax checking; however, the statements fail to execute due to some serious issue. You can cause run-time errors by attempting to do impossible arithmetic operations, such as calculate with nonnumeric data, divide by zero, or find the square root of a negative number.

In Chapter 3 you will learn to catch exceptions so that the program does not come to a halt when an error occurs.

Logic Errors

When your program contains logic errors, your project runs but produces incorrect results. Perhaps the results of a calculation are incorrect or the wrong text appears or the text is okay but appears in the wrong location.

Beginning programmers often overlook their logic errors. If the project runs, it must be right—right? All too often, that statement is not correct. You may need to use a calculator to check the output. Check all aspects of the project output: computations, text, and spacing.

For example, the Hello World project in this chapter has event procedures for displaying "Hello World" in English and in Spanish. If the contents of the two procedures were switched, the program would work but the results would be incorrect.

The following code does not give the proper instructions to display the message in Spanish:

```
Private Sub spanishButton_Click
   ' Display the Hello World Message in Spanish.

   Me.messageLabel.Text = "Hello World"
End Sub
```

Project Debugging

If you talk to any computer programmer, you will learn that programs don't have errors, but that programs get "bugs" in them. Finding and fixing these bugs is called **debugging**.

For syntax errors and run-time errors, your job is easier. Visual Basic displays the Editor window with the offending line highlighted. However, you must identify and locate logic errors yourself.

VB .NET 2005 brings back a feature that was very popular with VB 6 programmers: edit-and-continue. If you are able to identify the run-time error and fix it, you can continue project execution from that location by clicking on the Run button, pressing F5, or choosing *Debug / Start*. You also can correct the error and restart from the beginning.

The Visual Studio IDE has some very helpful tools to aid in debugging your projects. The debugging tools are covered in Chapter 4.

A Clean Compile

When you start executing your program, the first step is called *compiling*, which means that the VB statements are converted to Microsoft Intermediate Language (MSIL). Your goal is to have no errors during the compile process: a **clean compile**. Figure 1.53 shows the Error List window for a clean compile: 0 Errors; 0 Warnings; 0 Messages.

TIP

If you get the message "There were build errors. Continue?" always say No. If you say Yes, the last cleanly compiled version runs, rather than the current version. ■

Figure 1.53

Zero errors, warnings, and messages means that you have a clean compile.

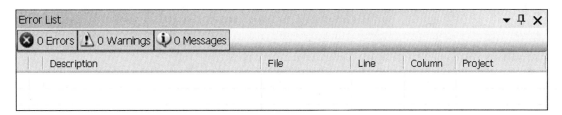

Naming Rules and Conventions for Objects

Using good consistent names for objects can make a project easier to read and understand, as well as easier to debug. You *must* follow the Visual Basic rules for naming objects, procedures, and variables. In addition, conscientious programmers also follow certain naming conventions.

Most professional programming shops have a set of standards that their programmers must use. Those standards may differ from the ones you find in this book, but the most important point is this: *Good programmers follow standards. You should have a set of standards and always follow them.*

The Naming Rules

When you select a name for an object, Visual Basic requires the name to begin with a letter or an underscore. The name can contain letters, digits, and underscores. An object name cannot include a space or punctuation mark and cannot be a reserved word, such as Button or Close, but can contain one. For example, exitButton and closeButton are legal.

The Naming Conventions

This text follows standard naming conventions, which help make projects more understandable. When naming controls, use **camel casing**, which means that you begin the name with a lowercase character and capitalize each additional word in the name. Make up a meaningful name and append the full name of the control's class. Do not use abbreviations unless it is a commonly used term that everyone will understand. All names must be meaningful and indicate the purpose of the object.

Examples
messageLabel
exitButton
dataEntryForm
discountRateLabel

Do not keep the default names assigned by Visual Basic, such as Button1 and Label3. Also, do not name your objects with numbers. The exception to this rule is for labels that never change during project execution. These labels usually hold items such as titles, instructions, and labels for other controls. Leaving these labels with their default names is perfectly acceptable and is practiced in this text.

Refer to Table 1.2 for sample object names.

Visual Studio Help

Visual Studio has an extensive Help facility, which contains much more information than you will ever use. You can look up any Basic statement, class, property, method, or programming concept. Many coding examples are available, and you can copy and paste the examples into your own project, modifying them if you wish.

The VS Help facility includes all of the Microsoft Developer Network library (MSDN), which contains several books, technical articles, and the Microsoft Knowledge Base, a database of frequently asked questions and their answers. MSDN includes reference materials for the VS IDE, the .NET Framework, Visual Basic, C#, J#, and C++. You will want to filter the information to display only the VB information.

Recommended Naming Conventions for Visual Basic Objects.

Table 1.2

Object Class	Example
Form	dataEntryForm
Button	exitButton
Label	totalLabel
TextBox	paymentAmountTextBox
Radio button	boldRadioButton
CheckBox	printSummaryCheckBox
Horizontal scroll bar	rateHorizontalScrollBar
Vertical scroll bar	temperatureVerticalScrollBar
PictureBox	landscapePictureBox
ComboBox	bookListComboBox
ListBox	ingredientsListBox
SoundPlayer	introPageSoundPlayer

Discuss in Class [handwritten annotation]

Installing and Running MSDN

You can run MSDN from a hard drive, from a network drive, or from the Web. Of course, if you plan to access MSDN from the Web, you must have a live Internet connection as you work.

When you install Visual Studio, by default MSDN is installed on the hard drive. If you don't want to install it there, you must specifically choose this option. You can access MSDN on the Web at http://msdn.microsoft.com.

Or, if you want to go directly to VB Help, add this link to your favorites:

http://msdn.microsoft.com/library/default.asp?url=/library/en-us/vblr7/html/vboriVBlangRefTopNode.asp

The extensive Help is a two-edged sword: You have available a wealth of materials, but it may take some time to find the topic you want.

Viewing Help Topics

The Help system display is greatly changed and improved in Visual Studio 2005. You view the Help topics in a separate window from the VS IDE, so you can have both windows open at the same time. When you choose *How Do I*, *Search*, *Contents*, *Index*, or *Help Favorites* from the *Help* menu, a new window opens on top of the IDE window (Figure 1.54). You can switch from one window to the other, or resize the windows to view both on the screen if your screen is large enough.

You can choose to filter the Help topics, so that you don't have to view topics for all of the languages when you search for a particular topic. In the Index or Contents window, drop down the *Filtered By* list and choose *Visual Basic* (Figure 1.55).

Figure 1.54

The Help window. **How Do I** *and* **Search** *appear in tabbed windows in the main Document window;* **Index**, **Contents**, *and* **Help Favorites** *appear in tabbed windows docked at the left of the main window.*

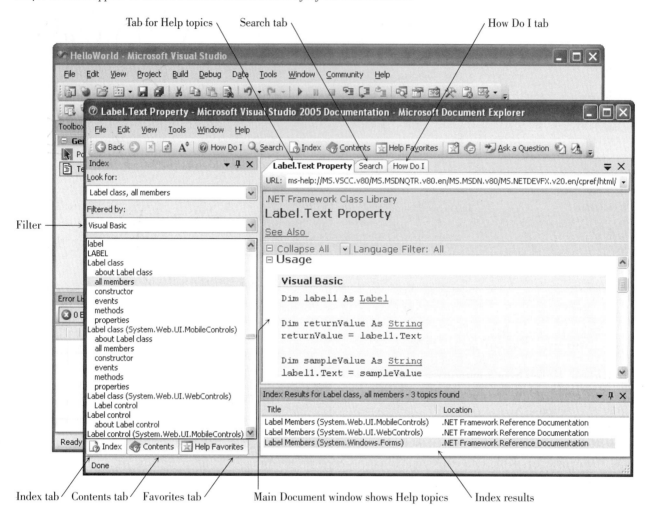

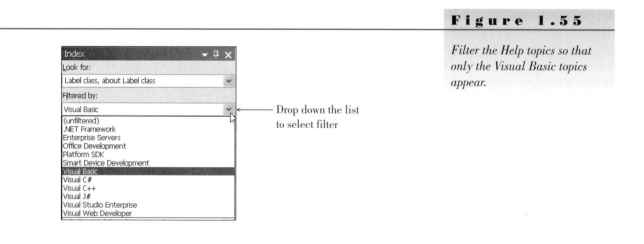

Figure 1.55

Filter the Help topics so that only the Visual Basic topics appear.

In the Search window, you can choose additional filter options, such as the technology and topic type. Drop down a list and select any desired options (Figure 1.56).

In class

Figure 1.56

Drop down the Topic Type list to make selections for the Search window.

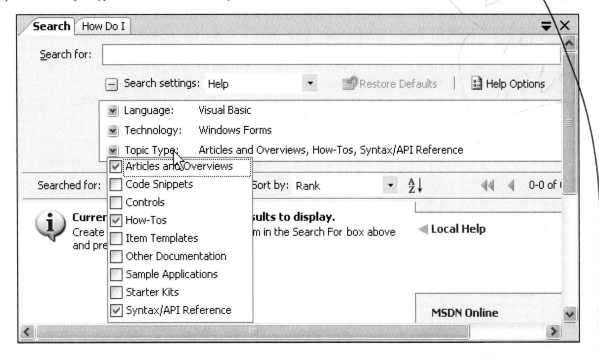

In the Help Index window, you see main topics and subtopics (indented beneath the main topics). All main topics and some subtopics have multiple entries available. When you choose a topic that has more than one possible entry, the choices appear in the Index Results window (Figure 1.57). Double-click on the entry of your choice to display its Help topic in the main Document window (Figure 1.58).

Many Help topics have entries for both Windows Forms and Web Forms (and some even Mobile Forms). For now, always choose Windows Forms. Chapters 1 to 8 deal with Windows Forms exclusively; Web Forms are introduced in Chapter 9.

A good way to start using Help is to view the topics that demonstrate how to look up topics in Help. On the *Help Contents* tab, select *Help on Help (Microsoft Document Explorer Help)*. Then choose *Microsoft Document Explorer Overview* and *What's New in Document Exploration*. Make sure to visit *Managing Help Topics and Windows*, which has subtopics describing how to copy topics and print topics.

When an Index topic has a choice of subtopics, the choices appear in a popup window. Double-click the desired subtopic.

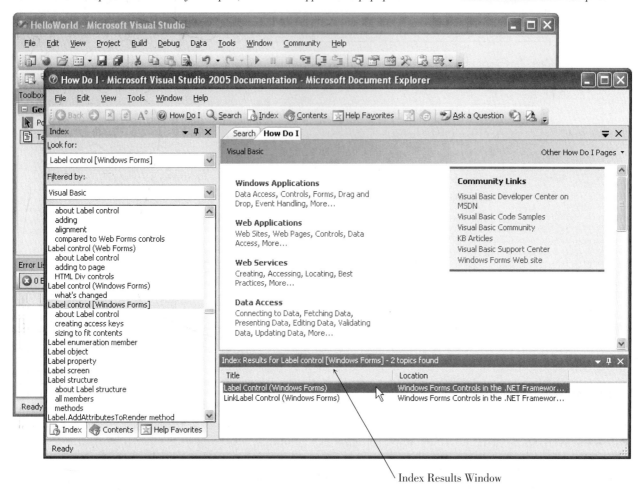

Index Results Window

Context-Sensitive Help

A quick way to view Help on any topic is to use **context-sensitive Help**. Select a VB object, such as a form or control, or place the insertion point in a word in the editor and press F1. The Help window pops up with the corresponding Help topic displayed, if possible, saving you a search. You can display context-sensitive Help about the environment by clicking in an area of the screen and pressing Shift + F1.

Managing Windows

At times you may have more windows and tabs open than you want. You can hide or close any window, or switch to a different window.

To close a window that is a part of a tabbed window, click the window's Close button. Only the top window will close.

To switch to another window that is part of a tabbed window, click on its tab.

For additional help with the environment, see Appendix C, "Tips and Shortcuts for Mastering the Visual Studio Environment."

Figure 1.58

Selected Help topics appear in the main Document window.

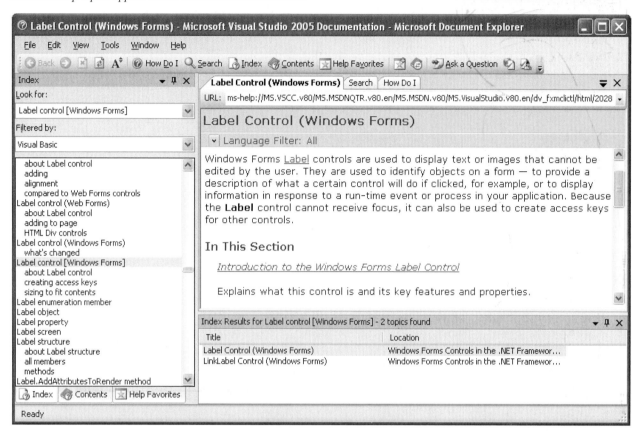

Feedback 1.1

Note: Answers for Feedback questions appear in Appendix A.

1. Display the Help Index, filter by *Visual Basic*, and type "button control". In the Index list, notice multiple entries for button controls, including HTML, Web Forms, and Windows Forms. Locate the main topic *Button control [Windows Forms]* and click on the entry for *about Button control*; multiple entries appear in the Index Results. Double-click on "Introduction to the Windows Forms Button Control" and the topic displays in the Document window. Notice that additional links appear in the text in the Document window. You can click on a link to view another topic.

2. Display the Editor window of your Hello World project. Click on the `Close` method to place the insertion point. Press the F1 key to view context-sensitive help.

3. Select each of the options from the VS IDE's *Help* menu to see how they respond.

Summary

1. Visual Basic is an object-oriented language used to write application programs that run in Windows or on the Internet using a graphical user interface (GUI).

2. In the OOP object model, classes are used to create objects that have properties, methods, and events.

3. The current release of Visual Basic is called .NET 2005. Visual Basic .NET is part of Visual Studio .NET. VB .NET has an Express Edition, a Standard Edition, a Professional Edition, and a Team System Edition.

4. The .NET Framework provides an environment for the objects from many languages to interoperate. Each language compiles to Microsoft Intermediate Language (MSIL) and runs in the Common Language Runtime (CLR).

5. To plan a project, first sketch the user interface and then list the objects and properties needed. Then plan the necessary event procedures.

6. The three steps to creating a Visual Basic project are (1) define the user interface, (2) set the properties, and (3) write the Basic code.

7. A Visual Basic application is called a *solution*. Each solution can contain multiple projects, and each project may contain multiple forms and additional files. The solution file has an extension of .sln, a project file has an extension of .vbproj, and form files and additional VB files have an extension of .vb. In addition, the Visual Studio environment and the VB compiler both create several more files.

8. The Visual Studio integrated development environment (IDE) consists of several tools, including a form designer, an editor, a compiler, a debugger, an object browser, and a Help facility.

9. VB has three modes: design time, run time, and debug time.

10. You can customize the Visual Studio IDE and reset all customizations back to their default state.

11. You create the user interface for an application by adding controls from the toolbox to a form. You can move, resize, and delete the controls.

12. The Name property of a control is used to refer to the control in code. The Text property holds the words that the user sees on the screen.

13. Visual Basic code is written in procedures. Sub procedures begin with the word `Sub` and end with `End Sub`.

14. Project remarks are used for documentation. Good programming practice requires remarks in every procedure and in the Declarations section of a file.

15. Assignment statements assign a value to a property or a variable. Assignment statements work from right to left, assigning the value on the right side of the equal sign to the property or variable named on the left side of the equal sign.

16. The `Me.Close()` method terminates program execution.

17. Each event to which you want to respond requires an event procedure.

18. You can print out the Visual Basic code for documentation.

19. Three types of errors can occur in a Visual Basic project: syntax errors, which violate the syntax rules of the Basic language; run-time errors, which contain a statement that cannot execute properly; and logic errors, which produce erroneous results.

20. Finding and fixing program errors is called *debugging*.

21. You should have a clean compile before you run the program.

22. Following good naming conventions can help make a project easier to debug.

23. Visual Basic Help has very complete descriptions of all project elements and their uses. You can use the *How Do I*, *Contents*, *Index*, *Search*, or context-sensitive Help.

Key Terms

assignment statement *29*
AutoCorrect *45*
Button *18*
camel casing *48*
class *4*
clean compile *47*
code *6*
context menu *21*
context-sensitive Help *52*
control *3*
debug time *13*
debugging *47*
Declarations section *40*
design time *13*
Document window *12*
Express Edition *5*
event *4*
event procedure *29*
form *3*
Form Designer *12*
graphical user interface (GUI) *2*
handle *12*
Help *12*
integrated development environment (IDE) *8*
Label *18*
logic error *43*
Me *30*
method *4*

namespace *22*
object *4*
object-oriented programming (OOP) *3*
procedure *28*
Professional Edition *5*
project file *7*
Properties window *12*
property *4*
pseudocode *6*
remark *29*
resizing handle *20*
run time *13*
run-time error *43*
snap lines *20*
solution *7*
Solution Explorer window *12*
solution file *7*
Standard Edition *5*
sub procedure *28*
syntax error *43*
Team System Edition *5*
Text property *24*
toolbar *11*
toolbox *12*
user interface *6*
Visual Studio environment *8*

Review Questions

1. What are objects and properties? How are they related to each other?
2. What are the three steps for planning and creating Visual Basic projects? Describe what happens in each step.
3. What is the purpose of these Visual Basic file types: .sln, .suo, and .vb?
4. When is Visual Basic in design time? run time? debug time?
5. What is the purpose of the Name property of a control?
6. Which property determines what appears on the form for a Label control?
7. What is the purpose of the Text property of a button? the Text property of a form?
8. What does pushButton_Click mean? To what does pushButton refer? To what does Click refer?
9. What is a Visual Basic event? Give some examples of events.
10. What property must be set to center text in a label? What should be the value of the property?
11. What is the Declarations section of a file? What belongs there?
12. What is meant by the term *debugging*?
13. What is a syntax error, when does it occur, and what might cause it?
14. What is a run-time error, when does it occur, and what might cause it?
15. What is a logic error, when does it occur, and what might cause it?
16. Tell the class of control and the likely purpose of each of these object names:

    addressLabel
    exitButton
    nameTextBox
    textBlueRadioButton
17. What does context-sensitive Help mean? How can you use it to see the Help page for a button?

Programming Exercises

1.1 For your first Visual Basic exercise, you must first complete the Hello World project. Then add buttons and event procedures to display the "Hello World" message in two more languages. You may substitute any other languages for those shown. Feel free to modify the user interface to suit yourself (or your instructor).

   Make sure to use meaningful names for your new buttons, following the naming conventions in Table 1.2. Include remarks at the top of every procedure and at the top of the file.

   | "Hello World" in French: | Bonjour tout le monde |
   | "Hello World" in Italian: | Ciao Mondo |

1.2 Write a new Visual Basic project that displays a different greeting, or make it display the name of your school or your company. Include at least two buttons to display the greeting, and exit the project.

Include a label that holds your name at the bottom of the form and change the Text property of the form to something meaningful.

Follow good naming conventions for object names; include remarks at the top of every procedure and at the top of the file.

Select a different font name and font size for the greeting label. If you wish, you also can select a different color for the font. Select each font attribute from the *Font* dialog box from the Properties window.

1.3   Write a project that displays four sayings, such as "The early bird gets the worm" or "A penny saved is a penny earned." (You will want to keep the sayings short, as each must be entered on one line.) When the saying displays on your form, long lines will run off the form if the label's AutoSize property is set to True. To wrap text within the label, change the AutoSize property to False and use the sizing handles to make the label large enough.

Make a button for each saying with a descriptive Text property for each, as well as a button to exit the project.

Include a label that holds your name at the bottom of the form. Also, make sure to change the form's title bar to something meaningful.

You may change the Font properties of the large label to the font and size of your choice.

Make sure the buttons are large enough to hold their entire Text properties.

Follow good naming conventions for object names; include remarks at the top of every procedure and at the top of the file.

1.4   Write a project to display company contact information. Include buttons and labels for the contact person, department, and phone. When the user clicks on one of the buttons, display the contact information in the corresponding label. Include a button to exit.

Include a label that holds your name at the bottom of the form and change the title bar of the form to something meaningful.

You may change the Font properties of the labels to the font and size of your choice.

Follow good naming conventions for object names; include remarks at the top of every procedure and at the top of the file.

1.5   Create a project to display the daily specials for "your" diner. Make up a name for your diner and display it in a label at the top of the form. Add a label to display the appropriate special depending on the button that is pressed. The buttons should be

- Soup of the Day

- Chef's Special

- Daily Fish

Also include an Exit button.

Sample Data: Dorothy's Diner is offering Tortilla Soup, a California Cobb Salad, and Hazelnut Coated Mahi Mahi.

Case Studies

Very Busy (VB) Mail Order

If you don't have the time to look for all those hard-to-find items, tell us what you're looking for. We'll send you a catalog from the appropriate company or order for you.

We can place an order and ship it to you. We also help with shopping for gifts; your order can be gift wrapped and sent anywhere you wish.

The company title will be shortened to VB Mail Order. Include this name on the title bar of the first form of each project that you create for this case study.

Your first job is to create a project that will display the name and telephone number for the contact person for the customer relations, marketing, order processing, and shipping departments.

Include a button for each department. When the user clicks on the button for a department, display the name and telephone number for the contact person in two labels. Also include identifying labels with Text "Department Contact" and "Telephone Number".

Be sure to include a button for Exit.

Include a label at the bottom of the form that holds your name.

Test Data

Department	Department Contact	Telephone Number
Customer Relations	Tricia Mills	500-1111
Marketing	Michelle Rigner	500-2222
Order Processing	Kenna DeVoss	500-3333
Shipping	Eric Andrews	500-4444

Valley Boulevard (VB) Auto Center

Valley Boulevard Auto Center will meet all of your automobile needs. The center has facilities with everything for your vehicles including sales and leasing for new and used cars and RVs, auto service and repair, detail shop, car wash, and auto parts.

The company title will be shortened to VB Auto Center. This name should appear as the title bar on the first form of every project that you create throughout the text for this case study.

Your first job is to create a project that will display current notices.

Include four buttons labeled "Auto Sales", "Service Center", "Detail Shop", and "Employment Opportunities". One label will be used to display the information when the buttons are clicked. Be sure to include a button for Exit.

Include your name in a label at the bottom of the form.

Test Data

Button	Label Text
Auto Sales	Family wagon, immaculate condition $12,995
Service Center	Lube, oil, filter $25.99
Detail Shop	Complete detail $79.95 for most cars
Employment Opportunities	Sales position, contact Mr. Mann 551-2134 x475

Video Bonanza

This neighborhood store is an independently owned video rental business. The owners would like to allow their customers to use the computer to look up the aisle number for movies by category.

Create a form with a button for each category. When the user clicks on a button, display the corresponding aisle number in a label. Include a button to exit.

Include a label that holds your name at the bottom of the form and change the title bar of the form to Video Bonanza.

You may change the font properties of the labels to the font and size of your choice. Include additional categories, if you wish.

Follow good programming conventions for object names; include remarks at the top of every procedure and at the top of the file.

Test Data

Button	Location
Comedy	Aisle 1
Drama	Aisle 2
Action	Aisle 3
Sci-Fi	Aisle 4
Horror	Aisle 5
New Releases	Back Wall

Very Very Boards

This chain of stores features a full line of clothing and equipment for snowboard and skateboard enthusiasts. Management wants a computer application to allow their employees to display the address and hours for each of their branches.

Create a form with a button for each store branch. When the user clicks on a button, display the correct address and hours.

Include a label that holds your name at the bottom of the form and change the title bar of the form to Very Very Boards.

You may change the font properties of the labels to the font and size of your choice.

Follow good programming conventions for object names; include remarks at the top of every procedure and at the top of the file.

Store Branches: The three branches are Downtown, Mall, and Suburbs. Make up hours and locations for each.

2

User Interface Design

1. Use text boxes, masked text boxes, group boxes, check boxes, radio buttons, and picture boxes effectively.

2. Set the BorderStyle property to make controls appear flat or three-dimensional.

3. Select multiple controls and move them, align them, and set common properties.

4. Make your projects easy for the user to understand and operate by defining access keys, setting an accept and a cancel button, controlling the tab sequence, resetting the focus during program execution, and causing ToolTips to appear.

5. Clear the contents of text boxes and labels.

6. Change text color during program execution.

7. Code multiple statements for one control using the With and End With statements.

8. Concatenate (join) strings of text.

9. Make a control visible or invisible at run time by setting its Visible property.

Introducing More Controls

In Chapter 1 you learned to use labels and buttons. In this chapter you will learn to use several more control types: text boxes, group boxes, check boxes, radio buttons, and picture boxes. Figure 2.1 shows the toolbox, with the *Containers* and *Common Controls* tabs open, to show the tools for these new controls. Figure 2.2 shows some of these controls on a form.

Figure 2.1

The toolbox with two tabs open, showing the controls that are covered in this chapter. Click the plus and minus signs on the tabs to open and close each section.

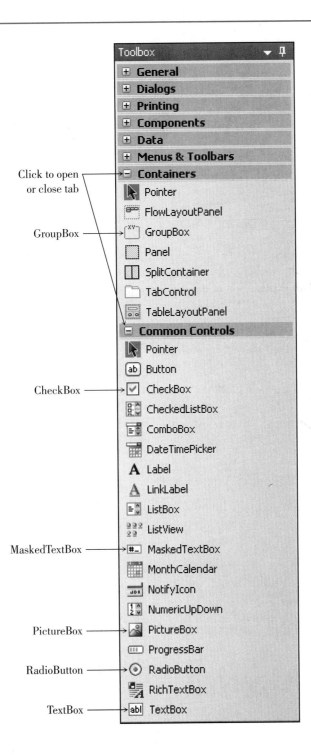

Click to open or close tab

GroupBox

CheckBox

MaskedTextBox

PictureBox

RadioButton

TextBox

Figure 2.2

This form uses labels, text boxes, a check box, radio buttons, group boxes, and a picture box.

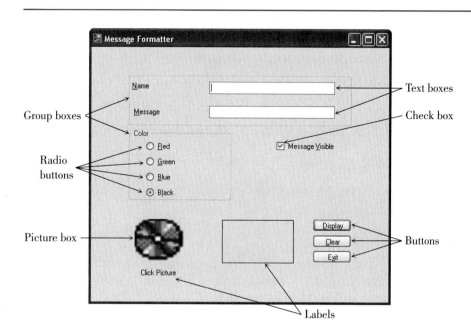

Each class of controls has its own set of properties. To see a complete list of the properties for any class of control, you can (1) place a control on a form and examine the properties list or (2) click on a tool or a control and press F1 for context-sensitive Help. Visual Studio will display the Help page for that control, and you can view a list of the properties and an explanation of their use.

Text Boxes

Use a **text box** control when you want the user to type some input. The form in Figure 2.2 has two text boxes. The user can move from one box to the next, make corrections, cut and paste if desired, and click the Display button when finished. In your program code you can use the **Text property** of each text box.

Example

```
nameLabel.Text = nameTextBox.Text
```

or

```
Me.nameLabel.Text = Me.nameTextBox.Text
```

In this example, whatever the user enters into the text box is assigned to the Text property of nameLabel. If you want to display some text in a text box during program execution, assign a literal to the Text property:

```
Me.messageTextBox.Text = "Watson, come here."
```

You can set the **TextAlign property** of text boxes to change the alignment of text within the box. In the Properties window, set the property to *Left*, *Right*, or *Center*. In code, you can set the property using these values:

HorizontalAlignment.Left
HorizontalAlignment.Right
HorizontalAlignment.Center

```
Me.messageTextBox.TextAlign = HorizontalAlignment.Left
```

Example Names for Text Boxes

```
titleTextBox
companyTextBox
```

Masked Text Boxes

A specialized form of the TextBox control is the MaskedTextBox. You can specify the format (the Mask property) of the data required of the user. For example, you can select a mask for a ZIP code, a date, a phone number, or a social security number. Figure 2.3 shows the *Input Mask* dialog box where you can select the mask and even try it out. At run time the user cannot enter characters that do not conform to the mask. For example, the phone number and social security number masks do not allow input other than numeric digits.

Example Names for Masked Text Boxes

```
dateMaskedTextBox
phoneMaskedTextBox
```

Note: For a date or time mask, the user can enter only numeric digits but may possibly enter an invalid value; for example, a month or hour greater than 12. The mask will accept any numeric digits, which could possibly cause your program to generate a run-time error. You will learn to check the input values in Chapter 4.

Group Boxes

Group boxes are used as containers for other controls. Usually, groups of radio buttons or check boxes are placed in group boxes. Using group boxes to group controls can make your forms easier to understand by separating the controls into logical groups.

Set a group box's Text property to the words you want to appear on the top edge of the box.

Example Names for Group Boxes

```
colorGroupBox
styleGroupBox
```

Figure 2.3

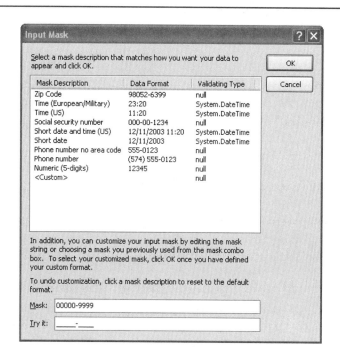

Select a format for the input mask in the Input Mask dialog box, which supplies the Mask property of the MaskedTextBox control.

Check Boxes

Check boxes allow the user to select (or deselect) an option. In any group of check boxes, any number can be selected. The **Checked property** of a check box is set to False if unchecked or True if checked.

You can write an event procedure for the CheckedChanged event, which executes when the user clicks in the box. In Chapter 4, when you learn about If statements, you can take one action when the box is checked and another action when it is unchecked.

Use the Text property of a check box for the text you want to appear next to the box.

Example Names for Check Boxes

```
boldCheckBox
italicCheckBox
```

Radio Buttons

Use **radio buttons** when only one button of a group may be selected. Any radio buttons that you place directly on the form (not in a group box) function as a group. A group of radio buttons inside a group box function together. The best method is to first create a group box and then create each radio button inside the group box.

The Checked property of a radio button is set to True if selected or to False if unselected. You can write an event procedure to execute when the user selects a radio button using the control's CheckedChanged event. In Chapter 4 you will learn to determine in your code whether or not a button is selected.

Set a radio button's Text property to the text you want to appear next to the button.

Example Names for Radio Buttons

```
redRadioButton
blueRadioButton
```

Picture Boxes

A **PictureBox control** can hold an image. You can set a picture box's **Image property** to a graphic file with an extension of .bmp, .gif, .jpg, .jpeg, .png, .ico, .emf, or .wmf. You first add your images to the project's resources; then you can assign the resource to the Image property of a PictureBox control.

Place a PictureBox control on a form and then select its Image property in the Properties window. Click on the Properties button (Figure 2.4) to display a **Select Resource dialog box** where you can select images that you have already added or add new images (Figure 2.5).

Click on the *Import* button of the *Select Resource* dialog box to add images. An *Open* dialog box appears (Figure 2.6), where you can navigate to your image files. A preview of the image appears in the preview box.

Note: To add files with an ico extension, select *All Files* for the *Files of type* in the *Open* dialog box.

You can use any graphic file (with the proper format) that you have available. You will find many icon files included with Visual Studio. This is the default location:

```
Program Files
 Microsoft Visual Studio 8
   Common7
     Graphics
      icons
```

Note: The Standard and Express editions of Visual Basic .NET do not include the graphic files. You will find many icon files in StudentData\Graphics on the textbook CD.

Figure 2.4

Click on the Image property for a PictureBox control, and a Properties button appears. Click on the Properties button to view the Select Resource dialog box.

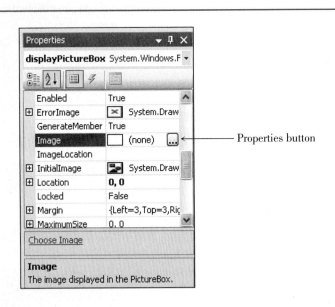

Properties button

Figure 2.5

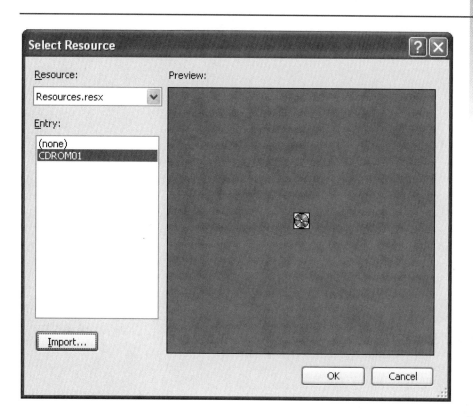

The Select Resource dialog box. Make your selection here for the graphic file you want to appear in the PictureBox control; click Import to add an image to the list.

Figure 2.6

Find the Visual Basic icon files in several folders beneath the Program Files\Microsoft Visual Studio 8\Common7\Graphics\icons folder.

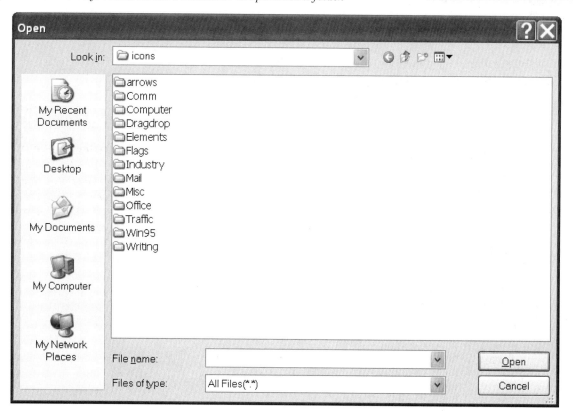

PictureBox controls have several useful properties that you can set at design time or run time. For example, set the **SizeMode property** to *StretchImage* to make the picture resize to fill the control. You can set the **Visible property** to False to make the picture box disappear.

For example, to make a picture box invisible at run time, use this code statement:

```
Me.logoPictureBox.Visible = False
```

Setting a Border and Style

Most controls can appear to be three-dimensional or flat. Labels, text boxes, and picture boxes all have a **BorderStyle property** with choices of *None*, *FixedSingle*, or *Fixed3D*. Text boxes default to *Fixed3D*; labels and picture boxes default to *None*. Of course, you can change the property to the style of your choice.

Feedback 2.1

Create a picture box control that displays an enlarged icon and appears in a 3D box. Make up a name that conforms to this textbook's naming convention.

Property	Setting
Name	
BorderStyle	
SizeMode	
Visible	

Drawing a Line

You can draw a line on a form by using the Label control. You may want to include lines when creating a logo or you may simply want to divide the screen by drawing a line. To create the look of a line, set the AutoSize property of your label to False, set the Text property to blank, set the BorderStyle to *None*, and change the Backcolor to the color you want for the line. You can control the size of the line with the Width and Height properties, located beneath the Size property.

You also can draw a line on the form using the graphics methods. Drawing graphics is covered in Chapter 13.

Working with Multiple Controls

You can select more than one control at a time, which means that you can move the controls as a group, set similar properties for the group, and align the controls.

Selecting Multiple Controls

There are several methods of selecting multiple controls. If the controls are near each other, the easiest technique is to use the mouse to drag a selection box around the controls. Point to a spot that you want to be one corner of a box surrounding the controls, press the mouse button, and drag to the opposite corner (Figure 2.7). When you release the mouse button, the controls will all be selected (Figure 2.8). Note that selected labels and check boxes with AutoSize set to True do not have resizing handles; other selected controls do have resizing handles.

You also can select multiple controls, one at a time. Click on one control to select it, hold down the Ctrl key or the Shift key, and click on the next control. You can keep the Ctrl or Shift key down and continue clicking on controls you wish to select. Ctrl-click (or Shift-click) on a control a second time to deselect it without changing the rest of the group.

When you want to select most of the controls on the form, use a combination of the two methods. Drag a selection box around all of the controls to select them and then Ctrl-click on the ones you want to deselect. You also can select all of the controls using the *Select All* option on the *Edit* menu or its keyboard shortcut: Ctrl + A.

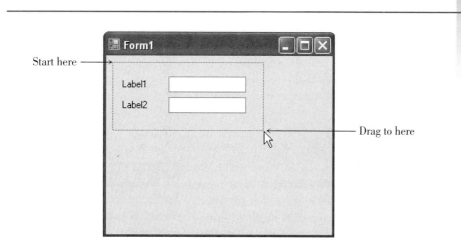

Figure 2.7

Use the pointer to drag a selection box around the controls you wish to select.

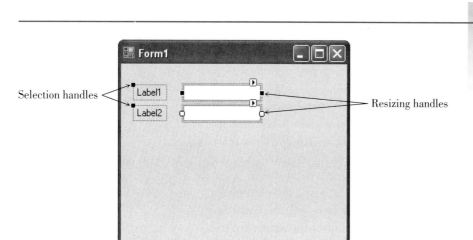

Figure 2.8

When multiple controls are selected, each has resizing handles (if resizable).

Deselecting a Group of Controls

When you are finished working with a group of controls, it's easy to deselect them. Just click anywhere on the form (not on a control) or select another previously unselected control.

Moving Controls as a Group

After selecting multiple controls, you can move them as a group. To do this, point inside one of the selected controls, press the mouse button, and drag the entire group to a new location (Figure 2.9).

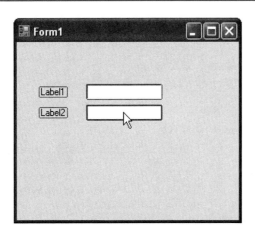

Figure 2.9

Drag a group of selected controls to move the entire group to a new location.

Make sure to read Appendix C for tips and shortcuts for working with controls. ■

Setting Properties for Multiple Controls

You can set some common properties for groups of controls. After selecting the group, check the Properties window. Any properties that appear in the window are shared by all of the controls and can be changed all at once. For example, you may want to set the BorderStyle property for a group of controls to three-dimensional or change the font used for a group of labels. Some properties appear empty; those properties do not share a common value. You can enter a new value that will apply to all selected controls.

Setting the font for the form changes the default font for all controls on the form. ■

Aligning Controls

After you select a group of controls, it is easy to resize and align them using the buttons on the Layout toolbar (Figure 2.10) or the corresponding items on the *Format* menu. Select your group of controls and choose any of the resizing buttons. These can make the controls equal in width, height, or both. Then select another button to align the tops, bottoms, or centers of the controls. You also can move the entire group to a new location.

Note: The alignment options align the group of controls to the control that is active (the sizing handles are white). Referring to Figure 2.8, the lower text box is the active control. To make another selected control the active control, simply click on it.

Figure   2.10

Resize and align multiple controls using the Layout toolbar.

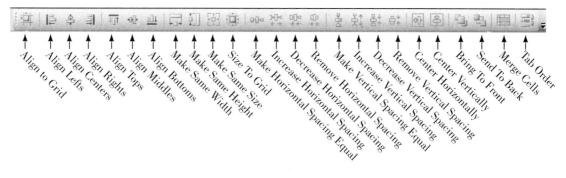

To set the spacing between controls, use the buttons for horizontal and/or vertical spacing. These buttons enable you to create equal spacing between controls or to increase or decrease the space between controls.

Note: If the Layout toolbar is not displaying, select *View / Toolbars / Layout*.

Designing Your Applications for User Convenience

One of the goals of good programming is to create programs that are easy to use. Your user interface should be clear and consistent. One school of thought says that if users misuse a program, it's the fault of the programmer, not the users. Because most of your users will already know how to operate Windows programs, you should strive to make your programs look and behave like other Windows programs. Some of the ways to accomplish this are to make the controls operate in the standard way, define keyboard access keys, set a default button, and make the Tab key work correctly. You also can define ToolTips, which are those small labels that pop up when the user pauses the mouse pointer over a control.

Designing the User Interface

The design of the screen should be easy to understand and "comfortable" for the user. The best way to accomplish these goals is to follow industry standards for the color, size, and placement of controls. Once users become accustomed to a screen design, they will expect (and feel more familiar with) applications that follow the same design criteria.

You should design your applications to match other Windows applications. Microsoft has done extensive program testing with users of different ages, genders, nationalities, and disabilities. We should take advantage of this research and follow their guidelines. Take some time to examine the screens and dialog boxes in Microsoft Office as well as those in Visual Studio.

One recommendation about interface design concerns color. You have probably noticed that Windows applications are predominantly gray. A reason for this choice is that many people are color blind. Also, research shows that gray is easiest for the majority of users. Although you may personally prefer brighter colors, you will stick with gray, or the system palette the user chooses, if you want your applications to look professional.

Colors can indicate to the user what is expected. Use a white background for text boxes to indicate that the user should input information. Use a gray background for labels, which the user cannot change. Labels that will display a message should have a border around them; labels that provide text on the screen should have no border (the default).

Group your controls on the form to aid the user. A good practice is to create group boxes to hold related items, especially those controls that require user input. This visual aid helps the user understand the information that is being presented or requested.

Use a sans serif font on your forms, such as the default MS Sans Serif, and do not make them boldface. Limit large font sizes to a few items, such as the company name.

Defining Keyboard Access Keys

Many people prefer to use the keyboard, rather than a mouse, for most operations. Windows is set up so that most functions can be done with either the keyboard or a mouse. You can make your projects respond to the keyboard by defining **access keys**, also called *hot keys*. For example, in Figure 2.11 you can select the OK button with Alt + o and the Exit button with Alt + x.

Figure 2.11

The underlined character defines an access key. The user can select the OK button by pressing Alt + o and the Exit button with Alt + x.

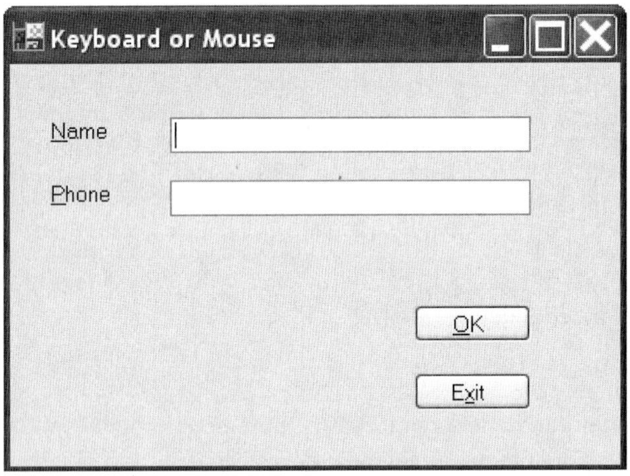

You can set access keys for buttons, radio buttons, and check boxes when you define their Text properties. Type an ampersand (&) in front of the character you want for the access key; Visual Basic underlines the character. You also can set an access key for a label; see "Setting the Tab Order for Controls" later in this chapter.

For examples of access keys on buttons, type the following for the button's Text property:

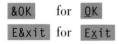

`&OK`   for   `OK`

`E&xit`   for   `Exit`

When you define access keys, you need to watch for several pitfalls. First, try to use the Windows-standard keys whenever possible. For example, use the x of Exit and the S of Save. Second, make sure you don't give two controls the same access key. It confuses the user and doesn't work correctly. Only the next control (from the currently active control) in the tab sequence is activated when the user presses the access key.

Note: To view the access keys on controls or menus in Windows 2000 or Windows XP, you may have to press the Alt key, depending on your system settings.

> **✔TIP**
>
> **U**se two ampersands when you want to make an ampersand appear in the Text property: &Health && Welfare for "Health & Welfare". ■

Setting the Accept and Cancel Buttons

Are you a keyboard user? If so, do you mind having to pick up the mouse and click a button after typing text into a text box? Once a person's fingers are on the keyboard, most people prefer to press the Enter key, rather than to click the mouse. If one of the buttons on the form is the accept button, pressing Enter is the same as clicking the button.

You can make one of your buttons the accept button by setting the **AcceptButton property** of the form to the button name. When the user presses Enter, that button is automatically selected.

You also can select a *cancel button*. The cancel button is the button that is selected when the user presses the Esc key. You can make a button the cancel button by setting the form's **CancelButton property**. An example of a good time to set the CancelButton property is on a form with OK and Cancel buttons. You may want to set the form's AcceptButton to OKButton and the CancelButton property to cancelButton.

Setting the Tab Order for Controls

In Windows programs, one control on the form always has the **focus**. You can see the focus change as you tab from control to control. For controls such as buttons, the focus appears as a thick blue border. For text boxes, the insertion point (also called the *cursor*) appears inside the box.

Some controls can receive the focus; others cannot. For example, text boxes and buttons can receive the focus, but labels and picture boxes cannot.

The Tab Order

Two properties determine whether the focus stops on a control and the order in which the focus moves. Controls that are capable of receiving focus have a **TabStop property**, which you can set to True or False. If you do not want the focus to stop on a control when the user presses the Tab key, set the TabStop property to False.

The **TabIndex property** determines the order the focus moves as the Tab key is pressed. As you create controls on your form, Visual Studio assigns the TabIndex property in sequence. Most of the time that order is correct, but if you want to tab in some other sequence or if you add controls later, you will need to modify the TabIndex properties of your controls.

When your program begins running, the focus is on the control with the lowest TabIndex (usually 0). Since you generally want the insertion point to appear in the first control on the form, its TabIndex should be set to 0. The next control should be set to 1; the next to 2; and so forth.

You may be puzzled by the properties of labels, which have a TabIndex property but not a TabStop. A label cannot receive focus, but it has a location in the tab sequence. This fact allows you to create keyboard access keys for text boxes. When the user types an access key that is in a label, such as Alt + N, the focus jumps to the first TabIndex following the label (the text box). See Figure 2.12.

F i g u r e   2 . 1 2

To use a keyboard access key for a text box, the TabIndex of the label must precede the TabIndex of the text box.

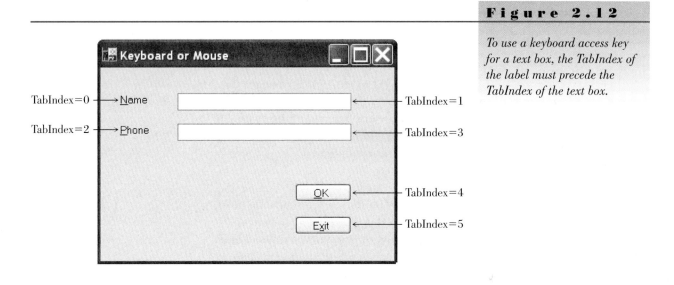

By default, buttons and text boxes have their TabStop property set to True, but radio buttons have their TabStop property set to False. If you want the tab sequence to include radio buttons, you must set their TabStop property to True. Be aware that the behavior of radio buttons in the tab sequence is different from other controls: The Tab key takes you only to one radio button in a group (the selected button), even though all buttons in the group have their TabStop and TabIndex properties set. If you are using the keyboard to select radio buttons, you must tab to the group and then use your Up and Down arrow keys to select the correct button.

☑ **TIP**

Make sure to not have duplicate numbers for the TabIndex properties or duplicate keyboard access keys. The result varies depending on the location of the focus and is very confusing. ■

Setting the Tab Order

To set the tab order for controls, you can set each control's TabIndex property in the Properties window. Or you can use Visual Studio's great feature that helps you set TabIndexes automatically. To use this feature, make sure that the Design window is active and select *View / Tab Order* or click the Tab Order button on the Layout toolbar. (The *Tab Order* item does not appear on the menu and is not available on the Layout toolbar unless the Design window is active.) Small numbers appear in the upper-left corner of each control; these are the current TabIndex properties of the controls. Click first in the control that you want to be TabIndex zero, then click on the control for TabIndex one, then click on the next control until you have set the TabIndex for all controls (Figure 2.13).

When you have finished setting the TabIndex for all controls, the white numbered boxes change to blue. Select *View / Tab Order* again to hide the sequence numbers or press the Esc key. If you make a mistake and want to change the tab order, turn the option off and on again, and start over with TabIndex zero again, or you can keep clicking on the control until the number wraps around to the desired value.

Label cannot receive focus, but Keyboard Hot Keys can access it, if Hot Key used it goes to

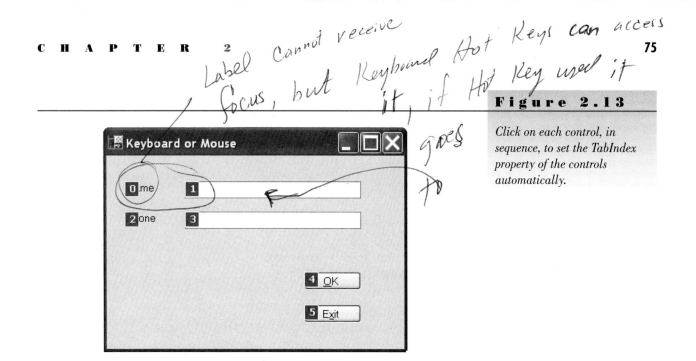

Figure 2.13

Click on each control, in sequence, to set the TabIndex property of the controls automatically.

Setting the Form's Location on the Screen

When your project runs, the form appears in the upper-left corner of the screen by default. You can set the form's screen position by setting the **StartPosition property** of the form. Figure 2.14 shows your choices for the property setting. To center your form on the user's screen, set the StartPosition property to *CenterScreen*.

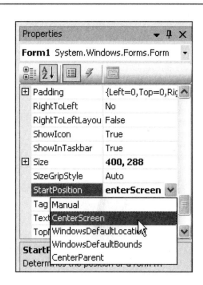

Figure 2.14

Set the StartPosition property of the form to CenterScreen to make the form appear in the center of the user's screen when the program runs.

Creating ToolTips

If you are a Windows user, you probably appreciate and rely on **ToolTips**, those small labels that pop up when you pause your mouse pointer over a toolbar button or control. You can easily add ToolTips to your projects by adding a **ToolTip component** to a form. After you add the component to your form, each of the form's controls has a new property: **ToolTip on ToolTip1**, assuming that you keep the default name, ToolTip1, for the control.

To define ToolTips, select the ToolTip tool from the toolbox (Figure 2.15) and click anywhere on the form or double-click the ToolTip tool in the toolbox. The new control appears in a new pane that opens at the bottom of the Form Designer (Figure 2.16). This pane, called the **component tray**, holds controls that do not have a visual representation at run time. You will see more controls that use the component tray later in this text.

Figure 2.15

Add a ToolTip component to your form; each of the form's controls will have a new property to hold the text of the ToolTip.

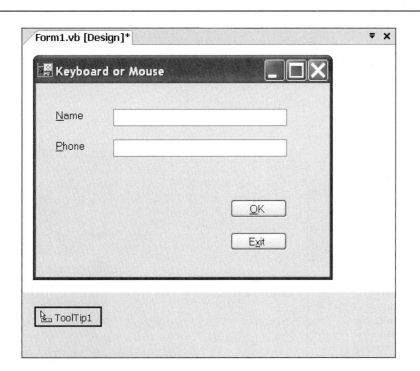

Figure 2.16

The new ToolTip component goes in the component tray at the bottom of the Form Designer window.

After you add the ToolTip component, examine the properties list for other controls on the form, such as buttons, text boxes, labels, radio buttons, check boxes, and even the form itself. Each has a new ToolTip on ToolTip1 property.

Try this example: Add a button to any form and add a ToolTip component. Change the button's Text property to Exit and set its ToolTip on ToolTip1 property to *Close and Exit the program.* Now run the project, point to the Exit button, and pause; the ToolTip will appear (Figure 2.17).

You also can add multiline ToolTips. In the ToolTip on ToolTip1 property, click the drop-down arrow. This drops down a white box in which you enter the text of the ToolTip. Type the first line and press Enter to create a second line; press Ctrl + Enter to accept the text (or click somewhere outside the Property window).

Coding for the Controls

You already know how to set initial properties for controls at design time. You also may want to set some properties in code, as your project executes. You can clear out the contents of text boxes and labels, reset the focus (the active control), change the color of text, or change the text in a ToolTip.

Clearing Text Boxes and Labels

You can clear out the contents of a text box or label by setting the property to an **empty string**. Use "" (no space between the two quotation marks). This empty string is also called a *null string* or *zero-length string*. You also can clear out a text box using the `Clear` method or set the Text property to `String.Empty`. Note that the `Clear` method works for text boxes but not labels.

Examples

```
' Clear the contents of text boxes and labels.
Me.nameTextBox.Text = ""
Me.messageLabel.Text = ""
Me.dataTextBox.Clear()
Me.messageLabel.Text = String.Empty
```

Resetting the Focus

As your program runs, you want the insertion point to appear in the text box where the user is expected to type. The focus should therefore begin in the first text box. But what about later? If you clear the form's text boxes, you should reset the focus to the first text box. The **Focus method** handles this situation. Remember, the convention is Object.Method, so the statement to set the insertion point in the text box called nameTextBox is as follows:

```
' Make the insertion point appear in this text box.
Me.nameTextBox.Focus()
```

Setting the Checked Property of Radio Buttons and Check Boxes

Of course, the purpose of radio buttons and check boxes is to allow the user to make selections. However, at times you need to select or deselect a control in code. You can select or deselect radio buttons and check boxes at design time (to set initial status) or at run time (to respond to an event).

To make a radio button or check box appear selected initially, set its Checked property to True in the Properties window. In code, assign True to its Checked property:

```
' Make button selected.
Me.redRadioButton.Checked = True

' Make check box checked.
Me.displayCheckBox.Checked = True

' Make check box unchecked.
Me.displayCheckBox.Checked = False
```

At times, you need to reset the selected radio button at run time, usually for a second request. You only need to set the Checked property to True for one button of the group; the rest of the buttons in the group will set to False automatically. Recall that only one radio button of a group can be selected at one time.

Setting Visibility at Run Time

You can set the visibility of a control at run time.

```
' Make label invisible.
Me.messageLabel.Visible = False
```

You may want the visibility of a control to depend on the selection a user makes in a check box or radio button. This statement makes the visibility match the check box: When the check box is checked (Checked = True), the label is visible (Visible = True).

```
' Make the visibility of the label match the setting in the check box.
Me.messageLabel.Visible = Me.displayCheckBox.Checked
```

> ## Feedback 2.2
>
> 1. Write the Basic statements to clear the text box called companyTextBox and reset the insertion point into the box.
> 2. Write the Basic statements to clear the label called customerLabel and place the insertion point into a text box called orderTextBox.
> 3. What will be the effect of each of these Basic statements?
>   (a) `Me.printCheckBox.Checked = True`
>   (b) `Me.colorRadioButton.Checked = True`
>   (c) `Me.drawingPictureBox.Visible = False`
>   (d) `Me.locationLabel.BorderStyle = BorderStyle.Fixed3D`
>   (e) `Me.cityLabel.Text = Me.cityTextBox.Text`

Changing the Color of Text

You can change the color of text by changing the **ForeColor property** of a control. Actually, most controls have a ForeColor and a BackColor property. The ForeColor property changes the color of the text; the BackColor property determines the color around the text.

The Color Constants

Visual Basic provides an easy way to specify a large number of colors. These **color constants** are in the Color class. If you type the keyword `Color` and a period in the editor, you can see a full list of colors. Some of the colors are listed below.

```
Color.AliceBlue
Color.AntiqueWhite
Color.Bisque
Color.BlanchedAlmond
Color.Blue
```

Examples

```
Me.nameTextBox.ForeColor = Color.Red
Me.messageLabel.ForeColor = Color.White
```

Changing Multiple Properties of a Control

By now you can see that there are times when you will want to change several properties of a single control. In versions of Visual Basic previous to version 4, you had to write out the entire name (Object.Property) for each statement.

Examples

```
Me.titleTextBox.Visible = True
Me.titleTextBox.ForeColor = Color.White
Me.titleTextBox.Focus()
```

Of course, you can still specify the statements this way, but Visual Basic provides a better way: the **With and End With statements**.

The With and End With Statements—General Form

```
With ObjectName
    ' Statement(s)
End With
```

You specify an object name in the With statement. All subsequent statements until the End With relate to that object.

The With and End With Statements—Example

```
With Me.titleTextBox
   .Visible = True
   .ForeColor = Color.White
   .Focus()
End With
```

The statements beginning with With and ending with End With are called a ***With** block*. The statements inside the block are indented for readability. Although indentation is not required by VB, it *is* required by good programming practices and aids in readability.

The real advantage of using the With statement, rather than spelling out the object for each statement, is that With is more efficient. Your Visual Basic projects will run a little faster if you use With. On a large, complicated project, the savings can be significant.

You can simplify including the Me keyword for the form's controls by using a With block.

```
With Me
   .titleTextBox.Clear()
   .nameTextBox.Clear()
   .resultLabel.Text = ""
End With
```

You also can nest With blocks; that is, one With block can be completely contained inside another. If you choose to nest With blocks, make sure that each block is indented one level, with the innermost block indented the farthest.

```
With Me
   With .titleTextBox
      .Visible = True
      .ForeColor = Color.White
      .Focus()
   End With
End With
```

Concatenating Text

At times you need to join strings of text. For example, you may want to join a literal and a property. You can "tack" one string of characters to the end of another in the process called ***concatenation***. Use an ampersand (&), preceded and followed by a space, between the two strings.

Examples

```
Me.messageLabel.Text = "Your name is: " & Me.nameTextBox.Text
Me.nameAndAddressLabel.Text = Me.nameTextBox.Text & " " & Me.addressTextBox.Text
```

Continuing Long Program Lines

Basic interprets the code on one line as one statement. You can type very long lines in the Editor window; the window scrolls sideways to allow you to keep typing. However, this method is inconvenient; it isn't easy to see the ends of the long lines.

When a Basic statement becomes too long for one line, use a **line-continuation character**. You can type a space and an underscore, press Enter, and continue the statement on the next line. It is OK to indent the continued lines. The only restriction is that the line-continuation character must appear between elements; you cannot place a continuation in the middle of a literal or split the name of an object or property.

> ☑ **TIP**
>
> Although in some situations Basic allows concatenation with the + operator, the practice is not advised. Depending on the contents of the text box, the compiler may interpret the + operator as an addition operator rather than a concatenation operator, giving unpredictable results or an error. ■

Example

```
Me.greetingsLabel.Text = "Greetings " & Me.nameTextBox.Text & ": " & _
    "You have been selected to win a free prize. " & _
    "Just send us $100 for postage and handling."
```

Your Hands-On Programming Example

For this example, you will write a program that uses many of the new controls and topics introduced in this chapter. The program will input the user's name and a message and display the two items concatenated in a label. The user can change the color of the label's text by selecting the color with radio buttons and hide or display the output by checking a check box.

In your program, you will include buttons to display the message in the label, clear the text boxes and label, and exit. Include keyboard access keys; make the Display button the accept button and make the Clear button the cancel button.

Place a logo on the form. Actually, you will place two picture boxes with different sizes for the logo on the form. Each time the user clicks on the logo, it will toggle the large and small versions of the logo.

Add a ToolTip to the logo that says "Click here".

Planning the Project

Sketch a form (Figure 2.18), which your users sign off as meeting their needs.

Note: Although this step may seem unnecessary, having your users sign off is standard programming practice and documents that your users have been involved and have approved the design.

Figure 2.18

A planning sketch of the form for the hands-on programming example.

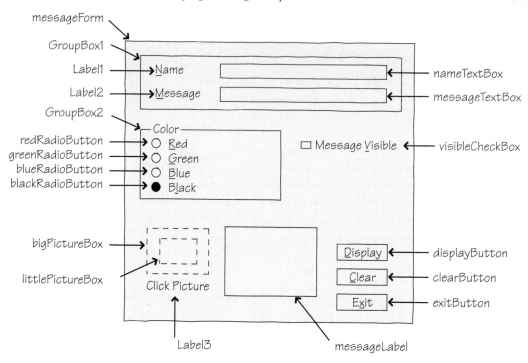

Plan the Objects and Properties

Plan the property settings for the form and for each control.

Object	Property	Setting
messageForm	Name	messageForm
	Text	Message Formatter
	AcceptButton	displayButton
	CancelButton	clearButton
	StartPosition	CenterScreen
GroupBox1	Text	(blank)
Label1	Text	&Name *Hint*: Do not change the name of this label.
nameTextBox	Name	nameTextBox
	Text	(blank)
Label2	Text	&Message
messageTextBox	Name	messageTextBox
	Text	(blank)
GroupBox2	Text	Color
redRadioButton	Name	redRadioButton
	Text	&Red

Object	Property	Setting
greenRadioButton	Name	greenRadioButton
	Text	&Green
blueRadioButton	Name	blueRadioButton
	Text	&Blue
blackRadioButton	Name	blackRadioButton
	Text	B&lack
	Checked	True
visibleCheckBox	Name	visibleCheckBox
	Text	Message &Visible
	Checked	True
bigPictureBox	Name	bigPictureBox
	SizeMode	StretchImage
	Image	Program Files\Microsoft Visual Studio 8\Common7\Graphics\Icons\Computer\ Cdrom01.ico (or StudentData folder on text CD)
	ToolTip on ToolTip1	Click here
	Visible	True
littlePictureBox	Name	littlePictureBox (Note that the two picture boxes are in the same location, one on top of the other.)
	SizeMode	StretchImage
	Image	Program Files\Microsoft Visual Studio 8\Common7\Graphics\Icons\Computer\ Cdrom02.ico (or StudentData folder on text CD)
	ToolTip on ToolTip1	Click here
	Visible	False
Label3	Text	Click Picture
ToolTip1	Name	ToolTip1
messageLabel	Name	messageLabel
	Text	(blank)
	AutoSize	False
	TextAlign	MiddleCenter
	BorderStyle	Fixed Single
displayButton	Name	displayButton
	Text	&Display
clearButton	Name	clearButton
	Text	&Clear
exitButton	Name	exitButton
	Text	E&xit

Plan the Event Procedures You will need event procedures for each button, radio button, check box, and picture box.

Procedure	Actions-Pseudocode
displayButton_Click	Set messageLabel to both the name and message from the text boxes (concatenate them).
clearButton_Click	Clear the two text boxes and label.
	Reset the focus in the first text box.
exitButton_Click	End the project.
redRadioButton_CheckedChanged	Make the ForeColor of messageLabel red.
greenRadioButton_CheckedChanged	Make the ForeColor of messageLabel green.
blueRadioButton_CheckedChanged	Make the ForeColor of messageLabel blue.
blackRadioButton_CheckedChanged	Make the ForeColor of messageLabel black.
bigPictureBox_Click	Make bigPictureBox invisible (Visible = False).
	Make littlePictureBox visible (Visible = True).
littlePictureBox_Click	Make littlePictureBox invisible.
	Make bigPictureBox visible.
visibleCheckBox_CheckedChanged	Make label's visibility match that of check box.

Write the Project Follow the sketch in Figure 2.18 to create the form. Figure 2.19 shows the completed form.

- Set the properties of each object, as you have planned. Make sure to set the tab order of the controls.

- Working from the pseudocode, write each event procedure.

- When you complete the code, thoroughly test the project.

Figure 2.19

The form for the hands-on programming example.

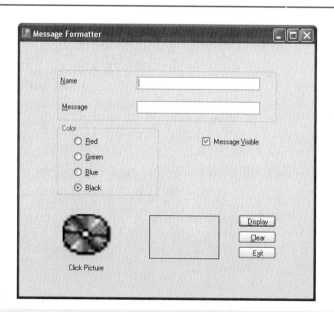

The Project Coding Solution

```
'Project:      Ch02HandsOn
'Programmer:   Bradley/Millspaugh
'Date:         June 2005
'Description:  This project uses labels, text boxes, radio buttons,
'              a check box, images in picture boxes, and buttons
'              to change the display.

Public Class messageForm

    Private Sub displayButton_Click(ByVal sender As System.Object, _
      ByVal e As System.EventArgs) Handles displayButton.Click
        ' Display the text in the message area.

        With Me
           .messageLabel.Text = .nameTextBox.Text & ": " & .messageTextBox.Text
        End With
    End Sub

    Private Sub clearButton_Click(ByVal sender As System.Object, _
      ByVal e As System.EventArgs) Handles clearButton.Click
          'Clear the text controls.

        With Me
          With .nameTextBox
            ' Clear the text box.
            .Clear()
            ' Reset the insertion point.
            .Focus()
          End With
          .messageTextBox.Clear()
          .messageLabel.Text = ""
        End With
    End Sub

    Private Sub exitButton_Click(ByVal sender As System.Object, _
      ByVal e As System.EventArgs) Handles exitButton.Click
        ' Exit the project.

        Me.Close()
    End Sub

    Private Sub blackRadioButton_CheckedChanged(ByVal sender As System.Object, _
      ByVal e As System.EventArgs) Handles blackRadioButton.CheckedChanged
        ' Make the label black.

        Me.messageLabel.ForeColor = Color.Black
    End Sub

    Private Sub blueRadioButton_CheckedChanged(ByVal sender As System.Object, _
      ByVal e As System.EventArgs) Handles blueRadioButton.CheckedChanged
        ' Make the label blue.

        Me.messageLabel.ForeColor = Color.Blue
    End Sub
```

```vbnet
Private Sub greenRadioButton_CheckedChanged(ByVal sender As System.Object, _
  ByVal e As System.EventArgs) Handles greenRadioButton.CheckedChanged
  ' Make the label green.

  Me.messageLabel.ForeColor = Color.Green
End Sub

Private Sub redRadioButton_CheckedChanged(ByVal sender As System.Object, _
  ByVal e As System.EventArgs) Handles redRadioButton.CheckedChanged
  ' Make the label red.

  Me.messageLabel.ForeColor = Color.Red
End Sub

Private Sub bigPictureBox_Click(ByVal sender As System.Object, _
  ByVal e As System.EventArgs) Handles bigPictureBox.Click
  ' Switch the icon.

  Me.bigPictureBox.Visible = False
  Me.littlePictureBox.Visible = True
End Sub

Private Sub littlePictureBox_Click(ByVal sender As System.Object, _
  ByVal e As System.EventArgs) Handles littlePictureBox.Click
  ' Switch the icon.

  With Me
    .littlePictureBox.Visible = False
    .bigPictureBox.Visible = True
  End With
End Sub

Private Sub visibleCheckBox_CheckedChanged(ByVal sender As System.Object, _
  ByVal e As System.EventArgs) Handles visibleCheckBox.CheckedChanged
  ' Set Visibility for messageLabel.

  Me.messageLabel.Visible = visibleCheckBox.Checked
End Sub
End Class
```

Good Programming Habits

1. Always test the tab order on your forms. Fix it if necessary by changing the TabIndex properties of the controls.
2. Provide visual separation for input fields and output fields and always make it clear to the user which are which.
3. Make sure that your forms can be navigated and entered from the keyboard. Always set a default button (AcceptButton property) for every form.
4. To make a label maintain its size regardless of the value of the Text property, set AutoSize to False.
5. To make the text in a text box right justified or centered, set the TextAlign property.
6. You can use the Checked property of a check box to set other properties that must be True or False.

Summary

1. Text boxes are used primarily for user input. The Text property holds the value input by the user. You also can assign a literal to the text property during design time or run time.

2. Group boxes are used as containers for other controls and to group like items on a form.

3. Check boxes and radio buttons allow the user to make choices. In a group of radio buttons, only one can be selected; but in a group of check boxes, any number of the boxes may be selected.

4. The current state of check boxes and radio buttons is stored in the Checked property; the CheckedChanged event occurs when the user clicks on one of the controls.

5. Picture box controls hold a graphic, which is assigned to the Image property. Set the SizeMode property to *StretchImage* to make the image resize to fit the control.

6. The BorderStyle property of many controls can be set to *None*, *FixedSingle*, or *Fixed3D* to determine whether the control appears flat or three-dimensional.

7. Use a Label control to create a line on a form.

8. You can select multiple controls and treat them as a group, including setting common properties at once, moving them, or aligning them.

9. Make your programs easier to use by following Windows standard guidelines for colors, control size and placement, access keys, default and cancel buttons, and tab order.

10. Define keyboard access keys by including an ampersand in the Text property of buttons, radio buttons, check boxes, and labels.

11. Set the AcceptButton property of the form to the desired button so that the user can press Enter to select the button. If you set the form's CancelButton property to a button, that button will be selected when the user presses the Esc key.

12. The focus moves from control to control as the user presses the Tab key. The sequence for tabbing is determined by the TabIndex properties of the controls. The Tab key stops only on controls that have their TabStop property set to True.

13. Add a ToolTip control to a form and then set the ToolTip on ToolTip1 property of a control to make a ToolTip appear when the user pauses the mouse pointer over the control.

14. Clear the Text property of a text box or a label by setting it to an empty string. Text boxes also can be cleared using the `Clear` method.

15. To make a control have the focus, which makes it the active control, use the `Focus` method. Using the `Focus` method of a text box makes the insertion point appear in the text box.

16. You can set the Checked property of a radio button or check box at run time and also set the Visible property of controls in code.

17. Change the color of text in a control by changing its ForeColor property.

18. You can use the color constants to change colors during run time.

19. The `With` and `End With` statements provide an easy way to refer to an object multiple times without repeating the object's name.

20. Joining two strings of text is called *concatenation* and is accomplished by placing an ampersand between the two elements. (A space must precede and follow the ampersand.)

21. Use a space and an underscore to continue a long statement on another line.

Key Terms

AcceptButton property   *73*
access key   *72*
BorderStyle property   *68*
CancelButton property   *73*
check box   *65*
Checked property   *65*
color constant   *79*
component tray   *76*
concatenation   *80*
empty string   *77*
focus   *73*
Focus method   *78*
ForeColor property   *79*
group box   *64*
Image property   *66*
line-continuation character   *81*

PictureBox control   *66*
radio button   *65*
Select Resource dialog box   *66*
SizeMode property   *68*
StartPosition property   *75*
StretchImage   *68*
TabIndex property   *73*
TabStop property   *73*
text box   *63*
Text property   *63*
TextAlign property   *64*
ToolTip   *75*
ToolTip component   *75*
ToolTip on ToolTip1 property   *75*
Visible property   *68*
With and End With statements   *79*

Review Questions

1. You can display program output in a text box or a label. When should you use a text box? When is a label appropriate?
2. How does the behavior of radio buttons differ from the behavior of check boxes?
3. If you want two groups of radio buttons on a form, how can you make the groups operate independently?
4. Explain how to make a graphic appear in a picture box control.
5. Describe how to select several labels and set them all to 12-point font size at once.
6. What is the purpose of keyboard access keys? How can you define them in your project? How do they operate at run time?
7. Explain the purpose of the AcceptButton and CancelButton properties of the form. Give an example of a good use for each.
8. What is a ToolTip? How can you make a ToolTip appear?
9. What is the focus? How can you control which object has the focus?
10. Assume you are testing your project and don't like the initial position of the insertion point. Explain how to make the insertion point appear in a different text box when the program begins.
11. During program execution, you want to return the insertion point to a text box called addressTextBox. What Basic statement will you use to make that happen?

12. What Basic statements will clear the current contents of a text box and a label?
13. How are the `With` and `End With` statements used? Give an example.
14. What is concatenation and when would it be useful?
15. Explain how to continue a very long Basic statement onto another line.

Programming Exercises

Graphics Files: When you install any edition of Visual Basic .NET other than the Standard or Express edition, the graphic files are installed by default in Program Files\Microsoft Visual Studio 8\Common7\Graphics\Icons. You may need to find the exact location of the Graphics folder on your system. If you are using the Standard Edition, the graphic files are not included. You can find the icon files in the StudentData\Graphics folder of the text CD.

 2.1 Create a project that will switch a light bulb on and off, using the user interface shown below as a guide.

Form: Include a text box for the user to enter his or her name. Create two picture boxes, one on top of the other. Only one will be visible at a time. Use radio buttons to select the color of the text in the label beneath the light bulb picture box.

Include keyboard access keys for the radio buttons and the buttons. Make the Exit button the cancel button. Create ToolTips for both light bulb picture boxes; make the ToolTips say "Click here to turn the light on or off."

Project Operation: The user will enter a name and click a radio button for the color (not necessarily in that order). When the light bulb is clicked, display the other picture box and change the message below it. Concatenate the user name to the end of the message.

The two icon files are Lightoff.ico and Lighton.ico and are found in the following folder:

```
Icons\Misc
```

(See the note at the top of the exercises for graphic file locations.)

Coding: In the click event procedure for each Color radio button, change the color of the message below the light bulb.

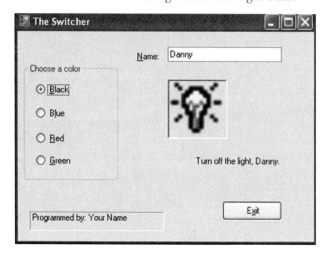
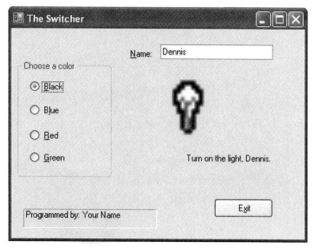

2.2. Write a project to display the flags of four different countries, depending on the setting of the radio buttons. In addition, display the name of the country in the large label under the flag picture box. The user also can choose to display or hide the form's title, the country name, and the name of the programmer. Use check boxes for the display/hide choices.

Include keyboard access keys for all radio buttons, check boxes, and buttons. Make the Exit button the cancel button. Include ToolTips.

You can choose the countries and flags. You will find more than 20 flag icons in Icons\Flags. (See the note at the top of the exercises for graphic file locations.)

Hints: When a project begins running, the focus goes to the control with the lowest TabIndex. Because that control likely is a radio button, one button will appear selected. You must either display the first flag to match the radio button or make the focus begin in a different control. You might consider beginning the focus on the button.

Set the Visible property of a control to the Checked property of the corresponding check box. That way when the check box is selected, the control becomes visible.

Because all three selectable controls will be visible when the project begins, set the Checked property of the three check boxes to True at design time. Set the flag picture boxes to `Visible = False` so they won't appear at startup. (If you plan to display one picture box at startup, its Visible property must be set to True.)

Rather than stacking the picture boxes as was done in the chapter example, consider another method of setting up the four flag picture boxes. Try placing four small invisible flag icons near the bottom of the form. When the user selects a different country's flag, set the Image property of the large flag picture box to the Image property of one of the small, invisible picture boxes. For example:

```
flagPictureBox.Image = mexicoPictureBox.Image
```

Make sure to set the SizeMode property of the large picture box control to *StretchImage.*

2.3 Write a project to display a weather report. The user can choose one of the radio buttons and display an icon and a message. The message should give the weather report in words and include the person's name (taken from the text box at the top of the form). For example, if the user chooses the Sunny button, you might display "It looks like sunny weather today, John" (assuming that the user entered *John* in the text box).

Include keyboard access keys for the button and radio buttons. Make the Exit button the cancel button and include ToolTips.

You might consider the method of hiding and displaying picture boxes described in the hints for exercise 2. The four icons displayed are in the Icons\Elements folder and are called Cloud.ico, Rain.ico, Snow.ico, and Sun.ico. (See the note at the top of the exercises for graphic file locations.)

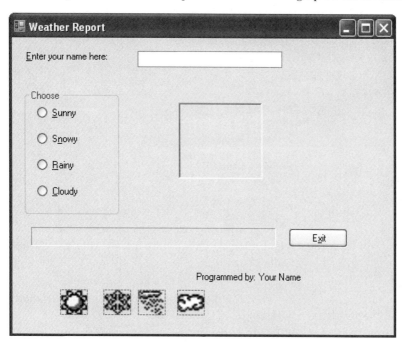

2.4 Write a project that will input the user name and display a message of the day in a label, along with the user's name. Include buttons (with keyboard access keys) for Display, Clear, and Exit. Make the Display button the accept button and the Clear button the cancel button. Include ToolTips where appropriate.

Include a group of radio buttons for users to select the color of the message. Give them a choice of four different colors.

Make your form display a changeable picture box. You can use the happy face icon files or any other images you have available (Icons\Misc\Face01.ico, Face02.ico, and Face03.ico). (See the note at the top of the exercises for graphic file locations.)

You may choose to have only one message of the day, or you can have several that the user can select with radio buttons. You might want to choose messages that go with the different face icons.

2.5 Create a project that allows the user to input information and then display the lines of output for a mailing label.

Remember that fields to be input by the user require text boxes, but display the output in labels. Use text boxes for the first name, last name, street address, city, state, and ZIP code; give meaningful names to the text boxes and set the initial Text properties to blank. Add appropriate labels to each text box to tell the user which data will be entered into each box and also provide ToolTips.

Use buttons for Display Label Info, Clear, and Exit. Make the Display button the accept button and the Clear button the cancel button.

Use three labels for displaying the information for Line 1, Line 2, and Line 3.

Use a masked text box for the ZIP code.

A click event on the Display Label Info button will display the following:

Line 1—The first name and last name concatenated together with a space between.
Line 2—The street address.
Line 3—The city, state, and ZIP code concatenated together. (Make sure to concatenate a comma and a space between the city and state, using ", " and two spaces between the state and ZIP code.)

Case Studies

VB Mail Order

Design and code a project that displays shipping information.

Use an appropriate image in a picture box in the upper-left corner of the form.

Use text boxes with identifying labels for Catalog Code, Page Number, and Part Number.

Use two groups of radio buttons on the form; enclose each group in a group box. The first group box should have a Text property of *Shipping* and contain radio buttons for Express and Ground. Make the second group box have a Text property of *Payment Type* and include radio buttons for Charge, COD, and Money Order.

Use a check box for New Customer.

Add buttons for Clear and Exit. Make the Clear button the cancel button.

Add ToolTips as appropriate.

VB Auto Center

Modify the project from the Chapter 1 VB Auto Center case study, replacing the buttons with images in picture boxes. (See "Copy and Move Projects" in Appendix C for help in making a copy of the Chapter 1 project to use for this project.) Above each picture box, place a label that indicates which department or command the graphic represents. A click on a picture box will produce the appropriate information in the special notices label.

Add an image in a picture box that clears the special notices label. Include a ToolTip for each picture box to help the user understand the purpose of the graphic.

Add radio buttons that will allow the user to view the special notices label in different colors.

Include a check box labeled Hours. When the check box is selected, a new label will display the message "Open 24 Hours—7 days a week".

By default, the images are all stored in the Icons folder. (See the note at the top of the exercises for graphic file locations.)

Department/Command	Image for Picture box
Auto Sales	Industry\Cars.ico
Service Center	Industry\Wrench.ico
Detail Shop	Elements\Water.ico
Employment Opportunities	Mail\MAIL12.ico
Exit	Computer\MSGBOX01.ico

Video Bonanza

Design and code a project that displays the location of videos using radio buttons. Use a radio button for each of the movie categories and a label to display the aisle number. A check box will allow the user to display or hide a message for members. When the check box is selected, a message stating "All Members Receive a 10% Discount" will appear.

Include buttons (with keyboard access keys) for Clear and Exit. The Clear button should be set as the accept button and the Exit as the cancel button.

Place a label on the form in a 24-point font that reads "Video Bonanza". Use a line to separate the label from the rest of the interface. Include an image in a picture box.

Radio Button	Location
Comedy	Aisle 1
Drama	Aisle 2
Action	Aisle 3
Sci-Fi	Aisle 4
Horror	Aisle 5

Very Very Boards

Create a project to display an advertising screen for Very Very Boards. Include the company name, a slogan (use "The very best in boards" or make up your own slogan), and a graphic image for a logo. You may use the graphic included with the text materials (Skateboard.gif) or one of your own.

Allow the user to select the color for the slogan text using radio buttons. Additionally, the user may choose to display or hide the company name, the slogan, and the logo. Use check boxes for the display options so that the user can select each option independently.

Include keyboard access keys for the radio buttons and the buttons. Make the Exit button the cancel button. Create ToolTips for the company name ("Our company name"), the slogan ("Our slogan"), and the logo ("Our logo").

When the project begins execution, the slogan text should be red and the Red radio button selected. When the user selects a new color, change the color of the slogan text to match.

Each of the check boxes must appear selected initially, since the company name, slogan, logo, and programmer name display when the form appears. Each time the user selects or deselects a check box, make the corresponding item display or hide.

Make the form appear in the center of the screen.

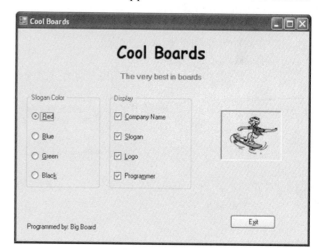

3

Variables, Constants, and Calculations

at the completion of this chapter, you will be able to . . .

1. Distinguish between variables, constants, and controls.

2. Differentiate among the various data types.

3. Apply naming conventions incorporating standards and indicating the data type.

4. Declare variables and constants.

5. Select the appropriate scope for a variable.

6. Convert text input to numeric values.

7. Perform calculations using variables and constants.

8. Convert between numeric data types using implicit and explicit conversions.

9. Round decimal values using the `Decimal.Round` method.

10. Format values for output using the `ToString` method.

11. Use `Try/Catch` blocks for error handling.

12. Display message boxes with error messages.

13. Accumulate sums and generate counts.

In this chapter you will learn to do calculations in Visual Basic. You will start with text values input by the user, convert them to numeric values, and perform calculations on them. You will also learn to format the results of your calculations and display them for the user.

Although the calculations themselves are quite simple (addition, subtraction, multiplication, and division), there are some important issues to discuss first. You must learn about variables and constants, the various types of data used by Visual Basic, and how and where to declare variables and constants. Variables are declared differently, depending on where you want to use them and how long you need to retain their values.

The code below is a small preview to show the calculation of the product of two text boxes. The first group of statements (the Dims) declares the variables and their data types. The second group of statements converts the text box contents to numeric and places the values into the variables. The last line performs the multiplication and places the result into a variable. The following sections of this chapter describe how to set up your code for calculations.

```
' Dimension the variables.
Dim quantityInteger As Integer
Dim priceDecimal, extendedPriceDecimal As Decimal

' Convert input text to numeric and assign values to variables.
quantityInteger = Integer.Parse(Me.quantityTextBox.Text)
priceDecimal = Decimal.Parse(Me.priceTextBox.Text)

' Calculate the product.
extendedPriceDecimal = quantityInteger * priceDecimal
```

Data—Variables and Constants

So far, all data you have used in your projects have been properties of objects. You have worked with the Text property of text boxes and labels. Now you will work with values that are not properties. Basic allows you to set up locations in memory and give each location a name. You can visualize each memory location as a scratch pad; the contents of the scratch pad can change as the need arises. In this example, the memory location is called *maximumInteger*.

```
maximumInteger = 100
```

maximumInteger
100

After executing this statement, the value of maximumInteger is 100. You can change the value of maximumInteger, use it in calculations, or display it in a control.

In the preceding example, the memory location called maximumInteger is a **variable**. Memory locations that hold data that can be changed during project execution are called *variables*; locations that hold data that cannot change during execution are called **constants**. For example, the customer's name will vary as the information for each individual is processed. However, the name of the company and the sales tax rate will remain the same (at least for that day).

When you declare a variable or a **named constant**, Visual Basic reserves an area of memory and assigns it a name, called an *identifier*. You specify identifier names according to the rules of Basic as well as some recommended naming conventions.

The **declaration** statements establish your project's variables and constants, give them names, and specify the type of data they will hold. The statements are not considered executable; that is, they are not executed in the flow of instructions during program execution. An exception to this rule occurs when you initialize a variable on the same line as the declaration.

Here are some sample declaration statements:

```
' Declare a string variable.
Dim nameString As String

' Declare integer variables.
Dim counterInteger As Integer
Dim maxInteger As Integer = 100

' Declare a named constant.
Const DISCOUNT_RATE_Decimal As Decimal = .15D
```

The next few sections describe the data types, the rules for naming variables and constants, and the format of the declarations.

Data Types

The **data type** of a variable or constant indicates what type of information will be stored in the allocated memory space: perhaps a name, a dollar amount, a date, or a total. The data types in VB .NET are actually classes and the variables are objects of the class. Table 3.1 shows the VB data types.

The Visual Basic Data Types, the Kind of Data Each Type Holds, and the Amount of Memory Allocated for Each

Table 3.1

Data Type	Use For	Storage Size in bytes
Boolean	True or False values	2
Byte	0 to 255, binary data	1
Char	Single Unicode character	2
Date	1/1/0001 through 12/31/9999	8
Decimal	Decimal fractions, such as dollars and cents	16
Single	Single-precision floating-point numbers with six digits of accuracy	4
Double	Double-precision floating-point numbers with 14 digits of accuracy	8
Short	Small integer in the range −32,768 to 32,767	2
Integer	Whole numbers in the range −2,147,483,648 to +2,147,483,647	4
Long	Larger whole numbers	8
String	Alphanumeric data: letters, digits, and other characters	Varies
Object	Any type of data	4

The most common types of variables and constants we will use are String, Integer, and Decimal. When deciding which data type to use, follow this guideline: If the data will be used in a calculation, then it must be numeric (usually Integer or Decimal); if it is not used in a calculation, it will be String. Use Decimal as the data type for any decimal fractions in business applications; Single and Double data types are generally used in scientific applications.

Consider the following examples:

Contents	Data Type	Reason
Social Security number	String	Not used in a calculation.
Pay rate	Decimal	Used in a calculation; contains a decimal point.
Hours worked	Decimal	Used in a calculation; may contain a decimal point. (Decimal can be used for any decimal fraction, not just dollars.)
Phone number	String	Not used in a calculation.
Quantity	Integer	Used in calculations; contains a whole number.

Naming Rules

A programmer has to name (identify) the variables and named constants that will be used in a project. Basic requires identifiers for variables and named constants to follow these rules: names may consist of letters, digits, and underscores; they must begin with a letter; they cannot contain any spaces or periods; and they may not be reserved words. (Reserved words, also called *keywords*, are words to which Basic has assigned some meaning, such as *print*, *name*, and *value*.)

Identifiers in VB are not case sensitive. Therefore, the names sumInteger, SumInteger, suminteger, and SUMINTEGER all refer to the same variable.

Note: In some earlier versions of VB, the maximum length of an identifier was 255 characters. In VB .NET, you can forget about the length limit, since the maximum is now 16,383 characters.

Naming Conventions

When naming variables and constants, you *must* follow the rules of Basic. In addition, you *should* follow some naming conventions. Conventions are the guidelines that separate good names from bad (or not so good) names. The meaning and use of all identifiers should always be clear.

Just as we established conventions for naming objects in Chapter 1, in this chapter we adopt conventions for naming variables and constants. The following conventions are widely used in the programming industry:

1. *Identifiers must be meaningful.* Choose a name that clearly indicates its purpose. Do not abbreviate unless the meaning is obvious and do not use very short identifiers, such as *X* or *Y*.
2. *Include the class (data type) of the variable.*

3. Begin with a lowercase letter and then capitalize each successive word of the name. Always use mixed case for variables; uppercase for constants.

Sample Identifiers

Field of Data	Possible Identifier
Social Security number	socialSecurityNumberString
Pay rate	payRateDecimal
Hours worked	hoursWorkedDecimal
Phone number	phoneNumberString
Quantity	quantityInteger
Tax rate (constant)	TAX_RATE_Decimal
Quota (constant)	QUOTA_Integer
Population	populationLong

Feedback 3.1

Indicate whether each of the following identifiers conforms to the rules of Basic and to the naming conventions. If the identifier is invalid, give the reason. Remember, the answers to Feedback questions are found in Appendix A.

1. omitted
2. #SoldInteger
3. Number Sold Integer
4. Number.Sold.Integer
5. amount$Decimal
6. Sub
7. subString
8. Text
9. maximum
10. minimumRateDecimal
11. maximumCheckDecimal
12. companyNameString

Constants: Named and Intrinsic

Constants provide a way to use words to describe a value that doesn't change. In Chapter 2 you used the Visual Studio constants Color.Blue, Color.Red, Color.Yellow, and so on. Those constants are built into the environment and called *intrinsic constants*; you don't need to define them anywhere. The constants that you define for yourself are called *named constants*.

Named Constants

You declare named constants using the keyword Const. You give the constant a name, a data type, and a value. Once a value is declared as a constant, its value cannot be changed during the execution of the project. The data type that you declare and the data type of the value must match. For example, if you declare an integer constant, you must give it an integer value.

You will find two important advantages to using named constants rather than the actual values in code. The code is easier to read; for example, seeing the identifier MAXIMUM_PAY_Decimal is more meaningful than seeing a number, such as 1,000. In addition, if you need to change the value at a later time, you need to change the constant declaration only once; you do not have to change every reference to it throughout the code.

Const Statement—General Form

```
Const Identifier [As Datatype] = Value
```

Naming conventions for constants require that you include the data type in the name as well as the As clause that actually declares the data type. Use all uppercase for the name with individual words separated by underscores.

This example sets the company name, address, and the sales tax rate as constants:

Const Statement—Examples

```
Const COMPANY_NAME_String As String = "R 'n R for Reading 'n Refreshment"
Const COMPANY_ADDRESS_String As String = "101 S. Main Street"
Const SALES_TAX_RATE_Decimal As Decimal = .08D
```

Assigning Values to Constants

The values you assign to constants must follow certain rules. You have already seen that a text (string) value must be enclosed in quotation marks; numeric values are not enclosed. However, you must be aware of some additional rules.

Numeric constants may contain only the digits (0-9), a decimal point, and a sign (+ or –) at the left side. You cannot include a comma, dollar sign, any other special characters, or a sign at the right side. You can declare the data type of numeric constants by appending a type-declaration character. If you do not append a type-declaration character to a numeric constant, any whole number is assumed to be Integer and any fractional value is assumed to be Double. The type-declaration characters are

Decimal	D
Double	R
Integer	I
Long	L
Short	S
Single	F

String literals (also called string constants) may contain letters, digits, and special characters, such as $#@%&*. You may have a problem when you want to include quotation marks inside a string literal since quotation marks enclose the literal. The solution is to use two quotation marks together inside the literal. Visual Basic will interpret the pair as one symbol. For example, "He said, ""I like it.""" produces this string: He said, "I like it."

Although you can use numeric digits inside a string literal, remember that these numbers are text and cannot be used for calculations.

The string values are referred to as ***string literals*** because they contain exactly (literally) whatever is inside the quotation marks.

The following table lists example constants.

Data Type	Constant Value Example
Integer	5 125 2170 2000 −100 12345678I
Single	101.25F −5.0F
Decimal	850.50D −100D
Double	52875.8 52875.8R −52875.8R
Long	134257987L −8250758L
String literals	"Visual Basic" "ABC Incorporated" "1415 J Street" "102" "She said ""Hello."""

Intrinsic Constants

Intrinsic constants are system-defined constants. Many sets of intrinsic constants are declared in system class libraries and are available for use in your VB programs. For example, the color constants that you used in Chapter 2 are intrinsic constants.

You must specify the class name or group name as well as the constant name when you use intrinsic constants. For example, Color.Red is the constant "Red" in the class "Color". Later in this chapter you will learn to use constants from the MessageBox class for displaying message boxes to the user.

Declaring Variables

Although there are several ways to declare a variable, inside a procedure you must use the Dim statement. Later in this chapter you will learn to declare variables outside of a procedure, using the Public, Private, or Dim statement.

Declaration Statements—General Form

```
Public|Private|Dim Identifier [As Datatype]
```

If you omit the optional data type, the variable's type defaults to Object. It is recommended practice to *always* declare the data type.

Note: If Option Strict is On, you receive a syntax error if you omit the data type.

Declaration Statement—Examples

Examples

```
Dim customerNameString As String
Private totalSoldInteger As Integer
Dim temperatureSingle As Single
Dim priceDecimal As Decimal
Private costDecimal As Decimal
```

The reserved word `Dim` is really short for dimension, which means "size." When you declare a variable, the amount of memory reserved depends on its data type. Refer to Table 3.1 (page 97) for the size of each data type.

You also can declare several variables in one statement; the data type you declare in the `As` clause applies to all of the variables on the line. Separate the variable names with commas. Here are some sample declarations:

```
Dim nameString, addressString, phoneString As String
Dim priceDecimal, totalDecimal As Decimal
```

Entering Declaration Statements

Visual Basic's IntelliSense feature helps you enter `Private`, `Public`, and `Dim` statements. After you type the space that follows `VariableName As`, a list pops up (Figure 3.1). This list shows the possible entries to complete the statement. The easiest way to complete the statement is to begin typing the correct entry; the list automatically scrolls to the correct section (Figure 3.2). When the correct entry is highlighted, press Enter, Tab, or the spacebar to select the entry, or double-click if you prefer using the mouse.

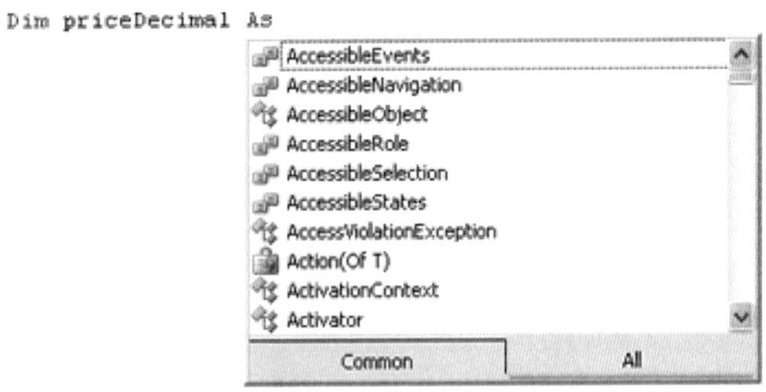

Figure 3.1

As soon as you type the space after As, *the IntelliSense menu pops up. You can make a selection from the list with your mouse or the keyboard.*

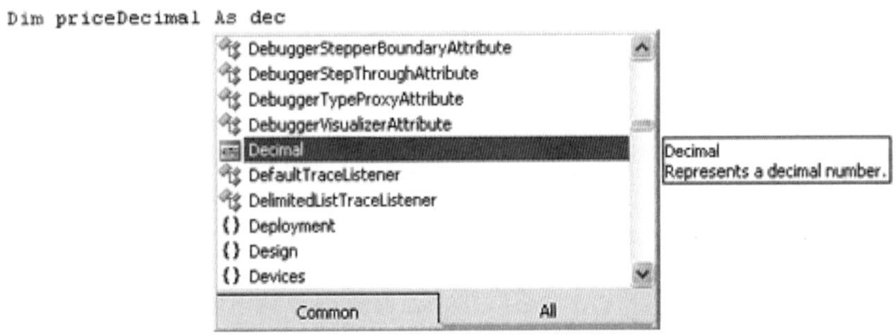

Figure 3.2

Type the first few characters of the data type and the IntelliSense list quickly scrolls to the correct section. When the correct word is highlighted, press Enter, Tab, or the spacebar to select the entry.

Note: Some people find the IntelliSense feature annoying rather than helpful. You can turn off the feature by selecting *Tools / Options*. In the *Options* dialog box, make sure that *Show All Settings* is selected and choose *Text Editor / Basic / General*; deselect *Auto list members* and *Parameter information*.

Feedback 3.2

Write a declaration using the `Dim` statement for the following situations; make up an appropriate variable identifier.

1. You need variables for payroll processing to store the following:
   (a) Number of hours, which can hold a decimal value.
   (b) Employee's name.
   (c) Department number (not used in calculations).
2. You need variables for inventory control to store the following:
   (a) Integer quantity.
   (b) Description of the item.
   (c) Part number.
   (d) Cost.
   (e) Selling price.

Scope and Lifetime of Variables

A variable may exist and be visible for an entire project, for only one form, or for only one procedure. The visibility of a variable is referred to as its **scope**. Visibility really means "this variable can be used or 'seen' in this location." The scope is said to be namespace, module level, local, or block. A **namespace-level variable** may be used in all procedures of the namespace, which is generally the entire project. **Module-level variables** are accessible from all procedures of a form. A **local variable** may be used only within the procedure in which it is declared and a **block-level variable** is used only within a block of code inside a procedure.

You declare the scope of a variable by choosing where to place the declaration statement.

Note: Previous versions of VB and some other programming languages refer to namespace variables as *global variables*.

Variable Lifetime

When you create a variable, you must be aware of its **lifetime**. The *lifetime* of a variable is the period of time that the variable exists. The lifetime of a local or block variable is normally one execution of a procedure. For example, each time you execute a sub procedure, the local `Dim` statements are executed. Each variable is created as a "fresh" new one, with an initial value of 0 for numeric variables and an empty string for string variables. When the procedure finishes, its variables disappear; that is, their memory locations are released.

The lifetime of a module-level variable is the entire time the form is loaded, generally the lifetime of the entire project. If you want to maintain the value of a variable for multiple executions of a procedure—for example, to calculate a running total—you must use a module-level variable (or a variable declared as `Static`, which is discussed in Chapter 7).

Local Declarations

Any variable that you declare inside a procedure is local in scope, which means that it is known only to that procedure. Use the keyword `Dim` for local declarations. A `Dim` statement may appear anywhere inside the procedure as long as it appears prior to the first use of the variable in a statement. However, good programming practices dictate that all `Dims` appear at the top of the procedure, prior to all other code statements (after the remarks).

```
' Module-level declarations.
Const DISCOUNT_RATE_Decimal As Decimal = 0.15D

Private Sub calculateButton_Click(ByVal sender As System.Object, _
    ByVal e As System.EventArgs) _
    Handles calculateButton.Click)
    ' Calculate the price and discount.
    Dim quantityInteger As Integer
    Dim priceDecimal, extendedPriceDecimal, discountDecimal, discountedPriceDecimal _
      As Decimal

    ' Convert input values to numeric variables.
    quantityInteger = Integer.Parse(Me.quantityTextBox.Text)
    priceDecimal = Decimal.Parse(Me.priceTextBox.Text)

    ' Calculate values.
    extendedPriceDecimal = quantityInteger * priceDecimal
    discountDecimal = Decimal.Round( _
      (extendedPriceDecimal * DISCOUNT_RATE_Decimal), 2)
    discountedPriceDecimal = extendedPriceDecimal – discountDecimal
```

Notice the `Const` statement in the preceding example. Although you can declare named constants to be local, block, module level, or namespace in scope, just as you can variables, good programming practices dictate that constants should be declared at the module level. This technique places all constant declarations at the top of the code and makes them easy to find in case you need to make changes.

Note: A new feature of VB 2005 marks any variables that you declare but do not use with a gray squiggle underline. You can ignore the marks if you have just declared the variable and not yet written the code.

Module-Level Declarations

At times you need to be able to use a variable or constant in more than one procedure of a form. When you declare a variable or constant as module level, you can use it anywhere in that form. When you write module-level declarations, you can use the `Dim`, `Public`, or `Private` keyword. The preferred practice is to use either the `Public` or `Private` keyword for module-level variables rather than `Dim`. In Chapter 6 you will learn how and why to choose `Public` or `Private`. Until then we will declare all module-level variables using the `Private` keyword.

Place the declarations (`Private` or `Const`) for module-level variables and constants in the Declarations section of the form. (Recall that you have been using the Declarations section for remarks since Chapter 1.) **If you wish to accumulate a sum or count items for multiple executions of a procedure, you should declare the variable at the module level.**

Figure 3.3 illustrates the locations for coding local variables and module-level variables.

Figure 3.3

The variables you declare inside a procedure are local. Variables that you declare in the Declarations section are module level.

```
(Declarations section)

Private ModuleLevelVariables
Const NamedConstants

Private Sub calculateButton_Click
    Dim LocalVariables

    ...
End Sub

Private Sub summaryButton_Click
    Dim LocalVariables

    ...
End Sub

Private Sub clearButton_Click
    Dim LocalVariables

    ...
End Sub
```

```
' Declarations section of a form.

' Dimension module-level variables and constants.
Private quantitySumInteger, saleCountInteger As Integer
Private discountSumDecimal As Decimal
Const MAXIMUM_DISCOUNT_Decimal As Decimal = 100.0D
```

Coding Module-Level Declarations

To enter module-level declarations, you must be in the Editor window at the top of your code (Figure 3.4). Place the `Private` and `Const` statements after the Class declaration but before your first procedure.

Figure 3.4

Code module-level declarations in the Declarations section at the top of your code.

```
'                Uses variables, constants, calculations, error
'                handling, and a message box to the user.
'Folder:         Ch03HandsOn

Public Class bookSaleForm

    ' Dimension module-level variables and constants.
    Private quantitySumInteger, saleCountInteger As Integer
    Private discountSumDecimal, discountedPriceSumDecimal As Decimal
    Const DISCOUNT_RATE_Decimal As Decimal = 0.15D

    Private Sub calculateButton_Click(ByVal sender As System.Object, _
      ByVal e As System.EventArgs) Handles calculateButton.Click
        ' Calculate the price and discount.
```

Block-Level and Namespace-Level Declarations

You won't use block-level or namespace-level declarations in this chapter. Block-level variables and constants have a scope of a block of code, such as `If` / `End If` or `Do` / `Loop`. These statements are covered later in this text.

Namespace-level variables and constants can sometimes be useful when a project has multiple forms and/or modules, but good programming practices exclude the use of namespace-level variables.

TIP

If you use the Me object on all of your controls, it is easy to distinguish between controls and variables in your code. ∎

Feedback 3.3

Write the declarations (`Dim`, `Private`, or `Const` statements) for each of the following situations and indicate where each statement will appear.

1. The total of the payroll that will be needed in a Calculate event procedure and in a Summary event procedure.
2. The sales tax rate that cannot be changed during execution of the program but will be used by multiple procedures.
3. The number of participants that are being counted in the Calculate event procedure but not displayed until the Summary event procedure.

Calculations

In programming you can perform calculations with variables, with constants, and with the properties of certain objects. The properties you will use, such as the Text property of a text box or a label, are usually strings of text characters. These character strings, such as "Howdy" or "12345", cannot be used directly in calculations unless you first convert them to the correct data type.

Converting Strings to a Numeric Data Type

You can use a `Parse` method to convert the Text property of a control to its numeric form before you use the value in a calculation. The class that you use depends on the data type of the variable to which you are assigning the value. For example, to convert text to an integer, use the `Integer.Parse` method; to convert to a decimal value, use `Decimal.Parse`. Pass the text string that you want to convert as an **argument** of the `Parse` method.

```
' Convert input values to numeric variables.
quantityInteger = Integer.Parse(Me.quantityTextBox.Text)
priceDecimal = Decimal.Parse(Me.priceTextBox.Text)

' Calculate the extended price.
extendedPriceDecimal = quantityInteger * priceDecimal
```

Converting from one data type to another is sometimes called *casting*. In the preceding example, the String value from the quantityTextBox.Text property is cast into an Integer data type and the String from priceTextBox.Text is cast into a Decimal data type.

Using the Parse Methods

As you know, objects have methods that perform actions, such as the `Focus` method for a text box. The data types that you use to declare variables are classes, which have properties and methods. Each of the numeric data type classes has a `Parse` method, which you will use to convert text strings into the correct numeric value for that type. The Decimal class has a `Parse` method that converts the value inside the parentheses to a decimal value while the Integer class has a `Parse` method to convert the value to an integer.

The Parse Methods—General Forms

```
' Convert to Integer.
Integer.Parse(StringToConvert)

' Convert to Decimal
Decimal.Parse(StringToConvert)
```

The expression you wish to convert can be the property of a control, a string variable, or a string constant. The `Parse` method returns (produces) a value that can be used as a part of a statement, such as the assignment statements in the following examples.

The Parse Methods—Examples

```
quantityInteger = Integer.Parse(Me.quantityTextBox.Text)
priceDecimal = Decimal.Parse(Me.priceTextBox.Text)
wholeNumberInteger = Integer.Parse(digitString)
```

The `Parse` methods examine the value stored in the argument and attempt to convert it to a number in a process called *parsing*, which means to pick apart, character by character, and convert to another format.

When a `Parse` method encounters a value that it cannot parse to a number, such as a blank or nonnumeric character, an error occurs. You will learn how to avoid those errors later in this chapter in the section titled "Handling Exceptions."

You will use the `Integer.Parse` and `Decimal.Parse` methods for most of your programs. But in case you need to convert to Long, Single, or Double, VB also has a `Parse` method for each data type class.

Converting to String

When you assign a value to a variable, you must take care to assign like types. For example, you assign an integer value to an Integer variable and a decimal value to a Decimal variable. Any value that you assign to a String variable or the Text property of a control must be string. You can convert any of the numeric data types to a string value using the `ToString` method. Later in this chapter you will learn to format numbers for output using parameters of the `ToString` method.

Note: The rule about assigning only like types has some exceptions. See "Implicit Conversions" later in this chapter.

Examples

```
resultTextBox.Text = resultDecimal.ToString()
countTextBox.Text = countInteger.ToString()
idString = idInteger.ToString()
```

Arithmetic Operations

The arithmetic operations you can perform in Visual Basic include addition, subtraction, multiplication, division, integer division, modulus, and exponentiation.

Operator	Operation
+	Addition
–	Subtraction
*	Multiplication
/	Division
\	Integer division
Mod	Modulus—Remainder of division
^	Exponentiation

The first four operations are self-explanatory, but you may not be familiar with \, Mod, or ^.

Integer Division (\)

Use integer division (\) to divide one integer by another, giving an integer result and truncating (dropping) any remainder. For example, if totalMinutesInteger = 150, then

```
hoursInteger = totalMinutesInteger \ 60
```

returns 2 for hoursInteger.

Mod

The Mod operator returns the remainder of a division operation. For example, if totalMinutesInteger = 150, then

```
minutesInteger = totalMinutesInteger Mod 60
```

returns 30 for minutesInteger.

Exponentiation (^)

The exponentiation operator (^) raises a number to the power specified and returns (produces) a result of the Double data type. The following are examples of exponentiation.

```
squaredDouble = numberDecimal ^ 2     ' Square the number--Raise to the 2nd power.
cubedDouble = numberDecimal ^ 3       ' Cube the number--Raise to the 3rd power.
```

Order of Operations

The order in which operations are performed determines the result. Consider the expression 3 + 4 * 2. What is the result? If the addition is done first, the result is 14. However, if the multiplication is done first, the result is 11.

The hierarchy of operations, or **order of precedence**, in arithmetic expressions from highest to lowest is

1. Any operation inside parentheses
2. Exponentiation
3. Multiplication and division
4. Integer division
5. Modulus
6. Addition and subtraction

In the previous example, the multiplication is performed before the addition, yielding a result of 11. To change the order of evaluation, use parentheses. The expression

(3 + 4) * 2

will yield 14 as the result. One set of parentheses may be used inside another set. In that case, the parentheses are said to be *nested*. The following is an example of nested parentheses:

```
((score1Integer + score2Integer + score3Integer) / 3) * 1.2
```

Extra parentheses can always be used for clarity. The expressions

```
2 * costDecimal * rateDecimal
```

and

```
(2 * costDecimal) * rateDecimal
```

are equivalent, but the second is easier to understand.

Multiple operations at the same level (such as multiplication and division) are performed from left to right. The example 8 / 4 * 2 yields 4 as its result, not 1. The first operation is 8 / 4, and 2 * 2 is the second.

Evaluation of an expression occurs in this order:

1. All operations within parentheses. Multiple operations within the parentheses are performed according to the rules of precedence.
2. All exponentiation. Multiple exponentiation operations are performed from left to right.
3. All multiplication and division. Multiple operations are performed from left to right.
4. All integer division. Multiple operations are performed from left to right.
5. Mod operations. Multiple operations are performed from left to right.
6. All addition and subtraction are performed from left to right.

TIP

Use extra parentheses to make the precedence clearer. The operation will be easier to understand and the parentheses have no negative effect on execution. ■

Although the precedence of operations in Basic is the same as in algebra, take note of one important difference: There are no implied operations in Basic. The following expressions would be valid in mathematics, but they are not valid in Basic:

Mathematical Notation	Equivalent Basic Function
2A	2 * A
3(X + Y)	3 * (X + Y)
(X + Y)(X − Y)	(X + Y) * (X − Y)

Feedback 3.4

What will be the result of the following calculations using the order of precedence?
        Assume that: xInteger = 2, yInteger = 4, zInteger = 3

1. xInteger + yInteger ^ 2
2. 8 / yInteger / xInteger
3. xInteger * (xInteger + 1)
4. xInteger * xInteger + 1
5. yInteger ^ xInteger + zInteger * 2
6. yInteger ^ (xInteger + zInteger) * 2
7. (yInteger ^ xInteger) + zInteger * 2
8. ((yInteger ^ xInteger) + zInteger) * 2

Using Calculations in Code

You perform calculations in assignment statements. Recall that whatever appears on the right side of an = (assignment operator) is assigned to the item on the left. The left side may be the property of a control or a variable. It cannot be a constant.

Examples

```
averageDecimal = sumDecimal / countInteger
amountDueLabel.Text = (priceDecimal − (priceDecimal * discountRateDecimal)).ToString()
Me.commissionTextBox.Text = (salesTotalDecimal * commissionRateDecimal).ToString()
```

In the preceding examples, the results of the calculations were assigned to a variable, the Text property of a label, and the Text property of a text box. In most cases you will assign calculation results to variables or to the Text properties of text boxes. When you assign the result of a calculation to a Text property, you must place parentheses around the entire calculation and convert the result of the calculation to a string.

Assignment Operators

In addition to the equal sign (=) as an **assignment operator**, VB .NET has several operators that can perform a calculation and assign the result as one operation. The assignment operators are +=, − =, *=, /=, \=, and &=. Each of these assignment operators is a shortcut for the standard method; you can use the standard (longer) form or the shortcut. The shortcuts allow you to type a variable name only once instead of having to type it on both sides of the equal sign.

For example, to add salesDecimal to totalSalesDecimal, the long version is

```
' Accumulate a total.
totalSalesDecimal = totalSalesDecimal + salesDecimal
```

Instead you can use the shortcut assignment operator:

```
' Accumulate a total.
totalSalesDecimal += salesDecimal
```

The two statements have the same effect.

To subtract 1 from a variable, the long version is

```
' Subtract 1 from a variable.
countDownInteger = countDownInteger − 1
```

And the shortcut, using the − = operator:

```
' Subtract 1 from a variable.
countDownInteger −= 1
```

The assignment operators that you will use most often are += and − =. The following are examples of other assignment operators:

```
' Multiply resultInteger by 2 and assign the result to resultInteger.
resultInteger *= 2

' Divide sumDecimal by countInteger and assign the result to sumDecimal.
sumDecimal /= countInteger

' Concatenate smallString to the end of bigString.
bigString &= smallString
```

Feedback 3.5

1. Write two statements to add 5 to countInteger, using (*a*) the standard, long version and (*b*) the assignment operator.
2. Write two statements to subtract withdrawalDecimal from balanceDecimal, using (*a*) the standard, long version and (*b*) the assignment operator.
3. Write two statements to multiply priceDecimal by countInteger and place the result into priceDecimal. Use (*a*) the standard, long version and (*b*) the assignment operator.

Option Explicit and Option Strict

Visual Basic provides two options that can significantly change the behavior of the editor and compiler. Not using these two options, **Option Explicit** and **Option Strict**, can make coding somewhat easier but provide opportunities for hard-to-find errors and very sloppy programming.

Option Explicit

When Option Explicit is turned off, you can use any variable name without first declaring it. The first time you use a variable name, VB allocates a new variable of Object data type. For example, you could write the line

```
Z = myTotal + 1
```

without first declaring either Z or myTotal. This is a throwback to very old versions of Basic that did not require variable declaration. In those days, programmers spent many hours debugging programs that had just a small misspelling or typo in a variable name.

You should always program with Option Explicit turned on. In VB .NET, the option is turned on by default for all new projects. If you need to turn it off (not a recommended practice), place the line

```
Option Explicit Off
```

before the first line of code in a file.

Option Strict

Option Strict is an option that makes VB more like other **strongly typed** languages, such as C++, Java, and C#. When Option Strict is turned on, the editor and compiler try to help you keep from making hard-to-find mistakes. Specifically, Option Strict does not allow any implicit (automatic) conversions from a wider data type to a narrower one, or between String and numeric data types.

All of the code you have seen so far in this text has been written with Option Strict turned on. With this option, you must convert to the desired data type from String or from a wider data type to a narrower type, such as from Decimal to Integer.

With Option Strict turned off, code such as this is legal:

```
quantityInteger = Me.quantityTextBox.Text
```

and

```
amountInteger = amountLong
```

and

```
totalInteger += saleAmountDecimal
```

With each of these legal (but dangerous) statements, the VB compiler makes assumptions about your data. And the majority of the time, the assumptions are correct. But bad input data or very large numbers can cause erroneous results or run-time errors.

The best practice is to always turn on Option Strict. This technique will save you from developing poor programming habits and will also likely save you hours of debugging time. You can turn on Option Strict either in code or in the Project Designer. Place the line

```
Option Strict On
```

before the first line of code, after the general remarks at the top of a file.

Example

```
'Project:       MyProject
'Date:          Today
'Programmer:    Your Name
'Description:    This project calculates correctly.

Option Strict On

Public Class myForm
```

To turn on Option Strict or Option Explicit for all files of a project, open the Project Designer by selecting *Project / Properties* or double-clicking My Project in the Solution Explorer. On the *Compile* tab you will find settings for both Option Explicit and Option Strict. By default, Option Explicit is turned on and Option Strict is turned off. Select *On* for Option Strict.

New to VB .NET 2005, you can set Option Strict on by default, which is better than setting it for each project: Select *Tools / Options / Project* and set the defaults.

Note: If *Show all settings* is checked in the *Options* dialog box, select *Projects and Solutions / VB Defaults* to find the default settings.

Note: Option Strict includes all of the requirements of Option Explicit. If Option Strict is turned on, variables must be declared, regardless of the setting of Option Explicit.

Converting Between Numeric Data Types

In VB you can convert data from one numeric data type to another. Some conversions can be performed implicitly (automatically) and some you must specify explicitly. And some cannot be converted if the value would be lost in the conversion.

Implicit Conversions

If you are converting a value from a narrower data type to a wider type, where there is no danger of losing any precision, the conversion can be performed by an **implicit conversion**. For example, the statement

```
bigNumberDouble = smallNumberInteger
```

does not generate any error message, assuming that both variables are properly declared. The value of smallNumberInteger is successfully converted and stored in bigNumberDouble. However, to convert in the opposite direction could cause problems and cannot be done implicitly.

The following list shows selected data type conversions that can be performed implicitly in VB:

From	To
Byte	Short, Integer, Long, Single, Double, or Decimal
Short	Integer, Long, Single, Double, or Decimal
Integer	Long, Single, Double, or Decimal
Long	Single, Double, or Decimal
Decimal	Single, Double
Single	Double

Notice that Double does not convert to any other type and you cannot convert implicitly from floating point (Single or Double) to Decimal.

Explicit Conversions

If you want to convert between data types that do not have implicit conversions, you must use an **explicit conversion**, also called *casting*. But beware: If you perform a conversion that causes significant digits to be lost, an exception is generated. (Exceptions are covered later in this chapter in the section titled "Handling Exceptions.")

Use methods of the Convert class to convert between data types. The Convert class has methods that begin with "To" for each of the data types: `ToDecimal`, `ToSingle`, and `ToDouble`. However, you must specify the integer data types using their .NET class names rather than the VB data types.

For the VB data type:	Use the method for the .NET data type:
Short	`ToInt16`
Integer	`ToInt32`
Long	`ToInt64`

The following are examples of explicit conversion. For each, assume that the variables are already declared following the textbook naming standards.

```
numberDecimal = Convert.ToDecimal(numberSingle)
valueInteger = Convert.ToInt32(valueDouble)
amountSingle = Convert.ToSingle(amountDecimal)
```

You should perform a conversion from a wider data type to a narrower one only when you know that the value will fit, without losing significant digits. Fractional values are rounded to fit into integer data types, and a single or double value converted to decimal is rounded to fit in 28 digits.

Performing Calculations with Unlike Data Types

When you perform calculations with unlike data types, VB performs the calculation using the wider data type. For example, `countInteger / numberDecimal` produces a decimal result. If you want to convert the result to a different data type, you must perform a cast: `Convert.ToInt32(countInteger / numberDecimal)` or `Convert.ToSingle(countInteger / numberDecimal)`. Note, however, that VB does not convert to a different data type until it is necessary. The expression `countInteger / 2 * amountDecimal` is evaluated as integer division for `countInteger / 2`, producing an integer intermediate result; then the multiplication is performed on the integer and decimal value (amountDecimal), producing a decimal result.

Rounding Numbers

At times you may want to round decimal fractions. You can use the `Decimal.Round` method to round decimal values to the desired number of decimal positions.

The Round Method—General Form

```
Decimal.Round(DecimalValue, IntegerNumberOfDecimalPositions)
```

The `Decimal.Round` method returns a decimal result, rounded to the specified number of decimal positions, which can be an integer in the range 0–28.

The Round Method—Examples

```
' Round to two decimal positions.
resultDecimal = Decimal.Round(amountDecimal, 2)

' Round to zero decimal positions.
wholeDollarsDecimal = Decimal.Round(dollarsAndCentsDecimal, 0)

' Round the result of a calculation.
discountDecimal = Decimal.Round(extendedPriceDecimal * DISCOUNT_RATE_Decimal, 2)
```

The `Decimal.Round` method and the `Convert` methods round using a technique called "rounding toward even." If the digit to the right of the final digit is exactly 5, the number is rounded so that the final digit is even.

Examples

Decimal Value to Round	Number of Decimal Positions	Result
1.455	2	1.46
1.445	2	1.44
1.5	0	2
2.5	0	2

In addition to the `Decimal.Round` method, you can use the `Round` method of the Math class to round either decimal or double values. See Appendix B for the methods of the Math class.

Note: Visual Basic provides many functions for mathematical operations, financial calculations, and string manipulation. These functions can simplify many programming tasks. When Microsoft created Visual Basic .NET and moved to object-oriented programming, they made the decision to keep many functions from previous versions of VB, although the functions do not follow the OOP pattern of *object.method*. You can find many of these helpful functions in Appendix B. The authors of this text elected to consistently use OOP methods rather than mix methods and functions.

Formatting Data for Display

When you want to display numeric data in the Text property of a label or text box, you must first convert the value to string. You also can **format** the data for display, which controls the way the output looks. For example, 12 is just a number, but $12.00 conveys more meaning for dollar amounts. Using the `ToString` method and formatting codes, you can choose to display a dollar sign, a percent sign, and commas. You also can specify the number of digits to appear to the right of the decimal point. VB rounds the value to return the requested number of decimal positions.

If you use the `ToString` method with an empty argument, the method returns an unformatted string. This is perfectly acceptable when displaying integer values. For example, the following statement converts numberInteger to a string and displays it in displayTextBox.Text.

```
Me.displayTextBox.Text = numberInteger.ToString()
```

Using Format Specifier Codes

You can use the **format specifier** codes to format the display of output. These predefined codes can format a numeric value to have commas and dollar signs, if you wish.

Note: The default format of each of the formatting codes is based on the computer's regional setting. The formats presented here are for the default English (United States) values.

```
' Display as currency.
Me.extendedPriceTextBox.Text = (quantityInteger * priceDecimal).ToString("C")
```

The "C" code specifies *currency*. By default, the string will be formatted with a dollar sign, commas separating each group of 3 digits, and 2 digits to the right of the decimal point.

```
' Display as numeric.
Me.discountTextBox.Text = discountDecimal.ToString("N")
```

The "N" code stands for *number*. By default, the string will be formatted with commas separating each group of 3 digits, with 2 digits to the right of the decimal point.

You can specify the number of decimal positions by placing a numeric digit following the code. For example, "C0" displays as currency with zero digits to the right of the decimal point. The value is rounded to the specified number of decimal positions.

Format Specifier Codes	Name	Description
C or c	Currency	Formats with a dollar sign, commas, and 2 decimal places. Negative values are enclosed in parentheses.
F or f	Fixed-point	Formats as a string of numeric digits, no commas, 2 decimal places, and a minus sign at the left for negative values.
N or n	Number	Formats with commas, 2 decimal places, and a minus sign at the left for negative values.
D or d	Digits	Use only for *integer* data types. Formats with a left minus sign for negative values. Usually used to force a specified number of digits to display.
P or p	Percent	Multiplies the value by 100, adds a space and a percent sign, rounds to 2 decimal places; negative values have a minus sign at the left.

Examples

Variable	Value	Format Specifier Code	Output
totalDecimal	1125.6744	"C"	$1,125.67
totalDecimal	1125.6744	"N"	1,125.67
totalDecimal	1125.6744	"N0"	1,126
balanceDecimal	1125.6744	"N3"	1,125.674
balanceDecimal	1125.6744	"F0"	1126
pinInteger	123	"D6"	000123
rateDecimal	0.075	"P"	7.50 %
rateDecimal	0.075	"P3"	7.500 %
rateDecimal	0.075	"P0"	8 %
valueInteger	–10	"C"	($10.00)
valueInteger	–10	"N"	–10.00
valueInteger	–10	"D3"	–010

Note that the formatted value returned by the `ToString` method is no longer purely numeric and cannot be used in further calculations. For example, consider the following lines of code:

```
amountDecimal += chargesDecimal
Me.amountTextBox.Text = amountDecimal.ToString("C")
```

Assume that amountDecimal holds 1050 after the calculation and amount-TextBox.Text displays $1,050.00. If you want to do any further calculations with this amount, such as adding it to a total, you must use amountDecimal, not amountTextBox.Text. The variable amountDecimal holds a numeric value; amountTextBox.Text holds a string of (nonnumeric) characters.

You also can format DateTime values using format codes and the `ToString` method. Unlike the numeric format codes, the date codes are case sensitive. The strings returned are based on the computer's regional settings and can be changed. The following are default values for US-English in Windows XP.

Date Specifier Code	Name	Description	Example of Default Setting
d	short date	Mm/dd/yyyy	6/13/2005
D	long date	Day, Month dd, yyyy	Monday, June 13, 2005
t	short time	hh:mm AM|PM	4:55 PM
T	long time	hh:mm:ss AM|PM	4:55:45 PM
f	full date/time (short time)	Day, Month dd, yyyy hh:mm AM|PM	Monday, June 13, 2005 4:55 PM
F	full date/time (long time)	Day, Month dd, yyyy hh:mm:ss AM|PM	Monday, June 13, 2005 4:55:45 PM
g	general (short time)	Mm/dd/yyyy hh:mm AM|PM	6/13/2003 11:00 AM
G	general (long time)	Mm/dd/yyyy hh:mm:ss AM|PM	6/13/2003 11:00:15 AM
M or m	month	Month dd	June 13
R or r	GMT pattern	Day, dd mmm yyyy hh:mm:ss GMT	Mon, 13 Jun 2005 11:00:15 GMT

Note that you can also use methods of the DateTime structure for formatting dates: `ToLongDateString`, `ToShortDateString`, `ToLongTimeString`, `ToShortTimeString`. See Appendix B or MSDN for additional information.

Choosing the Controls for Program Output

Some programmers prefer to display program output in labels; others prefer text boxes. Both approaches have advantages, but whichever approach you use, you should clearly differentiate between (editable) input areas and (uneditable) output areas.

Users generally get clues about input and output fields from their color. By Windows convention, input text boxes have a white background; output text has a gray background. The default background color of text boxes (BackColor property) is set to white; the default BackColor of labels is gray. However, you can change the BackColor property and the BorderStyle property of both text boxes and labels so that the two controls look very similar. You might wonder why a person would want to do that, but there are some very good reasons.

Using text boxes for output can provide some advantages: The controls do not disappear when the Text property is cleared and the borders and sizes of the output boxes can match those of the input boxes, making the form more visually uniform. Also, the user can select the text and copy it to another program using the Windows clipboard.

If you choose to display output in labels (the traditional approach), set the AutoSize property to False so that the label does not disappear when the Text property is blank. You also generally set the BorderStyle property of the labels to *Fixed3D* or *FixedSingle*, so that the outline of the label appears.

To use a text box for output, set its ReadOnly property to True (to prevent the user from attempting to edit the text) and set its TabStop property to False, so that the focus will not stop on that control when the user tabs from one control to the next. Notice that when you set ReadOnly to true, the BackColor property automatically changes to *Control*, which is the system default for labels.

The example programs in this chapter use text boxes, rather than labels, for output.

Feedback 3.6

Give the line of code that assigns the formatted output and tell how the output will display for the specified value.

1. A calculated variable called averagePayDecimal has a value of 123.456 and should display in a text box called averagePayTextBox.
2. The variable quantityInteger, which contains 176123, must be displayed in the text box called quantityTextBox.
3. The total amount collected in a fund drive is being accumulated in a variable called totalCollectedDecimal. What statement will display the variable in a text box called totalTextBox with commas and two decimal positions but no dollar signs?

A Calculation Programming Example

R 'n R—for Reading 'n Refreshment needs to calculate prices and discounts for books sold. The company is currently having a big sale, offering a 15 percent discount on all books. In this project you will calculate the amount due for a quantity of books, determine the 15 percent discount, and deduct the discount, giving the new amount due—the discounted amount. Use text boxes with the ReadOnly property set to True for the output fields.

Planning the Project

Sketch a form (Figure 3.5) that meets the needs of your users.

Figure 3.5

A planning sketch of the form for the calculation programming example.

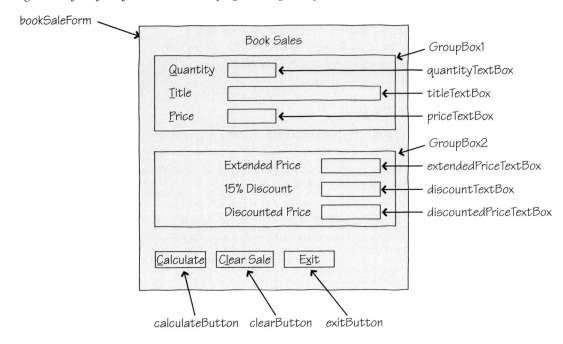

Plan the Objects and Properties

Plan the property settings for the form and each of the controls.

Object	Property	Setting
bookSaleForm	Name Text AcceptButton CancelButton	bookSaleForm R 'n R for Reading 'n Refreshment calculateButton clearButton
Label1	Text Font	Book Sales Bold, 12 point
GroupBox1	Name Text	GroupBox1 (blank)
Label2	Text	&Quantity
quantityTextBox	Name Text	quantityTextBox (blank)
Label3	Text	&Title
titleTextBox	Name Text	titleTextBox (blank)
Label4	Text	&Price
priceTextBox	Name Text	priceTextBox (blank)

Object	Property	Setting
GroupBox2	Name Text	GroupBox2 (blank)
Label5	Text	Extended Price
extendedPriceTextBox	Name TextAlign ReadOnly TabStop	extendedPriceTextBox Right True False
Label6	Text	15% Discount
discountTextBox	Name TextAlign ReadOnly TabStop	discountTextBox Right True False
Label7	Text	Discounted Price
discountedPriceTextBox	Name TextAlign ReadOnly TabStop	discountedPriceTextBox Right True False
calculateButton	Name Text	calculateButton &Calculate
clearButton	Name Text	clearButton C&lear Sale
exitButton	Name Text	exitButton E&xit

Plan the Event Procedures

Since you have three buttons, you need to plan the actions for three event procedures.

Event Procedure	Actions-Pseudocode
calculateButton_Click	Dimension the variables. Convert the input Quantity and Price to numeric. Calculate Extended Price = Quantity * Price. Calculate and round: Discount = Extended Price * Discount Rate. Calculate Discounted Price = Extended Price – Discount. Format and display the output in text boxes.
clearButton_Click	Clear each text box. Set the focus in the first text box.
exitButton_Click	Exit the project.

Write the Project

Follow the sketch in Figure 3.5 to create the form. Figure 3.6 shows the completed form.

1. Set the properties of each object, as you have planned.
2. Write the code. Working from the pseudocode, write each event procedure.
3. When you complete the code, use a variety of test data to thoroughly test the project.

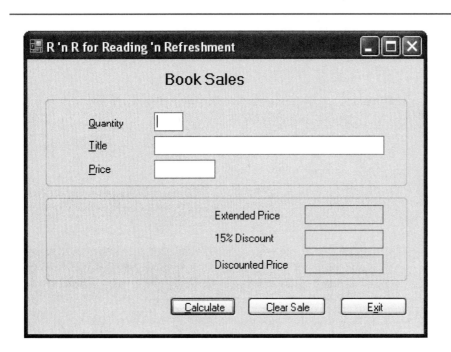

Figure 3.6

The form for the calculation programming example

Note: If the user enters nonnumeric data or leaves a numeric field blank, the program will cancel with a run-time error. In the "Handling Exceptions" section that follows this program, you will learn to handle the errors.

The Project Coding Solution

```
'Project:       Chapter Example BookSale
'Date:          June 2005
'Programmer:    Bradley/Millspaugh
'Description:   This project inputs sales information for books.
'               It calculates the extended price and discount for
'               a sale.
'               Uses variables, constants, and calculations.
'               Note that no error trapping is included in this version
'               of the program.
'Folder:        Ch03BookSale

Public Class bookSaleForm

    ' Declare the constant.
    Const DISCOUNT_RATE_Decimal As Decimal = 0.15D
```

```
        Private Sub calculateButton_Click(ByVal sender As System.Object, _
          ByVal e As System.EventArgs) Handles calculateButton.Click
          ' Calculate the price and discount.

          Dim quantityInteger As Integer
          Dim priceDecimal, extendedPriceDecimal, discountDecimal, _
            discountedPriceDecimal As Decimal

          With Me
            ' Convert input values to numeric variables.
            quantityInteger = Integer.Parse(.quantityTextBox.Text)
            priceDecimal = Decimal.Parse(.priceTextBox.Text)

            ' Calculate values.
            extendedPriceDecimal = quantityInteger * priceDecimal
            discountDecimal = Decimal.Round( _
              (extendedPriceDecimal * DISCOUNT_RATE_Decimal), 2)
            discountedPriceDecimal = extendedPriceDecimal - discountDecimal

            ' Format and display answers.
            .extendedPriceTextBox.Text = extendedPriceDecimal.ToString("C")
            .discountTextBox.Text = discountDecimal.ToString("N")
            .discountedPriceTextBox.Text = discountedPriceDecimal.ToString("C")
          End With
        End Sub

        Private Sub clearButton_Click(ByVal sender As System.Object, _
          ByVal e As System.EventArgs) Handles clearButton.Click
          ' Clear previous amounts from the form.

          With Me
            .titleTextBox.Clear()
            .priceTextBox.Clear()
            .extendedPriceTextBox.Clear()
            .discountTextBox.Clear()
            .discountedPriceTextBox.Clear()
            With .quantityTextBox
              .Clear()
              .Focus()
            End With
          End With
        End Sub

        Private Sub exitButton_Click(ByVal sender As System.Object, _
          ByVal e As System.EventArgs) Handles exitButton.Click
          ' Exit the project.

          Me.Close()
        End Sub
      End Class
```

Handling Exceptions

When you allow users to input numbers and use those numbers in calculations, lots of things can go wrong. The Parse methods, Integer.Parse and Decimal.Parse, fail if the user enters nonnumeric data or leaves the text box blank. Or your user may enter a number that results in an attempt to divide by zero. Each of those situations causes an **exception** to occur, or, as programmers like to say, *throws an exception*.

You can easily "catch" program exceptions by using structured exception handling. You catch the exceptions before they can cause a run-time error, and handle the situation, if possible, within the program. Catching exceptions as they happen is generally referred to as *error trapping*, and coding to take care of the problems is called *error handling*. The error handling in Visual Studio .NET is standardized for all of the languages using the Common Language Runtime, which greatly improves on the old error trapping in previous versions of VB.

Try/Catch Blocks

To trap or catch exceptions, enclose any statement(s) that might cause an error in a **Try/Catch block**. If an exception occurs while the statements in the Try block are executing, program control transfers to the Catch block; if a Finally statement is included, the code in that section executes last, whether or not an exception occurred.

The Try Block—General Form

```
Try
    ' Statements that may cause error.
Catch [VariableName As ExceptionType]
    ' Statements for action when exception occurs.
[Finally
    ' Statements that always execute before exit of Try block]
End Try
```

The Try Block—Example

```
Try
    quantityInteger = Integer.Parse(Me.quantityTextBox.Text)
    Me.quantityTextBox.Text = quantityInteger.ToString()
Catch
    Me.messageLabel.Text = "Error in input data."
End Try
```

The Catch as it appears in the preceding example will catch any exception. You also can specify the type of exception that you want to catch, and even write several Catch statements, each to catch a different type of exception. For example, you might want to display one message for bad input data and a different message for a calculation problem.

To specify a particular type of exception to catch, use one of the predefined exception classes, which are all based on, or derived from, the SystemException class. Table 3.2 shows some of the common exception classes.

To catch bad input data that cannot be converted to numeric, write this Catch statement:

```
Catch theException As FormatException
    Me.messageLabel.Text = "Error in input data."
```

The Exception Class

Each exception is an instance of the Exception class. The properties of this class allow you to determine the code location of the error, the type of error, and the cause. The Message property contains a text message about the error and the Source property contains the name of the object causing the error. The Stack-Trace property can identify the location in the code where the error occurred.

Common Exception Classes   Table 3.2

Exception	Caused By
FormatException	Failure of a numeric conversion, such as `Integer.Parse` or `Decimal.Parse`. Usually blank or nonnumeric data.
InvalidCastException	Failure of a conversion operation. May be caused by loss of significant digits or an illegal conversion.
ArithmeticException	A calculation error, such as division by zero or overflow of a variable.
System.IO.EndofStreamException	Failure of an input or output operation such as reading from a file.
OutOfMemoryException	Not enough memory to create an object.
Exception	Generic.

You can include the text message associated with the type of exception by specifying the Message property of the Exception object, as declared by the variable you named on the `Catch` statement. Be aware that the messages for exceptions are usually somewhat terse and not oriented to users, but they can sometimes be helpful.

```
Catch theException As FormatException
    messageLabel.Text = "Error in input data: " & theException.Message
```

Handling Multiple Exceptions

If you want to trap for more than one type of exception, you can include multiple `Catch` blocks (handlers). When an exception occurs, the `Catch` statements are checked in sequence. The first one with a matching exception type is used.

```
Catch theException As FormatException
    ' Statements for nonnumeric data.
Catch theException As ArithmeticException
    ' Statements for calculation problem.
Catch theException As Exception
    ' Statements for any other exception.
```

The last `Catch` will handle any exceptions that do not match either of the first two exception types. Note that it is acceptable to use the same variable name for multiple `Catch` statements; each `Catch` represents a separate code block, so the variable's scope is only that block.

Later in this chapter in the "Testing Multiple Fields" section, you will see how to nest one `Try/Catch` block inside another one.

Displaying Messages in Message Boxes

You may want to display a message when the user has entered invalid data or neglected to enter a required data value. You can display a message to the user in a message box, which is a special type of window. You can specify the message, an optional icon, title bar text, and button(s) for the message box (Figure 3.7).

Figure 3.7

Two sample message boxes created with the MessageBox class.

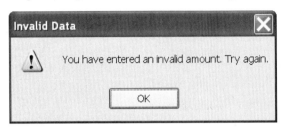

a.

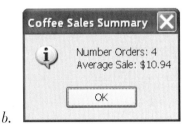

b.

You use the **Show method** of the **MessageBox** object to display a message box. The MessageBox object is a predefined instance of the MessageBox class that you can use any time you need to display a message.

The MessageBox Object—General Forms

There is more than one way to call the Show method. Each of the following statements is a valid call; you can choose the format you want to use. It's very important that the arguments you supply exactly match one of the formats. For example, you cannot reverse, transpose, or leave out any of the arguments. When there are multiple ways to call a method, the method is said to be *overloaded*. See the section "Using Overloaded Methods" later in this chapter.

General Forms

```
MessageBox.Show(TextMessage)
MessageBox.Show(TextMessage, TitlebarText)
MessageBox.Show(TextMessage, TitlebarText, MessageBoxButtons)
MessageBox.Show(TextMessage, TitlebarText, MessageBoxButtons, MessageBoxIcon)
```

The TextMessage is the message you want to appear in the message box. The TitlebarText appears on the title bar of the MessageBox window. The MessageBoxButtons argument specifies the buttons to display. And the MessageBoxIcon determines the icon to display.

The MessageBox Statement—Examples

Examples

```
MessageBox.Show("Enter numeric data.")

MessageBox.Show("Try again.", "Data Entry Error")

MessageBox.Show("This is a message.", "This is a title bar", MessageBoxButtons.OK)

Try
    quantityInteger = Integer.Parse(Me.quantityTextBox.Text)
    Me.quantityTextBox.Text = quantityInteger.ToString()
Catch err As FormatException
    MessageBox.Show("Nonnumeric Data.", "Error", _
      MessageBoxButtons.OK, MessageBoxIcon.Exclamation)
End Try
```

The TextMessage String

The message string you display may be a string literal enclosed in quotes or it may be a string variable. You also may want to concatenate several items, for example, combining a literal with a value from a variable. If the message you specify is too long for one line, Visual Basic will wrap it to the next line.

The Titlebar Text

The string that you specify for TitlebarText will appear in the title bar of the message box. If you choose the first form of the Show method, without the TitlebarText, the title bar will appear empty.

MessageBoxButtons

When you show a message box, you can specify the button(s) to display. In Chapter 4, after you learn to make selections using the If statement, you will display more than one button and take alternate actions based on which button the user clicks. You specify the buttons using the MessageBoxButtons constants from the MessageBox class. The choices are OK, OKCancel, RetryCancel, YesNo, YesNoCancel, and AbortRetryIgnore. The default for the Show method is OK, so unless you specify otherwise, you will get only the OK button in your message box.

MessageBoxIcon

The easy way to select the icon to display is to type MessageBoxIcon and a period into the editor; the IntelliSense list pops up with the complete list. The actual appearance of the icons varies from one operating system to another. You can see a description of the icons in Help under "MessageBoxIcon Enumeration."

Constants for MessageBoxIcon
Asterisk
Error
Exclamation
Hand
Information
None
Question
Stop
Warning

Using Overloaded Methods

As you saw earlier, you can call the Show method with several different argument lists. This OOP feature, called ***overloading***, allows the Show method to act differently for different arguments. Each argument list is called a ***signature***, so you can say that the Show method has several signatures.

When you call the Show method, the arguments that you supply must exactly match one of the signatures provided by the method. You must supply the correct number of arguments of the correct data type and in the correct sequence.

Fortunately, the smart Visual Studio editor helps you enter the arguments; you don't have to memorize or look up the argument lists. Type "MessageBox.Show(" and IntelliSense pops up with the first of the signatures for the Show method (Figure 3.8). Notice in the figure that there are 21 possible forms of the argument list, or 21 signatures for the Show method. (We only showed 4 of the 21 signatures in the previous example, to simplify the concept.)

To select the signature that you want to use, use the up or down arrows at the left end of the IntelliSense popup. For example, to select the signature that needs only the text of the message and the title bar caption, select the 14th format (Figure 3.9). The argument that you are expected to enter is shown in bold and a description of that argument appears in the last line of the popup. After you type the text of the message and a comma, the second argument appears in bold and the description changes to tell you about that argument (Figure 3.10).

TIP

Use the keyboard Up and Down arrow keys rather than the mouse to view and select the signature. The on-screen arrows jump around from one signature to the next, making mouse selection difficult. ∎

Figure 3.8

IntelliSense pops up the first of 21 signatures for the Show *method. Use the up and down arrows to see the other possible argument lists.*

```
1 of 21  Show (text As String, caption As String, buttons As System.Windows.Forms.MessageBoxButtons, icon As System.Windows.Forms.MessageBoxIcon,
        defaultButton As System.Windows.Forms.MessageBoxDefaultButton, options As System.Windows.Forms.MessageBoxOptions, displayHelpButton As Boolean) As System.Windows.Forms.DialogResult
text: The text to display in the message box.
```

Figure 3.9

Select the 14th signature to see the argument list. The currently selected argument is shown in bold and the description of the argument appears in the last line of the popup.

```
14 of 21  Show (text As String, caption As String) As System.Windows.Forms.DialogResult
text: The text to display in the message box.
```

Figure 3.10

Type the first argument and a comma, and IntelliSense bolds the second argument and displays a description of the needed data.

```
1 of 10  Show (text As String, caption As String, buttons As System.Windows.Forms.MessageBoxButtons, icon As System.Windows.Forms.MessageBoxIcon,
        defaultButton As System.Windows.Forms.MessageBoxDefaultButton, options As System.Windows.Forms.MessageBoxOptions, displayHelpButton As Boolean) As System.Windows.Forms.DialogResult
caption: The text to display in the title bar of the message box.
```

Testing Multiple Fields

When you have more than one input field, each field presents an opportunity for an exception. If you would like your exception messages to indicate the field that caused the error, you can nest one `Try/Catch` block inside another one.

Nested Try/Catch Blocks

One `Try/Catch` block that is completely contained inside another one is called a **nested `Try/Catch` block**. You can nest another `Try/Catch` block within the `Try` block or the `Catch` block.

```
Try      ' Outer try block for first field.
         ' Convert first field to numeric .

    Try      ' Inner Try block for second field.
             ' Convert second field to numeric.

        ' Perform the calculations for the fields that passed conversion.

    Catch secondException As FormatException
        ' Handle any exceptions for the second field.

        ' Display a message and reset the focus for the second field.

    End Try ' End of inner Try block for second field.

Catch firstException As FormatException
    ' Handle exceptions for first field.

    ' Display a message and reset the focus for the first field.

Catch anyOtherException as Exception
    ' Handle any generic exceptions.

    ' Display a message.

End Try
```

You can nest the `Try/Catch` blocks as deeply as you need. Make sure to place the calculations within the most deeply nested `Try`; you do not want to perform the calculations unless all of the input values are converted without an exception.

By testing each `Parse` method individually, you can be specific about which field caused the error and set the focus back to the field in error. Also, by using the `SelectAll` method of the text box, you can make the text appear selected to aid the user. Here are the calculations from the earlier program, rewritten with nested `Try/Catch` blocks.

```
Private Sub calculateButton_Click(ByVal sender As System.Object, _
    ByVal e As System.EventArgs) Handles calculateButton.Click
    ' Calculate the price and discount.
    Dim quantityInteger As Integer
    Dim priceDecimal, extendedPriceDecimal, discountDecimal, _
        discountedPriceDecimal, averageDiscountDecimal As Decimal
```

```
        With Me
            Try
                ' Convert quantity to numeric variables.
                quantityInteger = Integer.Parse(.quantityTextBox.Text)
                Try
                    ' Convert price if quantity was successful.
                    priceDecimal = Decimal.Parse(.priceTextBox.Text)

                    ' Calculate values for sale.
                    extendedPriceDecimal = quantityInteger * priceDecimal
                    discountDecimal = Decimal.Round( _
                        (extendedPriceDecimal * DISCOUNT_RATE_Decimal), 2)
                    discountedPriceDecimal = extendedPriceDecimal - discountDecimal

                    ' Format and display answers for sale.
                    .extendedPriceTextBox.Text = extendedPriceDecimal.ToString("C")
                    .discountTextBox.Text = discountDecimal.ToString("N")
                    .discountedPriceTextBox.Text = discountedPriceDecimal.ToString("C")

                Catch priceException As FormatException
                    ' Handle price exception.
                    MessageBox.Show("Price must be numeric.", "Data Entry Error", _
                        MessageBoxButtons.OK, MessageBoxIcon.Exclamation)
                    With.priceTextBox
                        .Focus()
                        .SelectAll()
                    End With
                End Try
            Catch quantityException As FormatException
                ' Handle quantity exception.
                MessageBox.Show("Quantity must be numeric.", "Data Entry Error", _
                    MessageBoxButtons.OK, MessageBoxIcon.Exclamation)
                With. quantityTextBox
                    .Focus()
                    .SelectAll()
                End With
            Catch anyException As Exception
                MessageBox.Show("Error: " & anyException.Message)
            End Try
        End With
End Sub
```

Counting and Accumulating Sums

Programs often need to calculate the sum of numbers. For example, in the previous programming exercise, each sale is displayed individually. If you want to accumulate totals of the sales amounts, of the discounts, or of the number of books sold, you need some new variables and new techniques.

As you know, the variables you declare inside a procedure are local to that procedure. They are re-created each time the procedure is called; that is, their lifetime is one time through the procedure. Each time the procedure is entered, you have a new fresh variable with an initial value of 0. If you want a variable to retain its value for multiple calls, in order to accumulate totals, you must declare the variable as module level. (Another approach, using Static variables, is discussed in Chapter 7.)

Summing Numbers

The technique for summing the sales amounts for multiple sales is to declare a module-level variable for the total. Then, in the calculateButton_Click event procedure for each sale, add the current amount to the total:

```
discountedPriceSumDecimal += discountedPriceDecimal
```

This assignment statement adds the current value for discountedPriceDecimal into the sum held in discountedPriceSumDecimal.

Counting

If you want to count something, such as the number of sales in the previous example, you need another module-level variable. Declare a counter variable as integer:

```
Private saleCountInteger as Integer
```

Then, in the calculateButton_Click event procedure, add 1 to the counter variable:

```
saleCountInteger += 1
```

This statement adds 1 to the current contents of saleCountInteger. The statement will execute one time for each time the calculateButton_Click event procedure executes. Therefore, saleCountInteger will always hold a running count of the number of sales.

Calculating an Average

To calculate an average, divide the sum of the items by the count of the items. In the R 'n R book example, we can calculate the average sale by dividing the sum of the discounted prices by the count of the sales:

```
averageDiscountedSaleDecimal = discountedPriceSumDecimal / saleCountInteger
```

Your Hands-On Programming Example

In this project, R 'n R—for Reading 'n Refreshment needs to expand the book sale project done previously in this chapter. In addition to calculating individual sales and discounts, management wants to know the total number of books sold, the total number of discounts given, the total discounted amount, and the average discount per sale.

Help the user by adding ToolTips wherever you think they will be useful.

Add error handling to the program, so that missing or nonnumeric data will not cause a run-time error.

Planning the Project

Sketch a form (Figure 3.11) that your users sign off as meeting their needs.

Figure 3.11

A planning sketch of the form for the hands-on programming example.

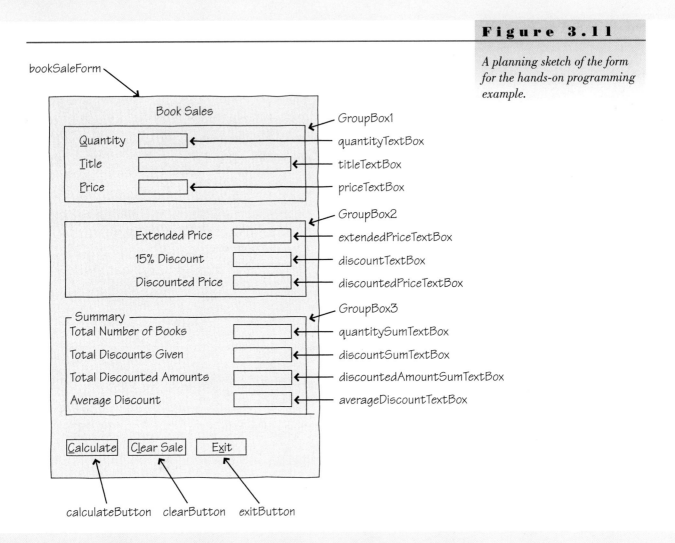

Plan the Objects and Properties Plan the property settings for the form and each control. These objects and properties are the same as the previous example, with the addition of the summary information beginning with GroupBox3.

Note: The ToolTips have not been added to the planning forms. Make up and add your own.

Object	Property	Setting
bookSaleForm	Name	bookSaleForm
	Text	R 'n R—for Reading 'n Refreshment
	AcceptButton	calculateButton
	CancelButton	clearButton
Label1	Text	Book Sales
	Font	Bold, 12 point
GroupBox1	Name	GroupBox1
	Text	(blank)
Label2	Text	&Quantity

Object	Property	Setting
quantityTextBox	Name	quantityTextBox
	Text	(blank)
Label3	Text	&Title
titleTextBox	Name	titleTextBox
	Text	(blank)
Label4	Text	&Price
priceTextBox	Name	priceTextBox
	Text	(blank)
GroupBox2	Name	GroupBox2
	Text	(blank)
Label5	Text	Extended Price
extendedPriceTextBox	Name	extendedPriceTextBox
	Text	(blank)
	ReadOnly	True
	TextAlign	Right
Label6	Text	15% Discount
discountTextBox	Name	discountTextBox
	Text	(blank)
	ReadOnly	True
	TextAlign	Right
Label7	Text	Discounted Price
discountedPriceTextBox	Name	discountedPriceTextBox
	Text	(blank)
	TextAlign	Right
	ReadOnly	True
calculateButton	Name	calculateButton
	Text	&Calculate
clearButton	Name	clearButton
	Text	C&lear Sale
exitButton	Name	exitButton
	Text	E&xit
GroupBox3	Name	GroupBox3
	Text	Summary
Label8	Text	Total Number of Books
quantitySumTextBox	Name	quantitySumTextBox
	Text	(blank)
	ReadOnly	True
	TextAlign	Right

Object	Property	Setting
Label9	Text	Total Discounts Given
discountSumTextBox	Name	discountSumTextBox
	Text	(blank)
	ReadOnly	True
	TextAlign	Right
Label10	Text	Total Discounted Amounts
discountedAmountSumTextBox	Name	discountedAmountSumTextBox
	Text	(blank)
	ReadOnly	True
	TextAlign	Right
Label11	Text	Average Discount
averageDiscountTextBox	Name	averageDiscountTextBox
	Text	(blank)
	ReadOnly	True
	TextAlign	Right

Plan the Event Procedures The planning that you did for the previous example will save you time now. The only procedure that requires more steps is the calculateButton_Click event.

Event Procedure	Actions-Pseudocode
calculateButton_Click	Declare the variables.
	Try
	Convert the input Quantity to numeric.
	Try
	Convert the input Price to numeric
	Calculate Extended Price = Quantity * Price.
	Calculate Discount = Extended Price * Discount Rate.
	Calculate Discounted Price = Extended Price − Discount.
	Calculate the summary values:
	Add Quantity to Quantity Sum.
	Add Discount to Discount Sum.
	Add Discounted Price to Discounted Price Sum.
	Add 1 to Sale Count.
	Calculate Average Discount = Discount Sum / Sale Count.
	Format and display sale output.
	Format and display summary values.
	Catch any Price exception
	Display error message and reset the focus to Price.
	Catch any Quantity exception
	Display error message and reset the focus to Quantity.
	Catch any generic exception
	Display error message.
clearButton_Click	Clear each text box except Summary fields.
	Set the focus in the first text box.
exitButton_Click	Exit the project.

Write the Project Following the sketch in Figure 3.11 create the form. Figure 3.12 shows the completed form.

- Set the properties of each of the objects, as you have planned.

- Write the code. Working from the pseudocode, write each event procedure.

- When you complete the code, use a variety of test data to thoroughly test the project. Test with nonnumeric data and blank entries.

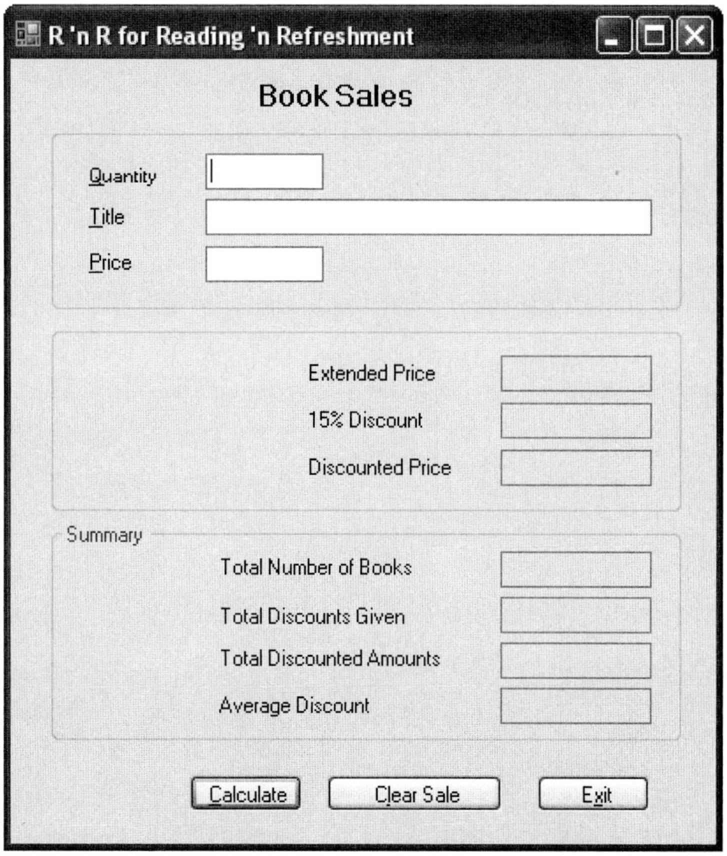

Figure 3.12

The form for the hands-on programming example.

The Project Coding Solution

```
'Project:      Chapter Example Totals and Exceptions
'Date:         June 2005
'Programmer:   Bradley/Millspaugh
'Description:  This project inputs sales information for books.
'              It calculates the extended price and discount for
'              a sale and maintains summary information for all
'              sales.
'              Uses variables, constants, calculations, error
'              handling, and a message box to the user.
'Folder:       Ch03HandsOn
```

```vb
Public Class bookSaleForm

    ' Dimension module-level variables and constants.
    Private quantitySumInteger, saleCountInteger As Integer
    Private discountSumDecimal, discountedPriceSumDecimal As Decimal
    Const DISCOUNT_RATE_Decimal As Decimal = 0.15D

  Private Sub calculateButton_Click(ByVal sender As System.Object, _
    ByVal e As System.EventArgs) Handles calculateButton.Click
    ' Calculate the price and discount.
    Dim quantityInteger As Integer
    Dim priceDecimal, extendedPriceDecimal, discountDecimal, _
      discountedPriceDecimal, averageDiscountDecimal As Decimal

    With Me
      Try
        ' Convert quantity to numeric variable.
        quantityInteger = Integer.Parse(.quantityTextBox.Text)
        Try
            ' Convert price if quantity was successful.
            priceDecimal = Decimal.Parse(.priceTextBox.Text)

            ' Calculate values for sale.
            extendedPriceDecimal = quantityInteger * priceDecimal
            discountDecimal = Decimal.Round( _
              (extendedPriceDecimal * DISCOUNT_RATE_Decimal), 2)
            discountedPriceDecimal = extendedPriceDecimal – discountDecimal

            ' Calculate summary values.
            quantitySumInteger += quantityInteger
            discountSumDecimal += discountDecimal
            discountedPriceSumDecimal += discountedPriceDecimal
            saleCountInteger += 1
            averageDiscountDecimal = discountSumDecimal / saleCountInteger

            ' Format and display answers for the sale.
            .extendedPriceTextBox.Text = extendedPriceDecimal.ToString("C")
            .discountTextBox.Text = discountDecimal.ToString("N")
            .discountedPriceTextBox.Text = discountedPriceDecimal.ToString("C")

            ' Format and display summary values.
            .quantitySumTextBox.Text = quantitySumInteger.ToString()
            .discountSumTextBox.Text = discountSumDecimal.ToString("C")
            .discountAmountSumTextBox.Text = discountedPriceSumDecimal.ToString("C")
            .averageDiscountTextBox.Text = averageDiscountDecimal.ToString("C")

        Catch priceException As FormatException
            ' Handle a price exception.
            MessageBox.Show("Price must be numeric.", "Data Entry Error", _
              MessageBoxButtons.OK, MessageBoxIcon.Exclamation)
            With .priceTextBox
                    .Focus()
                    .SelectAll()
            End With
        End Try
```

```
            Catch quantityException As FormatException
               ' Handle a quantity exception.
               MessageBox.Show("Quantity must be numeric.", "Data Entry Error", _
                  MessageBoxButtons.OK, MessageBoxIcon.Exclamation)
               With .quantityTextBox
                    .Focus()
                    .SelectAll()
               End With

            Catch anException As Exception
               ' Handle any other exception.
               MessageBox.Show("Error: " & anException.Message)
            End Try
         End With
      End Sub

      Private Sub clearButton_Click(ByVal sender As System.Object, _
         ByVal e As System.EventArgs) Handles clearButton.Click
         ' Clear previous amounts from the form.

         With Me
            .titleTextBox.Clear()
            .priceTextBox.Clear()
            .extendedPriceTextBox.Clear()
            .discountTextBox.Clear()
            .discountedPriceTextBox.Clear()
            With .quantityTextBox
               .Clear()
               .Focus()
            End With
         End With
      End Sub

      Private Sub exitButton_Click(ByVal sender As System.Object, _
         ByVal e As System.EventArgs) Handles exitButton.Click
         ' Exit the project.

         Me.Close()
      End Sub
End Class
```

Summary

1. Variables are temporary memory locations that have a name (called an *identifier*), a data type, and a scope. A constant also has a name, data type, and scope, but it also must have a value assigned to it. The value stored in a variable can be changed during the execution of the project; the values stored in constants cannot change.
2. The data type determines what type of values may be assigned to a variable or constant. The most common data types are String, Integer, Decimal, Single, and Boolean.
3. Identifiers for variables and constants must follow the Visual Basic naming rules and should follow good naming standards, called *conventions*. An identifier should be meaningful and have the data type appended at the

end. Variable names should begin with a lowercase character and be mixed upper- and lowercase, while constants are all uppercase.

4. Intrinsic constants, such as Color.Red and Color.Blue, are predefined and built into the .NET Framework. Named constants are programmer-defined constants and are declared using the `Const` statement. The location of the `Const` statement determines the scope of the constant.

5. Variables are declared using the `Private` or `Dim` statement; the location of the statement determines the scope of the variable. Use the `Dim` statement to declare local variables inside a procedure; use the `Private` statement to declare module-level variables at the top of the program, outside of any procedure.

6. The scope of a variable may be namespace level, module level, local, or block level. Block-level and local variables are available only within the procedure in which they are declared; module-level variables are accessible in all procedures within a form; namespace variables are available in all procedures of all classes in a namespace, which is usually the entire project.

7. The lifetime of local and block-level variables is one execution of the procedure in which they are declared. The lifetime of module-level variables is the length of time that the form is loaded.

8. Identifiers should include the data type of the variable or constant.

9. Use the `Parse` methods to convert text values to numeric before performing any calculations.

10. Calculations may be performed using the values of numeric variables, constants, and the properties of controls. The result of a calculation may be assigned to a numeric variable or to the property of a control.

11. A calculation operation with more than one operator follows the order of precedence in determining the result of the calculation. Parentheses alter the order of operations.

12. To explicitly convert between numeric data types, use the Convert class. Some conversions can be performed implicitly.

13. The `Decimal.Round` method rounds a decimal value to the specified number of decimal positions.

14. The `ToString` method can be used to specify the appearance of values for display. By using formatting codes, you can specify dollar signs, commas, percent signs, and the number of decimal digits to display. The method rounds values to fit the format.

15. `Try/Catch/Finally` statements provide a method for checking for user errors such as blank or nonnumeric data or an entry that might result in a calculation error.

16. A run-time error is called an *exception*; catching and taking care of exceptions is called *error trapping* and *error handling*.

17. You can trap for different types of errors by specifying the exception type on the `Catch` statement, and you can have multiple `Catch` statements to catch more than one type of exception. Each exception is an instance of the Exception class; you can refer to the properties of the Exception object for further information.

18. A message box is a window for displaying information to the user.

19. The `Show` method of the MessageBox class is overloaded, which means that the method may be called with different argument lists, called signatures.

20. You can calculate a sum by adding each transaction to a module-level variable. In a similar fashion, you can calculate a count by adding to a module-level variable.

Key Terms

Review Questions

1. Name and give the purpose of five data types available in Visual Basic.
2. What does *declaring a variable* mean?
3. What effect does the location of a declaration statement have on the variable it declares?
4. Explain the difference between a constant and a variable.
5. What is the purpose of the `Integer.Parse` method? The `Decimal.Parse` method?
6. Explain the order of precedence of operators for calculations.
7. What statement(s) can be used to declare a variable?
8. Explain how to make an interest rate stored in rateDecimal display in rate-TextBox as a percentage with three decimal digits.
9. What are implicit conversions? Explicit conversions? When would each be used?
10. When should you use `Try/Catch` blocks? Why?
11. What is a message box and when should you use one?
12. Explain why the `MessageBox.Show` method has multiple signatures.
13. Why must you use module-level variables if you want to accumulate a running total of transactions?

Programming Exercises

3.1 Create a project that calculates the total of fat, carbohydrate, and protein calories. Allow the user to enter (in text boxes) the grams of fat, the grams of carbohydrates, and the grams of protein. Each gram of fat is nine calories; a gram of protein or carbohydrate is four calories.

Display the total calories for the current food item in a text box. Use two other text boxes to display an accumulated sum of the calories and a count of the items entered.

Form: The form should have three text boxes for the user to enter the grams for each category. Include labels next to each text box indicating what the user is to enter.

Include buttons to Calculate, to Clear the text boxes, and to Exit.

Make the form's Text property "Calorie Counter".

Code: Write the code for each button. Make sure to catch any bad input data and display a message box to the user.

3.2 Lennie McPherson, proprietor of Lennie's Bail Bonds, needs to calculate the amount due for setting bail. Lennie requires something of value as collateral, and his fee is 10 percent of the bail amount. He wants the screen to provide boxes to enter the bail amount and the item being used for collateral. The program must calculate the fee.

Form: Include text boxes for entering the amount of bail and the description of the collateral. Label each text box.

Include buttons for Calculate, Clear, and Exit.

The text property for the form should be "Lennie's Bail Bonds".

Code: Include event procedures for the click event of each button. Calculate the amount due as 10 percent of the bail amount and display it in a text box, formatted as currency. Make sure to catch any bad input data and display a message to the user.

3.3 In retail sales, management needs to know the average inventory figure and the turnover of merchandise. Create a project that allows the user to enter the beginning inventory, the ending inventory, and the cost of goods sold.

Form: Include labeled text boxes for the beginning inventory, the ending inventory, and the cost of goods sold. After calculating the answers, display the average inventory and the turnover formatted in text boxes.

Include buttons for Calculate, Clear, and Exit. The formulas for the calculations are

$$\text{Average inventory} = \frac{\text{Beginning inventory} + \text{Ending inventory}}{2}$$

$$\text{Turnover} = \frac{\text{Cost of goods sold}}{\text{Average inventory}}$$

Note: The average inventory is expressed in dollars; the turnover is the number of times the inventory turns over.

Code: Include procedures for the click event of each button. Display the results in text boxes. Format the average inventory as currency and the turnover as a number with one digit to the right of the decimal. Make sure to catch any bad input data and display a message to the user.

Test Data

Beginning	Ending	Cost of Goods Sold	Average Inventory	Turnover
58500	47000	400000	$52,750.00	7.6
75300	13600	515400	44,450.00	11.6
3000	19600	48000	11,300.00	4.2

3.4 A local recording studio rents its facilities for $200 per hour. Management charges only for the number of minutes used. Create a project in which the input is the name of the group and the number of minutes it used the studio. Your program calculates the appropriate charges, accumulates the total charges for all groups, and computes the average charge and the number of groups that used the studio.

Form: Use labeled text boxes for the name of the group and the number of minutes used. The charges for the current group should be displayed formatted in a text box. Create a group box for the summary information. Inside the group box, display the total charges for all groups, the number of groups, and the average charge per group. Format all output appropriately. Include buttons for Calculate, Clear, and Exit.

Code: Use a constant for the rental rate per hour; divide that by 60 to get the rental rate per minute. Do not allow bad input data to cancel the program.

Test Data

Group	Minutes
Pooches	95
Hounds	5
Mutts	480

Check Figures

Total Charges for Group	Total Number of Groups	Average Charge	Total Charges for All Groups
$316.67	1	$316.67	$316.67
$16.67	2	$166.67	$333.33
$1,600.00	3	$644.44	$1,933.33

3.5 Create a project that determines the future value of an investment at a given interest rate for a given number of years. The formula for the calculation is

Future value = Investment amount * (1 + Interest rate) ^ Years

Form: Use labeled text boxes for the amount of investment, the interest rate (as a decimal fraction), and the number of years the investment will be held. Display the future value in a text box formatted as currency.

Include buttons for Calculate, Clear, and Exit. Format all dollar amounts. Display a message to the user for nonnumeric or missing input data.

Test Data

Amount	Rate	Years
2000.00	.15	5
1234.56	.075	3

Check Figures

Future Value

$4.022.71

$1,533.69

Hint: Remember that the result of an exponentiation operation is a Double data type.

3.6 Write a project that calculates the shipping charge for a package if the shipping rate is $0.12 per ounce.

Form: Use labeled text boxes for the package-identification code (a six-digit code) and the weight of the package—one box for pounds and another one for ounces. Use a text box to display the shipping charge.

Include buttons for Calculate, Clear, and Exit.

Code: Include event procedures for each button. Use a constant for the shipping rate, calculate the shipping charge, and display it formatted in a text box. Display a message to the user for any bad input data.

Calculation hint: There are 16 ounces in a pound.

ID	Weight	Shipping Charge
L5496P	0 lb. 5 oz.	$0.60
J1955K	2 lb. 0 oz.	$3.84
Z0000Z	1 lb. 1 oz.	$2.04

3.7 Create a project for the local car rental agency that calculates rental charges. The agency charges $15 per day plus $0.12 per mile.

Form: Use text boxes for the customer name, address, city, state, ZIP code, beginning odometer reading, ending odometer reading, and the number of days the car was used. Use text boxes to display the miles driven and the total charge. Format the output appropriately.

Include buttons for Calculate, Clear, and Exit.

Code: Include an event procedure for each button. For the calculation, subtract the beginning odometer reading from the ending odometer reading to get the number of miles traveled. Use a constant for the $15 per day charge and the $0.12 mileage rate. Display a message to the user for any bad input data.

3.8   Create a project that will input an employee's sales and calculate the gross pay, deductions, and net pay. Each employee will receive a base pay of $900 plus a sales commission of 6 percent of sales.

After calculating the net pay, calculate the budget amount for each category based on the percentages given.

Pay

Base pay	$900; use a named constant
Commission	6% of sales
Gross pay	Sum of base pay and commission
Deductions	18% of gross pay
Net pay	Gross pay minus deductions

Budget

Housing	30% of net pay
Food and clothing	15% of net pay
Entertainment	50% of net pay
Miscellaneous	5% of net pay

Form: Use text boxes to input the employee's name and the dollar amount of the sales. Use text boxes to display the results of the calculations.

Provide buttons for Calculate, Clear, and Exit. Display a message to the user for any bad input data.

Case Studies

VB Mail Order

The company has instituted a bonus program to give its employees an incentive to sell more. For every dollar the store makes in a four-week period, the employees receive 2 percent of sales. The amount of bonus each employee receives is based upon the percentage of hours he or she worked during the bonus period (a total of 160 hours).

The screen will allow the user to enter the employee's name, the total hours worked, and the amount of the store's total sales. The amount of sales needs to be entered only for the first employee. (*Hint:* Don't clear it.)

The Calculate button will determine the bonus earned by this employee, and the Clear button will clear only the name and hours-worked fields. Do not allow missing or bad input data to cancel the program; instead display a message to the user.

VB Auto Center

Salespeople for used cars are compensated using a commission system. The commission is based on the costs incurred for the vehicle:

Commission = Commission rate *
(Sales price – Cost value)

The form will allow the user to enter the salesperson's name, the selling price of the vehicle, and the cost value of the vehicle. Use a constant of 20 percent for the commission rate.

The Calculate button will determine the commission earned by the salesperson; the Clear button will clear the text boxes. Do not allow bad input data to cancel the program; instead display a message to the user.

Video Bonanza

Design and code a project to calculate the amount due and provide a summary of rentals. All movies rent for $1.80 and all customers receive a 10 percent discount.

The form should contain input for the member number and the number of movies rented. Inside a group box, display the rental amount, the 10 percent discount, and the amount due. Inside a second group box, display the number of customers served and the total rental income (after discount).

Include buttons for Calculate, Clear, and Exit. The Clear button clears the information for the current rental but does not clear the summary information. Do not allow bad input data to cancel the program; instead display a message to the user.

Very Very Boards

Very Very Boards rents snowboards during the snow season. A person can rent a snowboard without boots or with boots. Create a project that will calculate and display the information for each rental. In addition, calculate the summary information for each day's rentals.

For each rental, input the person's name, the driver's license or ID number, the number of snowboards, and the number of snowboards with boots. Snowboards without boots rent for $20; snowboards with boots rent for $30.

Calculate and display the charges for snowboards and snowboards with boots, and the rental total. In addition, maintain summary totals. Use constants for the snowboard rental rate and the snowboard with boots rental rate.

Create a summary frame with boxes to indicate the day's totals for the number of snowboards and snowboards with boots rented, total charges, and average charge per customer.

Include buttons for Calculate Order, Clear, Clear All, and Exit. The Clear All command should clear the summary totals to begin a new day's summary. *Hint*: You must set each of the summary variables to zero as well as clear the summary boxes.

Make your buttons easy to use for keyboard entry. Make the Calculate button the accept button and the Clear button the cancel button.

Do not allow bad input data to cancel the program; instead display a message to the user.

4

Decisions and Conditions

1. Use If statements to control the flow of logic.

2. Understand and use nested If statements.

3. Read and create action diagrams that illustrate the logic in a selection process.

4. Evaluate conditions using the comparison operators.

5. Combine conditions using And, Or, AndAlso, and OrElse.

6. Test the Checked property of radio buttons and check boxes.

7. Perform validation on numeric fields.

8. Use a Case structure for multiple decisions.

9. Use one event procedure to respond to the events for multiple controls and determine which control caused the event.

10. Call an event procedure from another procedure.

11. Create message boxes with multiple buttons and choose alternate actions based on the user response.

12. Debug projects using breakpoints, stepping program execution, and displaying intermediate results.

In this chapter you will learn to write applications that can take one action or another, based on a condition. For example, you may need to keep track of sales separately for different classes of employees, different sections of the country, or different departments. You also will learn alternate techniques for checking the validity of input data and how to display multiple buttons in a message box and take different actions depending on the user response.

If Statements

A powerful capability of the computer is its ability to make decisions and to take alternate courses of action based on the outcome.

A decision made by the computer is formed as a question: Is a given condition true or false? If it is true, do one thing; if it is false, do something else.

If *the sun is shining* Then	(condition)
go to the beach	(action to take if condition is true)
Else	
go to class	(action to take if condition is false)
End If	(See Figure 4.1.)

or

If *you don't succeed* Then	(condition)
try, try again	(action)
End If	(See Figure 4.2.)

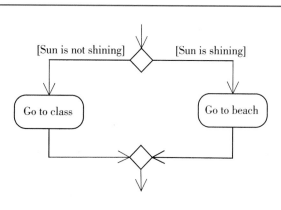

Figure 4.1

The logic of an If . . . Then . . . Else *statement in UML activity diagram form.*

Figure 4.2

The logic of an If *statement without an* Else *action in UML activity diagram form.*

Notice in the second example that no action is specified if the condition is not true.

In an `If` statement, when the condition is true, only the `Then` clause is executed. When the condition is false, only the `Else` clause, if present, is executed.

If . . . Then . . . Else Statement—General Form

```
If (condition) Then
    statement(s)
[ElseIf (condition) Then
    statement(s)]
[Else
    statements(s)]
End If
```

A block **If...Then...Else** must always conclude with **End If**. The word `Then` must appear on the same line as the `If` with nothing following `Then` (except a remark). `End  If` and `Else` (if used) must appear alone on a line. The statements under the `Then` and `Else` clauses are indented for readability and clarity.

Notice that the keyword `ElseIf` is all one word but that `End If` is two words.

If . . . Then . . . Else Statement—Example

When the number of units in unitsDecimal is less than 32, select the radio button for Freshman; otherwise, make sure the radio button is deselected (see Figure 4.3). Remember that when a radio button is selected, the Checked property has a Boolean value of True.

```
With Me
    unitsDecimal = Decimal.Parse(.unitsTextBox.Text)
    If unitsDecimal < 32D Then
        .freshmanRadioButton.Checked = True
    Else
        .freshmanRadioButton.Checked = False
    End If
End With
```

Figure 4.3

The `If` statement logic in UML activity diagram form. If the number of units is fewer than 32, the Freshman radio button will be selected; otherwise the Freshman radio button will be deselected.

Charting If Statements

A Uniform Modeling Language (UML) activity diagram is a useful tool for showing the logic of an If statement. It has been said that one picture is worth a thousand words. Many programmers find that a diagram helps them organize their thoughts and design projects more quickly.

The UML specification includes several types of diagrams. The activity diagram is a visual planning tool for decisions and actions for an entire application or a single procedure. The diamond-shape symbol (called a *decision symbol*) represents a condition. The branches from the decision symbol indicate which path to take for different results of the decision (Figure 4.4).

The UML activity diagram symbols used for program decisions and activities.

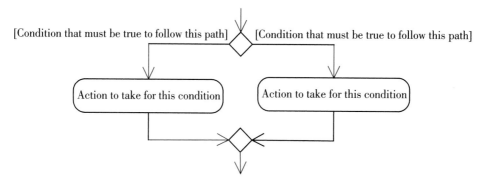

The Helpful Editor

You will find that the VS code editor is very helpful as you enter If statements. When you type an If statement and press Enter, the editor automatically adds the Then and End If statements and places the insertion point on a blank line, indented from the If. And if you type EndIf without the space, the editor adds the space for you.

The editor also attempts to correct some errors for you. If you type the word Else and another statement on the same line, which is illegal syntax, the editor adds a colon. A colon is a statement terminator, which allows you to have multiple statements on one line. However, good programming practices dictate that you should have only one statement per line, so if you find an extra colon in your code, remove it and correct the syntax.

Here is an example of illegal syntax:

```
' Illegal syntax.
If unitsDecimal < 32D Then
    Me.freshmanRadioButton.Checked = True
Else Me.freshmanRadioButton.Checked = False
End If
```

The editor's automatic correction, which you will fix, is

```
' The editor's automatic correction.
If unitsDecimal < 32D Then
    Me.freshmanRadioButton.Checked = True
Else : Me.freshmanRadioButton.Checked = False
End If
```

Fix this poor solution by separating the two statements into two separate lines:

```
' The preferred syntax.
If unitsDecimal < 32D Then
    Me.freshmanRadioButton.Checked = True
Else
    Me.freshmanRadioButton.Checked = False
End If
```

Conditions

The test in an If statement is based on a **condition**. To form conditions, you use **comparison operators** (Table 4.1), also called **relational operators**. The comparison is evaluated and the result is either True or False.

The conditions to be tested can be formed with numeric variables and constants, string variables and constants, object properties, and arithmetic expressions. However, it is important to note that comparisons must be made on like types; that is, strings can be compared only to other strings, and numeric values can be compared only to other numeric values, whether a variable, constant, property, or arithmetic expression.

The Comparison Operators   Table 4.1

Symbol	Relation Tested	Examples
>	greater than	`Decimal.Parse(Me.amountTextBox.Text) > limitDecimal` `correctInteger > 75`
<	less than	`Integer.Parse(Me.salesTextBox.Text) < 10000` `Me.nameTextBox.Text < nameString`
=	equal to	`Me.passwordTextBox.Text = "101"`
<>	not equal to	`Me.freshmanRadioButton.Checked <> True` `Me.nameTextBox.Text <> ""`
>=	greater than or equal to	`Integer.Parse(Me.quantityTextBox.Text) >= 500`
<=	less than or equal to	`Me.name1TextBox.Text <= Me.name2TextBox.Text`

Comparing Numeric Variables and Constants

When numeric values are involved in a test, an algebraic comparison is made; that is, the sign of the number is taken into account. Therefore, negative 20 is less than 10, and negative 2 is less than negative 1.

An equal sign (=) means replacement in an assignment statement. In a comparison, the equal sign is used to test for equality. For example, the condition

```
If Decimal.Parse(Me.priceTextBox.Text) = maximumDecimal Then
```

means "Is the current numeric value stored in priceTextBox.Text equal to the value stored in maximumDecimal?"

Sample Comparisons

alphaInteger	bravoInteger	charlieInteger
5	4	–5

Condition	Evaluates
alphaInteger = bravoInteger	False
charlieInteger < 0	True
bravoInteger > alphaInteger	False
charlieInteger <= bravoInteger	True
alphaInteger >= 5	True
alphaInteger <> charlieInteger	True

Comparing Strings

String variables can be compared to other string variables, string properties, or string literals enclosed in quotation marks. The comparison begins with the left-most character and proceeds one character at a time from left to right. As soon as a character in one string is not equal to the corresponding character in the second string, the comparison is terminated, and the string with the lower-ranking character is judged less than the other.

The determination of which character is less than another is based on the code used to store characters internally in the computer. The code, called the **ANSI code**, has an established order (called the *collating sequence*) for all letters, numbers, and special characters. (ANSI stands for American National Standards Institute.) In Table 4.2, A is less than B, L is greater than K, and all numeric digits are less than all letters. Some special symbols are lower than the numbers, some are higher, and the blank space is lower than the rest of the characters shown.

Note: VB actually stores string characters in Unicode, a coding system that uses 2 bytes to store every character. Using Unicode, all characters and symbols in foreign languages can be represented. For systems that do not use the foreign symbols, only the first byte of each character is used. And the first byte of Unicode is the same as the ANSI code. For comparison, Unicode can store 65,536 unique characters, ANSI code can store 256 unique characters, and ASCII, the earlier coding method, can store 128 unique characters. The first 128 characters of ANSI and Unicode are the same as the ASCII characters.

person1TextBox.Text	person2TextBox.Text
JOHN	JOAN

The condition `person1TextBox.Text < person2TextBox.Text` evaluates False. The *A* in JOAN is lower ranking than the *H* in JOHN.

The ANSI collating sequence

Code	Character	Code	Character	Code	Character
32	Space (blank)	64	@	96	`
33	!	65	A	97	a
34	"	66	B	98	b
35	#	67	C	99	c
36	$	68	D	100	d
37	%	69	E	101	e
38	&	70	F	102	f
39	' (apostrophe)	71	G	103	g
40	(	72	H	104	h
41	)	73	I	105	i
42	*	74	J	106	j
43	+	75	K	107	k
44	, (comma)	76	L	108	l
45	-	77	M	109	m
46	.	78	N	110	n
47	/	79	O	111	o
48	0	80	P	112	p
49	1	81	Q	113	q
50	2	82	R	114	r
51	3	83	S	115	s
52	4	84	T	116	t
53	5	85	U	117	u
54	6	86	V	118	v
55	7	87	W	119	w
56	8	88	X	120	x
57	9	89	Y	121	y
58	:	90	Z	122	z
59	;	91	[	123	{
60	<	92	\	124		
61	=	93	]	125	}
62	>	94	^	126	~
63	?	95	_	127	Del

word1TextBox.Text		word2TextBox.Text
HOPE		HOPELESS

The condition `word1TextBox.Text < word2TextBox.Text` evaluates True. When one string is shorter than the other, it compares as if the shorter string is padded with blanks to the right of the string, and the blank space is compared to a character in the longer string.

car1Label.Text		car2Label.Text
300ZX		Porsche

The condition `car1Label.Text < car2Label.Text` evaluates True. When the number 3 is compared to the letter P, the 3 is lower, since all numbers are lower ranking than all letters.

Feedback 4.1

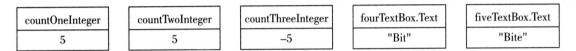

countOneInteger	countTwoInteger	countThreeInteger	fourTextBox.Text	fiveTextBox.Text
5	5	–5	"Bit"	"Bite"

Determine which conditions will evaluate True and which ones will evaluate False.

1. `countOneInteger >= countTwoInteger`
2. `countThreeInteger < 0`
3. `countThreeInteger < countTwoInteger`
4. `countOneInteger <> countTwoInteger`
5. `countOneInteger + 2 > countTwoInteger + 2`
6. `fourTextBox.Text < fiveTextBox.Text`
7. `fourTextBox.Text <> fiveTextBox.Text`
8. `fourTextBox.Text > "D"`
9. `"2" <> "Two""`
10. `"$" <= "?"`

Testing for True or False

You can use shortcuts when testing for True or False. Visual Basic evaluates the condition in an `If` statement. If the condition is a Boolean variable, it holds the values True or False.

For example:

```
If successfulOperationBoolean = True Then . . .
```

is equivalent to

```
If successfulOperationBoolean Then . . .
```

Comparing Uppercase and Lowercase Characters

When comparing strings, the case of the characters is important. An uppercase *Y* is not equal to a lowercase *y*. Because the user may type a name or word in uppercase, in lowercase, or as a combination of cases, we must check all possibilities. The best way is to use the **ToUpper** and **ToLower methods** of the

String class, which return the uppercase or lowercase equivalent of a string, respectively.

The ToUpper and ToLower Methods—General Forms

```
TextString.ToUpper()
TextString.ToLower()
```

The ToUpper and ToLower Methods—Examples

nameTextBox.Text Value	nameTextBox.Text.ToUpper()	nameTextBox.Text.ToLower()
Basic	BASIC	basic
PROGRAMMING	PROGRAMMING	programming
Robert Jones	ROBERT JONES	robert jones
hello	HELLO	hello

An example of a condition using the `ToUpper` method follows.

```
If nameTextBox.Text.ToUpper() = "BASIC" Then
    ' Do something.
End If
```

Note: When you convert nameTextBox.Text to uppercase, you must compare it to an uppercase literal ("BASIC") if you want it to evaluate as True.

Compound Conditions

You can use **compound conditions** to test more than one condition. Create compound conditions by joining conditions with **logical operators**, which compare Boolean expressions and return a Boolean result. The logical operators are `Or`, `And`, `Not`, `AndAlso`, `OrElse`, and `Xor`.

Logical Operator	Meaning	Example	Explanation
Or	If one condition or both conditions are True, the entire condition is True.	`Integer.Parse(Me.numberLabel.Text) = 1 Or _` `    Integer.Parse(Me.numberLabel.Text) = 2`	Evaluates True when numberLabel.Text is either "1" or "2".
And	Both conditions must be True for the entire condition to be True.	`Integer.Parse(Me.numberTextBox.Text) > 0 And _` `    Integer.Parse(Me.numberTextBox.Text) < 10`	Evaluates True when numberTextBox.Text is "1", "2", "3", "4", "5", "6", "7", "8", or "9".
Not	Reverses the condition so that a True condition will evaluate False and vice versa.	`Not Integer.Parse(Me.numberLabel.Text) = 0`	Evaluates True when numberLabel.Text is any value other than "0".
AndAlso	Short-circuiting version of And. If the first expression is False the condition returns False and the second expression is not evaluated.	`balanceDecimal > 0D AndAlso withinLimitBoolean`	If balanceDecimal is not greater than 0, the condition evaluates False and the second condition is not tested; otherwise works the same as an And.

continued

Logical Operator	Meaning	Example	Explanation
OrElse	Short-circuiting version of Or. If the first expression is True, the condition returns True and the second expression is not evaluated.	`numberCorrectInteger > 70 OrElse waiverBoolean`	If numberCorrectInteger is greater than 70, the conditions evaluates True and the second condition is not tested.
Xor	Exclusive Or; evaluates True if one or the other expression is True, but not both.	`countInteger > 10 Xor vipBoolean`	Evaluates True when countInteger > 10 or vipBoolean is True. If *both* conditions evaluate either True or False, this condition evaluates False.

Compound Condition—Examples

Examples

```
With Me
    If .maleRadioButton.Checked And Integer.Parse(.ageTextBox.Text) < 21 Then
        minorMaleCountInteger += 1
    End If

    If .juniorRadioButton.Checked Or .seniorRadioButton.Checked Then
        upperClassmanInteger += 1
    End If
End With
```

The first example requires that both the radio button test and the age test be True for the count to be incremented. In the second example, only one of the conditions must be True.

One caution when using compound conditions: Each side of the logical operator must be a complete condition. For example,

```
countInteger > 10 Or < 0
```

is incorrect. Instead, it must be

```
countInteger > 10 Or countInteger < 0
```

Combining Logical Operators

You can create compound conditions that combine multiple logical conditions. When you have both an And and an Or, the And is evaluated before the Or. However, you can change the order of evaluation by using parentheses; any condition inside parentheses will be evaluated first.

For example, will the following condition evaluate True or False? Try it with various values for saleDecimal, discountRadioButton, and stateTextBox.Text.

```
If saleDecimal > 1000.0D Or discountRadioButton.Checked And stateTextBox.Text.ToUpper() <> "CA" Then
    ' Code here to calculate the discount.
End If
```

saleDecimal	discountRadioButton.Checked	stateTextBox.Text.ToUpper	Evaluates
1500.0	False	CA	True
1000.0	True	OH	True
1000.0	True	CA	False
1500.0	True	NY	True
1000.0	False	CA	False

Short-Circuit Operations

Visual Basic .NET has two operators that provide **short-circuit** evaluation for compound conditions: the AndAlso and OrElse. When evaluating a compound condition formed with an And, VB evaluates both expressions for True or False, then evaluates the And. But you might prefer to not evaluate the second expression if the first expression evaluates False. For example, the following two statements both evaluate False when countInteger = 0, but the first statement evaluates both conditions and the second one stops after evaluating the first condition:

```
countInteger >= 0 And countInteger <= 10 ' Always tests both conditions.
countInteger >= 0 AndAlso countInteger <= 10 ' Short circuits when the first
                                    ' condition evaluates False.
```

The OrElse is designed to short circuit when the first condition evaluates True. In a regular Or operation, if one or the other condition is True, the entire compound condition is True. So if the first condition is True, it really isn't necessary to test the second condition. These two examples both evaluate False if totalInteger = −1 (negative 1), but the second example will perform one less comparison:

```
totalInteger < 0 Or totalInteger > 10
totalInteger < 0 OrElse totalInteger > 10
```

You may be wondering whether to use these short-circuit operators, which are included here for completeness. Generally, the AndAlso and OrElse are used for more advanced programming, when the second expression should not be executed for some reason. For your programs in this chapter, you can stick with the And and Or operators.

Nested If Statements

In many programs, another If statement is one of the statements to be executed when a condition tests True or False. If statements that contain additional If statements are said to be **nested If** statements. The following example shows a nested If statement in which the second If occurs in the Then portion of the first If (Figure 4.5).

Figure 4.5

Diagramming a nested If *statement.*

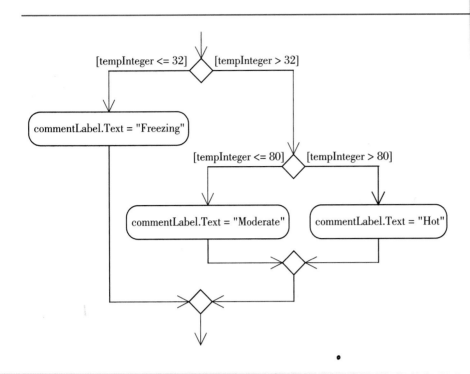

```
With Me
    If tempInteger > 32 Then
        If tempInteger > 80 Then
            .commentLabel.Text = "Hot"
        Else
            .commentLabel.Text = "Moderate"
        End If
    Else
        .commentLabel.Text = "Freezing"
    End If
End With
```

To nest If statements in the Else portion, you may use either of the following approaches; however, your code is simpler if you use the second method (using ElseIf . . . Then).

```
' One approach.
With Me
    If tempInteger <= 32 Then
        .commentLabel.Text = "Freezing"
    Else
        If tempInteger > 80 Then
            .commentLabel.Text = "Hot"
        Else
            .commentLabel.Text = "Moderate"
        End If
    End If
End With
```

```
' A simpler approach.
With Me
    If tempInteger <= 32 Then
        .commentLabel.Text = "Freezing"
    ElseIf tempInteger > 80 Then
        .commentLabel.Text = "Hot"
    Else
        .commentLabel.Text = "Moderate"
    End If
End With
```

You can nest Ifs in both the Then and Else. In fact, you may continue to nest Ifs within Ifs as long as each If has an End If. However, projects become very difficult to follow (and may not perform as intended) when Ifs become too deeply nested (Figure 4.6).

Figure 4.6

A diagram of a nested If statement with Ifs nested on both sides of the original If.

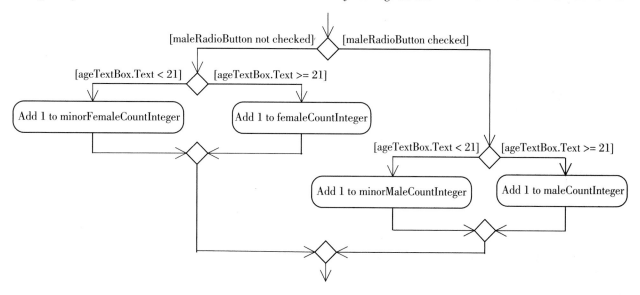

```
With Me
    If .maleRadioButton.Checked Then
        If Integer.Parse(.ageTextBox.Text) < 21 Then
            minorMaleCountInteger += 1
        Else
            maleCountInteger += 1
        End If
    Else
        If Integer.Parse(.ageTextBox.Text) < 21 Then
            minorFemaleCountInteger += 1
        Else
            femaleCountInteger += 1
        End If
    End If
End With
```

Feedback 4.2

Assume that `frogsInteger = 10`, `toadsInteger = 5`, and `polliwogsInteger = 6`. What will be displayed for each of the following statements?

> **TIP**
>
> **I**ndentation can help you catch errors. Visual Basic always matches an `Else` with the last unmatched `If` regardless of the indentation. ∎

```
1. If frogsInteger > polliwogsInteger Then
        Me.frogsRadioButton.Checked = True
   Else
        Me.frogsRadioButton.Checked = False
   End If
2. If frogsInteger > toadsInteger + polliwogsInteger Then
        Me.resultTextBox.Text = "It's the frogs"
   Else
        Me.resultTextBox.Text = "It's the toads and the polliwogs"
   End If
3. If polliwogsInteger > toadsInteger And frogsInteger <> 0 _
     Or toadsInteger = 0 Then
        Me.resultTextBox.Text = "It's true"
   Else
        Me.resultTextBox.Text = "It's false"
   End If
```

4. Write the statements necessary to compare the numeric values stored in applesTextBox.Text and orangesTextBox.Text. Display in most-TextBox.Text which has more, the apples or the oranges.
5. Write the Basic statements that will test the current value of balanceDecimal. When balanceDecimal is greater than zero, the check box for Funds Available, called fundsCheckBox, should be selected, the balanceDecimal set back to zero, and countInteger incremented by one. When balanceDecimal is zero or less, fundsCheckBox should not be selected (do not change the value of balanceDecimal or increment the counter).

Using If Statements with Radio Buttons and Check Boxes

In Chapter 2 you used the CheckedChanged event for radio buttons and check boxes to carry out the desired action. Now that you can use `If` statements, you should not take action in the CheckedChanged event procedures for these controls. Instead, use `If` statements to determine which options are selected.

To conform to good programming practice and make your programs consistent with standard Windows applications, place your code in the Click event of buttons, such as an OK button or an Apply button. For example, refer to the Visual Studio *Tools / Options* dialog box (Figure 4.7); no action will occur when you click on a radio button or check box. Instead, when you click on the OK button, VS checks to see which options are selected.

Figure 4.7

The Options *dialog box. When the user clicks OK, the program checks the state of all radio buttons and check boxes.*

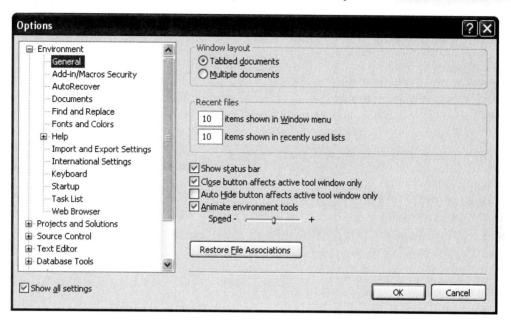

In an application such as the message formatter project in Chapter 2 (refer to Figure 2.19), you could modify the code for the Display button to include code similar to the following:

```
With Me
    If .redRadioButton.Checked Then
        .nameLabel.ForeColor = Color.Red
    ElseIf .greenRadioButton.Checked Then
        .nameLabel.ForeColor = Color.Green
    ElseIf .blueRadioButton.Checked Then
        .nameLabel.ForeColor = Color.Blue
    Else
        .nameLabel.ForeColor = Color.Black
    End If
End With
```

Additional Examples

```
With Me
    If .fastShipCheckBox.Checked Then
        totalDecimal += fastShipRateDecimal
    End If

    If .giftWrapCheckBox.Checked Then
        totalDecimal += WRAP_AMOUNT_Decimal
    End If
End With
```

A "Simple Sample"

Test your understanding of the use of the `If` statement by coding some short examples.

Test the Value of a Check Box

Create a small project that contains a check box, a label, and a button. Name the button testButton, the check box testCheckBox, and the label messageLabel. In the Click event procedure for testButton, check the value of the check box. If the check box is currently checked, display "Check box is checked" in messageLabel.

```
Private Sub testButton_Click(ByVal sender As System.Object, ByVal e As System.EventArgs) _
    Handles testButton.Click
        'Test the value of the check box.

        With Me
            If .testCheckBox.Checked Then
                .messageLabel.Text = "Check box is checked."
            End If
        End With
```

Test your project. When it works, add an `Else` to the code that displays "Check box is not checked."

Test the State of Radio Buttons

Remove the check box from the previous project and replace it with two radio buttons, named freshmanRadioButton and sophomoreRadioButton and labeled "<= 32 units" and "> 32 units". Now change the `If` statement to display "Freshman" or "Sophomore" in the label.

```
With Me
    If .freshmanRadioButton.Checked Then
        .messageLabel.Text = "Freshman"
    Else
        .messageLabel.Text = "Sophomore"
    End If
End With
```

Can you modify the sample to work for Freshman, Sophomore, Junior, and Senior? In the sections that follow, you will see code for testing multiple radio buttons and check boxes.

Checking the State of a Radio Button Group

Nested `If` statements work very well for determining which button of a radio button group is selected. Recall that in any group of radio buttons, only one button can be selected. Assume that your form has a group of radio buttons for Freshman, Sophomore, Junior, or Senior. In a calculation procedure, you want to add 1 to one of four counter variables, depending on which radio button is selected:

```
With Me
    If .freshmanRadioButton.Checked Then
        freshmanCountInteger += 1
    ElseIf .sophomoreRadioButton.Checked Then
        sophomoreCountInteger += 1
    ElseIf .juniorRadioButton.Checked Then
        juniorCountInteger += 1
    ElseIf .seniorRadioButton.Checked Then
        seniorCountInteger += 1
    End If
End With
```

Note that in most situations, the final condition is unnecessary. You should be able to use an `Else` and add to seniorRadioButton if the first three conditions are false. You might prefer to code the condition to make the statement more clear, or if no radio button is set initially, or if the program sets all radio buttons to False.

Checking the State of Multiple Check Boxes

Although nested `If` statements work very well for groups of radio buttons, the same is not true for a series of check boxes. Recall that if you have a series of check boxes, any number of the boxes may be selected. In this situation, assume that you have check boxes for Discount, Taxable, and Delivery. You will need separate `If` statements for each condition.

```
With Me
    If .discountCheckBox.Checked Then
        ' Calculate the discount.
    End If
    If .taxableCheckBox.Checked Then
        ' Calculate the tax.
    End If
    If .deliveryCheckBox.Checked Then
        ' Deliver it.
    End If
End With
```

Enhancing Message Boxes

In Chapter 3 you learned to display a message box to the user. Now it's time to add such features as controlling the format of the message, displaying multiple buttons, checking which button the user clicks, and performing alternate actions depending on the user's selection.

Displaying the Message String

The message string you display in a message box may be a string literal enclosed in quotes or it may be a string variable. You also may want to concatenate several items, for example, combining a literal with a value from a variable. It's usually a good idea to create a variable for the message and format the message before calling the Show method; if nothing else, it makes your code easier to read and follow.

Combining Values into a Message String

You can concatenate a literal such as "Total Sales:" with the value from a variable. You may need to include an extra space inside the literal to make sure that the value is separated from the literal.

```
Dim messageString As String

messageString = "Total Sales: " & totalSalesDecimal.ToString("C")
MessageBox.Show(messageString, "Sales Summary", MessageBoxButtons.OK)
```

Creating Multiple Lines of Output

If your message is too long for one line, VB wraps it to a second line. But if you would like to control the line length and position of the split, you can insert a **NewLine character** into the string message. Use the Visual Studio intrinsic constant ControlChars.NewLine to determine line endings. You can concatenate this constant into a message string to set up multiple lines.

In this example, a second line is added to the MessageBox from the previous example.

```
Dim formattedTotalString          As String
Dim formattedAvgString            As String
Dim messageString                 As String

formattedTotalString = totalSalesDecimal.ToString("N")
formattedAvgString = averageSaleDecimal.ToString("N")
messageString = "Total Sales:  " & formattedTotalString & ControlChars.NewLine _
   & "Average Sale:  " & formattedAvgString

MessageBox.Show(messageString, "Sales Summary", MessageBoxButtons.OK)
```

You can combine multiple NewLine constants to achieve double spacing and create multiple message lines (Figure 4.8).

Figure 4.8

A message box with multiple lines of output, created by concatenating two NewLine characters at the end of each line.

```
' Concatenate the message string.
messageString = "Number of Orders:  " & customerCount.ToString() _
  & ControlChars.NewLine & ControlChars.NewLine _
  & "Total Sales:  " & grandTotalDecimal.ToString("C") _
  & ControlChars.NewLine & ControlChars.NewLine _
  & "Average Sale:  " & averageDecimal.ToString("C")

' Display the message box.
MessageBox.Show(messageString, "Coffee Sales Summary", MessageBoxButtons.OK, _
  MessageBoxIcon.Information)
```

Using the ControlChars Constants

You can use several other intrinsic constants from the ControlChars list in addition to the `NewLine` constant. Type "ControlChars" and a period into the editor to see the complete list.

ControlChar Constant	Description
CrLf	Carriage return/linefeed character combination.
Cr	Carriage return.
Lf	Line feed.
NewLine	New line character. Same effect as a carriage return/line feed character combination.
NullChar	Character with a value of zero.
Tab	Tab character.
Back	Backspace character.
FormFeed	Formfeed character (not useful in Microsoft Windows).
VerticalTab	Vertical tab character (not useful in Microsoft Windows).
Quote	Quotation mark character.

Displaying Multiple Buttons

You can choose the buttons to display on the message box using the `Message-BoxButtons` constants (Figure 4.9). Figure 4.10 shows a MessageBox with two buttons using the `MessageBoxButtons.YesNo` constant. The `Show` method returns a **DialogResult object** that you can check to see which button the user clicked.

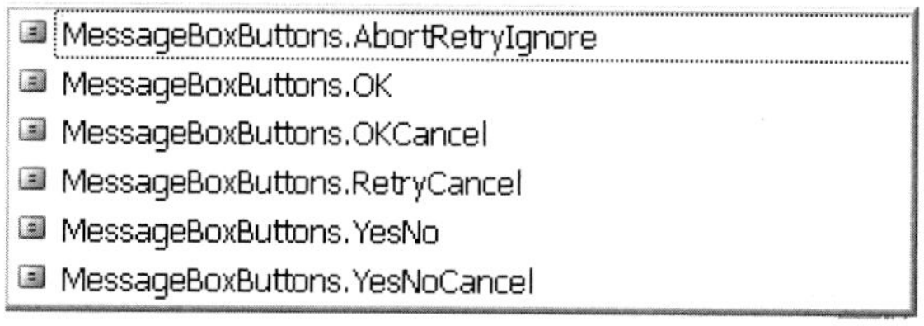

Figure   4.9

Choose the button(s) to display from the `MessageBoxButtons` *constants.*

```
MessageBoxButtons.AbortRetryIgnore
MessageBoxButtons.OK
MessageBoxButtons.OKCancel
MessageBoxButtons.RetryCancel
MessageBoxButtons.YesNo
MessageBoxButtons.YesNoCancel
```

Figure 4.10

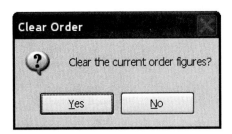

Determining the Return Type of a Method

How do you know that the `Show` method returns an object of the DialogResult class? An easy way is to point to the `Show` keyword and pause; the argument list that you are using pops up (Figure 4.11).

Figure 4.11

```
MessageBox.Show(messageString, "Coffee Sales Summary")
Public Shared Function Show(text As String, caption As String) As System.Windows.Forms.DialogResult
```

Declaring an Object Variable for the Method Return

To capture the information about the outcome of the `Show` method, you must declare a variable that can hold an instance of the DialogResult type.

```
Dim whichButtonDialogResult As DialogResult
```

Then you assign the return value of the `Show` method to the new variable.

```
whichButtonDialogResult = MessageBox.Show("Clear the current order figures?", "Clear Order", _
    MessageBoxButtons.YesNo, MessageBoxIcon.Question)
```

The next step is to check the value of the return, comparing to the DialogResult constants, such as `Yes`, `No`, `OK`, `Retry`, `Abort`, and `Cancel`.

```
If whichButtonDialogResult = DialogResult.Yes Then
  ' Code to clear the order.
End If
```

Specifying a Default Button and Options

Two additional signatures for the `MessageBox.Show` method are as follows:

```
MessageBox.Show(TextMessage, TitlebarText, MessageBoxButtons, MessageBoxIcons, _
    MessageBoxDefaultButton)
MessageBox.Show(TextMessage, TitlebarText, MessageBoxButtons, MessageBoxIcons, _
    MessageBoxDefaultButton, MessageBoxOptions)
```

When you display multiple buttons, you may want one of the buttons to be the default (the accept button). For example, to make the second button (the *No* button) the default, use this statement:

```
responseDialogResult = MessageBox.Show("Clear the current order figures?", "Clear Order", _
    MessageBoxButtons.YesNo, MessageBoxIcon.Question, MessageBoxDefaultButton.Button2)
```

You can right-align the message in the message box by setting the Message-BoxOptions argument:

```
responseDialogResult = MessageBox.Show("Clear the current order figures?", "Clear Order", _
    MessageBoxButtons.YesNo, MessageBoxIcon.Question, MessageBoxDefaultButton.Button2, _
    MessageBoxOptions.RightAlign)
```

Input Validation

Careful programmers check the values entered into text boxes before beginning the calculations. Validation is a form of self-protection; it is better to reject bad data than to spend hours (and sometimes days) trying to find an error only to discover that the problem was caused by a "user error." Finding and correcting the error early can often keep the program from producing erroneous results or halting with a run-time error.

Checking to verify that appropriate values have been entered for a text box is called **validation**. The validation may include making sure that the input is numeric, checking for specific values, checking a range of values, or making sure that required items are entered.

In Chapter 3 you learned to use `Try/Catch` blocks to trap for nonnumeric values. This chapter presents some additional validation techniques using `If` statements.

Note: Chapter 14 has some advanced validation techniques using the Validating event and error providers.

Checking for a Range of Values

Data validation may include checking the reasonableness of a value. Assume you are using a text box to input the number of hours worked in a day. Even with overtime, the company does not allow more than 10 work hours in a single day. You could check the input for reasonableness with this code:

```
If Integer.Parse(Me.hoursTextBox.Text) <= 10 Then
    ' Code to perform calculations.
Else
    MessageBox.Show("Too many hours", "Invalid Data", MessageBoxButtons.OK)
End If
```

Checking for a Required Field

Sometimes you need to be certain that a value has been entered into a text box before proceeding. You can compare a text box value to an empty string literal.

```
If nameTextBox.Text <> "" Then
    ' Code to perform some action.
Else
    MessageBox.Show("Required Entry", "Sales Summary", MessageBoxButtons.OK)
End If
```

By checking separately for blank or nonnumeric data, you can display a better message to the user. Make sure to check for blanks first, since a blank field will throw an exception with a parsing method. For example, if you reverse the order of the If and Try blocks in the following example, blanks in quantityTextBox will always trigger the nonnumeric message in the Catch block.

```
If Me.quantityTextBox.Text <> "" Then          ' Not blank.
    Try
        quantityDecimal = Decimal.Parse(Me.quantityTextBox.Text)
    Catch ' Nonnumeric data.
        messageString = "Nonnumeric data entered for quantity."
        MessageBox.Show(messageString, "Data Entry Error")
    End Try
Else                        ' Missing data.
    messageString = "Enter the quantity."
    MessageBox.Show(messageString, "Data entry error")
End If
```

Performing Multiple Validations

When you need to validate several input fields, how many message boxes do you want to display for the user? Assume that the user has neglected to fill five text boxes or make a required selection and clicked on Calculate. You can avoid displaying multiple message boxes in a row by using a nested If statement. This way you check the second value only if the first one passes, and you can exit the processing if a problem is found with a single field.

```
With Me
    If .nameTextBox.Text <> "" Then
        Try
            unitsDecimal = Decimal.Parse(.unitsTextBox.Text)
            If .freshmanRadioButton.Checked Or .sophomoreRadioButton.Checked _
                Or .juniorRadioButton.Checked Or .seniorRadioButton.Checked Then

                ' Data valid - Do calculations or processing here.

            Else
                MessageBox.Show ("Please select a Grade Level.", "Data Entry Error", _
                    MessageBoxButtons.OK)
            End If
        Catch anException As FormatException
            MessageBox.Show ("Enter number of units.", "Data Entry Error", _
                MessageBoxButtons.OK)
            .unitsTextBox.Focus()
        End Try
    Else
        MessageBox.Show ("Please enter a name", "Data Entry Error", _
            MessageBoxButtons.OK)
        .nameTextBox.Focus()
    End If
End With
```

Limiting User Actions by Disabling Controls

At times you can save errors or additional error checking by limiting the choices that you offer to the user. You have seen disabled buttons and menu choices that are "grayed" for some operations and enabled at other times. You can disable or gray a control by setting its Enabled property to False. Then, when the time is appropriate, set the property to True to enable the control.

As an example, consider an application that calculates an average. You don't want the user to attempt a calculation before the first item is entered, since dividing by zero throws an exception. You already know how to use a Try/Catch block to trap for the error or use an If statement to check for zero. But how about not allowing the user to click on the Average button until the first value is entered? This is often the most civilized approach.

In Figure 4.12 the Average button is disabled at design time. After the first score is entered, the button is enabled.

```
Private Sub addButton_Click(ByVal sender As System.Object, _
    ByVal e As System.EventArgs) Handles addButton.Click
    ' Add score to sum and count.

    With Me
        sumInteger += Integer.Parse(.scoreTextBox.Text)
        countInteger += 1
        .scoreTextBox.Clear()
        .averageButton.Enabled = True
    End With
End Sub
```

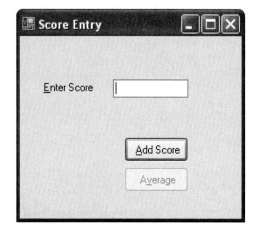

Figure 4.12

The Average button is disabled at design time and enabled during program execution, to limit the user's choices to legal operations.

The Case Structure

Earlier you used the If statement for testing conditions and making decisions. Whenever you want to test a single variable for multiple values, the **Case structure** provides a flexible and powerful solution. Any decisions that you can code with a Case structure also can be coded with nested If statements, but usually the Case structure is simpler and clearer.

The Select Case Statement—General Form

General Form

```
Select Case expression
     Case ConstantList
          [Statement(s)]
     [Case ConstantList
          [Statement(s)]]
          .
          .
          .
     [Case Else]
          [Statement(s)]
End Select
```

The expression in a **Case** structure is usually a variable or property that you wish to test.

The constant list is the value that you want to match; it may be a numeric or string constant or variable, a range of values, a relational condition, or a combination of these.

There is no limit to the number of statements that can follow a **Case** statement.

The Select Case Statement—Examples

Examples

```
With Me
     Select Case scoreInteger
          Case Is >= 100
               .messageLabel1.Text = "Excellent Score"
               .messageLabel2.Text = "Give yourself a pat on the back."
          Case 80 To 99
               .messageLabel1.Text = "Very Good"
               .messageLabel2.Text = "You should be proud."
          Case 60 To 79
               .messageLabel1.Text = "Satisfactory Score"
               .messageLabel2.Text = "You should have a nice warm feeling."
          Case Else
               .messageLabel1.Text = "Your score shows room for improvement."
               .messageLabel2.Text = ""
     End Select
End With

Select Case listIndexInteger
     Case 0
          ' Code to handle item zero.
     Case 1, 2, 3
          ' Code to handle items 1, 2, or 3.
     Case Else
          ' Code to handle any other value.
End Select
```

The examples show a combination of comparison operators, constant ranges, and multiple constants. Notice these points from the examples:

When using a comparison operator (e.g., **Is >= 100**), the word **Is** must be used.

To indicate a range of constants, use the word To (e.g., 80 To 99). Multiple constants should be separated by commas.

The elements used for the constant list may have any of these forms:

```
constant [, constant...]              Case 2, 5, 9
constant To constant                  Case 25 To 50
Is comparison-operator constant       Case Is > 100
```

You could also use all these forms in one case statement to test for multiple conditions:

```
Case 2, 5, 9, 25 To 50, Is > 100
```

When you want to test for a string value, you must include quotation marks around the literals.

Example

```
Select Case Me.teamNameTextBox.Text
    Case "Tigers"
        ' Code for Tigers.
    Case "Leopards"
        ' Code for Leopards.
    Case "Cougars", "Panthers"
        ' Code for Cougars and Panthers.
    Case Else
        ' Code for any nonmatch.
End Select
```

Note that in the previous example, the capitalization must also match exactly. A better solution would be

```
Select Case Me.teamNameTextBox.Text.ToUpper()
    Case "TIGERS"
        ' Code for Tigers.
    Case "LEOPARDS"
        ' Code for Leopards.
    Case "COUGARS", "PANTHERS"
        ' Code for Cougars and Panthers.
    Case Else
        ' Code for any nonmatch.
End Select
```

Although the Case Else clause is optional, generally you will want to include it in **Select Case** statements. The statements you code beneath Case Else execute only if none of the other Case conditions is matched. This clause provides checking for any invalid or unforeseen values of the expression being tested. If the Case Else clause is omitted and none of the Case conditions is True, the program continues execution at the statement following the End Select.

If more than one Case value is matched by the expression, only the statements in the *first* matched Case clause execute.

Feedback 4.3

Convert the following `If` statements to `Select Case` statements.

1. ```
If tempInteger <= 32 Then
    Me.commentLabel.Text = "Freezing"
ElseIf tempInteger > 80 Then
    Me.commentLabel.Text = "Hot"
Else
    Me.commentLabel.Text = "Moderate"
End If
```

2. ```
If countInteger = 0 Then
    MessageBox.Show("No items were entered.")
ElseIf countInteger < 11 Then
    MessageBox.Show("1 — 10 items were entered.")
ElseIf countInteger < 21 Then
    MessageBox.Show("11 — 20 items were entered.")
Else
    MessageBox.Show("More than 20 items were entered.")
End If
```

Sharing an Event Procedure

A very handy feature of VB .NET is the ability to share an event procedure for several controls. For example, assume that you have a group of five radio buttons to allow the user to choose a color (Figure 4.13). Each of the radio buttons must have its own name and will ordinarily have its own event procedure. But you can add events to the `Handles` clause at the top of an event procedure to make the procedure respond to events of other controls.

```
Private Sub blueRadioButton_CheckedChanged(ByVal sender As System.Object, _
    ByVal e As System.EventArgs) _
    Handles blueRadioButton.CheckedChanged, blackRadioButton.CheckedChanged, _
    redRadioButton.CheckedChanged, whiteRadioButton.CheckedChanged, _
    yellowRadioButton.CheckedChanged
```

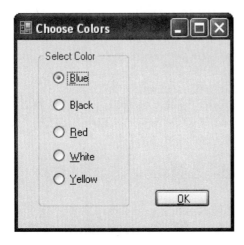

Figure 4.13

The five radio buttons allow the user to choose the color.

After you have added the additional events to the Handles clause, this event procedure will execute when the user selects *any* of the radio buttons.

A good, professional technique is to set up a module-level variable to hold the selection that the user makes. Then, in the OK button's event procedure you can take action based on which of the buttons was selected.

The key to using the shared event procedure is the sender argument that is passed to the CheckedChanged event procedure. The sender is defined as an object, which has a Name property. However, if you refer to sender.Name with Option Strict turned on, you generate a compiler error telling you that late binding is not allowed. **Late binding** means that the type cannot be determined at compile time but must be determined at run time. Late binding is allowed with Option Strict turned off but should be avoided if possible for performance reasons.

You can use the properties of the sender argument if you first cast (convert) sender to a specific object type instead of the generic object. You can use VB's **CType function** to convert from one object type to another:

```
CType(ValueToConvert, NewType)
```

The CType function returns an object of the new type. If the *ValueToConvert* is not in the range of legal values for *NewType*, an exception is generated at run time.

For the radio button example, declare a variable as RadioButton data type, cast the sender argument to a RadioButton object type, and assign it to the new variable:

```
Dim selectedRadioButton As RadioButton
selectedRadioButton = CType(sender, RadioButton)
```

After these statements, you can refer to selectedRadioButton.Name to determine which radio button was selected:

```
Select Case selectedRadioButton.Name
    Case "blueRadioButton"
        ' Code for blue button.
```

You can declare a module-level variable as a Color data type, assign the chosen color in the shared event procedure, and then apply the color in the OK button's click event.

```
' Declare a module-level variable.
 Private selectedColor As Color

Private Sub blueRadioButton_CheckedChanged(ByVal sender As System.Object, _
  ByVal e As System.EventArgs)  Handles yellowRadioButton.CheckedChanged, _
  whiteRadioButton.CheckedChanged, redRadioButton.CheckedChanged, _
  blackRadioButton.CheckedChanged, blueRadioButton.CheckedChanged
     ' Save the name of the selected button.

    Dim selectedRadioButton As RadioButton

    selectedRadioButton = CType(sender, RadioButton)
```

```
    Select Case selectedRadioButton.Name
        Case "blueRadioButton"
            selectedColor = Color.Blue
        Case "blackRadioButton"
            selectedColor = Color.Black
        Case "redRadioButton"
            selectedColor = Color.Red
        Case "whiteRadioButton"
            selectedColor = Color.White
        Case "yellowRadioButton"
            selectedColor = Color.Yellow
    End Select
End Sub

Private Sub okButton_Click(ByVal sender As System.Object, _
    ByVal e As System.EventArgs) Handles okButton.Click
        ' Change the color based on the selected radio button.

    Me.BackColor = selectedColor
End Sub
```

Calling Event Procedures

If you wish to perform a set of instructions in more than one location, you don't have to duplicate the code. Write the instructions once, in an event procedure, and "call" the procedure from another procedure. When you **call** an event procedure, the entire procedure is executed and then execution returns to the statement following the call.

The Call Statement—General Form

General Form

```
[Call] ProcedureName()
```

Notice that the keyword `Call` is optional and rarely used. You must include the parentheses; if the procedure that you are calling requires arguments, then place the arguments within the parentheses; otherwise leave them empty. Note that all procedure calls in this chapter do require arguments.

The Call Statement—Examples

Examples

```
Call clearButton_Click(sender, e)
clearButton_Click(sender, e)       ' Equivalent to the previous statement.
```

Notice the arguments for both of the example `Call` statements. You are passing the same two arguments that were passed to the calling procedure. If you examine any of the editor-generated event procedure headers, you can see that every event procedure requires these two arguments, which can be used to track the object that generated the event.

```
Private Sub summaryButton_Click( _
    ByVal sender As System.Object, ByVal e As System.EventArgs) Handles summaryButton.Click
...
    newOrderButton_Click(sender, e) ' Call the newOrderButton_Click event procedure.
```

In the programming example that follows, you will accumulate individual items for one customer. When that customer's order is complete, you need to clear the entire order and begin an order for the next customer. Refer to the interface in Figure 4.14; notice the two buttons: *Clear for Next Item* and *New Order*. The button for next item clears the text boxes on the screen. The button for a new order must clear the screen text boxes and clear the subtotal fields. Rather than repeat the instructions to clear the individual screen text boxes, we can call the event procedure for clearButton_Click from the newOrderButton_Click procedure.

```
Private Sub newOrderButton_Click(ByVal sender As System.Object, ByVal e As System.EventArgs) _
    Handles newOrderButton.Click
        ' Clear the current order and add to totals.

    clearButton_Click(sender, e)   ' Call the clearButton_Click event procedure.
        ' Continue with statements to clear subtotals.
```

In the newOrderButton_Click procedure, all the instructions in clearButton_Click are executed. Then execution returns to the next statement following the call.

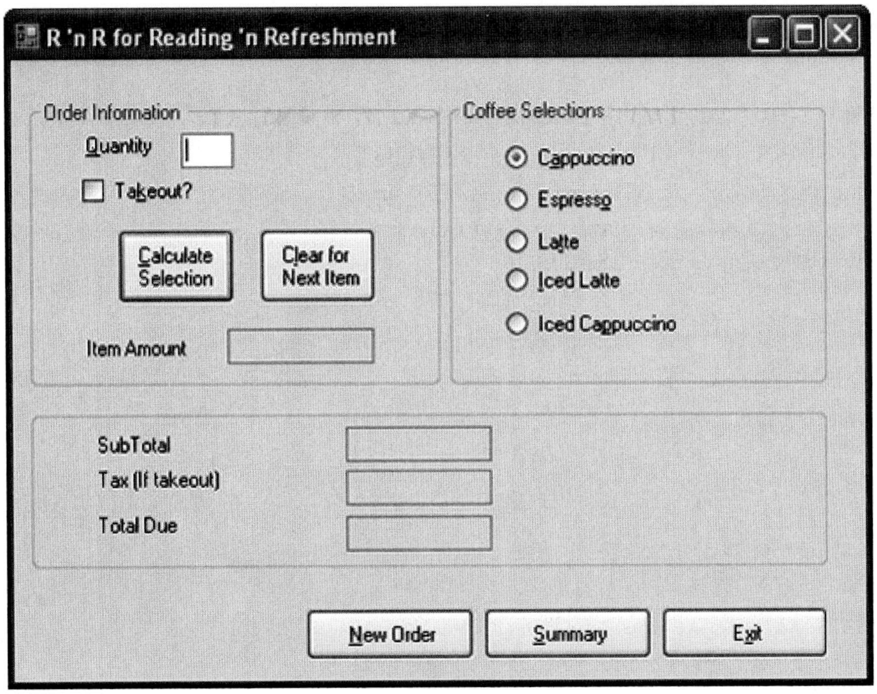

Figure 4.14

A form with buttons that perform overlapping functions. The New Order button must do the same tasks as Clear for Next Item.

Your Hands-On Programming Example

Create a project for R 'n R—for Reading 'n Refreshment that calculates the amount due for individual orders and maintains accumulated totals for a summary. Have a check box for takeout items, which are taxable at 8 percent; all other orders are nontaxable. Include radio buttons for the five coffee selections: Cappuccino, Espresso, Latte, Iced Cappuccino, and Iced Latte. The prices for each will be assigned using these constants:

Cappuccino	2.00
Espresso	2.25
Latte	1.75
Iced (either)	2.50

Use a button for *Calculate Selection*, which will calculate and display the amount due for each item. Display appropriate error messages for missing or nonnumeric data.

A button for *Clear for Next Item* will clear the selections and the amount for the current item and set the focus back to the quantity. The Clear button should be disabled when the program begins and be enabled after the user begins an order.

Additional text boxes in a separate group box will display the summary information for the current order, including subtotal, tax, and total.

Buttons at the bottom of the form will be used for *New Order*, *Summary*, and *Exit*. The *New Order* button will confirm that the user wants to clear the current order. If the user agrees, clear the current order and add to the summary totals. The *Summary* button should display a message box with the number of orders, the total dollar amount, and the average sale amount per order.

Planning the Project

Sketch a form (Figure 4.15), which your users sign as meeting their needs.

Plan the Objects and Properties Plan the property settings for the form and each of the controls.

Object	Property	Setting
billingForm	Name	billingForm
	Text	R 'n R for Reading 'n Refreshment
	AcceptButton	calculateButton
	CancelButton	clearButton
GroupBox1	Text	Order Information
GroupBox2	Text	Coffee Selections
GroupBox3	Text	(blank)
cappuccinoRadioButton	Name	cappuccinoRadioButton
	Text	C&appuccino
	Checked	True
espressoRadioButton	Name	espressoRadioButton
	Text	Espress&o

Figure 4.15

The planning sketch of the form for the hands-on programming exercise example.

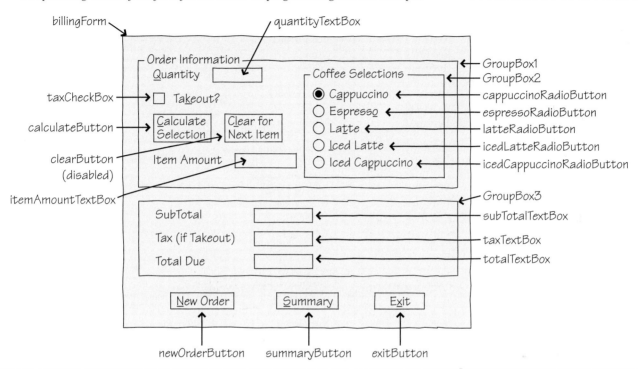

Object	Property	Setting
latteRadioButton	Name	latteRadioButton
	Text	La&tte
icedLatteRadioButton	Name	icedLatteRadioButton
	Text	&Iced Latte
icedCappuccinoRadioButton	Name	icedCappuccinoRadioButton
	Text	Iced Ca&ppuccino
Label1	Text	&Quantity
quantityTextBox	Name	quantityTextBox
	Text	(blank)
taxCheckBox	Name	taxCheckBox
	Text	Ta&keout ?
Label2	Text	Item Amount
Label3	Text	SubTotal
Label4	Text	Tax (if Takeout)
Label5	Text	Total Due
itemAmountTextBox	Name	itemAmountTextBox
	ReadOnly	True
	TabStop	False

Object	Property	Setting
subTotalTextBox	Name ReadOnly TabStop	subTotalTextBox True False
taxTextBox	Name ReadOnly TabStop	taxTextBox True False
totalTextBox	Name ReadOnly TabStop	totalTextBox True False
calculateButton	Name Text	calculateButton &Calculate Selection
clearButton	Name Text Enabled	clearButton C&lear for Next Item False
newOrderButton	Name Text	newOrderButton &New Order
summaryButton	Name Text	summaryButton &Summary
exitButton	Name Text	exitButton E&xit

Plan the Event Procedures You need to plan the actions for five event procedures for the buttons.

Object	Procedure	Action
calculateButton	Click	Validate for blank or nonnumeric amount. Find price of drink selection. Multiply price by quantity. Add amount to subtotal. Calculate tax if needed. Calculate total = subtotal + tax. Format and display the values. Disable the Takeout check box. Enable the Clear button.
clearButton	Click	Check that there are values to clear. Clear the coffee selections. Clear the quantity and the item price. Disable the Takeout check box. Set the focus to the quantity.
newOrderButton	Click	Confirm clearing current order. Clear the current order. Accumulate total sales and count. Set subtotal and total due to 0. Enable Takeout check box.
summaryButton	Click	If current order not added to totals Call newOrderButton_Click. Calculate the average. Display the summary totals in a message box.
exitButton	Click	Terminate the project.

Write the Project Follow the sketch in Figure 4.15 to create the form. Figure 4.16 shows the completed form.

- Set the properties of each object as you have planned.

- Write the code. Working from the pseudocode, write each event procedure.

- When you complete the code, use a variety of data to thoroughly test the project. Make sure the tab order is set correctly so that the insertion point begins in quantityTextBox.

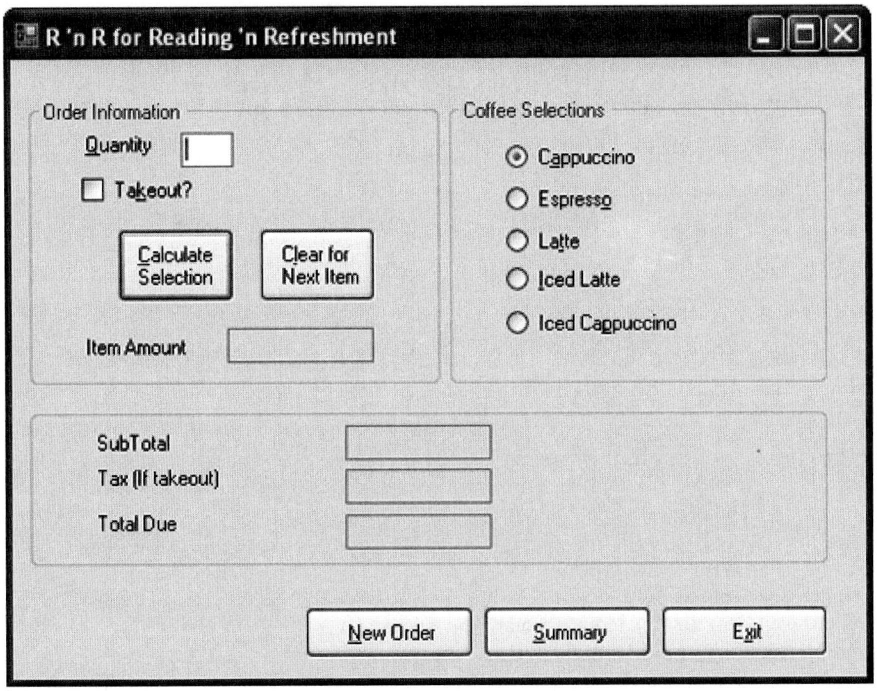

Figure 4.16

The form for the hands-on programming exercise.

The Project Coding Solution

```
'Program Name:    Ch04HandsOn
'Programmer:      Bradley/Millspaugh
'Date:            June 2005
'Description:     This project calculates the amount due
'                 based on the customer selection
'                 and accumulates summary data for the day.
'Folder:          Ch04HandsOn

Option Strict On

Public Class billingForm
    ' Declare constants.
    Const TAX_RATE_Decimal As Decimal = 0.08D
    Const CAPPUCCINO_PRICE_Decimal As Decimal = 2D
    Const ESPRESSO_PRICE_Decimal As Decimal = 2.25D
    Const LATTE_PRICE_Decimal As Decimal = 1.75D
    Const ICED_PRICE_Decimal As Decimal = 2.5D
```

```vb
' Declare variables for summary information.
Dim subtotalDecimal, totalDecimal, grandTotalDecimal As Decimal
Dim customerCountInteger As Integer

Private Sub calculateButton_Click(ByVal sender As System.Object, _
    ByVal e As System.EventArgs) Handles calculateButton.Click
        ' Calculate and display the current amounts and add to totals.

    Dim priceDecimal, taxDecimal, itemAmountDecimal As Decimal
    Dim quantityInteger As Integer
    With Me

        ' Find the price.
        If .cappuccinoRadioButton.Checked Then
            priceDecimal = CAPPUCCINO_PRICE_Decimal
        ElseIf .espressoRadioButton.Checked Then
            priceDecimal = ESPRESSO_PRICE_Decimal
        ElseIf .latteRadioButton.Checked Then
            priceDecimal = LATTE_PRICE_Decimal
        ElseIf .icedCappuccinoRadioButton.Checked _
                Or icedLatteRadioButton.Checked Then
            priceDecimal = ICED_PRICE_Decimal
        End If

        ' Calculate extended price and add to order total.
        Try
            quantityInteger = Integer.Parse(.quantityTextBox.Text)
            itemAmountDecimal = priceDecimal * quantityInteger
            subtotalDecimal += itemAmountDecimal
            If .taxCheckBox.Checked Then
                taxDecimal = subtotalDecimal * TAX_RATE_Decimal
            Else
                taxDecimal = 0
            End If
            totalDecimal = subtotalDecimal + taxDecimal
            .itemAmountTextBox.Text = itemAmountDecimal.ToString("C")
            .subTotalTextBox.Text = subtotalDecimal.ToString("N")
            .taxTextBox.Text = taxDecimal.ToString("N")
            .totalTextBox.Text = totalDecimal.ToString("C")
            ' Allow a change only for new order.
            .taxCheckBox.Enabled = False
            ' Allow Clear after an order is begun.
            .clearButton.Enabled = True

        Catch quantityException As FormatException
            MessageBox.Show("Quantity must be numeric.", _
                "Data Entry Error", MessageBoxButtons.OK, _
                MessageBoxIcon.Information)
            With .quantityTextBox
                .Focus()
                .SelectAll()
            End With
        End Try
    End With
End Sub

Private Sub clearButton_Click(ByVal sender As System.Object, _
    ByVal e As System.EventArgs) Handles clearButton.Click
        ' Clear the appropriate controls.
```

```vbnet
            With Me
                .cappuccinoRadioButton.Checked = True     ' All others are false.
                .itemAmountTextBox.Clear()
                With .quantityTextBox
                    .Clear()
                    .Focus()
                End With
            End With
        End Sub


        Private Sub newOrderButton_Click(ByVal sender As System.Object, _
          ByVal e As System.EventArgs) Handles newOrderButton.Click
            ' Clear the current order and add to the totals.

            Dim returnDialogResult As DialogResult
            Dim messageString As String

            With Me

            ' Confirm clear of current order.
                messageString = "Clear the current order figures?"
                returnDialogResult = MessageBox.Show(messageString, "Clear Order", _
                  MessageBoxButtons.YesNo, MessageBoxIcon.Question, _
                  MessageBoxDefaultButton.Button2)

                If returnDialogResult = DialogResult.Yes Then ' User said Yes.
                    clearButton_Click(sender, e) ' Clear the screen fields.
                    .subTotalTextBox.Clear()
                    .taxTextBox.Clear()
                    .totalTextBox.Clear()

                    Try
                        ' Add to Totals.
                        ' Add only if not a new order/customer.
                        If subtotalDecimal <> 0 Then
                            grandTotalDecimal += totalDecimal
                            customerCountInteger += 1
                            ' Reset totals for next customer.
                            subtotalDecimal = 0
                            totalDecimal = 0
                        End If
                    Catch
                        messageString = "Error in calculations."
                        MessageBox.Show(messageString, "Error", _
                          MessageBoxButtons.OK, MessageBoxIcon.Error)
                    End Try

                    ' Clear appropriate display items and enable check box.
                    With .taxCheckBox
                        .Enabled = True
                        .Checked = False
                    End With
                    .clearButton.Enabled = False
                End If
            End With
        End Sub
```

```vb
Private Sub summaryButton_Click(ByVal sender As System.Object, _
    ByVal e As System.EventArgs) Handles summaryButton.Click
    ' Calculate the average and display the totals.

    Dim averageDecimal As Decimal
    Dim messageString As String

    If totalDecimal <> 0 Then
        ' Make sure last order is counted.
        newOrderButton_Click(sender, e)
    End If

    If customerCountInteger > 0 Then
        Try
            ' Calculate the average.
            averageDecimal = grandTotalDecimal / customerCountInteger

            ' Concatenate the message string.
            messageString = "Number of Orders:   " _
              & customerCountInteger.ToString() _
              & ControlChars.NewLine & ControlChars.NewLine _
              & "Total Sales:   " & grandTotalDecimal.ToString("C") _
              & ControlChars.NewLine & ControlChars.NewLine _
              & "Average Sale:   " & averageDecimal.ToString("C")
            MessageBox.Show(messageString, "Coffee Sales Summary", _
              MessageBoxButtons.OK, MessageBoxIcon.Information)
        Catch
            messageString = "Error in calculations."
            MessageBox.Show(messageString, "Error", _
              MessageBoxButtons.OK, MessageBoxIcon.Error)
        End Try
    Else
        messageString = "No sales data to summarize."
        MessageBox.Show(messageString, "Coffee Sales Summary", _
          MessageBoxButtons.OK, MessageBoxIcon.Information)
    End If
End Sub
Private Sub exitButton_Click(ByVal sender As System.Object, _
    ByVal e As System.EventArgs) Handles exitButton.Click
    ' Terminate the project.

    Me.Close()
End Sub
End Class
```

Debugging Visual Basic Projects

One of the advantages of programming in the Visual Studio environment is the availability of debugging tools. You can use these tools to help find and eliminate logic and run-time errors. The debugging tools also can help you to follow the logic of existing projects to better understand how they work.

Sometimes it's helpful to know the result of a condition, the value of a variable or property, or the sequence of execution of your program. You can follow program logic in Debugging mode by single-stepping through code; you also can get information about execution without breaking the program run, using the WriteLine method of the Debug class.

In the following sections, you will learn to use many of the debugging tools on the VB standard toolbar (Figure 4.17) and the *Debug* menu (Figure 4.18).

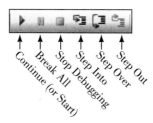

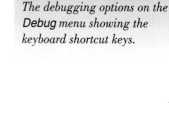

Figure 4.17

The debugging buttons on the VB standard toolbar.

Figure 4.18

The debugging options on the Debug menu showing the keyboard shortcut keys.

Writing Debug Output

You can place a **Debug.WriteLine method** in your code, which sends output to the Immediate window during program execution. In the argument for the WriteLine method, you can specify a message to write or an object that you want tracked.

The Debug.WriteLine Method—General Form

```
Debug.WriteLine(TextString)
Debug.WriteLine(Object)
```

The Debug.WriteLine method is overloaded, so you can pass it a string argument or the name of an object.

The Debug.WriteLine Method—Examples

```
Debug.WriteLine("calculateButton procedure entered.")
Debug.WriteLine(quantityTextBox)
Debug.WriteLine("quantityInteger = " & quantityInteger.ToString())
```

When the `Debug.WriteLine` method executes, its output appears in the Immediate window. Figure 4.19 shows the output of the three example statements above. Notice the second line of output, for quantityTextBox—the class of the object displays along with its current contents.

The Output window shows the output of the `Debug.WriteLine` *method.*

You may find it useful to place `WriteLine` methods in `If` statements, so that you can see which branch the logic followed.

```
If countInteger > 10 Then
    Debug.WriteLine("Count is greater than 10.")
    ' Other processing.
Else
    Debug.WriteLine("Count is not greater than 10.")
    ' Other processing.
End If
```

An advantage of using `WriteLine`, rather than the other debugging techniques that follow, is that you do not have to break program execution.

Note: By default, VS sends debug output to the Immediate window. You can choose to send the output to the Output window in *Tools / Options / Debugging* (with *Show All Options* selected); deselect *Redirect all Output Window text to the Immediate window*.

Clearing the Immediate Window

You can clear the Immediate window: Right-click in the window and choose *Clear All*.

Pausing Execution with the Break All Button

You can click on the Break All toolbar button to pause execution. This step places the project into debug time at whatever line the program is executing. However, you will generally prefer to break in the middle of a procedure. To choose the location of the break, you can force a break with a breakpoint.

Forcing a Break

During the debugging process, often you want to stop at a particular location in code and watch what happens (e.g., which branch of an `If...Then...Else`; which procedures were executed; the value of a variable just before or just after a calculation). You can force the project to break by inserting a **breakpoint** in code.

```
Try
    Me.amountDueLabel.Text = (priceDecimal* Decimal.Parse(Me.quantityTextBox.Text)).ToString()
Catch
    MessageBox.Show( "Please Enter a Numeric Value.", "Error", MessageBoxButtons.OK)
End Try
```

To set a breakpoint, place the mouse pointer in the gray margin indicator area at the left edge of the Editor window and click; the line will be highlighted in red and a large red dot will display in the margin indicator (Figure 4.20).

After setting a breakpoint, start execution. When the project reaches the breakpoint, it will halt, display the line, and go into debug time.

You can remove a breakpoint by clicking again in the gray margin area, or clear all breakpoints from the *Debug* menu.

TIP

Place the insertion point in the code line you want as a breakpoint and press F9. Press F9 again to toggle the breakpoint off. ∎

Checking the Current Values of Expressions

You can quickly check the current value of an expression such as a variable, a control, a condition, or an arithmetic expression. During debug time, display the Editor window and point to the expression that you want to view; a small label, called a *DataTip*, pops up and displays the current contents of the expression.

The steps for viewing the contents of a variable during run time are as follows:

1. Break the execution using a breakpoint.
2. If the code does not appear in the Editor, click on the Editor's tab in the Document window.
3. Point to the variable or expression you wish to view.

The current contents of the expression will pop up in a DataTip (Figure 4.21).

F i g u r e 4 . 2 0

A program statement with a breakpoint set appears highlighted, and a dot appears in the gray margin indicator area.

```
bookSaleForm.vb*                                              ▾ ✕
◇ calculateButton              ▾   ⚡ Click                    ▾
        Try
            ' Convert quantity to numeric variable.
 ●      quantityInteger = Integer.Parse(.quantityTextBox.Text)
        Try
                ' Convert price if quantity was successful.
            priceDecimal = Decimal.Parse(.priceTextBox.Text)
```

F i g u r e 4 . 2 1

Point to a variable name in code and its current value displays in a DataTip.

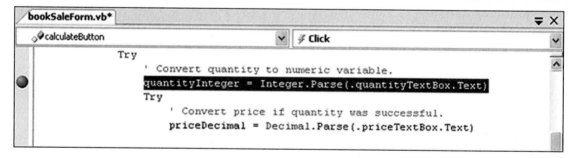

Stepping through Code

The best way to debug a project is to thoroughly understand what the project is doing every step of the way. In early programming days, this task was performed by following each line of code manually to understand its effect. But you can now use the Visual Studio debugging tools to trace program execution line by line and see the progression of the program as it executes through your code.

You step through code at debug time. You can use one of the techniques already mentioned to break execution or choose one of the stepping commands at design time; the program will begin running and immediately transfer to debug time.

The three stepping commands on the *Debug* menu in Debugging mode are *Step Into*, *Step Over*, and *Step Out*. You also can use the toolbar buttons for stepping or the keyboard shortcuts shown on the menu (refer to Figure 4.18).

These commands force the project to execute a single line at a time and to display the Editor window with the current statement highlighted. As you execute the program, by pressing a button, for example, the Click event occurs. Execution transfers to the Click event procedure, the Editor window for that procedure appears on the screen, and you can follow line-by-line execution.

Step Into

Most likely you will use the **Step Into** command more than the other two stepping commands. When you choose *Step Into* (from the menu, the toolbar button, or F8), the next line of code executes and the program pauses again in debug time. If the line of code is a call to another procedure, the first line of code of the other procedure displays.

To continue stepping through your program execution, continue choosing the *Step Into* command. When a procedure is completed, your form will display again, awaiting an event. You can click on one of the form's buttons to continue stepping through code in an event procedure. If you want to continue rapid execution without stepping, choose the *Continue* command (from the menu, the toolbar button, or F5).

Step Over

The **Step Over** command also executes one line of code at a time. The difference between *Step Over* and *Step Into* occurs when your code has calls to other procedures. *Step Over* displays only the lines of code in the current procedure being analyzed; it does not display lines of code in the called procedures.

You can choose *Step Over* from the menu, from the toolbar button, or by pressing Shift + F8. Each time you choose the command, one more program statement executes.

Step Out

You use the third stepping command when you are stepping through a called procedure. The **Step Out** command continues rapid execution until the called procedure completes and then returns to Debugging mode at the statement following the `Call`, that is, the next line of the calling procedure.

Continuing Program Execution

When you have seen what you want to see, continue rapid execution by pressing F5 or choosing *Continue* from the toolbar or the *Debug* menu.

Stopping Execution

Once you have located a problem in the program's code, usually you want to stop execution, correct the error, and run again. Stop execution by selecting *Stop Debugging* from the *Debug* menu or the toolbar button, or press the keyboard shortcut: Ctrl + Alt + Break.

Note: The keyboard shortcuts differ depending on the keyboard mapping scheme selected in *Tools / Options / Show All Options*.

Edit and Continue

VB 2005 reintroduces a feature that was present in VB6: Edit-and-Continue. You can use this feature to save time when debugging programs. When your program goes into Debugging mode and you make minor modifications to the code in the Editor, you may be able to continue execution without stopping to recompile. Press F5 or choose *Debug / Continue*. If the changes to the code are too major to continue without recompiling, the debugger displays a message (Figure 4.22). Choose *Restart* to recompile and run the program; click *Edit Code* to return to the Editor.

To use any of the debugging windows, you must be in debug mode or run time. ■

The Locals Window

Sometimes you may find that the **Locals window** displays just the information that you want (Figure 4.23). The Locals window displays all objects and variables that are within scope at debug time. That means that if you break execution in the calculateButton_Click event procedure, all variables local to that

Figure 4.22

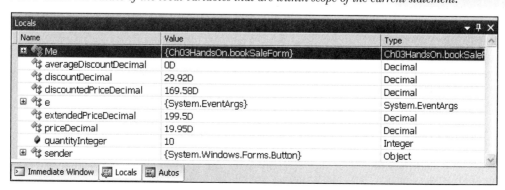

When you attempt to continue execution after making changes in Debugging mode, this dialog box appears if the edits were too major. Click Restart to recompile and run again.

Figure 4.23

The Locals window shows the values of the local variables that are within scope of the current statement.

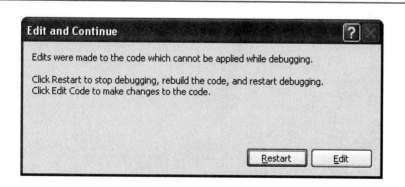

procedure display. You also can expand the Me entry to see the state of the form's controls and the values of module-level variables. Display the Locals window from the toolbar button or the *Debug / Windows / Locals* menu item, which appears only when a program is running, either in run time or debug mode.

The Autos Window

Another helpful debugging window is the **Autos window**. The Autos window "automatically" displays all variables and control contents that are referenced in the current statement and a few statements on either side of the current one (Figure 4.24). Note that the highlighted line is about to execute next; the "current" statement is the one just before the highlighted one.

You can view the Autos window when your program stops at a breakpoint. Click on the Autos window tab if it appears, or open it using the *Debug / Windows / Autos* menu item. Again, you must be in either run time or debug mode to see the menu item.

Figure 4.24

The Autos window automatically adjusts to show the variables and properties that appear in the previous few lines and the next few lines.

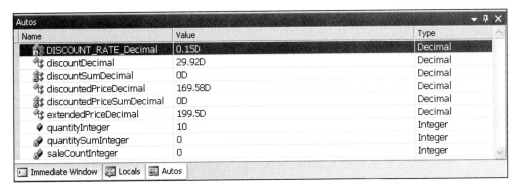

Name	Value	Type
DISCOUNT_RATE_Decimal	0.15D	Decimal
discountDecimal	29.92D	Decimal
discountSumDecimal	0D	Decimal
discountedPriceDecimal	169.58D	Decimal
discountedPriceSumDecimal	0D	Decimal
extendedPriceDecimal	199.5D	Decimal
quantityInteger	10	Integer
quantitySumInteger	0	Integer
saleCountInteger	0	Integer

Immediate Window | Locals | Autos

Debugging Step-by-Step Tutorial

In this exercise you will learn to set a breakpoint; pause program execution; single step through program instructions; display the current values in properties, variables, and conditions; and debug a Visual Basic project.

Test the Project

STEP 1: Open the debugging project on your student CD. The project is found in the Ch04Debug folder.

STEP 2: Run the program.

STEP 3: Enter color Blue, quantity "100", and press Enter or click on the Calculate button.

STEP 4: Enter another color Blue, quantity "50", and press Enter. Are the totals correct?

STEP 5: Enter color Red, quantity "30", and press Enter.

STEP 6: Enter color Red, quantity "10", and press Enter. Are the totals correct?

STEP 7: Enter color White, quantity "50", and press Enter.

STEP 8: Enter color White, quantity "100", and press Enter. Are the totals correct?

STEP 9: Exit the project. You are going to locate and correct the errors in the red and white totals.

Break and Step Program Execution

STEP 1: Display the program code. Scroll to locate this line, which is the first calculation line in the calculateButton_Click event procedure:
`quantityDecimal = Decimal.Parse(.quantityTextBox.Text)`

STEP 2: Click in the gray margin indicator area to set a breakpoint on the selected line. Your screen should look like Figure 4.25.

Figure 4.25

A program statement with a breakpoint set appears highlighted and a dot appears in the gray margin indicator area.

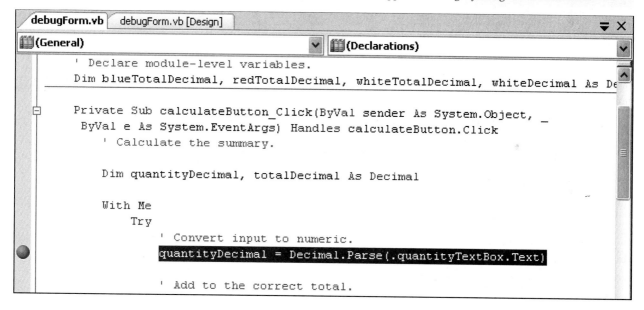

STEP 3: Run the project, enter Red, quantity "30", and press Enter.
The project will transfer control to the calculateButton_Click procedure, stop when it reaches the breakpoint, highlight the current line, and enter debug mode (Figure 4.26).

Note: The highlighted line has not yet executed.

STEP 4: Press the F8 key, which causes VB to execute the current program statement (the assignment statement). (F8 is the keyboard shortcut for *Debug / Step Into.*) The statement is executed and the highlight moves to the next statement (the `If` statement).

Note: If the F8 key is not the correct shortcut key, the keyboard defaults likely have been modified. Select *Tools / Options / Environment / Keyboard.* Click the Reset button to reset the keyboard mappings to their default values.

STEP 5: Press F8 again; the condition (`.blueRadioButton.Checked`) is tested and found to be False.

STEP 6: Continue pressing F8 a few more times and watch the order in which program statements execute.

Figure 4.26

When a breakpoint is reached during program execution, Visual Basic enters debug time, displays the Editor window, and highlights the breakpoint line.

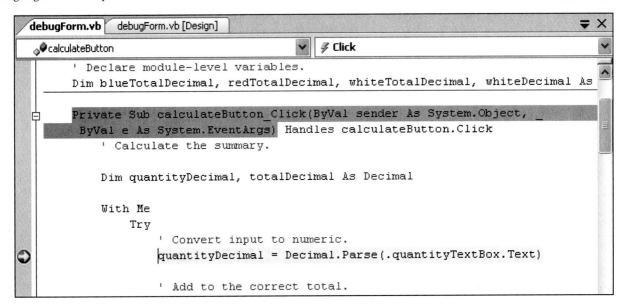

View the Contents of Properties, Variables, and Conditions

STEP 1: Scroll up if necessary and point to `quantityTextBox.Text` in the breakpoint line; the contents of the Text property pops up (Figure 4.27).

Figure 4.27

Point to a property reference in code and the current content pops up.

```
        Try
            ' Convert input to numeric.
            quantityDecimal = Decimal.Parse(.quantityTextBox.Text)
                                             Me.quantityTextBox.Text  🔍 ▾ "30"
            ' Add to the correct total.
            If .blueRadioButton.Checked Then
                blueTotalDecimal += quantityDecimal
```

STEP 2: Point to quantityDecimal and view the contents of that variable. Notice that the Text property is enclosed in quotes and the numeric variable is not. The 30D means 30 Decimal.

STEP 3: Point to `.blueRadioButton.Checked` in the `If` statement; then point to `.redRadioButton.Checked`. You can see the Boolean value for each of the radio buttons.

STEP 4: Point to redTotalDecimal to see the current value of that total variable. This value looks correct, since you just entered 30, which was added to the total.

Continue Program Execution

STEP 1: Press F5, the keyboard shortcut for the *Continue* command. The *Continue* command continues rapid execution.

STEP 2: Enter color Red and quantity "10". When you press Enter, program execution will again break at the breakpoint. (If the VS IDE window does not appear on top of your form, click its Taskbar button.)

The 10 you just entered should be added to the 30 previously entered for Red, producing 40 in the Red total.

STEP 3: Use the *Step Into* button on the toolbar to step through execution. Keep pressing *Step Into* until the 10 is added to redTotalDecimal. Display the current contents of the total. Can you see what the problem is?

Hint: redTotalDecimal has only the current amount, not the sum of the two amounts. The answer will appear a little later; try to find it yourself first.

You will fix this error soon, after testing the White total.

Test the White Total

STEP 1: Press F5 to continue execution. If the form does not reappear, click the project's Taskbar button.

STEP 2: Enter color White, quantity "100", and press Enter.

STEP 3: When execution halts at the breakpoint, press F5 to continue. This returns to rapid execution until the next breakpoint is reached.

STEP 4: Enter color White, quantity "50", and press Enter.

STEP 5: Press F8 several times when execution halts at the breakpoint until you execute the line for the white total. Remember that the highlighted line has not yet executed; press *Step Into* (F8) one more time, if necessary, to execute the addition statement.

STEP 6: Point to each variable name to see the current values (Figure 4.28). Can you see the problem?

> ☑ **TIP**
>
> **S**witch between the IDE window and your running application using the Taskbar buttons. ■

Figure 4.28

Point to the variable name in code and its current value displays as 2 Decimal.

```
                  ' Add to the correct total.
              If .blueRadioButton.Checked Then
                    blueTotalDecimal += quantityDecimal
              ElseIf .redRadioButton.Checked Then
                    redTotalDecimal = quantityDecimal
              ElseIf .whiteRadioButton.Checked Then
                    whiteTotalDecimal += 1
              End If            whiteTotalDecimal 2D
```

STEP 7: Display the Autos window by clicking on its tab. If the tab does not appear, select *Debug / Windows / Autos*. The Autos window displays the current value of all properties and variables referred to by a few statements before and after the current statement (Figure 4.29).

STEP 8: Identify all the errors. When you are ready to make the corrections, continue to the next step.

Figure 4.29

The Autos window displays the current contents of variables and properties in the statements before and after the current statement.

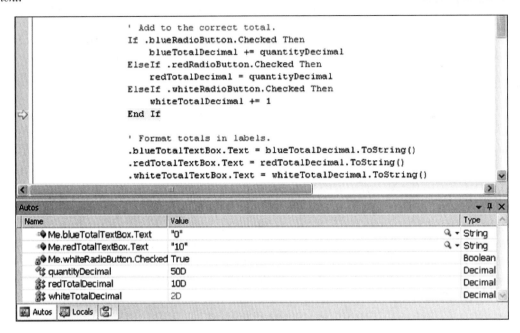

Correct the Red Total Error

STEP 1: Stop program execution by clicking on the *Stop Debugging* toolbar button (Figure 4.30).

Figure 4.30

Click on the Stop Debugging button on the Debug toolbar to halt program execution.

STEP 2: Locate this line:

```
redTotalDecimal = quantityDecimal
```

This statement replaces the value of redTotalDecimal with quantityDecimal rather than adding to the total.

STEP 3: Change the line to read:

```
redTotalDecimal += quantityDecimal
```

✓ TIP

Display keyboard shortcuts on ToolTips, as in Figure 4.30, by selecting *Tools / Customize / Show shortcut keys in ScreenTips.* ∎

Correct the White Total Error

STEP 1: Locate this line:

```
whiteTotalDecimal += 1
```

Do you see the problem with this line? It adds 1 to the total, rather than adding the quantity.

✓ TIP

You can change the current line of execution in Debugging mode by dragging the current line indicator arrow on the left side of the Editor window. ∎

STEP 2: Change the statement to read:

```
whiteTotalDecimal += quantityDecimal
```

STEP 3: Press F5 to start program execution. Enter color White and "100" and press Enter.

STEP 4: Press F5 to continue when the project halts at the breakpoint.

STEP 5: Enter White, "50", and Enter.

STEP 6: At the breakpoint, clear the breakpoint by clicking on the red margin dot for the line.

STEP 7: Press F5 to continue and check the total on the form. It should be correct now.

STEP 8: Test the totals for all three colors carefully and then click Exit.

Test the Exception Handling

STEP 1: Set a breakpoint again on the first calculation line in the calculate-Button_Click event procedure.

STEP 2: Run the program, this time entering nonnumeric characters for the amount. Click on Calculate; when the program stops at the breakpoint, press F8 repeatedly and watch program execution. The message box should appear.

Force a Run-Time Error

For this step, you will use a technique called *commenting out* code. Programmers often add apostrophes to the beginning of code lines to test the code without those lines. Sometimes it works well to copy a section of code, comment out the original to keep it unchanged, and modify only the copy. You'll find it easy to uncomment the code later, after you finish testing.

STEP 1: Select *Delete All Breakpoints* from the *Debug* menu if the menu item is available. The item is available only when there are breakpoints set in the program.

STEP 2: At the left end of the line with the `Try` statement, add an apostrophe, turning the line into a comment.

STEP 3: Scroll down and locate the exception-handling code. Highlight the lines beginning with `Catch` and ending with `End Try` (Figure 4.31).

Figure 4.31

Select the lines to convert to comments for debugging.

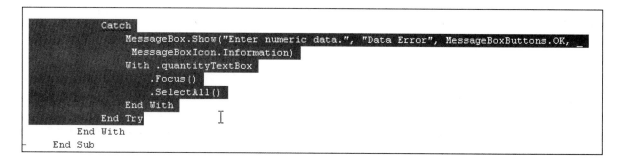

STEP 4:   Click on the *Comment out the selected lines* button on the Editing toolbar (Figure 4.32). The Editor adds an apostrophe to the start of each
of the selected lines.

Figure 4.32

*Click the Comment out the
selected lines toolbar button
to temporarily make program
lines into comments.*

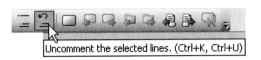

Comment out the selected lines. (Ctrl+K, Ctrl+C)

STEP 5:   Run the project. This time click the Calculate button without entering
a quantity. A run-time error will occur (Figure 4.33).
     You can click OK or Continue, if you wish. Either will cancel
execution.

Figure 4.33

The missing data causes an exception and run-time error.

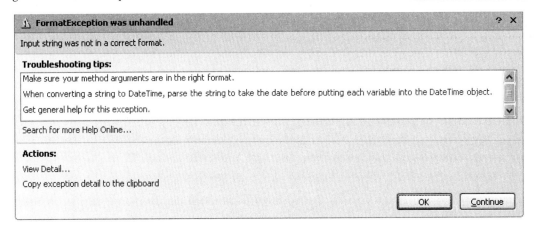

STEP 6:   After you are finished testing the program, select the commented lines
and click on *Uncomment the selected lines* button (Figure 4.34).
     Note: You can just click an insertion point in a line or select the en-
tire line when you comment and uncomment lines.

Figure 4.34

*Click the Uncomment the
selected lines toolbar button
after testing the program.*

Uncomment the selected lines. (Ctrl+K, Ctrl+U)

Summary

1. Visual Basic uses the `If...Then...Else` statement to make decisions. An `Else` clause is optional and specifies the action to be taken if the condition evaluates as False. An `If...Then...Else` statement must conclude with an `End If`.

2. UML activity diagrams can help visualize the logic of an `If...Then...Else` statement.

3. The conditions for an `If` statement are evaluated for True or False.

4. Conditions can be composed of the comparison operators, which compare items for equality, greater than, or less than. The comparison of numeric values is based on the quantity of the number, while string comparisons are based on the ANSI code table.

5. The `ToUpper` and `ToLower` methods of the String class can convert a text value to upper- or lowercase.

6. The `And`, `Or`, `AndAlso`, and `OrElse` logical operators may be used to combine multiple conditions. With the `And` operator, both conditions must be true for the entire condition to evaluate True. For the `Or` operator, if either or both conditions are true, the entire condition evaluates as True. When both `And` and `Or` are used in a condition, the `And` condition is evaluated before the `Or` condition. `AndAlso` and `OrElse` short circuit the condition so that the second part of a compound condition may not have to be tested.

7. A nested `If` statement contains an `If` statement within either the true or false actions of a previous `If` statement. Nesting an `If` statement inside of another requires the use of the `End If` clause. An `Else` clause always applies to the last unmatched `If` regardless of indentation.

8. The state of radio buttons and check boxes is better tested with `If` statements in the event procedure for a button rather than coding event procedures for the radio button or check box. Use individual `If` statements for check boxes and nested `If` statements for radio buttons.

9. The `MessageBox.Show` method can display a multiple-line message if you concatenate a NewLine character to specify a line break.

10. You can choose to display multiple buttons in a message box. The `MessageBox.Show` method returns an object of the DialogResult class, which you can check using the DialogResult constants.

11. Data validation checks the reasonableness or appropriateness of the value in a variable or property.

12. The same event procedure can be assigned to multiple controls, so that the controls share the procedure.

13. You can use the `sender` argument in an event procedure to determine which control caused the procedure to execute.

14. One procedure can call another procedure. To call an event procedure, you must supply the `sender` and `e` arguments.

15. A variety of debugging tools are available in Visual Studio. These include writing to the Immediate window, breaking program execution, displaying the current contents of variables, and stepping through code.

Key Terms

ANSI code   *150*
Autos window   *186*
breakpoint   *182*
call   *172*
Case structure   *167*
comparison operator   *149*
compound condition   *153*
condition   *149*
CType function   *171*
Debug.WriteLine method   *181*
DialogResult object   *163*
End If   *147*
If...Then...Else   *147*
late binding   *171*

Locals window   *185*
logical operator   *153*
nested If   *155*
NewLine character   *162*
relational operator   *149*
Select Case   *169*
short circuit   *155*
Step Into   *184*
Step Out   *184*
Step Over   *184*
ToLower method   *152*
ToUpper method   *152*
validation   *165*

Review Questions

1. What is the general format of the statement used to code decisions in an application?
2. What is a condition?
3. Explain the purpose of comparison operators and logical operators.
4. Differentiate between a comparison performed on numeric data and a comparison performed on string data.
5. How does Visual Basic compare the Text property of a text box?
6. Why would it be useful to include the ToUpper method in a comparison?
7. Name the types of items that can be used in a comparison.
8. Explain a Boolean variable test for True and False. Give an example.
9. Give an example of a situation where nested Ifs would be appropriate.
10. Define the term *validation*. When is it appropriate to do validation?
11. Define the term *checking a range*.
12. When would it be appropriate to use a Case structure? Give an example.
13. Explain the difference between *Step Into* and *Step Over*.
14. What steps are necessary to view the current contents of a variable during program execution?

Programming Exercises

4.1   Lynette Rifle owns an image consulting shop. Her clients can select from the following services at the specified regular prices: Makeover $125, Hair Styling $60, Manicure $35, and Permanent Makeup $200. She has distributed discount coupons that advertise discounts of 10 percent and 20 percent off the regular price. Create a project that will allow the receptionist to select a discount rate of 10 percent, 20 percent, or none, and then select a service. Display the price for the individual service and the total due after each visit is completed. A visit may include several services. Include buttons for *Calculate*, *Clear*, and *Exit*.

4.2   Modify Programming Exercise 4.1 to allow for sales to additional patrons. Include buttons for *Next Patron* and *Summary*. When the receptionist clicks the *Summary* button, display in a summary message box the number of clients and the total dollar value for all services rendered. For *Next Patron*, confirm that the user wants to clear the totals for the current customer.

4.3   Create a project to compute your checking account balance.

    Form: Include radio buttons to indicate the type of transaction: deposit, check, or service charge. A text box will allow the user to enter the amount of the transaction. Display the new balance in a ReadOnly text box or a label. Calculate the balance by adding deposits and subtracting service charges and checks. Include buttons for *Calculate*, *Clear*, and *Exit*.

4.4   Add validation to Programming Exercise 4.3. Display a message box if the new balance would be a negative number. If there is not enough money to cover a check, do not deduct the check amount. Instead, display a message box with the message "Insufficient Funds" and deduct a service charge of $10.

4.5   Modify Programming Exercise 4.3 or 4.4 by adding a *Summary* button that will display the total number of deposits, the total dollar amount of deposits, the number of checks, and the dollar amount of the checks. Do not include checks that were returned for insufficient funds, but do include the service charges. Use a message box to display the summary information.

4.6   (Select Case) Piecework workers are paid by the piece. Workers who produce a greater quantity of output are often paid at a higher rate.

    Form: Use text boxes to obtain the person's name and the number of pieces completed. Include a *Calculate* button to display the dollar amount earned. You will need a *Summary* button to display the total number of pieces, the total pay, and the average pay per person. A *Clear* button should clear the name and the number of pieces for the current employee and a *Clear All* button should clear the summary totals after confirming the operation with the user.

    Include validation to check for missing data. If the user clicks on the *Calculate* button without first entering a name and the number of pieces, display a message box. Also, you need to make sure to not display a summary before any data are entered; you cannot calculate an average when no items have been calculated. You can check the number of employees in the Summary event procedure or disable the *Summary* button until the first order has been calculated.

Pieces Completed	Price Paid per Piece for All Pieces
1–199	.50
200–399	.55
400–599	.60
600 or more	.65

4.7   Modify Programming Exercise 2.3 (the weather report) to treat radio buttons the proper way. Do not change the image and message in an event procedure for each radio button; instead use an *OK* button to display the correct image and message.

Note: For help in basing a new project on an existing project, see "Copy and Move a Project" in Appendix C.

4.8 Modify Programming Exercise 2.2 (the flag viewer) to treat radio buttons and check boxes in the proper way. Include a *Display* button and check the settings of the radio buttons and check boxes in the button's event procedure, rather than making the changes in event procedures for each radio button and check box.

Note: For help in basing a new project on an existing project, see "Copy and Move a Project" in Appendix C.

4.9 Create an application to calculate sales for Catherine's Catering. The program must determine the amount due for an event based on the number of guests, the menu selected, and the bar options. Additionally, the program maintains summary figures for multiple events.

Form: Use a text box to input the number of guests and radio buttons to allow a selection of Prime Rib, Chicken, or Pasta. Check boxes allow the user to select an Open Bar, and/or Wine with Dinner. Include buttons for *Calculate*, *Clear*, *Summary*, and *Exit*. Display the amount due for the event in a label or a ReadOnly text box.

Rates per Person

Prime Rib	25.95
Chicken	18.95
Pasta	12.95
Open Bar	25.00
Wine with dinner	8.00

Summary: Display the number of events and the total dollar amount in a message box. Prompt the user to determine if he or she would like to clear the summary information. If the response is Yes, set the number of events and the total dollar amount to zero. Do not display the summary message box if there is no summary information. (Either disable the *Summary* button until a calculation has been made or test the total for a value.)

Case Studies

VB Mail Order

Calculate the amount due for an order. For each order, the user should enter the following information into text boxes: customer name, address, city, state (two-letter abbreviation), and ZIP code. An order may consist of multiple items. For each item, the user will enter the product description, quantity, weight, and price into text boxes.

You will need buttons for *Add This Item*, *Clear*, *Update Summary*, and *Exit*.

For the *Add This Item* button, validate the quantity, weight, and price. Each must be present and numeric. For any bad data, display a message box. Calculate the charge for the current item and add the charge and weight into the appropriate totals. Do not calculate shipping and handling on individual items; rather, calculate shipping and handling on the entire order.

The *Clear* button should clear the fields for the current order.

When the *Update Summary* button is clicked, calculate the sales tax, shipping and handling, and the total amount due for the order. Sales tax is 8 percent of the total charge and is charged only for shipments to a California address. Do not charge sales tax on the shipping and handling charges. The shipping and handling should be calculated only for a complete order.

Optional: Disable the *Add This Item* button when the summary button is pressed.

The shipping and handling charges depend on the weight of the products. Calculate the shipping charge as $.25 per pound and add that amount to the handling charge (taken from the following table).

Weight	Handling
Less than 10 pounds	$1.00
10 to 100 pounds	$3.00
Over 100 pounds	$5.00

Display the entire amount of the bill in controls titled Dollar amount due, Sales tax, Shipping and handling, and Total amount due.

Test Data

Description	Quantity	Weight	Price
Planter	2	3	19.95
Mailbox	1	2	24.95
Planter	2	3	19.95

Test Data Output for Taxable (if shipped to a California address)

Dollar Amount Due	$104.75
Sales Tax	8.38
Shipping and Handling	6.50
Total Amount Due	$119.63

Test Data Output for Nontaxable (if shipped outside of California)

Dollar Amount Due	$104.75
Sales Tax	0.00
Shipping and Handling	6.50
Total Amount Due	$111.25

VB Auto Center

Create a project that determines the total amount due for the purchase of a vehicle. Include text boxes for the base price and the trade-in allowance. Check boxes will indicate if the buyer wants additional accessories: stereo system, leather interior, and/or computer navigation. A group box for the exterior finish will contain radio buttons for Standard, Pearlized, or Customized detailing.

Have the trade-in allowance default to zero; that is, if the user does not enter a trade-in value, use zero in your calculation. Validate the values from the text boxes, displaying a message box if necessary.

To calculate, add the price of selected accessories and finish to the base price and display the result in a control called Subtotal. Calculate the sales tax on the subtotal and display the result in a Total control. Then subtract any trade-in value from the total and display the result in an Amount Due control.

Include buttons for *Calculate*, *Clear*, and *Exit*. The *Calculate* button must display the total amount due after trade-in.

Hint: Recall that you can make an ampersand appear in the Text property of a control by including two ampersands. See the tip on page 73 (Chapter 2).

Item	Price
Stereo System	425.76
Leather Interior	987.41
Computer Navigation	1,741.23
Standard	No additional charge
Pearlize	345.72
Customized Detailing	599.99
Tax Rate	8%

Video Bonanza

Design and code a project to calculate the amount due for rentals. Movies may be in VHS (videotape) format or DVD format. Videotapes rent for $1.80 each and DVDs rent for $2.50. New releases are $3 for DVD and $2 for videotape.

On the form include a text box to input the movie title and radio buttons to indicate whether the movie is in DVD or videotape format. Use one check box to indicate whether the person is a member; members receive a 10 percent discount. Another check box indicates a new release.

Use buttons for *Calculate*, *Clear for Next Item*, *Order Complete*, *Summary*, and *Exit*. The *Calculate* button should display the item amount and add to the subtotal. The *Clear for Next Item* clears the check box for new releases, the movie title, and the radio buttons; the member check box cannot be changed until the current order is complete. Include validation to check for missing data. If the user clicks on the *Calculate* button without first entering the movie title and selecting the movie format, display a message box.

For the *Order Complete* button, first confirm the operation with the user and clear the controls on the form for a new customer.

The *Summary* button displays the number of customers and the sum of the rental amounts in a message box. Make sure to add to the customer count and rental sum for each customer order.

Very Very Boards

Very Very Boards does a big business in shirts, especially for groups and teams. They need a project that will calculate the price for individual orders, as well as a summary for all orders.

The store employee will enter the orders in an order form that has text boxes for customer name and order number. To specify the shirts, use a text box for the quantity, radio buttons to select the size (small, medium, large, extra large, and XXL), and check boxes to specify a monogram and/or a pocket. Display the shirt price for the current order and the order total in ReadOnly text boxes or labels.

Include buttons to add a shirt to an order, clear the current item, complete the order, and display the summary of all orders. Do not allow the summary to display if the current order is not complete. Also, disable the text boxes for customer name and order number after an order is started; enable them again when the user clicks on the button to begin a new order. Confirm the operation before clearing the current order.

When the user adds shirts to an order, validate the quantity, which must be greater than zero. If the entry does not pass the validation, do not perform any calculations but display a message box and allow the user to correct the value. Determine the price of the shirts from the radio buttons and check boxes for the monogram and pockets. Multiply the quantity by the price to determine the extended price, and add to the order total and summary total.

Use constants for the shirt prices.

Prices for the Shirts

Small, medium, and large	$10
Extra large	11
XXL	12
Monogram	Add $2
Pocket	Add $1

Display the order summary in a message box. Include the number of shirts, the number of orders, and the dollar total of the orders.

5

Menus, Common Dialog Boxes, Sub Procedures, and Function Procedures

at the completion of this chapter, you will be able to . . .

1. Create menus and submenus for program control.

2. Display and use the Windows common dialog boxes.

3. Create context menus for controls and the form.

4. Write reusable code in sub procedures and function procedures and call the procedures from other locations.

Menus

You have undoubtedly used menus quite extensively while working with the computer. **Menus** consist of a menu bar that contains menus, each of which drops down to display a list of menu items. You can use menu items in place of or in addition to buttons to execute a procedure.

Menu items are actually controls; they have properties and events. Each menu item has a Name property, a Text property, and a Click event, similar to a button. When the user selects a menu item, with either the mouse or the keyboard, the menu item's Click event procedure executes.

It is easy to create menus for a Windows form using the Visual Studio environment's **Menu Designer**. Your menus will look and behave like standard Windows menus.

Defining Menus

Visual Studio 2005 introduces new components for defining menus. You add a **MenuStrip component** to a form. The MenuStrip is a container to which you can add ToolStripMenuItems. You also can add ToolStripComboBoxes, ToolStripSeparators, and ToolStripTextBoxes, making the new menus considerably more powerful than those in previous versions of VB.

The Visual Studio Menu Designer allows you to add menus and menu items to your forms. You must add a MenuStrip component from the *Menus & Toolbars* tab of the toolbox (Figure 5.1), which appears in the component tray below the form. Once you have added the MenuStrip component, it is extremely easy to create the menu items for your menu. The words *Type Here* appear at the top of the form, so that you can enter the text for your first menu (Figure 5.2). After you type the text for the first menu name and press Enter, the words *Type Here*

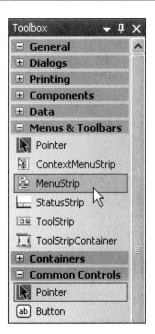

Figure 5.1

Add a MenuStrip component to the form using the MenuStrip tool from the toolbox.

appear both below the menu name and to the right of the menu name. You can choose next to enter menu items for the first menu or to type the words for the second menu (Figure 5.3). Each time you type the text for a new menu, you are automatically adding a ToolStripMenuItem to the MenuStrip's Items collection.

Note: If you click elsewhere on the form, you deactivate the Menu Designer. You can click on the menu at the top of the form or on the MenuStrip component to activate the Menu Designer again.

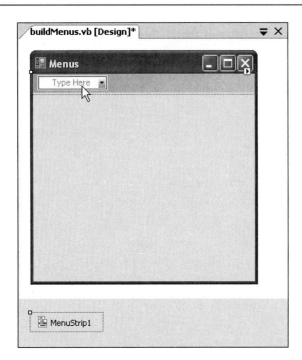

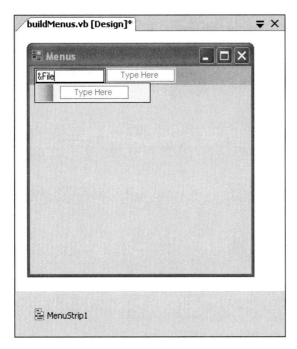

The Text Property

When you type the words for a menu or menu item, you are entering the Text property for an item. The Text property holds the words that you want to appear on the screen (just like the Text property of a button or label). To conform to Windows standards, your first menu's Text property should be <u>F</u>ile, with a keyboard access key. Use the ampersand (&) in the text to specify the key to use for keyboard access, as you learned to do in Chapter 2. For example, for <u>F</u>ile, the Text property should be &File.

You can enter and change the Text property for each of your menus and menu items using the Menu Designer. You also can change the Text property using the Properties window (Figure 5.4). Click on a menu or menu item to make its properties appear in the Properties window.

Figure 5.4

Modify the Text property of a menu item in the Properties window or the Menu Designer.

The Name Property

Another big improvement to VB 2005 menus is that the Menu Designer is now smart enough to give good names to the menu items. The *File* menu item that you add is automatically named *FileToolStripMenuItem*. Since the new items are named so well, you won't have to change the Name property of any menu component. However, if you change the Text property of any menu item, the item is not automatically renamed; you'll have to rename it yourself.

The MenuStrip Items Collection

As you create new menus using the Menu Designer, each menu is added to the Items collection that belongs to the MenuStrip. You can display the ToolStripMenuItems in the collection, set other properties of the items, as well as reorder, add, and delete items, using the Items Collection Editor (Figure 5.5). To display the Items Collection Editor, first select the MenuStrip (be sure you've selected the MenuStrip and not one of the ToolStripMenuItems) and then use one of these three techniques: (1) in the Items property in the

Figure 5.5

Use the MenuStrip's Items Collection Editor to display and modify properties of the menus. You also can add new menus to the collection or modify the order of the menus.

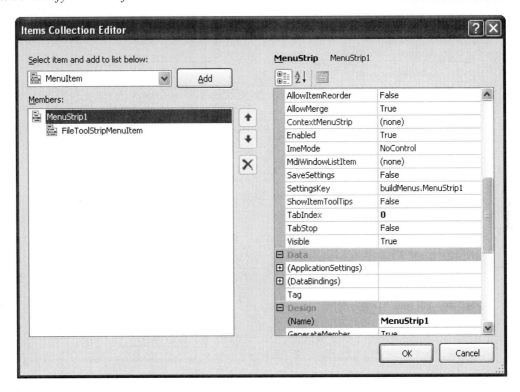

Properties window, click on the ellipses button; (2) right-click on the MenuStrip in the Menu Designer and select *Edit Items* from the context menu; or (3) click on the MenuStrip's smart-tag arrow (at the right end of the strip) to display the smart tag and select *Edit Items*.

A Menu's DropDownItems Collection

The MenuStrip's Items collection holds the top-level menus; each of the menus has its own collection of the menu items that appear in that menu. The Tool-StripMenuItems that appear below a menu name belong to the menu's Drop-DownItems collection. Therefore, if the *File* menu contains menu items for *Print*, *Save*, and *Exit*, the menu's DropDownItems collection will contain three Tool-StripMenuItems. Notice the title bar in Figure 5.6, which shows the Drop-DownItems collection for the *File* menu (FileToolStripMenuItem).

You can use the Items Collection Editor to rearrange or delete a menu item. You also can accomplish the same tasks using the MenuDesigner; just drag a menu item to a new location or right-click a menu item and select *Delete*.

Submenus

The drop-down list of items below a menu name is called a *menu item*. When an item on the menu has another list of items that pops up, the new list is called a ***submenu***. A filled triangle to the right of the item indicates that a menu item has a submenu (Figure 5.7). You create a submenu in the Menu Designer by moving to the right of a menu item and typing the next item's text (Figure 5.8).

Figure 5.6

*The Items Collection Editor for the DropDownItems collection, a property of the **File** menu's ToolStripMenuItem.*

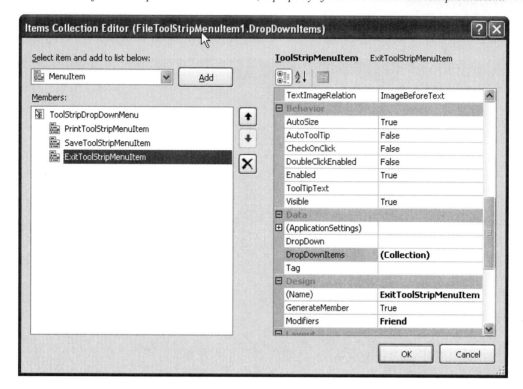

Figure 5.7

A filled triangle on a menu item indicates that a submenu will appear.

Separator Bars

When you have many items in a menu, you should group the items according to their purpose. You can create a **separator bar** in a menu, which draws a bar across the entire menu.

To create a separator bar, add a new menu item and click on its drop-down arrow (Figure 5.9). Drop down the list and select Separator (Figure 5.10).

Figure 5.8

Create a submenu by typing to the right of the parent menu item.

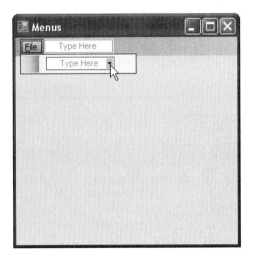

Enter submenu here

Figure 5.9

To create a menu item separator bar, click on the drop-down arrow for an item.

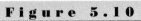

Figure 5.10

Select Separator from the smart tag's list.

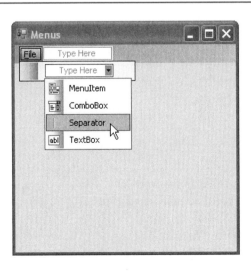

Other Features of ToolStrip Controls

You also can select ComboBox and TextBox for the type of menu item from the
drop-down list. Using these features you can create very powerful and professional menus and toolbars.

Another nice feature of the MenuStrip component is that you can now add
a menu to other components within your interface. For example, you could add
a menu to a group box if it was appropriate.

Creating a Menu—Step-by-Step

You are going to create a project with one form and a menu bar that contains
these menu items:

<u>F</u>ile	<u>H</u>elp
E<u>x</u>it	<u>A</u>bout

Create the Menu Items

STEP 1: Begin a new Windows Forms project (or open an existing one to which
you want to add a menu).

STEP 2: Add a MenuStrip component to the form. You can double-click or drag
the tool to the form; the component will appear in the component tray
at the bottom of the form (Figure 5.11).

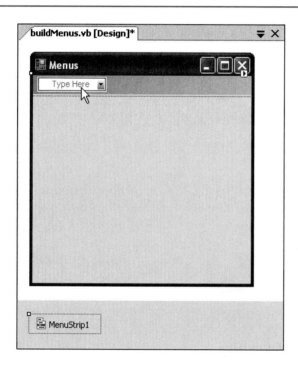

Figure 5.11

*Add a MenuStrip component to
the form. It will appear in the
component tray at the bottom
of the form.*

STEP 3: With the words *Type Here* selected, type "&File" over the words.

STEP 4: Move down to the *Type Here* words below the *File* menu and type
"E&xit".

STEP 5: Move up and to the right and add the *Help* menu ("&Help").

STEP 6: Below the *Help* menu, add the *About* menu item ("&About").

Coding for Menu Items

After you create your form's menu bar, it appears on the form in design time. Double-click any menu item and the Editor window opens in the item's Click event procedure where you can write the code. For example, in design time, open your form's *File* menu and double-click on *Exit*. The Editor window will open with the ExitToolStripMenuItem_Click procedure displayed.

Write the Code

STEP 1: Code the procedure for the *Exit* by pulling down the menu and double-clicking on the word *Exit*. Type a remark and a `Me.Close()` statement.

STEP 2: Open the AboutToolStripMenuItem_Click event procedure. Use a `MessageBox.Show` statement to display the *About* box. The message string should say "Programmer:" followed by your name (Figure 5.12).

Figure 5.12

Display a message box for an About box.

STEP 3: Run the program and test your menu items.

The Enabled Property

By default, all new menu items have their **Enabled property** set to True. An enabled menu item appears in black text and is available for selection, whereas the grayed out or **disabled** (Enabled = False) items are not available (Figure 5.13). You can set the Enabled property at design time or run time, in code.

```
DisplayInstructionsToolStripMenuItem.Enabled = False
```

Figure 5.13

Menu items can be disabled (grayed) or checked. A check mark usually indicates that the item is currently selected.

The Checked Property

A menu item may contain a check mark beside it (indicating that the item is **checked**). Usually a check mark next to a menu item indicates that the option is currently selected (refer to Figure 5.13). By default, the **Checked property** is set to False; you can change it at design time or in code.

```
DisplaySummaryMenuItem.Checked = True
```

Toggling Check Marks On and Off

If you create a menu item that can be turned on and off, you should include a check mark to indicate its current state. Set the initial state of the Checked property in the Properties window (Figure 5.14).

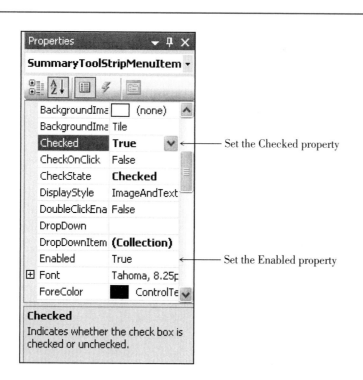

To change a menu item's state in code, set its Checked property to True or False. For example, for a menu item that displays or hides a summary, called *DisplaySummaryToolStripMenuItem*, a check mark indicates that the summary is currently selected. Choosing the menu item a second time should remove the check mark and hide the summary.

```
Private Sub DisplaySummaryToolStripMenuItem_Click(ByVal sender As System.Object, _
    ByVal e As System.EventArgs) Handles DisplaySummaryMenuItem.Click
    ' Hide or display the summary.

    If DisplaySummaryToolStripMenuItem.Checked Then
        ' Hide the summary information.
        DisplaySummaryToolStripMenuItem.Checked = False
    Else
        ' Show the summary information.
        DisplaySummaryToolStripMenuItem.Checked = True
    End If
End Sub
```

Setting Keyboard Shortcuts

Many computer users prefer to use keyboard shortcuts for selecting menu items. For example, most applications from Microsoft use Ctrl + P for the *Print* menu item and Ctrl + S for *Save*. You can create keyboard shortcuts for your menu items and choose whether or not to display the shortcuts on the menu. (For example, you can exit most Windows applications using Alt + F4, but the keyboard shortcut rarely appears on the menu.)

To set a keyboard shortcut for a menu item, first select the menu item in the designer. Then in the Properties window, select the ShortcutKeys property. Drop down the list to see the available choices and make your selection. You can use many combinations of function keys, the Alt key, the Shift key, and the Ctrl key. By default, the ShowShortcutKeys property is set to True; you can change it to False if you don't want the shortcut to show up on the menu.

You can toggle a Boolean value on and off using the Not operator: DisplaySummaryToolStripMenuItem. Checked = Not DisplaySummary-ToolStripMenuItem.Checked ■

Standards for Windows Menus

When you write applications that run under Windows, your programs should follow the Windows standards. You should always include keyboard access keys; if you include keyboard shortcuts, such as Ctrl + key, stick with the standard keys, such as Ctrl + P for printing. Also follow the Windows standards for placing the *File* menu on the left end of the menu bar and ending the menu with an *Exit* command. If you have a *Help* menu, it belongs at the right end of the menu bar.

Any menu item that will display a dialog box asking for more information from the user should have "..." appended to its Text property. Following Windows standards, the "..." indicates that a dialog box with further choices will appear if the user selects the menu item. You do not use the "..." for menu items that display dialog boxes that are informational only, such as an *About* box or a Summary form.

Plan your menus so that they look like other Windows programs. Your users will thank you.

Common Dialog Boxes

You can use a set of predefined standard dialog boxes in your projects for such tasks as specifying colors and fonts, printing, opening, and saving. Use the **common dialog** components in the *Dialogs* tab of the toolbox to display the dialog boxes that are provided as part of the Windows environment. The common dialog components provided with Visual Studio are ColorDialog, Folder-BrowserDialog, FontDialog, OpenFileDialog, SaveFileDialog (Figure 5.15).

To use a common dialog component, add the component to the form, placing it in the component tray. You can keep the default names for the components, such as ColorDialog1 and FontDialog1, since you will have only one component of each type.

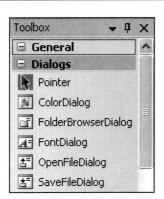

Displaying a Windows Common Dialog Box

After you place a common dialog component on your form, you can display the dialog box at run time using the **ShowDialog** method.

ShowDialog Method—General Form

```
DialogObject.ShowDialog()
```

The DialogObject is the name of the common dialog component that you placed on the form. The name will be the default name, such as ColorDialog1 or FontDialog1.

ShowDialog Method—Examples

```
ColorDialog1.ShowDialog()
FontDialog1.ShowDialog()
```

Place the code to show the dialog in the event procedure for a menu item or button.

Modal versus Modeless Windows

You probably have noticed that when you display a Windows dialog box, it remains on top until you respond. But in many applications, you can display additional windows and switch back and forth between the windows. A dialog box is said to be **modal**, which means that it stays on top of the application and must be responded to. You use the ShowDialog method to display a dialog box, which is just a window displayed modally. In Chapter 6 you will learn to display additional windows that are **modeless**, which do not demand that you respond. You will use the Show method to display a modeless window.

Using the Information from the Dialog Box

Displaying the *Color* dialog box (Figure 5.16) doesn't make the color of anything change. You must take care of that in your program code. When the user

Figure 5.16

The Color common dialog box.

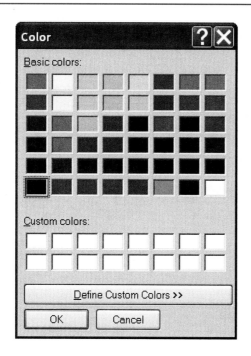

clicks on OK, the selected color is stored in a property that you can access. You can assign the value to the properties of controls in your project.

Using the Color Dialog Box

The color selected by the user is stored in the Color property. You can assign this property to another object, such as a control.

```
With Me
    .titleLabel.BackColor = .ColorDialog1.Color
End With
```

Because Basic executes the statements in sequence, you would first display the dialog box with the ShowDialog method. (Execution then halts until the user responds to the dialog box.) Then you can use the Color property:

```
Public Sub ColorToolStripMenuItem_Click(ByVal sender As System.Object, _
  ByVal e As System.EventArgs) Handles ColorToolStripMenuItem.Click
    ' Change the color of the total labels.

    With Me
        With .ColorDialog1
            .ShowDialog()
            subTotalLabel.ForeColor = .Color
            taxLabel.ForeColor = .Color
            totalLabel.ForeColor = .Color
        End With
    End With
End Sub
```

Using the Font Dialog Box

When you display the *Font* common dialog box (Figure 5.17), the available fonts for the system display. After the user makes a selection, you can use the Font property of the dialog box object. You may want to assign the Font property to the Font property of other objects on your form.

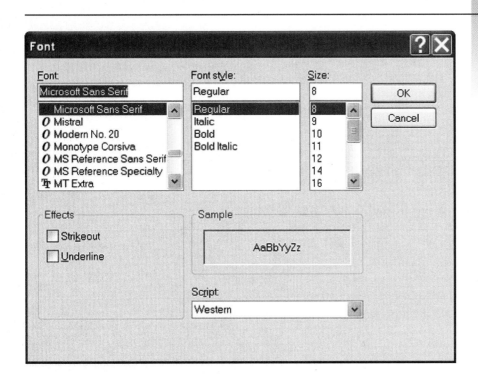

Figure 5.17

The Font common dialog box. The fonts that display are those installed on the user's system.

```
Public Sub FontToolStripMenuItem_Click(ByVal sender As System.Object, _
   ByVal e As System.EventArgs) Handles FontToolStripMenuItem.Click
   ' Change the font name for the labels.

   With FontDialog1
      .ShowDialog()
      subTotalLabel.Font = .Font
      taxLabel.Font = .Font
      totalLabel.Font = .Font
   End With
End Sub
```

When the user clicks on the *Font* menu item, the *Font* dialog box appears on the screen. Execution halts until the user responds to the dialog box, either by clicking OK or Cancel.

Setting Initial Values

When a common dialog box for colors or fonts appears, what color or font do you want to display? It's best to assign initial values before showing the dialog box. Before executing the ShowDialog method, you should assign the existing values of the object's properties that will be altered. This step makes the current values selected when the dialog box appears. It also means that if the user

selects the Cancel button, the property settings for the objects will remain unchanged.

```
With Me
    .FontDialog1.Font =.subTotalLabel.Font
End With
```

or

```
With Me
    .colorDialog1.Color = .BackColor
End With
```

Creating Context Menus

You also can add **context menus** to your applications. Context menus are the
shortcut menus that pop up when you right-click. Generally, the items in a
context menu are specific to the component to which you are pointing, reflect-
ing the options available for that component or that situation.

Creating a context menu is similar to creating a menu. You add a
ContextMenuStrip component, which appears in the component tray below the form. At the top of the form, in the Menu Designer, the words say
ContextMenuStrip (Figure 5.18). A context menu does not have a top-level
menu, only the menu items. Click on the words *Type Here* to type the text of
your first menu item.

Your application can have more than one context menu. You assign the
context menu to the form or control by setting its ContextMenuStrip property.

Figure 5.18

*Add a ContextMenuStrip
component to the component
tray and create the context
menu using the Menu
Designer.*

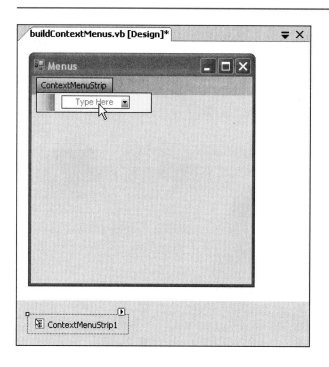

For example, a form has a ContextMenuStrip property, a button has a ContextMenuStrip property, and all visible controls have ContextMenuStrip properties. You can assign the same ContextMenuStrip to the form and each of the
controls, or a different context menu to each. If you have only one context
menu, attach it to the form—it will pop up if the user right-clicks anywhere on
the form, including on a control. However, some controls have an "automatic"
context menu. For example, a text box has an automatic context menu that allows the user to cut, copy, and paste text. If you set the ContextMenuStrip property of a text box to your own context menu, your context menu will appear
instead of the original (automatic) context menu.

Creating a Context Menu—Step-by-Step

You are going to create a context menu that contains these menu items:

<u>C</u>olor...
<u>F</u>ont...
E<u>x</u>it

Add the Context Menu Strip to a Form

STEP 1: Begin a new Windows project (or open an existing one to which you
want to add a context menu). Change the form's filename and form
name.

STEP 2: Add a ContextMenuStrip component from the *Menus & Toolbars* tab of
the toolbox; the component will appear in the component tray at the
bottom of the form (refer to Figure 5.18).

STEP 3: Click on the words *ContextMenuStrip* in the Menu Designer to make a
Type Here menu item appear.

STEP 4: Click on the words *Type Here* and type the text for the first menu item:
"&Color...".

STEP 5: Type the text for the second and third menu items: "&Font..." and
"E&xit".

STEP 6: Add a label named messageLabel to your form and set the Text property to "Right-click for the Context Menu".

STEP 7: Set the form's ContextMenuStrip property to ContextMenuStrip1. Notice that the property box has a drop-down list. If you have more than
one context menu defined, you can choose from the list.

STEP 8: Add a ColorDialog component from the *Dialogs* tab of the toolbox.

STEP 9: Add a FontDialog component.

In this example, right-clicking anywhere on the form allows you to change
the foreground color or the font of the form. As you know, if you haven't set
those properties for individual controls, the form's properties apply to all controls on the form.

STEP 10: Code the form as follows:

> ☑**TIP**
>
> It's a good idea to set a Con-
> textMenu property for all controls
> and for the form to allow users the
> option of using context menus. ■

```
'Program:        Ch05ContextMenus
'Programmer:     Your Name
'Date:           today's date
'Description:    Create and apply a context menu.
```

```
Public Class contextMenuForm
    Private Sub ColorToolStripMenuItem_Click(ByVal sender As System.Object, _
        ByVal e As System.EventArgs) Handles ColorToolStripMenuItem.Click
        ' Change the form's ForeColor.
        ' Applies to all controls on the form that haven't had their
        '    ForeColor explicitly modified.

        With Me.ColorDialog1
            ' Initialize the dialog box.
            .Color = Me.ForeColor
            .ShowDialog()
            ' Assign the new color.
            Me.ForeColor = .Color
        End With
    End Sub

    Private Sub FontToolStripMenuItem_Click(ByVal sender As System.Object, _
        ByVal e As System.EventArgs) Handles FontToolStripMenuItem.Click
        ' Change the label's font.

        With Me.FontDialog1
            ' Initialize the dialog box.
            .Font = Me.messageLabel.Font
            .ShowDialog()
            ' Assign the new font.
            Me.messageLabel.Font = .Font
        End With
    End Sub

    Private Sub ExitToolStripMenuItem_Click(ByVal sender As System.Object, _
        ByVal e As System.EventArgs) Handles ExitToolStripMenuItem.Click
        ' Terminate the project.

        Me.Close()
    End Sub
End Class
```

Test the Program

STEP 1: Experiment with right-clicking on the form and on the label. Test each of the options.

After you have the program working, experiment with adding more controls, adding more ContextMenuStrip components, and setting the ContextMenuStrip property of controls.

Sharing Procedures

Most frequently a context menu is added as an additional way to access a feature that is also available from another menu or a button. Recall from Chapter 4 that you can use the same procedure for several events by adding to the Handles clause.

```
Private Sub FontToolStripMenuItem_Click (ByVal sender As System.Object, _
    ByVal e As System.EventArgs) _
    Handles FontToolStripMenuItem.Click, fontButton.Click
    ' Change the label's font.
```

```
      With Me.FontDialog1
         ' Initialize the dialog box.
         .Font = Me.messageLabel.Font
         .ShowDialog()
         ' Assign the new font.
         Me.messageLabel.Font = .Font
      End With
End Sub
```

Writing General Procedures

Often you will encounter programming situations in which multiple procedures perform the same operation. This condition can occur when the user can select either a button or a menu item to do the same thing. Rather than retyping the code, you can write reusable code in a **general procedure** and call it from both event procedures.

General procedures are also useful in breaking down large sections of code into smaller units that perform a specific task. By breaking down your calculations into smaller tasks, you simplify any maintenance that needs to be done in a program in the future. For example, bowling statistics for a league may require calculations for handicap and series total. If the formula for calculating handicaps changes, wouldn't it be nice to have a procedure that calculates handicaps only instead of one that performs all the calculations?

You can choose from two types of general procedures: **sub procedures** and **function procedures**:

- A sub procedure performs actions.

- A function procedure performs actions and returns a value (the **return value**).

You will likely use a sub procedure if you need to set property values for a series of objects. However, if you need to calculate a result, then a function procedure is the appropriate choice. Both sub procedures and function procedures are considered the **methods** of object-oriented programming.

Creating a New Sub Procedure

You can create a sub procedure in your code window by enclosing the desired lines of code within a set of Sub and End Sub statements.

Sub...End Sub Statements—General Form

General Form

```
Private Sub ProcedureName()
    '... Statements in the procedure.
End Sub
```

When you type the line

```
Private Sub ProcedureName
```

and press Enter, the editor automatically adds the parentheses to the Sub statement, adds the End Sub statement, and places the insertion point on the line between the two new lines.

Sub...End Sub Statements—Example

```
Private Sub SelectColor()
    ' Display the color dialog box.

    ColorDialog1.ShowDialog()
End Sub
```

Note that VB .NET has choices other than Private for the access, such as Public, Friend, and Protected. In a later chapter, you will learn about the other types of procedures; for now use Private for all general procedures.

The coding for the new procedure is similar to the other procedures we have been coding but is not yet attached to any event. Therefore, this code cannot be executed unless we specifically **call** the procedure from another procedure. To call a sub procedure, just give the procedure name, which in this case is SelectColor.

```
Private Sub changeMessageButton_Click(ByVal sender As System.Object, _
   ByVal e As System.EventArgs) Handles changeMessageButton.Click
    ' Change the color of the message.

    SelectColor()
    With Me
      .messageLabel.ForeColor = .ColorDialog1.Color
    End With
End Sub

Private Sub changeTitleButton_Click(ByVal sender As System.Object, _
   ByVal e As System.EventArgs) Handles changeTitleButton.Click
    ' Change the color of the title.

    SelectColor()
    With Me
      .titleLabel.ForeColor = .ColorDialog1.Color
    End With
End Sub
```

Passing Arguments to Procedures

At times you may need to use the value of a variable in one procedure and then again in a second procedure that is called from the first. In this situation, you could declare the variable as module level, but that approach makes the variable visible to all other procedures. To keep the scope of a variable as narrow as possible, consider declaring the variable as local and passing it to any called procedures.

As an example, we will expand the capabilities of the previous SelectColor sub procedure to display the original color when the dialog box appears. Because the SelectColor procedure can be called from various locations, the original color must be passed to the procedure.

```vb
Private Sub SelectColor(incomingColor As Color)
    ' Allow the user to select a color.

    With ColorDialog1
        ' Set the initial color.
        .Color = incomingColor
        .ShowDialog()
    End With
End Sub

Private Sub changeMessageButton_Click(ByVal sender As System.Object, _
    ByVal e As System.EventArgs) Handles changeMessageButton.Click
        ' Change the color of the message.
        Dim originalColor As Color

    With Me
        originalColor = .messageLabel.ForeColor
        SelectColor(originalColor)
        .messageLabel.ForeColor = .colorDialog1.Color
    End With
End Sub

Private Sub changeTitleButton_Click(ByVal sender As System.Object, _
    ByVal e As System.EventArgs) Handles changeTitleButton.Click
        ' Change the color of the title.
        Dim originalColor As Color

    With Me
        originalColor = .titleLabel.ForeColor
        SelectColor(originalColor)
        .titleLabel.ForeColor = .ColorDialog1.Color
    End With
End Sub
```

Notice that in this example the SelectColor procedure now has an argument inside the parentheses. This syntax specifies that when called, an argument must be supplied.

When a sub procedure definition names an argument, any call to that procedure must supply the argument. In addition, the argument value must be the same data type in both locations. Notice that in the two calling procedures (changeMessageButton_Click and changeTitleButton_Click), the variable originalColor is declared as a Color data type.

Another important point is that the name of the argument does not have to be the same in both locations. The ShowColor sub procedure will take whatever Color value it is passed and refer to it as incomingColor inside the procedure.

You may specify multiple arguments in both the sub procedure header and the call to the procedure. The number of arguments, their sequence, and their data types must match in both locations! You will see some examples of multiple arguments in the sections that follow.

Passing Arguments ByVal or ByRef

When you pass a value to a procedure, you may pass it **ByVal** or **ByRef** (for by value or by reference). ByVal sends a copy of the argument's value to the procedure so that the procedure cannot alter the original value. ByRef sends a reference indicating where the value is stored in memory, allowing the called procedure to actually change the argument's original value. You can specify how you want to pass the argument by using the `ByVal` or `ByRef` keyword before the argument. If you don't specify `ByVal` or `ByRef`, arguments are passed by value.

```
' Argument passed by reference.
Private Sub SelectColor(ByRef incomingColor As Color)

' Argument passed by value.
Private Sub SelectColor(ByVal incomingColor As Color)

' Argument passed by value (the default).
Private Sub SelectColor(incomingColor As Color)
```

Writing Function Procedures

As a programmer, you may need to calculate a value that will be needed in several different procedures or programs. You can write your own function that will calculate a value and call the function from the locations where it is needed. As an example, we will create a function procedure called `Commission` that calculates and returns a salesperson's commission.

Typing in a block of code using the `Function...End Function` statements creates a function procedure. Since the procedure returns a value, you must specify a data type for the value.

Function...End Function Statements—General Form

General Form

```
Private Function ProcedureName() As Datatype

End Function
```

Functions also can be declared as `Public`, `Protected`, or `Friend`, which you will learn about later. `Private` is appropriate for all functions for now.

Function...End Function Statements—Example

Example

```
Private Function Commission() As Decimal
    ' Statements in function.
End Function
```

Notice that this procedure looks just like a sub procedure except that the word `Function` replaces the word `Sub` on both the first line and the last line. The procedure header also includes a data type, which is the type of the value returned by the function.

Remember that functions also have arguments. You supply arguments to a function when you call the function by placing a value or values inside the parentheses. You can choose to pass the arguments `ByVal` or `ByRef`.

When you write a function, you declare the argument(s) that the function needs. You give each argument an identifier and a data type. The name that you give an argument in the function procedure header is the identifier that you will use inside the function to refer to the value of the argument (Figure 5.19).

Examples

```
Private Function Commission(ByVal salesAmountDecimal As Decimal) As Decimal
Private Function Payment(rateDecimal As Decimal, timeDecimal As Decimal, _
  amountDecimal As Decimal) As Decimal
```

In the function procedure, the argument list you enter establishes the number of arguments, their type, and their sequence. When using multiple arguments, the sequence of the arguments is critical, just as when you use the predefined Visual Basic functions.

Returning the Result of a Function

The main difference between coding a function procedure and coding a sub procedure is that in a function procedure you must set up the return value. This return value is placed in a variable that Visual Basic names with the same name as the function name. In the example in Figure 5.19, the variable name is Commission.

Figure 5.19

A procedure header for a function procedure.

You can choose from two techniques for returning the result of the function:

- Somewhere inside the Commission function, set the function name to a value. Example: Commission = 0.15D * salesAmountDecimal

- Use the Return statement. If you use the Return statement, you do not use the function's name as a variable name.
  Example: Return 0.15D * salesAmountDecimal

Writing a Commission Function

Here is the Commission function procedure coded using the first technique for returning a value.

```
Private Function Commission(ByVal salesAmountDecimal As Decimal) As Decimal
  ' Calculate the sales commission.

  If salesAmountDecimal < 1000D Then
    Commission = 0D
  ElseIf salesAmountDecimal <= 2000D Then
    Commission = 0.15D * salesAmountDecimal
  Else
    Commission = 0.2D * salesAmountDecimal
  End If
End Function
```

And here is the same Commission function procedure using the Return statement.

```
Private Function Commission(ByVal salesAmountDecimal As Decimal) As Decimal
    ' Calculate the sales commission.

    If salesAmountDecimal < 1000D Then
        Return 0D
    ElseIf salesAmountDecimal <= 2000D Then
        Return 0.15D * salesAmountDecimal
    Else
        Return 0.2D * salesAmountDecimal
    End If
End Function
```

Calling the Commission Function

In another procedure in the form, you can call your function by using it in an expression.

```
Private Sub calculateButton_Click(ByVal sender As System.Object, _
    ByVal e As System.EventArgs) Handles calculateButton.Click
    ' Calculate the commission.
    Dim salesDecimal As Decimal

    With Me
        salesDecimal = Decimal.Parse(.salesTextBox.Text)
        .commissionLabel.Text = Commission(salesDecimal).ToString("C")
    End With
End Sub
```

Notice in the preceding example that the argument named in the function call does not have the same name as the argument named in the function definition. When the function is called, a copy of salesDecimal is passed to the function and is assigned to the named argument, in this case salesAmountDecimal. As the calculations are done (inside the function), for every reference to salesAmountDecimal, the value that was passed in for salesDecimal is actually used.

You can combine the functions, if you wish:

```
With Me
    .commissionLabel.Text = _
        Commission(Decimal.Parse(.salesTextBox.Text)).ToString("C")
End With
```

To read this statement, begin with the inner parentheses: salesTextBox.Text is passed to `Decimal.Parse` for conversion to Decimal; the result of that conversion is passed as an argument to the `Commission` function; the value returned by the `Commission` function is formatted as it is converted to a string and then assigned to commissionLabel.Text.

Converting SelectColor to a Function Procedure

The SelectColor procedure that we wrote earlier is a good candidate for a function procedure, since we need to return one argument: the color.

```vb
Private Function SelectColor(incomingColor As Color) As Color
    ' Allow the user to select a color.

    With ColorDialog1
        ' Set the initial color.
        .Color = incomingColor
        .ShowDialog()
        Return .Color
    End With
End Function

Private Sub changeMessageButton_Click(ByVal sender As System.Object, _
  ByVal e As System.EventArgs) Handles changeMessageButton.Click
    ' Call the new SelectColor function (with a single line of code).

    With Me
        .messageLabel.ForeColor = SelectColor(.messageLabel.ForeColor)
    End With
End Sub
```

Functions with Multiple Arguments

A function can have multiple arguments. The sequence and data type of the arguments in the `call` must exactly match the arguments in the function procedure header.

Writing a Function with Multiple Arguments

When you create a function with multiple arguments such as a `Payment` function, you enclose the list of arguments within the parentheses. The following example indicates that three arguments are needed in the call: The first argument is the annual interest rate, the second is the time in years, and the third is the loan amount. All three argument values will have a data type of decimal, and the return value will be decimal. Look carefully at the following formula and notice how the identifiers in the parentheses are used.

```vb
Private Function Payment(ByVal rateDecimal As Decimal, ByVal timeDecimal As Decimal, _
  ByVal amountDecimal As Decimal) As Decimal
    ' Calculate the monthly payment on an amortized loan.

    Dim ratePerMonthDecimal As Decimal
    ratePerMonthDecimal = rateDecimal / 12D

    ' Calculate and set the return value of the function.
    Payment = Convert.ToDecimal((amountDecimal * ratePerMonthDecimal) _
        / ((1 - (1 / (1 + ratePerMonthDecimal) ^ (timeDecimal * 12D)))))
End Function
```

Calling a Function with Multiple Arguments

To call this function from another procedure, use these statements:

```vb
With Me
    principalDecimal = Decimal.Parse(.principalTextBox.Text)
    rateDecimal = Decimal.Parse(.rateTextBox.Text)
    yearsDecimal = Decimal.Parse(.yearsTextBox.Text)
End With
paymentDecimal = Payment(rateDecimal, yearsDecimal, principalDecimal)
```

You can pass the value of the text boxes as well as format the result by combining functions:

```
With Me
  .paymentLabel.Text = Payment(Decimal.Parse(.rateTextBox.Text), _
    Decimal.Parse(.yearsTextBox.Text), _
    Decimal.Parse(.principalTextBox.Text)).ToString("C")
End With
```

When you call the function, the VS smart editor shows you the arguments of your function (Figure 5.20), just as it does for built-in functions (assuming that you have already entered the function procedure).

Figure 5.20

The Visual Studio IntelliSense feature pops up with the list of arguments for your own newly written procedure.

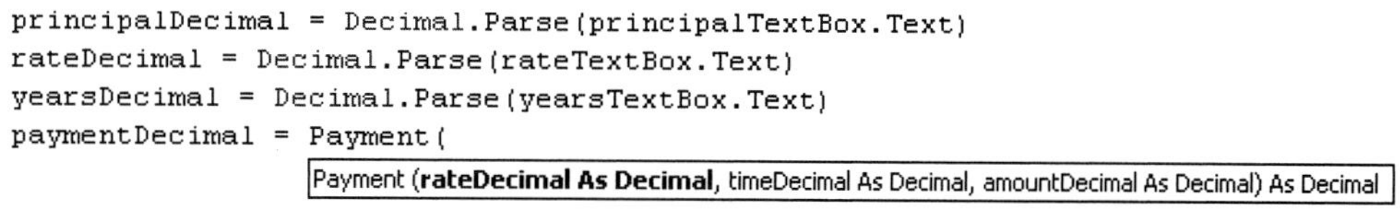

```
principalDecimal = Decimal.Parse(principalTextBox.Text)
rateDecimal = Decimal.Parse(rateTextBox.Text)
yearsDecimal = Decimal.Parse(yearsTextBox.Text)
paymentDecimal = Payment(
```
```
Payment (rateDecimal As Decimal, timeDecimal As Decimal, amountDecimal As Decimal) As Decimal
```

Breaking Calculations into Smaller Units

A project with many calculations can be easier to understand and to write if you break the calculations into small units. Each unit should perform one program function or block of logic. In the following example that calculates bowling statistics, separate function procedures calculate the average, handicap, and series total, and find the high game.

```
'Project:        Chapter 5 Bowling Example
'Programmer:     Bradley/Millspaugh
'Date:           June 2005
'Folder:         Ch05Bowling
'Description:     This project calculates bowling statistics using
'                 multiple function procedures.

Public Class bowlingForm

    Private Function FindAverage(ByVal score1Integer As Integer, _
      ByVal score2Integer As Integer, ByVal score3Integer As Integer) As Decimal
        ' Return the average of three games.

        Return (score1Integer + score2Integer + score3Integer) / 3D
    End Function

    Private Function FindHandicap(ByVal averageDecimal As Decimal) As Decimal
        ' Calculate the handicap.

        Return (200D - averageDecimal) * 0.8D
    End Function

    Private Function FindSeries(ByVal game1Integer As Integer, _
      ByVal game2Integer As Integer, ByVal game3Integer As Integer) As Integer
        ' Calculate the series total.

        Return game1Integer + game2Integer + game3Integer
    End Function
```

```vb
Private Function FindHighGame(ByVal game1Integer As Integer, _
  ByVal game2Integer As Integer, ByVal game3Integer As Integer) As String
    ' Find the highest game in the series.

    If game1Integer > game2Integer And game1Integer > game3Integer Then
      Return "1"
    ElseIf game2Integer > game1Integer And game2Integer > game3Integer Then
      Return "2"
    ElseIf game3Integer > game1Integer And game3Integer > game2Integer Then
      Return "3"
    Else
      Return "Tie"
    End If
End Function

Private Sub CalculateToolStripMenuItem_Click(ByVal sender As System.Object, _
  ByVal e As System.EventArgs) Handles CalculateToolStripMenuItem.Click
    ' Calculate individual and summary info.

    Dim averageDecimal, handicapDecimal As Decimal
    Dim seriesInteger, game1Integer, game2Integer, game3Integer As Integer
    Dim highGameString As String
    Try
      With Me
        game1Integer = Integer.Parse(.score1TextBox.Text)
        game2Integer = Integer.Parse(.score2TextBox.Text)
        game3Integer = Integer.Parse(.score3TextBox.Text)

        ' Perform all calculations.
        averageDecimal = FindAverage(game1Integer, game2Integer, game3Integer)
        seriesInteger = FindSeries(game1Integer, game2Integer, game3Integer)
        highGameString = FindHighGame(game1Integer, game2Integer, game3Integer)
        handicapDecimal = FindHandicap(averageDecimal)

        ' Format the output.
        .averageTextBox.Text = averageDecimal.ToString("N1")
        .highGameTextBox.Text = highGameString
        .seriesTextBox.Text = seriesInteger.ToString()
        .handicapTextBox.Text = handicapDecimal.ToString("N1")
      End With
    Catch
      MessageBox.Show("Please Enter three numeric scores", "Missing Data", _
        MessageBoxButtons.OK)
    End Try
End Sub

Private Sub ExitToolStripMenuItem_Click(ByVal sender As System.Object, _
  ByVal e As System.EventArgs) Handles ExitToolStripMenuItem.Click
    ' Terminate the project.

    Me.Close()
End Sub

Private Sub ClearToolStripMenuItem_Click(ByVal sender As System.Object, _
  ByVal e As System.EventArgs) Handles ClearToolStripMenuItem.Click
    With Me
      With .nameTextBox
        .Clear()
        .Focus()
      End With
```

```
          .maleRadioButton.Checked = False
          .femaleRadioButton.Checked = False
          .scoreaverageTextBox.Clear()
          .scorehandicapTextBox.Clear()
          .scorehighGameTextBox.Clear()
          .seriesTextBox.Clear()
          .averageTextBox.Clear()
          .highGameTextBox.Clear()
          .handicapTextBox.Clear()
       End With
    End Sub
End Class
```

Feedback 5.1

You need to write a procedure to calculate and return the average of three integer values.

1. Should you write a sub procedure or a function procedure?
2. Write the header line of the procedure.
3. Write the calculation.
4. How is the calculated average passed back to the calling procedure?

Basing a New Project on an Existing Project

In this chapter you will base a new project on an existing project but keep the previous project unchanged. To create a new project based on a previous one, you should copy the project folder. Then you can move it as necessary.

You can copy an entire Windows project folder from one location to another using My Computer. Make sure that the project is not open in Visual Studio and copy the entire folder.

- Make sure the project is not open (very important).

- Copy the folder to a new location using My Computer.

- Rename the new folder for the new project name, still using My Computer.

- Open the new project (the copy) in the Visual Studio IDE.

- In the IDE's Solution Explorer, rename the solution and the project. The best way to do this is to right-click on the name and choose the *Rename* command from the shortcut menu.

- Rename the forms, if desired. (If VS can't find the startup form, you must open the *Project Designer* and set the Startup Object. Select *Project / ProjectName Properties* or double-click on the *My Project* entry in the Solution Explorer.)

- Open the *Project Designer* and change the Assembly Name and Root Namespace entries to match your new project name.

Warning: Do not try to copy a project that is open using the *Save As* command, attempting to place a copy in a new location. The original solution and project files are modified, and you won't be able to open the original project.

Your Hands-On Programming Example

Modify the hands-on programming example from Chapter 4 by replacing some of the buttons with menus. Write a function procedure to calculate the sales tax and allow the user to select the font and color of the summary text boxes.

The project for R 'n R—for Reading 'n Refreshment calculates the amount due for individual orders and maintains accumulated totals for a summary. Use a check box for takeout items, which are taxable (8 percent); all other orders are nontaxable. Include radio buttons for the five coffee selections: Cappuccino, Espresso, Latte, Iced Latte, and Iced Cappuccino. The prices for each will be assigned using these constants:

Cappuccino	2.00
Espresso	2.25
Latte	1.75
Iced (either)	2.50

Use a button for *Calculate Selection*, which will calculate and display the amount due for each item. A button for *Clear for Next Item* will clear the selections and amount for the single item. Additional text boxes in a separate frame will maintain the summary information for the current order to include subtotal, tax, and total.

The *New Order* menu item will clear the bill for the current customer and add to the totals for the summary. The menu item for *Summary* should display the total of all orders, the average sale amount per customer, and the number of customers in a message box.

The *Edit* menu contains options that duplicate the Calculate and Clear buttons. The *Font* and *Color* options change the properties of the subtotal, tax, and total text boxes.

The *About* selection on the *Help* menu will display a message box with information about the programmer.

File	Edit	Help
New Order	Calculate Selection	About
Summary	Clear Item	
Exit	———	
	Font...	
	Color...	

Planning the Project

Sketch a form (Figure 5.21) that your users sign as meeting their needs.

Plan the Objects and Properties Plan the property settings for the form and each of the controls.

Object	Property	Setting
billingForm	Name	billingForm
	Text	R 'n R for Reading 'n Refreshment
	AcceptButton	calculateButton
	CancelButton	clearButton

Figure 5.21

A sketch of the form for the hands-on programming example.

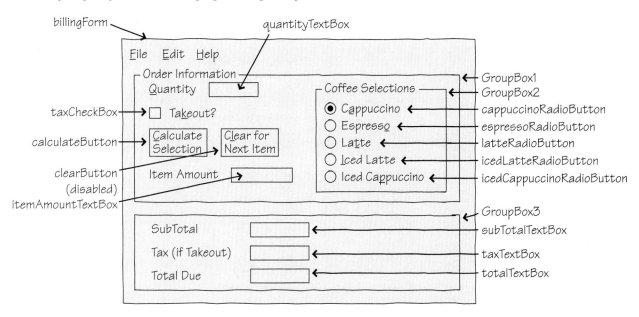

Object	Property	Setting
GroupBox1	Text	Order Information
GroupBox2	Text	Coffee Selections
GroupBox3	Text	(blank)
cappuccinoRadioButton	Name	cappuccinoRadioButton
	Text	C&appuccino
	Checked	True
espressoRadioButton	Name	espressoRadioButton
	Text	Espress&o
latteRadioButton	Name	latteRadioButton
	Text	La&tte
icedLatteRadioButton	Name	icedLatteRadioButton
	Text	&Iced Latte
icedCappuccinoRadioButton	Name	icedCappuccinoRadioButton
	Text	Iced Ca&ppuccino
Label1	Text	&Quantity
quantityTextBox	Name	quantityTextBox
	Text	(blank)
taxCheckBox	Name	taxCheckBox
	Text	Ta&keout?
Label2	Text	Item Amount

Object	Property	Setting
Label3	Text	SubTotal
Label4	Text	Tax (if Takeout)
Label5	Text	Total Due
itemAmountTextBox	Name TabStop ReadOnly	itemAmountTextBox False True
subTotalTextBox	Name TabStop ReadOnly	subTotalTextBox False True
taxTextBox	Name TabStop ReadOnly	taxTextBox False True
totalTextBox	Name TabStop ReadOnly	totalTextBox False True
calculateButton	Name Text	calculateButton &Calculate Selection
clearButton	Name Text	clearButton C&lear for Next Item
FileToolStripMenuItem	Text	&File
NewOrderToolStripMenuItem	Text	&New Order
SummaryToolStripMenuItem	Text	&Summary
ExitToolStripMenuItem	Text	E&xit
EditToolStripMenuItem	Text	&Edit
CalculateSelectionToolStripMenuItem	Text	&Calculate Selection
ClearItemToolStripMenuItem	Text	Clear &Item
FontToolStripMenuItem	Text	&Font . . .
ColorToolStripMenuItem	Text	C&olor . . .
HelpToolStripMenuItem	Text	&Help
AboutToolStripMenuItem	Text	&About
ColorDialog1	Name	ColorDialog1
FontDialog1	Name	FontDialog1

Plan the Event Procedures　You need to plan the actions for the buttons and the actions of the menu items, as well as the function for the sales tax.

Object	Procedure	Action
calculateButton	Click	Validate for blank or nonnumeric amount.
		Find price of drink selection.
		Multiply price by quantity.
		Add amount to subtotal.
		Call tax function if needed.
		Calculate total = subtotal + tax.
		Format and display the values.
		Enable the Clear button.
		Disable the Takeout check box.
clearButton	Click	Check that there are data to clear.
		Clear the coffee selections.
		Clear the quantity and the item price.
		Set the focus to the quantity.
		Disable the Clear button.
NewOrderToolStripMenuItem	Click	Confirm clearing the current order.
		Clear the current order.
		Accumulate total sales and count.
		Set subtotal and total due to 0.
		Enable Takeout check box.
		Disable the Clear button.
SummaryToolStripMenuItem	Click	If current order not added to totals
		Call NewOrderToolStripMenuItem_Click.
		Calculate the average.
		Display the summary totals in a message box.
ExitToolStripMenuItem	Click	Terminate the project.
CalculateSelectionToolStripMenuItem	Click	Share the event procedure for calculateButton.
ClearItemToolStripMenuItem	Click	Share the event procedure for clearButton.
AboutToolStripMenuItem	Click	Display the About message box.
FontToolStripMenuItem	Click	Allow user to change fonts.
ColorToolStripMenuItem	Click	Allow user to change colors.
(Function procedure)	FindTax	Calculate the sales tax.

Write the Project Follow the sketch in Figure 5.21 to create the form. Figure 5.22 shows the completed form.

- If you are basing your project on the project from Chapter 4, first copy the project folder, as described in the section "Basing a New Project on an Existing Project."

- Set the properties of each object according to your plan. If you are modifying the project from Chapter 4, add the menus and the common dialog components, and remove the extra buttons.

- Write the code. Working from the pseudocode, write each event procedure.

- When you complete the code, use a variety of data to thoroughly test the project.

Figure 5.22

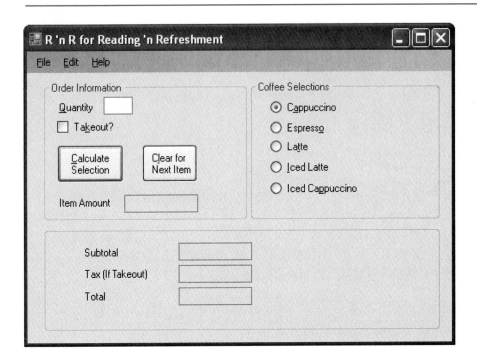

The form for the hands-on programming example.

The Project Coding Solution

```
'Program Name    Ch05HandsOn
'Programmer:     Bradley/Millspaugh
'Date:           June 2005
'Description:     This project calculates the amount due
'                 based on the customer selection
'                 and accumulates summary data for the day.
'                 Incorporates menus and common dialog boxes,
'                 which allow the user to change the font and
'                 color of labels.
'Folder:          Ch05HandsOn

Public Class billingForm

    ' Declare module-level variables for summary information.
    Dim subtotalDecimal, totalDecimal, grandTotalDecimal As Decimal
    Dim customerCountInteger As Integer

    ' Declare  constants.
    Const TAX_RATE_Decimal As Decimal = 0.08D
    Const CAPPUCCINO_PRICE_Decimal As Decimal = 2D
    Const ESPRESSO_PRICE_Decimal As Decimal = 2.25D
    Const LATTE_PRICE_Decimal As Decimal = 1.75D
    Const ICED_PRICE_Decimal As Decimal = 2.5D
```

```vbnet
Private Sub calculateButton_Click(ByVal sender As System.Object, _
    ByVal e As System.EventArgs) _
    Handles calculateButton.Click, CalculateSelectionToolStripMenuItem.Click
        ' Calculate and display the current amounts and add to totals.
        Dim priceDecimal, taxDecimal, itemAmountDecimal As Decimal
        Dim quantityInteger As Integer

    With Me
        ' Find the price.
        If .cappuccinoRadioButton.Checked Then
            priceDecimal = CAPPUCCINO_PRICE_Decimal
        ElseIf .espressoRadioButton.Checked Then
            priceDecimal = ESPRESSO_PRICE_Decimal
        ElseIf .latteRadioButton.Checked Then
            priceDecimal = LATTE_PRICE_Decimal
        ElseIf .icedCappuccinoRadioButton.Checked Or .icedLatteRadioButton.Checked Then
            priceDecimal = ICED_PRICE_Decimal
        End If

        ' Calculate the extended price and add to order total.
        Try
            quantityInteger = Integer.Parse(.quantityTextBox.Text)
            itemAmountDecimal = priceDecimal * quantityInteger
            subtotalDecimal += itemAmountDecimal
            If .taxCheckBox.Checked Then
                ' Call a function procedure.
                taxDecimal = FindTax(subtotalDecimal)
            Else
                taxDecimal = 0
            End If
            totalDecimal = subtotalDecimal + taxDecimal
            .itemAmountTextBox.Text = itemAmountDecimal.ToString("C")
            .subTotalTextBox.Text = subtotalDecimal.ToString("N")
            .taxTextBox.Text = taxDecimal.ToString("N")
            .totalTextBox.Text = totalDecimal.ToString("C")
            ' Allow change for new order only.
            .taxCheckBox.Enabled = False
            ' Allow Clear after an order is begun.
            .clearButton.Enabled = True
        Catch quantityException As FormatException
            MessageBox.Show("Quantity must be numeric.", "Data entry error", _
                MessageBoxButtons.OK, MessageBoxIcon.Information)
            With .quantityTextBox
                .Focus()
                .SelectAll()
            End With
        End Try
    End With
End Sub

Private Function FindTax(ByVal amountDecimal As Decimal) As Decimal
    ' Calculate the sales tax.

    Return amountDecimal * TAX_RATE_Decimal
End Function
```

```vb
Private Sub clearButton_Click(ByVal sender As System.Object, _
   ByVal e As System.EventArgs) _
   Handles clearButton.Click, ClearItemToolStripMenuItem.Click
      ' Clear the appropriate controls.

   With Me
         .cappuccinoRadioButton.Checked = True
         .itemAmountTextBox.Clear()
         With .quantityTextBox
             .Clear()
             .Focus()
         End With
      End With
End Sub

Private Sub NewOrderToolStripMenuItem_Click(ByVal sender As System.Object, _
   ByVal e As System.EventArgs) Handles NewOrderToolStripMenuItem.Click
      ' Clear the current order and add to the totals.
      Dim responseDialogResult As DialogResult
      Dim messageString As String

      ' Confirm clear of the current order.
      messageString = "Clear the current order figures?"
      responseDialogResult = MessageBox.Show(messageString, "Clear Order", _
         MessageBoxButtons.YesNo, MessageBoxIcon.Question, _
         MessageBoxDefaultButton.Button2)

      With Me
         If responseDialogResult = DialogResult.Yes Then
             ' User said Yes; clear the screen fields.
             clearButton_Click(sender, e)
             .subTotalTextBox.clear()
             .taxTextBox.clear()
             .totalTextBox.clear()

             Try
                 ' Add to the totals only if not a new order/customer.
                 If subtotalDecimal <> 0 Then
                     grandTotalDecimal += totalDecimal
                     customerCountInteger += 1
                     ' Reset totals for the next customer.
                     subtotalDecimal = 0
                     totalDecimal = 0
                 End If
             Catch
                 messageString = "Error in calculations."
                 MessageBox.Show(messageString, "Error", _
                    MessageBoxButtons.OK, MessageBoxIcon.Error)
             End Try

             ' Clear the appropriate display items and enable the check box.
             With .taxCheckBox
                 .Enabled = True
                 .Checked = False
             End With
             .clearButton.Enabled = False
         End If
      End With
End Sub
```

```vb
Private Sub SummaryToolStripMenuItem_Click(ByVal sender As System.Object, _
   ByVal e As System.EventArgs) Handles SummaryToolStripMenuItem.Click
      ' Calculate the average and display the totals.

      Dim averageDecimal As Decimal
      Dim messageString As String

      If totalDecimal <> 0 Then
         ' Make sure the last order is counted.
         NewOrderToolStripMenuItem_Click(sender, e)
      End If

      If customerCountInteger > 0 Then
         Try
               ' Calculate the average.
               averageDecimal = grandTotalDecimal / customerCountInteger

               ' Concatenate the message string.
               messageString = "Number of Orders:  " _
                  & customerCountInteger.ToString() _
                  & ControlChars.NewLine & ControlChars.NewLine _
                  & "Total Sales:  " & grandTotalDecimal.ToString("C") _
                  & ControlChars.NewLine & ControlChars.NewLine _
                  & "Average Sale:  " & averageDecimal.ToString("C")
               MessageBox.Show(messageString, "Coffee Sales Summary", _
                  MessageBoxButtons.OK, MessageBoxIcon.Information)
         Catch
               messageString = "Error in calculations."
               MessageBox.Show(messageString, "Error", _
                  MessageBoxButtons.OK, MessageBoxIcon.Error)
         End Try
      Else
         messageString = "No sales data to summarize."
         MessageBox.Show(messageString, "Coffee Sales Summary", _
            MessageBoxButtons.OK, MessageBoxIcon.Information)
      End If
End Sub

Private Sub ExitToolStripMenuItem_Click(ByVal sender As System.Object, _
   ByVal e As System.EventArgs) Handles ExitToolStripMenuItem.Click
      ' Terminate the project.

      Me.Close()
End Sub

Private Sub AboutToolStripMenuItem_Click(ByVal sender As System.Object, _
   ByVal e As System.EventArgs) Handles AboutToolStripMenuItem.Click
      ' Display the About message box.
      Dim messageString As String

      messageString = "R 'n R Billing" & ControlChars.NewLine _
         & ControlChars.NewLine & "Programmed by Bradley and Millspaugh"

      MessageBox.Show(messageString, "About R 'n R Billing", MessageBoxButtons.OK, _
         MessageBoxIcon.Information)
   End Sub
```

```vb
Private Sub FontToolStripMenuItem_Click(ByVal sender As System.Object, _
    ByVal e As System.EventArgs) Handles FontToolStripMenuItem.Click
    ' Allow the user to select a new font for the summary totals.

    With Me.FontDialog1
        .Font = Me.subTotalTextBox.Font
        .ShowDialog()
        Me.subTotalTextBox.Font = .Font
        Me.taxTextBox.Font = .Font
        Me.totalTextBox.Font = .Font
    End With
End Sub

Private Sub ColorToolStripMenuItem_Click(ByVal sender As System.Object, _
    ByVal e As System.EventArgs) Handles ColorToolStripMenuItem.Click
    ' Allow the user to select a new color for the summary totals.

    With Me.ColorDialog1
        .Color = Me.subTotalTextBox.ForeColor
        .ShowDialog()
        Me.subTotalTextBox.ForeColor = .Color
        Me.taxTextBox.ForeColor = .Color
        Me.totalTextBox.ForeColor = .Color
    End With
End Sub
End Class
```

Summary

1. The Visual Studio Menu Designer enables you to create menus by using MenuStrips that contain ToolStrip menu items with keyboard access keys.
2. In the Menu Designer you can set and modify the order and level of menu items.
3. Each menu item has a Click event. The code to handle selection of a menu item belongs in the item's Click event procedure.
4. Common dialog boxes allow Visual Basic programs to display the predefined Windows dialog boxes for *Color*, *Font*, *Open File*, and *Save File*. These dialog boxes are part of the operating environment; therefore, it is an unnecessary duplication of effort to have each programmer create them again.
5. Context menus, or shortcut menus, are created using a ContextMenuStrip component and the Menu Designer. Context menus pop up when the user right-clicks.
6. The programmer can write reusable code in general procedures. These procedures may be sub procedures or function procedures and may be called from any other procedure in the form module.
7. Both sub procedures and function procedures can perform an action. However, function procedures return a value and sub procedures do not. The value returned by a function procedure has a data type.
8. Arguments can be passed ByRef or ByVal (the default). ByRef passes a reference to the actual data item; ByVal passes a copy of the data.
9. A function procedure must return a value, which can be accomplished using the Return statement or by setting the name of the function to the result.

Key Terms

ByRef *220*
ByVal *220*
Call (procedure call) *219*
checked *210*
Checked property *210*
common dialog *211*
context menu *215*
ContextMenuStrip component *215*
disabled *209*
Enabled property *209*
function procedure *218*
general procedure *218*

menu *202*
Menu Designer *202*
MenuStrip component *202*
method *218*
modal *212*
modeless *212*
return value *218*
separator bar *206*
shortcut menu *215*
ShowDialog method *212*
sub procedure *218*
submenu *205*

Review Questions

1. Explain the difference between a menu and a submenu.
2. How can the user know if a menu item contains a submenu?
3. What is a separator bar and how is it created?
4. Name at least three types of common dialog boxes.
5. What is a context menu? How would you attach a context menu to a control?
6. Why would you need procedures that are not attached to an event?
7. Code the necessary statements to produce a color dialog box and use it to change the background color of a label.
8. Explain the difference between a sub procedure and a function procedure.
9. What is a return value? How can it be used?
10. Explain the differences between ByRef and ByVal. When would each be used?

Programming Exercises

5.1 Modify Programming Exercise 4.6 (piecework pay) to replace buttons with menus and add a function procedure.

This project will input the number of pieces and calculate the pay for multiple employees. It also must display a summary of the total number of pieces, the total pay, and the average pay for all employees.

Menu: The menu bar must have these items:

```
File              Edit              Help
  Calculate Pay     Clear             About
  Summary           ─────
  Exit              Font...
                    Color...
```

Piecework workers are paid by the piece. Workers who produce a greater quantity of output may be paid at a higher rate.

Use text boxes to obtain the name and the number of pieces completed. The *Calculate Pay* menu item calculates and displays the dollar amount earned. The *Summary* menu item displays the total number of pieces, the total pay, and the average pay per person in a message box. The *Clear* menu choice clears the name and the number of pieces for the current employee and resets the focus.

The *Color* and *Font* items should change the color and font of the information displayed in the Amount Earned control.

Use a message box to display the program name and your name for the *About* option on the *Help* menu.

Write a function procedure to find the pay rate and return a value to the proper event procedure.

Pieces Completed	Price Paid per Piece for All Pieces
1 to 199	.50
200 to 399	.55
400 to 599	.60
600 or more	.65

Note: For help in basing a new project on an existing project, see "Basing a New Project on an Existing Project" in this chapter.

5.2   Redo the checking account programming exercises from Chapter 4 (4.3, 4.4, and 4.5) using menus and sub procedures.

Menu:

File	Edit	Help
Transaction	Clear	About
Summary		
Exit	Font...	
	Color...	

Form: Use radio buttons to indicate the type of transaction—deposit, check, or service charge. Use a text box to allow the user to enter the amount of the transaction. Display the balance in a ReadOnly text box or a label.

Include validation that displays a message box if the amount of the transaction is a negative number. If there is not enough money to cover a check, display a message box with the message "Insufficient Funds." Do not pay the check, but deduct a service charge of $10.

Write function procedures for processing deposits, checks, and service charges. The deposit function adds the deposit to the balance; the check function subtracts the transaction amount from the balance; the service charge function subtracts the transaction amount from the balance. Each of the functions must return the updated balance.

The *Summary* menu item displays the total number of deposits and the dollar amount of deposits, the number of checks, and the dollar amount of the checks in a message box.

The *Clear* menu item clears the radio buttons and the amount and resets the focus.

The *Color* and *Font* menu items change the color and font of the information displayed in the balance label.

Use a message box to display the program name and your name as the programmer for the *About* option on the *Help* menu.

Note: For help in basing a new project on an existing project, see "Basing a New Project on an Existing Project" in this chapter.

5.3 A salesperson earns a weekly base salary plus a commission when sales are at or above quota. Create a project that allows the user to input the weekly sales and the salesperson name, calculates the commission, and displays summary information.

Form: The form should have text boxes for the salesperson's name and his or her weekly sales.

Menu:

```
File            Edit            Help
  Pay             Clear           About
  Summary         _____
  Exit            Font...
                  Color...
```

Use constants to establish the base pay, the quota, and the commission rate.

The *Pay* menu item calculates and displays the commission and the total pay for that person. However, if there is no commission, do not display the commission amount (do not display a zero-commission amount).

Write a function procedure to calculate the commission. The function must compare sales to the quota. When the sales are equal to or greater than the quota, calculate the commission by multiplying sales by the commission rate.

Each salesperson receives the base pay plus the commission (if one has been earned). Format the dollar amounts to two decimal places; do not display a dollar sign.

The *Summary* menu item displays a message box that holds total sales, total commissions, and total pay for all salespersons. Display the numbers with two decimal places and dollar signs.

The *Clear* menu item clears the name, sales, and pay for the current employee and then resets the focus.

The *Color* and *Font* menu items should change the color and font of the information displayed in the total pay text box.

Use a message box to display the program name and your name as programmer for the *About* option on the *Help* menu.

Test Data: Quota = 1000; Commission rate = .15; and Base pay = $250.

Name	Sales
Sandy Smug	1,000.00
Sam Sadness	999.99
Joe Whiz	2,000.00

Totals should be

Sales	$3,999.99
Commissions	450.00
Pay	1,200.00

5.4 The local library has a summer reading program to encourage reading. The staff keeps a chart with readers' names and bonus points earned. Create a project using a menu and a function procedure that determines and returns the bonus points.
Menu:

File	Edit	Help
Points	Clear	About
Summary		
Exit	Font...	
	Color...	

Form: Use text boxes to obtain the reader's name and the number of books read. Use a ReadOnly text box or a label to display the number of bonus points.

The *Points* menu item should call a function procedure to calculate the points using this schedule: The first three books are worth 10 points each. The next three books are worth 15 points each. All books over six are worth 20 points each.

The *Summary* menu item displays the average number of books read for all readers that session.

The *Clear* menu item clears the name, the number of books read, and the bonus points and then resets the focus.

The *Color* and *Font* menu items change the color and font of the bonus points.

Use a message box to display the program name and your name as programmer for the *About* option on the *Help* menu.

5.5 Modify Programming Exercise 2.2 (the flag viewer) to use a menu instead of radio buttons, check boxes, and buttons. Include check marks next to the name of the currently selected country and next to the selected display options.
Menu:

File	Country	Display	Help
Exit	United States	Title	About
	Canada	Country Name	
	Japan	Programmer	
	Mexico		

Note: For help in basing a new project on an existing project, see "Basing a New Project on an Existing Project" in this chapter.

Case Studies

VB Mail Order

Modify the case study project from Chapter 4 to use menus and a function procedure. Refer to Chapter 4 for project specifications.

Write a function procedure to calculate and return the shipping and handling based on the weight for an entire order. (Do not calculate shipping and handling on individual items—wait until the order is complete.)

Apply the user's font and color changes to the Total Due, or another control of your choice.

Menu:

```
File            Edit            Help
  Update Summary  Add This Item   About
  Exit            Clear
                  _____
                  Font...
                  Color...
```

Note: For help in basing a new project on an existing project, see "Basing a New Project on an Existing Project" in this chapter.

VB Auto Center

Modify the case study project from Chapter 4 to use menus and a function procedure. Refer to Chapter 4 for project specifications.

Write a function procedure to calculate and return the sales tax.

Apply the user's font and color changes to the Amount Due, or other control of your choice.

Menu:

```
File            Edit            Help
  Exit            Calculate       About
                  Clear
                  _____
                  Font...
                  Color...
```

Consider adding keyboard shortcuts to the menu commands.

Note: For help in basing a new project on an existing project, see "Basing a New Project on an Existing Project" in this chapter.

Video Bonanza

Modify the case study project from Chapter 4 to use menus and a function procedure. Refer to Chapter 4 for project specifications.

Use a function procedure to calculate the rental fee based on the type of video.

The *Help* menu *About* option should display a message box with information about the program and the programmer. The *Color* option should change the background color of the form; the font changes can change the control of your choice.

Menu:

```
File        Edit                    Help
  Summary     Calculate               About
  Exit        Clear for Next Item
            Order Complete
            _____
            Color...
            Font...
```

Optional extra: Set keyboard shortcuts for the menu commands.

Note: For help in basing a new project on an existing project, see "Basing a New Project on an Existing Project" in this chapter.

Very Very Boards

Modify your case study project from Chapter 4 to add a menu and a function procedure. Refer to Chapter 4 for the project specifications.

Write a function procedure to calculate and return the price of shirts; display the *About* box in a message box.

Allow the user to change the font size and font color of the label that displays the company slogan.

Include keyboard shortcuts for the menu commands.

Menu:

```
File        Sale                Display     Help
  Summary     Add to Order        Font...     About
  _____     Clear This Item     Color...
  Exit        Order Complete      _____
                                  Slogan
                                  Logo
```

The Slogan and Logo: Make up a slogan for the company, such as "We're Number One" or "The Best in Boards." The logo should be a graphic; you can use an icon, any graphic you have available, or a graphic you create yourself with a draw or paint program.

The *Slogan* and *Logo* menu choices must toggle and display a check mark when selected. For example, when the slogan is displayed, the *Slogan* menu command is checked. If the user selects the *Slogan* command again, hide the slogan and uncheck the menu command. The *Slogan* and *Logo* commands operate independently; that is, the user may select either, both, or neither item.

When the project begins, the slogan and logo must both be displayed and their menu commands appear checked.

Note: For help in basing a new project on an existing project, see "Basing a New Project on an Existing Project" in this chapter.

6

Multiform Projects

Try
'Convert quantity to numeric variables.

'Calculate values for sale.
extendedPriceDecimal = quantityInteger
discountDecimal = extendedPriceDecimal
discountedPriceDecimal = extendedPrice
'Calculate summary values.
quantitySumInteger += quantityInteger
discountSumDecimal += discountDecimal
discountedPriceSumDecimal += discounte
saleCountInteger += 1

at the completion of this chapter, you will be able to . . .

1. Include multiple forms in an application.

2. Use templates to create splash screens and about boxes.

3. Use the Show, ShowDialog, and Hide methods to display and hide forms.

4. Understand the various form events and select the best procedure for your code.

5. Declare variables with the correct scope and access level for multiform projects.

Using Multiple Forms

All the projects that you have created up to now have operated from a single form. It has probably occurred to you that the project could appear more professional if you could use different windows for different types of information. Consider the example in Chapter 5 in which summary information is displayed in a message box when the user presses the *Summary* button. You have very little control over the appearance of the message box. The summary information could be displayed in a much nicer format in a new window with identifying labels. Another window in Visual Basic is actually another form.

The first form a project displays is called the ***startup form***. You can add more forms to the project and display them as needed. A project can have as many forms as you wish.

Creating New Forms

To add a new form to a project, select *Add Windows Form* from the *Project* menu. The *Add New Item* dialog box appears (Figure 6.1), in which you can select from many installed templates. You will learn about some of the other form types later in the chapter. For now, choose *Windows Form* to add a regular new form.

F i g u r e   6 . 1

Select the Windows Form template to add a new form to a project. Your dialog box may have more or fewer item templates, depending on the version of VB you are using.

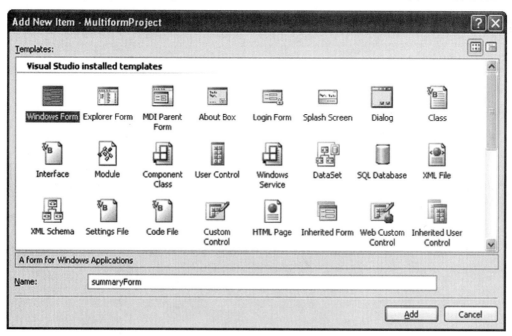

Adding a New Form to a Project

You can add a new form to a project by following these steps:

STEP 1: Select *Add Windows Form* from the *Project* menu.
STEP 2: In the *Add New Item* dialog box select *Windows Form* from the template list.
STEP 3: Enter a name for the new form and click on *Add*.

The new form will display on the screen and be added to the Solution Explorer window (Figure 6.2).

Figure   6.2

View Code   View Designer

After adding a new form, the Solution Explorer shows the filename of the new form.

While in design time, you can switch between forms in several ways. In the Solution Explorer window, you can select a form name and click the *View Designer* button or the *View Code* button. Double-clicking a form name opens the form in the designer. But the easiest way to switch between forms is to use the tabs at the top of the Document window that appear after the form has been displayed (Figure 6.3). If there isn't room to display tabs for all open documents, you can click the *Open Files* button to drop down a list and make a selection (Figure 6.4).

Each form is a separate file and a separate class. Later in this chapter you will learn to display and hide each of the forms in a project.

Figure   6.3

Open Files button

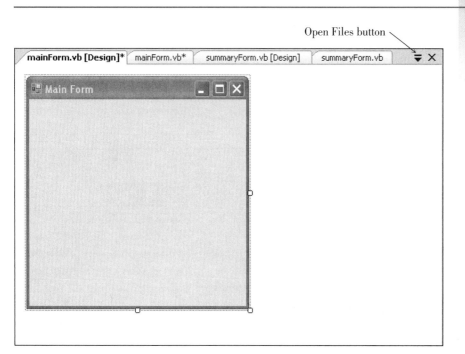

Click on the tabs at the top of the Document window to switch among the Form Designer and Editor windows.

Figure 6.4

You can drop down the list of available windows and select a form to which to switch.

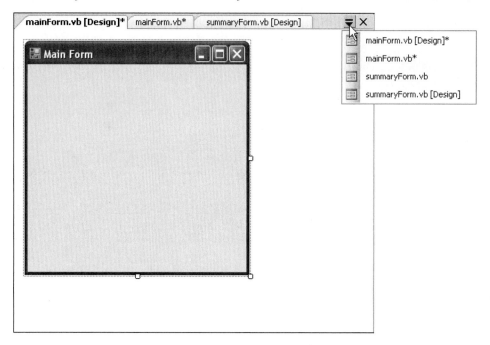

Adding and Removing Forms

The Solution Explorer window shows the files that are included in a project. You can add new files and remove files from a project.

Adding Existing Form Files to a Project

Forms may be used in more than one project. You might want to use a form that you created for one project in a new project.

Each form is saved as three separate files. All of the information for the form resides in the files, which includes the code procedures and the visual interface as well as all property settings for the controls.

To add an existing form to a project, use the *Add Existing Item* command on the *Project* menu and navigate to the form file to be added. You select only one filename: FormName.vb; all three files are automatically copied into the project folder.

You can add an existing form to a project by following these steps:

STEP 1: Select *Add Existing Item* from the *Project* menu.
STEP 2: In the *Add Existing Item* dialog box, locate the folder and file desired.
STEP 3: Click on *Add*.

Removing Forms from a Project

If you want to remove a file from a project, select its name in the Solution Explorer window. You can then either click the Delete key or right-click on the filename to display the context menu and choose *Delete*. You also can choose *Exclude from project* to remove the form from the project but not delete the files.

Use the Ctrl + F6 key combination to toggle between the *Form Designer Window* tab and the *Form Code* tab. Use Ctrl + Tab to cycle through all open files and IDE windows: while holding Ctrl, press Tab multiple times; when you reach the item you want, release the Ctrl key. ■

An About Box

One popular type of form in a project is an **About box**, such as the one you find in most Windows programs under *Help / About*. Usually an About box gives the name and version of the program as well as information about the programmer or company.

You can create your own About box by creating a new form and entering the information in labels. Of course, you may use any of the Windows controls on this new form, but About boxes typically hold labels and perhaps a picture box for a logo. Figure 6.5 shows a typical About box.

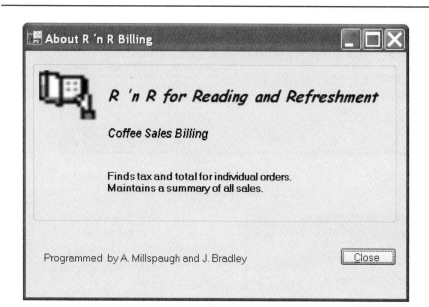

Figure 6.5

A typical About box that contains labels, a group box, a picture box, and a button.

Using the About Box Template

You also can use Visual Studio's About Box template to create a new About box. Choose *Add Windows Form* from the *Project* menu and select *About Box* (Figure 6.6). A new form named AboutBox1 is added to your project (Figure 6.7) with controls you can modify. You can change the captions and image by setting the properties as you would on any other form. Once you create the form in your project, it is yours and may be modified as you please.

Setting Assembly Information

Notice in Figure 6.7 that the About Box template form includes the product name, version, copyright, company name, and description. You can manually set the Text properties of the controls, but there's a better way that provides this information for the entire project. Open the Project Designer (Figure 6.8) from *Project / ProjectName Properties* or double-click *My Project* in the Solution Explorer. Click on the *Assembly Information* button and fill in the desired information in the *Assembly Information* dialog box (Figure 6.9).

Select the About Box template to add a preformatted About Box form to a project.

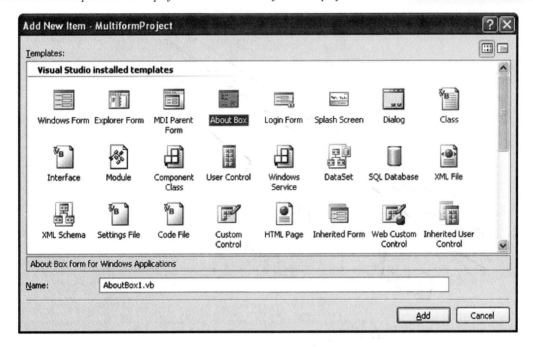

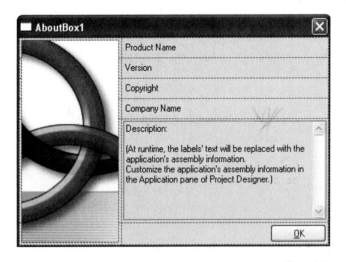

A new form created with the About Box template. You can customize the form by setting properties of the controls, adding controls, or removing controls.

Once the information is entered into the *Assembly Information*, you can retrieve it by using the My.Application object. The following code is automatically included in the AboutBox form's code:

```
Me.LabelProductName.Text = My.Application.Info.ProductName
Me.LabelVersion.Text = String.Format("Version {0}", _
  My.Application.Info.Version.ToString)
Me.LabelCopyright.Text = My.Application.Info.Copyright
Me.LabelCompanyName.Text = My.Application.Info.CompanyName
Me.TextBoxDescription.Text = My.Application.Info.Description
```

Typically you find much of this same information on the application's splash screen.

Figure 6.8

Open the Project Designer and click on the Assembly Information button to display the project's assembly information.

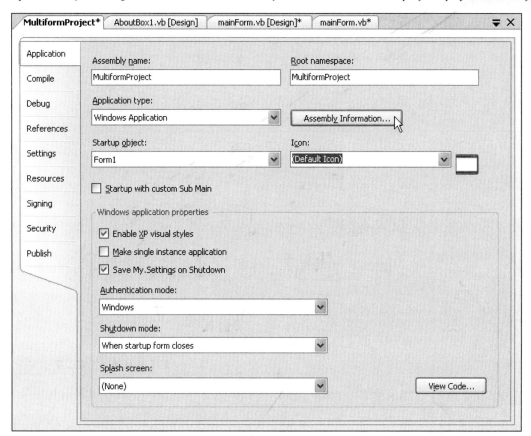

Figure 6.9

Enter or modify the project's information on the Assembly Information dialog box.

A Splash Screen

Perhaps you have noticed the logo or window that often appears while a program is loading, such as the one in Figure 6.10. This initial form is called a **splash screen**. Professional applications use splash screens to tell the user that the program is loading and starting. It can make a large application appear to load and run faster, since something appears on the screen while the rest of the application loads.

Figure 6.10

A custom splash screen created from a standard Windows form.

Using the Splash Screen Template

You can create your own splash screen or use the splash screen template included with Visual Studio (Figure 6.11). Select *Project / Add New Item* to display the *Add New Item* dialog box (refer to Figure 6.6). Choose *Splash Screen* to add the new form; then modify the form to fit your needs. You may want to make modifications to the labels and to the code.

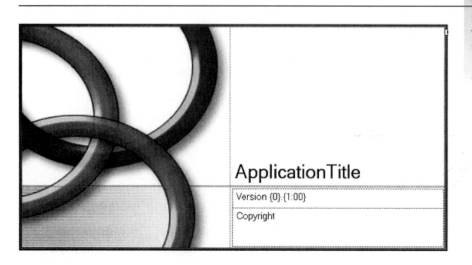

Figure 6.11

A splash form created using the Splash Screen template. You can customize the form as much as you wish.

The predefined code in the splash screen template may be more complicated than you need. It includes code to fill in the application title, version, and copyright information from the project's assembly information (refer to "Setting Assembly Information" in the preceding section for the About box). You can either set the assembly information or modify the labels to display the text that you want.

Making the Splash Form Display First

Whether you create your own splash screen or use the VB template, you must take one more step to make the splash screen appear before the startup form. Display the Project Designer from the *Project* menu and set the *Splash screen* drop-down list to your splash screen (Figure 6.12). Do not change the setting for *Startup object* or *Shutdown mode*, which would require coding techniques that go beyond the scope of this chapter.

When you run the project, the splash screen should display while the startup form is loading and then disappear. For small applications such as you

Figure 6.12

Set the Splash screen drop-down list to your new form in the Project Designer.

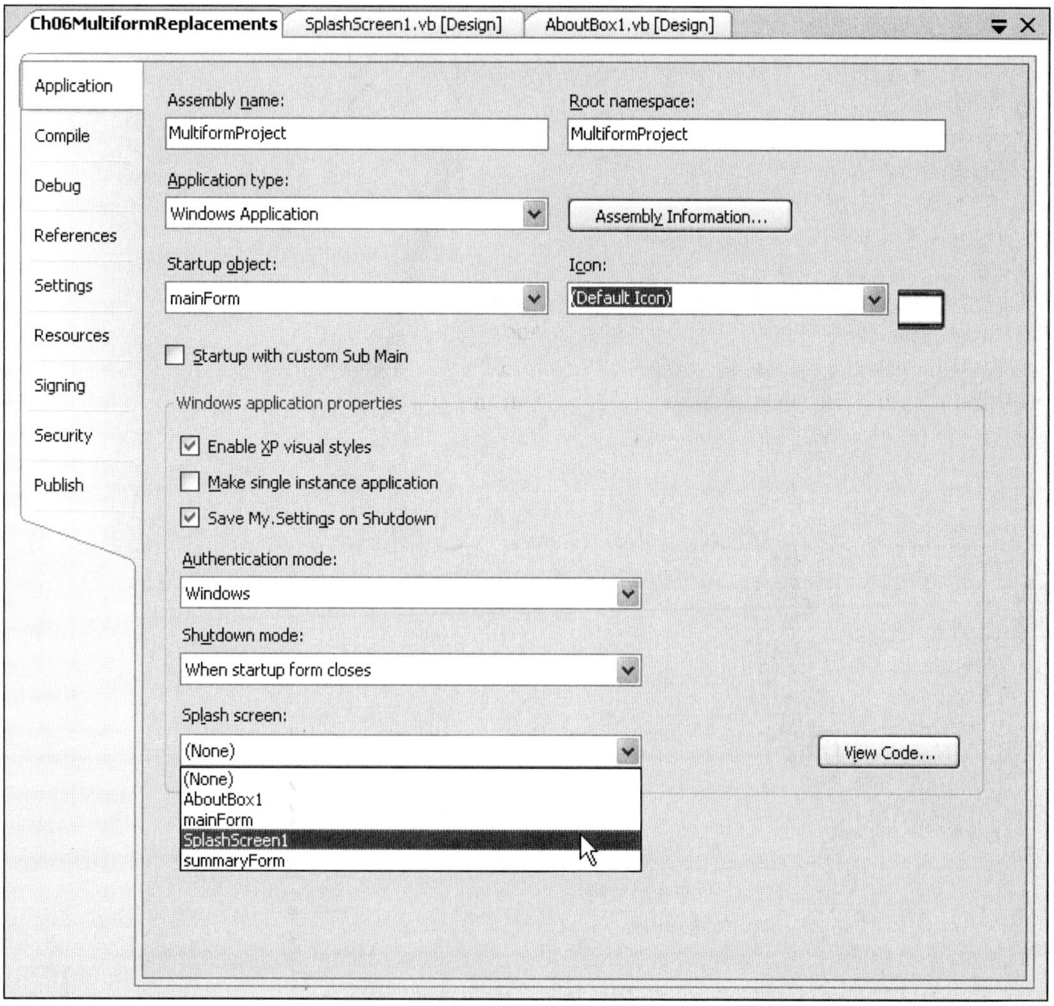

are writing, the startup form loads so quickly that it is nearly impossible to see the splash screen. Later in this chapter, in the section "Holding the Splash Screen Display," you will see a technique to force the splash screen to display long enough to read its contents.

Other Template Forms

Take a look at the other templates in the *Add New Item* dialog. Some others that you might find of interest are the Login Form and the Explorer Form. Note that the templates vary depending on the version of Visual Studio. The Express Edition has the fewest templates; see the Student Data CD if you are missing the Splash Screen template.

Using the Methods and Events of Forms

In code, you can use several methods to show, hide, and close forms.

Showing a Form

You generally display a new form in response to a user clicking a button or a menu item. In the event procedure for the button or menu item, you can use either the `Show` method or the `ShowDialog` method to display the new form.

Modal versus Modeless Forms

The **Show method** displays a form as **modeless**, which means that both forms are open and the user can navigate from one form to the other. When you use the **ShowDialog method**, the new form displays as **modal**; the user must respond to the form in some way, usually by clicking a button. No other program code can execute until the user responds to and hides or closes the modal form. However, if you display a modeless form, the user may switch to another form in the project without responding to the form.

Note: Even with a modal form, the user can switch to another application within Windows.

The Show Method—General Form

```
formName.Show()
```

The `Show` method creates a form object from the specified class and displays it modelessly. The formName is the name of the form you wish to display.

The Show Method—Example

```
summaryForm.Show()
```

The ShowDialog Method—General Form

```
formName.ShowDialog()
```

Use the `ShowDialog` method when you want the user to notice, respond to, and close the form before proceeding with the application.

The ShowDialog Method—Example

```
summaryForm.ShowDialog()
```

You generally place this code in a menu item or a button's click event procedure:

```
Private Sub summaryButton_Click(ByVal sender As System.Object, _
   ByVal e As System.EventArgs) Handles summaryButton.Click
      'Show the summary form.

      summaryForm.ShowDialog()
End Sub
```

Note: Form handling in VB .NET 2005 is significantly different than form handling in VB .NET 2003 and earlier versions. VB 2005 automatically creates a form object for each of the form classes that you create. You can show, hide, and close forms without explicitly declaring a new object. This default form object is not actually instantiated until you access one of the form's objects (such as a text box) or a form method (such as the `Show` method). You also can declare and instantiate a new form object like this:

```
Dim aNewSummaryForm as New summaryForm
aNewSummaryForm.ShowDialog()
```

Hiding or Closing a Form

You already know how to close the current form: `Me.Close()`. You also can use the `Close` method to close any other form: `summaryForm.Close()`.

The `Close` method behaves differently for a modeless form (using the `Show` method) compared to a modal form (using the `ShowDialog` method). For a modeless form, `Close` destroys the form instance and removes it from memory; for a modal form, the form is only hidden. A second `ShowDialog` method displays the same form instance, which can have data left from the previous time the form was displayed. In contrast, a second `Show` method creates a new instance, so no leftover data can appear.

You also can choose to use a form's **Hide method**, which sets the form's Visible property to False and keeps the form instance in memory.

The Hide Method—General Form

```
formName.Hide()
```

Hiding conceals a form but keeps it in memory, ready to be redisplayed. Use the `Hide` method rather than `Close` when the user is likely to display the form again. A good example might be a form with instructions or Help text, which the user may display multiple times.

The Hide Method—Example

```
summaryForm.Hide()
```

Responding to Form Events

The two primary events for which you may need to write code are the *FormName*.Load and *FormName*.Activated. The first time a form is shown in an application, the form generates both the Load and Activated events. The Load event occurs when the form is loaded into memory; the Activated event occurs after the Load event, just as control is passed to the form. Each subsequent time the form is shown, the Activated event occurs, but not the Load event. Therefore, if a form may be displayed multiple times, you may want to place initializing steps into the Activated event procedure rather than into the Load. Also, if you wish to set the focus in a particular place on the new form, place the Focus method in the FormName_Activated procedure.

The Sequence of Form Events

Although you don't need to write event procedures for all of these form events, it's helpful to know the order in which they occur:

Load	Occurs before the form is displayed for the first time. Happens only once for any one form unless the form is closed rather than hidden.
Activated	Occurs each time the form is shown. This event procedure is the correct location for initialization or Focus.
Paint	Occurs each time any portion of the form is redrawn, which happens each time a change is made or the form is moved or uncovered.
Deactivate	Occurs when the form is no longer the active form, such as when the user clicks on another window or the form is about to be hidden or closed.
FormClosing	Occurs as the form is about to close.
FormClosed	Occurs after the form is closed.

Writing Event Procedures for Selected Events

You are accustomed to double-clicking a control or form to open an event procedure for its default event. If you double-click a form, the default event is *FormName*.Load. To open an event procedure for the other events, you can use either of two easy techniques.

From the Code Editor

In the Editor, drop down the Class Name list and choose the entry that shows the events for the selected form (Figure 6.13). Then in the Method Name list (Figure 6.14), select the event for which you want to write a procedure. Any events that already have an event procedure written appear in bold in the list.

Figure 6.13

Select the (FormName Events) entry to see the list of possible events for which to write a procedure.

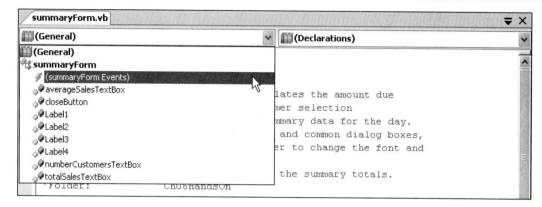

Figure 6.14

Select the event from the Method Name list to create an empty event procedure.

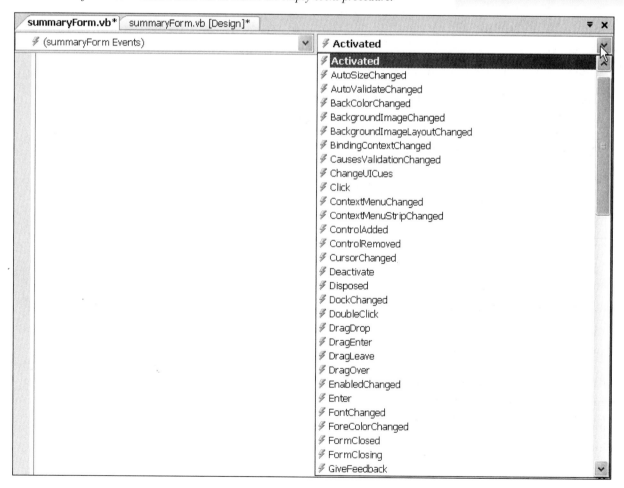

Notice in Figure 6.14 that there are *many* more events for forms than those covered in this chapter.

From the Properties Window in the Designer

You can select an event using the Properties window in the form designer, which is a feature new to VB .NET 2005. Click on the form to show its properties in the Properties window and click on the Events button (Figure 6.15) to display the available events (Figure 6.16). The default event appears selected, but you can double-click any other event to create its event procedure. You also can select a previously written procedure from the drop-down list for any event. When you want to switch the Properties window back to viewing properties, click on the Properties button.

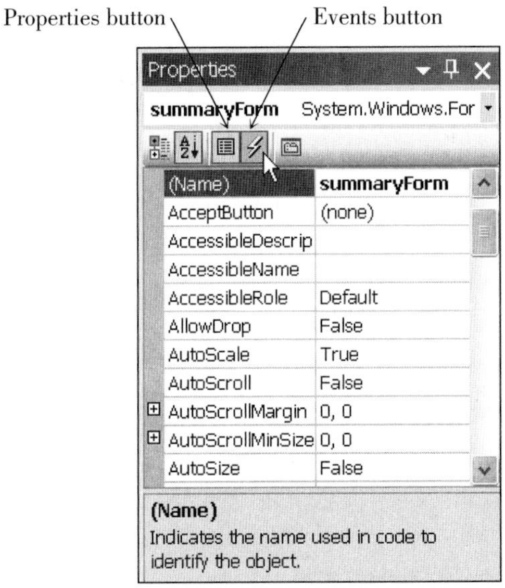

Properties button   Events button

Figure 6.15

Click on the Events button in the Properties window to see the list of possible events for which to write a procedure.

Figure 6.16

Double-click on the event to create an empty event procedure.

Holding the Splash Screen Display

As you learned earlier in this chapter, the splash screen should display only as long as it takes for the rest of the application to load. But our applications are so small that the splash screen disappears before the user can read it. You can write code to hold the splash screen longer, but it takes a technique not covered until the advanced text. You can just enter this code if you wish, even if you don't completely understand the statements.

First use one of the two techniques in the preceding section to create an event procedure for the FormClosing event. The FormClosing event occurs just before the form actually closes.

```
Private Sub SplashScreen_FormClosing(ByVal sender As Object, _
   ByVal e As System.Windows.Forms.FormClosingEventArgs) Handles Me.FormClosing
      ' Hold the form on the screen approximately 5 seconds before closing.

   System.Threading.Thread.Sleep(5000)      ' Sleep 5000 milliseconds.
End Sub
```

Note: A VB program can have multiple threads, which allows for multiple processes to execute simultaneously. The Sleep method pauses the current thread (the one and only thread in all programs in this text). Threading is covered in *Advanced Programming Using Visual Basic .NET* by Bradley and Millspaugh and in MSDN.

Variables and Constants in Multiform Projects

When you have multiple forms in a project, the scope, access level, and lifetime of the variables and constants become a little more complicated. If you want module-level variables to be available in more than one form in a project, you must declare them as Friend or Public, not as Private.

Example

```
Friend grandTotalDecimal As Decimal
```

Scope

Chapter 3 defined **scope** as the area of the program that can "see" and "use" the variable or constant. To expand the definition of scope for multiform projects: Scope is the set of statements that can access a variable or constant *without qualifying its name*. For example, if a variable is declared as Friend or Public in one form, another form can refer to that variable only by adding the form name (qualifying the name).

Example
In billingForm:

```
Friend grandTotalDecimal As Decimal
```

In summaryForm:

```
Me.grandTotalTextBox.Text = billingForm.grandTotalDecimal.ToString("C")
```

Access Level

Access level specifies the permission required to make use of the variable or constant. For example, the hands-on project for Chapter 5 used module-level variables for the grand total and number of customers. Those variables were declared as **Private**, so they were available only to the one form. If you want to display the summary information on another form, which would look more professional, you must allow the summary form permission to use the variables. To make a variable available to other forms, you must use either Public or Friend in place of Private. Use **Friend** to allow other forms in your project to access the variable; use **Public** to allow all other programs to access the variables (generally considered a poor practice).

Note: The true access level of Friend is the entire *assembly*, rather than the entire project. An assembly can consist of multiple projects. In this text, all applications consist of a single project, so it makes sense to think of Friend access as projectwide.

By default, variables and constants are Private. You can use the following keywords to set the access level of module-level variables:

Private   Available only in the class (form) in which it is declared.
Friend   Available to all classes (forms) in the assembly, (project).
Public   Available to all code in this project or any other.

Examples

```
Private runningCountInteger As Integer  ' Accessible only by this form.
Friend totalDecimal As Decimal  ' Accessible by all forms in this project.
Public dailyCountInteger As Integer   ' Accessible by any code in any project.
```

You can use the access-level keywords only for module-level variables. Local and block-level variables are declared inside a procedure and are always private.

Lifetime

Lifetime is the period of time that a variable or constant remains in existence. Recall from Chapter 3 that local and block variables exist only as long as that procedure executes and are re-created for each execution of the procedure. Module and namespace variables exist as long as the application runs.

Static Variables

Another statement you can use to declare local and block-level variables is the **Static** statement. Static variables retain their value for the life of the project, rather than being reinitialized for each call to the procedure. If you need to retain the value in a variable for multiple calls to a procedure, such as a running count, declare it as Static. However, if you need to use the variable in multiple procedures, declare it at the module level. (Using a static local variable is better than using a module-level variable because it is always best to keep the scope of a variable as narrow as possible.)

The Static Statement—General Form

```
Static Identifier As DataType
```

The format of the Static statement is the same as the format of the Dim statement. However, Static statements can appear only inside procedures; Static statements never appear at the module level.

The Static Statement—Examples

```
Static personCountInteger As Integer
Static reportTotalDecimal As Decimal
```

You never use access-level qualifiers on static variables since all static variables are local.

Namespaces

A VB project is automatically assigned to a **namespace**, which defaults to the name of the project. You can view and modify the project's namespace, called the *root namespace*, in the Project Designer (Figure 6.17).

Figure 6.17

Change the project's root namespace in the Project Designer.

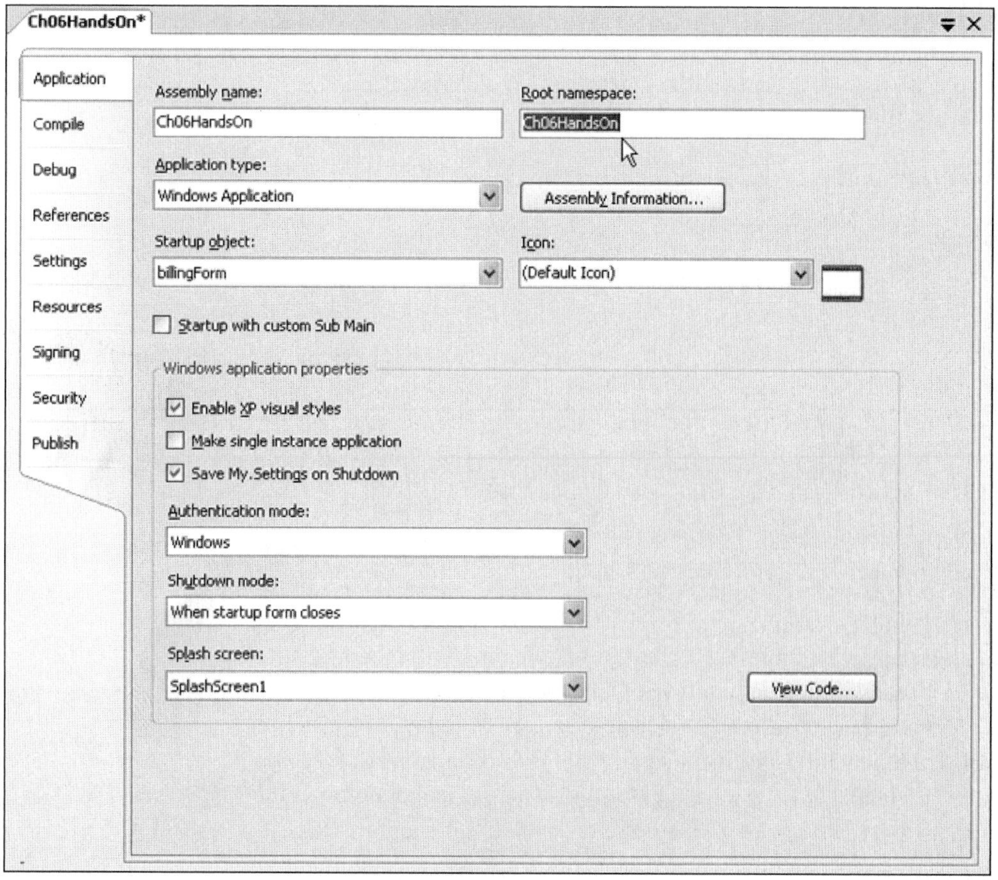

Declaration Summary for Variables and Constants

Keyword	Location of Declaration Statement	Lifetime	Accessibility
Dim	Module level (outside of any procedure). *Note:* The default for Dim is the same as for Private. The Private keyword is preferred over Dim.	As long as the form is loaded.	All procedures in the class (form).
Dim	Inside a procedure but not inside a block such as If / End If or Try / End Try.	One execution of the procedure.	Local to that procedure.
Dim	Inside a block of code such as If / End If or Try / End Try.	One execution of the procedure.	Only the code within the block.
Private	Module level.	As long as the form is loaded.	All procedures in the class (form).
Friend	Module level.	As long as any form in the project is loaded.	Any code in the project. To refer to it in any other form, must qualify with form name: *formName.variableName*.
Public	Module level.	As long as any form in the project is loaded.	Any code in any program. However, any references from outside the form must be qualified.
Const	Module level (outside of any procedure).	As long as the form is loaded.	Any code in the form. (Const is Private by default.)
Const	Inside a procedure.	As long as the form is loaded.	Any code in the procedure. (Behaves like a read-only static variable.)
Const	Inside a block.	As long as the form is loaded.	Any code in the block. (Behaves like a read-only static variable.)
Friend Const	Module level.	As long as the form is loaded.	Any code in the project, but any references from outside the form must be qualified.
Static	Inside a procedure	As long as the form is loaded.	Local to that procedure.

Guidelines for Declaring Variables and Constants

When you declare variables and constants, select the location of the declaration carefully. These general guidelines will help you decide where to place declarations:

1. Place all local declarations (Dim, Static) at the top of a procedure. Although VB will accept declarations placed further down in the code, such placement is considered a poor practice. Your code will be easier to read, debug, modify, and maintain if you follow this guideline.

2. Use named constants for any value that doesn't change during program execution. It is far more clear to use named constants such as MAXIMUM_RATE_Decimal and COMPANY_NAME_String than to

place the values into your code; and if in the future the values must be modified, having a constant name (at the top of your code) makes the task much easier.

3. Keep the scope of variables and constants as narrow as possible. Don't declare them all to be module level for convenience. There are books full of horror stories about strange program bugs popping up because the value of a variable was changed in an unknown location.

4. Consider making variables local if possible.

5. If you need to keep the value of a variable for multiple executions of a procedure, but don't need the variable in any other procedure, make it `Static`.

6. If you need to use a variable both in a procedure and also in a second procedure called by the first procedure, declare the variable as local and pass it as an argument. (Refer to "Passing Variables to Procedures" in Chapter 5.)

7. If you need to use a variable in multiple procedures, such as to add to the variable in one procedure and to display it in another, use `Private` module-level variables.

8. Finally, if you need to use the value of a variable in more than one form, declare it as `Friend`.

► Feedback 6.1

For each of these situations, write the declaration statement and tell where it should appear. Assume the project will have multiple forms.

1. The number of calories in a gram of fat (nine), to use in the calculations of a procedure.

2. The name of the person with the highest score, which will be determined in one procedure and displayed in a label on a different form. (The value must be retained for multiple executions of the procedure.)

3. The name of the company ("Bab's Bowling Service"), which will appear in several forms.

4. A total dollar amount to be calculated in one procedure of a form, added to a grand total in a procedure of a second form, and formatted and displayed in a third form.

5. A count of the number of persons entered using a single form. The count will be used to help calculate an average in a second form.

6. The formatted version of a dollar total, which will be displayed in a text box in the next statement.

Running Your Program Outside the IDE

Every time that you create and run an application, the executable file is placed in the project's bin\Debug folder. You can move that .exe file to another computer, place the file on the system desktop, or use it as a shortcut just like any other application on your system. If you copy the executable file to another system, you must make sure that the computer has the Microsoft .NET Framework 2.0. It is possible to download the framework for free from the Microsoft Web site.

You also may want to change the icon for your program. The default icon is a standard window image. To change the icon to something more interesting, open the Project Designer. On the *Application* tab, drop down the list for Icon (Figure 6.18) and browse to find another file with an .ico extension. Many icon files are in the Professional version of Visual Studio and in various folders in Windows; a few are on the text StudentData CD. You must recompile (build) the project again after setting the icon.

Select a different icon for your project in the Project Designer.

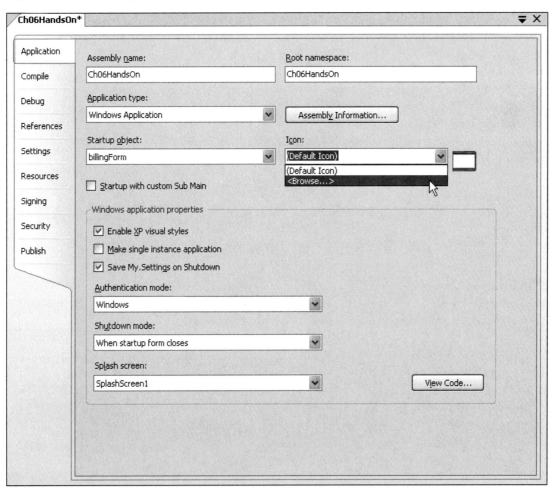

Your Hands-On Programming Example

Modify the hands-on project from Chapter 5 to include multiple forms. This version of the project requires four forms: billingForm, aboutForm, splashForm, and summaryForm.

Note: Follow the instructions in Chapter 5, "Basing a New Project on an Existing Project," or Appendix C, "Copy and Move a Project," to begin this hands-on example.

• billingForm: Use the billingForm form from Chapter 5 with a few modifications to display output on new forms rather than in message boxes.

- summaryForm: Create a form with the appropriate labels and text boxes for the summary information.

- aboutForm: Replace the MessageBox for the *Help / About* menu item from Chapter 5 with a new form using the About Box template.

- splashForm: Create a splash screen using the Splash Screen template.

Reviewing the Project Requirements from Chapter 5 For the billingForm, the user enters the number of items, selects the coffee type from radio buttons, and selects the check box for taxable items. The price for each coffee is calculated according to these prices:

Cappuccino	2.00
Espresso	2.25
Latte	1.75
Iced (either)	2.50

The *Calculate Selection* button calculates and displays the amount due for each item, adds the current item to the order, and calculates and displays the order information in text boxes. The *Clear for Next Item* button clears the selections and amount for the single item.

The *New Order* menu item clears the bill for the current customer and adds to the totals for the summary. The *Summary* menu item shows the summary form that displays the total of all orders, the average sale amount per customer, and the number of customers.

The *Edit* menu contains options that duplicate the *Calculate* and *Clear* buttons. The *Font* and *Color* options change the contents of the subtotal, tax, and total text boxes.

The *About* selection on the *Help* menu displays the About box, which contains information about the program.

```
File                Edit                        Help
  New Order           Calculate Selection         About
  Summary             Clear Item
  Exit               _____
                      Font...
                      Color...
```

Planning the Project

Sketch the four forms (Figure 6.19). The users approve and sign off the forms as meeting their needs.

Plan the Objects and Properties for the Billing Form See the hands-on exercise for Chapter 5 for the objects and properties of billingForm, which are unchanged for this project.

Plan the Procedures for the Billing Form Most of the procedures for billingForm are unchanged from the project in Chapter 5. You must change the accessibility of the variables that must be displayed on the summary form; you

Figure 6.19

The planning sketches of the forms for the hands-on programming example. a. the billing form; b. the summary form; c. the splash form; and d. the About box.

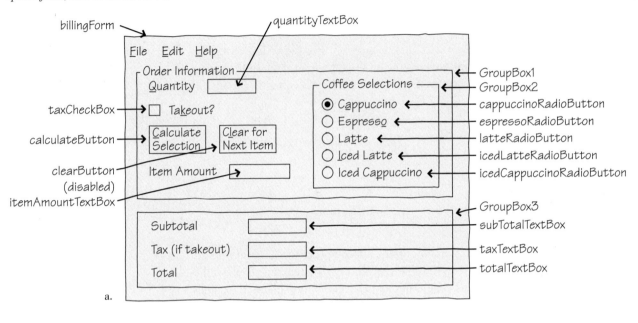

a.

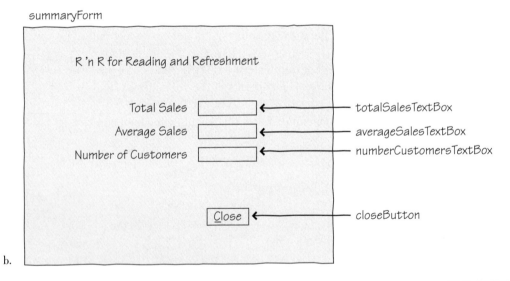

b.

also must change the variable used for the average (averageDecimal) to a module-level `Friend` variable.

Object	Procedure	Actions
SummaryToolStripMenuItem	Click	If current order not added to totals Call newOrderToolStripMenuItem_Click. Calculate the average (in a `Friend` variable). Display the summary form.
AboutToolStripMenuItem	Click	Display the About Box form.

Figure 6.19

(continued)

c.

d.

Plan the Objects and Properties for the Summary Form

Object	Property	Setting
summaryForm	Name	summaryForm
	Text	R 'n R Billing Summary
	AcceptButton	closeButton
Label1	Name	Label1
	Text	Total Sales
totalSalesTextBox	Name	totalSalesTextBox
	ReadOnly	true
Label2	Name	Label2
	Text	Average Sales
averageSalesTextBox	Name	averageSalesTextBox
	ReadOnly	true
Label3	Name	Label3
	Text	Number of Customers
numberCustomersTextBox	Name	numberCustomersTextBox
	ReadOnly	true
closeButton	Name	closeButton
	Text	&Close

Plan the Procedures for the Summary Form

Object	Procedure	Actions
summaryForm	Activated	Assign values from billing form to text boxes
closeButton	Click	Close this form

Plan the Objects and Properties for the Splash Screen

Use the Splash Screen template and consider changing the graphic. Fill in the Assembly Information in the Project Designer so that the screen fields appear filled.

Plan the Procedures for the Splash Screen

If you use the Splash Screen template, you don't need to write any code for the form.

Object	Procedure	Actions
SplashScreen	FormClosing	Sleep for a few seconds

Plan the Objects and Properties for the About Box

Use the About Box template and consider changing the graphic. Fill in the Assembly Information in the Project Designer so that the screen fields appear filled.

Plan the Procedures for the About Box

If you use the About Box template, you don't need to write any code for the form.

Plan the Project Properties Changes

Splash Screen　Set to the name of your splash screen form in the Project Designer.

Assembly Information　Fill in fields to display in splash screen and About box.

Write the Project

Follow the instructions in Chapter 5, "Basing a New Project on an Existing Project," or Appendix C, "Copy and Move a Project," to base this project on Ch05HandsOn. If you have not written Ch05HandsOn, do so first before beginning this project.

　　Follow the sketches in Figure 6.19 to create the forms. Use the Splash Screen and About Box templates. Figure 6.20 shows the completed forms.

- Set the properties of each of the objects according to your plan.

- Write the code. Working from the pseudocode, write each procedure.

- Make sure to change the module-level variables needed for the summary form to Friend access level. Move the declaration of averageDecimal from the local level to the module level.

- When you complete the code, use a variety of data to thoroughly test the project.

Figure 6.20

The completed forms for the hands-on programming example. a. the billing form; b. the summary form; c. the splash screen; and d. the About box.

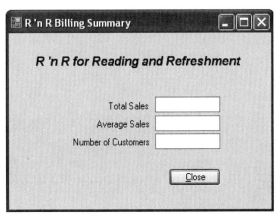

a.

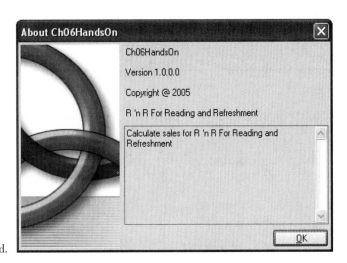

b.

c.

d.

The Project Coding Solution

billingForm

```
'Program Name:    Ch06HandsOn
'Programmer:      Bradley/Millspaugh
'Date:            June 2005
'Description:     This project calculates the amount due
'                 based on the customer selection
'                 and accumulates summary data for the day.
'                 Incorporates menus and common dialog boxes,
'                 which allow the user to change the font and
'                 color of controls.
'                 This version of the project includes a splash form,
'                 a summary form, and an About box form.
'Folder:          Ch06HandsOn
'Form:            billingForm

Public Class billingForm
    ' Declare project wide variables.
    Friend grandTotalDecimal, averageDecimal As Decimal
    Friend customerCountInteger As Integer

    ' Declare module-level variables.
    Private subTotalDecimal, totalDecimal As Decimal

    ' Declare constants.
    Const TAX_RATE_Decimal As Decimal = 0.08D
    Const CAPPUCCINO_PRICE_Decimal As Decimal = 2D
    Const ESPRESSO_PRICE_Decimal As Decimal = 2.25D
    Const LATTE_PRICE_Decimal As Decimal = 1.75D
    Const ICED_PRICE_Decimal As Decimal = 2.5D

    Private Sub calculateButton_Click(ByVal sender As System.Object, _
      ByVal e As System.EventArgs) Handles calculateButton.Click, _
    CalculateSelectionToolStripMenuItem.Click
        ' Calculate and display the current amounts and add to totals.
        Dim priceDecimal, taxDecimal, itemAmountDecimal As Decimal
        Dim quantityInteger As Integer

        With Me
            ' Find the price.
            If .cappuccinoRadioButton.Checked Then
                priceDecimal = CAPPUCCINO_PRICE_Decimal
            ElseIf .espressoRadioButton.Checked Then
                priceDecimal = ESPRESSO_PRICE_Decimal
            ElseIf .latteRadioButton.Checked Then
                priceDecimal = LATTE_PRICE_Decimal
            ElseIf .icedCappuccinoRadioButton.Checked Or .icedLatteRadioButton.Checked Then
                priceDecimal = ICED_PRICE_Decimal
            Else
                MessageBox.Show("Please make a drink selection", "Selection Required", _
                    MessageBoxButtons.OK, MessageBoxIcon.Information)
            End If

            ' Calculate the extended price and add to order total.
            Try
                quantityInteger = Integer.Parse(.quantityTextBox.Text)
                itemAmountDecimal = priceDecimal * quantityInteger
```

```
                        subTotalDecimal += itemAmountDecimal
                        If .taxCheckBox.Checked Then
                            ' Call a function procedure.
                            taxDecimal = FindTax(subTotalDecimal)
                        Else
                            taxDecimal = 0
                        End If
                        totalDecimal = subTotalDecimal + taxDecimal
                        .itemAmountTextBox.Text = itemAmountDecimal.ToString("C")
                        .subTotalTextBox.Text = subTotalDecimal.ToString("N")
                        .taxTextBox.Text = taxDecimal.ToString("N")
                        .totalTextBox.Text = totalDecimal.ToString("C")
                        ' Allow change for new order only.
                        .taxCheckBox.Enabled = False
                        ' Allow Clear after an order is begun.
                        .clearButton.Enabled = True
                    Catch quantityException As FormatException
                        MessageBox.Show("Enter the quantity.", "Data entry error", _
                            MessageBoxButtons.OK, MessageBoxIcon.Information)
                        With .quantityTextBox
                            .Focus()
                            .SelectAll()
                        End With
                    End Try
            End With
    End Sub

    Private Function FindTax(ByVal amountDecimal As Decimal) As Decimal
        ' Calculate the sales tax.

        Return amountDecimal * TAX_RATE_Decimal
    End Function

    Private Sub clearButton_Click(ByVal sender As System.Object, _
      ByVal e As System.EventArgs) Handles clearButton.Click, _
      ClearItemToolStripMenuItem.Click
        ' Clear the appropriate controls.

        With Me
            .cappuccinoRadioButton.Checked = True
            .itemAmountTextBox.Clear()
            With .quantityTextBox
                .Clear()
                .Focus()
            End With
        End With
    End Sub

    Private Sub NewOrderToolStripMenuItem_Click(ByVal sender As System.Object, _
      ByVal e As System.EventArgs) Handles NewOrderToolStripMenuItem.Click
        ' Clear the current order and add to the totals.
        Dim responseDialogResult As DialogResult
        Dim messageString As String

        ' Confirm clear of the current order.
        messageString = "Clear the current order figures?"
        responseDialogResult = MessageBox.Show(messageString, "Clear Order", _
          MessageBoxButtons.YesNo, MessageBoxIcon.Question, _
          MessageBoxDefaultButton.Button2)
```

```
        With Me
            If responseDialogResult = DialogResult.Yes Then
                ' User said Yes; clear the screen fields.
                clearButton_Click(sender, e)
                .subTotalTextBox.Text = ""
                .taxTextBox.Text = ""
                .totalTextBox.Text = ""
                Try
                    ' Add to the totals only if not a new order/customer.
                    If subTotalDecimal <> 0 Then
                        grandTotalDecimal += totalDecimal
                        customerCountInteger += 1
                        ' Reset totals for the next customer.
                        subTotalDecimal = 0
                        totalDecimal = 0
                    End If
                Catch
                    messageString = "Error in calculations."
                    MessageBox.Show(messageString, "Error", _
                        MessageBoxButtons.OK, MessageBoxIcon.Error)
                End Try

                ' Clear the appropriate display items and enable the check box.
                With .taxCheckBox
                    .Enabled = True
                    .Checked = False
                End With
                .clearButton.Enabled = False
            End If
        End With
End Sub

Private Sub SummaryToolStripMenuItem_Click(ByVal sender As System.Object, _
    ByVal e As System.EventArgs) Handles SummaryToolStripMenuItem.Click
        ' Calculate the average and display the totals.
        Dim messageString As String

        If totalDecimal <> 0 Then
            ' Make sure the last order is counted.
            NewOrderToolStripMenuItem_Click(sender, e)
            ' Pass incoming arguments to the called procedure.
        End If

        If customerCountInteger > 0 Then
            Try
                ' Calculate the average.
                averageDecimal = grandTotalDecimal / customerCountInteger
                summaryForm.ShowDialog()
            Catch
                messageString = "Error in calculations."
                MessageBox.Show(messageString, "Error", MessageBoxButtons.OK, _
                    MessageBoxIcon.Error)
            End Try
        Else
            messageString = "No sales data to summarize."
            MessageBox.Show(messageString, "Coffee Sales Summary", MessageBoxButtons.OK, _
                MessageBoxIcon.Information)
        End If
End Sub
```

```vb
    Private Sub ExitToolStripMenuItem_Click(ByVal sender As System.Object, _
      ByVal e As System.EventArgs) Handles ExitToolStripMenuItem.Click
        ' Terminate the project.

        Me.Close()
    End Sub

    Private Sub AboutToolStripMenuItem_Click(ByVal sender As System.Object, _
      ByVal e As System.EventArgs) Handles AboutToolStripMenuItem.Click
        ' Display the About Box form.

        AboutBox1.ShowDialog()
    End Sub

    Private Sub FontToolStripMenuItem_Click(ByVal sender As System.Object, _
      ByVal e As System.EventArgs) Handles FontToolStripMenuItem.Click
        ' Allow the user to select a new font for the summary totals.

        With Me.FontDialog1
            .Font = Me.subTotalTextBox.Font
            .ShowDialog()
            Me.subTotalTextBox.Font = .Font
            Me.taxTextBox.Font = .Font
            Me.totalTextBox.Font = .Font
        End With
    End Sub

    Private Sub ColorToolStripMenuItem_Click(ByVal sender As System.Object, _
      ByVal e As System.EventArgs) Handles ColorToolStripMenuItem.Click
        ' Allow the user to select a new color for the summary totals.

        With Me.ColorDialog1
            .Color = Me.subTotalTextBox.ForeColor
            .ShowDialog()
            Me.subTotalTextBox.ForeColor = .Color
            Me.taxTextBox.ForeColor = .Color
            Me.totalTextBox.ForeColor = .Color
        End With
    End Sub
End Class
```

summaryForm

```vb
'Program Name:    Ch06HandsOn
'Programmer:      Bradley/Millspaugh
'Date:            June 2005
'Description:     This project calculates the amount due
'                 based on the customer selection
'                 and accumulates summary data for the day.
'                 Incorporates menus and common dialog boxes,
'                 which allow the user to change the font and
'                 color of controls.
'                 This form displays the summary totals.
'Folder:          Ch06HandsOn
'Form:            summaryForm
```

```
Public Class summaryForm

    Private Sub summaryForm_Activated(ByVal sender As System.Object, _
      ByVal e As System.EventArgs) Handles MyBase.Activated
       ' Get the data.

       With Me
          .totalSalesTextBox.Text = billingForm.grandTotalDecimal.ToString("C")
          .averageSalesTextBox.Text = billingForm.averageDecimal.ToString("C")
          .numberCustomersTextBox.Text = billingForm.customerCountInteger.ToString()
       End With
    End Sub

    Private Sub closeButton_Click(ByVal sender As System.Object, _
      ByVal e As System.EventArgs) Handles closeButton.Click
         ' Close this summary form.

         Me.Hide()
    End Sub
End Class
```

SplashScreen

Note: Nearly all of the code is generated by the template. Add one event procedure to hold the splash screen long enough to read it.

```
    Private Sub SplashScreen1_FormClosing(ByVal sender As Object, _
      ByVal e As System.Windows.Forms.FormClosingEventArgs) Handles Me.FormClosing
         ' Hold the form on the screen approximately 5 seconds before closing.

         System.Threading.Thread.Sleep(5000)
    End Sub
```

AboutBox

Note: All of the About Box code is generated by the template.

S u m m a r y

1. Projects may need more than one form; there is virtually no limit to the number of forms that can be used within a single project.
2. Forms used for one project can be added to another project. Forms also can be removed from a project.
3. An About box, which typically contains information about the version of an application and the programmer and copyrights, may be created by adding a new form. VB has an About Box template form that you can use to create an About box.
4. A splash screen may be displayed while a program loads. VB provides a Splash Screen template that you can use to create a new splash screen form.

5. Both the Splash Screen and About Box templates automatically insert information that you can enter in the *Assembly Information* dialog box.

6. The `Show` (modeless) and `ShowDialog` (modal) methods are used to display a form on the screen.

7. A form displayed as modal requires a response from the user; it must be closed or unloaded before any execution continues. When a form is displayed as modeless, the user can switch to another form without closing the form.

8. The `Form.Hide` method hides the form but keeps it loaded in memory; the `Form.Close` method removes a modeless form from memory; the `Form.Close` method for a modal form actually hides the form rather than closing it.

9. The `Form.Load` event occurs once for each loaded form; the `Form.Activated` event can occur multiple times—each time the form is shown.

10. The form's `FormClosing` event occurs just before the form closes. You can write event procedures for any of the form's events.

11. Variables that are visible to all forms in a project are declared using the keyword `Friend`. The `Private` keyword sets the access level to the current form, and the `Public` keyword makes the variable available to all classes in all programs.

12. To refer to a `Friend` variable in a different form, use the form name, a period, and the variable name.

13. Variables declared with the keyword `Static` retain their values for multiple calls to the procedure in which they are declared. Static variables are local or block-level.

14. Each project has a default namespace, called the *root namespace*. You can change the root namespace for a VB project in the Project Designer, which you display either by double-clicking *My Project* in the Solution Explorer or selecting *Project / ProjectName Properties*.

15. You can run a project outside the VS IDE by moving and running the .exe file.

Key Terms

access level   *258*

About Box   *247*

Friend   *258*

Hide method   *253*

modal   *252*

modeless   *252*

namespace   *259*

Private   *258*

Public   *258*

scope   *257*

Show method   *252*

ShowDialog method   *252*

splash screen   *250*

startup form   *244*

Static   *258*

R e v i e w   Q u e s t i o n s

1. List some of the items generally found in an About box.
2. What is the purpose of a splash screen?
3. What is the term used for the first form to display in a project?
4. How can you choose a different form as the startup form after the project has been created?
5. Explain how to include an existing form in a new project.
6. What is the *assembly information*? How can you change the information? How can you use the information?
7. Explain the difference between *modal* and *modeless*.
8. How does the `Show` method differ from the `ShowDialog` method?
9. Explain when the form's Load event and Activated event occur. In which event procedure should you place code to initialize screen fields? Is the answer always the same?
10. Explain the differences between `Public`, `Private`, and `Friend` access levels.
11. What is a static variable? When would it be useful?
12. How can you run a compiled VB program outside the Visual Studio IDE?

P r o g r a m m i n g   E x e r c i s e s

Note: For help in basing a new project on an existing project, see "Copy and Move a Project" in Appendix C.

6.1   Modify Programming Exercise 5.5 (the flag viewer) to include a splash screen and an About box.
      Menus

File	Country	Display	Help
Exit	United States	Title	About
	Canada	Country Name	
	Japan	Programmer	
	Mexico		

6.2   Create a project that will produce a summary of the amounts due for Pat's Auto Repair Shop. Display a splash screen first; then display the main form, which has only the menus. If you wish, you can add a graphic to the form.
      Main Form Menus

File	Process	Help
Exit	Job Information	About

Job Information
The *Job Information* menu item will display the Job Information form.

   Job Information Form The Job Information form must have text boxes for the user to enter the job number, customer name, amount charged for parts, and the hours of labor. Include labels and text boxes for Parts, Labor, Subtotal, Sales Tax, and Total.

Include buttons for Calculate, Clear, and OK.

The Calculate button finds the charges and displays them in controls. The tax rate and the hourly labor charge should be set up as named constants so that they can be easily modified if either changes. Current charges are $50 per hour for labor and 8 percent (.08) for the sales tax rate. Sales tax is charged only on parts, not on labor.

The Clear button clears the text boxes and resets the focus in the first text box.

The OK button hides the Job Information form and displays the main form.

6.3 Modify Programming Exercise 6.2 so that summary information is maintained for the total dollar amount for parts, labor, sales tax, and total for all customers.

Add a *Summary* menu item under the *Process* menu with a separator bar between the two menu items. When the user selects the *Summary* menu item, display the summary information in a Summary form. The Summary form should have an OK button that closes the Summary form and returns the user to the main form.

6.4 A battle is raging over the comparative taste of Prune Punch and Apple Ade. Each taste tester rates the two drinks on a scale of 1 to 10 (10 being best). The proof of the superiority of one over the other will be the average score for the two drinks.

Display a splash screen and then the main form. The main form has only the menus; you can add a graphic if you wish.

Main Form Menus

```
File            Help
  New Tester      About
  Summary
  ──────────
  Exit
```

New Tester Menu Item

The *New Tester* menu item displays a form that inputs the test results for each drink. The form contains an OK button and a Cancel button.

When the user clicks the OK button, add the score for each type of drink to the drink's total, clear the text boxes, and reset the focus. Leave the form on the screen in case the next tester is ready to enter scores. If either score is blank when the OK button is pressed, display a message in a message box and reset the focus to the box for the missing data.

The Cancel button returns to the main form without performing any calculation.

Summary Menu Item

The *Summary* item displays a form that contains the current results of the taste test. It should display the winner, the total number of taste testers, and the average rating for each drink. The form contains an OK button that returns to the main form. (The user will be able to display the summary at any time and as often as desired.)

About Box

The About box should display information about the program and the programmer. Include an OK button that returns the user to the main form.

6.5   Modify Programming Exercise 5.1 (piecework pay) to add a Splash form, an About box, and a Summary form. Add a slogan and a logo that the user can hide or display from menu choices on the main form.

Splash Form

The Splash form must appear when the project begins execution. It should display the project name, programmer name, and at least one graphic.

About Box

The About box should have the program name, version number, and programmer name, as well as a graphic and an OK button. It must be displayed as modal.

Summary Form

The Summary form should display the summary information. Note that in Chapter 5 the summary information was displayed in a message box. You must remove the message box and display the summary information only on the Summary form.

Slogan and Logo

Make up a slogan for the company, such as "We're Number One" or "We Do Chicken Right." For the logo, you can use an icon or any graphic you have available, or create one yourself with a draw or paint program.

The *Slogan* and *Logo* menu choices must toggle and display a check mark when selected. For example, when the slogan is displayed, the *Slogan* menu item is checked. If the user selects the *Slogan* command again, hide the slogan and uncheck the menu item. The *Slogan* and *Logo* commands operate independently; that is, the user may select either, both, or neither item.

When the project begins, the slogan and logo must both be displayed on the main form and their menu items appear checked.

Case Studies

VB Mail Order

Modify the VB Mail Order project from Chapter 5 to include a splash screen, an About box, and a summary form. Include an image on both the Splash form and the About box.

VB Auto Center

Create a project that uses four forms. Add the form from the Chapter 5 VB Auto case study and create a main form, a splash screen, and an About box.

Main Form: The main form should display a large label with the words: "Valley Boulevard Auto Center - Meeting all your vehicle's needs" and appropriate image(s).

Main Form Menus

File	Edit	Help
Input Sale	Color...	About
Exit	Font...	

The *Color* and *Font* items should allow the user to change the large label on the form.

The *Input Sale* item should display the form from Chapter 5.

Video Bonanza

Modify the Video Bonanza project from Chapter 5 to separate the project into multiple forms. Include a summary form, a splash screen, and an About box.

Very Very Boards

Modify the Very Very Boards project from Chapter 5 to separate the project into multiple forms. Include a summary form, a splash screen, and an About box.

CHAPTER

7

Lists, Loops, and Printing

Calculate values for sale.
extendedPriceDecimal = quantityInteger
discountDecimal = extendedPriceDecimal
discountedPriceDecimal = extendedPrice
Calculate summary values.
quantitySumInteger += quantityInteger
discountSumDecimal += discountDecimal
discountedPriceSumDecimal += discounte
saleCountInteger += 1

at the completion of this chapter, you will be able to . . .

1. Create and use list boxes and combo boxes.

2. Differentiate among the available types of combo boxes.

3. Enter items into list boxes using the Items collection in the Properties window.

4. Add and remove items in a list at run time.

5. Determine which item in a list is selected.

6. Use the Items.Count property to determine the number of items in a list.

7. Display a selected item from a list.

8. Use Do/Loops and For/Next statements to iterate through a loop.

9. Terminate a loop with the Exit statement.

10. Skip to the next iteration of a loop by using the Continue statement.

11. Send information to the printer or the Print Preview window using the PrintDocument class.

Often you will want to offer the user a list of items from which to choose. You can use the Windows ListBox and ComboBox controls to display lists on a form. You may choose to add items to a list during design time, during run time, or perhaps a combination of both. Several styles of list boxes are available; the style you use is determined by design and space considerations as well as by whether you will allow users to add items to the list.

List Boxes and Combo Boxes

Both list boxes and combo boxes allow you to have a list of items from which the user can make a selection. Figure 7.1 shows the toolbox tools for creating the controls; Figure 7.2 shows several types of list boxes and combo boxes, including **simple list boxes**, **simple combo boxes**, **drop-down combo boxes**, and **drop-down lists**. The list boxes on the left of the form in Figure 7.2 are all created with the list box tool; the boxes on the right of the form are created with the combo box tool. Notice the three distinct styles of combo boxes.

    ListBox controls and **ComboBox controls** have most of the same properties and operate in a similar fashion. One exception is that a combo box control has a DropDownStyle property, which determines whether or not the list box also has a text box for user entry and whether or not the list will drop down (refer to Figure 7.2).

    Both list boxes and combo boxes have a great feature. If the box is too small to display all the items in the list at one time, VB automatically adds a scroll bar. You do not have to be concerned with the location of the scroll box in the scroll bar; the scrolling is handled automatically.

Figure 7.1

Use the ListBox tool and ComboBox tool to create list boxes and combo boxes on your forms.

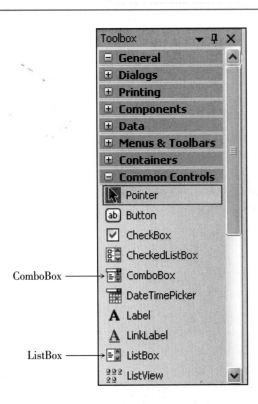

ComboBox ⟶

ListBox ⟶

Figure 7.2

Various styles of list boxes and combo boxes.

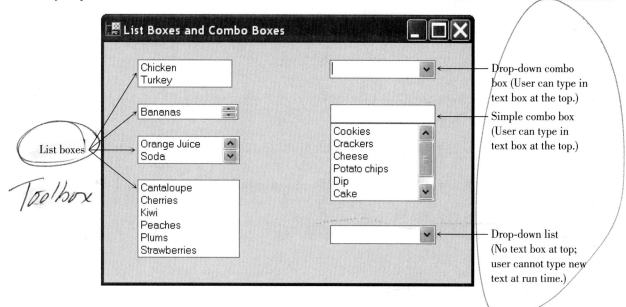

When you add a list control to a form, choose the style according to the space you have available and how you want the box to operate. Do you want the user to select from an existing list? If so, use a simple list box or a drop-down list (ComboBox DropDownStyle = DropDownList). Do you want the user to be able to type a new entry if necessary? In this case, use one of the two styles with an added text box: the drop-down combo box (DropDownStyle = DropDown) or the simple combo box (DropDownStyle = Simple).

At design time, the behavior of list boxes and combo boxes differs. For list boxes Visual Basic displays the Name property in the control; for combo boxes, the Text property displays, which is blank by default. Don't spend any time trying to make a list box appear empty during design time; the box will appear empty at run time. Combo boxes have a Text property, which you can set at design time if you wish. List boxes also have a Text property, but you can access it only at run time.

The Items Collection

The list of items that displays in a list box or combo box is a **collection**. VB collections are objects that have properties and methods to allow you to add items, remove items, refer to individual elements, count the items, and clear the collection. In the sections that follow, you will learn to maintain and refer to the Items collection.

You can refer to the items in a collection by an index, which is zero based. For example, if a collection holds 10 items, the indexes to refer to the items range from 0 to 9. To refer to the first item in the Items collection, use Items(0).

Filling a List

You can use several methods to fill the Items collection of a list box and combo box. If you know the list contents at design time and the list never changes, you can define the Items collection in the Properties window. If you must add items to the list during program execution, you will use the `Items.Add` or `Items.Insert` method in an event procedure. In Chapter 11 you will learn to fill a list from a data file on disk. This technique allows the list contents to vary from one run to the next.

Using the Properties Window

The **Items property**, which is a collection, holds the list of items for a list box or combo box. To define the Items collection at design time, select the control and scroll the Properties window to the Items property (Figure 7.3). Click on the ellipses button to open the String Collection Editor (Figure 7.4) and type your list items, ending each line with the Enter key. Click OK when finished. You can open the editor again to modify the list, if you wish.

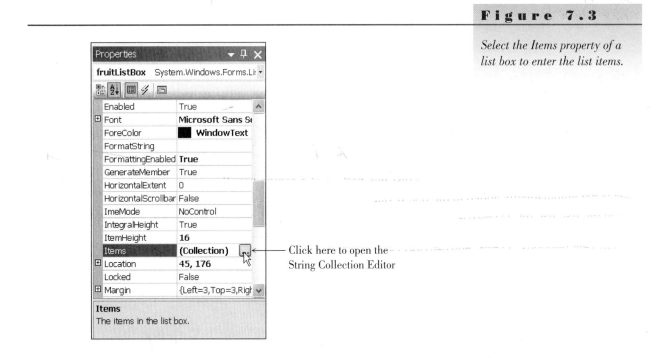

Figure 7.3

Select the Items property of a list box to enter the list items.

Click here to open the String Collection Editor

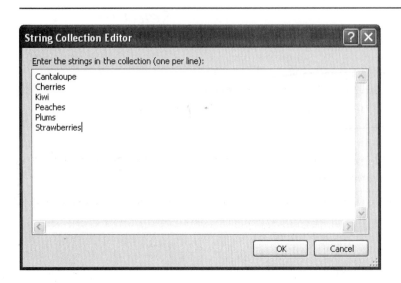

Figure 7.4

In the String Collection Editor that opens, type each list item and press Enter to go to the next line.

Using the Items.Add Method

To add an item to a list at run time, use the **Items.Add method**. You can choose to add a variable, a constant, the contents of the text box at the top of a combo box, or the Text property of another control.

The Items.Add Method—General Form

```
Object.Items.Add(ItemValue)
```

ItemValue is the string value to add to the list. If the value is a string literal, enclose it in quotation marks.

The new item generally goes at the end of the list. However, you can alter the placement by setting the control's **Sorted property** to True. Then the new item will be placed alphabetically in the list.

The Items.Add Method—Examples

```
Me.schoolsListBox.Items.Add("Harvard")
Me.schoolsListBox.Items.Add("Stanford")
Me.schoolsListBox.Items.Add(schoolsTextBox.Text)
Me.majorsComboBox.Items.Add(majorsComboBox.Text)
Me.majorsComboBox.Items.Add(majorString)
```

When the user types a new value in the text box portion of a combo box, that item is not automatically added to the list. If you want to add the newly entered text to the list, use the `Items.Add` method:

```
Me.coffeeComboBox.Items.Add(Me.coffeeComboBox.Text)
```

or the preferable form:

```
With Me.coffeeComboBox
   .Items.Add(.Text)
End With
```

You also can add the contents of a text box to a list box.

```
Me.schoolsListBox.Items.Add(Me.schoolTextBox.Text)
```

Using the Items.Insert Method

You can choose the location for a new item added to the list. In the **Items.Insert method**, you specify the index position for the new item.

The Items.Insert Method—General Form

```
Object.Items.Insert(IndexPosition, ItemValue)
```

The index position is zero based. To insert a new item in the first position, use index position = 0.

The Items.Insert Method—Examples

```
Me.schoolsListBox.Items.Insert(0, "Harvard")
Me.majorsComboBox.Items.Insert(1, Me.majorsComboBox.Text)
```

If you choose the index position of an item using the Insert method, do not set the list control's Sorted property to True. A sorted list is always sorted into alphabetic order, regardless of any other order that you request.

The SelectedIndex Property

When a project is running and the user selects (highlights) an item from the list, the index number of that item is stored in the **SelectedIndex property** of the list box. Recall that the index of the first item in the list is 0. If no list item is selected, the SelectedIndex property is set to negative 1 (–1).

You can use the SelectedIndex property to select an item in the list or deselect all items in code.

Examples

```
' Select the fourth item in list.
Me.coffeeTypesListBox.SelectedIndex = 3

' Deselect all items in list.
Me.coffeeTypesListBox.SelectedIndex = –1
```

The Items.Count Property

You can use the Count property of the Items collection to determine the number of items in the list. We will use the **Items.Count property** later in this chapter to process each element in the list. Items.Count is also handy when you need to display the count at some point in your project.

Remember: Items.Count is always one more than the highest possible SelectedIndex, since the indexes begin with 0. For example, if there are five items in a list, Items.Count is 5 and the highest index is 4 (Figure 7.5).

Examples

```
totalItemsInteger = Me.itemsListBox.Items.Count
MessageBox.Show("The number of items in the list is " & _
    Me.itemsListBox.Items.Count.ToString())
```

F i g u r e   7 . 5

For a list of five items, the indexes range from 0 to 4.

Items.SelectedIndex	Items.Count = 5
(0)	Harvard
(1)	Stanford
(2)	University of California
(3)	Miami University
(4)	University of New York

Referencing the Items Collection

If you need to display one item from a list, you can refer to one element of the Items collection. The Items collection of a list box or combo box holds the text of all list elements. You specify which element you want by including an index. This technique can be useful if you need to display a list item in a label or on another form. Later in this chapter we will use the Items property to send the contents of the list box to the printer.

Using the Items Collection—General Form

```
Object.Items(IndexPosition) [ = Value]
```

The index of the first list element is 0, so the highest index is Items.Count − 1.

Note: If you use an *IndexPosition* less than 0 or greater than Items.Count −1, an exception will be thrown.

You can retrieve the value of a list element or set an element to a new value.

Using the Items Collection—Examples

```
Me.schoolsListBox.Items(5) = "University of California"
Me.majorLabel.Text = Me.majorsComboBox.Items(indexInteger)
Me.selectedMajorLabel.Text = Me.majorsComboBox.Items(Me.majorsComboBox.SelectedIndex)
Me.selectedMajorLabel.Text = Me.majorsComboBox.Text
```

To refer to the currently selected element of a list, you must combine the Items property and the SelectedIndex property:

```
selectedFlavorString = Me.flavorListBox.Items(Me.flavorListBox.SelectedIndex).ToString()
```

You also can retrieve the selected list item by referring to the Text property of the control:

```
Me.selectedMajorLabel.Text = Me.majorsComboBox.Text
```

Note: If you assign a value to a particular item, you replace the previous contents of that position. For example,

```
Me.schoolsListBox.Items(0) = "My School"
```

places "My School" into the first position, replacing whatever was there already. It does not insert the item into the list or increase the value in Items.Count.

Removing an Item from a List

You can remove individual items from a list either by specifying the index of the item or the text of the item. Use the **Items.RemoveAt method** to remove an item by index and the **Items.Remove method** to remove by specifying the text.

The Items.RemoveAt Method—General Form

```
Object.Items.RemoveAt(IndexPosition)
```

The index is required; it specifies which element to remove. The index of the first list element is 0, and the index of the last element is Items.Count − 1. If you specify an invalid index, the system throws an IndexOutOfRange exception.

The Items.RemoveAt Method—Examples

```
' Remove the first name from the list.
Me.namesListBox.Items.RemoveAt(0)
' Remove the item in position indexInteger.
Me.schoolsComboBox.Items.RemoveAt(indexInteger)
' Remove the currently selected item.
Me.coffeeComboBox.Items.RemoveAt(coffeeComboBox.SelectedIndex)
```

The Items.Remove Method—General Form

```
Object.Items.Remove(TextString)
```

The `Items.Remove` method looks for the specified string in the Items collection. If the string is found, it is removed; however, if it is not found, no exception is generated.

The Items.Remove Method—Examples

```
' Remove the specified item.
Me.namesListBox.Items.Remove("My School")
' Remove the matching item.
Me.schoolsComboBox.Items.Remove(schoolTextBox.Text)
' Remove the currently selected item.
Me.coffeeComboBox.Items.Remove(coffeeComboBox.Text)
```

If you remove the currently selected item using either the `RemoveAt` or `Remove` method, make your code more efficient and easier to read by using the `With` statement.

```
With Me.coffeeComboBox
    If .SelectedIndex <> -1 Then
        .Items.RemoveAt(.SelectedIndex)     ' Remove by Index.
        '.Items.Remove(.Text)               ' Alternate - remove by Text.
    Else
        MessageBox.Show("First select the coffee to remove", "No selection made", _
            MessageBoxButtons.OK, MessageBoxIcon.Exclamation)
    End If
End With
```

Clearing a List

In addition to removing individual items at run time, you can also clear all items from a list. Use the **Items.Clear method** to empty a combo box or list box.

The Items.Clear Method—General Form

```
Object.Items.Clear()
```

The Clear Method—Examples

```
Me.schoolsListBox.Items.Clear()
Me.majorsComboBox.Items.Clear()
```

```
' Confirm clearing the majors list.
Dim responseDialogResult As DialogResult

responseDialogResult = MessageBox.Show("Clear the majors list?", "Clear Majors List", _
    MessageBoxButtons.YesNo, MessageBoxIcon.Question)

If responseDialogResult = DialogResult.Yes Then
    Me.majorsComboBox.Items.Clear()
End If
```

List Box and Combo Box Events

Later in the chapter we will perform actions in event procedures for events of list boxes and combo boxes. Some useful events are the SelectedIndexChanged, TextChanged, Enter, and Leave.

   Note: Although we haven't used these events up until this point, many other controls have similar events. For example, you can code event procedures for the Enter, Leave, and TextChanged events of text boxes.

The TextChanged Event

As the user types text into the text box portion of a combo box, the TextChanged event occurs. Each keystroke generates another TextChanged event.

The Enter Event

When a control receives the focus, an Enter event occurs. As the user tabs from control to control, an Enter event fires for each control. Later you will learn to make any existing text appear selected when the user tabs to a text box or the text portion of a combo box.

The Leave Event

You can also write code for the Leave event of a control. When the user tabs from one control to another, the Leave event is triggered as the control loses focus, before the Enter event of the next control. Programmers often use Leave event procedures to validate input data.

☑ **TIP**

To write a procedure for an event that isn't the default event, you cannot just double-click the control. Instead, in the Editor window, select the control name in the Class Name list (at the top-left of the window), drop down the Method Name list, and select the event for which you want to write code *or* double-click the event name in the Properties window after clicking the Events button. The Editor will create the procedure header for you. ∎

Feedback 7.1

Describe the purpose of each of the following methods or properties for a list box or combo box control.

1. Sorted
2. SelectedIndex
3. Items
4. DropDownStyle
5. Items.Count
6. Items.Add
7. Items.Insert
8. Items.Clear
9. Items.RemoveAt
10. Items.Remove

Do/Loops

Until now, there has been no way to repeat the same steps in a procedure without calling them a second time. The computer is capable of repeating a group of instructions many times without calling the procedure for each new set of data. The process of repeating a series of instructions is called *looping*. The group of repeated instructions is called a ***loop***. An **iteration** is a single execution of the statement(s) in the loop. In this section, you will learn about the Do/Loop. Later in this chapter, you will learn about another type of loop—a For/Next loop.

A **Do/Loop** terminates based on a condition that you specify. Execution of a Do/Loop continues *while* a condition is True or *until* a condition is True. You can choose to place the condition at the top or the bottom of the loop. Use a Do/Loop when the exact number of iterations is unknown.

Align the **Do** and **Loop statements** with each other and indent the lines of code to be repeated in between.

The Do and Loop Statements—General Form

```
Do {While | Until} Condition
   ' Statements in loop.

Loop

or

Do
   ' Statements in loop.

Loop {While | Until} Condition
```

The first form of the Do/Loop tests for completion at the top of the loop. With this type of loop, also called a ***pretest*** or ***entry test***, the statements inside the loop may never be executed if the terminating condition is True the first time it is tested.

Example

```
totalInteger = 0
Do Until totalInteger = 0
    ' These statements in loop will never execute.
Loop
```

Because totalInteger is 0 the first time the condition is tested, the condition is True and the statements inside the loop will not execute. Control will pass to the statement following the `Loop` statement.

The second form of the `Do/Loop` tests for completion at the bottom of the loop, which means that the statements inside the loop will *always* be executed at least once. This form of loop is sometimes called a **posttest** or **exit test**. Changing the example to a posttest, you can see the difference.

```
totalInteger = 0
Do
    ' Statements in loop will execute at least once.

Loop Until totalInteger = 0
```

In this case the statements inside the loop will be executed at least once. Assuming the value for totalInteger does not change inside the loop, the condition (totalInteger = 0) will be True the first time it is tested and control will pass to the first statement following the `Loop` statement. Figure 7.6 shows UML action diagrams of pretest and posttest loops, using both `While` and `Until`.

The Do and Loop Statements—Examples

```
Do Until itemIndexInteger = Me.itemsListBox.Items.Count — 1
    ' Statements in loop.

Loop

Do While amountDecimal >= 10D And amountDecimal <= 20D
    ' Statements in loop.

Loop

Do
    ' Statements in loop.
Loop Until totalInteger < 0
```

The Boolean Data Type Revisited

In Chapter 2 you learned about the Boolean data type, which holds only the values True and False. You will find Boolean variables very useful when setting and testing conditions for a loop. You can set a Boolean variable to True when a specific circumstance occurs and then write a loop condition to continue until the variable is True.

An example of using a Boolean variable is when you want to search through a list for a specific value. The item may or may not be found, and you want to quit looking when a match is found.

Figure 7.6

UML action diagrams of pretest and posttest loops.

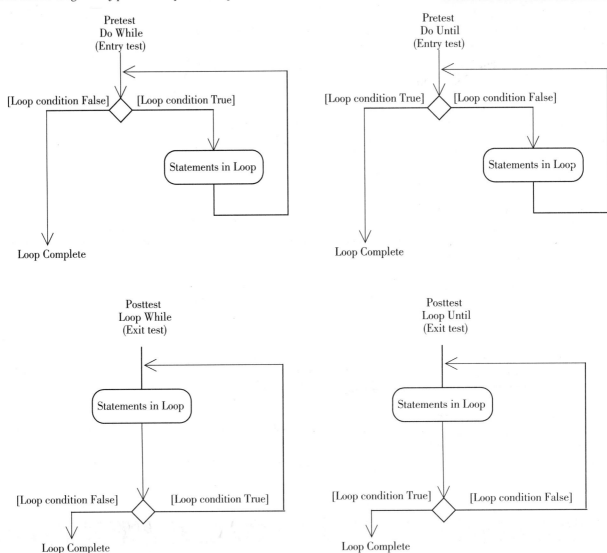

Using a Boolean variable is usually a three-step process. First you must dimension a variable and set its initial value (or use the default VB setting of False). Then, when a particular situation occurs, you set the variable to True. A loop condition can then check for True.

```
Dim itemFoundBoolean as Boolean = False

Do Until itemFoundBoolean    ' Checks for True.
    ' ...
```

A Boolean variable is always in one of two states: True or False. Many programmers refer to Boolean variables as *switches* or *flags*. Switches have two states—on or off; flags are considered either up or down.

Using a Do/Loop with a List Box

This small example combines a Boolean variable with a Do/Loop. Inside the loop, each element of the list is compared to newItemTextBox.Text for a match. The loop will terminate when a match is found or when all elements have been tested. Follow through the logic to see what happens when there is a match, when there isn't a match, when the match occurs on the first list element, and when the match occurs on the last list element.

```
Private Sub findButton_Click(ByVal sender As System.Object, _
    ByVal e As System.EventArgs) Handles findButton.Click
      ' Look for a match between text box and list items.
      Dim itemFoundBoolean As Boolean = False
      Dim itemIndexInteger As Integer = 0

      With Me
        Do Until itemFoundBoolean Or itemIndexInteger = .itemsListBox.Items.Count
          If .newItemTextBox.Text = .itemsListBox.Items(itemIndexInteger).ToString() Then
              itemFoundBoolean = True     'A match was found.
          Else
              itemIndexInteger += 1
          End If
        Loop
      End With

      If itemFoundBoolean Then
        MessageBox.Show("Item is in the list", "Item match", _
          MessageBoxButtons.OK, MessageBoxIcon.Information)
      Else
        MessageBox.Show("Item is not is the list", "No item match", _
          MessageBoxButtons.OK, MessageBoxIcon.Information)
      End If
End Sub
```

> ### Feedback 7.2

Explain the purpose of each line of the following code:

```
  itemFoundBoolean = False
  itemIndexInteger = 0
  With Me
      Do Until itemFoundBoolean Or itemIndexInteger = .itemsListBox.Items.Count
        If .newItemTextBox.Text = .itemsListBox.Items(itemIndexInteger).ToString() Then
            itemFoundBoolean = True
        Else
            itemIndexInteger += 1
        End If
      Loop
  End With
```

For/Next Loops

When you want to repeat the statements in a loop a specific number of times, the **For/Next loop** is ideal. The For/Next loop uses the **For** and **Next statements** and a counter variable, called the ***loop index***. The loop index is tested to determine the number of times the statements inside the loop will execute.

```
Dim loopIndexInteger as Integer
Dim maximumInteger as Integer
maximumInteger = Me.schoolsListBox.Items.Count — 1

For loopIndexInteger = 0 To maximumInteger
    ' The statements inside of the loop are indented
    ' and referred to as the body of the loop
Next loopIndexInteger
```

When the For statement is reached during program execution, several things occur. The loop index, loopIndexInteger, is established as the loop counter and is initialized to 0 (the initial value). The final value for the loop index is set to the value of maximumInteger, which was assigned the value of schoolsListBox.Items.Count −1 in the previous statement.

Execution is now "controlled by" the For statement. After the value of loopIndexInteger is set, it is tested to see whether loopIndexInteger is *greater than* maximumInteger. If not, the statements in the body of the loop are executed. The Next statement causes the loopIndexInteger to be incremented by 1. Then control passes back to the For statement. Is the value of loopIndexInteger greater than maximumInteger? If not, the loop is again executed. When the test is made and the loop index *is* greater than the final value, control passes to the statement immediately following the Next.

A counter-controlled loop generally has three elements (see Figure 7.7 for a UML action diagram of loop logic).

1. Initialize the counter.
2. Increment the counter.
3. Test the counter to determine when it is time to terminate the loop.

A For/Next loop handles all three steps for you.

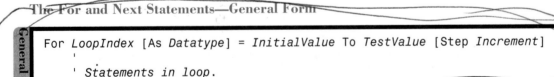

The For and Next Statements—General Form

```
For LoopIndex [As Datatype] = InitialValue To TestValue [Step Increment]

    ' Statements in loop.

Next [LoopIndex]
```

LoopIndex must be a numeric variable; InitialValue and TestValue may be constants, variables, numeric property values, or numeric expressions. The optional word Step may be included, along with the value to be added to the loop index for each iteration of the loop. When the Step is omitted, the increment is assumed to be 1.

The optional As Datatype entry allows you to declare the index variable as part of the For statement. This technique creates a block-level variable that is available only inside the For/Next loop. Declaring and using a block-level

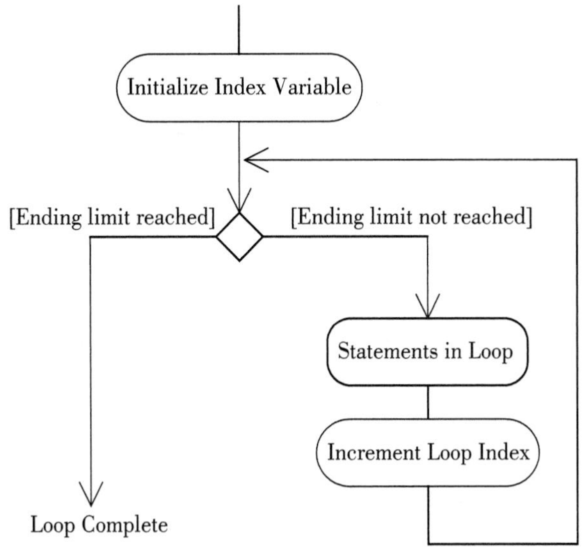

Figure 7.7

A UML action diagram of the logic of a For/Next *loop.*

```
Initialize Index Variable
```

[Ending limit reached]   [Ending limit not reached]

```
Statements in Loop
```

```
Increment Loop Index
```

Loop Complete

variable for the loop index is a new feature of VB 2005 and is the preferred approach.

The For and Next Statements—Examples

```
For indexInteger As Integer = 2 To 100 Step 2
For countInteger As Integer = startInteger To endInteger Step incrementInteger
For countInteger = 0 To Me.coffeeComboBoxType.Items.Count − 1
For numberInteger = (numberCorrectInteger − 5) To totalPossibleInteger
For rateDecimal As Decimal = 0.05D To 0.25D Step 0.05D
For countDownInteger As Integer = 10 To 0 Step −1
```

Each For statement has a corresponding Next statement, which must follow the For. All statements between the For and Next statements are considered to be the body of the loop and will be executed the specified number of times.

The first For statement example will count from 2 to 100 by 2. The statements in the body of the loop will be executed 50 times: first with indexInteger = 2, next with indexInteger = 4, next with indexInteger = 6, and so forth.

When the comparison is done, the program checks for *greater than* the test value—not equal to. When indexInteger = 100 in the preceding example, the body of the loop will execute one more time. Then, at the Next statement, indexInteger will be incremented to 102, the test will be made, and control will pass to the statement following the Next.

Negative Increment or Counting Backward

You can use a negative number for the Step increment to decrease the loop index rather than increase it. When the Step is negative, VB tests for *less than* the test value instead of greater than.

```
' Count Backwards.
For countInteger As Integer = 10 To 1 Step −1
   ' Statements in body of loop.
Next countInteger
```

☑TIP

Use a For/Next loop when you know the number of iterations needed for the loop. Use a Do/Loop when the loop should end based on a condition. ■

Conditions Satisfied before Entry

At times the final value will be reached before entry into the loop. In that case, the statements in the body of the loop will not be executed at all.

```
' An unexecutable loop.
finalInteger = 5
For indexInteger As Integer = 6 to finalInteger
   ' The execution will never reach here.
Next indexInteger
```

Altering the Values of the Loop Control Variables

Once a For loop has been entered, the values for InitialValue, TestValue, and Increment have already been set. Changing the value of these control variables within the loop will have no effect on the number of iterations of the loop. Many texts admonish against changing the values within the loop. However, Visual Basic just ignores you if you try.

```
' Bad Example — Changing the Control Variable.
finalInteger = 10
increaseInteger = 2
For indexInteger As Integer = 1 to finalInteger Step increaseInteger
    finalInteger = 25
    increaseInteger = 5
Next indexInteger
```

If you tried this example and displayed the values of indexInteger, you would find that the final value remains 10 and the increment value is 2.

The value that you *can* change within the loop is the loop index. However, this practice is considered poor programming.

```
' Poor Programming.
For indexInteger = 1 To 10 Step 1
  indexInteger += 5
Next indexInteger
```

Endless Loops

Changing the value of a loop index variable is not only considered a poor practice but also may lead to an endless loop. Your code could get into a loop that is impossible to exit. Consider the following example; when will the loop end?

```
' More Poor Programming.
For indexInteger = 1 To 10 Step 1
    indexInteger = 1
Next indexInteger
```

Exiting Loops

In the previous example of an endless loop, you will have to break the program execution manually. You can click on your form's close box or use the Visual

Basic menu bar or toolbar to stop the program. If you can't see the menu bar or toolbar, you can usually move or resize your application's form to bring it into view. If you prefer, press Ctrl + Break to enter break time; you may want to step program execution to see what is causing the problem.

Usually loops should proceed to normal completion. However, on occasion you may need to terminate a loop before the loop index reaches its final value. Visual Basic provides `Exit For` and `Exit Do` statements for this situation. Generally, the `Exit` statement is part of an `If` statement.

The Exit Statement—General Form

```
Exit For
Exit Do
```

The `Exit For` and `Exit Do` transfer control to the statement following the loop termination—the `Next` or `Loop` statement at the bottom of the loop structure.

The Exit Statement—Examples

```
For indexInteger As Integer = 1 To maxInteger
    If indexInteger > 1000 Then
        Exit For
    End If
    ' Statements in loop.
Next indexInteger

With Me
    Do Until itemIndexInteger = .itemsListBox.Items.Count
        If .newItemTextBox.Text = _
            .itemsListBox.Items(itemIndexInteger).ToString() Then
            itemFoundBoolean = True
            Exit Do
        Else
            itemIndexInteger += 1
        End If
    Loop
End With
```

Skipping to the Next Iteration of a Loop

At times you may be finished in the current iteration of a loop and want to skip to the next. The new `Continue` statement transfers control to the last statement in the loop and retests the loop exit condition. This effectively skips to the next iteration of the loop. Generally, the `Continue` statement is part of an `If` statement.

The Continue Statement—General Form

```
Continue For
Continue Do
```

The Continue Statement—Examples

```
With Me
    For loopInteger As Integer = 0 To .nameListBox.Items.Count — 1
        If .nameListBox.Items(loopInteger).ToString() = String.Empty Then
            Continue For
        End If
        ' Code to do something with the name found.
        Debug.WriteLine("Name = " & .nameListBox.Items(loopInteger).ToString())
    Next
End With

With Me
    loopInteger = —1
    Do Until loopInteger = .nameListBox.Items.Count — 1
        loopInteger += 1
        If .nameListBox.Items(loopInteger).ToString() = String.Empty Then
            Continue Do
        End If
        ' Code to do something with the name found.
        Debug.WriteLine("Name = " & .nameListBox.Items(loopInteger).ToString())
    Loop
End With
```

Note: The two above examples do the same thing, but you'll notice that the For loop has less code. Because the number of iterations is known (Items.Count), the For statement is the preferred solution.

Feedback 7.3

1. Identify the statements that are correctly formed and those that have errors. For those with errors, state what is wrong and how to correct it.
   (a) `For indexDecimal = 3.5D To 6.0D, Step 0.5D`
       `Next indexDecimal`
   (b) `For indexInteger = beginInteger To endInteger Step incrementInteger`
       `Next endInteger`
   (c) `For 4 = 1 To 10 Step 2`
       `Next For`
   (d) `For indexInteger = 100 To 0 Step —25`
       `Next indexInteger`
   (e) `For indexInteger = 0 To —10 Step —1`
       `Next indexInteger`
   (f) `For indexInteger = 10 To 1`
       `Next indexInteger`
2. How many times will the body of the loop be executed for each of these examples? What will be the value of the loop index after normal completion of the loop?
   (a) `For countInteger = 1 To 3`
   (b) `For countInteger = 2 To 11 Step 3`
   (c) `For countInteger = 10 To 1 Step —1`
   (d) `For counterDecimal = 3.0D To 6.0D Step 0.5D`
   (e) `For countInteger = 5 To 1`

Making Entries Appear Selected

You can use several techniques to make the text in a text box or list appear selected.

Selecting the Entry in a Text Box

When the user tabs into a text box that already has an entry, how do you want the text to appear? Should the insertion point appear at either the left or right end of the text? Or should the entire entry appear selected? You can also apply this question to a text box that failed validation: Shouldn't the entire entry be selected? The most user-friendly approach is to select the text, which you can do with the SelectAll method of the text box. A good location to do this is in the text box's Enter event procedure, which occurs when the control receives the focus.

```
Private Sub nameTextBox_Enter(ByVal sender As Object, _
   ByVal e As System.EventArgs) Handles nameTextBox.Enter
      ' Select any existing text.

   nameTextBox.SelectAll()
End Sub
```

Selecting an Entry in a List Box

You can make a single item in a list box appear selected by setting the SelectedIndex property.

```
Me.coffeeListBox.SelectedIndex = indexInteger
```

When a list box has a very large number of entries, you can help users by selecting the matching entry as they type in a text box. This method is similar to the way the Help Topics list in Visual Basic works. For example, when you type *p*, the list quickly scrolls and displays words beginning with *p*. Then if you next type *r*, the list scrolls down to the words that begin with *pr* and the first such word is selected. If you type *i* next, the first word beginning with *pri* is selected. The following example implements this feature. See if you can tell what each statement does.

Notice that this is coded in the TextChanged event procedure for the control into which the user is typing; the event occurs once for every keystroke entered.

```
Private Sub coffeeTextBox_TextChanged(ByVal sender As System.Object, _
   ByVal e As System.EventArgs) Handles coffeeTextBox.TextChanged

      ' Locate first matching occurrence in the list.

      Dim indexInteger As Integer = 0
      Dim foundBoolean As Boolean = False
      Dim listCompareString As String
      Dim textCompareString As String
```

```
      With Me
          Do While Not foundBoolean And indexInteger < .coffeeListBox.Items.Count
              listCompareString = .coffeeListBox.Items(indexInteger).ToString().ToUpper()
              textCompareString = .coffeeTextBox.Text.ToUpper()
              If listCompareString.StartsWith(textCompareString) Then
                  .coffeeListBox.SelectedIndex = indexInteger
                  foundBoolean = True
              Else
                  indexInteger += 1
              End If
          Loop
      End With
End Sub
```

Sending Information to the Printer

So far, all program output has been on the screen. You can use the .NET Print-Document and PrintPreviewDialog components to produce output for the printer and also to preview the output on the screen. These components appear in the *Printing* tab of the toolbox.

Visual Basic was designed to run under Windows, which is a highly interactive environment. It is extremely easy to create forms for interactive programs, but it is not easy at all to print on the printer. Most professional programmers using Visual Basic use a separate utility program to format printer reports. Several companies sell utilities that do a nice job of designing and printing reports. The VB Professional Edition and Enterprise Edition include Crystal Reports for creating reports from database files.

The PrintDocument Component

You set up output for the printer using the methods and events of the **Print-Document component**. Add a PrintDocument component to a form; the component appears in the component tray below the form (Figure 7.8).

Figure 7.8

Add a PrintDocument component to your application. The component appears in the form's component tray.

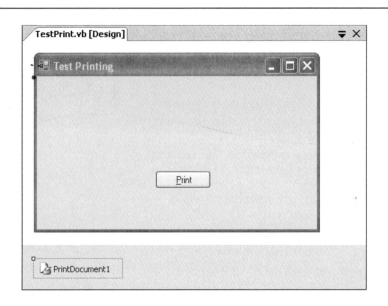

Beginning the Print Operation

To start printing output, you execute the **Print method** of the PrintDocument component. This code belongs in the Click event procedure for the *Print* button or menu item that the user selects to begin printing.

```
Private Sub printButton_Click(ByVal sender As System.Object, _
   ByVal e As System.EventArgs) Handles printButton.Click
      ' Print output on the printer.

      PrintDocument1.Print()    ' Start the print process.
End Sub
```

Setting Up the Print Output

The logic for the actual printing belongs in the PrintDocument's **PrintPage event procedure**. The PrintPage event is fired once for each page to be printed. This technique is referred to as a ***callback*** and is different from anything we have done so far. In a callback, the object notifies the program that it needs to do something or that a situation exists that the program needs to handle. The object notifies the program of the situation by firing an event.

The PrintDocument object is activated when you issue its `Print` method (usually from a menu option or a button click). It then sets up the graphics page that corresponds to your printer and fires a PrintPage event for each page to print. It also fires events for BeginPrint and EndPrint, for which you can write code if you wish.

```
Private Sub PrintDocument1_PrintPage(ByVal sender As System.Object, _
   ByVal e As System.Drawing.Printing.PrintPageEventArgs) _
   Handles PrintDocument1.PrintPage
      ' Set up actual output to print.

End Sub
```

Notice the argument: `e As System.Drawing.Printing.PrintPage-EventArgs`. We will use some of the properties and methods of the PrintPage-EventArgs argument for such things as determining the page margins and sending a string of text to the page.

The Graphics Page

You set up a graphics page in memory and then the page is sent to the printer. The graphics page can contain strings of text as well as graphic elements.

You must specify the exact location on the graphics page for each element that you want to print. You can specify the upper-left corner of any element by giving its X and Y coordinates, or by using a Point structure or a Rectangle structure. We will stick with the X and Y coordinates in these examples (Figure 7.9).

You can use multiple PrintDocument objects if you have more than one type of output or report. Each PrintDocument has its own PrintPage event. Code the graphics commands to precisely print the page in each document's PrintPage event procedure.

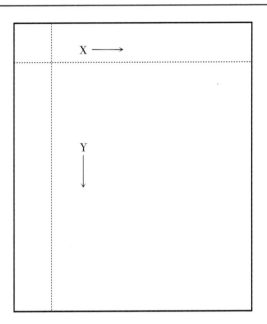

Using the DrawString Method

You use the **DrawString method** to send a line of text to the graphics page. The DrawString method belongs to the Graphics object of the PrintPage-EventArgs argument. Refer back to the procedure header for the PrintPage event in "Setting Up the Print Output."

The DrawString Method—General Form

The DrawString method is overloaded, which means that there are several forms for calling the method. The form presented here is the least complicated and requires that page coordinates be given in X and Y format.

General Form

```
DrawString(StringToPrint, Font, Brush, Xcoordinate, Ycoordinate)
```

You supply the arguments of the DrawString method: what to print, what font and color to print it in, and where to print it.

The DrawString Method—Examples

Examples

```
e.Graphics.DrawString(printLineString, printFont, Brushes.Black, _
    horizontalPrintLocationSingle, verticalPrintLocationSingle)
e.Graphics.DrawString("My text string", myFont, Brushes.Black, 100.0, 100.0)
e.Graphics.DrawString(nameTextBox.Text, New Font("Arial", 10), Brushes.Red, _
    leftMarginSingle, currentLineSingle)
```

Before you execute the DrawString method, you should set up the font that you want to use and the X and Y coordinates.

Setting the X and Y Coordinates

For each line that you want to print, you must specify the X and Y coordinates. It is helpful to set up some variables for setting these values, which should be declared as Single data type.

```
Dim horizontalPrintLocationSingle As Single
Dim verticalPrintLocationSingle As Single
```

The PrintPageEventArgs argument has several useful properties (Figure 7.10), such as MarginBounds, PageBounds, and PageSettings. You can use these properties to determine the present settings. For example, you may want to set the X coordinate to the current left margin and the Y coordinate to the top margin.

```
horizontalPrintLocationSingle = e.MarginBounds.Left
verticalPrintLocationSingle = e.MarginBounds.Top
```

Figure 7.10

Use the properties of the PrintPageEventArgs argument to determine the current margin settings.

To send multiple lines to the print page, you must increment the Y coordinate. You can add the height of a line to the previous Y coordinate to calculate the next line's Y coordinate.

```
' Declarations at the top of the procedure.
Dim printFont As New Font("Arial", 12)
Dim lineHeightSingle As Single = printFont.GetHeight
horizontalPrintLocationSingle = e.MarginBounds.Left
verticalPrintLocationSingle = e.MarginBounds.Top
' ... More declarations here.

  ' Print a line.
  e.Graphics.DrawString(printLineString, printFont, Brushes.Black, _
    horizontalPrintLocationSingle, verticalPrintLocationSingle)
  ' Increment the Y position for the next line.
  verticalPrintLocationSingle += lineHeightSingle
```

Printing the Contents of a List Box

You can combine the techniques for printing, a loop, and the list box properties to send the contents of a list box to the printer. You know how many iterations to make, using the Items.Count property. The Items collection allows you to print out the actual values from the list.

```
' Print out all items in the coffeeComboBox list.

For listIndexInteger as Integer = 0 To Me.coffeeComboBox.Items.Count - 1
    ' Set up a line.
    printLineString = Me.coffeeComboBox.Items(listIndexInteger)
    ' Send the line to the graphics page object.
    e.Graphics.DrawString(printLineString, printFont, Brushes.Black, _
        horizontalPrintLocationSingle, verticalPrintLocationSingle)

    ' Increment the Y position for the next line.
    verticalPrintLocationSingle += lineHeightSingle
Next listIndexInteger
```

Printing the Selected Item from a List

When an item is selected in a list box or a combo box, the Text property holds the selected item. You can use the Text property to print the selected item.

```
' Set up the line for the list selections.
printLineString = "Coffee: " & Me.coffeeComboBox.Text _
    & "    Syrup: " & Me.syrupListBox.Text
' Send the line to the graphics page object.
e.Graphics.DrawString(printLineString, printFont, Brushes.Black, _
    horizontalPrintLocationSingle, verticalPrintLocationSingle)
```

Aligning Decimal Columns

When the output to the printer includes numeric data, the alignment of the decimal points is important. Alignment can be tricky with proportional fonts, where the width of each character varies. The best approach is to format each number as you want it to print and then measure the length of the formatted string. This technique requires a couple more elements: You need an object declared as a SizeF structure, which has a Width property, and you need to use the MeasureString method of the Graphics class. Both the SizeF structure and the MeasureString method work with pixels, which is what you want. It's the same unit of measure as used for the X and Y coordinates of the DrawString method.

The following example prints a left-aligned literal at position 200 on the line and right-aligns a formatted number at position 500. (Assume that all variables are properly declared.)

```
' SizeF structure for font size info.
Dim fontSizeF As New SizeF()

' Set X for left-aligned column.
horizontalPrintLocationSingle = 200
' Set ending position for right-aligned column.
columnEndSingle = 500

' Format the number.
formattedOutputString= amountDecimal.ToString("C")

' Calculate the X position of the amount.
```

```
' Measure string in this font.
fontSizeF= e.Graphics.MeasureString(formattedOutputString, printFont)
' Subtract width of string from the column position.
columnXSingle = columnEndSingle — fontSizeF.Width

' Set up the line — each element separately.
e.Graphics.DrawString("The Amount = ", printFont, Brushes.Black, _
   horizontalPrintLocationSingle, verticalPrintLocationSingle)
e.Graphics.DrawString(formattedOutputString, printFont, Brushes.Black, _
   columnXSingle, verticalPrintLocationSingle)
' Increment line for next line.
verticalPrintLocationSingle += lineHeightSingle
```

Displaying a Print Preview

A really great feature of the new VB .NET printing model is **print preview**. You can view the printer's output on the screen and then choose to print or cancel. This is especially helpful for testing and debugging a program, so that you don't have to keep sending pages to the printer and wasting paper.

The **PrintPreviewDialog component** is the key to print preview. You add the control to your form's component tray; the default name is PrintPreviewDialog1 (Figure 7.11). Since you can use the same dialog for all print previews, you do not need to rename the component.

You write two lines of code in the event procedure for the button or menu item where the user selects the print preview option. The PrintPreviewDialog component uses the same PrintDocument component that you declared for printer output. You assign the PrintDocument to the Document property of the PrintPreviewDialog and execute the ShowDialog method. The same PrintPage event procedure executes as for the PrintDocument.

Figure 7.11

Add a PrintPreviewDialog component to your form's component tray.

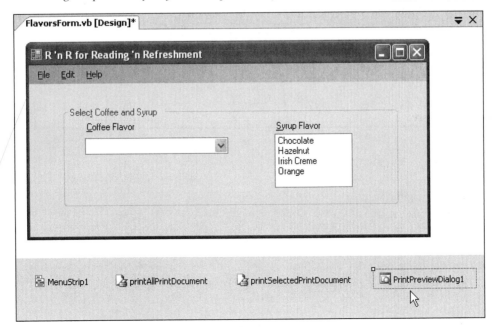

```
Private Sub filePrintPreviewMenu_Click(ByVal sender As Object, _
  ByVal e As System. EventArgs) Handles filePrintPreviewMenu.Click
      ' Begin the process for print preview.

      Me.PrintPreviewDialog1.Document = reportPrintDocument
      Me.PrintPreviewDialog1.ShowDialog()
End Sub
```

The Using Block

When you are using system resources such as fonts, you can access the resources inside of a **Using block**. Any variables that are declared in a Using block are only accessible within that block, as with any other block-level variable. The advantage of declaring a variable inside a Using block is that system resources are released as soon as the block terminates.

```
Using headingFont as New Font("Arial", 14, FontStyle.Bold)
   e.Graphics.DrawString("Flavors", headingFont, Brushes.Black, horizontalPrintLocationSingle, _
      verticalPrintLocationSingle)
End Using
```

Printing Multiple Pages

You can easily print multiple pages, both to the printer and to the *Print Preview* dialog box. Recall that the PrintDocument's PrintPage event fires once for each page. You indicate that you have more pages to print by setting the HasMorePages property of the PrintPageEventArgs argument to True.

The following example prints four pages full of the same line, just to illustrate multiple-page output. Normally you will have a certain amount of data to print and stop when you run out.

```
Private Sub reportPrintDocument_PrintPage(ByVal sender As Object, _
  ByVal e As System.Drawing.Printing.PrintPageEventArgs) _
  Handles reportPrintDocument.PrintPage

    ' Print multiple-page output.
    Dim printFont As New Font("Arial", 12)
    Dim lineHeightSingle As Single = printFont.GetHeight + 2
    Dim horizontalPrintLocationSingle As Single = e.MarginBounds.Left
    Dim verticalPrintLocationSingle As Single = e.MarginBounds.Top
    Dim printLineString As String

    ' Count pages for multiple-page output.
    ' Initialize the page number at 1.
    Static pageCountInteger As Integer = 1

    verticalPrintLocationSingle = e.MarginBounds.Top
    printLineString = "This is a line of output"

    ' Print the page number.
    e.Graphics.DrawString("Page " & pageCountInteger.ToString(), printFont, _
      Brushes.Black, 600, verticalPrintLocationSingle)
    verticalPrintLocationSingle += lineHeightSingle * 2
```

```
    ' Print a page full of the same line.
    Do
        ' Print a line.
        e.Graphics.DrawString(printLineString, printFont, Brushes.Black, _
            horizontalPrintLocationSingle, verticalPrintLocationSingle)
        verticalPrintLocationSingle += lineHeightSingle
        ' Stop at the bottom margin.
    Loop Until verticalPrintLocationSingle >= e.MarginBounds.Bottom

    ' Increment the page number.
    pageCountInteger += 1

    ' Indicate whether there are more pages to print.
    If pageCountInteger <= 4 Then         ' Print only 4 pages.
        e.HasMorePages = True
    Else
        e.HasMorePages = False
        ' Reset the page counter for the next report.
        pageCountInteger = 1
    End If
End Sub
```

Declaring the Page Counter as Static

As you learned in Chapter 6, static local variables keep their values from one execution of the procedure to the next. When you print multiple pages, you must keep track of the current page number, but you don't need that value in any procedure but the PrintPage procedure. This is the perfect time to use a static local variable.

```
' Count pages for multiple-page output.
' Initialize the page number at 1.
Static pageCountInteger As Integer = 1
```

Feedback 7.4

What is the purpose of each of these elements? Where and how is each used?

1. The PrintDocument component.
2. The `Print` method.
3. The PrintPage event.
4. The `DrawString` method.
5. `System.Drawing.Printing.PrintPageEventArgs`.
6. `MarginBounds.Left`.
7. The PrintPreviewDialog component.

Your Hands-On Programming Example

Create a project for R 'n R—for Reading 'n Refreshment that contains a drop-down combo box of the coffee flavors and a list box of the syrup flavors. Adjust the size of the boxes as needed when you test the project. The controls should have labels above them with the words *Coffee* and *Syrup*. Enter the initial values for the syrup flavors and coffee flavors in the Properties window. Set the

Sorted property of both lists to True. The user will be able to add more coffee flavors to the list at run time by typing in the top portion of the combo box and selecting a menu item.

Coffee Flavors	**Syrup Flavors**
Espresso Roast	(None)
Jamaica Blue Mountain	Chocolate
Kona Blend	Hazelnut
Chocolate Almond	Irish Cream
Vanilla Nut	Orange

Include one menu item to print all the flavors and another to print only a selected item from each list. Then include submenus for each of the print options to allow the user to send the output to the printer or the Print Preview window. These print commands belong on the *File* menu, along with the *Exit* command. Use a separator bar between the *Prints* and the *Exit*.

Include an *Edit* menu with items to *Add coffee flavor*, *Remove coffee flavor*, *Clear coffee list*, and *Display coffee count*.

Add an About form to your project and add a *Help* menu with an *About* command.

After you have completed the project, try using different styles for the combo box and rerun the project. As an added challenge, modify the *Add coffee flavor* routine so that no duplicates are allowed.

Planning the Project

Sketch a form (Figure 7.12), which your users sign off as meeting their needs.

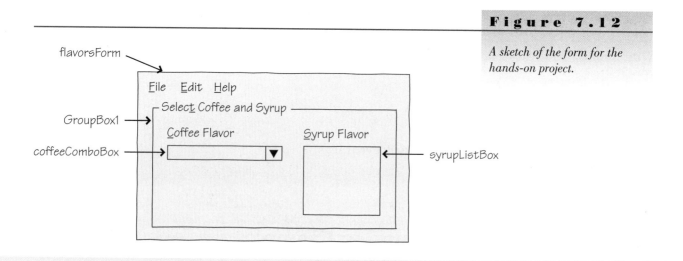

Figure 7.12

A sketch of the form for the hands-on project.

Plan the Objects and Properties

Object	Property	Setting
flavorsForm	Name	flavorsForm
	Text	R 'n R for Reading 'n Refreshment
GroupBox1	Text	Selec&t Coffee and Syrup
Label1	Text	&Coffee Flavor
Label2	Text	&Syrup Flavor
coffeeComboBox	Name	coffeeComboBox
	DropDownStyle	DropDown
	Items	Chocolate Almond
		Espresso Roast
		Jamaica Blue Mountain
		Kona Blend
		Vanilla Nut
	Sorted	True
syrupListBox	Name	syrupListBox
	Items	(None)
		Chocolate
		Hazelnut
		Irish Creme
		Orange
	Sorted	True
FileToolStripMenuItem	Text	&File
PrintSelectedFlavorsToolStripMenuItem	Text	Print &Selected Flavors
PrintAllFlavorsToolStripMenuItem	Text	Print &All Flavors
PrintAllToolStripMenuItem	Text	&Print All
PreviewAllToolStripMenuItem	Text	Pre&view All
PrintSelectedToolStripMenuItem	Text	&Print Selected
PreviewSelectedToolStripMenuItem	Text	Pre&view Selected
ExitToolStripMenuItem	Text	E&xit
EditToolStripMenuItem	Text	&Edit
AddCoffeeFlavorToolStripMenuItem	Text	&Add Coffee Flavor
RemoveCoffeeFlavorToolStripMenuItem	Text	&Remove Coffee Flavor
ClearCoffeeListToolStripMenuItem	Text	&Clear Coffee List
DisplayCoffeeCountToolStripMenuItem	Text	Count Coffee &List
HelpToolStripMenuItem	Text	&Help
AboutToolStripMenuItem	Text	&About
printAllPrintDocument	Name	printAllPrintDocument
printSelectedPrintDocument	Name	printSelectedPrintDocument
PrintPreviewDialog1	Name	PrintPreviewDialog1

Different (handwritten annotation with arrow)

Plan the Event Procedures

Main Form

Procedure	Actions

PreviewSelectedToolStripMenuItem_Click	If both coffee and syrup selected
	    Set Boolean variable for selected item.
	    Set the print preview document.
	    Show the print preview dialog.
	Else
	    Display error message.

PrintSelectedToolStripMenuItem_Click	If both coffee and syrup selected
	    Set Boolean variable for selected item.
	    Start the print operation.
	Else
	    Display error message.

PreviewAllToolStripMenuItem_Click	Set the print preview document. Show the print preview dialog.
PrintAllToolStripMenuItem_Click	Start the print operation.
printAllPrintDocument_PrintPage	Use a loop to send all flavor names to the printer.

printSelectedPrintDocument_PrintPage	If item is selected
	    Send selected item to the printer.
	Else
	    Display error message.

ExitToolStripMenuItem_Click	Terminate the Project.

AddCoffeeFlavorToolStripMenuItem_Click	If a selection is made
	If duplicate item
	    Display "Duplicate" message.
	Else
	    Add item to the list.
	    Clear the list's Text property.

RemoveCoffeeFlavorToolStripMenuItem_Click	If coffee flavor selected then
	    Remove selected item.
	Else
	    Display error message.

ClearCoffeeListToolStripMenuItem_Click	Display a message box to confirm the clear. If user clicks Yes Clear the coffee list.
DisplayCoffeeCountToolStripMenuItem_Click	Display list count in message box.
AboutToolStripMenuItem_Click	Display the About box.

About Form

Procedure	Actions
okButton_Click	Close the About box.

Write the Project

Follow the sketch in Figure 7.12 to create the form. Figure 7.13 shows the completed form.

- Set the properties of each object as you have planned.

- Write the code. Working from the pseudocode, write each event procedure.

- When you complete the code, use a variety of data to thoroughly test the project.

Figure 7.13

The main form for the hands-on project.

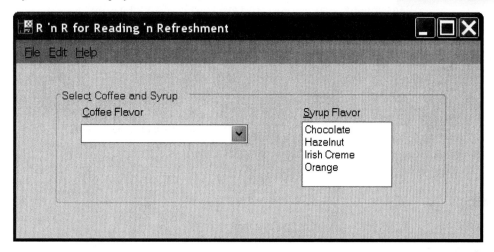

The Project Coding Solution

Main Form

```
'Project:       Ch07HandsOn
'Programmer:    Bradley/Millspaugh
'Date:          June 2005
'Description:   Maintain a list of coffee flavors; print the selected flavor
'               of coffee and syrup or print a list of all of the coffee flavors.
'Folder:        Ch07HandsOn

Public Class FlavorsForm

    Private Sub ExitToolStripMenuItem_Click(ByVal sender As System.Object, _
        ByVal e As System.EventArgs) Handles ExitToolStripMenuItem.Click
            'End the program.

        Me.Close()
    End Sub

    Private Sub AddCoffeeFlavorToolStripMenuItem_Click(ByVal sender As System.Object, _
        ByVal e As System.EventArgs) Handles AddCoffeeFlavorToolStripMenuItem.Click
            ' Add a new coffee flavor to the coffee list.
```

```vbnet
        With Me.coffeeComboBox
            ' Test for blank input.
            If .Text <> "" Then
                ' Make sure item is not already on the list.
                Dim itemFoundBoolean As Boolean
                Dim itemIndexInteger As Integer
                Do Until itemFoundBoolean Or itemIndexInteger = .Items.Count
                    If .Text = .Items(itemIndexInteger).ToString() Then
                        itemFoundBoolean = True
                        Exit Do
                    Else
                        itemIndexInteger += 1
                    End If
                Loop
                If itemFoundBoolean Then
                    MessageBox.Show("Duplicate item.", "Add Failed", _
                        MessageBoxButtons.OK, MessageBoxIcon.Exclamation)
                Else
                    ' If it's not in the list, add it.
                    .Items.Add(.Text)
                    .Text = ""
                End If
            Else
                MessageBox.Show("Enter a coffee flavor to add", _
                    "Missing Data", MessageBoxButtons.OK, _
                    MessageBoxIcon.Exclamation)
            End If
            .Focus()
        End With
    End Sub

    Private Sub PrintAllToolStripMenuItem_Click(ByVal sender As System.Object, _
      ByVal e As System.EventArgs) Handles PrintAllToolStripMenuItem.Click
      ' Begin the print process to print all items.

        printAllPrintDocument.Print()
    End Sub

    Private Sub PreviewAllToolStripMenuItem_Click(ByVal sender As Object, _
      ByVal e As System.EventArgs) Handles PreviewAllToolStripMenuItem.Click
      ' Begin the process for print preview of all items.

        PrintPreviewDialog1.Document = printAllPrintDocument
        PrintPreviewDialog1.ShowDialog()
    End Sub

    Private Sub PrintSelectedToolStripMenuItem1_Click(ByVal sender As System.Object, _
      ByVal e As System.EventArgs) Handles PrintSelectedToolStripMenuItem1.Click
      ' Begin the print process to print the selected item.

        With Me
            If .syrupListBox.SelectedIndex = -1 Then
                ' Select (None) if nothing selected.
                .syrupListBox.SelectedIndex = 0
            End If
            If .coffeeComboBox.SelectedIndex <> -1 Then
                ' Items selected.
                .printSelectedPrintDocument.Print()
```

Done

```
                    Else
                        ' No item selected.
                        MessageBox.Show("Select a flavor from the coffee list", _
                            "Print Selection", MessageBoxButtons.OK, MessageBoxIcon.Exclamation)
                    End If
                End With
        End Sub

        Private Sub PreviewSelectedToolStripMenuItem1_Click(ByVal sender As Object, _
          ByVal e As System.EventArgs) _
          Handles PreviewSelectedToolStripMenuItem1.Click
         ' Begin the process for print preview of the selected item.

                With Me
                    If .syrupListBox.SelectedIndex = -1 Then
                        ' Select (None) if nothing selected.
                        .syrupListBox.SelectedIndex = 0
                    End If
                    If .coffeeComboBox.SelectedIndex <> -1 Then
                        ' Item selected.
                        .PrintPreviewDialog1.Document = printSelectedPrintDocument
                        .PrintPreviewDialog1.ShowDialog()
                    Else
                        ' No item selected.
                        MessageBox.Show("Select a flavor from the coffee list", "Print Selection", _
                            MessageBoxButtons.OK, MessageBoxIcon.Exclamation)
                    End If
                End With
        End Sub

        Private Sub printAllPrintDocument_PrintPage(ByVal sender As Object, _
          ByVal e As System.Drawing.Printing.PrintPageEventArgs) _
          Handles printAllPrintDocument.PrintPage

         ' Handle printing and print previews when printing all.

                Dim printFont As New Font("Arial", 12)
                Dim lineHeightSingle As Single = printFont.GetHeight + 2
                Dim horizontalPrintLocationSingle As Single = e.MarginBounds.Left
                Dim verticalPrintLocationSingle As Single = e.MarginBounds.Top
                Dim printLineString As String
                Dim listIndexInteger As Integer

                ' Print the heading.
                Using headingFont As New Font("Arial", 14, FontStyle.Bold)
                    e.Graphics.DrawString("Flavors", headingFont, _
                        Brushes.Black, horizontalPrintLocationSingle, _
                        verticalPrintLocationSingle)
                End Using

                ' Loop through the entire list.
                For listIndexInteger = 0 To Me.coffeeComboBox.Items.Count - 1
                    ' Increment the Y position for the next line.
                    verticalPrintLocationSingle += lineHeightSingle

                    ' Set up a line.
                    printLineString = Me.coffeeComboBox.Items(listIndexInteger).ToString()
```

```vb
            ' Send the line to the graphics page object.
            e.Graphics.DrawString(printLineString, printFont, _
              Brushes.Black, horizontalPrintLocationSingle, verticalPrintLocationSingle)

        Next listIndexInteger
End Sub

Private Sub printSelectedPrintDocument_PrintPage(ByVal sender As System.Object, _
    ByVal e As System.Drawing.Printing.PrintPageEventArgs) _
    Handles printSelectedPrintDocument.PrintPage
        ' Handle printing and print previews when printing selected items.

        Dim printFont As New Font("Arial", 12)
        Dim headingFont As New Font("Arial", 14, FontStyle.Bold)
        Dim lineHeightSingle As Single = printFont.GetHeight + 2
        Dim horizontalPrintLocationSingle As Single = e.MarginBounds.Left
        Dim verticalPrintLocationSingle As Single = e.MarginBounds.Top
        Dim printLineString As String

        ' Set up and display heading lines.
        printLineString = "Print Selected Item"
        e.Graphics.DrawString(printLineString, headingFont, _
          Brushes.Black, horizontalPrintLocationSingle, verticalPrintLocationSingle)
        printLineString = "by Programmer Name"
        verticalPrintLocationSingle += lineHeightSingle
        e.Graphics.DrawString(printLineString, headingFont, _
          Brushes.Black, horizontalPrintLocationSingle, verticalPrintLocationSingle)

        ' Leave a blank line between the heading and detail line.
        verticalPrintLocationSingle += lineHeightSingle * 2
        ' Set up the selected line.
        printLineString = "Coffee: " & Me.coffeeComboBox.Text & _
          "     Syrup: " & Me.syrupListBox.Text
        ' Send the line to the graphics page object.
        e.Graphics.DrawString(printLineString, printFont, _
          Brushes.Black, horizontalPrintLocationSingle, verticalPrintLocationSingle)
End Sub

Private Sub ClearCoffeeListToolStripMenuItem_Click(ByVal sender As Object, _
    ByVal e As System.EventArgs) Handles ClearCoffeeListToolStripMenuItem.Click
        ' Clear the coffee list.
        Dim responseDialogResult As DialogResult

        responseDialogResult = MessageBox.Show("Clear the coffee flavor list?", _
          "Clear coffee list", MessageBoxButtons.YesNo, MessageBoxIcon.Question)
        If responseDialogResult = DialogResult.Yes Then
            Me.coffeeComboBox.Items.Clear()
        End If
End Sub

Private Sub RemoveCoffeeFlavorToolStripMenuItem_Click(ByVal sender As Object, _
    ByVal e As System.EventArgs) Handles RemoveCoffeeFlavorToolStripMenuItem.Click
        ' Remove the selected coffee from list.

        With Me.coffeeComboBox
            If .SelectedIndex <> -1 Then
                .Items.RemoveAt(.SelectedIndex)
```

```
                Else
                    MessageBox.Show("First select the coffee to remove", _
                        "No selection made", MessageBoxButtons.OK, _
                        MessageBoxIcon.Exclamation)
                End If
        End With
    End Sub

    Private Sub DisplayCoffeeCountToolStripMenuItem_Click(ByVal sender As Object, _
        ByVal e As System.EventArgs) _
        Handles DisplayCoffeeCountToolStripMenuItem.Click
            ' Display a count of the coffee list.

            MessageBox.Show("The number of coffee types is " & _
                Me.coffeeComboBox.Items.Count, "R 'n R Coffee Type Count", _
                MessageBoxButtons.OK, MessageBoxIcon.Information)
    End Sub

    Private Sub AboutToolStripMenuItem_Click(ByVal sender As Object, _
        ByVal e As System.EventArgs) Handles AboutToolStripMenuItem.Click
            ' Display the About form.

            aboutForm.ShowDialog()
    End Sub
End Class
```

About Form

```
'Class:        AboutForm
'Programmer:   Bradley/Millspaugh
'Date:         June 2005
'Description:  Display information about the program
'              and the programmer.
'Folder:       Ch07HandsOn

Public Class aboutForm

    Private Sub okButton_Click(ByVal sender As System.Object, _
        By Val e As System.EventArgs) Handles okButton.Click
            ' Close the form.

            Me.Close()
    End Sub
End Class
```

Summary

1. List boxes and combo boxes hold lists of values. The three styles of combo boxes are simple combo boxes, drop-down combo boxes, and drop-down lists.

2. The size of a list box or combo box is determined at design time. If all of the items will not fit into the box, VB automatically adds scroll bars.

3. The values for the items in a list are stored in the Items property, which is a collection. The items can be entered in the Items property in the Properties window. At run time, items are added to lists using the `Items.Add` or `Items.Insert` method.

4. The SelectedIndex property can be used to select an item in the list or to determine which item is selected.

5. The Items.Count property holds the number of elements in the list.

6. The Items collection holds all elements of the list. The individual elements can be referenced by using an index.

7. The `Items.Remove` and `Items.RemoveAt` methods remove one element from a list.

8. The `Items.Clear` method may be used to clear all of the contents of a list box's Items collection at once.

9. Code can be written for several events of list boxes and combo boxes. Combo boxes have a TextChanged event; both combo boxes and list boxes have Enter and Leave events.

10. A loop allows a statement or series of statements to be repeated. `Do/Loops` continue to execute the statements in the loop until a condition is met. Each pass through a loop is called an iteration.

11. `Do/Loops` can have the condition test at the top or the bottom of the loop and can use a `While` or `Until` to test the condition.

12. A `Do/Loop` can be used to locate a selected item in a combo box.

13. A loop index controls `For/Next` loops; the index is initialized to an initial value. After each iteration, the loop index is incremented by the `Step` value (the increment), which defaults to 1. The loop is terminated when the loop index is greater than the ending value.

14. The PrintDocument and PrintPreviewDialog components can be used to send program output to the printer or the screen.

15. The `Print` method of the PrintDialog control begins a print operation. The control's PrintPage event fires once for each page to print. All printing logic belongs in the PrintPage event procedure. The PrintPage event continues to fire as long as the HasMorePages property of the PrintDocument component has a value of True.

16. The page to print or display is a graphics object. Use the `DrawString` method to send a string of text to the page, specifying X and Y coordinates for the string.

17. Aligning columns of numbers is difficult using proportional fonts. Numbers can be right aligned by formatting the number, measuring the length of the formatted string in pixels, and subtracting the length from the right end of the column for the X coordinate.

Key Terms

Review Questions

1. What is a list box? a combo box?
2. Name and describe the three styles of combo boxes.
3. How can you make scroll bars appear on a list box or combo box?
4. Explain the purpose of the SelectedIndex property and the Items.Count property.
5. When and how is information placed inside a list box or a combo box?
6. In what situation would a loop be used in a procedure?
7. Explain the difference between a pretest and a posttest in a Do/Loop.
8. Explain the differences between a Do/Loop and a For/Next loop.
9. What are the steps in processing a For/Next loop?
10. Discuss how and when the values of the loop index change throughout the processing of the loop.
11. What is the purpose of the PrintDocument component? the PrintPreview-Dialog component?
12. In what procedure do you write the logic for sending output to the printer?
13. What is the purpose of the X and Y coordinates on a print page?

Programming Exercises

7.1   Create a project for obtaining student information.
Startup form controls are as follows:

- Text boxes for entering the name and units completed.

- Radio buttons for Freshman, Sophomore, Junior, and Senior.

- Check box for Dean's List.

- A list box for the following majors: Accounting, Business, Computer Information Systems, and Marketing.

- A simple combo box for the name of the high school—initially loaded with Franklin, Highland, West Highland, and Midtown. If the user types in a new school name, it should be added to the list.

- Print button that prints the data from the form. Use the *Print Preview* dialog box.

- An OK button that clears the entries from the form and resets the focus. The button should be the Accept button for the form.

Menus

The *File* menu should have an item for *Print Schools* and *Exit*. The *Edit* menu should have an item for *Add High School*; the *Help* menu should have an item for the *About* box. Include appropriate access keys on your menu items.

Note: Print your name at the top of the printer output for the schools. Display the printer output in the *Print Preview* dialog box.

7.2   R 'n R—for Reading 'n Refreshment needs a project that contains a form for entering book information.

Form Controls

- Text boxes for author and title.

- Radio buttons for type: fiction or nonfiction.

- Drop-down list for Subject that will include Best-Seller, Fantasy, Religion, Romance, Humor, Science Fiction, Business, Philosophy, Education, Self-Help, and Mystery.

- List box for Shelf Number containing RC-1111, RC-1112, RC-1113, and RC-1114.

- *Print* button that prints the data from the form. Use the *Print Preview* dialog box.

- An OK button that clears the entries from the form and resets the focus. Make this the Accept button.

Menus

The *File* menu will have items for *Print Subjects* and *Exit*. The *Help* menu will have an item for *About* that displays the About box. Include appropriate access keys on your menu items.

Note: Print your name at the top of the printer output for the subjects. Display the printer output in the *Print Preview* dialog box.

7.3   Create a project to input chartering information about yachts and print a summary report showing the total revenue, number of charters, and average hours per charter.

Menus

The *File* menu will contain items for *Print Summary*, *Print Yacht Types*, and *Exit*. Place a separator before *Exit*. The *Edit* menu should have items for *Clear for Next Charter*, *Add Yacht Type*, *Remove Yacht Type*, and *Display Count of Yacht Types*. Include a separator after the *Clear* item. The *Help* menu will contain an *About* item that displays an About form. Include appropriate access keys on your menu items.

The Form

- The form should contain text boxes for responsible party, hours chartered, and the calculated price of the charter.

- A drop-down combo box will contain the type of yacht: Ranger, Wavelength, Catalina, Coronado, Hobie, C & C, Hans Christian, and Excalibur. Any items that are added to the text box during processing must be added to the list.

- A drop-down list will contain the sizes: 22, 24, 30, 32, 36, 38, 45. (No new sizes can be entered at run time.)

- An OK button will calculate and display the price and add to the totals. The calculations will require price per hour. Use the following chart:

Size	Hourly Rate
22	95.00
24	137.00
30	160.00
32	192.00
36	250.00
38	400.00
45	550.00

- A *Clear* button will clear the contents of the screen controls. The functions of the *Clear* button are the same as for the *Clear for Next Charter* menu item.

- Make the OK button the Accept button and the *Clear* button the form's Cancel button.

Summary Report

The summary report will print the summary information and send the report to a *Print Preview* dialog box. The summary information will include Number of Charters, Total Revenue, and Average Hours Chartered. Include your name on the output and identifying labels for the summary information.

Yacht Types Report
Display the yacht types in the combo box in the *Print Preview* dialog box.
Include your name and a title at the top of the report.

7.4   Create a project that contains a list box with the names of all U.S. states
and territories. When the user types the first letters of the state into a text
box, set the SelectedIndex property of the list box to display the appropriate name. Include an *Exit* menu item.

Alabama	Kentucky	Oklahoma
Alaska	Louisiana	Oregon
American Samoa	Maine	Pennsylvania
Arizona	Maryland	Puerto Rico
Arkansas	Massachusetts	Rhode Island
California	Michigan	South Carolina
Colorado	Minnesota	South Dakota
Connecticut	Mississippi	Tennessee
Delaware	Missouri	Texas
District of Columbia	Montana	Trust Territories
Florida	Nebraska	Utah
Georgia	Nevada	Vermont
Guam	New Hampshire	Virgin Islands
Hawaii	New Jersey	Virginia
Idaho	New Mexico	Washington
Illinois	New York	West Virginia
Indiana	North Carolina	Wisconsin
Iowa	North Dakota	Wyoming
Kansas	Ohio	

7.5   Maintain a list of bagel types for Bradley's Bagels. Use a drop-down
combo box to hold the bagel types and use buttons or menu choices to
Add Bagel Type, *Remove Bagel Type*, *Clear Bagel List*, *Print Bagel List*, *Display Bagel Type Count*, and *Exit*. Keep the list sorted in alphabetic order.
Include appropriate access keys on your menu items.

Do not allow a blank type to be added to the list. Display an error message if the user selects *Remove* without first selecting a bagel type.

Before clearing the list, display a message box to confirm the operation.
Here are some suggested bagel types. You can make up your own list.

Plain	Poppy seed
Egg	Sesame seed
Rye	Banana nut
Salt	Blueberry

7.6   Modify Programming Exercise 7.5 to not allow duplicate bagel types to be added to the list.

Case Studies

VB Mail Order

Create a project for VB Mail Order to maintain a list of catalogs. Use a drop-down combo box for the catalog names and allow the user to enter new catalog names, delete catalog names, display a count of the number of catalogs, clear the catalog list, or print the catalog list.

Do not allow a blank catalog name to be added to the list. Display an error message if the user selects *Remove* without first selecting a catalog name. Before clearing the list, display a message box to confirm the operation.

To begin, the catalog list should hold these catalog names: Odds and Ends, Solutions, Camping Needs, ToolTime, Spiegel, The Outlet, and The Large Size.

Display the printed output in the *Print Preview* dialog box. Include your name and a heading at the top of the report.

VB Auto Center

Create an application for the car wash located at VB Auto Center.

The form will contain three list box or combo box controls that do not permit the user to type in items at run time. The first list will contain the names of the packages available for detailing a vehicle: Standard, Deluxe, Executive, or Luxury.

The contents of the other two lists will vary depending upon the package selected. Display one list for the interior work and one list for the exterior work. Store the descriptions of the items in string constants. You must clear the lists for the interior and exterior for each order and add new items to the lists each time the user makes a selection from the package list.

Use a drop-down list to allow the user to select the fragrance. The choices are Hawaiian Mist, Baby Powder, Pine, Country Floral, Pina Colada, and Vanilla.

Include menu items for *Print Order*, *Clear*, and *Exit* with appropriate access keys. The print option should send its output to the *Print Preview* window. Include your name and a heading at the top of the report.

The Order printout will contain the package name (Standard, Deluxe, Executive, or Luxury), the interior and exterior items included, and the fragrance selected. Use a For/Next loop when printing the interior and exterior lists.

	Item Description	S	D	E	L
Exterior	Hand Wash	✓	✓	✓	✓
	Hand Wax		✓	✓	✓
	Check Engine Fluids			✓	✓
	Detail Engine Compartment				✓
	Detail Under Carriage				✓
Interior	Fragrance	✓	✓	✓	✓
	Shampoo Carpets		✓	✓	✓
	Shampoo Upholstery				✓
	Interior Protection Coat (dashboard and console)			✓	
	Scotchgard™				✓

Note: S—Standard; D—Deluxe; E—Executive; L—Luxury

Video Bonanza

Maintain a list of movie categories. Use a drop-down combo box to hold the movie types, keeping the list in alphabetic order. Use buttons or menu choices to *Add a Category*, *Remove a Category*, *Clear All Categories*, *Print the Category List*, *Display the Movie Category Count*, and *Exit*. Include appropriate access keys on your form and/or menu items.

Do not allow a blank type to be added to the list. Display an error message if the user selects *Remove* without first selecting a movie category. Before clearing the list, display a message box to confirm the operation.

The starting categories are

- Comedy
- Drama
- Action
- Sci-Fi
- Horror

Display the printed output in the *Print Preview* dialog box. Include your name and a heading at the top of the report.

Very Very Boards

Write a project to maintain a list of shirt styles. Keep the styles in a drop-down combo box, with styles such as crew, turtleneck, or crop top.

Add a *Style* menu with options to *Add Style*, *Remove Style*, *Clear Style List*, and *Count Styles*. Add a

Print Style List option to the *File* menu and include access keys and keyboard shortcuts for the menu items.

Display the printed output in the *Print Preview* dialog box. Include your name and a heading at the top of the report.

Arrays

Try
Convert quantity to numeric variables.

Calculate values for sale.
extendedPriceDecimal = quantityInteger
discountDecimal = extendedPriceDecimal
discountedPriceDecimal = extendedPrice
' Calculate summary values.
quantitySumInteger += quantityInteger
discountSumDecimal += discountDecimal
discountedPriceSumDecimal += discounte
saleCountInteger += 1

at the completion of this chapter, you will be able to . . .

1. Establish an array and refer to individual elements in the array with subscripts.

2. Use the For Each/Next to traverse the elements of an array.

3. Create a structure for multiple fields of related data.

4. Accumulate totals using arrays.

5. Distinguish between direct access and indirect access of a table.

6. Write a table lookup for matching an array element.

7. Combine the advantages of list box controls with arrays.

8. Store and look up data in multidimensional arrays.

Single-Dimension Arrays

An **array** is a list or series of values, similar to a list box or a combo box. You can think of an array as a list box without the box—without the visual representation. Any time you need to keep a series of variables for later processing, such as reordering, calculating, or printing, you need to set up an array.

Consider an example that has a form for entering product information one product at a time. After the user has entered many products, you will need to calculate some statistics, perhaps use the information in different ways, or print it. Of course, each time the user enters the data for the next product, the previous contents of the text boxes are replaced. You could assign the previous values to variables, but they also would be replaced for each new product. Another approach might be to create multiple variables, such as product1String, product2String, product3String, and so on. This approach might be reasonable for a few entries, but what happens when you need to store 50 or 500 products?

When you need to store multiple values, use an array. An array is a series of individual variables, all referenced by the same name. Sometimes arrays are referred to as **tables** or **subscripted variables**. For an array for storing names, you may have nameString(0), nameString(1), nameString(2), and so on.

Each individual variable is called an *element* of the array. The individual elements are treated the same as any other variable and may be used in any statement, such as an assignment statement. The **subscript** (which also may be called an *index*) inside the parentheses is the position of the element within the array. Figure 8.1 illustrates an array of 10 elements with subscripts from 0 to 9.

Figure 8.1

An array of string variables with 10 elements. Subscripts are 0 through 9.

nameString array

(0)	Janet Baker
(1)	George Lee
(2)	Sue Li
(3)	Samuel Hoosier
(4)	Sandra Weeks
(5)	William Macy
(6)	Andy Harrison
(7)	Ken Ford
(8)	Denny Franks
(9)	Shawn James

Subscripts

The real advantage of using an array is not realized until you use variables for subscripts in place of the constants.

```
nameString(indexInteger) = ""
Debug.WriteLine(nameString(indexInteger))
```

Subscripts may be constants, variables, or numeric expressions. Although the subscripts must be integers, Visual Basic rounds any noninteger subscript.

A question has probably occurred to you by now: How many elements are there in the nameString array? The answer is that you must declare the array name and the number of elements.

The Declaration Statements for Arrays—General Forms

You can declare arrays by using the `Dim`, `Public`, `Private`, or `Friend` keyword. Just as with any other variable, the location of the declaration determines the scope and lifetime of the array variables.

General Forms

```
Private ArrayName(UpperSubscript) As Datatype
Dim ArrayName() As Datatype  = {InitialValueList}
Dim ArrayName As Datatype() = {InitialValueList}
```

The first declaration above creates storage for the specified number of elements and initializes each numeric variable to 0. In the case of string arrays, each element is set to an empty string (zero characters).

In the second and third forms of the declaration statements, you specify initial values for the array elements, which determines the number of elements. You cannot declare the upper subscript *and* initial values.

The Declaration Statements for Arrays—Examples

Examples

```
Dim nameString(25) As String
Dim balanceDecimal(10) As Decimal
Dim productString(99) As String
Dim indexInteger() As Integer = {1, 5, 12, 18, 20}
Dim indexInteger As Integer() = {1, 5, 12, 18, 20}
Dim departmentsString() As String = {"Accounting", "Marketing", "Human Relations"}
Private categoryString(10) As String
Friend idNumbersString(5) As String
```

Array subscripts are zero based, so the first element is always element zero. The upper subscript is the highest subscript—one less than the number of elements. For example, the statement

```
Dim categoryString(10) As String
```

creates an array of 11 elements with subscripts 0 through 10.

Notice that you declare a data type for the array. All of the array elements must be the same data type. If you omit the data type (by having Option Strict off), just as with single variables, the type defaults to Object.

Valid Subscripts

A subscript must reference a valid element of the array. If a list contains 10 names, it wouldn't make sense to ask: What is the 15th name on the list? *or* What is the 2½th name on the list? Visual Basic rounds fractional subscripts and throws an exception for a subscript that is out of range.

Note: Arrays are based on System.Array, which is a collection.

Feedback 8.1

```
Dim nameString(20) As String
Const INDEX_Integer As Integer = 10
```

After execution of the preceding statements, which of the following are valid subscripts?

1. nameString(20)
2. nameString(INDEX_Integer)
3. nameString(INDEX_Integer * 2)
4. nameString(INDEX_Integer * 3)
5. nameString(0)
6. nameString(INDEX_Integer – 20)
7. nameString(INDEX_Integer / 3)
8. nameString(INDEX_Integer / 5 – 2)

For Each/Next Statements

When you use an array, you need a way to reference each element in the array. For/Next loops, which you learned to use in Chapter 7, work well to traverse the elements in an array. Another handy loop construct is the For Each and Next. The significant advantages of using the **For Each** and **Next** are that you don't have to manipulate the subscripts of the array or know how many elements there are in the array.

The For Each and Next Statements—General Form

```
General Form
For Each ElementName [As Datatype] In ArrayName
      ' Statement(s) in loop.
Next [ElementName]
```

Visual Basic automatically references each element of the array, assigns its value to ElementName, and makes one pass through the loop. If the array has 12 elements, for example, the loop will execute 12 times. The variable used for ElementName must be the same data type as the array elements or an Object data type. It's best to declare the variable for *ElementName* as part of the For Each statement, which creates a block-level variable.

In the following example, assume that the array nameString has already been dimensioned and holds data and the variable oneNameString will hold the individual values of nameString, one element at a time.

The For Each and Next Statements—Example

```
Example
For Each oneNameString As String In nameString
      ' Write one element of the array.
      Debug.WriteLine(oneNameString)
Next oneNameString
```

The For Each loop will execute if the array has at least one element. All the statements within the loop are executed for the first element. If the array has more elements, the loop continues to execute until all the elements are processed. When the loop finishes, execution of code continues with the line following the `Next` statement.

Note: You may use an `Exit For` statement within the loop to exit early.

Structures

You have been using the VB data types, such as Integer, String, and Decimal, since Chapter 3. Now you will learn to combine multiple fields of related data to create a new **structure**. In many ways, a structure is similar to defining a new data type. For example, an Employee structure may contain last name, first name, Social Security number, street, city, state, ZIP code, date of hire, and pay code. A Product structure might contain a description, product number, quantity, and price. You can combine the fields into a structure using the `Structure` and `End Structure` statements.

The Structure and End Structure Statements—General Form

```
[Public | Private | Friend] Structure NameOfStructure
    Dim FirstField As DataType
    Dim SecondField As DataType
    ...
End Structure
```

The `Structure` declaration cannot go inside a procedure. You generally place the `Structure` statement at the top of a file with the module-level declarations. You also can place a `Structure` in a separate file.

The Structure and End Structure Statements—Examples

```
Structure Employee
    Dim lastNameString As String
    Dim firstNameString As String
    Dim socialSecurityNumberString As String
    Dim streetString As String
    Dim cityString As String
    Dim stateString As String
    Dim zipCodeString As String
    Dim hireDate As Date
    Dim payCodeInteger As Integer
End Structure

Friend Structure Product
    Dim descriptionString As String
    Dim productNumberString As String
    Dim quantityInteger As Integer
    Dim priceDecimal As Decimal
End Structure

Structure SalesDetail
    Dim saleDecimal() As Decimal
End Structure
```

By default, a structure is public. You can declare the structure to be `Friend` or `Private` if you wish.

If you include an array inside a structure, you cannot specify the number of elements. You must use a `ReDim` statement in your code to declare the number of elements.

Declaring Variables Based on a Structure

Once you have created a structure, you can declare variables of the structure, just as if it were another data type.

```
Dim officeEmployee As Employee
Dim warehouseEmployee As Employee
Dim widgetProduct As Product
Dim inventoryProduct(100) As Product
Dim houseWaresSalesDetail As SalesDetail
Dim homeFurnishingsSalesDetail As SalesDetail
```

Accessing the Elements in a Structure Variable

Each field of data in a variable declared as a structure is referred to as an *element* of the structure. To access elements, use the dot notation similar to that used for objects: Specify *Variable.Element*.

```
officeEmployee.lastNameString
officeEmployee.hireDate
warehouseEmployee.lastNameString
widgetProduct.descriptionString
widgetProduct.quantityInteger
widgetProduct.priceDecimal
inventoryProduct(indexInteger).descriptionString
inventoryProduct(indexInteger).quantityInteger
inventoryProduct(indexInteger).priceDecimal
```

Notice the use of indexes in the preceding examples. Each example was taken from the preceding `Structure` and `Dim` statements. A variable that is not an array, such as widgetProduct, does not need an index. However, for inventoryProduct, which was dimensioned as an array of 101 elements (0 through 100), you must specify not only the inventoryProduct item but also the element within the structure.

Including an Array in a Structure

The SalesDetail structure is a little more complicated than the other structures described above. In this structure, we want to include an array of seven variables, one for each day of the week. However, VB does not allow you to declare the number of elements in the `Structure` declaration. You must use the `ReDim` statement inside a procedure to give the array a size.

```
' Module-level declarations.
Structure SalesDetail
    Dim saleDecimal() As Decimal
End Structure

Private houseWaresSalesDetail As SalesDetail
```

```
' Inside a procedure:
'     Establish the number of elements in the array.
ReDim houseWaresSalesDetail.saleDecimal(6)

' In processing.
houseWaresSalesDetail.saleDecimal(dayIndexInteger) = currentDaySalesDecimal
```

Because the saleDecimal element of the SalesDetail structure is declared as an array, you must use a subscript to refer to each individual element within the structure.

Feedback 8.2

1. Write a `Structure` statement to hold student data containing last name, first name, student number, number of units completed, and GPA. The new structure should be called "Student".
2. Declare an array of 100 students that will use the structure for student information.
3. Write the `Structure` statement for a structure called "Project" containing a project name, form name, and folder name.
4. Declare a variable called "myProject" based on the Project structure.
5. Declare an array of 100 elements called "ourProjects", based on the Project structure.

Using Array Elements for Accumulators

Array elements are regular variables and perform in the same ways as all variables used so far. You may use the subscripted variables in any way you choose, such as for counters or total accumulators.

To demonstrate the use of array elements as total accumulators, eight totals will be accumulated. For this example, eight scout troops are selling raffle tickets. A separate total must be accumulated for each of the eight groups. Each time a sale is made, the number of tickets must be added to the correct total. The statement

```
Dim totalInteger(7) As Integer
```

declares the eight accumulators with subscripts 0 to 7.

Adding to the Correct Total

Assume that your user inputs a group number into groupTextBox.Text and the number of tickets sold into saleTextBox.Text. The sales may be input in any order with multiple sales for each group. Your problem is to add each ticket sale to the correct total, numbered 0 to 7, for groups numbered 1 to 8.

You can subtract one from the group number to use as the subscript to add to the correct total. For example, if the first sale of 10 tickets is for group 4, the 10 must be added to totalInteger(3). (Figure 8.2 shows the form and the variables used for this example.)

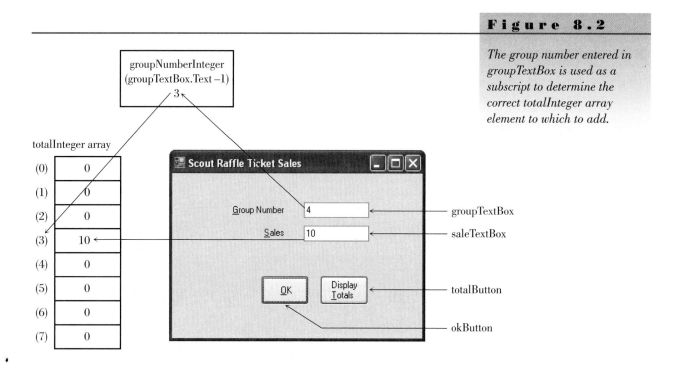

The group number entered in groupTextBox is used as a subscript to determine the correct totalInteger array element to which to add.

```
With Me
    ' Convert input group number to subscript.
    groupNumberInteger = Integer.Parse(.groupTextBox.Text) — 1
    ' Add sale to the correct total.
    saleInteger = Integer.Parse(.saleTextBox.Text)
    totalInteger(groupNumberInteger) += saleInteger
End With
```

Of course, the user might enter an incorrect group number. Because you don't want the program to cancel with an exception, you must validate the group number.

```
Try
    ' Convert input group number to a subscript.
    With Me
        groupNumberInteger = Integer.Parse(.groupTextBox.Text) — 1
        If groupNumberInteger >= 0 And groupNumberInteger <= 7 Then
            ' Add sale to correct total.
            saleInteger = Integer.Parse(.saleTextBox.Text)
            totalInteger(groupNumberInteger) += saleInteger
        Else
            MessageBox.Show("Enter a valid group number (1-8)", "Data Entry Error", _
                MessageBoxButtons.OK, MessageBoxIcon.Exclamation)
        End If
    End With
Catch
    MessageBox.Show("Numeric entries required for both group number and sales", _
        "Data Entry Error", MessageBoxButtons.OK, MessageBoxIcon.Exclamation)
End Try
```

Using the group number as an index to the array is a technique called ***direct reference***. The groups are assigned numbers from 1 to 8. You can subtract 1 from the group number to create the subscripts, which are 0 to 7.

Debugging Array Programs

You can view the contents of array elements when your program is in debugging time. Set a breakpoint and view the Autos window (Figure 8.3). You will need to click on the plus sign to the left of the array name to view the individual array elements.

Figure 8.3

View the contents of an array in the Autos window at debugging time.

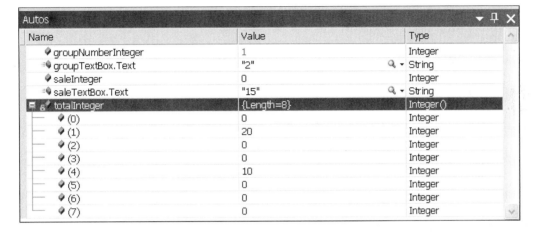

Table Lookup

Things don't always work out so neatly as having sequential group numbers that can be used to access the table directly. Sometimes you will have to do a little work to find (look up) the correct value and reference the array elements indirectly. Reconsider the eight scout troops and their ticket sales. Now the groups are not numbered 1 to 8, but 101, 103, 110, 115, 121, 123, 130, and 145. The group number and the number of tickets sold are still input, and the number of tickets must be added to the correct total. But now you must do one more step: determine to which array element to add the ticket sales, using a **table lookup**.

The first step in the project is to establish a structure with the group numbers and totals and then dimension an array of the structure. Before any processing is done, you must load the group numbers into the table; the best place to do this is in the Form_Load event procedure, which is executed once as the form is loaded into memory.

Place the following statements at the top of a form class:

```
' Declare structure and module-level variables.
Structure Group
    Dim groupNumberString As String
    Dim totalInteger As Integer
End Structure

' Hold group number and total for 8 groups.
Private arrayGroup(7) As Group
```

Then initialize the values of the array elements by placing these statements into the Form_Load event procedure:

```
Private Sub salesForm_Load(ByVal sender As System.Object, _
  ByVal e As System.EventArgs) Handles MyBase.Load
      ' Initialize group numbers.

      arrayGroup(0).groupNumberString = "101"
      arrayGroup(1).groupNumberString = "103"
      arrayGroup(2).groupNumberString = "110"
      arrayGroup(3).groupNumberString = "115"
      arrayGroup(4).groupNumberString = "121"
      arrayGroup(5).groupNumberString = "123"
      arrayGroup(6).groupNumberString = "130"
      arrayGroup(7).groupNumberString = "145"
End Sub
```

During program execution, the user still enters the group number and the number of tickets sold into text boxes.

The technique used to find the subscript is called a *table lookup*. In this example, the object is to find the element number (0 to 7) of the group number and add to the corresponding group total. If the user enters the third group number ("110"), the subscript is 2 and the sale is added to the total for subscript 2. If the seventh group number ("130") is entered, the sale is added to the total with the subscript 6, and so on. Hence, you need a way, given the group number in groupTextBox.Text, to find the corresponding subscript of the arrayGroup array.

When Visual Basic executes the statement

```
arrayGroup(indexInteger).totalInteger += saleInteger
```

the value of indexInteger must be a number in the range 0 to 7. The task for the lookup operation is to find the number to place in indexInteger, based on the value of groupTextBox.Text. Figure 8.4 shows the variables used for the lookup. Figure 8.5 shows the UML action diagram of the lookup logic.

Coding a Table Lookup

For a table lookup, you will find that a Do/Loop works better than For Each. As you compare to each element in the array and eventually find a match, you need to know the subscript of the matching element.

Figure 8.4

A lookup operation: The group number is looked up in the arrayGroup array; the correct subscript is found and used to add the sale to the correct totalInteger.

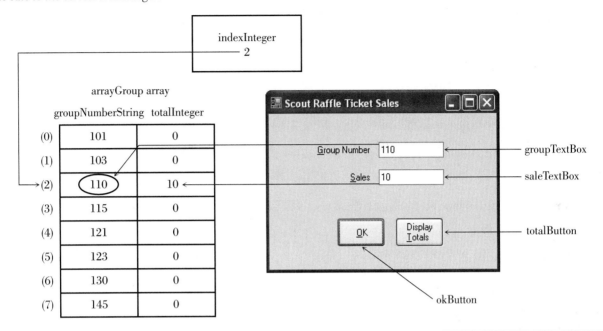

Figure 8.5

A UML action diagram of the logic of a lookup operation.

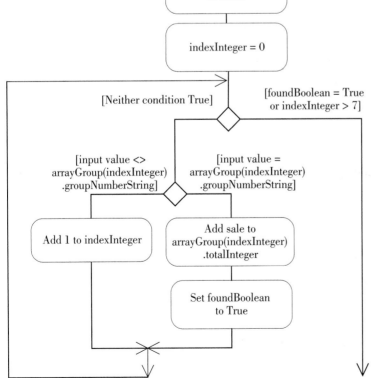

```
' Accumulate the sales by group number.
Dim saleInteger As Integer
Dim indexInteger As Integer = 0
Dim foundBoolean As Boolean = False

' Look up input group number to find subscript.
Do Until foundBoolean Or indexInteger > 7
    With Me
        If .groupTextBox.Text = arrayGroup(indexInteger).groupNumberString Then
            ' Add sale to correct total.
            saleInteger = Integer.Parse(.saleTextBox.Text)
            arrayGroup(indexInteger).totalInteger += saleInteger
            foundBoolean = True
        Else
            indexInteger += 1
        End If
    End With
Loop
```

Once again, you should do some form of validation. If the user enters an invalid group number, you should display a message box. You can check the value of the Boolean variable foundBoolean after completion of the loop to determine whether the loop terminated because of a match or without a match.

```
If Not foundBoolean Then
    MessageBox.Show("Enter a valid group number", "Data Entry Error", _
        MessageBoxButtons.OK, MessageBoxIcon.Exclamation)
    With Me.groupTextBox
        .Focus()
        .SelectAll()
    End With
End If
```

The table-lookup technique will work for any table, numeric or string. It isn't necessary to arrange the fields being searched in any particular sequence. The comparison is made to one item in the list, then the next, and the next—until a match is found. In fact, you can save processing time in a large table by arranging the elements with the most-often-used entries at the top so that fewer comparisons must be made.

Using List Boxes with Arrays

In the previous example of a lookup, the user had to type some information into a text box, which was used to look up the information in an array. A more efficient and friendly solution might be to substitute a list box for the text box. You can store the eight group numbers in a list box and allow the user to select from the list (Figure 8.6).

The initial Items collection can contain the values 101, 103, 110, 115, 121, 123, 130, and 145.

You have probably already realized that you can use the SelectedIndex property to determine the array subscript. Remember that the SelectedIndex property holds the position or index of the selected item from the list.

In place of the lookup operation, we can use this code:

```
' Declare module-level variables.
Private totalInteger(7) As Integer  ' Hold totals for 8 groups.

Private Sub okButton_Click(ByVal sender As System.Object, _
  ByVal e As System.EventArgs) Handles okButton.Click
  ' Accumulate the sales by group number.
      Dim saleInteger As Integer
      Dim indexInteger As Integer
      Try
          With Me
              indexInteger = .groupListBox.SelectedIndex
              If indexInteger <> -1 Then       ' Selection made.
                  ' Add to correct total.
                  saleInteger = Integer.Parse(.saleTextBox.Text)
                  totalInteger(indexInteger) += saleInteger

                  ' Clear the screen fields.
                  .groupListBox.SelectedIndex = -1
                  .saleTextBox.Text = ""
              Else
                  MessageBox.Show("Select a group number from the list.", _
                      "Data Entry Error", MessageBoxButtons.OK, _
                      MessageBoxIcon.Exclamation)
              End If
          End With
      Catch
          MessageBox.Show("Sales must be numeric.")
      End Try
End Sub
```

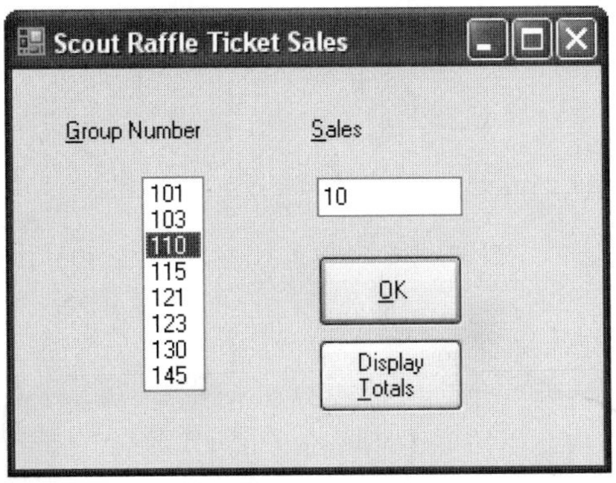

Figure 8.6

Allow the user to select from a list and you can use the list's SelectedIndex property as the subscript of the total array.

Multidimensional Arrays

You generally need to use two subscripts to identify tabular data, where data are arranged in **rows** and **columns**.

Many applications of two-dimensional tables quickly come to mind: insurance rate tables, tax tables, addition and multiplication tables, postage rates, foods and their nutritive value, population by region, rainfall by state.

To define a two-dimensional array or table, the `Dim` statement specifies the number of rows and columns in the array. The row is horizontal and the column is vertical. The following table has three rows and four columns:

The Declaration Statements for Two-Dimensional Arrays—General Forms

General Forms

```
Dim ArrayName(HighestRowSubscript, HighestColumnSubscript) As Datatype
Dim ArrayName( , ) As Datatype = {ListOfValues}
```

The Declaration Statements for Two-Dimensional Arrays—Examples

Examples

```
Dim nameString(2, 3) As String
Dim nameString( , ) As String = { {"James", "Mary", "Sammie", "Sean"}, _
    {"Tom", "Lee", "Leon", "Larry"}, {"Maria", "Margaret", "Jill", "John"} }
```

Both of these two statements establish an array of 12 elements, with three rows and four columns. Just as with single-dimension arrays, you cannot specify the number of elements within parentheses *and* specify initial values.

Notice the comma inside the parentheses in the second example: You must use a comma to specify that there are two dimensions to the array. Specify the initial values with the first dimension (the row) first and the second dimension (the column) second. The compiler determines the number of elements from the initial values that you supply. The second example above fills the table in this sequence:

(0, 0) James	(0, 1) Mary	(0, 2) Sammie	(0, 3) Sean
(1, 0) Tom	(1, 1) Lee	(1, 2) Leon	(1, 3) Larry
(2, 0) Maria	(2, 1) Margaret	(2, 2) Jill	(2, 3) John

You must always use two subscripts when referring to individual elements of the table. Specify the row with the first subscript and the column with the second subscript.

The elements of the array may be used in the same ways as any other variable—in accumulators, counts, and reference fields for lookup; in statements like assignment and printing; and as conditions. Some valid references to the table include

```
nameString(1, 2) = "New Name"
nameString(rowInteger, columnInteger) = "New Name"
Me.displayLabel.Text = nameString(1, 2)
DrawString(nameString(rowInteger, columnInteger), printFont, Brushes.Black, 100.0, 100.0)
```

Invalid references for the nameString table would include any value greater than 2 for the first subscript, greater than 3 for the second subscript, or less than 0 for either subscript.

Initializing Two-Dimensional Arrays

Numeric array elements are initially set to 0 and string elements are set to empty strings. And, of course, you can assign initial values when you declare the array. But many situations require that you reinitialize arrays to 0 or some other value. You can use nested For/Next loops to set each array element to an initial value.

Nested For/Next Example

The assignment statement in the inner loop will be executed 12 times, once for each element of nameString.

```
For rowInteger As Integer = 0 To 2
    For columnInteger As Integer = 0 To 3
        ' Initialize each element.
        nameString(rowInteger, columnInteger) = ""
    Next columnInteger
Next rowInteger
```

Printing a Two-Dimensional Table

When you want to print the contents of a two-dimensional table, you can use a For Each/Next loop. This example prints one array element per line.

```
' Print one name per line.
For Each elementString As String In nameString
    ' Set up a line.
    e.Graphics.DrawString(elementString, printFont, _
      Brushes.Black, horizontalPrintLocationSingle, verticalPrintLocationSingle)

    ' Increment the Y position for the next line.
    verticalPrintLocationSingle += lineHeightSingle
Next elementString
```

If you wish to print an entire row in one line, use a For/Next loop and set up the X and Y coordinates to print multiple elements per line.

```
' Print one line per row .
For rowInteger As Integer = 0 To 2
    For columnInteger As Integer = 0 To 3
        e.Graphics.DrawString(nameString(rowInteger, columnInteger), printFont, _
          Brushes.Black, horizontalPrintLocationSingle, verticalPrintLocationSingle)
        ' Move across the line.
        horizontalPrintLocationSingle += 200
    Next columnInteger

    ' Start next line; Reset to left margin.
    horizontalPrintLocationSingle = e.MarginBounds.Left
    ' Move down to next line.
    verticalPrintLocationSingle += lineHeightSingle
Next rowInteger
```

Summing a Two-Dimensional Table

You can find the sum of a table in various ways. You may sum either the columns or the rows of the table; or, as in a cross-foot, you can sum the figures in both directions and double-check the totals.

To sum the array in both directions, each column needs one total variable and each row needs one total variable. Two one-dimensional arrays will work well for the totals. Figure 8.7 illustrates the variables used in this example.

```
' Crossfoot total a 2D table.

' Give the 6 x 4 array values for testing.
'   (Normally you would total values that are accumulated in a program.)
Dim amountDecimal(,) As Decimal = _
    {{2.5D, 3D, 1.2D, 2.2D, 4.5D, 3.5D}, _
    {2D, 2D, 2D, 2D, 2D, 2D}, _
    {3D, 3.1D, 3.2D, 3.3D, 3.4D, 3.5D}, _
    {4.4D, 4.5D, 4.6D, 4.7D, 4.8D, 4.9D}}
Dim amountDecimal(3, 5) As Decimal
Dim rowTotalDecimal(3) As Decimal
Dim columnTotalDecimal(5) As Decimal

For rowInteger As Integer = 0 To 3
    For columnInteger As Integer = 0 To 5
        rowTotalDecimal(rowInteger) += amountDecimal(rowInteger, columnInteger)
        columnTotalDecimal(columnInteger) += amountDecimal(rowInteger, columnInteger)
    Next columnInteger
Next rowInteger
```

Figure 8.7

Two one-dimensional arrays hold totals for the two-dimensional array.

Feedback 8.3

Write VB statements to do the following:

1. Dimension a table called temperatureDecimal with five columns and three rows.

2. Set each element in the first row to 0.
3. Set each element in the second row to 75.
4. For each column of the table, add together the elements in the first and second rows, placing the sum in the third row.
5. Print the entire table. (Write only the logic for printing inside the Print-Document_PrintPage event procedure.)

Lookup Operation for Two-Dimensional Tables

When you look up items in a two-dimensional table, you can use the same techniques discussed with single-dimensional arrays: direct reference and table lookup. The limitations are the same.

1. To use a direct reference, row and column subscripts must be readily available. For example, you can tally the hours used for each of five machines (identified by machine numbers 1 to 5) and each of four departments (identified by department numbers 1 to 4).

```
With Me
    rowInteger = Integer.Parse(.machineTextBox.Text) - 1
    columnInteger = Integer.Parse(.departmentTextBox.Text) - 1
    hoursDecimal = Decimal.Parse(.hoursTextBox.Text)
    machineTotalDecimal(rowInteger, columnInteger) += hoursDecimal
End With
```

2. A table lookup is the most common lookup technique.

Many two-dimensional tables used for lookup require additional one-dimensional arrays or lists to aid in the lookup process. For an example, use a shipping rate table (Figure 8.8) to look up the rate to ship a package. The shipping rate depends on the weight of the package and the zone to which it is being shipped. You could design the project with the weight and zones in list boxes, or you could use a text box and let the user input the data.

F i g u r e   8 . 8

This shipping rate table in a two-dimensional array can be used to look up the correct shipping charge.

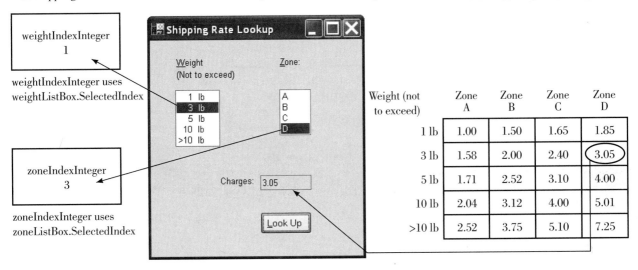

Weight (not to exceed)	Zone A	Zone B	Zone C	Zone D
1 lb	1.00	1.50	1.65	1.85
3 lb	1.58	2.00	2.40	3.05
5 lb	1.71	2.52	3.10	4.00
10 lb	2.04	3.12	4.00	5.01
>10 lb	2.52	3.75	5.10	7.25

Using List Boxes

In the example illustrated in Figure 8.8, a list box holds the weight limits, and another list holds the zones. The values for the two lists are set in the Items properties at design time. The five-by-four rate table is two-dimensional, and the values are set when the table is declared.

```vb
' Look up values from list boxes.

' Declare module-level variables.
Dim rateDecimal( , ) As Decimal = _
    {{1D, 1.5D, 1.65D, 1.85D}, _
     {1.58D, 2D, 2.4D, 3.05D}, _
     {1.71D, 2.52D, 3.1D, 4D}, _
     {2.04D, 3.12D, 4D, 5.01D}, _
     {2.52D, 3.75D, 5.1D, 7.25D}}

Private Sub lookupButton_Click(ByVal sender As System.Object, _
    ByVal e As System.EventArgs) Handles lookupButton.Click
        ' Look up the shipping rate.

    Dim weightIndexInteger As Integer
    Dim zoneIndexInteger As Integer

    With Me
        weightIndexInteger = .weightListBox.SelectedIndex
        zoneIndexInteger = .zoneListBox.SelectedIndex
        If weightIndexInteger <> -1 And zoneIndexInteger <> -1 Then
            .chargesTextBox.Text _
                = rateDecimal(weightIndexInteger, zoneIndexInteger).ToString("N")
        Else
            MessageBox.Show("Select the weight and zone.", "Information Missing", _
                MessageBoxButtons.OK, MessageBoxIcon.Exclamation)
        End If
    End With
End Sub
```

Using Text Boxes

If you are using text boxes rather than list boxes for data entry, the input requires more validation. You must look up both the weight and zone entries before you can determine the correct rate. The valid zones and weight ranges will be stored in two separate one-dimensional arrays. The first step in the project is to establish and fill the arrays. The five-by-four rate table is two-dimensional, and the values should be preloaded, as in the previous example.

Note that the Try/Catch blocks were omitted to clarify the logic. You should always use error trapping when converting input to numeric values.

```vb
' Look up values from text boxes.

' Declare module-level variables.
Dim rateDecimal(,) As Decimal = _
    {{1D, 1.5D, 1.65D, 1.85D}, _
     {1.58D, 2D, 2.4D, 3.05D}, _
     {1.71D, 2.52D, 3.1D, 4D}, _
     {2.04D, 3.12D, 4D, 5.01D}, _
     {2.52D, 3.75D, 5.1D, 7.25D}}
```

```
Dim weightInteger() As Integer = {1, 3, 5, 10}
Dim zoneString() As String = {"A", "B", "C", "D"}

Private Sub lookupButton_Click(ByVal sender As System.Object, _
  ByVal e As System.EventArgs) Handles lookupButton.Click
     ' Look up the shipping rate.

     Dim weightIndexInteger As Integer
     Dim zoneIndexInteger As Integer
     Dim indexInteger As Integer = 0
     Dim weightInputInteger As Integer
     Dim weightFoundBoolean As Boolean = False
     Dim zoneFoundBoolean As Boolean = False

     ' Look up the weight to find the weightIndexInteger.
     weightInputInteger = Integer.Parse(Me.weightTextBox.Text)
     Do Until weightFoundBoolean Or indexInteger > 3
         If weightInputInteger <= weightInteger(indexInteger) Then
             weightIndexInteger = indexInteger
             weightFoundBoolean = True
         Else
             indexInteger += 1
         End If
     Loop
     If Not weightFoundBoolean Then
         ' Weight above 10 pounds.
         weightIndexInteger = 4
         weightFoundBoolean = True
     End If

     ' Look up the zone to find the zoneIndexInteger.
     indexInteger = 0
     Do Until zoneFoundBoolean Or indexInteger > 3
         If Me.zoneTextBox.Text.ToUpper() = zoneString(indexInteger) Then
             zoneIndexInteger = indexInteger
             zoneFoundBoolean = True
         Else
             indexInteger += 1
         End If
     Loop

     ' Display the appropriate rate.
     If weightFoundBoolean And zoneFoundBoolean Then
         Me.chargesTextBox.Text = _
             rateDecimal(weightIndexInteger, zoneIndexInteger).ToString("N")
     Else
         MessageBox.Show("Enter the weight and zone.", "Information Missing", _
             MessageBoxButtons.OK, MessageBoxIcon.Exclamation)
     End If
End Sub
```

Your Hands-On Programming Example

Create a project for R 'n R—for Reading 'n Refreshment that determines the price per pound for bulk coffee sales. The coffees are divided into categories: regular, decaf, and special blend. The prices are set by the quarter pound, half pound, and full pound. Use a *Find Price* button to search for the appropriate price based on the selections.

	Regular	Decaffeinated	Special Blend
¼ pound	2.60	2.90	3.25
½ pound	4.90	5.60	6.10
Full pound	8.75	9.75	11.25

Create a structure that contains the coffee type, amount, and price. Set up a module-level variable that is an array of 20 elements of your structure; this array will hold the transactions. Each time the *Find Price* button is pressed, look up and display the price of the coffee selection and add the data to the array.

Include a *Clear* button to clear the selections from the screen and a *Print* button that prints all of the transactions. Using *Print Preview*, print appropriate headings and the data from the transaction array.

When the *Exit* button is pressed, give the user another opportunity to print all the transactions.

Planning the Project

Sketch a form (Figure 8.9), which your users sign off as meeting their needs.

Figure 8.9

A planning sketch of the form for the hands-on programming example.

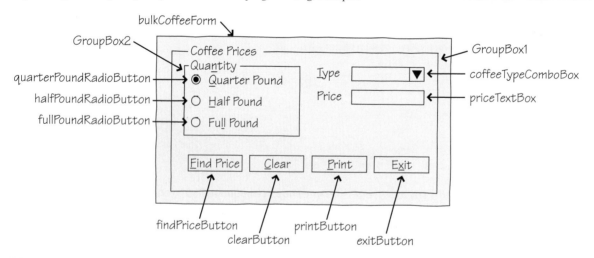

Plan the Objects and Properties

Object	Property	Setting
bulkCoffeeForm	Name	bulkCoffeeForm
	Text	R 'n R for Reading and Refreshment
	AcceptButton	findPriceButton
GroupBox1	Text	Coffee Prices

GroupBox2	Text	Qua&ntity
coffeeTypeComboBox	Name	coffeeTypeComboBox
	Items	Regular
		Decaffeinated
		Special Blend
	DropDownStyle	DropDownList
Label1	Text	&Type
Label2	Text	Price
priceTextBox	Name	priceTextBox
	ReadOnly	True
	TabStop	False
quarterPoundRadioButton	Name	quarterPoundRadioButton
	Text	&Quarter Pound
	Checked	True
halfPoundRadioButton	Name	halfPoundRadioButton
	Text	&Half Pound
fullPoundRadioButton	Name	fullPoundRadioButton
	Text	Fu&ll Pound
findPriceButton	Name	findPriceButton
	Text	&Find Price
clearButton	Name	clearButton
	Text	&Clear
printButton	Name	printButton
	Text	&Print
exitButton	Name	exitButton
	Text	E&it
PrintDocument1	Name	PrintDocument1
PrintPreviewDialog1	Name	PrintPreviewDialog1

Plan the Event Procedures   You need to plan the actions for the event procedures.

Procedure	Actions
findPriceButton_Click	Find the column from the list selection.
	Find the row from the radio button selection.
	Look up the price in the table.
	Display the price in the label.
	Store the type, quantity, and price in the transaction array.
clearButton_Click	Select the first radio button.
	Deselect the list entry.
	Clear the price label.
printButton_Click	Set up print preview.
	Print the report.

Procedure	Actions
exitButton_Click	Display message box giving the user opportunity to print. If the user wants to print Execute printButton_Click procedure. End If Terminate the project.
All radio buttons_Click	Save the name of the selected button.
PrintDocument1_PrintPage	Print title. Loop to print all of the stored transactions.

Write the Project
Follow the sketch in Figure 8.9 to create the form. Figure 8.10 shows the completed form and Figure 8.11 shows sample report output.

* Set the properties of each object, according to your plan.

* Write the code. Working from the pseudocode, write each event procedure.

* When you complete the code, use a variety of data to thoroughly test the project.

Figure 8.10

The form for the hands-on programming example.

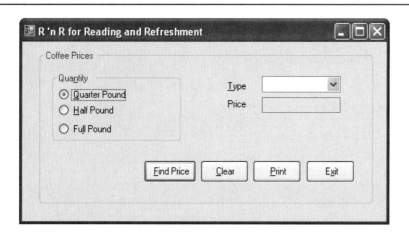

Figure 8.11

A sample report created by the program.

R 'n R Coffee Sales
by Programmer Name

Quarter Pound	Regular	2.60
Quarter Pound	Special Blends	3.25
Full Pound	Decaffeinated	9.75

The Project Coding Solution

```
' Program:           Ch08HandsOn
' Programmer:        Bradley/Millspaugh
' Date:              June 2005
' Description:        Look up the price for bulk coffee
'                     based upon quantity and type.
'                     Uses a structure and arrays, and prints a report
'                     of the transactions from the array.
' Folder:            Ch08HandsOn

Public Class bulkCoffeeForm
    ' Declare structure and module-level variables
    Structure CoffeeSale
        Dim typeString As String
        Dim quantityString As String
        Dim priceDecimal As Decimal
    End Structure

    Private transactionCoffeeSale(20) As CoffeeSale
    Private numberTransactionsInteger As Integer
    Private priceDecimal( , ) As Decimal = _
        {{2.6D, 2.9D, 3.25D}, {4.9D, 5.6D, 6.1D}, {8.75D, 9.75D, 11.25D}}
    Private selectedButtonString As String

    Private Sub clearButton_Click(ByVal sender As System.Object, _
      ByVal e As System.EventArgs) Handles clearButton.Click
        ' Remove the selection from the list and
        ' clear the price.

        ' Select first radio button.
        quarterPoundRadioButton.Select()
        ' Clear coffee type selection.
        coffeeTypeComboBox.SelectedIndex = -1
        priceTextBox.Clear()
    End Sub

    Private Sub exitButton_Click(ByVal sender As System.Object, _
      ByVal e As System.EventArgs) Handles exitButton.Click
        ' Terminate the project.
        Dim responseDialogResult As DialogResult

        responseDialogResult = MessageBox.Show("Print the report?", _
          "Terminate the Application", MessageBoxButtons.YesNo, _
          MessageBoxIcon.Question)
        If responseDialogResult = DialogResult.Yes Then
            printButton_Click(sender, e)
        End If
        Me.Close()
    End Sub

    Private Sub findPriceButton_Click(ByVal sender As System.Object, _
      ByVal e As System.EventArgs) Handles findPriceButton.Click
        ' Look up the price using the quantity and type.

        Dim rowInteger, columnInteger As Integer
        Dim salePriceDecimal As Decimal
```

```
      With Me
         ' Allow only 20 transactions.
         If numberTransactionsInteger < 20 Then
            columnInteger = .coffeeTypeComboBox.SelectedIndex
            If columnInteger <> -1 Then
               ' Coffee selection made, determine quantity selected.
               Select Case selectedButtonString
                  Case "quarterPoundRadioButton"
                     rowInteger = 0
                     transactionCoffeeSale(numberTransactionsInteger).quantityString _
                        = "Quarter Pound"
                  Case "halfPoundRadioButton"
                     rowInteger = 1
                     transactionCoffeeSale(numberTransactionsInteger).quantityString _
                        = "Half Pound"
                  Case "fullPoundRadioButton"
                     rowInteger = 2
                     transactionCoffeeSale(numberTransactionsInteger).quantityString _
                        = "Full Pound"
                  Case Else
                     ' No selection made; use quarter pound.
                     rowInteger = 0
                     transactionCoffeeSale(numberTransactionsInteger).quantityString _
                        = "Quarter Pound"
               End Select

               ' Retrieve price of selection.
               salePriceDecimal = priceDecimal(rowInteger, columnInteger)
               priceTextBox.Text = salePriceDecimal.ToString("C")
               ' Save this transaction.
               transactionCoffeeSale(numberTransactionsInteger).typeString _
                  = .coffeeTypeComboBox.Text
               transactionCoffeeSale(numberTransactionsInteger).priceDecimal _
                  = salePriceDecimal
               numberTransactionsInteger += 1
            Else
               MessageBox.Show("Select the coffee type.", "Selection Incomplete", _
                  MessageBoxButtons.OK, MessageBoxIcon.Exclamation)
            End If
         Else
            MessageBox.Show("Sorry, only 20 transactions allowed.")
         End If
      End With
   End Sub

Private Sub printButton_Click(ByVal sender As Object, _
   ByVal e As System.EventArgs) Handles printButton.Click
      ' Print the report using Print Preview.

      With Me
         .PrintPreviewDialog1.Document = .PrintDocument1
         .PrintPreviewDialog1.ShowDialog()
      End With
   End Sub

Private Sub PrintDocument1_PrintPage(ByVal sender As Object, _
   ByVal e As System.Drawing.Printing.PrintPageEventArgs) _
      Handles PrintDocument1.PrintPage

      ' Handle print and print previews.
```

```
        Dim printFont As New Font("Arial", 12)
        Dim headingFont As New Font("Arial", 14, FontStyle.Bold)
        Dim lineHeightSingle As Single = printFont.GetHeight + 2
        Dim column1HorizontalLocationSingle As Single = e.MarginBounds.Left
        Dim verticalPrintLocationSingle As Single = e.MarginBounds.Top
        Dim column2HorizontalLocationSingle As Single = 300
        Dim column3HorizontalLocationSingle As Single
        Dim printLineString As String
        Dim fontSizeF As New SizeF
        Dim formattedPriceString As String

        ' Set up and display heading lines.
        printLineString = "R 'n R Coffee Sales"
        e.Graphics.DrawString(printLineString, headingFont, _
          Brushes.Black, column2HorizontalLocationSingle, verticalPrintLocationSingle)
        printLineString = "by Programmer Name"
        verticalPrintLocationString += lineHeightSingle
        e.Graphics.DrawString(printLineString, printFont, _
          Brushes.Black, column2HorizontalLocationSingle, verticalPrintLocationSingle)
        verticalPrintLocationString += lineHeightSingle * 2

        ' Loop through the transactions.
        For Each individualCoffeeSale As CoffeeSale In transactionCoffeeSale
            ' Don't print if blank.
            If individualCoffeeSale.quantityString <> "" Then
              ' Set up a line.

              ' Quantity.
              e.Graphics.DrawString(individualCoffeeSale.quantityString, printFont, _
                Brushes.Black, column1HorizontalLocationSingle, verticalPrintLocationSingle)

              ' Type.
              e.Graphics.DrawString(individualCoffeeSale.typeString, printFont, _
                Brushes.Black, column2HorizontalLocationSingle, verticalPrintLocationSingle)

              ' Right-align the price.
              formattedPriceString = individualCoffeeSale.priceDecimal.ToString("N")
              ' Measure string in this font.
              fontSizeF = e.Graphics.MeasureString(formattedPriceString, printFont)
              ' Subtract width of string from column position
              column3HorizontalLocationSingle = 550 - fontSizeF.Width
              e.Graphics.DrawString(formattedPriceString, printFont, _
                Brushes.Black, column3HorizontalLocationSingle, verticalPrintLocationSingle)

              ' Increment the Y position for the next line; Double space.
              verticalPrintLocationString += lineHeightSingle * 2
            End If
        Next
    End Sub

    Private Sub quarterPoundRadioButton_CheckedChanged(ByVal sender _
      As System.Object, ByVal e As System.EventArgs) _
      Handles fullPoundRadioButton.CheckedChanged, _
      halfPoundRadioButton.CheckedChanged, _
      quarterPoundRadioButton.CheckedChanged

      ' Save the name of the selected radio button.
      ' This procedure is executed each time any radio button is selected.

      selectedButtonString = CType(sender, RadioButton).Name
    End Sub
End Class
```

Summary

1. A series of variables with the same name is called an array. The individual values are referred to as elements, and each element is accessed by its subscript, which is a position number.
2. Array subscripts or indexes are zero based; they must be integers in the range of the array elements. VB rounds noninteger values.
3. You can assign initial values in the array declaration *or* specify the highest subscript allowed.
4. A special form of the For loop called For Each is available for working with arrays. The For Each eliminates the need for the programmer to manipulate the subscripts of the array.
5. You can declare a structure to combine related fields and then declare variables and arrays of the structure. Structure statements must appear in the declarations section at the top of a file.
6. Arrays can be used like any other variables; they can be used to accumulate a series of totals or to store values for a lookup procedure.
7. The information in arrays may be referenced directly by subscript, or a table lookup may be used to determine the correct table position.
8. You can use the SelectedIndex property of a list box as a subscript of an array.
9. Arrays may be multidimensional. A two-dimensional table contains rows and columns and is processed similarly to a one-dimensional array. Accessing a multidimensional array frequently requires the use of nested loops.

Key Terms

array *322*
column *333*
direct reference *328*
element *322*
For Each and Next *324*
index *322*

row *333*
structure *325*
subscript *322*
subscripted variable *322*
table *322*
table lookup *329*

Review Questions

1. Define the following terms:
   (a) Array
   (b) Element
   (c) Subscript
   (d) Index
   (e) Subscripted variable
2. What is a structure? When might a structure be useful?
3. Describe the logic of a table lookup.
4. Name some situations in which it is important to perform validation when working with subscripted variables.
5. Compare a two-dimensional table to an array of a structure.
6. How can you initialize values in a two-dimensional table?

Programming Exercises

8.1 *Array of a structure.* Create a project to analyze an income survey. The statistics for each home include an identification code, the number of members in the household, the yearly income, and the state of residence.

   A menu will contain *File*, *Reports*, and *Help*. The *File* menu will contain *Enter Data* and *Exit*. As the data are entered, they should be assigned from the text boxes to the elements of a structure.

   The reports for the project will be sent to the printer and include the following:
   (a) A four-column report displaying the input data.
   (b) A listing of the identification number and income for each household that exceeds the average income.
   (c) The percentage of households having incomes below the poverty level.

   Test Data

   Poverty Guidelines for 2004:

Family Size	48 Contiguous States	Alaska	Hawaii
1	9310	11630	10700
2	12490	15610	14360
3	15670	19590	18020
4	18850	23570	21680
5	22030	27550	25340
6	25210	35510	32660
7	28390	35510	32660
8	31570	39490	36320
For each additional person add	3180	3980	3660

ID Number	Number of Persons	Annual Income	Residence
2497	2	32500	Nevada
3323	5	23000	Illinois
4521	4	38210	Arizona
6789	2	38000	Maine
5476	1	26000	North Dakota
4423	3	16400	California
6587	4	25000	Alaska
3221	4	20500	Hawaii
5555	2	18000	Alaska
0085	3	19700	Hawaii
3097	8	30000	Washington
4480	5	23400	Florida
0265	2	19700	Texas
8901	3	13000	Michigan

8.2   *Two-dimensional table*. Modify Programming Exercise 8.1 to assign the data to a multidimensional array rather than use an array of a structure.

8.3   Create a project to keep track of concert ticket sales by your club. Ticket prices are based on the seating location. Your program should calculate the price for each sale, accumulate the total number of tickets sold in each section, display the ticket price schedule, and print a summary of all sales.

The form should contain a list box of the sections for seating.

Do not allow the user to receive an exception for subscript out-of-range.

Section	Price
Orchestra	40.00
Mezzanine	27.50
General	15.00
Balcony	10.00

8.4   *Array of a structure*. Create a project that will allow a user to look up state
      names and their two-letter abbreviations. The user will have the options to
      Look up the Abbreviation or *Look up the State Name.* In the event that a match
      cannot be found for the input, display an appropriate error message.

      Use radio buttons with a shared event procedure and a `Select Case`
      to determine which text box (state name or abbreviation) should have the
      focus and which should be set to ReadOnly.

Data			
AL	Alabama	MT	Montana
AK	Alaska	NE	Nebraska
AS	American Samoa	NV	Nevada
AZ	Arizona	NH	New Hampshire
AR	Arkansas	NJ	New Jersey
CA	California	NM	New Mexico
CO	Colorado	NY	New York
CT	Connecticut	NC	North Carolina
DE	Delaware	ND	North Dakota
DC	District of Columbia	OH	Ohio
FL	Florida	OK	Oklahoma
GA	Georgia	OR	Oregon
GU	Guam	PA	Pennsylvania
HI	Hawaii	PR	Puerto Rico
ID	Idaho	RI	Rhode Island
IL	Illinois	SC	South Carolina
IN	Indiana	SD	South Dakota
IA	Iowa	TN	Tennessee
KS	Kansas	TX	Texas
KY	Kentucky	TT	Trust Territories
LA	Louisiana	UT	Utah
ME	Maine	VT	Vermont
MD	Maryland	VA	Virginia
MA	Massachusetts	VI	Virgin Islands
MI	Michigan	WA	Washington
MN	Minnesota	WV	West Virginia
MS	Mississippi	WI	Wisconsin
MO	Missouri	WY	Wyoming

8.5 *Two-dimensional table*. Create a project that looks up the driving distance between two cities. Use two drop-down lists that contain the names of the cities. Label one list "Departure" and the other "Destination". Use a *Look Up* button to calculate the distance.

Store the distances in a two-dimensional table.

	Boston	Chicago	Dallas	Las Vegas	Los Angeles	Miami	New Orleans	Toronto	Vancouver	Washington DC
Boston	0	1004	1753	2752	3017	1520	1507	609	3155	448
Chicago	1004	0	921	1780	2048	1397	919	515	2176	709
Dallas	1753	921	0	1230	1399	1343	517	1435	2234	1307
Las Vegas	2752	1780	1230	0	272	2570	1732	2251	1322	2420
Los Angeles	3017	2048	1399	272	0	2716	1858	2523	1278	2646
Miami	1520	1397	1343	2570	2716	0	860	1494	3447	1057
New Orleans	1507	919	517	1732	1858	860	0	1307	2734	1099
Toronto	609	515	1435	2251	2523	1494	1307	0	2820	571
Vancouver	3155	2176	2234	1322	1278	3447	2734	2820	0	2887
Washington DC	448	709	1307	2420	2646	1057	1099	571	2887	0

8.6 *Two-dimensional table*. Create a project in which the user will complete a 10-question survey. Create a form containing labels with each of the questions and a group of radio buttons for each question with the following responses: Always, Usually, Sometimes, Seldom, and Never.

Use a two-dimensional array to accumulate the number of each response for each question.

Have a menu or button option that will print an item analysis on the printer that shows the question number and the count for each response.

Sample of partial output:

Question	Always	Usually	Sometimes	Seldom	Never
1	5	2	10	4	6
2	2	2	10	2	1
3	17	0	10	0	0

Case Studies

VB Mail Order

Create a project that will calculate shipping charges from a two-dimensional table of rates. The rate depends on the weight of the package and the zone to which it will be shipped. The Weight column specifies the maximum weight for that rate. All weights over 10 pounds use the last row.

	Zone			
Weight	A	B	C	D
1	1.00	1.50	1.65	1.85
3	1.58	2.00	2.40	3.05
5	1.71	2.52	3.10	4.00
10	2.04	3.12	4.00	5.01
>10	2.52	3.75	5.10	7.25

VB Auto Center

VB Auto sells its own brand of spark plugs. To cross-reference to major brands, it keeps a table of equivalent part numbers. VB Auto wants to computerize the process of looking up part numbers in order to improve its customer service.

The user should be able to enter the part number and brand and look up the corresponding VB Auto part number. You may allow the user to select the brand (Brand A, Brand C, or Brand X) from a list or from radio buttons.

You can choose from two approaches for the lookup table. Store the part numbers either in a two-dimensional table or in an array of a structure. In either case, use the part number and brand entered by the user; look up and display the VB Auto part number.

VB Auto	Brand A	Brand C	Brand X
PR214	MR43T	RBL8	14K22
PR223	R43	RJ6	14K24
PR224	R43N	RN4	14K30
PR246	R46N	RN8	14K32
PR247	R46TS	RBL17Y	14K33
PR248	R46TX	RBL12-6	14K35
PR324	S46	J11	14K38
PR326	SR46E	XEJ8	14K40
PR444	47L	H12	14K44

Video Bonanza

Create a project that displays the aisle number of a movie category in a label. The movie categories will be in a list box. Store the aisle numbers and categories in an array.

A *Search* button should locate the correct location from the array and display it in a label. Make sure that the user has selected a category from the list and use the list box SelectedIndex property to find the appropriate aisle number.

Table Data

Aisle 1	Comedy
Aisle 2	Drama
Aisle 3	Action
Aisle 4	Sci-Fi
Aisle 5	Horror
Back Wall	New Releases

Very Very Boards

Modify your project from Chapter 6 to keep track of each order in an array. You can then print out the entire order with detail lines for each type of shirt. Convert the event handling for the radio buttons to share an event procedure. Use a `Case` structure for selection.

Create an array of a structure, which holds the quantity, size, monogram (Boolean), pocket (Boolean), price, and extended price for each type of shirt ordered. As each shirt type is added to an order, store the information in the array. Add a menu option to print out the order, which will have the customer name and order number at the top, and one line for each shirt type ordered. Use the following layout as a rough guide for your list. Make sure to align the numeric columns correctly. For the two Boolean fields (Monogram and Pocket), print Yes or No. Do not allow the user to print an invoice until the order is complete.

Very Very Boards Shirt Orders

By Your Name

Customer name: xxxxxxxxxxxxxxxxxxxxxx

Order Number: xxxxx

Quantity	Size	Monogram	Pocket	Price Each	Extended Price
==
xxx	xxx	xxx	xxx	xx	x,xxx
Order Total:					xx,xxx

9

Programming with Visual Web Developer

at the completion of this chapter, you will be able to . . .

1. Explain the functions of the server and the client in Web programming.

2. Create a Web Form and run it in a browser.

3. Describe the differences among the various types of Web controls and the relationship of Web controls to controls used on Windows forms.

4. Understand the event structure required for Web programs.

5. Design a Web Form using tables.

6. Validate Web input using the validator controls.

7. Define ASP, XML, WSDL, and SOAP.

Visual Basic and Web Programming

So far, all of your projects are based on Windows Forms and run stand-alone in the Windows environment. In this chapter you learn to program for the Internet. In Visual Basic .NET you use **Web Forms** to create the user interface for Web projects. A Web Form displays as a document in a **browser** such as Netscape Navigator (NN) or Internet Explorer (IE). If you are using the VB Standard Edition, Professional Edition, or above (not Visual Web Developer), you can create documents that display on mobile devices such as cell phones and personal digital assistants (PDAs).

Important software note: Microsoft has released a new product for developing Web applications: Visual Web Developer 2005 Express Edition, which is a streamlined subset of Visual Studio. This chapter was created using Visual Web Developer (VWD) Beta and Visual Studio Standard Edition Beta. The steps and screen captures may differ slightly if you are using Visual Studio Professional or above.

Client/Server Web Applications

Most Windows applications are stand-alone applications; Web applications require a server and a client. The server sends Web pages to the client, where the pages display inside a browser application (Figure 9.1).

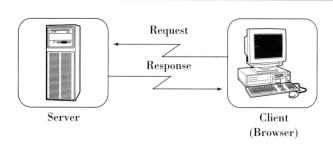

F i g u r e   9 . 1

A server delivers Web pages to a client, where the pages display in a browser window. The server can be on a remote machine or on the same machine as the client.

Server   Client
                                        (Browser)

Web Servers

To develop Web applications you can either use a remote Web server or make your local machine a Web server. Microsoft provides two pieces of software that can make the development machine function as a server: the new Visual Studio Web server and Internet Information Services (IIS). The server software handles the Web server functions and the browser acts as the client.

The Visual Studio Web server simplifies development testing and debugging. After you have debugged your Web application, you can use the tools in the IDE to transfer the application to an IIS Web server to share with others. The VS Web server is installed automatically when you install Visual Web Developer or Visual Studio.

Web Clients

Browsers display pages written in hypertext markup language (HTML). The pages also may contain programming logic in the form of script such as JavaScript, VBScript, or JScript; or as Java applets. The browser renders the page and displays it on the local system.

You have likely seen Web pages that look different when displayed in different browsers, or even in different versions of the same browser. Although many browser applications are available, the most common are Internet Explorer, Netscape Navigator, Mozilla and FireFox.

You may know which browser your users are using, such as when you are programming for a network within a company, called an ***intranet***. Or you may develop applications that run on the Internet and might display in any browser. If your projects will run on different browsers, you should test and check the output on multiple browsers.

Web Pages

One characteristic of HTML **Web pages** is that they are **stateless**. That is, a page does not store any information about its contents from one invocation to the next. Several techniques have been developed to get around this limitation, including storing cookies on the local machine and sending state information to the server as part of the page's address, called the *uniform resource locator* (URL). The server can then send the state information back with the next version of the page, if necessary.

When a user requests a Web page, the browser (client) sends a request to the server. The server may send a preformatted HTML file, or a program on the server may dynamically generate the necessary HTML to render the page. One Microsoft technology for dynamically generating HTML pages is active server pages (ASP).

ASP.NET

The latest Web programming technology from Microsoft is ASP.NET 2.0, which represents major advances over the earlier ASP.NET and ASP. ASP.NET provides libraries, controls, and programming support that allow you to write programs that interact with the user, maintain state, render controls, display data, and generate appropriate HTML. When you use Web Forms in Visual Basic .NET or Visual Web Developer, you are using ASP.NET.

Using VB and ASP.NET you can create object-oriented event-driven Web applications.

Visual Basic and ASP.NET

Each Web Form that you design has two distinct pieces: (1) the HTML and instructions needed to render the page and (2) the Visual Basic code. This separation is a big improvement over older methods that mix the HTML and programming logic (script or applets). A Web Form generates a file with an .aspx extension for the HTML and another file with an .aspx.vb extension for the Visual Basic code.

Don't panic if you don't know HTML; the HTML is generated automatically by the Visual Studio IDE. You visually create the document using the IDE's designer; you can then view and modify the HTML tags in the Visual Studio editor.

The VB code contains the program logic to respond to events. This code file is called the "code-behind" file. The code looks just like the code you have been writing for Windows applications, but many of the events for the controls on Web Forms are different from those of Windows Forms. Another change is that the VB code is not compiled into an executable (.exe) file as it is for Windows applications.

Types of Web Sites

Web applications are referred to as *Web sites* in Visual Studio 2005. VS provides four types of Web sites, which you can see in the *Open Web Site* dialog box (Figure 9.2). Notice the options down the left side of the dialog box: File System, Local IIS, FTP Site, and Remote Site. If you are using the full version of VS, the *Open Web Site* dialog box shows one more icon for Source Control.

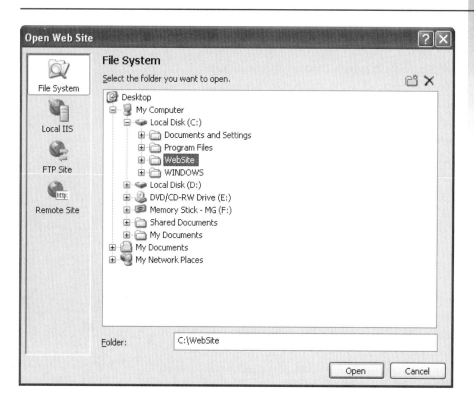

Figure 9.2

The four types of Web sites supported by Visual Web Developer appear on the left edge of the Open Web Site dialog box. Visual Studio supports one additional choice: Source Control.

File System Web Sites

A File System Web site stores the Web pages and associated files in any folder on the local computer or other computer on the network. The Web pages are then tested using the Visual Studio Web server. The examples in this chapter all use File System sites.

    The new features of File System sites and the Visual Studio Web server provide several advantages for Web developers over using IIS. The VS Web server does not expose the computer to security vulnerabilities and does not require administrative rights to create and debug a Web project. Also, the VS Web server can run on Windows XP Home, which most home users are running rather than XP Professional.

TIP

Use a File System Web site for development. You can use the *Copy Web Site* feature to convert to IIS or a remote server after you debug the application. ■

IIS Web Sites

Internet Information Services (IIS) is Microsoft's production Web server and is part of the operating system in Windows 2000, Windows XP Professional, and Windows Server 2003, but not in Windows XP Home Edition. IIS includes a

Web server, FTP server, e-mail server, and other services. When you run IIS on your local computer, you are hosting a Web server that you must take extra steps to secure.

You must have administrative rights on the computer to create IIS Web projects. If the security on your campus or corporate network does not allow the proper permissions, you cannot create IIS Web applications.

When you create a Web site using local IIS (instead of the new VS Web server), by default the files are stored in the C:\inetpub\wwwroot folder. However, you can create a virtual IIS directory elsewhere on your computer and store your Web site there.

Remote Sites and FTP Sites

It is possible that your campus network will be set up for you to do development on a remote Web server. However, you must be granted administrative rights on the host computer. You cannot use an FTP site to create a new Web site; you can only open a previously created FTP Web site in Visual Studio.

Follow your instructor's directions for the type of site to use.

Creating a Web Site

You can create a new Web site by selecting *New Web Site* from the *File* menu. In the *New Web Site* dialog box (Figure 9.3), you select *ASP.NET Web Site* for the template, *File System* for the location, and *Visual Basic* for the language. The *Location* field is set to a folder called WebSites in your My Documents folder, which is the default location for a File System site. You can browse to select a different folder if you wish. You give your project a name by changing the name in the *Location* box.

The default location for a File System Web site project location and name is C:\UserName\My Documents\WebSites*ProjectName*.

Note: The default for a Local IIS project location and name is http://*localhost*/*ProjectName* (localhost is translated by IIS to your local virtual directory, usually C:\Inetpub\wwwroot).

Caution: In a change from Visual Web Developer Beta 1 to an interim build of Visual Studio, the folder defaults changed. Hopefully, the defaults will change again before the final version of the software. As this text went to press, VB created the Web site in the default folder (C:\UserName\My Documents\WebSites\ *ProjectName*), but also created an additional folder with only the .sln and .suo files. This extra folder appeared in the location specified as the default location for Visual Studio projects, which you can check and modify in *Tools\Options\ Projects and Solutions\General.*

Web Page Files

A new Web site automatically contains one Web page, called Default.aspx, which contains the visual representation of the page. A second file, Default.aspx.vb, the code-behind file, holds the VB code for the project. This model is very similar to a Windows project, which also keeps the visual elements separate from the code. But in the case of Web pages, the visual elements are created with HTML tags rather than VB code.

Figure 9.3

Begin a new Web project by entering the location and project name on the New Web Site *dialog box. Note that this dialog box can vary depending on how the software was installed and configured.*

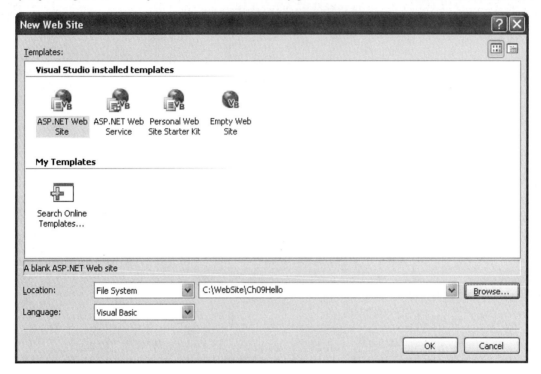

ASP.NET provides two models for managing controls and code. In addition to the **code separation model** described in the preceding paragraph, you also can use a **single-file model**, which combines the visible elements and the code in a single file. In early versions of ASP (before .NET), the single-file model was the only format available, so you may see old applications created in this style. We will use the code separation model for all programs in this text.

Web Forms in the Visual Studio IDE

As soon as you open a new Visual Basic Web application, you notice many differences from Windows Forms. Instead of a Windows Form, you see a new Web Form (Figure 9.4), also called a *Web page* or *Web document*. The toolbar is different, as is the list of files in the Solution Explorer. The toolbox has different controls, and even those that look the same, such as TextBoxes, Buttons, and Labels, are actually different from their Windows counterparts and have some different properties and events. For example, Web controls have an ID property rather than a Name property.

Note: If the IDE opens the Web page with the *Source* tab active, you will see HTML tags in the window. Click on the *Design* tab at the bottom of the window (Figure 9.4) to display the page. The Properties window may not appear automatically; press the Properties button or select *View/Properties Window* to display it. You can change the default to always display the *Source* tab first in *Tools/ Options/Show all settings/HTML Designer/Start Pages in Design View*.

Figure 9.4

The Visual Web Developer IDE with a new Web site opened. If the page's Source *tab is selected, click the* Design *tab.*

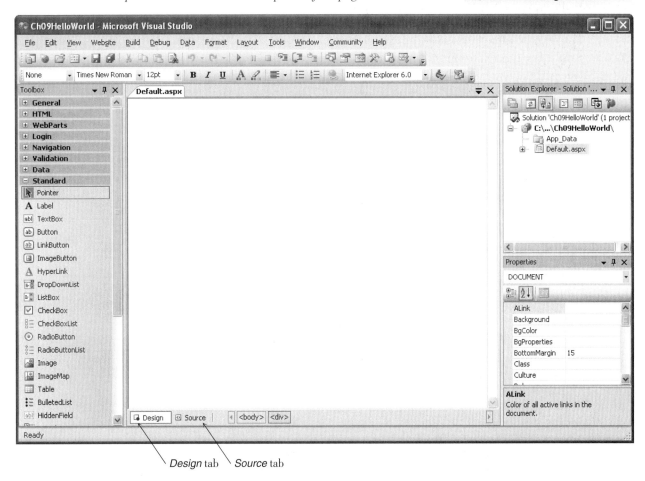

Design tab   \ *Source* tab

Creating Your First Web Form—Step-by-Step

This simple step-by-step exercise creates a Web application that displays a Hello message on a document in a browser window.

These instructions are written for Visual Web Developer. If you are using the full version of Visual Studio, the menu choices may be slightly different.

Begin the Project

STEP 1: Open Visual Web Developer 2005 Express Edition or the full version of Visual Studio .NET.

STEP 2: From the *File* menu select *New Web Site* and set the Web site name to "Ch09Hello" by changing the location to "C:\UserName\My Documents\WebSites\Ch09Hello". Click *OK*.

Note: You can use the folder of your choice in place of WebSites. If you are using a shared computer, select a folder in your My Documents folder or your own disk or flash drive.

STEP 3: If you don't see a blank page in the Document window, click on the *Design* tab at the bottom of the window or click on the *View Designer* button in the Solution Explorer (Shortcut: Shift + F7).

Create the User Interface

You add elements to a Web page in a manner similar to writing text in a word processor. You must press Enter to move to a new line and press the Spacebar to move across a line.

STEP 1: Press Enter a few times and type "Enter Name:".

STEP 2: Add a TextBox control from the Standard section of the toolbox. You can drag the text box onto the form or double-click the tool in the toolbox. Double-clicking makes the text box appear at the insertion point.
   Note: The text box is a server control and the text "Enter Name:" is static HTML. You will learn more about these elements later in this chapter.

STEP 3: Set the ID property of the text box to nameTextBox. You may want to click the *Alphabetic* button in the Properties window to sort the properties. The ID property appears at the top of the list due to the parentheses, just as the Name property appears at the top of the list in Windows forms.

STEP 4: Click after the text box, press Enter twice, and add a Label control.

STEP 5: Set the Label's ID property to messageLabel and delete the Text property. The label will display its ID property at design time but not at run time.

STEP 6: Click after the label, press Enter a couple of times, and add a Button control. Set the ID property to submitButton and the Text property to "Submit".

STEP 7: In the Properties window, drop down the list of objects and select DOCUMENT, which is the Web Form. Set the BgColor property (background color) to a color of your choice.

STEP 8: Set the document's Title property to "Hello Application". The Title property displays in the title bar of the browser when you run the application.

Add Code

STEP 1: Double-click on the *Submit* button and add the following code.

```
'Web Site:        Ch09Hello
'Web page:        Default.aspx
'Programmer:      Your Name
'Date:            June 2005
'Description:     Concatenate the name and display in a label.

Partial Class Default_aspx
    Inherits System.Web.UI.Page

    Protected Sub submitButton_Click(ByVal sender As Object, _
      ByVal e As System.EventArgs) Handles submitButton.Click
        ' Display the name and a message.

        With Me
            .messageLabel.Text = "Hello " & .nameTextBox.Text & "!"
        End With
    End Sub
End Class
```

Run the Web Application

The menu choices and toolbar buttons for running a Web application differ somewhat for Visual Web Developer and the full version of Visual Studio.

STEP 1: Run the project. In Visual Web Developer, run without debugging using Ctrl + F5 or select *Start without Debugging* from the *Debug* menu. In the full VS, you can still run without debugging using Ctrl + F5, even though it does not appear on the menu.

   Note: You also can right-click on the aspx file or on the page in the Document window and select *View in Browser*.

STEP 2: The Internet Explorer browser should launch and open the page with your page showing.

   Note: If you are running the Windows firewall, you may receive a message that the firewall has blocked the Web Server and asking what you would like to do; choose *Unblock* to permit the server to render your page and then refresh the page in the browser window.

STEP 3: Enter a name and press the Submit button. A "Hello" message should appear in the label.

STEP 4: Close the browser window to end execution.

Viewing the HTML Code

When you are viewing your Web Form in the designer, you can see two tabs at the bottom of the form: *Design* and *Source*. You can click on the *Source* tab to see the static HTML code. The HTML creates the visual elements on the page and is automatically generated, like the Windows-generated code in a Windows Form.

Controls

Several types of controls are available for Web Forms. You can mix the control types on a single form. Refer to Figure 9.4 to view the toolbox. For most of your work, you will use the controls in the Standard section of the toolbox.

• *Standard (ASP.NET server controls)*. These are the richest, most powerful controls provided by ASP.NET and the .NET framework. Web server controls do not directly correspond to HTML controls but are rendered differently for different browsers in order to achieve the desired look and feel. Some of the special-purpose Web server controls are Calendar, CheckBoxList, AdRotator, and RadioButtonList.

• *Data*. This list of controls includes the GridView and DataList for displaying data.

• *Validation*. These controls are used to validate the data before they are sent to the server.

• *Navigation*. This list includes a menu control.

• *Login*. Visual Studio 2005 includes login controls and wizards.

• *WebParts*. The WebParts set of components enables users to change the appearance and behavior of the interface from the browser.

- *HTML.* These are the standard HTML elements that operate only on the client. You cannot write any server-side programming logic for HTML controls. As you submit forms to the server, any HTML controls pass to the server and back as static text. You might want to use HTML controls if you have existing HTML pages that are working and you want to convert to ASP.NET for additional capabilities.

- *Others.* Depending on your version of VS 2005, you may have other sections, such as Crystal Reports.

You can see the available controls in the toolbox when a Web Form is in Design view. Generally, the Standard section is showing (Figure 9.5). Try selecting other toolbox tabs, such as *Data*, *Validation*, *Navigation*, *Login*, *WebParts*, and *HTML*.

In Design view, you can tell the difference between client-side HTML controls and server-side controls. The VS designer adds a small green arrow in the upper-left corner for all server controls (Figure 9.6).

Figure 9.5

The Standard section of the toolbox holds the ASP.NET server controls, which you will use primarily. Click on the tabs to view the other sections of the toolbox.

Figure 9.6

The small green arrow in the corner of a control indicates a server control.

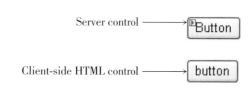

Server control ⟶ Button

Client-side HTML control ⟶ button

Event Handling

You write VB code for events of Web controls in the same way that you write for Windows controls. The events may actually occur on either the client or the server. The process of capturing an event, sending it to the server, and executing the required methods is all done for you automatically.

The events of Web Forms and controls are somewhat different from those of Windows Forms. For example, a Web Form has a Page_Load event rather than a Form_Load event. You can see the events of the page using the editor; in the *Class name* list on the left, select *(Page Events)* and drop down the *Method name* list (on the right) to see the list of events for the page. You also can select any control on the page to see the events of the control. For example, if you select a button control, you can see that you still have a Click event, but the list of events is much shorter than it is for Windows Forms.

Files

The files that you find in a Web application differ greatly from those in a Windows application (Figure 9.7). Two files make up the form: the aspx file and the aspx.vb file. The aspx file holds the specifications for the user interface that are used by the server to render the page. The aspx.vb file holds the Visual Basic code that you write to respond to events. The aspx.vb file is the code-behind file for the aspx file. When you are designing the user interface, you select the *FormName.aspx* tab and select the *Design* tab at the bottom of the window; when you are working on the code procedures, you select the *FormName.aspx.vb* tab.

Debugging

Running a Web application in the Visual Studio IDE is different from running a Windows application. The IDE does not automatically generate the code necessary for debugging a Web application. If you want to use the debugging tools, such as breakpoints and single-stepping, you must take steps to add the debugging functions to your project.

F i g u r e   9 . 7

The Solution Explorer for a Web application. The Web page called "Default" consists of two files: Default.aspx (the visual elements) and Default.aspx.vb (the VB code-behind file).

Run without Debugging

If you choose to run without debugging, you can press Ctrl + F5, or in Visual Web Developer, choose *Debug / Start Without Debugging*.

Run with Debugging

To add the necessary support for debugging, your project must have a Web.config file that contains the following line:

```
<compilation debug="true" />
```

If you try to run with debugging (F5), you receive an error telling you that it can't start with debug mode because debugging is not enabled in the Web.config file (Figure 9.8). It gives you two options: add a Web.config file with debugging enabled or run without debugging (equivilant to Ctrl + F5). If you choose to add the Web.config file, it will have the necessary statement for debugging.

Figure 9.8

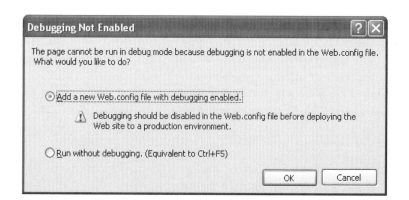

*This dialog box appears if you attempt to run with debugging. Select **Add a new Web.config file** if you want to use the debugging tools, otherwise select **Run without debugging.***

You also can create your own Web.config file: Select *Website / Add New Item* to open the *Add New Item* dialog box (Figure 9.9). Select the *Web Configuration File* template and click *Add*. You will see a Web.config file appear in the Solution Explorer.

Open the new Web.config file either by double-clicking the file in the Solution Explorer or by right-clicking and selecting *Open* from the context menu. Locate the following line:

```
<compilation debug="false" />
```

Change "false" to "true" and save the file. You also can close the file's window.

After you create the Web.config file, you can set breakpoints, single-step execution, and display the contents of variables and properties. Try setting a breakpoint in the submitButton event procedure and rerun the program. The project compiles and displays in the browser. After you click on the button, the breakpoint halts execution and you can view the code and the values of properties, just as you can in Windows applications. Single-step execution using the F8 key (see the *Debug* menu if you have changed your keyboard layout) and view your objects and properties in the Autos or Locals window.

Always remove debugging support before deploying an application. Debugging code slows the application considerably. ■

Figure 9.9

Add a Web.config file to your project in the **Add New Item** *dialog box.*

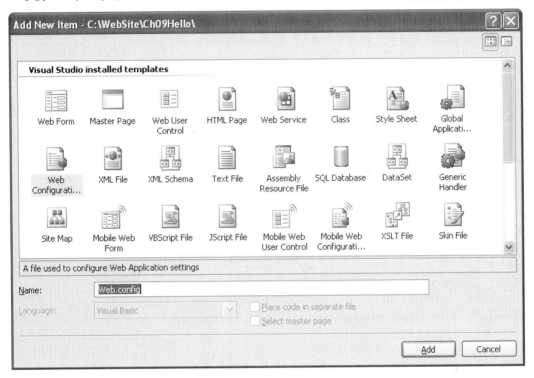

Testing in Other Browsers

You can test your project in another browser, such as Netscape Navigator. From the Solution Explorer window, right-click on the project name and select *Browse With*. You can select from browsers that are installed on your computer.

Feedback 9.1

1. What two files make up a Web Form? What is the purpose of each file?
2. How can you display a preview of how your Web Form will display in a browser without actually running the program?
3. What is the difference between an ASP.NET server control and an HTML control? When might you want to use each type?

Laying Out Web Forms

You must always be aware that users may have different browsers, different screen sizes, and different screen resolutions. ASP.NET generates appropriate HTML to render the page in various browsers but cannot be aware of the screen size, resolution, or window size on the target machine.

Using Tables for Layout

If you want to have more control over placement of elements on your Web page, you can add an HTML **table**. You can add controls and text to the table cells to align the columns as you want them.

The table is an HTML control, which doesn't need any server-side programming. Although there is a Web server Table control, that is generally used when you want to write code to add rows, columns, or controls at run time.

You can either add a table to a Web page by selecting the Table tool from the toolbox HTML section, or allow the IDE to give you more help. Select *Insert Table* from the *Layout* menu. In the *Insert Table* dialog box (Figure 9.10), you can choose the number of rows and columns, as well as set many attributes of the table and cells. You can even choose from a set of preformatted templates if you choose the *Template* option.

After you create a table, you can set properties, such as borders, alignment, and background color for the entire table, for individual rows, or for individual cells (Figure 9.11). Note that the HTML colors differ from the ones you can select for the document. You can adjust the column widths by dragging the bar between columns. If you want to move the table, you must click outside the table and insert or delete lines on the page.

To add or delete a table row, first select a row. Then right-click and use the context menu. You can use the same technique to add or delete a column.

Entering Controls or Text in a Table

You can add controls to any table cell or type text in a cell during design time. If you want to be able to refer to the text in a cell at run time, add a label and give it an ID; otherwise you can type text directly into the cell. Figure 9.12 shows a table in Design view. Although the table's border is set to zero, the borders appear at design time but not at run time (Figure 9.13).

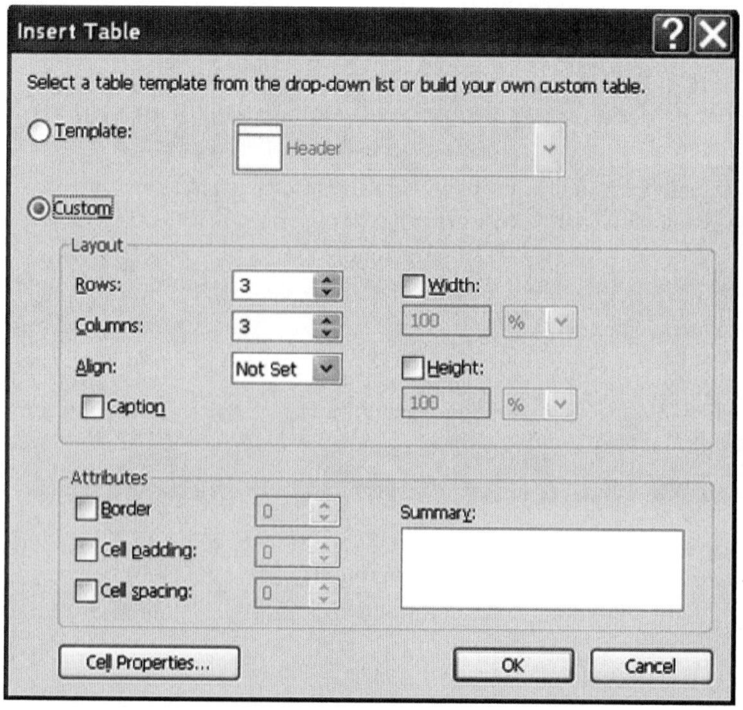

Figure 9.10

In the Insert Table dialog box, you can create a new table and set many properties of the table. Click on the Cell Properties button to set properties of the cells.

Figure 9.11

You can click on the arrows to select the entire table, a row, or a column. You also can resize the table by dragging the resizing handles.

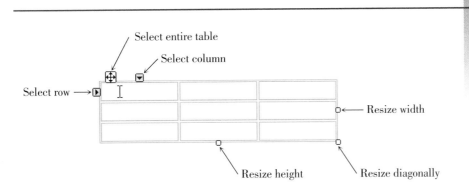

Figure 9.12

Add text and controls to the table cells. Although the Border property is set to zero, the borders still show at design time.

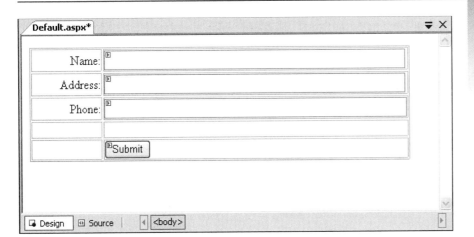

Figure 9.13

The table at run time. With the Border property set to zero, the borders do not appear.

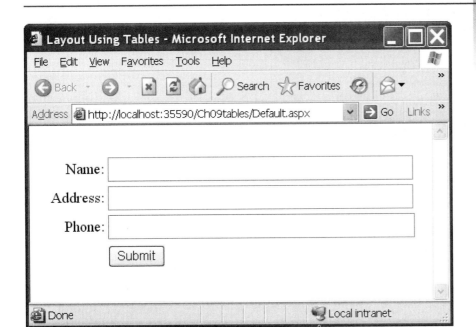

When you are working with a table, there are some menu options that may help you adjust your table. The *Layout* menu not only allows you to select the table and to insert columns, rows, or cells, but it also provides the ability to merge cells. This means that you can make the entire top row a single cell for your title or you may combine a couple of cells for a larger image.

Including Images on Web Pages

You can add graphics to a Web page using the Image control. The concept is similar to the PictureBox control on Windows Forms, but the graphic file is connected differently due to the nature of Web applications. Each Image control has an ImageUrl property that specifies the location of the graphic file.

To place an image on a Web page, you should first copy the graphic into the Web site folder. If the project is open in the IDE when you add the graphic files, click the *Refresh* button at the top of the Solution Explorer to make the files show up.

You can add an Image control to a cell in a table or directly on a Web page. In the ImageUrl property, click on the Property button (...) to open the *Select Image* dialog box (Figure 9.14). If you have added the graphic to the project folder and either clicked the Solution Explorer *Refresh* button or reopened the project, the graphic file will appear in the *Contents* pane.

Figure 9.14

Select the graphic for the ImageUrl property of the Image control in the Select Image dialog box.

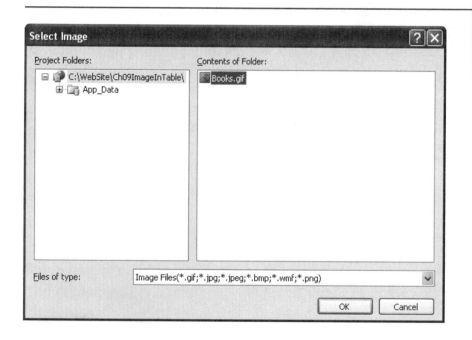

The page in Figure 9.15 is made up of a table of three rows and three columns. The image and company title are in the first row and the text box is in the second row. The hyperlink shown in the last row is discussed in the next section.

Figure 9.15

Place images, text, and controls where you want them by using a table. The elements on this page are inserted into table cells.

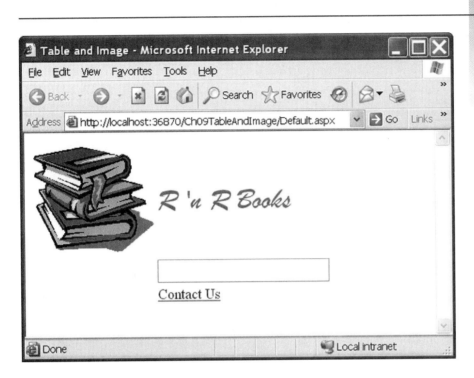

▶ **Feedback 9.2**

1. Name two ways to place a button at the bottom of a Web page.
2. What is the difference between an HTML Table control and a Web Table control?
3. Where should you store images for a Web application?

Navigating Web Pages

ASP .NET provides several techniques for navigating from one Web page to another. The easiest form of navigation is to use a HyperLink control.

Using Hyperlinks

You may need to allow your user to navigate to another site or to another page in your application. You can add a HyperLink to a Web page. The HyperLink control allows you to enter a Text property for the text to display for the user and a NavigateUrl property that specifies the URL to which to navigate.

When you select the NavigateUrl property for a HyperLink control, the *Select URL* dialog box appears (Figure 9.16). You can select the page from the list. If you want to navigate to another Web site, simply type the web address as the NavigateUrl property value.

Figure 9.16

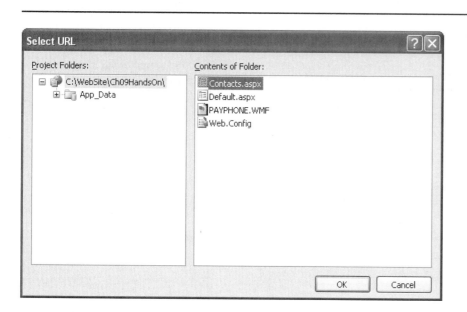

Adding a Second Web Page

Often you need to include multiple Web pages in your application. For example, you can have a separate page to display contact information for your company. You can create a Web Form that contains labels about the company and a HyperLink control to return to the company's home page. The following step-by-step exercise adds a page to the Hello project you created earlier and adds HyperLinks to each page to navigate back and forth.

Add a New Form to the Hello Project

STEP 1: Open the Ch09Hello Web site in the IDE if necessary.

STEP 2: Select *Add New Item* from the *Website* menu.

   Note: If the templates are not listed, make sure that the project is displaying in the Solution Explorer.

STEP 3: In the *Add New Item* dialog box (Figure 9.17), set the *Name* box to ContactInfo.aspx. Make sure the language is set to Visual Basic.

STEP 4: Make sure that the check box for *Place code in separate file* is selected. This option should be selected for all pages in a project.

STEP 5: Click *Add*. The ContactInfo.aspx file appears in the Document window.

STEP 6: If the source code for HTML is displaying, display Design view by selecting the tab at the bottom of the Document window or by clicking on the *View Designer* button in the Solution Explorer window.

Add Controls to the New Page

STEP 1: Set the document's Title property to "Hello Contact Information".

STEP 2: Add a HyperLink control to the top of the page.

STEP 3: Set the HyperLink's Text property to "Return to Home Page".

STEP 4: Click on the *Property* button for the HyperLink's NavigateUrl property to open the *Select URL* dialog box.

Figure 9.17

To add a new Web Form to a Web site, select Web Form *in the* Add New Item *dialog box. Make sure to choose Visual Basic for the language and select* Place code in separate file.

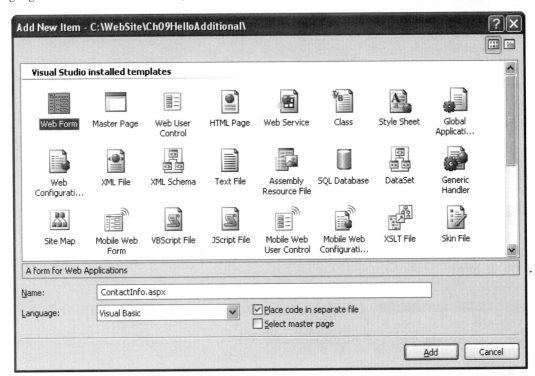

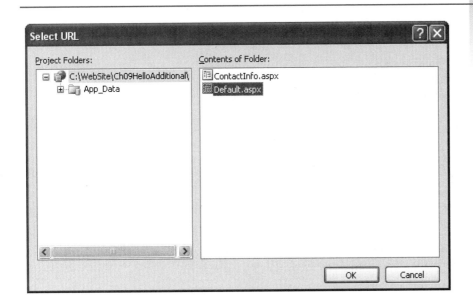

Figure 9.18

Select Default.aspx, the main page of the Web site, as the page to which to navigate.

STEP 5: Select Default.aspx (Figure 9.18), the main page of this Web site, and click OK.

STEP 6: Press Enter three or four times and enter the contact information. (Make up any information.)

Add a HyperLink to the Main Page

STEP 1: Display Default.aspx in the designer and add a HyperLink control to the bottom of the page.

STEP 2: Set the Text property of the control to "Contact Information".

STEP 3: Set the NavigateUrl property to ContactInfo.aspx.

STEP 4: Run the application. Test the links on both pages, which should navigate back and forth between the two pages.

> *Note:* If the Default.aspx page is not the first page in the browser, in the IDE right-click Default.aspx in the Solution Explorer window and select *Set as Start Page* from the context menu.

Feedback 9.3

1. What property of a HyperLink control indicates to which Web page the control is linked?
2. Describe how to set up the HyperLinks to navigate from a main page to a second page and back again to the main page.

Using the Validator Controls

ASP.NET provides several controls that can automatically validate input data. You add a **validator control**, attach it to an input control such as a text box, and set the error message. At run time, when the user inputs data, the error message displays if the validation rule is violated. These validation controls run on the client-side, so the page does not have to be submitted to the server to view and clear the message. Table 9.1 lists the ASP.NET validator controls.

Note that a blank entry passes the validation for each of the controls except the RequiredFieldValidator. If you want to ensure that the field is not blank *and* that it passes a range check, for example, attach both a RangeValidator and a RequiredFieldValidator control to a field.

For the ErrorMessage property of the validator controls, you can either enter a complete message or set the property to an asterisk. When the user leaves the field blank or enters invalid data, the asterisk will appear.

Feedback 9.4

Describe how to validate a text box called numberTextBox using validator controls. A numeric entry is required, in the range 0 to 1000. The field must not be blank.

Maintaining State

As you learned earlier, a Web page holds static data. Each time a page is displayed, or redisplayed, it is a new "fresh" copy of the page. In fact, each time the page is posted back to the server, a new fresh copy of the *program* is loaded. The server responds to the postback, handles any events that have occurred,

Validator Controls

Control	Purpose	Properties to Set
RequiredFieldValidator	Requires that the user enter something into the field.	ControlToValidate ErrorMessage
CompareValidator	Compares the value in the field to the value in another control or to a constant value. You also can set the Type property to a numeric type and the CompareValidator will verify that the input value can be converted to the correct type.	ControlToValidate ControlToCompare *or* ValueToCompare Type (To force type checking) ErrorMessage
RangeValidator	Makes sure that the input value falls in the specified range.	ControlToValidate MinimumValue MaximumValue Type (To force type checking) ErrorMessage
RegularExpressionValidator	Validates against a regular expression, such as a required number of digits, or a formatted value, such as a telephone number or Social Security number. Use the Regular Expression Editor to select or edit expressions; open by selecting the *Property* button on the ValidationExpression property.	ControlToValidate ValidationExpression ErrorMessage
ValidationSummary	Displays a summary of all of the messages from the other validation controls.	DisplayMode (Can be set to a list, bulleted list, or a single paragraph.)

sends the page back to the client (the browser), and releases the memory used by the program. Unless steps are taken to maintain the values of variables and the controls on the page, called the *state* of the page, all values will be lost in every postback.

Retaining the Contents of Controls

Although regular HTML does not retain the contents of controls during a post-back, ASP.NET *can* retain and redisplay control contents. Web controls have an EnableViewState property, which indicates that you want the server to send the control's contents back with the page. EnableViewState is set to True by default, so control contents reappear for each postback.

Retaining the Values of Variables

Local variables in a Web application work just like local variables in a Windows application: The variables are re-created each time the procedure begins. But module-level variables in Web applications do not work like the ones you are used to in Windows. Because the program is reloaded for each postback, the values of module-level variables are lost unless you take steps to save them. You can store the value of a module-level variable in a control on the Web page; the control's EnableViewState property takes care of holding the value during postback.

Note: More advanced techniques for maintaining state, such as cookies and session variables, are beyond the scope of this text. These techniques are covered in the authors' Advanced VB .NET text.

You can either set up a label with its Visible property set to False or use the new HiddenField control in the toolbox. Then assign the module-level variable to the invisible control. For an invisible label, use the Text property; for the hidden field, you must use the Value property, which is a string. In the following example, discountTotalHiddenField is a control on the page and discountTotalDecimal is a module-level variable.

```
' Declare a module-level variable
Private discountTotalDecimal As Decimal

Private Sub submitButton_Click(ByVal sender As System.Object, _
  ByVal e As System.EventArgs) Handles submitButton.Click
    ' Perform calculations.
    Dim discountDecimal As Decimal

    ' Omitted code to convert input to numeric and calculate a discount.

    ' Add to the discount total.
    discountTotalDecimal += discountDecimal
    ' Save the discount total in a hidden field.
    discountTotalHiddenField.Value = discountTotalDecimal.ToString()
End Sub
```

Checking for Postback

When an ASP.NET Web application loads, the Page_Load event occurs. But unlike Windows applications, the page is reloaded for each "round-trip" to the server (each postback). Therefore, the Page_Load event occurs many times in a Web application. The page's IsPostBack property is set to False for the initial page load and to True for all page loads following the first. If you want to perform an initialization task once, you can test for IsPostBack = False (or Not IsPostBack) in the Page_Load event procedure. And if you want to make sure that you perform an action only on postback (not the initial page load), you can check for IsPostBack = True.

```
Private Sub Page_Load(ByVal sender As System.Object, _
  ByVal e As System.EventArgs) Handles MyBase.Load

    ' If a value exists for the discount total...
    If IsPostBack And discountTotalHiddenField.Value <> "" Then
        discountTotalDecimal = Decimal.Parse(discountTotalHiddenField.Value)
    End If
```

Notice that the module-level variable discountTotalDecimal is assigned a value only on postback *and* discountTotalHiddenField already has been assigned a value.

▶ Feedback 9.5

Why is it necessary to check for a postback when writing Web applications?

Managing Web Projects

Moving and renaming Web projects is extremely easy when you are using File System Web sites, as opposed to IIS sites. Always make sure that the project is closed, and then you can rename the project folder, move it to another location on the computer, or copy it to another computer. To open the moved or renamed project, open the IDE first, select *File / Open Web site*, and navigate to the project's folder.

A potential problem exists with the files in the interim build of Visual Studio. As mentioned earlier, this version of the software creates a second folder that holds .sln and .suo files. If the folder arrangement continues in subsequent versions of Visual Studio and/or Visual Web Developer, you can handle these solution files in one of two ways: (1) You can ignore the files and continue to open the Web site folder using the *Open Web Site* menu item in the IDE; or (2) You can open the Web site from the .sln file. Unfortunately, the .sln file contains hard-coded paths that do not change when you copy or rename the Web site's folder. Unless you want to manually edit the .sln file in an editor, such as Notepad, it's best to just ignore these extra files.

Using the Copy Web Site Tool

You can use the Copy Web Site tool to copy an entire Web site from one location to another on the same computer, or to another computer on a network, or to a remote site. The tool can copy the Web site to a remote server where it can be accessed by multiple users. Select *Website / Copy Web Site* to begin the operation. For a demonstration, see the MSDN Help page "Walkthrough: Copying a Web Site Using the Copy Web Site Tool".

Some Web Acronyms

You have seen many acronyms in this chapter, such as HTML, ASP, IIS, and URL. But we have only scratched the surface. As you read the Help files for VB .NET and begin developing Web applications, you will want to know the meaning of many more. These include the following:

XML Extensible Markup Language. This popular tag-based notation is used to define data and their format and transmit the data over the Web. XML is entirely text based, does not follow any one manufacturer's specifications, and can pass through firewalls.
See the page "XML, about XML, XML in Visual Studio" in Help for further information.

SOAP Simple Object Access Protocol. An XML-based protocol for exchanging component information among distributed systems of many different types. Since it is based on XML, its messages can pass through network firewalls.
See http://www.w3.org/TR/SOAP/

HTTP	HyperText Transfer Protocol. The protocol used to send and receive Web pages over the Internet using standardized request and response messages.
Web Service	Code in classes used to provide middle-tier services over the Internet.
WSDL	Web Services Description Language. An XML document using specific syntax that defines how a Web service behaves and how clients interact with the service.

Your Hands-On Programming Example

R 'n R has decided to start selling books online. Create a Web site to calculate the amount due including discounts. Allow the user to display the total of the discounts.

The user enters the quantity, title, and price of a book, and the program calculates the extended price, a 15 percent discount, and the discounted price.

The input must be validated. The quantity and price are required fields, and the quantity must be an integer between 1 and 100.

Additionally, the program will maintain a total of all discounts given and display that total on the page in response to a button click.

Include a second page for contact information.

Note: This project is a Web version of the Book Sales program for R 'n R from Chapter 3.

Planning the Project

Sketch the Web forms (Figure 9.19), which your users sign off as meeting their needs.

Figure 9.19

Sketch the forms for the hands-on programming example; a. the main (default) page and b. the contacts page.

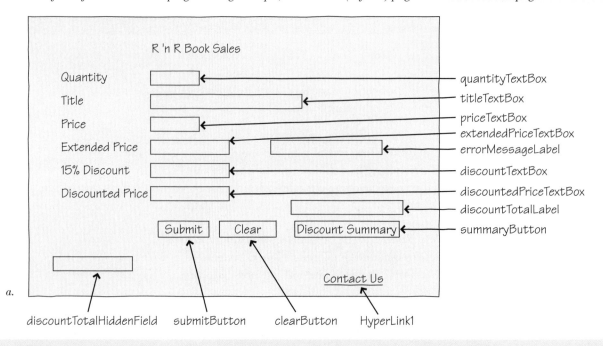

Figure 9.19

(continued)

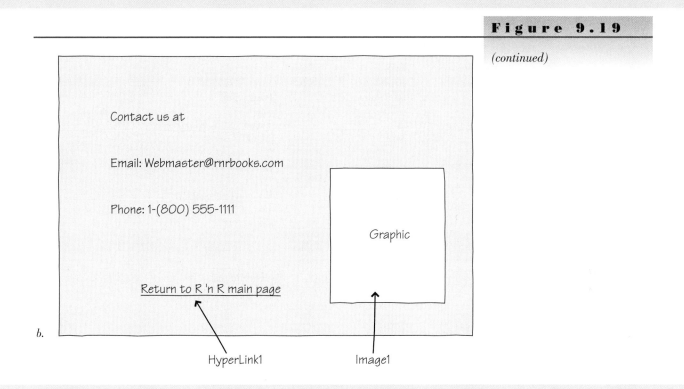

b.

Plan the Objects and Properties

Default Page

Object	Property	Setting
HTML Table (8 rows by 3 columns)		
Text entered directly in cells (not in controls)		R 'n R Book Sales (Font: Bold, Arial, Medium) Quantity Title Price Extended Price 15% Discount Discounted Price
quantityTextBox	ID Text	quantityTextBox (blank)
titleTextBox	ID Text	titleTextBox (blank)
priceTextBox	ID Text	priceTextBox (blank)
extendedPriceTextBox	ID Text ReadOnly BackColor	extendedPriceTextBox (blank) True Transparent (*Hint*: Select from Web colors)

Object	Property	Setting
discountTextBox	ID	discountTextBox
	Text	(blank)
	ReadOnly	True
	BackColor	Transparent
discountedPriceTextBox	ID	discountedPriceTextBox
	Text	(blank)
	ReadOnly	True
	BackColor	Transparent
discountTotalLabel	ID	discountTotalLabel
	Text	(blank)
	Visible	False
discountTotalHiddenField	ID	discountTotalHiddenField
submitButton	ID	submitButton
	Text	Submit
clearButton	ID	clearButton
	Text	Clear
summaryButton	ID	summaryButton
	Text	Discount Summary
quantityRequiredFieldValidator	ID	quantityRequiredFieldValidator
	ControlToValidate	quantityTextBox
	ErrorMessage	*
quantityRangeValidator	ID	quantityRangeValidator
	ControlToValidate	quantityTextBox
	Type	Integer
	MaximumValue	100
	MinimumValue	1
	ErrorMessage	1-100 Only.
priceRequiredFieldValidator	ID	priceRequiredFieldValidator
	ControlToValidate	priceTextBox
	ErrorMessage	Required Field
priceRangeValidator	ID	priceRangeValidator
	ControlToValidate	priceTextBox
	Type	Currency
	ErrorMessage	Must be numeric
errorMessageLabel	ID	errorMessageLabel
	Text	(blank)
	ForeColor	Red
Hyperlink1	Text	Contact Us
	NavigateUrl	Contact.aspx

Contact Page

Object	Property	Setting
Text entered directly in cells (not in controls)		Contact us at Email: Webmaster@rnr.com *Note*: This will convert to an e-mail link automatically. Phone: 1-(800) 555-1111
HyperLink1	Text NavigateUrl	Return to R 'n R main page HomePage.aspx
Image1	ImageUrl	Payphone.wmf (Stored in project folder) (Image found in StudentData\Graphics)

Plan the Procedures

Default Page

Procedure	Actions
Page_Load	If PostBack and hidden field has a value Load discount total from hidden field.
submitButton_Click	Clear any text in errorMessageLabel. Convert input text values to numeric. Calculate the extended price = price * quantity. Calculate the discount = extended price * discount rate. Calculate the discounted price = extended price − discount. Add the discount to the discount total. Assign the discount total to the hidden field. Format and display the results. Handle any conversion exceptions.
clearButton_Click	Clear all text boxes and labels.
summaryButton_Click	Display the discount total in a label.

Contact Page
The contact page has no event procedures.

Write the Project
Follow the sketch in Figure 9.19 to create the Web pages. Figure 9.20 shows the completed pages and Figure 9.21 shows the pages in Design view.

- Set the properties of each of the objects according to your plan.

- Write the code. Working from the pseudocode, write each procedure.

- When you complete the code, use a variety of data to thoroughly test the project. Make sure to test with empty fields, data out of range, and nonnumeric data in the numeric fields.

The finished Web application; a. the main (default) page and b. the contacts page.

Lay out the controls in Design view; a. the main (default) page and b. the contacts page.

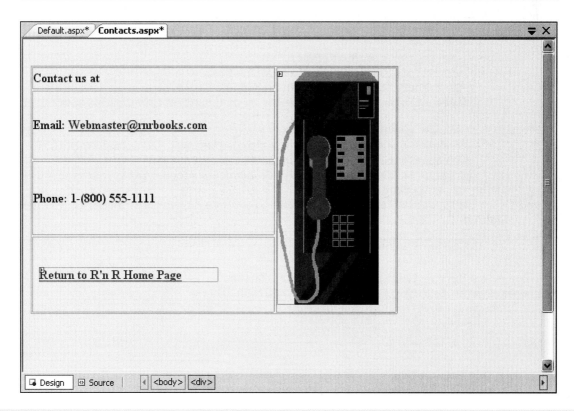

The Project Coding Solution

```vb
'Program:        Chapter 9 HandsOn
'Programmer:     Bradley/Millspaugh
'Date:           June 2005
'Description:    A Web site to calculate the extended price for books sold,
'                a discount, and the discounted amount. Calculates and displays
'                the total discounts.
'                Uses validator controls for input validation.
'Folder:         Ch09HandsOn

Partial Class Default_aspx
   Inherits System.Web.UI.Page

   Private discountTotalDecimal As Decimal
   Const DISCOUNT_RATE_Decimal As Decimal = 0.15D

   Sub submitButton_Click(ByVal sender As Object, _
     ByVal e As System.EventArgs) Handles submitButton.Click
        Dim quantityInteger As Integer
        Dim priceDecimal, extendedPriceDecimal As Decimal
        Dim discountDecimal, discountedPriceDecimal As Decimal

        With Me
            .errorLabel.Text = String.Empty
            Try
                ' Convert input values to numeric variables.
                quantityInteger = Integer.Parse(.quantityTextBox.Text)
                priceDecimal = Decimal.Parse(.priceTextBox.Text)
                ' Calculate values for sale.
                extendedPriceDecimal = quantityInteger * priceDecimal
                discountDecimal = extendedPriceDecimal * DISCOUNT_RATE_Decimal
                discountedPriceDecimal = extendedPriceDecimal – discountDecimal

                ' Add to the discount total.
                discountTotalDecimal += discountDecimal
                ' Save the discount total in a hidden field.
                .discountTotalHiddenField.Value = discountTotalDecimal.ToString()

                ' Format and display answers.
                .extendedPriceTextBox.Text = extendedPriceDecimal.ToString("C")
                .discountTextBox.Text = discountDecimal.ToString("N")
                .discountPriceTextBox.Text = discountedPriceDecimal.ToString("C")
            Catch ex As Exception
                .errorLabel.Text = "Unable to calculate. Check for numeric values."
            End Try
        End With
   End Sub

   Private Sub clearButton_Click(ByVal sender As Object, _
     ByVal e As System.EventArgs) Handles clearButton.Click
       ' Clear previous amounts from the page.
```

```
        With Me
            .quantityTextBox.Text = ""
            .TitleTextBox.Text = ""
            .priceTextBox.Text = ""
            .extendedPriceTextBox.Text = ""
            .discountTextBox.Text = ""
            .discountPriceTextBox.Text = ""
            .discountTotalLabel.Text = ""
            .errorLabel.Text = ""
        End With
    End Sub

    Sub Page_Load(ByVal sender As Object, _
      ByVal e As System.EventArgs) Handles Me.Load
            ' If a value exists for the discount total...

        With Me.discountTotalHiddenField
            If IsPostBack And .Value <> "" Then
                discountTotalDecimal = Decimal.Parse(.Value)
            End If
        End With
    End Sub

    Private Sub summaryButton_Click(ByVal sender As Object, _
      ByVal e As System.EventArgs) Handles summaryButton.Click
            ' Display the total discount.

        Me.discountTotalLabel.Text _
            = "Total Discounts: $" & Me.discountTotalHiddenField.Value
    End Sub
End Class
```

Summary

1. A Web application runs in a browser whereas most Windows applications run stand-alone.
2. A Web site has a client, which is the system running the Web page in a browser, and a server, which is the location of the Web page files.
3. Different browsers may display Web pages differently. Web developers must test their applications on multiple browsers unless they know that all users will use the same browser, such as in a company intranet.
4. Web pages are static and stateless. They require processing to change the appearance of the page and cannot store variables on their own.
5. ASP.NET is the Web technology included in Visual Studio .NET. Web Forms in Visual Basic use ASP.NET.
6. A Web Form consists of two files: the .aspx file that holds the code to render the user interface and the .aspx.vb file that holds the VB code.
7. The controls for Web pages are different from those used on Windows Forms.
8. In Design view, the *HTML* tab displays the HTML that is automatically generated.
9. You can display a page preview as it will appear in a browser.

10. Controls on Web pages may be HTML (client-side) controls or Web server controls, which are the controls provided by ASP.NET. Web server controls are rendered specifically for the browser being used.

11. Although the events of Web controls are somewhat different from those for Windows controls, coding for the events is the same.

12. A different set of files is generated for Web projects than for Windows projects.

13. In a Web page, controls are placed one after another, from top to bottom, similar to a word processing document.

14. You can use an HTML table to lay out controls and text in rows and columns.

15. Add graphics to a page using an Image control. The control's ImageUrl property holds the location of the file.

16. Validator controls allow testing for a required field, proper type of data, or a range of values.

17. The EnableViewState property of a Web control determines whether the control maintains its value during postback. To maintain the value of a program module-level variable, assign the variable's value to a hidden or invisible control.

18. A HyperLink control is used for navigation. Set the NavigateURL property to the page to which to navigate, which can be in the current project or another Web site.

19. You can add multiple pages to a Web application and set up navigation between the pages.

20. To move a Web project from one computer to another, make sure the project is not open in the IDE and copy the project's folder.

21. XML is used to store and transfer data on the Internet. XML is tag-based and text-only and can be transmitted through network firewalls. SOAP and WSDL are based on XML.

Key Terms

browser *354*

code separation model *358*

intranet *355*

single-file model *358*

stateless *355*

table *366*

validator control *372*

Web Form *354*

Web page *355*

1. Explain the differences between the execution of a Windows application and a Web site.
2. Differentiate between the client and the server for a Web application.
3. What is meant by the statement that Web pages are stateless?
4. What options are available for locations of Web site files?
5. What are the differences between HTML controls and standard controls?
6. How does event handling differ from that for Windows applications?
7. What functions are done by validator controls? How can you set up a validator control?
8. What is the purpose of XML? of SOAP?

Programming Exercises

9.1 Rewrite your project from Chapter 3 to be a Web project; include validation.

9.2 Rough Riders Rodeo wants to sell tickets online. Allow the user to enter the number of tickets needed. The data entry screen should also include the shipping address for the tickets, a credit card number, expiration date, and a drop-down box allowing the user to select the type of credit card. Also include a check box for attending the Awards Event. Include a hyperlink for confirming the order. Make the link invisible to begin but display it after the Submit button has been clicked.

The confirmation page should say "Thank you for your order".

The tickets are $15 for just the rodeo, $25 if they want to attend the event. Note that all members of the party must select the same type of tickets.

When the user selects the Submit button, display the amount due and display a link to confirm the order (make the existing link visible).

9.3 Create a Web page for entering new customer information. The fields include name, e-mail, username, and password. Include a second text box to confirm the password. Set the TextMode property of the two password fields to "Password". Use a table to lay out your controls.

Validate that all fields contain information. Display appropriate messages for any empty fields. Include a Submit button.

When all information is entered and the Submit button is pressed, compare the two password fields to see if they are equal. If not, clear both text boxes and display a message to reenter the password information. When the passwords match, display a message that says "Welcome" and the name of the customer.

Case Studies

VB Mail Order

Write the VB Mail Order project from Chapter 4 as a Web project. Use validator controls for the validation. Include a second page with contact information for the company.

VB Auto Center

Write the VB Auto Center project from Chapter 4 as a Web project. Use validator controls for the validation. Include a second page with contact information for the company.

Video Bonanza

Write the Video Bonanza project from Chapter 3 or Chapter 4 as a Web project. Use validator controls for the validation. Include a second page with contact information for the company.

Very Very Boards

Write the Very Very Boards project from Chapter 3 or Chapter 4 as a Web project. Use validator controls for the validation. Include a second page with contact information for the company.

CHAPTER

10

Accessing Database Files

Calculate values for sale.
extendedPriceDecimal = quantityInteger
discountDecimal = extendedPriceDecimal
discountedPriceDecimal = extendedPriceD
Calculate summary values.
quantitySumInteger += quantityInteger
discountSumDecimal += discountDecimal
discountedPriceSumDecimal += discounted
saleCountInteger += 1

at the completion of this chapter, you will be able to . . .

1. Use database terminology correctly.

2. Create Windows and Web projects that display database data.

3. Display data in a DataGridView control.

4. Bind data to text boxes and labels.

5. Allow the user to select from a combo box or list box and display the corresponding record in data-bound controls.

Database Files

Most data handling today is done with relational database files. Many manufacturers produce database management systems (DBMSs), each with its own proprietary format. One challenge for software developers has been accessing data from multiple sources that are stored in different formats. Most of the new tools available to developers, including Microsoft's Visual Studio .NET, attempt to handle data from multiple locations (servers) and data stored in different formats.

Visual Basic and Database Files

You can use Visual Basic to write projects that display and update the data from database files. Visual Basic .NET uses ADO.NET, which is the next generation of database technology, based on Microsoft's previous version called *ActiveX Data Objects (ADO)*. One big advantage of ADO.NET is that information is stored and transferred in Extensible Markup Language (XML). You will find more information about XML in the section "XML Data" later in this chapter.

ADO.NET allows you to access database data in many formats. The basic types of providers are OleDb, SQLClient for SQL Server (Microsoft's proprietary DBMS), Odbc, and Oracle. Using OleDb you can obtain data from sources such as Access, Oracle, Sybase, or DB2. The examples in this text use Microsoft's new SQL Server Express (SSE), which installs automatically with Visual Studio.

Database Terminology

To use database files, you must understand the standard terminology of relational databases. Although there are various definitions of standard database terms, we will stick with the most common terms, those used in SQL Server and Access.

A database file (with an .mdf or .mdb extension) can hold multiple tables. Each **table** can be viewed like a spreadsheet, with rows and columns. Each **row** in a table represents the data for one item, person, or transaction and is called a *record*. Each **column** in a table is used to store a different element of data, such as an account number, a name, an address, or a numeric amount. The elements represented in columns are called *fields*. You can think of the table in Figure 10.1 as consisting of rows and columns or of records and fields.

Most tables use a **key field** (or combination of fields) to identify each record. The key field is often a number such as employee number, account number, identification number, or Social Security number; or it may be a text field, such as last name, or a combination, such as last name and first name.

A relational database generally contains multiple tables and relationships between the tables. For example, an Employee table may have an Employee ID field and the Payroll table also will have an Employee ID field. The two tables are related by Employee ID. You can find the employee information for one payroll record by retrieving the record for the corresponding Employee ID in the Employee table. One reason to create relationships between tables is to keep the data compact and easy to maintain. By having multiple payroll records related to one employee record through the Employee ID, an employee's address, for example, can be changed in one spot without having to go to each payroll record to update it.

Figure 10.1

ISBN	Title	Author	Publisher
0-111-11111-1	89 Years in a Sand Trap	Beck, Fred	Hill and Wang
0-15-500139-6	Business Programming in C	Millspaugh, A. C.	The Dryden Press
0-394-75843-9	Cultural Literacy	Hirsch, E. D. Jr.	Vintage
0-440-22284-2	Five Days in Paris	Steel, Danielle	Dell Publishing
0-446-51251-6	Megatrends	Naisbitt, John	Warner Books
0-446-51652-X	Bridges of Madison County	Waller, Robert James	Warner Books
0-446-60274-4	The Rules	Fein/Schneider	Warner Books
0-451-16095-9	The Stand	King, Stephen	Signet
0-452-26011-6	Song of Solomon	Morrison, Toni	Plume/Penguin
0-517-59905-8	How to Talk to Anyone, Anytime, Anywhere	King, Larry	Crown
0-534-26076-4	A Quick Guide to the Internet	Bradley, Julia Case	Integrated Media Group

A database table consists of rows (records) and columns (fields).

— Record or row

Field or column

Any time a database table is open, one record is considered the current record. As you move from one record to the next, the current record changes.

XML Data

XML is an industry-standard format for storing and transferring data. You can find the specifications for XML at http://www.w3.org/XML, which is the site for the World Wide Web Consortium (W3C).

You don't need to know any XML to write database applications in VB. The necessary XML is generated for you automatically, like the automatically generated VB code and HTML. However, a few facts about XML can help you understand what is happening in your programs.

Most proprietary database formats store data in binary, which cannot be accessed by other systems or pass through Internet firewalls. Data stored in XML is all text, identified by tags, similar to HTML tags. An XML file can be edited by any text editor program, such as Notepad.

If you have seen or written any HTML, you know that opening and closing tags define elements and attributes. For example, any text between <b> and </b> is rendered in bold by the browser.

```
<b>This text is bold.</b> <i>This is italic.</i>
```

The tags in XML are not predefined as they are in HTML. The tags can identify fields by name. For example, following are three records of the

RnrBooks database file exported to XML. (Later in this chapter you will be using the RnrBooks database for VB projects.)

```xml
<?xml version="1.0" encoding="UTF-8"?><dataroot xmlns:od="urn:schemas-microsoft-com:officedata">
  <Books>
    <ISBN>0-15-500139-6</ISBN>
    <Title>Business Programming in C</Title>
    <Author>Millspaugh, A. C.</Author>
    <Publisher>The Dryden Press</Publisher>
  </Books>
  <Books>
    <ISBN>0-446-51652-X</ISBN>
    <Title>Bridges of Madison County</Title>
    <Author>Waller, Robert James</Author>
    <Publisher>Warner Books</Publisher>
  </Books>
  <Books>
    <ISBN>0-451-16095-9</ISBN>
    <Title>The Stand</Title>
    <Author>King, Stephen</Author>
    <Publisher>Signet</Publisher>
  </Books>
</dataroot>
```

In addition to an XML data file, you usually also have an XML schema file. The schema describes the fields, data types, and any constraints, such as required fields. ADO.NET validates the data against the schema and checks for constraint violations. The schema also is defined with XML tags and can be viewed or edited in a text editor. You will be able to see the schema for your data files in a VB project by viewing the .xsd file shown in the Solution Explorer.

The format of XML data offers several advantages for programming. Because an XML schema provides for strong data typing, the various data types can be handled properly. And ADO.NET can treat the XML data as objects, allowing the IntelliSense feature of the VS .NET environment to provide information for the programmer. In addition, data handling in XML and ADO.NET executes faster than in earlier forms of ADO.

Feedback 10.1

1. Assume you have a database containing the names and phone numbers of your friends. Describe how the terms *file*, *table*, *row*, *column*, *record*, *field*, and *key field* apply to your database.
2. What is an advantage of transferring data as XML rather than as a proprietary format such as Access or SQL Server?

Using ADO.NET and Visual Basic

In Visual Basic, you can display data from a database on a Windows Form or a Web Form. You add controls to the form and bind data to the controls. The controls may be labels or text boxes or one of the special controls designed just for data, such as the DataGridView or DataList. However, just as you found in

Chapter 9, the controls for a Windows application are different from the controls for a Web application and have different properties and events. In this chapter, you will write database applications using both Windows Forms and Web Forms. Figure 10.2 shows a data table displaying in a DataGridView on a Windows Form.

Figure 10.2

The DataGridView control is bound to a table in a dataset. The data fields display automatically in the cells of the grid.

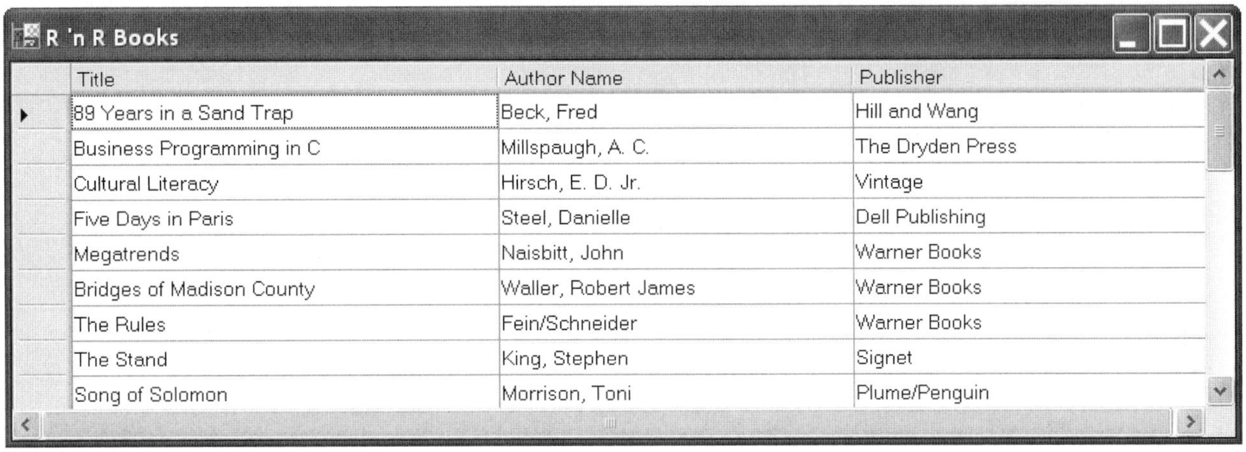

Title	Author Name	Publisher
89 Years in a Sand Trap	Beck, Fred	Hill and Wang
Business Programming in C	Millspaugh, A. C.	The Dryden Press
Cultural Literacy	Hirsch, E. D. Jr.	Vintage
Five Days in Paris	Steel, Danielle	Dell Publishing
Megatrends	Naisbitt, John	Warner Books
Bridges of Madison County	Waller, Robert James	Warner Books
The Rules	Fein/Schneider	Warner Books
The Stand	King, Stephen	Signet
Song of Solomon	Morrison, Toni	Plume/Penguin

R 'n R Books

You must use several classes and objects to set up data access in Visual Basic.

Data Access in Visual Studio 2005

A new feature to this version of Visual Studio is the Data Sources window. This new window provides an easy way to create data-bound controls on a form. As you will see later in this chapter, you can drag tables and fields from the window onto a form to automatically create controls that are bound to the data. You can display the data in grids or individual fields, which are referred to as *details*. You also can drag a field from the Data Sources window and drop it on an existing control, which causes **data binding** to be set up automatically. If you have done any database programming in previous versions of VB or other languages, you will be pleased with the significant improvements in VS 2005.

When you add data-bound controls to a form, two things occur: An .xsd file with the schema is added to the Server Explorer window and BindingSource, TableAdapter, and DataSet objects are added to the form's component tray.

The following list is an overview of database objects; each of the classes is further described in the sections that follow.

- *Binding source.* A binding source establishes a link to the actual data, which is a specific file and/or database.

- *Table adapter.* A table adapter handles retrieving and updating the data. A table adapter automatically generates SQL statements that you can use to access or update data. SQL, or Structured Query Language, is an industry-standard language that is used to select and update data in a relational database.

- *Dataset.* A dataset contains the actual data. The data in a single dataset may come from multiple binding sources and/or multiple table adapters.

Figure 10.3 shows a visual representation of the required steps.

Figure 10.3

To display database data in bound controls on a form, you need a binding source, a table adapter, and a dataset.

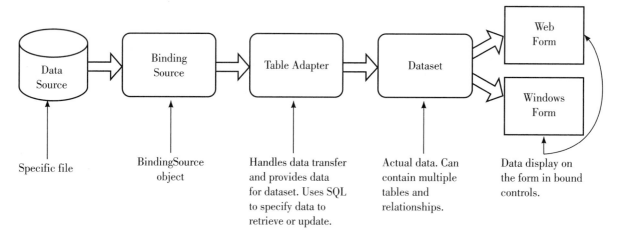

Specific file | BindingSource object | Handles data transfer and provides data for dataset. Uses SQL to specify data to retrieve or update. | Actual data. Can contain multiple tables and relationships. | Data display on the form in bound controls.

Binding Sources

A **Binding Source** object establishes a link from a specific file or database to your program. In this chapter, you will use a wizard to automatically create BindingSource objects. You also can add new BindingSource objects using the *Data Sources* window or the *Data* menu.

Note: Earlier versions of VB .NET used *Connection objects* rather than BindingSources.

Table Adapters

A **table adapter** does all of the work of passing data back and forth between a **data source** (the binding source) and a program (the dataset). The binding source for a table adapter does not have to be a database; it also can be a text file, an object, or even an array. No matter where the actual data (the source) for the binding source is, the table adapter transfers data from the source to the dataset (fills) or transfers data from the dataset to the source (updates) all via XML.

Datasets

A **dataset** is a temporary set of data stored in the memory of the computer. In ADO.NET, datasets are disconnected, which means that the copy of data in memory does not keep an active connection to the data source. This technique is a big improvement from the recordsets in earlier versions of ADO, which maintain open connections to the data source. A dataset may contain multiple tables; however, the examples in this chapter use only one table per dataset.

Any controls that you have bound to the dataset will automatically fill with data.

Creating a Database Application

In the following step-by-step exercise, you will create a Windows application that displays data from the Books table of the RnrBooks.mdf database file. You will display the fields from the table in a **DataGridView control** on a Windows Form. Refer to Figure 10.2 for the finished application.

A Windows Database Application—Step-By-Step

This step-by-step exercise uses the RnRBooks.mdf SQL Server database file, which is available in the StudentData folder from the student CD and from the text download site. Make sure that the file is available before starting this project.

Start a New Project

STEP 1: Start a new Windows Application project called "Ch10DataGrid-View".

STEP 2: Name the form "BooksForm" and set the Text property to "R 'n R Books". Widen the form to about three times the original size.

STEP 3: Select *Save All* from the *File* menu or the toolbar button.

Add a Grid to Display the Data

STEP 1: Add a DataGridView control to the form. You can find the control in the toolbox in both the *All Windows Forms* tab and the *Data* tab. Click the Smart Tag arrow to pop up the smart tag (Figure 10.4).

Add a DataGridView control to a form and pop up its smart tag.

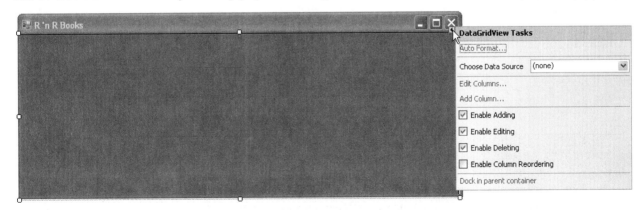

STEP 2: On the smart tag, drop down the list for *Choose Data Source*. Select *Add Project Data Source* from the drop-down (Figure 10.5), which activates the Data Source Configuration Wizard. Click *Next*.

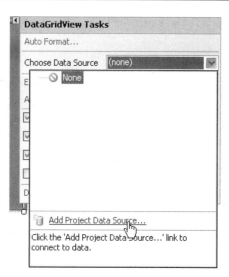

Note: If the smart tag is off the edge of the screen, select the form and drag it smaller, then select the DataGridView and click on the Smart Tag arrow to display the smart tag again.

STEP 3: Select *Database* (Figure 10.6) and click *Next*.

Note that it isn't necessary to copy the database .mdf file into the project folder; the wizard will ask you later if you want to add the data file to the project, which automatically copies the file to your project folder. You can select the file from anywhere it is available, including from the CD. When the project runs, it uses the copy in your project

Data Source Configuration Wizard

Choose a Data Source Type

This step provides you with different sources of data.

Where will the application get data from?

Database   Web Service   Object

Lets you choose the database objects you are interested in and creates a DataSet in the current project as a result.

[< Previous]   [Next >]   [Finish]   [Cancel]

folder. If you want to use a database file stored somewhere else, for example to share with other applications, you will not add the file to your project.

STEP 4: Select *New Connection* (Figure 10.7) to set up the connection for the Binding Source object.

Figure 10.7

Select New Connection *to set up the connection to the database file.*

STEP 5: In the *Add Connection* dialog box, the Data source should be set to "Microsoft SQL Server Database File (SqlClient)." Browse to select the RnRBooks.mdf file. You can find it anywhere it is available, including on the CD; later the file will be added to your project. Click *Open* and then *Test Connection*; you should see a message that the test connection succeeded. Click *OK*.

STEP 6: Your new connection should now appear selected; click *Next*.

A dialog pops up asking if you want to add the file to your project (Figure 10.8). Click *Yes*, which will make your project portable, so that you can run it on different computers without worrying about the file location.

Figure 10.8

This dialog gives you the option of making a copy of the database file in the current folder. Select Yes.

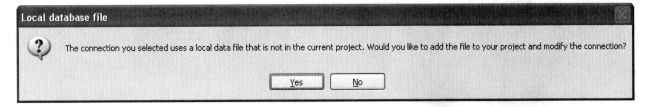

STEP 7: Click *Next*. The database objects in the RnRBooks database will appear.

STEP 8: Expand the Tables node and place a check mark in front of Books (Figure 10.9). Click *Finish*.

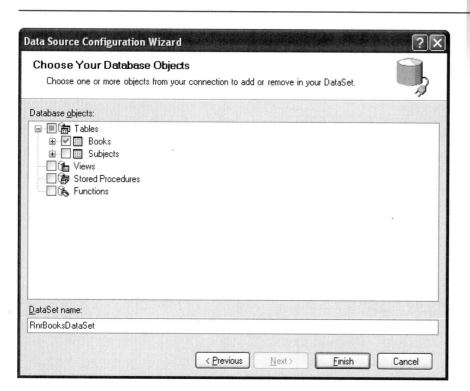

STEP 9: Notice that the grid column headings now have the names of the fields. Later you will learn to resize the widths of the columns.

Run the Data Application

STEP 1: Run your program. The grid should fill with data. At this point, the user can resize the columns by dragging the dividers between column headings.

STEP 2: Close the form or click the *Stop Debugging* button (Shift + F5) in the IDE to stop program execution.

Examine the Components

STEP 1: Take a look in the components tray (Figure 10.10). Your form now contains a TableAdapter component, a DataSet component, and a BindingSource component. The wizard automatically names the dataset with the name of the database source and the others using the name of the table.

STEP 2: Now look at the form's code. The Form_Load procedure automatically contains the code to fill the data set from the table adapter.

```
Me.BooksTableAdapter.Fill(Me.RnrBooksDataSet.Books)
```

Format the DataGridView

STEP 1: Switch back to the designer and click on the DataGridView and then click on the Smart Tag arrow—the small arrow on the right side of the grid or form. In the smart tag that pops up, select *Edit Columns* (Figure 10.11).

Figure 10.10

The data components that were generated by the Data Source Configuration Wizard appear in the component tray of the form.

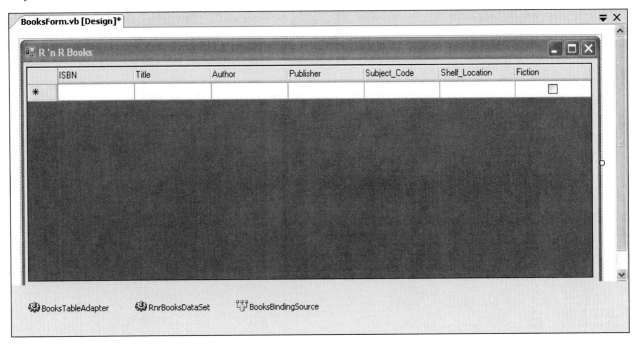

Figure 10.11

Pop up the smart tag and select Edit Columns to format the grid.

STEP 2: In the *Edit Columns* dialog box (Figure 10.12), you can add, remove, and reorder the columns. You also can select any of the columns on the left side of the dialog box and view or modify its properties on the right side. For example, you can set the width of a column and change its heading text (HeaderText property).

STEP 3: Delete the extra fields so that the grid displays only the title, author, and publisher. For the Title column, change the AutoSizeMode setting to "None" and set the Width to "250 pixels". For the Author column, set AutoSizeMode to "None", Width to "250 pixels", and header text to "Author Name". Set the Publisher column to AutoSizeMode = "None" and Width = "250 pixels".

Figure 10.12

Format the columns of the grid in the **Edit Columns** *dialog box.*

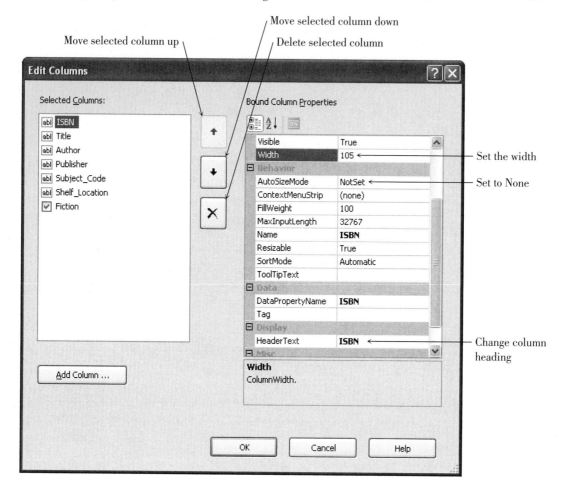

Move selected column down

Move selected column up

Delete selected column

Set the width

Set to None

Change column heading

Note: You cannot set the width without first setting AutoSizeMode.

STEP 4: Run the application and make note of any changes that would improve the layout.

STEP 5: Return to design time, make any further modifications, and run the application again.

The Smart Tag

Earlier you used the smart tag to select a data source and to edit the properties of grid columns. You also can use the smart tag to AutoFormat the grid, dock the grid in its parent container (the form), and add and edit columns.

When you select *AutoFormat*, you can choose from many predefined formats. Figure 10.13 shows the grid with a format applied.

The Database Schema File

When you add a new data source to a project, a file with the extension .xsd is added to the Solution Explorer. This file contains the XML schema definition, which has the description and properties of the data. You can double-click on

Figure 10.13

You can apply predefined formats from the AutoFormat *item on the smart tag.*

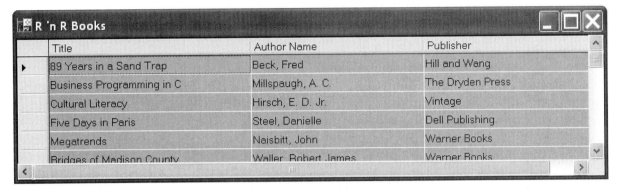

the .xsd file to open the **Data Designer** (Figure 10.14). The schema shows the names of the table(s) and fields, the primary keys for each table, and the relationships among the tables if more than one table is represented. You can click on the table name or a field name to display the properties in the Properties window.

Figure 10.14

The .xsd file holds the schema of the database, where you can view and modify the table elements, relationships, and keys.

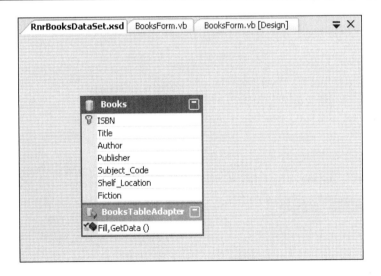

Notice in Figure 10.14 that at the bottom of the schema appears the TableAdapter for the table. The TableAdapter handles the `Fill` and `GetData` methods for the table. You can click on the *TableAdapter* row to display its properties in the Properties window, or click on the *Fill,GetData()* row to view the properties of the Fill Query.

Binding Individual Data Fields

You can bind table fields from your dataset to many types of controls, such as labels, text boxes, combo boxes, and check boxes. Controls that are connected to fields in the database are referred to as **bound controls** or **data-bound controls**. The easiest way to create bound controls is to use the automatic binding features of the Data Sources window. You can set the data to display as details and then drag the table to the form. This technique creates individual text box controls for each field of data and a navigation control, which allows the user to move from one record to another. Figure 10.15 shows a form with data-bound text boxes; you will create this form in the next section.

Figure 1 0 . 1 5

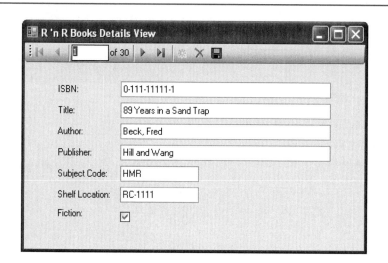

Each text box or check box is bound to one field from the table. As the user clicks the navigation buttons, all controls change to display the data for the next record.

The Data Sources Window

You can display the Data Sources window by selecting *Show Data Sources* from the *Data* menu or the *Data Sources* tab that usually appears docked with the Solution Explorer. In a new project, you can use the Data Sources window to add a new data source (Figure 10.16).

Figure 1 0 . 1 6

Add a new data source in the Data Sources window.

When you select the option to add a new data source, the Data Source Configuration Wizard opens and steps you through selecting the file and table, just as you did in the earlier step-by-step exercise. The new data source appears in the Data Sources window. You can click on the table name to make a drop-down list available, on which you can select *Details* (Figure 10.17). Note that the default view is DataGridView, which is the view that you used in the previous step-by-step exercise. After you select Details view, the table's icon changes to match the view (Figure 10.18).

Note: The form's designer must be open for the table's check mark to appear.

Figure 10.17

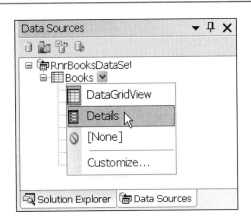

Drop down the list for the table name and select Details to bind each field to its own Text Box control.

Figure 10.18

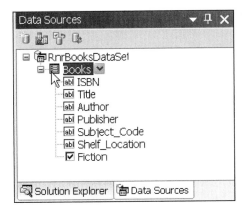

The table's icon changes to indicate Details view.

Database Details Program—Step-By-Step

This step-by-step exercise creates the data-bound Details view shown in Figure 10.15.

Begin a New Project

STEP 1: Create a new Windows project called "Ch10DetailsView".

STEP 2: Change the form's filename to "DetailsForm" and the form's Text property to "R 'n R Books Detail View".

STEP 3: Save the project.

Set Up the Data Source

STEP 1: Open the Data Sources window by using one of these two techniques: If the *Data Sources* tab appears docked with the Solution Explorer, click on the tab; or select *Show Data Sources* from the *Data* menu.

STEP 2: Click on *Add New Data Source* in the Data Sources window.

STEP 3: In the Data Source Configuration Wizard, click *Next*, select *Database*, and click *Next* again.

STEP 4: Click on *New Connection* and browse to locate a copy of RnRBooks.mdf database file. This file can be in any other folder or on your CD. Click *Open* and *OK*.

STEP 5: Click *Next*, which pops up the dialog box asking if you want to add the file to your project; click *Yes*, then click *Next* again.

STEP 6: Open the Tables node and click in the box for the Books table. Click *Finish*.

Create the Bound Controls

STEP 1: In the Data Sources window, click on *Books*, which makes a down arrow appear to the right of the name (Figure 10.19). *Warning:* The form designer must be open for the down arrow to appear.

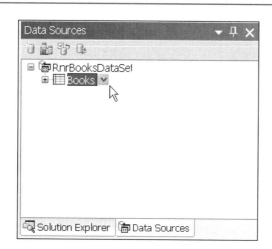

F i g u r e   1 0 . 1 9

Click on the table name to make the drop-down list available.

STEP 2: Click on the down arrow and select *Details* (refer to Figure 10.17).

STEP 3: Point to the Books table name and drag the table to the form to a position about an inch down from the top of the form.

STEP 4: Change the widths of the text boxes and the form as desired. Notice in Figure 10.20 that the component tray holds four new components: a DataSet, BindingSource, TableAdapter, and BindingNavigator, which provides the navigation buttons at the top of the form.

Also notice the text of the labels on the form. The new version of VS is smart enough to figure out multiple-word field names. For example, if your table names contain underscores or multiple capital letters, the smart labels will have the words separated by spaces. The Books table has fields called "Subject_Code" and "Shelf_Location", but the labels say "Subject Code" and "Shelf Location".

STEP 5: Run the project. Try the navigation buttons to step through the records.

Note: Remember that the ADO.NET dataset is loaded into memory and is disconnected from the database, so you can make changes to the records and use the navigation bar buttons for *Add New* (the record is added to the end of the dataset), *Delete*, and *Save*.

Figure 10.20

Resize the form and controls of
the automatically generated
controls.

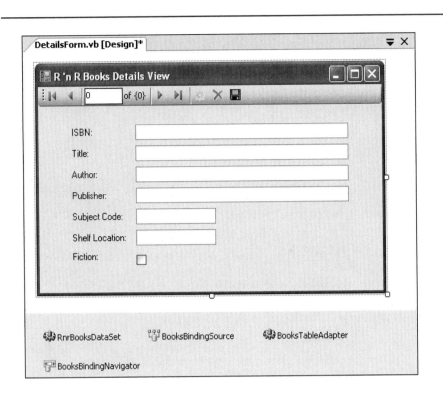

Selecting Records from a List

Many applications allow the user to select an item to display from a list. You can
fill a list box or combo box with values from a database. Consider the previous
program. A better approach might be to display the list of ISBN numbers in a
drop-down list and allow the user to make a selection. Then, after the ISBN is selected, the corresponding data elements fill remaining fields (Figure 10.21).

Figure 10.21

The user can select a book from
the combo box. The labels
automatically fill with the
field values that correspond to
that ISBN.

You can easily select the control type for a bound control in the Data Sources window. The choices are TextBox, ComboBox, Label, LinkLabel, and ListBox.

Converting to Combo Box Selection—Step-By-Step

This step-by-step exercise converts the previous exercise to a selection application. Figure 10.21 shows the output.

Begin the Project

STEP 1: Open your Ch10DetailsView project. It should contain text boxes for the data.

STEP 2: Click on the BindingNavigator component in the component tray and press the *Delete* key to delete the navigation bar from the form.

Set Up a Combo Box Control

STEP 1: Select the ISBN TextBox control and delete it.

STEP 2: In the Data Sources window, click on the ISBN field to make the down-arrow appear. Then click on the arrow to drop down the list of possible control types (Figure 10.22). Select *ComboBox*.

Figure 10.22

Select ComboBox for the ISBN field.

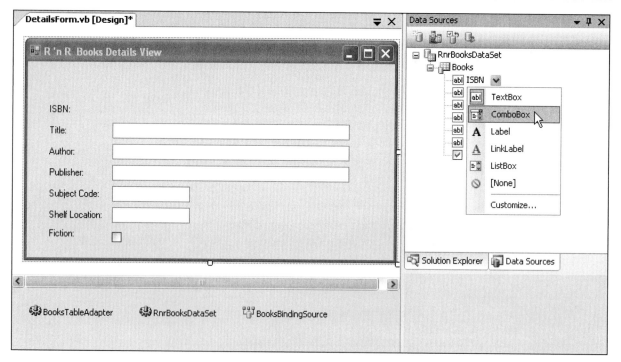

STEP 3: Drag the ISBN field from the Data Sources window to the form, which will automatically create a combo box control and an extra label for ISBN. Delete the extra label and resize the combo box to match the text boxes (refer to Figure 10.21).

STEP 4: Click on the smart tag arrow for the combo box and select *Use data bound items*, which pops up some new fields for *Data Binding Mode*

(Figure 10.23). Drop down the list for *Data Source* and select *Books-BindingSource*. Select *ISBN* for *Display Member* and *Selected Value*.

Figure 10.23

Set up the data binding for the ISBN combo box using the smart tag.

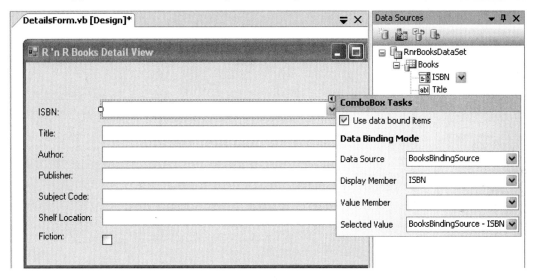

STEP 5: Set the TabIndex of the ISBN combo box to 2, which was the index of the text box that you deleted.

Run the Application

STEP 1: Run the program.

STEP 2: Drop down the combo box and select another ISBN. The other controls automatically fill with the data for the selected book.

Selecting Fields from the Table

Often you only need to display some of the fields from a database table. You can select individual fields when you create the new data source, or select the fields later, after you have created the data source.

Selecting Fields When You Create the Data Source

To set up a new dataset with selected fields, choose the *Add New Data Source* option from the *Data* menu or the Data Sources window. The Data Source Configuration Wizard appears as described earlier. When you get to the *Choose Your Database Objects*, expand the Tables node and place a check mark on just the fields that you want (Figure 10.24).

Selecting Fields after the Data Source Is Created

To modify the fields in a dataset after it has been created, select the dataset name in the Data Sources window. You can either click the *Configure DataSet with Wizard* button at the top of the window or right-click and choose the same option. You can make the field selection from the wizard as described in Figure 10.24, which will change the schema for your dataset.

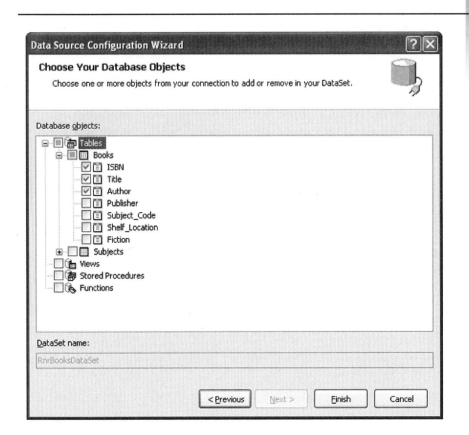

Sorting the List Data

You cannot sort bound data in a combo box or list box using the Sorted property of the control. However, you can sort the records in the query that selects the data for the dataset. Although the SQL SELECT statement is generated automatically by the designer, you can find and modify it. In the Solution Explorer, double-click on the dataset's schema file, with the .xsd extension. In the displayed schema (Figure 10.25), click on the *Fill,GetData()* entry at the bottom, which displays the properties of the Fill command in the Properties window. Click on the Property button (...) for the CommandText property; the Query-Builder window will open. If you have any experience creating queries in Access, this window will look very familiar to you.

In the QueryBuilder you can modify the SQL SELECT command that selects the data for the dataset. To sort by a field, drop down the *Sort Type* list for the desired field and choose *Ascending* or *Descending*. After you make the selection and press Enter, the SQL statement changes to include an ORDER BY clause (Figure 10.26), which sorts the data records as they are retrieved and makes the list items appear in sorted order. You also can type directly into the SELECT statement to make modifications, if you wish. Notice at the bottom of the Query-Builder window that you can execute the query to preview its output in the lower part of the window.

Choosing the Control Type for Fields

When you drag a Details view to a form, by default text fields are represented by text boxes. You saw earlier that you can select a different type of control in

Figure 10.25

Click on the Fill,GetData() entry in the dataset schema to display the properties of the Fill *command in the Properties window.*

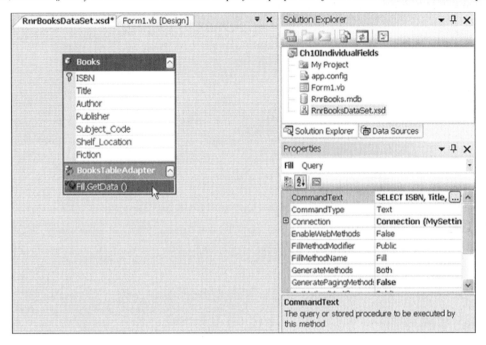

Figure 10.26

Select Ascending *for the* Sort Type *to sort the data by the Title field. The SQL statement changes to include an* ORDER BY *clause.*

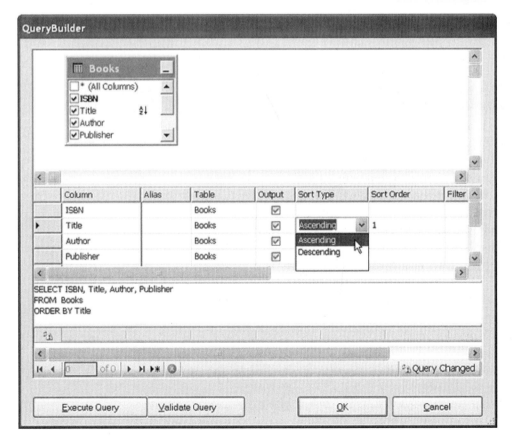

the Data Sources window before dragging it to the form. In the Data Sources window, click on a field name; a small down arrow appears to the right of the field name. Drop down the list and choose the control type (Figure 10.27). You can choose the control type for all controls and then drag the table to the form to create the Details view.

Note: You must have the form displayed in the form designer to select the control type for the field.

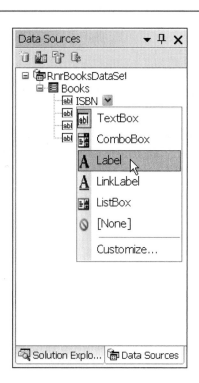

Figure 1 0 . 2 7

Select the control type for each control before creating the Details view.

▶ Feedback 10.3

1. You drag a table name from the Data Sources window onto a form. What determines whether the action produces a bound grid or a set of individual fields?
2. How can you create data-bound text boxes? Data-bound labels?
3. What properties of a ComboBox control must you set to bind the control to a data field?
4. How can you make the list items in a data-bound combo box appear in sorted order?

Selecting Records Using Web Forms

When you write database programs for the Web instead of Windows, you have a few more considerations. You still set up data sources and bind to controls, but the Web controls are considerably different from their Windows counterparts. You also have additional security issues for Web-based database applications.

A Web database application operates somewhat differently than a Windows application due to the nature of Web pages in a client/server environment. Remember that a Web page is stateless. Each time a page displays, it is a "new fresh page."

In the Web version of the list selection program (Figure 10.28), each time the user makes a selection from the list, a **postback** occurs. A postback is a round-trip to the server. After a postback, the Web page redisplays with only the selected data.

Figure 10.28

Allow the user to select a book title from the drop-down list; then display the corresponding Author and ISBN for the selected title.

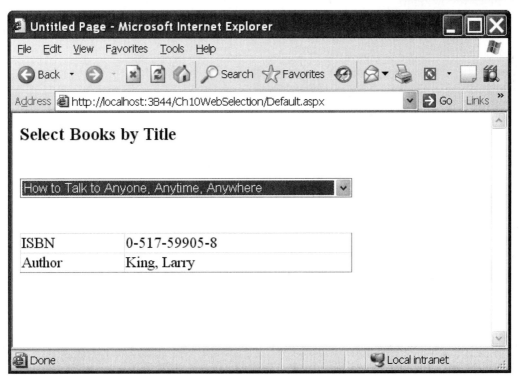

Security in Web Database Applications

Security is much tighter for Web database applications than for Windows applications. You wouldn't want an unauthorized user to be able to access data from the Web. If you set up a Web application that displays or allows modifications to data, you must require user authentication and set permission levels. Visual Studio 2005 integrates security features, which are generally strict by default, so that data will be secure unless you take steps to unprotect your files.

For the programs in this text, which introduce the basic features of Web programming, the challenge is to avoid security restrictions, rather than to secure your database. You will use a SQL Server database file, stored in the Data folder beneath the project folder. This folder has the necessary permissions for the default user of development projects.

Note: If you wish to use a database stored in a folder other than the ProjectName\Data folder, the folder must have read and write permissions for the ComputerName\ASPNET user.

Creating the Web Selection Application—Step-by-Step

This step-by-step exercise develops the Web version of the selection program that you created earlier in Windows. The Web version must use two data sources rather than one. The drop-down list must have a separate data source from the one used for the individual fields of data. The finished application appears in Figure 10.28.

Begin a New Web Site

STEP 1: Select *File / New Web Site* and set the *Location* to the folder of your choice and "Ch10WebSelection" for the name. *Example*: C:\My Documents\WebSites\Ch10WebSelection.

STEP 2: Switch to Windows Explorer or My Computer and copy RnRBooks.mdf into the project's App_Data folder. *Example*: C:\My Documents\WebSites\Ch10WebSelection\App_Data\RnRBooks.mdf. Or you can copy the file from another location and then click on the App_Data folder in the Solution Explorer window and paste the file. The database appears in the App_Data folder (Figure 10.29).

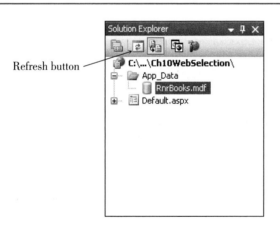

Refresh button

F i g u r e   1 0 . 2 9

Click the Refresh button after you have copied the file into the Data folder to see the changes in the Solution Explorer.

STEP 3: Select *Document* in the Properties window *Object* drop-down list and set the Web page's Title property to "R 'n R Book Selection".

STEP 4: Click at the top of the Web Form and type "Select Books by Title"; select the text and enlarge the font and make it bold. Click after the text and press Enter two or three times to move the insertion point down the page.

Set Up the Drop-Down List

STEP 1: Add a DropDownList control from the Standard tab of the toolbox. In the smart tag select *Choose Data Source*.

STEP 2: In the *Choose Data Source* dialog box, drop down the list for *Select a data source* and select *<New data source...>*.

STEP 3: In the Data Source Configuration, wizard select *SQL Database* (Figure 10.30). You can leave the ID of the data source set to SQLDataSource1. Click *OK*.

STEP 4: Next you set up the connection: Click on the *New Connection* button and click on the *Change* button for *Data source*. In the *Change Data Source* dialog box, select "Microsoft SQL Server Database File", which is the new SQL Express format. Click *OK*.

Figure 10.30

Set the data source to a SQL database file.

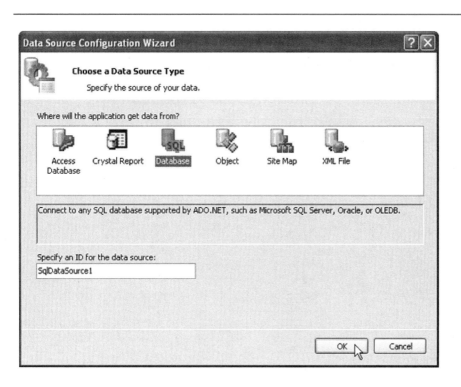

STEP 5: In the *Add Connection* dialog box, browse to select the RnrBooks.mdf file in the App_Data folder beneath the project folder. Click *OK* and *Next*. Click *Next* again.

STEP 6: On the Configure Data Source page, you will select the data fields for the dataset for the drop-down list. Click on (check) *ISBN* and *Title*. You need the ISBN because it is the table's primary key.

STEP 7: Click on the *ORDER BY* button (Figure 10.31).

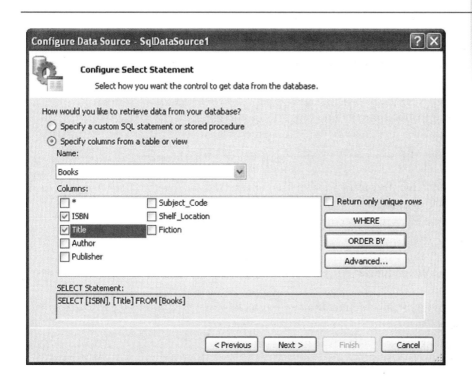

STEP 8: In the *Add ORDER BY Clause* dialog box, drop down the *Sort by* list and select *Title*. Click *OK*.

STEP 9: Back on the Configure Data Source page of the wizard, you can see the new ORDER BY clause added to the SQL SELECT statement (Figure 10.32).

Figure   10.32

An ORDER BY *clause is added to the SQL* SELECT *statement.*

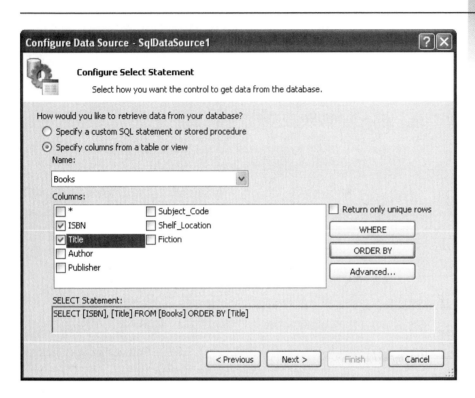

STEP 10: Click *Next*. Before you click *Finish*, you can click on the *Test Query* button if you would like to see the records returned from the query you just created. Click *Finish*.

The Data Source Configuration Wizard reappears.

STEP 11: Choose *Title* for *Select a data field to display in the DropDownList*. Keep *ISBN* as the value of the DropDownList (Figure 10.33). Click *OK*.

STEP 12: Display the smart tag for the drop-down list again and select *Enable AutoPostBack* (Figure 10.34). This important step specifies that each time the user makes a new selection from the list, the page should be sent back to the server. This step is necessary to select and display the data for the selected book.

STEP 13: Widen the DropDownList control so that it is wide enough to hold a book title.

STEP 14: Click after the SqlDataSource component (which will not appear at run time) and press Enter two or three times.

Set Up the Additional Fields

STEP 1: In the toolbox, open the Data tab and click to view the available controls and components.

You can see tools for data sources, which is another way to add a new data source. The controls near the top of the list are those that can be bound to data.

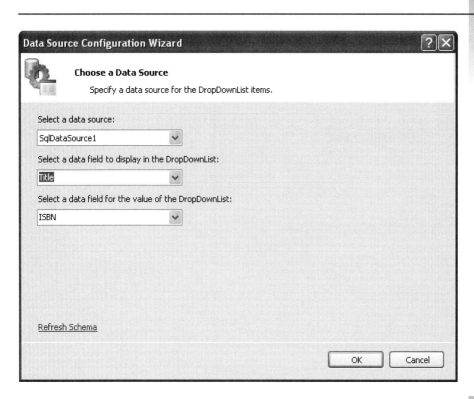

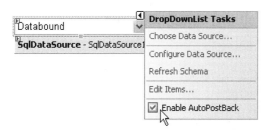

STEP 2: Add a DetailsView control to the Web page. In the smart tag, drop down the *Choose Data Source* list and select *<New data source...>*. Do *not* choose *SQLDataSource1*, which you just created. The data for the DetailsView must be different from the data for the list.

STEP 3: Select *SQL Database* and click *OK*. Then click on *New Connection*, change the Data Source to "Microsoft SQL Server Database File", and select *RnrBooks.mdf* from the App_Data folder, just like you did for the other data source. Click *OK*, then *Next*, and *Next* again.

STEP 4: On the Configure Data Source page of the wizard, select *ISBN* and *Author* for the fields. Then click on the *WHERE* button.

STEP 5: In the *Add WHERE Clause* dialog box, you will set up the parameter used to select the correct data for the individual fields. Drop down the *Column* list and select *ISBN*; leave the *Operator* drop-down as "=", then drop down the list for *Source* and select *Control*. The *Parameter properties* group box pops up on the right side of the dialog box. For *Control ID* select *DropDownList1* and notice the SQL Expression ([ISBN] = @ISBN) (Figure 10.35). This type of query is called a *parameterized query*.

STEP 6: Click on *Add* and view the WHERE clause at the bottom of the dialog box. It should say [ISBN] = @ISBN DropDownList1.SelectedValue. If it isn't correct, you can click *Remove* and repeat step 5. Click *OK*.

Back in the wizard, the SELECT statement should read:

```
SELECT [ISBN], [Author] FROM [Books] WHERE ([ISBN] = @ISBN)
```

STEP 7: Click *Next* and *Finish*.

Note: Don't bother with *Test Query* this time because you must supply an existing ISBN number—the parameter—to make the query work.

STEP 8: Resize the DetailsView control to be approximately the same width as the DropDownList control (Figure 10.36). *Note*: If your grid does not look like the figure, select *Refresh Schema* from the SqlDataSource's smart tag.

STEP 9: Click *Save All* (or press Ctrl + Shift + S).

Run the Application

STEP 1: Press Ctrl + F5 (or *Debug / Start without Debugging*) to test application.

STEP 2: Make new selections from the list; the data fields below should change to match the selection.

Moving Database Projects

You should be able to move the database projects in this chapter to another computer, open them in the IDE, and edit and/or run the applications. This is a huge improvement over earlier versions of VB .NET.

Make sure that the project is not open in the IDE and copy the complete folder from one computer or location to another. For Web projects, you must first open the IDE, select *Open Web Site*, and browse to the folder.

Figure 10.36

Widen the DetailsView control.

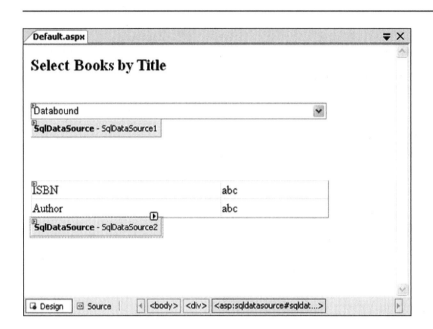

Your Hands-On Programming Example

Create a Windows application that contains a drop-down list of titles from the RnrBooks.mdf database file. When the user selects a title, display the corresponding ISBN, author, and publisher in labels. Include additional labels to identify the contents of the list box and the data fields.

Planning the Project

Sketch the form (Figure 10.37), which your users sign off as meeting their needs. Figure 10.38 shows the form in Design mode.

Select the control types for the controls in the Data Sources window before dragging the Details view to the form.

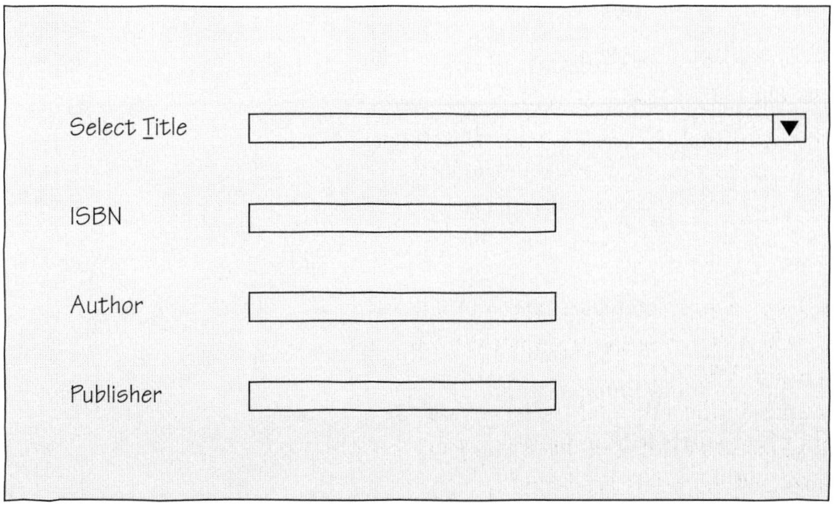

Figure 10.37

A planning sketch of the Windows form for the hands-on programming example.

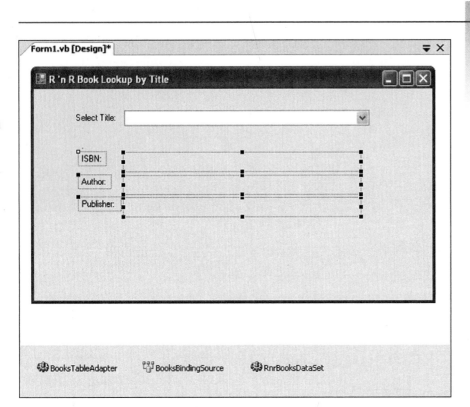

Plan the Objects and Properties

Object	Property	Setting
BooksBindingSource	Name	BooksBindingSource
RnrBooksDataset	Name	RnrBooksDataset
BooksTableAdapter	Name	BooksTableAdapter
TitleComboBox	Name	TitleComboBox
	BindingSource	BooksBindingSource
	DisplayMember	Title
Labels	Name	Keep default names

Plan the Procedures
No code is required if all properties are correctly set.

Write the Project

- Create a new Windows project.

- Create the new SQL Server data source based on the RnrBooks.mdf data file. Include only those fields that appear on the finished form.

- Set the control types to a combo box and labels for the fields.

- Drag a Details view of the data to the form and rearrange the controls to match the sketch in Figure 10.37. Figures 10.38 and 10.39 show the completed form.

- Set the properties of the combo box according to your plan.

- Thoroughly test the project.

Figure 10.39

The form for the hands-on programming example.

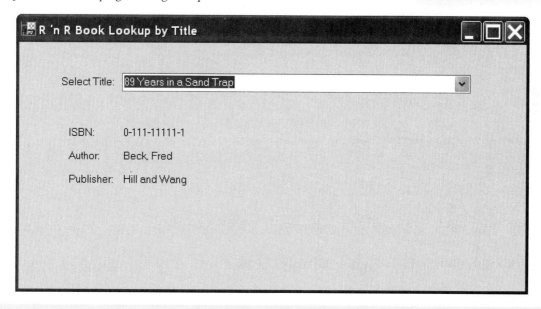

The Project Code

Isn't it amazing that so powerful a program doesn't require any code at all?

Summary

1. Visual Studio .NET uses Microsoft's ADO.NET technology to access databases in many different formats.
2. ADO.NET provides several types of connections for databases: OleDb, SQL Server, Odbc, and Oracle.
3. Databases are composed of tables of related information. Each table is organized into rows representing records and columns containing fields of data.
4. The primary key field uniquely identifies a row or record.
5. ADO.NET stores and transfers data using a format called XML (Extensible Markup Language), which can be used by many different platforms.

6. Many controls can be bound to a database including labels, text boxes, list boxes, or a DataGridView.

7. A binding source establishes a link to a data source, which is a specific data file or server.

8. A table adapter handles the transfer of data between a data source and a dataset.

9. A dataset stores information from the database in the memory of the computer. A dataset can contain multiple tables and their relationships.

10. You can create datasets by dragging tables from the Data Sources window or by using the Configuration Wizard that displays when *Add New Data Source* is selected from the *Data* menu.

11. A table adapter uses a SQL SELECT statement to specify the data to retrieve.

12. You can add a DataGridView to a form and automatically bind the grid to a data source.

13. The dataset's schema is defined in the .xsd file that appears in the project folder.

14. To bind individual controls to data fields, select *Details* for the table in the Data Sources window and drag the table to the form.

15. You can change the type of control used to display bound data in the control's smart tag.

16. It is common to allow the user to select a value from a list and then display the data values for the selected item in bound labels.

17. To use a bound combo box for selection, you must set its DataSource and DisplayMember properties.

18. You can select a subset of the fields in a table for a dataset.

19. In a Web database application, you must be very aware of the security requirements.

20. Each selection from a list requires a postback to the server to fill the bound controls. You must set the AutoPostBack property of the drop-down list to True to make the postback occur.

21. A Web selection program requires a parameterized query to retrieve the data matching the list selection. The Windows program does not have the same requirement.

Key Terms

Binding Source *392*	field *388*
bound controls *400*	key field *388*
column *388*	postback *409*
data binding *391*	record *388*
Data Designer *399*	row *388*
data source *392*	table *388*
data-bound controls *400*	table adapter *392*
DataGridView control *393*	XML *389*
dataset *392*	

Review Questions

1. Explain the purpose of a binding source.
2. Explain the purpose of the table adapter control.
3. What is a dataset?
4. How is a DataGridView control used?
5. Explain the steps to change a data source from DataGridView to Details.
6. What options are available for styles of a bound control?
7. What is the purpose of the Data Source's window?
8. How do a Windows and a Web version of a list selection program vary? Why?
9. What is a parameterized query? When would it be used?
10. What is a postback? When does it occur?

Programming Exercises

Note: Each of these exercises can be written as a Windows application or as a Web application.

10.1 The Rnrbooks.mdf database file holds two tables: the Books table used in this chapter and the Subjects table. The Subjects table has only two fields: the Subject Code (the key) and the Subject Name. Write a project that displays the Subjects table in a grid.

10.2 Write a project to display a list of the subject names in the Subjects table described in Programming Exercise 10.1. Use a drop-down combo box. Display in a label the subject code for the name selected from the list.

10.3 Write a project to display the Publishers table from the Contacts.mdf database from your StudentData\DatabaseFiles folder on the text CD. The Publishers table has the following fields: PubID (the key field), Name, Company Name, Address, City, State, ZIP, Telephone, and Fax.

Allow the user to select the publisher name from a drop-down list; display the rest of the fields in labels.

Case Studies

VB Mail Order

1. Create a Windows application to display the VB Mail Order Customer table from the VbMail.mdf database on your student CD in labels. Use the navigation bar to move from record to record.
2. Create a Web application to display the Customer table in a grid on a Web Form.

The Customers table holds these fields:

CustomerID

LastName

FirstName

Address

City

State

ZipCode

VB Auto Center

Create a Windows application or a Web application to display the VB Auto Center Vehicle table from the VBAuto.mdf database on your student CD. Display the InventoryID in a combo box. Display the remaining fields in individual controls.

The table holds these fields:

InventoryID

Manufacturer

ModelName

Year

VehicleID

CostValue

Video Bonanza

1. Create a Windows application to display the information from the Studio table in the VBVideo.mdf database. Allow the user to select the studio name from a drop-down list and display the rest of the fields in labels.
2. Create a Windows or Web application to display the Studio table in a grid.

The Studio table contains these fields:

Studio ID

Studio Name

Contact Person

Phone

Very Very Boards

1. Create a Windows application to display the Product table from the VeryBoards.mdf database file on your student CD. Allow the user to select the product ID from a drop-down list and display the rest of the fields in labels.
2. Create a Windows or a Web application to display the Product table in a grid.

The Product table contains these fields:

ProductID

Description

MfgID

Unit

Cost

LastOrderDate

LastOrderQuantity

CHAPTER

11

Saving Data in Files

Calculate values for sale.
extendedPriceDecimal = quantityInteger
discountDecimal = extendedPriceDecimal
discountedPriceDecimal = extendedPrice
' Calculate summary values.
quantitySumInteger += quantityInteger
discountSumDecimal += discountDecimal
discountedPriceSumDecimal += discounte
saleCountInteger += 1

at the completion of this chapter, you will be able to . . .

1. Declare and instantiate objects in code.

2. Store and retrieve data in files using streams.

3. Save the values from a list box and reload for the next program run.

4. Check for the end of file.

5. Test whether a file exists.

6. Display the standard *Open File* and *Save File* dialog box to allow the user to choose or name the file.

Creating Objects

You have worked with many objects, such as the forms and controls in your projects. These objects are created by the VB form designer. If you examine the code in the *FormName*.Designer.vb file in a project, you can see the statements that declare and instantiate each of the objects. In this chapter you will need to create some of your own objects in code.

Note: To view the *FormName*.Designer.vb file, click the *Show All Files* button at the top of the Solution Explorer and click the plus sign next to the *FormName*.vb file, which expands to show the *FormName*.Designer.vb file.

Declaring an Object Variable

In order to create a new object, you generally declare an object of the class. The rules for declaring an object variable are the same as those for declaring the numeric and string variables you are used to declaring. You can use `Dim`, `Public`, `Private`, and `Friend` for accessibility, and the location of the declaration determines the scope and lifetime of the object.

Examples

```
Dim headingFont As Font
Private namesStreamReader As StreamReader
```

Instantiating an Object

Declaring an object variable does not create the object; it only creates the identifier (name) and object type. To actually create the new object, you must create an instance of the class using the **New keyword**. This step is referred to as *instantiating* an object.

The New Keyword

You can use the `New` keyword in several different ways:

- *Declare the variable and instantiate in one statement*. You can use this technique to instantiate an object inside a procedure (a local object variable) or a module-level object variable. The location determines the scope and lifetime of the object.

```
Dim headingFont As New Font("Arial", 12)
Dim namesStreamWriter As New StreamWriter(fileNameString)
```

- *Declare the variable in one location and instantiate it in another*. The most common reason for using this technique is that you need the object to be available in more than one procedure, so it must be module-level. However, because the `New` statement could fail, it should be enclosed in a `Try/Catch` block, which must be inside a procedure.

```
' Declare a module-level variable.
Private namesStreamReader As StreamReader
```

```
' Inside a procedure, instantiate the object.
namesStreamReader = New StreamReader("Phone.txt")
```

- *Instantiate a new object without a variable name.* You may want to do this if you don't plan to refer to the object again in code.

```
Me.messageLabel.Font = New Font("Arial", 12)
```

Specifying a Namespace

If you have examined the designer-generated code for a form in the *Form-Name*.Designer.vb file, you may have noticed statements like this (which was copied from a program from this chapter):

```
Me.nameTextBox = New System.Windows.Forms.TextBox
```

The name of the class is TextBox; the **namespace** is System.Windows.Forms. Actually this is a bit of overkill; the entire namespace isn't needed for any classes in the namespaces that are automatically included in a Windows Forms project, which include System, System.Windows.Forms, and System.Drawing. A fully qualified name consists of the complete namespace and class name, such as System.Windows.Forms.TextBox.

When you refer to a class in a different namespace, you have two choices. You can write out the entire namespace and class, such as

```
Me.messageLabel.Font = New System.Drawing.Font("Arial", 12)
```

or you can add an `Imports` statement at the top of the code file to specify the namespace, and then refer only to the class name. For example:

```
Imports System.Drawing
```

```
Me.messageLabel.Font = New Font("Arial", 12)
```

For specifying fonts, both of these techniques are unnecessary, since the System.Drawing namespace is automatically imported into all Windows Forms projects. However, later in this chapter you will need to declare objects from the System.IO namespace, which is not automatically included in new projects.

Data Files

Many computer applications require that data be saved from one run to the next. Although the most common technique is to use a database, many times a database is overkill. Perhaps you just need to store a small amount of data, such as the date of the last program run, the highest ID number assigned, a user preference, or the property values of an object to transfer to another application. This chapter deals with techniques to store and retrieve **data files** on disk.

Note that the default security policy for the Internet and for intranets does not allow access to disk files. This chapter presents only basic file input and output (I/O) for Windows applications.

Data Files and Project Files

In computer terminology, any data/information that you store on disk is given its own unique name and is called a *file*. In other words, a file is a collection of related data stored together and assigned a name so that it can be accessed later. Each of your Visual Basic projects requires multiple files—for the forms, other classes, assembly information, and project information. However, the files you will create now are different; they contain actual data, such as names and addresses, inventory amounts, account balances, or even the contents of a list box.

Data File Terminology

The entire collection of data is called a *file*. The file is made up of **records**— one record for each entity in the file. Each record can be broken down further into **fields** (also called *data elements*). For example, in an employee file, the information for one employee is one record. In a name and address file, the information for one person is a record.

In the name and address file, each person has a last name field, a first name field, address fields, and a phone number field. Each field in a record pertains to the same person. Figure 11.1 illustrates a name and address file.

Figure 11.1

The rows in this data file represent records; the columns represent fields.

Last Name	First Name	Street	City	State	Zip	Phone	Email
Maxwell	Harry	795 W. J Street	Ontario	CA	91764	909-555-1234	
Helm	Jennifer	201 Cortez Way	Pomona	CA	91766	818-555-2222	JHelm@ms.org
Colton	Craig	1632 Granada Place	Pomona	CA	91766	909-555-3333	

A record | \ A field

File Handling Using Streams

Visual Studio handles data files using streams. A **stream** is designed to transfer a series of bytes from one location to another. Streams are objects that have methods and properties, just like any other object. The stream objects are found in the **System.IO namespace**. You can save the trouble of fully qualifying references by including an `Imports` statement at the top of the file, before the statement declaring the form's class.

```
Imports System.IO

Public Class fileIOForm
```

File I/O

You can read and write data in a disk file. You may have the user enter data into text boxes that you want to store in a file; that is called *writing* or *output*. At a later time, when you want to retrieve the data from the file, that is *reading* or *input* (Figure 11.2).

Figure 11.2

Write output from a program to a file; read input from the file into a program.

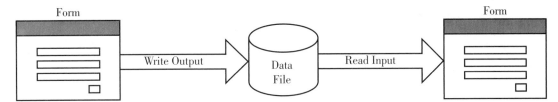

In VB, the simplest way to read and write small amounts of data is to use the **StreamReader** and **StreamWriter** objects. Generally, you write the StreamWriter code first, to create the data file. Then you can write the Stream-Reader code to read the file that you just created.

Writing Data in a File

To write data to a file, you first have the user input the data into text boxes and then write the data to the disk. The steps for writing data are

- Declare a new StreamWriter object, which also declares the name of the data file.

- Use the StreamWriter's `WriteLine` method to copy the data to a buffer in memory. (A buffer is just a temporary storage location.)

- Call the StreamWriter's `Close` method, which transfers the data from the buffer to the file and releases the system resources used by the stream.

Instantiating a StreamWriter Object—General Forms

General Forms

```
Dim ObjectName As New StreamWriter("FileName")
Dim ObjectName As New StreamWriter("FileName", BooleanAppend)
```

You declare a new StreamWriter object for writing data to a file. The first argument in the constructor specifies the name of the file. The default location for the file is where the program executable (.exe) is placed, which is the bin\Debug folder beneath the folder for the current project. You also can specify the complete path of the file.

In the second version of the StreamWriter constructor, you can specify that you want to append data to an existing file. Specify True to append. By default, the option is set to False, and the old data file is deleted and a new data file is created, in effect overwriting any existing data.

Declaring a new StreamWriter object opens the file. The file must be open before you can write in the file. If the file does not already exist, a new one is created. If you don't use a full qualifying path, then the file is opened or created in the project's bin\Debug folder where the program executable is located. Because no exception occurs whether or not the file exists, you can declare the StreamWriter object in the declarations section of your program or in a procedure. If you do use a full path in the filename, then you should instantiate the StreamWriter object in a `Try/Catch` block in case the path does not exist.

TIP

Use .txt as your extension to allow for easy viewing of the file in Notepad. ■

Declaring a StreamWriter Object—Examples

```
Dim phoneStreamWriter As New StreamWriter("Phone.txt")
Private namesStreamWriter As New StreamWriter("C:\MyFiles\Names.txt") ' Could throw
    ' an exception if the path doesn't exist.
Friend logFileStreamWriter As New StreamWriter("LogFile.txt", True)
```

The StreamWriter object has both a **Write** and a **WriteLine method**. The difference between the two is a carriage-return character. The Write method places items consecutively in the file with no delimiter (separator). The WriteLine method places an Enter (carriage return) between items. We will use the WriteLine in this chapter because we want to easily retrieve the individual data elements later.

The WriteLine Method—General Form

```
ObjectName.WriteLine(DataToWrite)
```

The DataToWrite argument may be string or numeric. The WriteLine method converts any numeric data to string and actually writes string data in the file.

The WriteLine Method—Examples

```
phoneStreamWriter.WriteLine(Me.nameTextBox.Text)
phoneStreamWriter.WriteLine(Me.phoneTextBox.Text)

namesStreamWriter.WriteLine("Sammy")

bankBalanceStreamWriter.WriteLine(balanceDecimal.ToString())
```

If you are inputting data from the user and writing in a file, you generally place the WriteLine in a button click event procedure. That way you can write one record at a time. Figure 11.3 shows the form for the following phone list example.

Figure 11.3

The user enters data into the text boxes and clicks the Save button, which writes this record in the stream's buffer.

```
Private Sub saveButton_Click(ByVal sender As System.Object, _
    ByVal e As System.EventArgs) Handles saveButton.Click
        ' Save the record to the file.

        ' Write to already-open stream.
        With Me
            phoneStreamWriter.WriteLine(.nameTextBox.Text)
            phoneStreamWriter.WriteLine(.phoneTextBox.Text)
            With .nameTextBox
                .Clear()
                .Focus()
            End With
            .phoneTextBox.Clear()
        End With
End Sub
```

The *Save* button writes the data from the screen to the StreamWriter object and then clears the screen.

Closing a File

After you finish writing data in a file, you must close the file. Closing a file is good housekeeping; it finishes writing all data from the stream's buffer to the disk and releases the system resources. Use the StreamWriter's **Close method**, which is similar to closing a form. A common location for the `Close` method is in your program's Exit command or the form's FormClosing event procedure (see page 438).

```
Private Sub exitButton_Click(ByVal sender As System.Object, _
    ByVal e As System.EventArgs) Handles exitButton.Click
        ' Close the file and the form.

        phoneStreamWriter.Close()
        Me.Close()
End Sub
```

If you fail to close a file when you are finished with it, the file may remain open for an indefinite time and sometimes may become unusable. See "The FormClosing Event Procedure" section later in this chapter.

Viewing the Contents of a File

After you run your project, you can view the new file using a text editor such as Notepad. You can also view the file in the Visual Studio IDE. In the Solution Explorer, select the project name. If you don't see the bin and obj folders listed, click on the *Show All Files* button at the top of the window. Then you can expand the bin folder and the Debug folder, find the data file's name, and open it. The contents of the file should appear in the Editor window (Figure 11.4).

TIP

It's best to open a file only when it is needed and close it as soon as you are done with it so that you don't tie up system resources unnecessarily. ■

Reading Data from a File

You use the StreamReader class to read the data from a file that you created with a StreamWriter.

Show All Files button

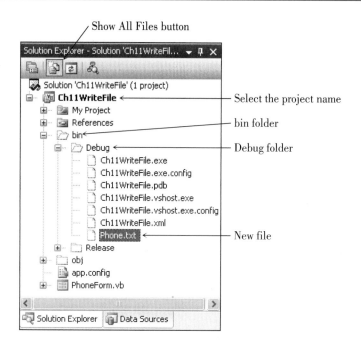

— Select the project name

— bin folder

— Debug folder

— New file

The steps for reading the data from a file are the following:

- Declare an object of the StreamReader class. The constructor declares the filename and optional path. This statement opens the file so that you can read from it.

- Use the `ReadLine` method to read the data. You may need to use a loop to retrieve multiple records.

- When finished, close the stream using the StreamReader's `Close` method.

Instantiating a StreamReader Object—General Form

General Form

```
Dim ObjectName As New StreamReader("FileName")
```

The StreamReader class works in much the same way as the StreamWriter. However, the file must exist in the location that the application expects it. If no such file exists, an exception occurs. For this reason, you must instantiate the StreamReader object in a procedure so that you can enclose it in a `Try/Catch` block.

Instantiating a StreamReader Object—Examples

Examples

```
Try
    Dim namesStreamReader As New StreamReader("C:\MyFiles\Names.txt")
Catch
    MessageBox.Show("File does not exist.")
End Try

' In declarations section, to create a module-level variable name.
Private phoneStreamReader As StreamReader
...
' In a procedure, to catch an exception for a missing file.
Try
    phoneStreamReader = New StreamReader("Phone.txt")
Catch
    MessageBox.Show("File does not exist.")
End Try
```

Using the ReadLine Method

Use the StreamReader's **ReadLine method** to read the previously saved data. Each time you execute the method, it reads the next line from the file. Assign the value from the read to the desired location, such as a label, a text box, or a string variable. The ReadLine method has no arguments.

```
Me.nameTextBox.Text = phoneStreamReader.ReadLine()
```

Checking for the End of the File

How can you tell when there is no more data in the file? One way is to use the StreamReader's **Peek method**. The Peek method looks at the next element without really reading it. The value returned when you peek beyond the last element is negative 1 (–1).

```
If phoneStreamReader.Peek <> —1 Then
  Me.nameTextBox.Text = phoneStreamReader.ReadLine()
  Me.phoneTextBox.Text = phoneStreamReader.ReadLine()
End If
```

Note that the ReadLine method does not throw an exception when you attempt to read past the end of the file.

You must always make sure to read the data elements in the same order in which they were written. Otherwise your output will display the wrong values. For example, if you reversed the two lines in the program segment above, the phone number would display for the name and vice-versa. The ReadLine method just reads the next line and assigns it to the variable or property that you specify.

The File Read Program

Here is the completed program that reads the name and phone numbers from a file and displays them on the form (Figure 11.5). Each time the user clicks *Next*, the program reads and displays the next record. Note that for this example program, we copied the Phone.txt file from the bin\Debug folder of the Write File

Figure 11.5

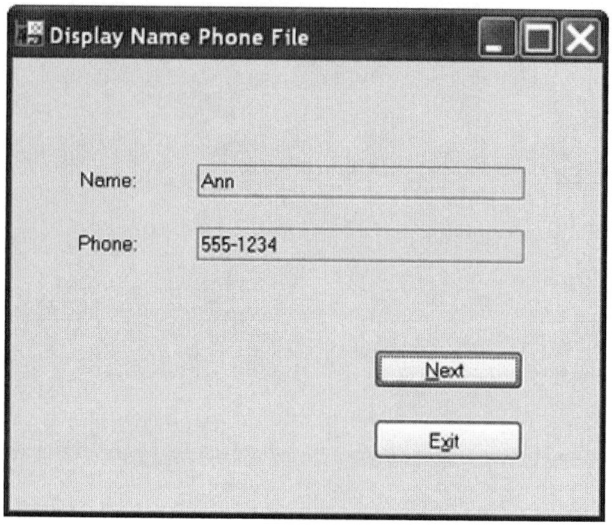

*Each time the user clicks Next,
the next record is read from the
file and displayed in the
labels.*

project, to the bin\Debug folder of this project. You also could specify the exact
path of the file.

```
'Program:        Ch11ReadFile
'Programmer:     Bradley/Millspaugh
'Date:           June 2005
'Description:    Retrieve the information stored in a data file
'                and display it on the screen.
'                Uses a StreamReader.
'                By default, the data file is expected to be in the
'                project's bin\Debug folder.

Imports System.IO

Public Class displayForm
    ' Declare module-level variable.
    Private phoneStreamReader As StreamReader

    Private Sub phoneForm_Load(ByVal sender As System.Object, _
      ByVal e As System.EventArgs) Handles MyBase.Load
        ' Open the file and display the first record.

        Try
            phoneStreamReader = New StreamReader("Phone.txt")
            DisplayRecord()
        Catch
            ' File is not found.
            MessageBox.Show("File does not exist.")
        End Try
    End Sub

    Private Sub nextButton_Click(ByVal sender As System.Object, _
      ByVal e As System.EventArgs) Handles nextButton.Click
        ' Read the next record.

        DisplayRecord()
    End Sub
```

```
Private Sub exitButton_Click(ByVal sender As System.Object, _
    ByVal e As System.EventArgs) Handles exitButton.Click
      ' End the project.

      phoneStreamReader.Close()
      Me.Close()
End Sub

Private Sub DisplayRecord()
    ' Read and display the next record.

    If phoneStreamReader.Peek <> -1 Then
       Me.nameTextBox.Text = phoneStreamReader.ReadLine()
       Me.phoneTextBox.Text = phoneStreamReader.ReadLine()
    Else
       MessageBox.Show("All names have been displayed.")
    End If
End Sub
End Class
```

Feedback 11.1

1. Write the statement to create an inventory StreamWriter object that will write data to a file called "Inventory.txt".
2. Code the statement to write the contents of descriptionTextBox into the inventory stream.
3. Why should the declaration statement for a StreamReader object be in a Try/Catch block? Does the declaration statement for a StreamWriter object need to be in a Try/Catch block? Why or why not?
4. Write the statement(s) to read a description and a product number from inventoryStreamReader assuming it has been opened as a StreamReader object. Make sure to test for the end of the file.

Using the File Common Dialog Box

In the preceding file read and write programs, the filenames are hard-coded into the programs. You may prefer to allow the user to browse and enter the filename at run time. You can display the standard Windows *Open File* dialog box, in which the user can browse for a folder and filename and/or enter a new filename. Use the **OpenFileDialog** common dialog component to display the dialog box, and then use the object's FileName property to open the selected file.

OpenFileDialog Component Properties

You will find the following properties of the OpenFileDialog component very useful:

Property	Description
Name	Name of the component. You can use the default OpenFileDialog1.
CheckFileExists	Display an error message if the file does not exist. Set to False for saving a file, since you want to create a new file if the file does not exist. Leave at the default True to read an existing file.
CheckPathExists	Display an error message if the path does not exist. Set to False for saving a file, since you want it to create the new folder if necessary.
FileName	The name of the file selected or entered by the user, which includes the file path. Use this property after displaying the dialog box to determine which file to open. You also can give this property an initial value, which places a default filename in the dialog box when it appears.
Filter	Filter file extensions to display. Example: `Text Files (*.txt)|*.txt|All files (*.*)|*.*`
InitialDirectory	Directory to display when the dialog box opens. Set this in code to Application.StartupPath to begin in the same folder as your application.
Title	Title bar of the dialog box.

Displaying the Open File Dialog Box

To display an *Open File to Read* dialog box (Figure 11.6), you must first add an OpenFileDialog component to your form. The component appears in the component tray. At design time, set initial properties for Name, CheckFileExists, CheckPathExists, Filter, and Title (see the preceding table for the values). In code, set the InitialDirectory property to **Application.StartupPath**, display the dialog box using the ShowDialog method, and retrieve the FileName property.

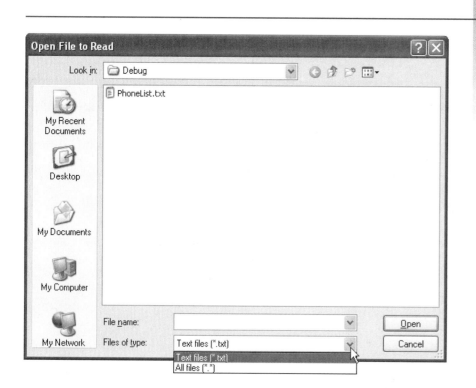

Figure 11.6

Display the Windows Open File to Read dialog box using the OpenFileDialog component. The Filter property determines the entries for Files of type.

```
Private Sub OpenToolStripMenuItem_Click(ByVal sender As System.Object, _
  ByVal e As System.EventArgs) Handles fileOpenMenuItem.Click
    ' Open the file.
    Dim responseDialogResult As DialogResult

    ' Begin in the project folder.
    OpenFileDialog1.InitialDirectory = Application.StartupPath
    ' Display the Open File dialog box.
    responseDialogResult = OpenFileDialog1.ShowDialog()
    ' Make sure that the user didn't click the Cancel button.
    If responseDialogResult <> DialogResult.Cancel Then
        ' Open the output file.
        phoneStreamWriter = New StreamWriter(OpenFileDialog1.FileName)
    End If
End Sub
```

Notice that the user may click on the Cancel button of the *Open File* dialog box. Check the DialogResult for Cancel. And if the user *does* click Cancel, that presents one more task for the program: You cannot close a StreamWriter object that isn't open.

Checking for Successful File Open

In the preceding file-open procedure, the statement

```
phoneStreamWriter = New StreamWriter(OpenFileDialog1.FileName)
```

may not execute. In that case, the StreamWriter is not instantiated. You can verify the object's instantiation using the VB keyword **Nothing**. An object variable that has not been instantiated has a value of Nothing. Notice the syntax: You must use the keyword IsNot rather than the not equal operator (<>).

```
' Is the file already open?
If phoneStreamWriter IsNot Nothing Then
  phoneStreamWriter.Close()
End If
```

Place this code in the form's FormClosing event procedure.

Checking for Already Open File

It's possible that the user may select the *File / Open* menu item twice, which can cause a problem. A second open instantiates another file stream, and the Close method never executes for the first file. It's best to check for an active instance of the file stream before instantiating a new one.

```
Private Sub OpenToolStripMenuItem_Click(ByVal sender As System.Object, _
    ByVal e As System.EventArgs) Handles OpenToolStripMenuItem.Click
    ' Open the file.
    Dim responseDialogResult As DialogResult

    ' Is the file already open?
    If phoneStreamWriter IsNot Nothing Then
      phoneStreamWriter.Close()
    End If
```

```
    ' Begin in the project folder.
    OpenFileDialog1.InitialDirectory = Application.StartupPath
    ' Display the File Open dialog box.
    responseDialogResult = OpenFileDialog1.ShowDialog()
    ' Make sure that the user didn't click the Cancel button.
    If responseDialogResult <> DialogResult.Cancel Then
      ' Open the output file.
      phoneStreamWriter = New StreamWriter(OpenFileDialog1.FileName)
    End If
End Sub
```

Using the Save File Dialog Component

In addition to the OpenFileDialog, you also can choose to display a SaveFile-
Dialog component, which displays the standard system *Save As* dialog box. The
SaveFileDialog allows the user to browse and enter a filename to save; it has
most of the same properties as the OpenFileDialog component. By default, the
SaveFileDialog component checks for an already existing file and displays a di-
alog box asking the user whether to replace the existing file.

The Open and Write File Program

Here is the complete listing of the Open and Write File program, which allows
the user to select the filename. The user can select the *Open* command from the
File menu. But if the *Save* button is clicked and the file is not yet open, the
Open File dialog box displays automatically.

```
'Program:        Ch11 Open and Write File
'Programmer:     Bradley/Millspaugh
'Date:           June 2005
'Description:    Allow the user to enter names and phone numbers and
'                save them in a file.
'                Display the File Open dialog box for the user to
'                enter the file and path.
'Folder:         Ch11OpenAndWriteFile

Imports System.IO

Public Class phoneForm
  ' Declare module-level variable.
  Private phoneStreamWriter As StreamWriter

  Private Sub saveButton_Click(ByVal sender As System.Object, _
    ByVal e As System.EventArgs) Handles saveButton.Click
    ' Save the record to the file.

    If phoneStreamWriter IsNot Nothing Then  ' Is the file open?
      With Me
        phoneStreamWriter.WriteLine(.nameTextBox.Text)
        phoneStreamWriter.WriteLine(.phoneTextBox.Text)
        With .nameTextBox
          .Clear()
          .Focus()
        End With
        .phoneTextBox.Clear()
      End With
```

```
            Else              ' File is not open.
                MessageBox.Show("You must open the file before you can save a record", _
                    "File Not Open", MessageBoxButtons.OK, MessageBoxIcon.Information)
                ' Display the File Open dialog box.
                OpenToolStripMenuItem_Click(sender, e)
            End If
    End Sub

    Private Sub OpenToolStripMenuItem_Click(ByVal sender As System.Object, _
      ByVal e As System.EventArgs) Handles OpenToolStripMenuItem.Click
            ' Open the file.
            Dim responseDialogResult As DialogResult

            ' Is the file already open?
            If phoneStreamWriter IsNot Nothing Then
                phoneStreamWriter.Close()
            End If

            ' Begin in the project folder.
            OpenFileDialog1.InitialDirectory = Application.StartupPath
            ' Display the File Open dialog box.
            responseDialogResult = OpenFileDialog1.ShowDialog()
            ' Make sure that the user didn't click the Cancel button.
            If responseDialogResult <> DialogResult.Cancel Then
                ' Open the output file.
                phoneStreamWriter = New StreamWriter(OpenFileDialog1.FileName)
            End If
    End Sub

    Private Sub ExitToolStripMenuItem_Click(ByVal sender As Object, _
      ByVal e As System.EventArgs) Handles ExitToolStripMenuItem.Click
            ' Close the file and the form.

            If phoneStreamWriter IsNot Nothing Then ' Is the file open?
                phoneStreamWriter.Close()
            End If
            Me.Close()
    End Sub
End Class
```

▶ Feedback 11.2

1. What is the Filter property setting to display only .txt files?
2. Write the statement to set OpenFileDialog1 to begin in the same folder as the application.
3. Write the statement to close phoneStreamWriter; make sure to allow for the possibility that the file is not open.

Saving the Contents of a List Box

In Chapter 7 you wrote a program to maintain a list. The user was allowed to add items and remove items, but the next time the program ran, the list changes were gone. The changes were not saved from one execution to the next.

Now that you know how to save data in a file, you can save the contents of a list when the program exits and reload the list when the program reopens. Use the following techniques for this project:

- Do not give any values to the list's Items collection at design time. Instead, when the program begins, open the data file and read the items into the Items collection.

- If the user makes any changes to the list, ask whether to save the list when the program ends.

- Include a menu option to save the list.

- If the file holding the list elements does not exist when the program begins, give the user the option of creating a new list by adding items.

The examples in this section use the hands-on example from Chapter 7, which allows the user to make changes to the Coffee Flavor list (Figure 11.7). We will load the list from a file in the Form_Load procedure and query the user to save the list if any changes are made.

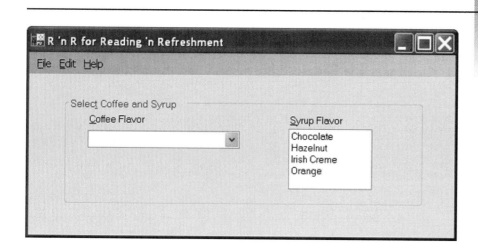

Figure 11.7

The form for the list save program, taken from Chapter 7.

Loading the List Box

Assuming that the list items are stored in a data file, you can read the file into the list in the Form_Load procedure. Loop through the file until all elements are read, placing each item in the list with the `Items.Add` method.

```
Dim coffeeFlavorString As String

' Read all elements into the list.
Do Until flavorsStreamReader.Peek = -1
    coffeeFlavorString = flavorsStreamReader.ReadLine()
    Me.coffeeComboBox.Items.Add(coffeeFlavorString)
Loop
```

Checking for Existence of the File

When you create a StreamReader object, the constructor checks to make sure the file exists. If the file does not exist, what do you want to do? Maybe the user wants to exit the program, locate the file, and try again. Or maybe the user prefers to begin with an empty list, add the list items, and create a new file. This technique is a good way to create the file in the first place.

You can catch the exception for a missing file and display a message box asking if the user wants to create a new file.

```vb
responseDialogResult = MessageBox.Show("Create a new file?", "File not Found", _
    MessageBoxButtons.YesNo, MessageBoxIcon.Question)
```

If the user says Yes, allow the program to begin running with an empty list; the file will be created when the program exits or the user saves the list. If the user says No, exit the program immediately.

```vb
Private Sub FlavorsForm_Load(ByVal sender As Object, _
    ByVal e As System.EventArgs) Handles Me.Load
    ' Load the items in the coffeeComboBox list.
    Dim responseDialogResult As DialogResult
    Dim coffeeFlavorString As String

    Try
        ' Open the file.
        Dim flavorsStreamReader As New StreamReader("Coffees.txt")
        ' Read all elements into the list.
        Do Until flavorsStreamReader.Peek = -1
            coffeeFlavorString = flavorsStreamReader.ReadLine()
            Me.coffeeComboBox.Items.Add(coffeeFlavorString)
        Loop
        ' Close the file.
        flavorsStreamReader.Close()
    Catch ex As Exception
        ' File missing.
        responseDialogResult = MessageBox.Show("Create a new file?", "File not Found", _
            MessageBoxButtons.YesNo, MessageBoxIcon.Question)
        If responseDialogResult = DialogResult.No Then
            ' Exit the program.
            Me.Close
        End If
    End Try
End Sub
```

Saving the File

In this program the user can choose a menu option to save the file. Open a StreamWriter object and loop through the Items collection of the list box, saving each element with a `WriteLine` method.

```vb
Private Sub SaveFlavorListToolStripMenuItem_Click(ByVal sender As System.Object, _
    ByVal e As System.EventArgs) Handles SaveFlavorListToolStripMenuItem.Click
    ' Save the flavor list in a file.
    Dim numberItemsInteger As Integer
```

```
      ' Open the file.
      Dim flavorsStreamWriter As New StreamWriter("Coffees.txt")
      ' Save the items in the file.
      numberItemsInteger = Me.coffeeComboBox.Items.Count - 1
      For indexInteger As Integer = 0 To numberItemsInteger
         flavorsStreamWriter.WriteLine(Me.coffeeComboBox.Items(indexInteger))
      Next indexInteger
      ' Close the file.
      flavorsStreamWriter.Close()
      isDirtyBoolean = False
End Sub
```

The last line in this procedure needs some explanation. The next section
explains the reason for isDirtyBoolean = False.

Querying the User to Save

If your program allows users to make changes to data during program execution, it's a good idea to ask them if they want to save the changes before the
program ends. This is similar to working in a word processing program or the
VB editor. If you close the file after making changes, you receive a message
asking if you want to save the file. But if you haven't made any changes since
the last save, no message appears.

To keep track of data changes during execution, you need a module-level
Boolean variable. Because the standard practice in programming is to refer to
the data as "dirty" if changes have been made, we will call the variable is-
DirtyBoolean. In each procedure that allows changes (Add, Remove, Clear),
you must set isDirtyBoolean to True. After saving the file, set the variable to
False. (The code for this appears in the preceding section.)

Just before the project ends, you must check the value of isDirtyBoolean; if
True, ask the user if he or she wants to save; if False, you can just exit without
a message.

The FormClosing Event Procedure

If you want to do something before the project ends, such as ask the user to
save the file, the best location is the form's **FormClosing event** procedure.
This is a much better place for such a question than your exit procedure,
because the user can quit the program in more than one way. The Form_
FormClosing event procedure executes before the form closes when the user
clicks on your Exit button or menu command, clicks on the window's Close button, or even exits Windows.

```
Private Sub FlavorsForm_FormClosing(ByVal sender As Object, _
   ByVal e As System.Windows.Forms.FormClosingEventArgs) Handles Me.FormClosing
      'Ask the user to save the file.
      Dim responseDialogResult As DialogResult
      Dim messageString As String = "Coffee list has changed. Save the list?"

      If isDirtyBoolean Then
         responseDialogResult = MessageBox.Show(messageString, "Coffee List Changed", _
            MessageBoxButtons.YesNo, MessageBoxIcon.Question)
```

```
        If responseDialogResult = DialogResult.Yes Then
            SaveFlavorListToolStripMenuItem_Click(sender, e)
        End If
    End If
End Sub
```

Feedback 11.3

1. Write the loop to save all of the elements from namesListBox using namesStreamWriter, which is a StreamWriter already opened and connected to Names.txt.
2. In what procedure should the code from Question 1 be placed?
3. Write the statements in the Form_Load event procedure to load the list of names into namesListBox.

Your Hands-On Programming Example

Modify the hands-on programming example from Chapter 7 to save the list changes from one run of the program to the next. The user can add items to the Coffee Flavor list, remove items, and clear the list. If there are any changes to the list, allow the user to save the list. When the program begins, load the list from the disk file, so that it displays the list as it appeared during the last run.

Do not give the Coffee Flavor list initial values; if the user has not entered any flavors, the list should be blank. If the file holding coffee flavors is not found, allow the user to enter the new flavors at run time.

Add a *Save Flavors List* menu item on the *File* menu. Also query the user to save the file if the list has changed when the program closes.

Note: We have removed the printing routines from the Ch07HandsOn program to better focus on the file-handling routines.

Planning the Project

Sketch the form (Figure 11.8), which your users sign off as meeting their needs.

Figure 11.8

A sketch of the form for the hands-on programming example.

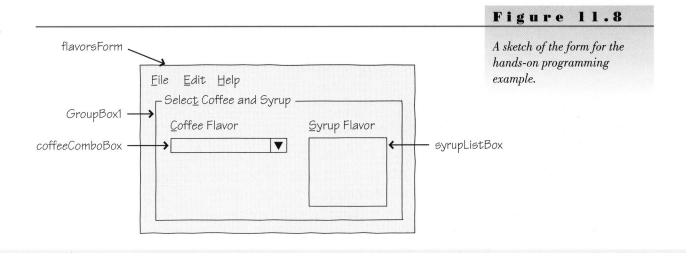

Plan the Objects and Properties

See the planning for the Chapter 7 hands-on programming example and make the following addition:

Object	Property	Setting
SaveFlavorListToolStripMenuItem	Name Text	SaveFlavorListToolStripMenuItem &Save Flavor List

Plan the Procedures

Refer to the planning for the Chapter 7 hands-on programming example and make the following changes. You can remove the controls and procedures for printing.

Procedure	Actions
SaveFlavorListToolStripMenuItem_Click	Open the file. Save the list items in the file. Close the file. Set isDirtyBoolean to False.

Form_Load	Try
	    Open the file.
	    Read the file contents into the Flavors list.
	    Close the file.
	Catch (File is missing)
	    Query the user to create the new file.
	    If answer is No
	        Exit the program.
	    End If
	End Try

Form_FormClosing	If list has changed (is dirty)
	    Query the user to save the list data.
	    If Yes
	        Call SaveFlavorListToolStripMenuItem_Click.

Write the Project

Begin with the Chapter 7 hands-on programming example. See "Basing a New Project on an Existing Project" in Chapter 5 (page 227) for help. Figure 11.8 shows the sketch and Figure 11.9 shows the completed form.

- Add the menu item and set the properties according to your plan.

- Make sure to add the new Imports statement:

```
Imports System.IO
```

- Add the module-level variable isDirtyBoolean.

- Write the code for the new menu item based on the pseudocode.

- Write the new code for the Form_Load and Form_FormClosing event procedures, based on the pseudocode.

- When you complete the code, thoroughly test the project. Fill the list, save the list, and rerun the program multiple times. Make sure that you can modify the list and have the changes appear in the next program run. Also test the option to not save changes and make sure that it works correctly.

Figure 11.9

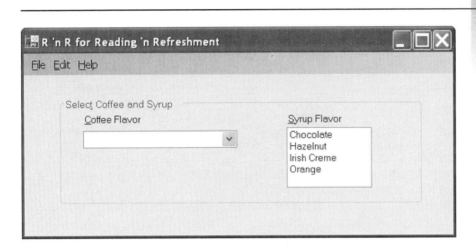

The completed form for the hands-on programming example.

The Project Coding Solution

```
'Project:          Ch11HandsOn
'Programmer:       Bradley/Millspaugh
'Date:             June 2005
'Description:       Maintain a list of coffee flavors.
'                  Note: This program extends Ch07HandsOn to save the modified list
'                  in a file. The printing has been removed for clarity.
'Folder:           Ch11HandsOn

Imports System.IO

Public Class FlavorsForm

    ' Declare module-level variable.
    Private isDirtyBoolean As Boolean

    Private Sub FlavorsForm_Load(ByVal sender As Object, _
        ByVal e As System.EventArgs) Handles Me.Load
            ' Load the items in the coffeeComboBox list.
        Dim responseDialogResult As DialogResult
        Dim coffeeFlavorString As String

        Try
            ' Open the file.
            Dim flavorsStreamReader As New StreamReader("Coffees.txt")
            ' Read all elements into the list.
            Do Until flavorsStreamReader.Peek = -1
                coffeeFlavorString = flavorsStreamReader.ReadLine()
                Me.coffeeComboBox.Items.Add(coffeeFlavorString)
            Loop
            ' Close the file.
            flavorsStreamReader.Close()
```

```vbnet
        Catch ex As Exception
          ' File missing.
          responseDialogResult = MessageBox.Show("Create a new file?", "File not Found", _
            MessageBoxButtons.YesNo, MessageBoxIcon.Question)
          If responseDialogResult = DialogResult.No Then
            ' Exit the program.
            Me.Close()
          End If
        End Try
    End Sub

    Private Sub FlavorsForm_FormClosing(ByVal sender As Object, _
      ByVal e As System.Windows.Forms.FormClosingEventArgs) Handles Me.FormClosing
        'Ask the user to save the file.
        Dim responseDialogResult As DialogResult
        Dim messageString As String = "Coffee list has changed. Save the list?"

        If isDirtyBoolean Then
          responseDialogResult = MessageBox.Show(messageString, "Coffee List Changed", _
            MessageBoxButtons.YesNo, MessageBoxIcon.Question)

          If responseDialogResult = DialogResult.Yes Then
            SaveFlavorListToolStripMenuItem_Click(sender, e)
          End If
        End If
    End Sub

    Private Sub SaveFlavorListToolStripMenuItem_Click(ByVal sender As System.Object, _
      ByVal e As System.EventArgs) Handles SaveFlavorListToolStripMenuItem.Click
        ' Save the flavor list in a file.
        Dim numberItemsInteger As Integer

        ' Open the file.
        Dim flavorsStreamWriter As New StreamWriter("Coffees.txt")
        ' Save the items in the file.
        numberItemsInteger = Me.coffeeComboBox.Items.Count — 1
        For indexInteger As Integer = 0 To numberItemsInteger
          flavorsStreamWriter.WriteLine(Me.coffeeComboBox.Items(indexInteger))
        Next indexInteger
        ' Close the file.
        flavorsStreamWriter.Close()
        isDirtyBoolean = False
    End Sub

    Private Sub ExitToolStripMenuItem_Click(ByVal sender As System.Object, _
      ByVal e As System.EventArgs) Handles ExitToolStripMenuItem.Click
        ' End the program.

        Me.Close()
    End Sub

    Private Sub AddCoffeeFlavorToolStripMenuItem_Click(ByVal sender As System.Object, _
      ByVal e As System.EventArgs) Handles AddCoffeeFlavorToolStripMenuItem.Click
        ' Add a new coffee flavor to the coffee list.
```

```vb
        With Me.coffeeComboBox
            ' Test for blank input.
            If .Text <> "" Then
                ' Make sure item is not already on the list.
                Dim itemFoundBoolean As Boolean
                Dim itemIndexInteger As Integer
                Do Until itemFoundBoolean Or itemIndexInteger = .Items.Count
                    If .Text = .Items(itemIndexInteger).ToString() Then
                        itemFoundBoolean = True
                        Exit Do
                    Else
                        itemIndexInteger += 1
                    End If
                Loop
                If itemFoundBoolean Then
                    MessageBox.Show("Duplicate item.", "Add Failed", MessageBoxButtons.OK, _
                        MessageBoxIcon.Exclamation)
                Else
                    ' If it's not in the list, add it.
                    .Items.Add(.Text)
                    .Text = ""
                    isDirtyBoolean = True
                End If
            Else
                MessageBox.Show("Enter a coffee flavor to add", _
                    "Missing Data", MessageBoxButtons.OK, _
                    MessageBoxIcon.Exclamation)
            End If
            Me.coffeeComboBox.Focus()
        End With
End Sub

Private Sub ClearCoffeeListToolStripMenuItem_Click(ByVal sender As Object, _
    ByVal e As System.EventArgs) Handles ClearCoffeeListToolStripMenuItem.Click
        ' Clear the coffee list.
        Dim responseDialogResult As DialogResult

        responseDialogResult = MessageBox.Show("Clear the coffee flavor list?", _
            "Clear coffee list", MessageBoxButtons.YesNo, MessageBoxIcon.Question)
        If responseDialogResult = DialogResult.Yes Then
            Me.coffeeComboBox.Items.Clear()
            isDirtyBoolean = True
        End If
End Sub

Private Sub RemoveCoffeeFlavorToolStripMenuItem_Click(ByVal sender As Object, _
    ByVal e As System.EventArgs) Handles RemoveCoffeeFlavorToolStripMenuItem.Click
        ' Remove the selected coffee from list.

        With Me.coffeeComboBox
            If .SelectedIndex <> -1 Then
                .Items.RemoveAt(.SelectedIndex)
                isDirtyBoolean = True
            Else
                MessageBox.Show("First select the coffee to remove", _
                    "No selection made", MessageBoxButtons.OK, _
                    MessageBoxIcon.Exclamation)
            End If
        End With
End Sub
```

```
Private Sub DisplayCoffeeCountToolStripMenuItem_Click(ByVal sender As Object, _
    ByVal e As System.EventArgs) Handles DisplayCoffeeCountToolStripMenuItem.Click
        ' Display a count of the coffee list.

        MessageBox.Show("The number of coffee types is " & _
            Me.coffeeComboBox.Items.Count, "R 'n R Coffee Type Count", _
            MessageBoxButtons.OK, MessageBoxIcon.Information)
    End Sub

    Private Sub AboutToolStripMenuItem_Click(ByVal sender As Object, _
        ByVal e As System.EventArgs) Handles AboutToolStripMenuItem.Click
            ' Display the About form.

            aboutForm.Show()
    End Sub
End Class
```

Summary

1. To create a new object, you generally declare an object variable and instantiate it using the New keyword. The declaration and instantiation can be in one statement or two. The location of the declaration determines the scope and lifetime of the object.

2. You can add an Imports statement to the top of a file to import the namespace, so that you do not have to fully qualify references to classes in the namespace.

3. A data file is made up of records, which can be further broken down into fields or data elements. The field used for organizing the file is the key field.

4. A stream object is used to transfer data to and from a data file. The StreamWriter outputs (writes) the data and the StreamReader inputs (reads) data.

5. The constructors for a StreamWriter and StreamReader take the name of the file, with an optional path, as a parameter.

6. The WriteLine method writes a data line to disk.

7. A Close method should be used as soon as you are done with the stream. Make sure the stream is closed prior to the termination of a program that uses streams.

8. The Peek method looks at the next element, which allows testing for the end of the file. The Peek method returns −1 at the end of file.

9. List box data may be saved to a stream. The Items collection should be filled in the Form_Load if the file exists. Any changes are saved back to the file when the program terminates.

10. A Boolean variable is used to track whether changes are made to the data.

11. The form's FormClosing event procedure is a good location for the code to prompt the users if they wish to save any changes.

12. The OpenFileDialog and SaveFileDialog components can be used to display the *Open File* and *Save As* dialog boxes and allow the user to select the filename.

Key Terms

Application.StartupPath *432*

Close method *427*

data file *423*

field *424*

file *424*

FormClosing event *438*

namespace *423*

New keyword *422*

Nothing *433*

OpenFileDialog *431*

Peek method *429*

ReadLine method *429*

record *424*

stream *424*

StreamReader *425*

StreamWriter *425*

System.IO namespace *424*

Write method *426*

WriteLine method *426*

Review Questions

1. Explain how to create a new object that should have module-level scope and be instantiated in a `Try/Catch` block.
2. What is the difference between a Visual Basic project file and a data file?
3. Explain what occurs when a stream object is instantiated.
4. Name two types of stream classes. What is the difference between the two?
5. What is the difference between a `Write` method and a `WriteLine` method?
6. What steps are necessary for storing the list items from a list box into a disk file?
7. What is the format for the statements to read and write streams?
8. What method can be used to determine the end of file?
9. When is exception handling necessary for stream handling?
10. Explain when a form's FormClosing event occurs and what code might be included in the FormClosing event procedure.

Programming Exercises

11.1 Rewrite Programming Exercise 8.4 using a file to store the state names and abbreviations. You need two projects: The first will allow the typist to enter the state name and the abbreviation in text boxes and store them in a file. The second project will perform the lookup functions specified in Programming Exercise 8.4.

Note: For help in basing a new project on an existing project, see "Basing a New Project on an Existing Project" in Chapter 5.

Optional extra: Allow the user to select the file to open using the *Open File* dialog box.

11.2 Create a file for employee information and call it Employee.txt. Each record will contain fields for first name, last name, employee number, and hourly pay rate.

Write a second project to process payroll. The application will load the employee data into an array of structures from the file with an extra field for the pay. The form will contain labels for the information from the array (display one record at a time) and a text box for the hours worked.

A button called *FindPay* will use a `For/Next` loop to process the array. You will calculate the pay and add the pay to the totals. Then display the labels for the next employee. (Place the pay into the extra field in the array.)

The *Exit* button will print a report on the printer and terminate the project. (Print the array.)

Processing: Hours over 40 receive time-and-a-half pay. Accumulate the total number of hours worked, the total number of hours of overtime, and the total amount of pay.

Sample Report

Ace Industries

Employee Name	Hours Worked	Hours Overtime	Pay Rate	Amount Earned
Janice Jones	40	0	5.25	210.00
Chris O'Connel	35	0	5.35	187.25
Karen Fisk	45	5	6.00	285.00
Tom Winn	42	2	5.75	247.25
Totals	162	7		929.50

Optional Extra: Allow the user to select the file to open using the *Open File* dialog box.

11.3 Modify Programming Exercise 7.5 to store the list box for Bradley's Bagels in a data file. Load the list during the Form_Load event procedure and then close the file. Be sure to use error checking in case the file does not exist.

In the FormClosing procedure, prompt the user to save the bagel list back to the disk.

Note: For help in basing a new project on an existing project, see "Basing a New Project on an Existing Project" in Chapter 5.

Optional Extra: Allow the user to select the file to open using the *Open File* dialog box.

11.4 Create a simple text editor that has one large text box (with its Multiline property set to True) or a RichTextBox control. Set the text control to fill the form and set its Anchor property to all four edges, so that the control fills the form even when it is resized.

Allow the user to save the contents of the text box in a data file and load a data file into the text box using the *Open File* dialog box.

11.5 Create a project that stores personal information for a little electronic "black book." The fields in the file should include name, phone number, pager number, cell phone number, voice mail number, and e-mail address. Create an object that contains the appropriate fields and text boxes to enter the data.

Create a second project to load the names into a list box. Perform a "look up" and display the appropriate information for the selected name.

Optional Extra: Allow the user to select the file to open using the *Open File* dialog box.

Case Studies

Note: For help in basing a new project on an existing project, see "Basing a New Project on an Existing Project" in Chapter 5.

VB Mail Order

Modify your project from Chapter 7 to save the changes to the catalog name combo box from one run to the next. When the program begins, load the list from the data file. If the file does not exist, display a message asking if the user wants to create it.

Allow the user to save changes from a *Save* menu item. When the program terminates, check to see if there are any unsaved changes. If so, prompt the user to save the changes.

Optional extra: Allow the user to select the file to open using the *Open File* dialog box.

VB Auto Center

Write a project to store vehicle information including model, manufacturer, year, and VIN number.

Create a second project that loads the data from the file into memory and loads a drop-down combo box with the VIN numbers. When a number is selected from the combo box, display the appropriate information regarding the vehicle in labels.

Optional extra: Allow the user to select the file to open using the *Open File* dialog box.

Video Bonanza

Modify your project from Chapter 7 to save the changes to the movie combo box from one run to the next. When the program begins, load the list from the data file. If the file does not exist, display a message asking if the user wants to create it.

Allow the user to save changes from a *Save* menu item. When the program terminates, check to see if there are any unsaved changes. If so, prompt the user to save the changes.

Optional extra: Allow the user to select the file to open using the *Open File* dialog box.

Very Very Boards

Modify your project from Chapter 7 to save the changes to the shirt style combo box from one run to the next. When the program begins, load the list from the data file. If the file does not exist, display a message asking if the user wants to create it.

Allow the user to save changes from a *Save* menu item. When the program terminates, check to see if there are any unsaved changes. If so, prompt the user to save the changes.

Optional extra: Allow the user to select the file to open using the *Open File* dialog box.

12

OOP: Creating Object-Oriented Programs

at the completion of this chapter, you will be able to . . .

1. Use object-oriented terminology correctly.

2. Create a two-tier application that separates the user interface from the business logic.

3. Differentiate between a class and an object.

4. Create a class that has properties and methods.

5. Declare object variables and use property procedures to set and retrieve properties of a class.

6. Assign values to the properties with a constructor.

7. Instantiate an object in a project using your class.

8. Differentiate between shared members and instance members.

9. Understand the purpose of the constructor and destructor methods.

10. Inherit a new class from your own class.

11. Use visual inheritance by deriving a form from another form.

Object-Oriented Programming

You have been using objects since Chapter 1. As you know quite well by now, **objects** have properties and methods and generate events that you can respond to (or ignore) if you choose. Up until now, the classes for all objects in your projects have been predefined; that is, you could choose to create a new object of the form class, a button class, a text box class, or any other class of control in the toolbox. In this chapter you will learn to define your own new class and create objects based on that class.

Object-oriented programming (OOP) is currently the most accepted style of programming. Some computer languages, such as Java, C#, and SmallTalk, were designed to be object oriented (OO) from their inception. Other languages, such as Visual Basic and C++, have been modified over the last few years to accommodate OOP. Visual Basic .NET is the first version of Visual Basic to be truly object oriented.

Writing object-oriented programs is a mind-set—a different way of looking at a problem. You must think in terms of using objects. As your projects become more complex, using objects becomes increasingly important.

Objects

Beyond the many built-in choices you have for objects to include in your projects, Visual Basic allows you to create your own new object type by creating a **class**. Just like other object types, your class may have both properties and methods. Your class can have events too, just like the Click event for the Button class. So remember: Properties are characteristics, and methods are actions that can be performed by a class of object.

An object is a *thing* such as a button. You create a button object from the button tool in the toolbox. In other words, *button* is a class but *exitButton* is an actual occurrence or **instance** of the class; the instance is the object. Just as you may have multiple buttons in a project, you may have many objects of a new class type.

Defining your own class is like creating a new tool for the toolbox; the process does not create the object, only a definition of what that type of object looks like and how it behaves. You may then create as many instances of the class as you need using the New keyword. Your class may be a student, an employee, a product, or any other type of object that would be useful in a project.

Many people use a cookie analogy to describe the relationship of a class and an object. The cookie cutter is the class. You can't eat a cookie cutter, but you can use it to make cookies; the cookie is the object. When you make a cookie using a cookie cutter, you **instantiate** an object of the cookie class. You can use the same cookie cutter to make various kinds of cookies. Although all the cookies made will have the same shape, some may be chocolate, others are lemon, or vanilla; some may be frosted or have colored sprinkles on top. The characteristics of the cookie, such as flavor and topping, are the properties of the object. You could refer to the properties of your cookie object as

```
Cookie1.Flavor = "Lemon"
Cookie1.Topping = "Cream Frosting"
```

What about methods? Recall that a method is an action or behavior—something the object can do or have done to it, such as Move, Clear, or Print. Possible methods for our cookie object might be Eat, Bake, or Crumble. Using object terminology, you can refer to Object.Method:

```
Cookie1.Crumble
```

Sometimes the distinction between a method and an event is somewhat fuzzy. Generally, anything you tell the object to do is a method; if the object does an action and needs to inform you, that's an event. So if you tell the cookie to crumble, that is a method; if the cookie crumbles on its own and needs to inform you of the fact, that's an event.

Object-Oriented Terminology

Key features of an object-oriented language are encapsulation, inheritance, and polymorphism.

Encapsulation

Encapsulation refers to the combination of characteristics of an object along with its behaviors. You have one "package" that holds the definition of all properties, methods, and events. For example, when you create a button, you can set or retrieve its properties, such as Text, Name, or BackColor. You can execute its methods, such as Focus, Hide, or Show, and you can write code for its events, such as Click or Double-click. But you cannot make up new properties or tell it to do anything that it doesn't already know how to do. It is a complete package; you can think of all of the parts of the package as being in a capsule.

You can witness encapsulation by looking at any program. The form is actually a class. All of the methods and events that you code are enclosed within the Class and End Class statements. The variables that you place in your code are actually properties of the specific form class that you are generating.

Encapsulation is sometimes referred to as data hiding. Each object keeps its data (properties) and procedures (methods) hidden. Through use of the Public, Private, Protected, and Friend keywords, an object can "expose" only those data elements and procedures that it wishes to allow the outside world to see.

Inheritance

Inheritance is the ability to create a new class from an existing class. You can add enhancements to an existing class without modifying the original. By creating a new class that inherits from an existing class, you can add or modify class variables and methods. For example, each of the forms that you create is inherited from, or derived from, the existing Form class. The original class is known as the **base class**, **superclass**, or **parent class**. The inherited class is called a **subclass**, **derived class**, or **child class**. Of course, a new class can inherit from a subclass—that subclass becomes a superclass as well as a subclass.

Look closely at the first lines of the *FormName*.Designer.vb code file for a form:

```
Partial Public Class Form1
    Inherits System.Windows.Forms.Form
```

The base class is System.Windows.Forms.Form and Form1 is the derived class. Inherited classes have an "is a" relationship with the base class. In the form example, the new Form1 "is a" Form.

The real purpose of inheritance is **reusability**. You may need to reuse or obtain the functionality from one class or object when you have another similar situation. The new Form1 class that you create has all of the characteristics and actions of the base class, System.Windows.Forms.Form. From there you can add the functionality for your own new form. Other classes that you have reused multiple times are the Button class and the TextBox class.

You can create your own hierarchy of classes. You place the code you want to be common in a base class. You then create other classes from it, which inherit the base class methods. This concept is very helpful if you have features that are similar in two classes. Rather than writing two classes that are almost identical, you can create a base class that contains the similar procedures.

An example of reusing classes could be a Person class, where you might have properties for name, address, and phone number. The Person class can be a base class from which you derive an Employee class, a Customer class, or a Student class (Figure 12.1). The derived classes could call shared procedures from the base class and contain any procedures that are unique to the derived class. In inheritance, typically the classes go from general to the more specific.

Figure 12.1

The derived classes inherit from the base class.

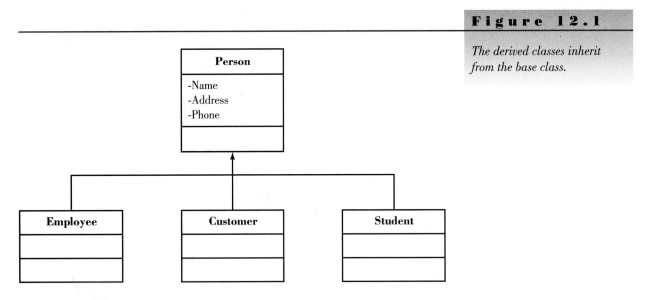

Polymorphism

The term *polymorphism* actually means the ability to take on many shapes or forms. As applied to OOP, polymorphism refers to methods that have identical names but different implementations, depending on the situation. For example, radio buttons, check boxes, and list boxes all have a `Select` method. In each case, the `Select` method operates appropriately for its class.

Polymorphism also allows a single class to have more than one method with the same name. When the method is called, the argument type determines which version of the method to use. Each of the identically named methods should perform the same task in a slightly different manner, depending on the arguments.

Later in this chapter you will use both **overloading** a method and **overriding** a method to implement polymorphism. You have already seen examples of *overloading*, such as the `MessageBox.Show` method that gives you several argument lists for calling the method. *Overriding* refers to a method that has the same name as a method in its base class. The method in the subclass, or derived class, takes precedence over, or overrides, the identically named method in the base class.

Reusable Classes

A big advantage of object-oriented programming over traditional programming is the ability to reuse classes. When you create a new class, you can then use that class in multiple projects. Each object that you create from the class has its own set of properties. This process works just like the built-in VB controls you have been using all along. For example, you can create two PictureBox objects: PictureBox1 and PictureBox2. Each has its own Visible property and Image property, which will probably be set differently from each other.

As you begin creating classes in your projects, you will find many situations in which classes are useful. You might want to create your own class to provide database access. You could include methods for adding and deleting data members. If you work frequently with sales, you might create a Product class. The Product class would likely have properties such as description, quantity, and cost. The methods would probably include finding the current value of the product.

Multitier Applications

A common practice for writing professional applications is to write independent components that work in multiple "tiers" or layers. Each of the functions of a **multitier application** can be coded in a separate component and the components may be stored and run on different machines.

One of the most popular approaches is a three-tier application. The tiers in this model are the Presentation tier, Business tier, and Data tier (Figure 12.2). You also hear the term "n-tier" application, which is an expansion of the three-tier model. The middle tier, which contains all of the business logic, may be written in multiple classes that can be stored and run from multiple locations.

Figure 12.2

The three-tier model for application design.

Presentation Tier	Business Tier	Data Tier
User Interface Forms, controls, menus	**Business Objects** Validation Calculations Business logic Business rules	**Data Retrieval** Data storage

In a multitier application, the goal is to create components that can be combined and replaced. If one part of an application needs to change, such as a redesign of the user interface or a new database format, the other components do not need to be replaced. A developer can simply "plug in" a new user interface and continue using the rest of the components of the application.

The Presentation tier refers to the user interface, which in VB is the form. Consider that in the future the user interface could be redesigned or even converted to a Web page.

The Business tier is a class or classes that handle the data. This layer can include validation to enforce business rules as well as the calculations.

The Data tier includes retrieving and storing the data in a database. Occasionally an organization will decide to change database vendors or will need to retrieve data from several different sources. The Data tier retrieves the data and passes the results to the Business tier, or takes data from the Business tier and writes them in the appropriate location.

Classes

The classes that you have worked with up until now have generated visual objects such as text boxes and labels. These were easily created from the toolbox at design time. You also can create objects at run time. In Chapter 11 you instantiated objects of the StreamWriter and StreamReader classes, and in Chapter 7 you instantiated objects of the Font class in your printing routines. In both cases you used the New keyword to instantiate the objects.

Before you can refer to most properties and methods of a class, you must instantiate an object of the class. The exception is shared members, which you will see later in this chapter. ■

Designing Your Own Class

To design your own class, you need to analyze the characteristics and behaviors that your object needs. The characteristics or properties are defined as variables, and the behaviors (methods) are sub procedures or function procedures. For a simple example, assume that you have a user interface (form) that gathers the price and the quantity of a product. You can design a class to perform the calculations. For the class to calculate the extended price, it must know the price and the quantity. The form needs to retrieve the extended price. The price, quantity, and extended price are stored in private variables in the class; those variables are accessed through property procedures. The form will instantiate the class, pass the price and quantity to it through property procedures, call a method to calculate the extended price, and then display the extended price on the form by retrieving it from a property procedure.

Creating Properties in a Class

Inside your class you define private member variables, which store the values for the properties of the class. Theoretically, you could declare all variables as Public so that all other project code could set and retrieve their values. However, this approach violates the rules of encapsulation that require each object to be in charge of its own data. Remember that encapsulation is also called *data hiding*. To accomplish encapsulation, you will declare all variables in a class as Private or Protected. Protected variables behave as private but are available in any class that inherits from this class. As a private or protected variable, the value is available only to procedures within the class, the same way that private module-level variables are available only to procedures within a form's class code.

When your program creates objects from your class, you will need to assign values to the properties. Because the properties are private variables, you will use special property procedures to pass the values to the class module and to return values from the class module.

Property Procedures

The way that your class allows its properties to be accessed is with **accessor methods** in a **property procedure**. The procedure may contain a `Get` accessor method to retrieve a property value and/or a `Set` accessor method to assign a value to the property. The name that you use for the `Property` procedure becomes the name of the property to the outside world. Create "friendly" property names that describe the property, such as LastName or EmployeeNumber. You do not include the data type as part of a property name.

The Property Procedure—General Form

General Form

```
{Private | Protected} ClassVariable As DataType

[Public] Property PropertyName() As DataType
     Get
          Return ClassVariable [| PropertyName = ClassVariable ]
     End Get
     Set(ByVal value As DataType)
          [statements, such as validation]
          ClassVariable = value
     End Set
End Property
```

The `Set` statement uses the **value keyword** to refer to the incoming value for the property. Property procedures are public by default, so you can omit the optional `Public` keyword. `Get` blocks are similar to function procedures in at least one respect: Somewhere inside the procedure, before the `End Get`, you must assign a return value to the procedure name or use a `Return` statement to return a value. The data type of the incoming value for a `Set` must match the type of the return value of the corresponding `Get`.

The Property Procedure—Example

Example

```
Private lastNameString As String

Property LastName() As String
     Get
          Return lastNameString
     End Get
     Set(ByVal value As String)
          lastNameString = value
     End Set
End Property
```

Remember, the private module-level variable holds the value of the property. The `Property` `Get` and `Set` retrieve the current value and assign a new value to the property.

Note: If you do not specify an access modifier, the default is `Public`.

Read-Only Properties

In some instances, you may wish to have a property that can be retrieved by an object but not changed. You can write a property procedure to create a read-only property: Use the **ReadOnly** modifier and write only the Get portion of the property procedure.

```
' Define the property at the module level.
Private totalPayDecimal As Decimal

' The property procedure for a read-only property.
ReadOnly Property TotalPay() As Decimal
    Get
        Return totalPayDecimal
    End Get
End Property
```

Write-Only Properties

At times you may need to have a property that can be assigned by an object but not retrieved. You can create a property block that contains only a Set to create a write-only property.

```
' Private module-level variable to hold the property value.
Private priceDecimal As Decimal

Public WriteOnly Property Price() As Decimal
    Set(ByVal value As Decimal)
        If value >= 0 Then
            priceDecimal = value
        End If
    End Set
End Property
```

Class Methods

You create methods of the new class by coding public methods within the class. Any methods that you declare with the Private keyword are available only within the class. Any methods that you declare with the Public keyword are available to external objects created from this class or other classes.

```
' Private method used for internal calculations.

Private Sub CalculateExtendedPrice()
    ' Calculate the extended price.

    extendedPriceDecimal = quantityInteger * priceDecimal
End Sub
```

Constructors and Destructors

A **constructor** is a method that executes automatically when an object is instantiated. A **destructor** is a method that executes automatically when an object is destroyed. In VB, the name of a constructor method is New.

Constructors

The constructor executes automatically when you instantiate an object of the class. Because the constructor method executes before any other code in the class, the constructor is an ideal location for any initialization tasks that you need to do, such as setting the initial values of variables and properties.

The constructor must be public, because the objects that you create must execute this method.

Note: If a class does not contain a constructor, the compiler creates an implicit method called the *default constructor*. The default constructor has an empty argument list.

Overloading the Constructor

Recall from Chapter 3 that *overloading* means that two methods have the same name but a different list of arguments (the signature). You can create overloaded procedures in your class by giving the same name to multiple procedures, each with a different argument list. The following example shows an empty constructor (one without arguments) and a constructor that passes arguments to the class.

```
Sub New()

    ' Empty constructor.

End Sub


Sub New(ByVal Title As String, ByVal Quantity As Integer, _
  ByVal Price As Decimal)

        ' Code statements to assign property values.

End Sub
```

Parameterized Constructor

The term ***parameterized constructor*** refers to a constructor that requires arguments. This popular technique allows you to pass arguments as you create the new object.

```
' Instantiate the object and set the properties.
aBookSale = New BookSale(Me.titleTextBox.Text, _
  Integer.Parse(Me.quantityTextBox.Text), _
  Decimal.Parse(Me.priceTextBox.Text))
```

Within the class code, use the Me keyword to refer to the current class. So Me.Quantity refers to the Quantity property of the current class. This technique is preferable to just assigning the passed argument to the class-level property variables, since validation is often performed in the Set methods.

```
Sub New(ByVal Title As String, ByVal Quantity As Integer, _
  ByVal Price As Decimal)
        ' Assign property values.
```

```
    With Me
        .Title = Title
        .Quantity = Quantity
        .Price = Price
    End With
    CalculateExtendedPrice()
End Sub
```

When your class has both an empty constructor and a parameterized constructor, the program that creates the object can choose which method to use.

Creating a New Class—Step-by-Step

In this step-by-step exercise, you will create a new class to hold book sale information for R 'n R.

Begin the Project

A class file is part of a Visual Basic project, so the first step is to create a new project.

STEP 1: Create a new Windows project called "Ch12SBS" (for *step-by-step*).

Begin a New Class

STEP 1: Select *Add Class* from the *Project* menu. The *Add New Item* dialog box will appear (Figure 12.3) with the Class template already selected.

STEP 2: In the *Add New Item* dialog box, type "BookSale.vb" for the class name and click on *Add*. You will see a new tab in the Document window for the new class.

Figure 12.3

Add a new class to a project in the **Add New Item** *dialog box.*

Add a new class

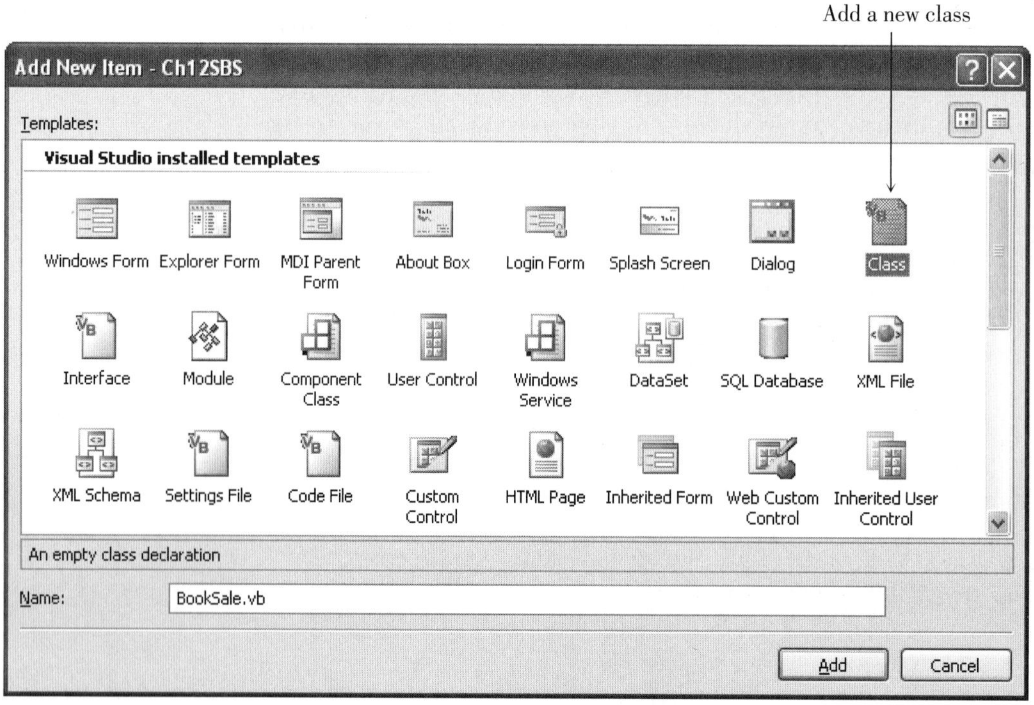

Define the Class Properties

STEP 1: In the Document window, in the line after the `Class` statement, declare the `Private` variables. These module-level variables will hold the values for the properties of your new class.

```
Private titleString As String
Private quantityInteger As Integer
Private priceDecimal, extendedPriceDecimal As Decimal
```

This class has private module-level variables: titleString, quantityInteger, priceDecimal, and extendedPriceDecimal (Figure 12.4). Because the variables are declared as `Private`, they can be accessed only by procedures within the class module. To allow access from outside the class module, you must add property procedures.

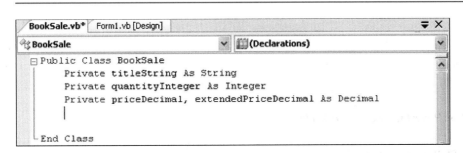

```
BookSale.vb*   Form1.vb [Design]                                   ⬇ ✕
⬛ BookSale                              ⬇  ▦ (Declarations)                  ⬇
⊟ Public Class BookSale                                                    ▲
       Private titleString As String
       Private quantityInteger As Integer
       Private priceDecimal, extendedPriceDecimal As Decimal
       |

  └ End Class
```

Figure 12.4

Declare module-level variables for the class properties.

☑**TIP**

Follow variable naming conventions for the module-level variable to hold the property value; use a friendly name for the property name in the Property procedure. ■

Add the Title Property Procedure

STEP 1: In the Editor window, after the property declarations, type "Property Title As String". Press Enter.

The `Get` and `Set` blocks will appear, as well as the parentheses on the property name.

Note: The smart editor takes care of the capitalization of keywords. However, the new property name that you declare will be capitalized exactly as you enter it. You can save a little time by typing the line "property Title as string".

STEP 2: Write the code for the Property procedures.

```
Property Title() As String
    Get
         Return titleString
    End Get
    Set(ByVal value As String)
         titleString = value
    End Set
End Property
```

Add the Quantity Property Procedure

STEP 1: On a new line after the `End Property` for Title, type "Property Quantity As Integer" and press Enter.
The `Get` and `Set` blocks will appear.

STEP 2: Write the code for the Property procedure.

```
Property Quantity() As Integer
    Get
        Return quantityInteger
    End Get
    Set(ByVal value As Integer)
        If value >= 0 Then
            quantityInteger = value
        End If
    End Set
End Property
```

Notice the code to validate the incoming `value` in the `Set`.

Add the Price Property Procedure

STEP 1: After the `End Property` for Quantity, add the property procedure for Price.

STEP 2: Write the code.

```
Property Price() As Decimal
    Get
        Return priceDecimal
    End Get
    Set(ByVal value As Decimal)
        If value >= 0 Then
            priceDecimal = value
        End If
    End Set
End Property
```

Add the ExtendedPrice Property Procedure

STEP 1: After the `End Property` for Price, add the property procedure for ExtendedPrice.

STEP 2: Write the code.

```
Property ExtendedPrice() As Decimal
    Get
        Return extendedPriceDecimal
    End Get
    Set(ByVal value As Decimal)
        If value >= 0 Then
            extendedPriceDecimal = value
        End If
    End Set
End Property
```

Write the Constructor

STEP 1: Following the Private module-level variables and above the property procedures, type in "Public Sub New(Title As String, Quantity As Integer, Price As Decimal)" and press Enter.

Notice that the editor adds the `ByVal` before each argument.

The constructor can actually appear anywhere in the code, as long as it's inside the class and not inside another procedure. A good convention is to place the constructors near the top of the class, right after the module-level declarations.

STEP 2: Type the code for the procedure.

```
Public Sub New(ByVal Title As String, ByVal Quantity As Integer, _
  ByVal Price As Decimal)
      ' Assign the property values.

    With Me
        .Title = Title
        .Quantity = Quantity
        .Price = Price
    End With
    CalculateExtendedPrice()
End Sub
```

The call to `CalculateExtendedPrice` is flagged as an error. You will code that procedure next.

Code a Method

You can create methods by adding sub procedures and functions for the behaviors needed by the class. For this class, you will add a sub procedure to calculate the extended price, which is the price per book multiplied by the quantity. Note that if you declare sub procedures and functions with the `Public` keyword, the methods are public; if you use the `Protected` keyword, the methods can be executed from the current class or any inherited classes; if you use the `Private` keyword, the methods are private and can be executed only from inside the class.

STEP 1: After the property procedures, type
         "Protected Sub CalculateExtendedPrice" and press Enter.
         Notice that the editor adds the parentheses after the procedure name.
STEP 2: Type the code for the procedure.

```
Protected Sub CalculateExtendedPrice()
      ' Calculate the extended price.

    extendedPriceDecimal = quantityInteger * priceDecimal
End Sub
```

Add General Remarks

STEP 1: Type the remarks at the top of the file, before the Class declaration line.

```
'Class Name:      BookSale
'Programmer:      Your Name
'Date:            Today's Date
'Description:     Handle book sale information.
'Folder:          Ch12SBS
```

STEP 2: Save your project.

The Complete Class Code

```
'Class Name:      BookSale
'Programmer:      Your Name
'Date:            Today's Date
'Description:     Handle book sale information.
'Folder:          Ch12SBS

Public Class BookSale
    Private titleString As String
    Private quantityInteger As Integer
    Private priceDecimal, extendedPriceDecimal As Decimal

    Sub New(ByVal Title As String, ByVal Quantity As Integer, _
        ByVal Price As Decimal)
        ' Assign the property values.

        With Me
            .Title = Title
            .Quantity = Quantity
            .Price = Price
        End With
        CalculateExtendedPrice()
    End Sub

    Property Title() As String
        Get
            Return titleString
        End Get
        Set(ByVal value As String)
            titleString = value
        End Set
    End Property

    Property Quantity() As Integer
        Get
            Return quantityInteger
        End Get
        Set(ByVal value As Integer)
            If value >= 0 Then
                quantityInteger = value
            End If
        End Set
    End Property

    Property Price() As Decimal
        Get
            Return priceDecimal
        End Get
        Set(ByVal value As Decimal)
            If value >= 0 Then
                priceDecimal = value
            End If
        End Set
    End Property

    Property ExtendedPrice() As Decimal
        Get
            Return extendedPriceDecimal
        End Get
```

```
            Set(ByVal value As Decimal)
                extendedPriceDecimal = value
            End Set
        End Property

        Protected Sub CalculateExtendedPrice()
            ' Calculate the extended price.

            extendedPriceDecimal = quantityInteger * priceDecimal
        End Sub
End Class
```

Property Procedures with Mixed Access Levels

It is possible to set the `Property` statement as `Public` and then to assign either
the `Get` or the `Set` procedure to a more restrictive level such as `Friend` or
`Private`. This mixed-level access is a welcome addition to VB .NET 2005.

```
Private titleString As String

Public Property Title() As String
    Get
        Return titleString
    End Get
    Private Set(ByVal value As String)
        titleString = value
    End Set
End Property
```

This code allows public access to the `Get` procedure, but the `Set` procedure is
private. This would work well with our programs where we call the `Set` only
from the constructor. Remember, if you do not specify the access, it defaults
to `Public`.

Feedback 12.1

1. What is the difference between an object and a class?
2. Given the statement

   ```
   Private aProduct As Product
   ```

   Is aProduct an object or class? What about Product?
3. What actions are performed by the following statement?

   ```
   aProduct.Quantity = Integer.Parse(Me.quantityTextBox.Text)
   ```

4. Write the property declarations for a class module for a Student
   class that will contain the properties: LastName, FirstName,
   StudentIDNumber, and GPA. Where will these statements appear?
5. Code the Property procedure to set and retrieve the value of the
   LastName property.
6. Code the Property procedure to retrieve the value of the read-only GPA
   property.

Creating a New Object Using a Class

Creating a new class defines a new type; it does not create any objects. This is similar to creating a new tool for the toolbox but not yet creating an instance of the class.

Generally you will create new objects of your class in a two-step operation: first declare a variable for the new object and then instantiate the object using the New keyword. Use Dim, Public, or Private to declare the identifier that refers to the object of the class.

```
Private aBookSale As BookSale
```

This line merely states that the name aBookSale is associated with the Book-Sale class, but it does not create an instance of the object. You must use the New keyword to actually create the object.

```
aBookSale = New BookSale()
```

In Visual Basic it is legal to declare and instantiate an object at the same time:

```
Dim aBookSale As New BookSale()
```

If you will need to use the object variable in multiple procedures, you should declare the object at the module level. But when you instantiate an object, you may need to include the New statement in a Try/Catch block to allow error checking, and a Try/Catch block *must* be inside a procedure. Make sure to enclose the instantiation in a Try/Catch block if you are converting and passing values that a user enters in a text box so that you catch any bad input data.

The preferred technique is to include the New statement inside of a procedure at the time the object is needed. And if the object is never needed, it won't be created needlessly.

If you *do* choose to declare the variable and instantiate it at the same time, these two statements are equivalent:

```
Private aBookSale As BookSale = New BookSale()
Private aBookSale as New BookSale()
```

The second statement is a coding shortcut for the first (more complete) statement.

If you are using a parameterized constructor, you must pass the values for the arguments when you instantiate the object.

```
Private aBookSale As BookSale

' Instantiate the BookSale object and set the properties.
With Me
    aBookSale = New BookSale(.titleTextBox.Text, _
       Integer.Parse(.quantityTextBox.Text), _
       Decimal.Parse(.priceTextBox.Text))
End With
```

Defining and Using a New Object—Step-by-Step

To continue the step-by-step tutorial for the BookSale class, the next step is to design the form for the user interface. The form has text boxes for the user to enter the title, quantity, and price; a menu choice to calculate the sale (the extended price); and another menu item to exit.

In the Calculate Sale event procedure, you will create an instance of the BookSale class and assign the input values for title, quantity, and price to the properties of the BookSale object. The ExtendedPrice property in the BookSale class retrieves the amount of the sale, which appears in a ReadOnly text box on the form. Figure 12.5 shows the completed form.

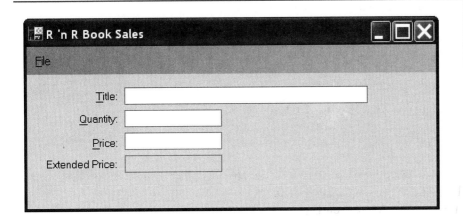

Figure 12.5

The user interface that uses the new BookSale class; the completed form for the step-by-step exercise.

Placing all calculations in a separate class is a good thing. You are seeing your first example of dividing a program into a Presentation tier and a Business tier.

Create the Form

This is a continuation of the step-by-step tutorial for this chapter. If the project is not still open, open it now.

STEP 1: Open the form designer for Form1. Referring to Figure 12.5, create the user interface with text boxes for the title, quantity, and price, and a ReadOnly text box for the extended price. Set appropriate properties for the form and the controls.

STEP 2: Change the form name to "salesForm".

STEP 3: Create menu items on the *File* menu for *Calculate Sale*, *Clear*, and *Exit*. You may want to create keyboard shortcuts for the menu items to simplify testing.

Add General Remarks

STEP 1: Type the remarks at the top of the form's code.

```
'Program:      Chapter 12 BookSale Step-by-Step
'Programmer:   Your Name
'Date:         Today's Date
'Description:  Calculate sales price using the BookSale class.
'              Instantiate aBookSale as a new object of the BookSale class.
'Folder:       Ch12SBS
```

Declare the New Object

STEP 1: Declare the object variable in the Declarations section, right under the Public Class salesForm statement.

```
' Declare the new object.
Private aBookSale As BookSale
```

Write the Code

STEP 1: In the CalculateSaleToolStripMenuItem event procedure, write the code to instantiate the BookSale object, assign the values to the properties, calculate the extended price, and assign the result to extendedPriceTextBox. Notice that IntelliSense pops up with the properties and method of your new BookSale class.

```
Private Sub CalculateSaleToolStripMenuItem_Click(ByVal sender As Object, _
  ByVal e As System.EventArgs) Handles CalculateSaleToolStripMenuItem.Click
     ' Calculate the extended price for the sale.

    Try
         ' Instantiate the object and set the properties.
        With Me
            aBookSale = New BookSale(.titleTextBox.Text, _
               Integer.Parse(.quantityTextBox.Text), Decimal.Parse(.priceTextBox.Text))
             ' Calculate and format the result.
            .extendedPriceTextBox.Text = aBookSale.ExtendedPrice.ToString("N")
        End With
    Catch ex As Exception
        MessageBox.Show("Enter numeric data.", "R 'n R Book Sales", _
           MessageBoxButtons.OK, MessageBoxIcon.Exclamation)
    End Try
End Sub
```

STEP 2: Code the ClearToolStripMenuItem_Click procedure.

```
Private Sub ClearToolStripMenuItem_Click(ByVal sender As Object, _
   ByVal e As System.EventArgs) Handles ClearToolStripMenuItem.Click
     ' Clear the screen controls.

    With Me
        .quantityTextBox.Clear()
        .priceTextBox.Clear()
        .extendedPriceTextBox.Clear()
        With .titleTextBox
            .Clear()
            .Focus()
        End With
    End With
End Sub
```

STEP 3: Code the ExitToolStripMenuItem_Click procedure.

```
Private Sub ExitToolStripMenuItem_Click(ByVal sender As Object, _
   ByVal e As System.EventArgs) Handles ExitToolStripMenuItem.Click
     ' Exit the program.

    Me.Close()
End Sub
```

Save Your Work

STEP 1: Click the *Save All* toolbar button to save the project, class, and form.

Run the Project

The next step is to watch the project run—hopefully without errors.

STEP 1: Run the program; your form should appear.

STEP 2: Fill in test values for the title, quantity, and price. Select the *Calculate Sale* menu item. What did you get for the extended price? Is it correct? Try putting in something other than a number for Quantity. What happened when you calculated the sale?

STEP 3: Stop program execution using the *File / Exit* menu item.

Single-Step the Execution

If you get an error message or an incorrect answer in the output, you will need to debug the project. The quickest and easiest way to debug is to single-step program execution. Single-stepping is an interesting exercise, even if you *did* get the right answer.

To single-step, you need to be in break time. Place a breakpoint on the first line in the CalculateSaleToolStripMenuItem_Click procedure (the `Try` statement). Run the program, enter test values for quantity and price, and select *File / Calculate Sale*. When the program stops at the breakpoint, press the F8 key repeatedly and watch each step; you will see execution transfer to the code for the BookSale class for each property and for the `CalculateExtendedPrice` method. If an error message halts program execution, point to the variable names and property names on the screen to see their current values.

When the Click event procedure finishes, if the form does not reappear, you can click on your project's Taskbar button.

Instance Variables versus Shared Variables

The class properties that you have created up to this point belong to each instance of the class. Therefore, if you create two BookSale objects, each object has its own set of properties. This is exactly what you want for properties such as quantity and price, but what if you need to find a total or count for all of the BookSales objects? You don't want each new object to have its own count property; there would be nothing to increment.

The variables and properties that we have declared thus far are called *instance variables*, or **instance properties**. A separate memory location exists for each instance of the object. Now we will create **shared variables**, also called *shared properties*. A shared property is a single variable that exists, or is available, for all objects of a class.

Terminology varies from one OOP language to another. In some languages, shared members are called *class variables* or *static variables*. Microsoft documentation refers to *instance members* and *shared members*, which include both properties and methods. In general, a shared member has one copy for all objects of the class, and an instance member has one copy for *each* instance or object of the class. Methods also can be declared as shared and are considered shared members.

Another important point is that you can access shared members without instantiating an object of the class. When you display class documentation in

MSDN Help, shared members display with a yellow *S* next to the name (Figure 12.6). You must reference these shared members with `ClassName.Property` or `ClassName.Method()`, whether or not you have instantiated an object from the class.

Figure 12.6

Shared members display in MSDN Help with a yellow S.

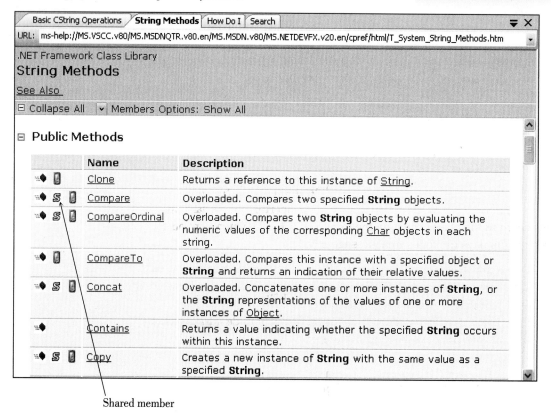

Shared member

Creating Shared Members

Use the `Shared` keyword to create a shared member.

```
[Public | Protected | Private] Shared VariableName As Datatype
[Public | Protected | Private] Shared Function FunctionName(ArgumentList) As Datatype
```

If we want to accumulate a total of all sales and a count of the number of sales for our BookSale class, we need shared properties:

```
Private Shared salesTotalDecimal As Decimal
Private Shared salesCountInteger As Integer
```

You will want to make these shared properties read-only, so that their values can be retrieved but not set directly. The values of the properties are accumulated inside the class; each time a new sale is calculated, the extended price is added to the total sales and the sales count is incremented by one.

```
Shared ReadOnly Property SalesTotal() As Decimal
    Get
        Return salesTotalDecimal
    End Get
End Property

Shared ReadOnly Property SalesCount() As Integer
    Get
        Return salesCountInteger
    End Get
End Property
```

Note that the `Shared` keyword on the `Private` module-level variable makes it a shared member and is required; the `Shared` keyword on the property procedure is optional. You need to use it if you plan to retrieve the property without first creating an instance of the class.

Adding Shared Properties to the Step-by-Step Exercise

You will now make the BookSale class calculate the total of all sales and a count of the number of sales. You will need shared properties for the sales total and sales count in the class. Then, on the form, you will add a menu option for *Summary* that displays the totals in a message box.

Add Shared Properties to the Class

If the chapter step-by-step exercise is not still open, open it now.

STEP 1: In the BookSale class, add the private module-level declarations for salesTotalDecimal and salesCountInteger.

```
Private Shared salesTotalDecimal As Decimal
Private Shared salesCountInteger As Integer
```

STEP 2: Add the property procedures for these two shared read-only properties.

```
Shared ReadOnly Property SalesTotal() As Decimal
    Get
        Return salesTotalDecimal
    End Get
End Property

Shared ReadOnly Property SalesCount() As Integer
    Get
        Return salesCountInteger
    End Get
End Property
```

Modify the Code to Calculate the Totals

STEP 1: Add a protected procedure for calculating the totals. This method will be called inside the class (or any classes that inherit from this class) but cannot be called from an object outside the class.

```
Protected Sub AddToTotals()
    ' Add to summary information.

    salesTotalDecimal += extendedPriceDecimal
    salesCountInteger += 1
End Sub
```

STEP 2: Modify the constructor procedure to call the `AddToTotals` procedure.

```
Sub New(ByVal Title As String, ByVal Quantity As Integer, _
  ByVal Price As Decimal)
    ' Assign property values.

    With Me
        .Title = Title
        .Quantity = Quantity
        .Price = Price
    End With
    CalculateExtendedPrice()
    AddToTotals()
End Sub
```

Modify the Form

STEP 1: Add a menu item for *File / Summary* to the form.

STEP 2: Write the event procedure for SummaryToolStripMenuItem to display the sales total and sales count from the properties of the class. Use a message box and format the sales total to display dollars and cents. Note that you retrieve the shared members of the BookSale class without using an instance of the class: `BookSale.SalesTotal`.

```
Private Sub SummaryToolStripMenuItem_Click(ByVal sender As Object, _
  ByVal e As System.EventArgs) Handles SummaryToolStripMenuItem.Click
    ' Display the sales summary information.
    Dim messageString As String

    messageString = "Sales Total: " & BookSale.SalesTotal.ToString("C") & _
        ControlChars.NewLine & "Sales Count: " & BookSale.SalesCount.ToString()
    MessageBox.Show(messageString, "R 'n R Book Sales Summary", _
        MessageBoxButtons.OK, MessageBoxIcon.Information)
End Sub
```

STEP 3: Test the program. Try entering several sales and checking the totals. Also try selecting *Summary* without first calculating a sale. If the program throws an exception, it means that you probably left the `Shared` modifier off the property procedures for the two shared properties.

Destructors

If there is special processing that you need to do when an object goes out of scope, you can write a `Finalize` procedure, which is also called a *destructor*. However, Microsoft recommends against writing `Finalize` procedures unless you need to do something special that the system doesn't know how to handle, such as closing some types of database connections.

Garbage Collection

The **garbage collection** feature of the .NET Common Language Runtime cleans up unused components. Periodically the garbage collector checks for unreferenced objects and releases all memory and system resources used by the objects. If you have written a `Finalize` procedure, it executes during garbage collection. Microsoft recommends that you rely on garbage collection to release resources and not try to finalize objects yourself. Using this technique, you don't know exactly when your objects will be finalized, since the CLR performs garbage collection on its own schedule, when it needs to recover the resources or has spare time.

Inheritance

When you create a class, the new class can be based on another class. You can make the new class inherit from one of the existing .NET classes or from one of your own classes. Recall that a form uses inheritance using the statement

```
Partial Public Class Form1
    Inherits System.Windows.Forms.Form
```

The `Inherits` statement must follow the class header prior to any comments.

```
Public Class NewClass
    Inherits BaseClass
```

Inheriting Properties and Methods

All public and protected data members and methods of the base class are inherited in the derived class. If you want the derived class to have a different implementation for a base-class method, you must write the method in the derived class that overrides the base-class method.

In the past you have used the `Public`, `Private`, and `Friend` keywords. You also can declare elements with the **Protected** keyword, which specifies that the element is accessible only within its own class or any class derived from that class.

Constructors in Inheritance

Although a derived class can inherit all public and protected methods, there is one exception: A subclass cannot inherit constructors from the base class. Each class must have its own constructors, unless the only constructor needed is an empty constructor. (Visual Basic automatically creates an empty constructor for all classes, so you don't need to write one if that's the only constructor that you need.)

Calling the Base Class Constructor

Often an inherited class needs to make sure that the constructor for the base class executes as well as the constructor for the inherited class. You can call the base class constructor with the statement

```
MyBase.New()
```

You generally place this code in the constructor for the inherited class, before any additional statements.

```
Sub New(ByVal Title As String, ByVal Quantity As Integer, ByVal Price As Decimal)
    ' Assign property values.

    ' Call the base class constructor.
    MyBase.New(Title, Quantity, Price)
End Sub
```

Overriding Methods

You can create a method with the same name and the same argument list as a method in the base class. The new method is said to override the base-class method. The derived class will use the new method rather than the method in the base class.

To override a method in Visual Basic .NET, you must declare the original method with the `Overridable` keyword and declare the new method with the `Overrides` keyword. The access modifier for the base-class procedure can be `Private` or `Protected` (not `Public`).

Base Class

```
Protected Overridable Sub CalculateExtendedPrice()
```

Inherited Class

```
Protected Overrides Sub CalculateExtendedPrice()
```

In a base class, you can actually use the `Overridable`, `Overrides`, or **`MustOverride`** keyword on a method that can be overridden. Use `Overridable` when you are writing a new method that has code. Use `MustOverride` for an **abstract method**, which is an empty method. Abstract methods are designed to be overridden by subclasses and have no implementation of their own. The only time that you declare a base-class method with the `Overrides` keyword is when the method is overriding a method in *its* base class.

When you use the keyword `Overridable` for a base-class method, in the derived class you have the option of using the base-class implementation for the method or overriding the method by supplying new code. However, if you use the `MustOverride` keyword on a base-class method, the method does not have any code; the derived class *must* provide its own code for the method. A class that has any method declared as `MustOverride` is considered an **abstract class**, which can be used only for inheritance. You cannot instantiate objects from a class that contains abstract methods.

Accessing Properties

Your derived class can set and retrieve the properties of the base class by using the property accessor methods. Usually your derived class needs to make use of properties and methods of the base class. You can call the base class constructor from the derived class constructor, which allows you to use the property values from the base class. In the following example, the derived StudentBookSale class inherits from BookSale. Notice the constructor, which uses the `MyBase.New()` statement to call the constructor of the base class. If the constructor requires arguments, you can pass the argument values when you call the constructor:

```
Sub New(ByVal Title As String, ByVal Quantity As Integer, _
   ByVal Price As Decimal)
        ' Assign property values.

        ' Call base-class constructor and pass the property values.
        MyBase.New(Title, Quantity, Price)
End Sub
```

After you have assigned values to the properties of the base class, you can refer to the properties in methods in the derived class. In the following example, the `CalculateExtendedPrice` method in the derived class uses properties of the base class by property name.

```
' Procedure in the derived class that overrides the procedure in the base class:
Protected Overrides Sub CalculateExtendedPrice()
      ' Calculate the extended price and add to the totals.

      discountDecimal = Quantity * Price * DISCOUNT_RATE_Decimal
      ExtendedPrice = Quantity * Price - discountDecimal
      discountTotalDecimal += discountDecimal
End Sub
```

Note that to use base-class properties in the derived class as in this example, the properties must have both a `Get` and a `Set` accessor method. Read-only or write-only properties cannot be accessed by name from a derived class.

Creating a Derived Class Based on BookSale

The BookSale class could be considered a generic class, which is appropriate for most sales. But now we want another similar class, but with some differences. The new class should have all of the same properties and methods of the BookSale class, but will calculate sales with a student discount of 15 percent. We also want a new shared property in the new class to hold the total of the student discounts.

Our new derived class will be called StudentBookSale; the base class is BookSale. Figure 12.7 shows the UML diagram to indicate the inherited class. The inherited class automatically has all public and protected properties and methods of the base class; in this case, StudentBookSale automatically has six properties and one method.

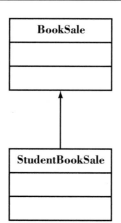

Adding Inheritance to the Step-by-Step Exercise

This continuation of the chapter step-by-step exercise includes adding a new subclass class, overriding a method, and adding a new property.

Add the New Class

STEP 1: Open your project, if necessary, and select *Add Class* from the *Project* menu.

STEP 2: In the *Add New Item* dialog, with *Class* selected, type "StudentBookSale" for the class name and click on *Add*. You will see a new tab in the Document window for the new class.

STEP 3: Add a new line after the class declaration and type the Inherits statement.

```
Public Class StudentBookSale
    Inherits BookSale
```

You can ignore the warning error message; it tells you that this subclass must have a constructor, which you will do in the next step.

All of the public and protected properties and methods of the base class will be inherited by the subclass.

Add the Constructor

STEP 1: The subclass must have its own constructors, since constructors are not inherited. Write the following code inside the new class:

```
Sub New(ByVal Title As String, ByVal Quantity As Integer, _
    ByVal Price As Decimal)
        ' Call the base class constructor.

    MyBase.New(Title, Quantity, Price)
End Sub
```

Add the New Property

STEP 1: Add a module-level variable to hold the value of a new shared property for the total of discounts.

```
Private Shared discountTotalDecimal As Decimal
```

STEP 2: Add the property procedure for `DiscountTotal`.

```
Shared ReadOnly Property DiscountTotal() As Decimal
    Get
        Return discountTotalDecimal
    End Get
End Property
```

Add a Constant

STEP 1: Add a constant at the module level to hold the discount rate of 15 percent.

```
Const DISCOUNT_RATE_Decimal As Decimal = 0.15D
```

Override a Method

When you override a method from the base class in an inherited class, the method name and the argument list must match exactly.

STEP 1: Open the BookSale base class in the editor and modify the procedure header for `CalculateExtendedPrice`.

```
Protected Overridable Sub CalculateExtendedPrice()
```

STEP 2: In the StudentBookSale inherited class, write the new `Calculate-ExtendedPrice` procedure, using the `Overrides` keyword.

```
Protected Overrides Sub CalculateExtendedPrice()
    ' Calculate the discount, extended price, and add to the total.
    Dim discountDecimal As Decimal

    discountDecimal = Quantity * Price * DISCOUNT_RATE_Decimal
    ExtendedPrice = Quantity * Price — discountDecimal
    discountTotalDecimal += discountDecimal
End Sub
```

Modify the Form to Use the Inherited Class

STEP 1: Add a check box to the form, named studentCheckBox, with the Text set to "Student". You can set the RightToLeft property to True, if you want the text to appear to the left of the box (Figure 12.8). Rearrange the controls to keep the input fields together and reset the tab sequence.

STEP 2: In the form's code editor window, add a module-level variable for an object of the new StudentBookSale class.

```
Private aStudentBookSale As StudentBookSale
```

Figure 12.8

Add a Student check box to the form.

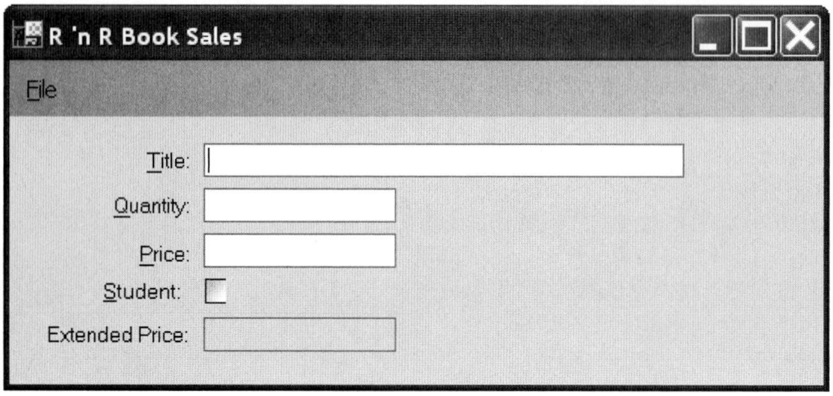

STEP 3: Modify the CalculateSaleToolStripMenuItem event procedure to create the correct object, depending on the state of studentCheckBox.

```
Try
    With Me
        If studentCheckBox.Checked Then
        ' Instantiate the StudentBookSale object and set the properties.
            aStudentBookSale = New StudentBookSale(.titleTextBox.Text, _
                Integer.Parse(.quantityTextBox.Text), Decimal.Parse(.priceTextBox.Text))
            ' Calculate and format the result.
            .extendedPriceTextBox.Text = aStudentBookSale.ExtendedPrice.ToString("C")
        Else
            ' Instantiate the BookSale object and set the properties.
            aBookSale = New BookSale(.titleTextBox.Text, Integer.Parse(.quantityTextBox.Text), _
                Decimal.Parse(.priceTextBox.Text))
            ' Calculate and format the result.
            .extendedPriceTextBox.Text = aBookSale.ExtendedPrice.ToString("C")
        End If
    End With
Catch ' Rest of code for procedure goes here.
```

Notice that the code uses the `ExtendedPrice` property in either case. But when studentCheckBox is checked, the `ExtendedPrice` of the subclass is retrieved; when the check box is not checked, the `ExtendedPrice` property of the base class is used. Both classes add to the shared `SalesTotal` and `SalesCount` properties of the base class, which will hold the totals for both classes.

STEP 4: Modify the SummaryToolStripMenuItem event procedure to include the discount total.

```
messageString = "Sales Total: " & BookSale.SalesTotal.ToString("C") & _
    ControlChars.NewLine & "Sales Count: " & BookSale.SalesCount.ToString() & _
    ControlChars.NewLine & "Total of Student Discounts: " & _
    StudentBookSale.DiscountTotal.ToString("C")
```

STEP 5: Run the program. Try both student and nonstudent sales; check the totals.

STEP 6: Close the project.

Creating a Base Class Strictly for Inheritance

Sometimes you may want to create a class solely for the purpose of inheritance by two or more similar classes. For example, you might create a Person class that you don't intend to instantiate. Instead you will create subclasses of the Person class, such as Employee, Customer, and Student.

For a base class that you intend to inherit, include the **MustInherit** modifier on the class declaration, which creates an abstract class. In each of the methods in the base class that must be overridden, include the MustOverride modifier. The method that must be overridden does not contain any code in the base class.

Base Class

```
MustInherit Class BaseClass
    Public MustOverride Sub SomeProcedure()
        ' No code allowed here, specifically, no End Sub statement.
End Class
```

Inherited Class

```
Class DerivedClass
    Inherits BaseClass
    Public Overrides Sub SomeProcedure()
        ' Code goes here.
    End Sub
End Class
```

Note: You must build (compile) the base class before using it for an inherited class.

Inheriting Form Classes

Some projects require that you have several forms. You may want to use a similar design from one form to the next. You can use **visual inheritance** by designing one form and then inheriting any other forms from the first (Figure 12.9).

Once you have designed the form that you want to use for a pattern, you can add more forms that inherit from your design master, called your *base class*. Your base class inherits from System.Windows.Forms.Form, and your new forms inherit from your base class.

When you design the base class, you can include design elements and other controls, such as labels, text boxes, and buttons. You also can write procedures and declare variables in the base class. Just as you saw earlier, all public and protected procedures and variables are inherited from the base class to the sub class. You can write procedures in the base class and specify Overridable or MustOverride, and then in the subclass write the identically named procedure with the Overrides keyword.

To create an inherited form to your project, first create the base class, save, and build the project. You cannot inherit from a form that has not been compiled. Then you can define the inherited form class in two ways:

1. Select *Project / Add Windows Form* and type the name of the new Windows form. In the Solution Explorer, show all files and open the

Figure 12.9

Create a base form and inherit the visual interface to new forms. a. The base form; b., c., and d., inherited forms.

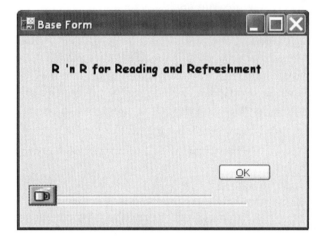

a.

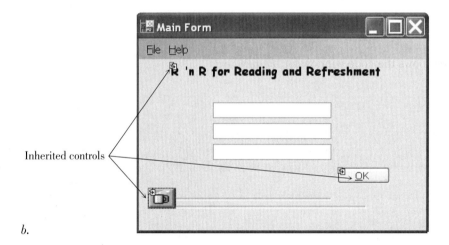

Inherited controls

b.

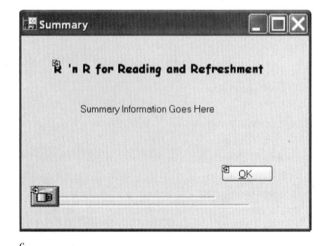

c.

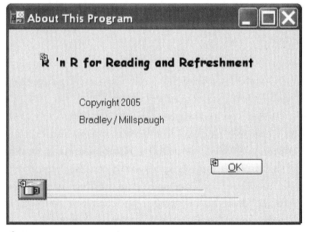

d.

designer-generated code file for the form. For example, if your form is called EntryForm, the Solution Explorer will have two files: Entry-Form.vb and EntryForm.Designer.vb. Change the `Inherits` clause to inherit from your base form using your project name as the namespace.

```
Public Partial Class EntryForm
    Inherits Ch12VisualInheritance.BaseForm
```

Open the new form in the designer and you should see the inherited visual elements.

2. Select *Project / Add Windows Form* and select the template for Inherited Form. Note that the Inherited Form template is not available in the Express Edition of VB, so the first technique must be used.

Type the name of the new form. After naming your form, you are shown a dialog displaying the compiled forms in the project from which to select.

Note: Using the second technique creates a form class in a different format than those to which you are accustomed. The inherited form is created in one file, with designer-generated code embedded in the file. The form behaves in the same way as the two-file model; you just must ignore the designer-generated code. Figure 12.10 shows the code window for the new form.

Figure   12.10

The code for an inherited form created by using **Project / Add Inherited Form.** *The designer-generated code appears in a section of the form's file, rather than in a separate file.*

Form Inheritance Example

This example has three forms that inherit from a base class. The base class has an OK button, a picture box, and labels. All forms that inherit from the base class will have all of these controls. You cannot delete any of the controls on the inherited forms, but you can make a control invisible. For example, in Main-Form, the OK button's Visible property is set to False.

The base class has an okButton_Click event procedure, which can be overridden in the sub classes. Note that the okButton_Click event procedure must be declared as `Public` or `Protected` to be inherited and overridden in derived classes.

All forms are in the same project, called Ch12VisualInheritance.

Make sure to open the Project Designer (*Project / ProjectName Properties*) and set the startup object to the form that you want to appear first.

Note that the forms in this example were created using the Inherited Form template, so the forms include their designer-generated code.

BaseForm

```
Public Class BaseForm

   Public Overridable Sub okButton_Click(ByVal sender As Object, _
     ByVal e As System.EventArgs) Handles okButton.Click
       ' Allow inherited classes to override this method.

       Me.Close()
   End Sub
End Class
```

AboutForm

```
Public Class AboutForm
   Inherits Ch12VisualInheritance.BaseForm

    ' No code needed; event procedure for okButton is inherited from the base class.

End Class
```

MainForm

Make sure to set this form as the startup object in the Project Designer (*Project /
ProjectName Properties*).

```
Public Class MainForm
   Inherits Ch12VisualInheritance.BaseForm

        ' This form will have additional procedures to perform some calculations.

    Private Sub MainForm_Load(ByVal sender As Object, _
      ByVal e As System.EventArgs) Handles MyBase.Load
        ' Hide the OK button for this form.

        Me.okButton.Hide()
    End Sub

    Private Sub AboutToolStripMenuItem_Click(ByVal sender As Object, _
      ByVal e As System.EventArgs) Handles AboutToolStripMenuItem.Click
        ' Show the About Box.

        AboutForm.ShowDialog()
    End Sub

    Private Sub SummaryToolStripMenuItem_Click(ByVal sender As Object, _
      ByVal e As System.EventArgs) Handles SummaryToolStripMenuItem.Click
        ' Show the Summary form.

        SummaryForm.ShowDialog()
    End Sub

    Private Sub ExitToolStripMenuItem_Click(ByVal sender As Object, _
      ByVal e As System.EventArgs) Handles ExitToolStripMenuItem.Click
        ' Exit the project.

        Me.Close()
    End Sub
End Class
```

SummaryForm

```
Public Class SummaryForm
  Inherits Ch12VisualInheritance.BaseForm

    Public Overrides Sub okButton_Click(ByVal sender As Object, _
      ByVal e As System.EventArgs) Handles okButton.Click
        ' Override the base class method.

        Me.Hide()
    End Sub

    Private Sub SummaryForm_Activated(ByVal sender As Object, _
      ByVal e As System.EventArgs) Handles Me.Activated
        ' Code to retrieve the summary data and fill the form's controls.

    End Sub
End Class
```

Note: If you have problems with creating inherited forms or want further information, see the MSDN topics "Walkthrough: Demonstrating Visual Inheritance" and "Windows Forms Inheritance".

Coding for Events of an Inherited Class

When you derive a new form class from an existing form, you often want to write code for events of inherited controls. Unfortunately, you can't double-click on an inherited control and have the event procedure open, as you can for most controls. In the previous example of form inheritance, for the okButton_Click event procedure header, we copied the procedure from the base class into the derived class and made the modifications.

Managing Multiclass Projects

This chapter has examples of projects with multiple forms and multiple classes. In each case, every class is stored in a separate file. Although you must keep form classes in separate files, other classes do not have that requirement. You can code multiple classes in one file.

Adding an Existing Class File to a Project

If you have an existing form or other class file that you want to include in a project, you can choose to reference the file in its original location or move or copy it into your project folder. Unless you need to share a class among several projects, it's best to place the class file into the project folder. After you move or copy the desired file into the project folder, add the file to the project by selecting *Project / Add Existing Item* (or right-click the project name in the Solution Explorer and select *Add / Existing Item* from the context menu).

Using the Object Browser

The Object Browser is an important tool for working with objects. The Object Browser can show you the names of objects, properties, methods, events, and constants for VB objects, your own objects, and objects available from other applications.

Select *View / Object Browser* or the *Object Browser* toolbar button (Figure 12.11) to open the Object Browser window (Figure 12.12). You can enter an item for which to search in the Search box.

The Object Browser uses several icons to represent items. Notice in Figure 12.12 the icons that represent properties, methods, events, constants, classes, and namespaces. In the lower-right corner of the window you can see a description of any item you select.

Figure 12.11

Open the Object Browser from the toolbar button.

Figure 12.12

The Object Browser window; notice the icons to indicate the member type.

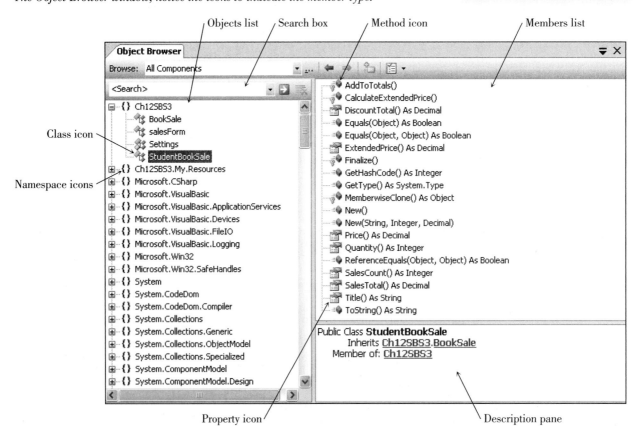

Objects list   Search box   Method icon   Members list

Class icon

Namespace icons

Property icon   Description pane

Examining VB Classes

You can look up the available properties, methods, events, or constants of a Visual Basic class. You can see which elements are defined in the class, what is the base class, and which properties, methods, and events are inherited. In Figure 12.13 notice the entries for System.Windows.Forms.MessageBox; the overloaded constructors appear in the *Members* list. And in Figure 12.14, you can see the constants for MessageBoxButtons.

Figure 12.13

Display the members of the System.Windows.Forms.MessageBox class.

Constant icon

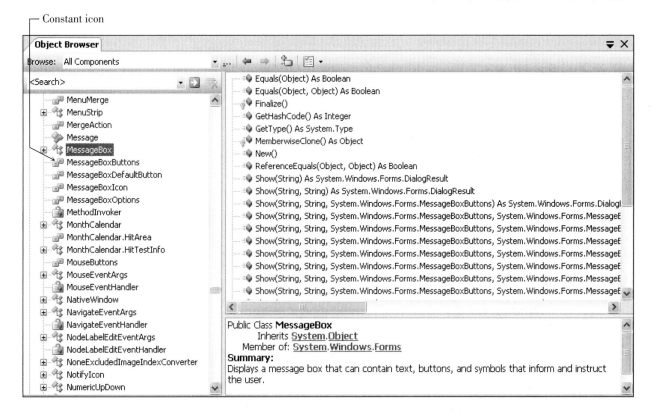

Figure 12.14

Display the MessageBoxButtons constants.

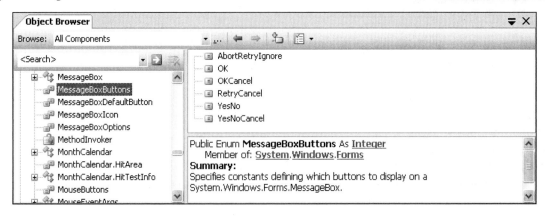

Examining Your Own Classes

You can see your own classes listed in the Object Browser. With the chapter step-by-step project open, select your project name in the Object Browser. Try clicking on each class name and viewing the list of properties and methods (Figure 12.15).

Figure 12.15

View the properties and methods for your own classes. Double-click on an item in the Members list to jump to its definition in code.

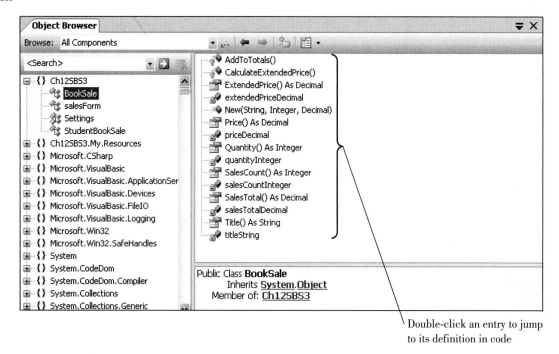

Double-click an entry to jump to its definition in code

You can use the Object Browser to jump to the definition of any property or method by double-clicking on its name in the *Members* list. This technique is also a great way to jump to any of the procedures in your forms. Select your form name in the *Objects* list and double-click on the name of the procedure you want to view.

Your Hands-On Programming Example

This program must calculate book sales for R 'n R, with a discount of 15 percent for students. The project will use the BookSale and StudentBookSale classes developed in the chapter step-by-step.

Create a project with multiple forms that have a shared design element. Include a main form, an About form, and a Summary form that displays the sales summary information.

Design a base form to use for inheritance and make the other three forms inherit from the base form. The About form and Summary form must have an OK button, which closes or hides the form. The main form will have menus and no OK button.

Main Form Menu

```
File                    Help
  Calculate Sale          About
  Clear
  Summary
  ─────────
  Exit
```

Planning the Project

Sketch a base form for inheritance, a main form, an About form, and a Summary form (Figure 12.16) for your users. The users approve and sign off the forms as meeting their needs.

Figure 12.16

The planning sketches of the forms for the hands-on programming example. a. The Base form; b. the Main form; c. the About form; and d. the Summary form.

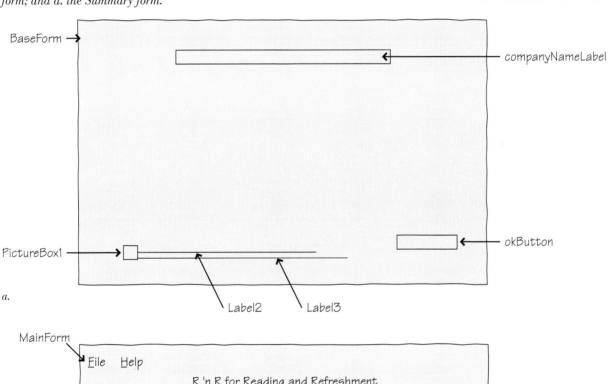

a.

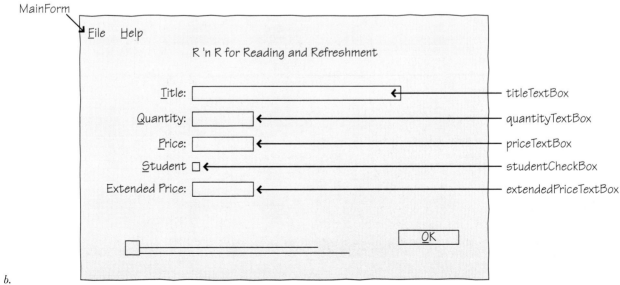

b.

Figure 12.16

(continued)

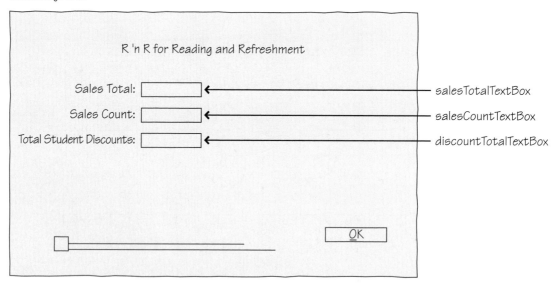

AboutForm

R 'n R for Reading and Refreshment

By Bradley and Millspaugh

Version 1.0

OK

c.

SummaryForm

R 'n R for Reading and Refreshment

Sales Total: ⬅——— salesTotalTextBox

Sales Count: ⬅——— salesCountTextBox

Total Student Discounts: ⬅——— discountTotalTextBox

OK

d.

Plan the Objects and Properties for the Base Form

Object	Property	Setting
BaseForm	Name	BaseForm
companyNameLabel	Name Text	companyNameLabel R 'n R for Reading and Refreshment
okButton	Name Text	okButton &OK
Label2	Name Size	Label2 250, 4
Label3	Name Size	Label3 300, 4
PictureBox1	Name Image	PictureBox1 Cup.bmp

Plan the Procedures for the Base Form

Procedure	Actions
okButton_Click	(Overridable) Close the form.

Plan the Objects and Properties for the Main Form

Object	Property	Setting
MainForm	Name Text	MainForm R 'n R Book Sales
Label1	Name Text	Label1 &Title:
titleTextBox	Name	titleTextBox
Label2	Name Text	Label2 &Quantity:
quantityTextBox	Name	quantityTextBox
Label3	Name Text	Label3 &Price:
priceTextBox	Name	priceTextBox
studentCheckBox	Name Text RightToLeft	studentCheckBox &Student Yes
Label4	Name Text	Label4 Extended Price:
extendedPriceTextBox	Name ReadOnly TabStop	extendedPriceTextBox True False

Object	Property	Setting
FileToolStripMenuItem	Name Text	FileToolStripMenuItem &File
CalculateSaleToolStripMenuItem	Name Text	CalculateSaleToolStripMenuItem &Calculate Sale
ClearToolStripMenuItem	Name Text	ClearToolStripMenuItem C&lear
SummaryToolStripMenuItem	Name Text	SummaryToolStripMenuItem &Summary
ExitToolStripMenuItem	Name Text	ExitToolStripMenuItem E&xit
HelpToolStripMenuItem	Name Text	HelpToolStripMenuItem &Help
AboutToolStripMenuItem	Name Text	AboutToolStripMenuItem &About

Plan the Procedures for the Main Form

Procedure	Actions
Form_Load	Hide the inherited OK button.

CalculateSaleToolStripMenuItem_Click	If student sale then
	    Create a StudentBookSale object.
	    Calculate and format the extended price.
	Else
	    Create a BookSale object.
	    Calculate and format the extended price.
	End If

ClearToolStripMenuItem_Click	Clear the text boxes. Uncheck the check box. Set the focus on first text box.
SummaryToolStripMenuItem_Click	Show the Summary form.
ExitToolStripMenuItem_Click	End the project.
AboutToolStripMenuItem_Click	Show the About form.

Plan the Objects and Properties for the About Form

Object	Property	Setting
AboutForm	Name Text	AboutForm About This Program
okButton	Name Text	(Inherited) okButton &OK

Plan the Procedures for the About Form

Procedure	Actions
okButton_Click	(No code; inherited from base class)

Plan the Objects and Properties for the Summary Form

Object	Property	Setting
SummaryForm	Name	SummaryForm
	Text	Summary
Label1	Name	Label1
	Text	Sales Total:
salesTotalTextBox	Name	salesTotalTextBox
	ReadOnly	True
	TabStop	False
Label2	Name	Label2
	Text	Sales Count:
salesCountTextBox	Name	salesCountTextBox
	ReadOnly	True
	TabStop	False
Label3	Name	Label3
	Text	Total Student Discounts:
discountTotalTextBox	Name	discountTotalTextBox
	ReadOnly	True
	TabStop	False
okButton	Name	(Inherited) okButton
	Text	&OK

Plan the Procedures for the Summary Form

Procedure	Actions
Form_Activated	Fill the form controls.
okButton_Click	(Override the base class method) Hide this form.

Plan the BookSale Object Class

Properties

Declare private module-level variables and write property procedures for all public properties:

    Instance:
        Title
        Quantity
        Price
    Shared:
        SalesTotal
        SalesCount

Methods

Procedure	Actions
ExtendedPrice	Calculate extended price = Quantity * Price. Add extended price to SalesTotal. Add 1 to SalesCount. Return extended price.

Plan the StudentBookSale Object Class

Inherit from BookSale.

Additional Properties

Shared:
DiscountTotal

Methods

Procedure	Actions
ExtendedPrice	Calculate discount = price * quantity * discount rate. Calculate extended price = quantity * price – discount. Add extended price to SalesTotal. Add 1 to SalesCount. Add discount to DiscountTotal. Return extended price.

Write the Project

Follow the sketches in Figure 12.16 to create the forms. Create the base form first and inherit the other three forms from the base form. Figure 12.17 shows the completed forms.

Figure 12.17

The completed forms for the hands-on programming example. a. The Base form; b. the Main form; c. the About form; and d. the Summary form.

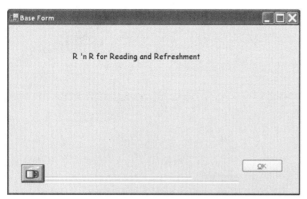

a.

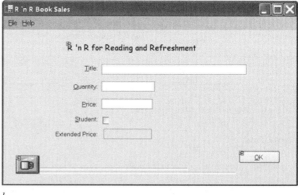

b.

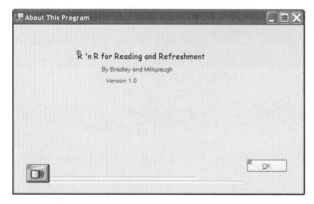

c.

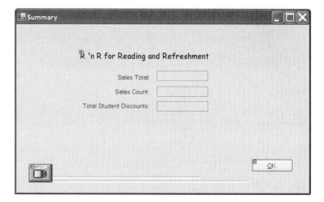

d.

- Set the project's startup object to the main form.

- Set the properties of each of the objects according to your plan.

- Create the BookSale and StudentBookSale classes, or copy them into your project folder and add them to the project.

- Write the code. Working from the pseudocode, write each procedure.

- When you complete the code, use a variety of data to thoroughly test the project.

The Project Coding Solution

BaseForm

```
'Program:      Chapter 12 BookSale Hands-On Program
'Programmer:   Bradley/Millspaugh
'Date:         June 2005
'Description:  Base form for hands-on project.
'Folder:       Ch12HandsOn

Public Class BaseForm

   Public Overridable Sub okButton_Click(ByVal sender As Object, _
      ByVal e As System.EventArgs) Handles okButton.Click
         ' Allow inherited classes to override this method.


   End Sub
End Class
```

MainForm

```
'Program:      Chapter 12 BookSale Hands-On Program
'Programmer:   Bradley/Millspaugh
'Date:         June 2005
'Description:  Calculate sales price using the BookSale and StudentBookSale classes.
'              Main form for hands-on project.
'Folder:       Ch12HandsOn

Public Class MainForm
   ' Declare the new objects.
      Private aBookSale As BookSale
      Private aStudentBookSale As StudentBookSale

      Private Sub mainForm_Load(ByVal sender As Object, _
         ByVal e As System.EventArgs) Handles MyBase.Load
            ' Make the OK button invisible on this form.

         Me.okButton.Visible = False
      End Sub

      Private Sub CalculateSaleToolStripMenuItem_Click(ByVal sender As Object, _
         ByVal e As System.EventArgs) Handles CalculateSaleToolStripMenuItem.Click
            ' Calculate the extended price for the sale.

         With Me
            Try
```

```
            If studentCheckBox.Checked Then

                ' Instantiate the StudentBookSale object and set the properties.
                aStudentBookSale = New StudentBookSale(.titleTextBox.Text, _
                  Integer.Parse(.quantityTextBox.Text), Decimal.Parse(.priceTextBox.Text))
                ' Calculate and format the result.
                .extendedPriceTextBox.Text = aStudentBookSale.ExtendedPrice.ToString("N")
            Else
                ' Instantiate the BookSale object and set the properties.
                aBookSale = New BookSale(.titleTextBox.Text, _
                  Integer.Parse(.quantityTextBox.Text), Decimal.Parse(.priceTextBox.Text))
                ' Calculate and format the result.
                .extendedPriceTextBox.Text = aBookSale.ExtendedPrice.ToString("N")
            End If
            Catch
            MessageBox.Show("Error in quantity or price field.", "R 'n R Book Sales", _
                MessageBoxButtons.OK, MessageBoxIcon.Exclamation)
            End Try
        End With
    End Sub

    Private Sub ClearToolStripMenuItem_Click(ByVal sender As Object, _
       ByVal e As System.EventArgs) Handles ClearToolStripMenuItem.Click
        ' Clear the screen controls.

        With Me
            .quantityTextBox.Clear()
            .priceTextBox.Clear()
            .extendedPriceTextBox.Clear()
            .studentCheckBox.Checked = False
            With .titleTextBox
                .Clear()
                .Focus()
            End With
        End With
    End Sub

    Private Sub SummaryToolStripMenuItem_Click(ByVal sender As Object, _
       ByVal e As System.EventArgs) Handles SummaryToolStripMenuItem.Click
        ' Display the sales summary information.

        SummaryForm.ShowDialog()
    End Sub

    Private Sub AboutToolStripMenuItem_Click(ByVal sender As Object, _
       ByVal e As System.EventArgs) Handles AboutToolStripMenuItem.Click
        ' Display the About form.

        AboutForm.ShowDialog()
    End Sub

    Private Sub ExitToolStripMenuItem_Click(ByVal sender As Object, _
       ByVal e As System.EventArgs) Handles ExitToolStripMenuItem.Click
        ' End the project.

        Me.Close()
    End Sub
End Class
```

AboutForm

```
'Program:         Chapter 12 BookSale Hands-On Program
'Programmer:      Bradley/Millspaugh
'Date:            June 2005
'Description:     Calculate sales price using the BookSale class.
'                 About form for hands-on project.
'Folder:          Ch12HandsOn

Public Class AboutForm

    Public Overrides Sub okButton_Click(ByVal sender As Object, _
        ByVal e As System.EventArgs) Handles okButton.Click
          ' Override the base class method.

        Me.Close()
    End Sub
End Class
```

SummaryForm

```
'Program:         Chapter 12 BookSale Hands-On Program
'Programmer:      Bradley/Millspaugh
'Date:            June 2005
'Description:     Calculate sales price using the BookSale class.
'                 Summary form for hands-on project.
'Folder:          Ch12HandsOn

Public Class SummaryForm

    Public Overrides Sub okButton_Click(ByVal sender As Object, _
        ByVal e As System.EventArgs) Handles okButton.Click
          ' Override the base class method.

        Me.Hide()
    End Sub

    Private Sub SummaryForm_Activated(ByVal sender As Object, _
        ByVal e As System.EventArgs) Handles Me.Activated
          ' Display the summary information on the form.

        Me.salesTotalTextBox.Text = BookSale.SalesTotal.ToString("C")
        Me.salesCountTextBox.Text = BookSale.SalesCount.ToString()
        Me.discountTotalTextBox.Text = StudentBookSale.DiscountTotal.ToString("C")
    End Sub
End Class
```

BookSale Class

```
'Class Name:      BookSale
'Programmer:      Bradley/Millspaugh
'Date:            June 2005
'Description:     Handle book sale information.
'Folder:          Ch12HandsOn

Public Class BookSale

    Private titleString As String
```

```vb
Private quantityInteger As Integer
Private priceDecimal, extendedPriceDecimal As Decimal
Private Shared salesTotalDecimal As Decimal
Private Shared salesCountInteger As Integer

' Parameterized Constructor.
Sub New(ByVal Title As String, ByVal Quantity As Integer, _
    ByVal Price As Decimal)
        ' Assign property values.

        With Me
            .Title = Title
            .Quantity = Quantity
            .Price = Price
        End With
        CalculateExtendedPrice()
        AddToTotals()
End Sub

Property Title() As String
    Get
            Return titleString
    End Get
    Set(ByVal Value As String)
            titleString = Value
    End Set
End Property

Property Quantity() As Integer
    Get
            Return quantityInteger
    End Get
    Set(ByVal Value As Integer)
            If Value >= 0 Then
                    quantityInteger = Value
            End If
    End Set
End Property

Property Price() As Decimal
    Get
            Return priceDecimal
    End Get
    Set(ByVal Value As Decimal)
            If Value >= 0 Then
                    priceDecimal = Value
            End If
    End Set
End Property

Property ExtendedPrice() As Decimal
    Get
            Return extendedPriceDecimal
    End Get
    Set(ByVal Value As Decimal)
            extendedPriceDecimal = Value
    End Set
End Property
```

```
        Shared ReadOnly Property SalesTotal() As Decimal
            Get
                Return salesTotalDecimal
            End Get
        End Property

        Shared ReadOnly Property SalesCount() As Integer
            Get
                Return salesCountInteger
            End Get
        End Property

        Protected Overridable Sub CalculateExtendedPrice()
            ' Calculate the extended price.

            extendedPriceDecimal = quantityInteger * priceDecimal
        End Sub

        Protected Sub AddToTotals()
            ' Add to the summary information.

            salesTotalDecimal += extendedPriceDecimal
            salesCountInteger += 1
        End Sub
End Class
```

StudentBookSale Class

```
'Class Name:    StudentBookSale
'Programmer:    Bradley/Millspaugh
'Date:          June 2005
'Description:   Handle book sale information for student sales,
'               which receive a discount.
'Folder:        Ch12HandsOn

Public Class StudentBookSale
  Inherits BookSale

    Const DISCOUNT_RATE_Decimal As Decimal = 0.15D
    Private discountDecimal As Decimal
    Private Shared discountTotalDecimal As Decimal

    Sub New(ByVal Title As String, ByVal Quantity As Integer, _
      ByVal Price As Decimal)
        ' Assign property values.

        ' Call base-class constructor and pass the property values.
        MyBase.New(Title, Quantity, Price)
    End Sub

    Shared ReadOnly Property DiscountTotal() As Decimal
        Get
            Return discountTotalDecimal
        End Get
    End Property
```

```
Protected Overrides Sub CalculateExtendedPrice()
    ' Calculate the extended price and add to the totals.

    discountDecimal = Quantity * Price * DISCOUNT_RATE_Decimal
    ExtendedPrice = Quantity * Price - discountDecimal
    discountTotalDecimal += discountDecimal
End Sub
End Class
```

S u m m a r y

1. Objects have properties and methods, and can trigger events.
2. You can create a new class that can then be used to create new objects.
3. Creating a new object is called *instantiating* the object; the object is called an *instance* of the class.
4. In object-oriented terminology, encapsulation refers to the combination of the characteristics and behaviors of an item into a single class definition.
5. Polymorphism allows different classes of objects in an inheritance hierarchy to have similarly named methods that behave differently for that particular object.
6. Inheritance provides a means to derive a new class based on an existing class. The existing class is called a *base class*, *superclass*, or *parent class*. The inherited class is called a *subclass*, *derived class*, or *child class*.
7. One of the biggest advantages of object-oriented programming is that classes that you create for one application may be reused in another application.
8. Multitier applications separate program functions into a Presentation tier (the user interface), Business tier (the logic of calculations and validation), and Data tier (accessing stored data).
9. The variables inside a class used to store the properties should be private, so that data values are accessible only by procedures within the class.
10. The way to make the properties of a class available to code outside the class is to use Property procedures. The `Get` portion returns the value of the property and the `Set` portion assigns a value to the property. Validation is often performed in the `Set` portion.
11. Read-only properties are declared with the `ReadOnly` keyword and have only a `Get` accessor method. Write-only properties are written with the `WriteOnly` keyword and have only a `Set` accessor method.
12. The public functions and sub procedures of a class module are its methods.
13. To instantiate an object of a class, you must use the `New` keyword either on the declaration statement or an assignment statement. The location of the `New` keyword determines when the object is created.
14. A constructor is a method that automatically executes when an object is created; a destructor method is triggered when an object is destroyed.

15. A constructor method must be named New and may be overloaded.

16. A parameterized constructor requires arguments to create a new object.

17. Shared members (properties and methods) have one copy that can be used by all objects of the class, generally used for totals and counts. Instance members have one copy for each instance of the object. Declare shared members with the Shared keyword.

18. The garbage collection feature periodically checks for unreferenced objects, destroys the object references, and releases resources.

19. A subclass inherits all public and protected properties and methods of its base class, except for the constructor.

20. To override a method from a base class, the original method must be declared as Overridable or MustOverride, and the new method must use the Overrides keyword.

21. A base class used strictly for inheritance is called an abstract class and cannot be instantiated. The class should be declared as MustInherit and the methods that must be overridden should be declared as MustOverride.

22. You can use visual inheritance to derive new forms from existing forms.

23. You can use the Object Browser to view classes, properties, methods, events, and constants in system classes as well as your own classes.

Key Terms

abstract class *472*

abstract method *472*

accessor methods *455*

base class *451*

child class *451*

class *450*

constructor *456*

derived class *451*

destructor *456*

encapsulation *451*

garbage collection *471*

inheritance *451*

instance *450*

instance property *467*

instance variable *467*

instantiate *450*

multitier application *453*

MustInherit *477*

MustOverride *472*

object *450*

overloading *452*

overriding *452*

parameterized constructor *457*

parent class *451*

polymorphism *452*

property procedure *455*

Protected *471*

ReadOnly *456*

reusability *452*

shared property *467*

shared variable *467*

subclass *451*

superclass *451*

value keyword *455*

visual inheritance *477*

Review Questions

1. What is an object? a property? a method?
2. What is the purpose of a class?
3. Why should property variables of a class be declared as private?
4. What are property procedures and what is their purpose?
5. Explain how to create a new object.
6. What steps are needed to assign property values to an object?
7. What actions trigger the constructor and destructor methods of an object?
8. How can you write methods for a new class?
9. What is a shared member? How is it created?
10. Explain the steps necessary to inherit a class from another class.
11. Differentiate between overriding and overloading.
12. What is a parameterized constructor?
13. When might you use the `Protected` keyword on a constructor?
14. What is visual inheritance?

Programming Exercises

Note: For help in basing a new project on an existing project, see "Copy and Move Projects" in Appendix C.

12.1 Modify the program for Programming Exercise 5.1 (the piecework pay) to separate the business logic into a separate class. The class should have properties for Name and Pieces, as well as shared read-only properties to maintain the summary information.

12.2 Modify Programming Exercise 12.1 to include multiple forms. Create a base form that you can use for visual inheritance. Display the summary information and the About box on separate forms, rather than in message boxes.

12.3 *Extra Challenge*: Modify Programming Exercise 12.2 to have an inherited class. Create a derived class for senior workers, who receive 10 percent higher pay for 600 or more pieces. Add a check box to the main form to indicate a senior worker.

12.4 Modify Programming Exercise 5.3 (the salesperson commissions) to separate the business logic into a separate class. The class should have properties for Name and Sales, as well as shared read-only properties to maintain the summary information.

12.5 Modify Programming Exercise 12.4 to include multiple forms. Create a base form that you can use for visual inheritance. Display the summary information and the About box on separate forms, rather than message boxes.

12.6 *Extra Challenge*: Modify Programming Exercise 12.5 to have an inherited class. Create a derived class for supervisors, who have a different pay scale. The supervisor quota is $2,000, the commission rate is 20 percent, and the base pay is $500. Include a check box on the main form to indicate a supervisor, and calculate separate totals for supervisors.

12.7   Modify Programming Exercise 5.2 (the check transactions) to separate the business logic from the user interface. Create a Transaction class and derived classes for Deposit, Check, and Service Charges. Display the summary information on a separate form rather than a message box.
       Optional Extra: Use visual inheritance for the forms.

12.8   Modify Programming Exercise 5.4 (the library reading program) to separate the business logic from the user interface. Create a class with properties for Name and Number of Books. Display the summary information and About box in separate forms rather than message boxes.
       Optional Extra: Use visual inheritance for the forms.

12.9   *Extra Challenge*: Modify Programming Exercise 12.8 to have inherited classes. Have separate classes and separate totals for elementary, intermediate, and high school. Include radio buttons on the form to select the level; display totals for all three groups on the summary.

12.10 Create a project that contains a class for sandwich objects. Each sandwich object should have properties for Name, Bread, Meat, Cheese, and Condiments. Use a form for user input. Assign the input values to the properties of the object, and display the properties on a separate form.

12.11 Create a project that contains a Pet class. Each object will contain pet name, animal type, breed, and color. The form should contain text boxes to enter the information for the pets. A button or menu item should display the pet information on a separate form.

12.12 Modify the project that you created in Chapter 3 to separate the user interface from the business logic (calculations) and return the results through a property.

Case Studies

VB Mail Order

Modify your VB Mail Order project from Chapter 5 to separate the user interface from the business logic. Create two new classes: one for customer information and one for order items. The order item class should perform the calculations and maintain the summary information.

Add a menu option to display the customer information. Display the properties of the Customer object on a separate form.

Display the About box and the summary information on forms, rather than message boxes.

Optional extra: Use visual inheritance for the forms.

Need a bigger challenge? Create an inherited class for preferred customers. Preferred customers receive an automatic 5 percent discount on all purchases. Use a check box to determine if the customer is a preferred customer and instantiate the appropriate class. Maintain and display separate totals for preferred customers.

Note: For help in basing a new project on an existing project, see "Copy and Move Projects" in Appendix C.

VB Auto Center

Modify your VB Auto Center project from Chapter 5 to separate the business logic from the user interface. Create a class for purchases, with properties for each of the options. The methods of the class will calculate the subtotal, total, and amount due.

Make the About box display on a separate form, rather than a message box.

Need a bigger challenge? Add summary totals for the number of sales, the total sales, and the total trade-ins. Maintain the totals as shared read-only properties of the class and display the summary information on a separate form.

Note: For help in basing a new project on an existing project, see "Copy and Move Projects" in Appendix C.

Video Bonanza

Modify the Video Bonanza project from Chapter 5 to separate the user interface from the business logic. Create a class for each rental. Include a property for Title, Boolean properties for Video format and Members, and shared read-only properties for the summary information.

Display the summary information and the About box on forms, rather than message boxes.

Note: For help in basing a new project on an existing project, see "Copy and Move Projects" in Appendix C.

Very Very Boards

Modify the Very Very Boards project from Chapter 5 to separate the user interface from the business logic. Create a class for each shirt sale with properties for Order Number, Quantity, and Size. Use Boolean properties for Monogram and Pocket and a method to calculate the price. Maintain shared read-only properties for the summary information.

Display the summary information and the About box on forms, rather than message boxes.

Optional extra: Use visual inheritance for the forms.

Note: For help in basing a new project on an existing project, see "Copy and Move Projects" in Appendix C.

13

Graphics, Animation, Sound, and Drag-and-Drop

1. Use Graphics methods to draw shapes, lines, and filled shapes.

2. Create a drawing surface with a Graphics object.

3. Instantiate Pen and Brush objects as needed for drawing.

4. Create animation by changing pictures at run time.

5. Create simple animation by moving images.

6. Use the Timer component to automate animation.

7. Use scroll bars to move an image.

8. Add sounds to a project.

9. Incorporate drag-and-drop events into your program.

10. Draw a pie chart using the methods of the Graphics object.

You had your first introduction to graphics when you learned to print documents in Chapter 7. In this chapter you will learn to draw shapes, such as lines, rectangles, and ellipses, using the methods of the Graphics object. You can use the Graphics methods to draw pictures and charts in a business application.

You will do simple animation by replacing and moving graphics. You also will use a Timer component to cause events to fire, so that you can create your own animation.

Graphics in Windows and the Web

The term *graphics* refers to any text, drawing, image, or icon that you display on the screen. You have placed a graphic image in a PictureBox control to display pictures on your forms. A picture box also can display animated .gif files, so you can easily produce animation on the screen.

You can display a graphics file on either a Web Form or a Windows Form. Recall that the Web control is an Image control and the Windows control is a PictureBox. Both display graphics files, but the Windows control accepts a few more file formats.

Using Windows Forms, you can draw graphics shapes such as circles, lines, and rectangles on a form or control. The Graphics methods work only on Windows Forms, not Web Forms. Therefore, the programs in the next section use Windows Forms only.

The Graphics Environment

The .NET Framework uses a technology called *GDI+* for drawing graphics. GDI+ is more advanced and an improvement over the previous Graphics Device Interface (GDI) used in previous versions of VB. GDI+ is designed to be device-independent, so that the programmer doesn't have to be concerned about the physical characteristics of the output device. For example, the code to draw a circle is the same whether the output goes to a large-screen monitor, a low-resolution monitor, or the printer.

Steps for Drawing Graphics

When you draw a picture, you follow these general steps. The sections that follow describe the steps in more detail.

- Create a Graphics object to use as a drawing surface.

- Instantiate a Pen or Brush object to draw with.

- Call the drawing methods from the Graphics object.

Looking over the steps, you realize that this is what you did for creating printer output in Chapter 7. In that chapter you used the `DrawString` method to place text on the Graphics object; in this chapter you will use methods that draw shapes.

The Paint Event Procedure

You draw lines and shapes on a form or control by drawing on a Graphics object. And where do you place the code for the drawing methods? In the Paint event procedure for the form or the control on which you are drawing.

Each time a window is displayed, resized, moved, maximized, restored, or uncovered, the form's Paint event executes. In the Paint event procedure, the form and its controls are redrawn. If you draw some graphics on the form, in say the Form_Load event procedure or the click event of a button, the graphics are not automatically redrawn when the form is repainted. The only way to make sure that the graphics appear is to create them in the Paint event procedure. Then they are redrawn every time the form is rendered.

So far we have ignored the Paint event and allowed the repainting to proceed automatically. Now we will place code in that event procedure. You can write code in the form's Paint event procedure to draw on the form, or code in a control's Paint event procedure to draw graphics on the control.

In the Paint event procedure, you can use the e.Graphics object or declare a Graphics object. You assign the Graphics property of the procedure's PaintEventArgs argument to the new Graphics object.

TIP

To write code for the form's Paint event, in the Editor window select *(FormName Events)* from the *Class Name* list and then drop down the *Method Name* list and click on *Paint*; or in the Form Designer, click on the *Events* button in the Properties window and double-click on *Paint*. ■

```
Private Sub Form1_Paint(ByVal sender As Object, _
   ByVal e As System.Windows.Forms.PaintEventArgs) Handles Me.Paint
      'Create a graphics object
      Dim gr As Graphics = e.Graphics
```

You also can create a graphic object by calling the `CreateGraphics` method of a form or control. You would use this method when you want to display a graphic from a procedure other than the Paint event.

```
' Draw on the form.
Me.CreateGraphics.DrawMethod

' Draw on a control.
Me.GroupBox1.CreateGraphics.DrawMethod
```

Pen and Brush Objects

Using a **Pen object** you can draw lines or outlined shapes such as rectangles or circles. A **Brush object** creates filled shapes. You can set the width of a Pen and the color for both a Pen and a Brush. Figure 13.1 shows some lines and shapes created with Pen and Brush objects.

When you create a new Pen object, you set the color using the Color constants, such as Color.Red, Color.Blue, and Color.Aquamarine. You also can set the pen's width, which is measured in pixels. The term **pixel** is an abbreviation of *picture element*—a dot that makes up a picture. You are probably most familiar with pixels in the determination of the resolution of a monitor. A display of 1,280 by 1,024 is a reference to the number of pixels horizontally and vertically.

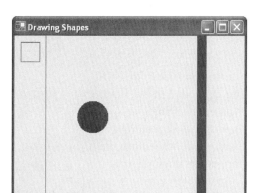

The Pen Class—Constructors

```
Pen(Color)
Pen(Color, Width)
```

If you don't set the width of the pen, it defaults to one pixel.

The Pen Class—Examples

```
Dim redPen As New Pen(Color.Red)
Dim widePen As New Pen(Color.Black, 10)
```

You may find that you want several different pens. For each different color or line width, you can create another Pen object or redefine an already dimensioned Pen variable if you are finished with it.

If you want to create filled figures, declare Brush objects—one for each different color that you want to use.

The SolidBrush Class—Constructor

```
SolidBrush(Color)
```

Use the Color constants to assign a color to your Brush objects.

The SolidBrush Class—Example

```
Dim blueBrush As New SolidBrush(Color.Blue)
```

You may have deduced from the name of the SolidBrush class that other types of brushes exist. See Help if you are interested in using a TextureBrush, Hatch-Brush, LinearGradientBrush, or PathGradientBrush.

The Coordinate System

Graphics are measured from a starting point of 0,0 for the x and y coordinates beginning in the upper-left corner. The x is the horizontal position, and the y is the vertical measurement. The starting point depends on where the graphic is being placed. If the graphic is going directly on a form, the 0,0 coordinates are the upper-left corner of the form, below the title bar and menu bar. You also can draw graphics in a container, such as a PictureBox, GroupBox, or Button. In this case, the container has its own 0,0 coordinates to be used as the starting point for measuring the location of items inside the container (Figure 13.2).

Figure 13.2

The coordinates for graphics begin with 0,0 in the upper-left corner of a form or container.

Each of the drawing methods allows you to specify the starting position using x and y coordinates. Most of the methods also allow you to specify the position using a Point structure. In some methods it is useful to use a Rectangle structure, and in others a Size structure comes in handy.

The Point Structure

A **Point structure** is designed to hold the x and y coordinates as a single unit. You can create a Point object, giving it values for the x and y. Then you can use the object anywhere that accepts a Point as an argument.

```
Dim myStartingPoint As New Point(20, 10)
```

You can see an example of a Point in the design of any of your forms. Examine the Location property of any control; the Location is assigned a Point object, with x and y properties.

The Size Structure

A **Size structure** has two components, the width and height. Both integers specify the size in pixels. Some Graphics methods accept a Size structure as an argument.

```
Dim myPictureSize As New Size(100, 20) ' Width is 100, height is 20.
```

You also can see an example of a Size structure by examining the design of any of your forms. Each of the controls has a Size property, which has width and height properties.

For an interesting exercise, examine the automatically generated code for a Button control in the *FormName*.Designer.vb file. The button's Location is set to a new Point object and the size is set to a new Size object.

The Rectangle Structure

A **Rectangle structure** defines a rectangular region, specified by its upper-left corner and its size.

```
Dim myRectangle As New Rectangle(myStartingPoint, myPictureSize)
```

The overloaded constructor also allows you to declare a new Rectangle by specifying its location in x and y coordinates and its width and height.

```
Dim myOtherRectangle As New Rectangle(xInteger, yInteger, widthInteger, heightInteger)
```

Note that you also can create Point, Size, and Rectangle structures for single-precision floating-point values. Specify the PointF, SizeF, and RectangleF structures.

Graphics Methods

The drawing methods fall into two basic categories: draw and fill. The draw methods create an outline shape and the fill methods are solid shapes. The first argument in a draw method is a Pen object; the fill methods use Brush objects. Each of the methods also requires the location for the upper-left corner, which you can specify as x and y coordinates or as a Point object. Some of the methods require the size, which you may supply as width and height, or as a Rectangle object.

Rather than declaring a pen or brush you can type `Pens.`*color* or `Brushes.`*color* directly in your Graphics method. You must declare the pen or brush object if you want to change the width. ∎

Graphics Methods—General Forms

```
DrawLine(Pen, x1Integer, y1Integer, x2Integer, y2Integer)
DrawLine(Pen, Point1, Point2)

DrawRectangle(Pen, xInteger, yInteger, widthInteger, heightInteger)
DrawRectangle(Pen, Rectangle)

FillRectangle(Brush, xInteger, yInteger, widthInteger, heightInteger)
FillRectangle(Brush, Rectangle)

FillEllipse(Brush, xInteger, yInteger, widthInteger, heightInteger)
FillEllipse(Brush, Rectangle)
```

The following code draws the outline of a rectangle in red using the **DrawRectangle method** and draws a line with the **DrawLine method**. The **FillEllipse method** is used to draw a filled circle.

```
Private Sub graphicsForm_Paint(ByVal sender As Object, _
    ByVal e As System.Windows.Forms.PaintEventArgs) Handles Me.Paint
    With e.Graphics
        ' Draw a red rectangle.
        '.DrawRectangle(Pens.Red, 10, 10, 30, 30)
        'or
        Dim smallRectangle as New Rectangle(10, 10, 30, 30)
        .DrawRectangle(Pens.Red, smallRectangle)

        ' Draw a green line.
        .DrawLine(Pens.Green, 50, 0, 50, 300)
```

```
      ' Draw a blue filled circle.
      ' If the width and height are equal, then the FillEllipse method
      ' draws a circle; otherwise it draws an ellipse.
      .FillEllipse(Brushes.Blue, 100, 100, 50, 50)

      ' Draw a fat blue line.
      .DrawLine(New Pen(Color.Blue, 15), 300, 0, 300, 300)
   End With
End Sub
```

Table 13.1 shows some of the methods in the Graphics class.

Selected Methods from the Graphics Class   Table 13.1

Method	Purpose
Clear()	Clear the drawing surface by setting it to the container's background color.
Dispose()	Release the memory used by a Graphics object.
DrawArc(*Pen*, *x1Integer*, *y1Integer*, *x2Integer*, *y2Integer*, *widthInteger*, *heightInteger*) DrawArc(*Pen*, *Rectangle*, *startAngleSingle*, *angleLengthSingle*)	Draw an arc (segment of an ellipse).
DrawLine(*Pen*, *x1Integer*, *y1Integer*, *x2Integer*, *y2Integer*) DrawLine(*Pen*, *Point1*, *Point2*)	Draw a line from one point to another.
DrawEllipse(*Pen*, *xInteger*, *yInteger*, *widthInteger*, *heightInteger*) DrawEllipse(*Pen*, *Rectangle*)	Draw an oval shape. A circle has equal width and height.
DrawRectangle(*Pen*, *xInteger*, *yInteger*, *widthInteger*, *heightInteger*) DrawRectangle(*Pen*, *Rectangle*)	Draw a rectangle.
DrawPie(*Pen*, *xInteger*, *yInteger*, *widthInteger*, *heightInteger*, *angleStartInteger*, *angleLengthInteger*) DrawPie(*Pen*, *Rectangle*, *angleStartSingle*, *angleLengthSingle*)	Draw a partial circle (segment of a pie).
DrawString(*textString*, *Font*, *Brush*, *xSingle*, *ySingle*) DrawString(*textString*, *Font*, *Brush*, *PointF*)	Draw a string of text. Note that coordinates are single-precision.
FillEllipse(*SolidBrush*, *xInteger*, *yInteger*, *widthInteger*, *heightInteger*) FillEllipse(*SolidBrush*, *Rectangle*)	Draw a filled oval; a circle for equal width and height.
FillPie(*Brush*, *xInteger*, *yInteger*, *widthInteger*, *heightInteger*, *angleStartInteger*, *angleLengthInteger*) FillPie(*Brush*, *Rectangle*, *angleStartSingle*, *angleLengthSingle*)	Draw a partial filled oval (segment of a pie).
FillRectangle(*SolidBrush*, *xInteger*, *yInteger*, *widthInteger*, *heightInteger*) FillRectangle(*SolidBrush*, *Rectangle*)	Draw a filled rectangle.

There are a number of other draw and fill methods, like `DrawCurve`, `Draw-Lines`, `DrawPath`, `FillClosedCurve`, `FillPolygon`, and so forth. See Help for all the draw and fill methods.

Random Numbers

Often it is useful to be able to generate random numbers. The **Random class** contains various methods for returning random numbers of different data types. A Random object is popular for use in games, as well as problems in probability and queuing theory.

```
Dim generateRandom As New Random()
```

Unfortunately, the computer can't really generate random numbers. Each time you run an application, the Random object produces the identical sequence of "random" numbers. To generate a different series for each run, use an integer value when you instantiate an object from the Random class. This is called *seeding* the random number generator. You can use the system date and time to get a different seed for each execution of the code.

```
' Instantiate and seed the random number generator.
Dim generateRandom As Random = New Random(DateTime.Now.Millisecond)
```

You seed the Random object once when you instantiate it and generate the random numbers using the Random object's **Next method**, which returns a positive integer number. You can use one of three overloaded argument lists to choose the range for the random numbers.

The Random.Next Method—General Forms

```
' Any positive integer number.
Object.Next()

' A positive integer up to the value specified.
Object.Next(MaximumValueInteger)

' A positive integer in the range specified.
Object.Next(minimumValueInteger, maximumValueInteger)
```

The Random.Next Method—Examples

```
' Return an integer in the range 0 - 10.
generateRandomInteger = generateRandom.Next(10)

' Return an integer in the range 1 to the width of the form.
randomNumberInteger = generateRandom.Next(1, Me.Width)
```

A Random Number Example

This example program draws graphics using the Graphics methods and generates snowflakes using the `Random.Next` method. Figure 13.3 shows the screen generated by this code.

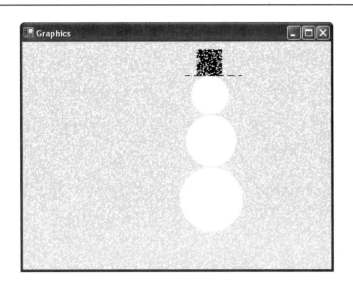

Figure 13.3

This output is produced by the Ch13RandomNumbers example program. The program draws the figure and generates random snowflakes in the form's Paint event handler.

```
'Program:      Chapter 13 Random Numbers
'Programmer:   Bradley/Millspaugh
'Date:         June 2005
'Description:  Draw a snowman using filled ellipses and then snow using
'              random locations.
'Folder:       Ch13RandomNumbers

Public Class graphicsForm

    ' Declare module-level variable.
    Private generateRandom As Random = New Random(DateTime.Now.Millisecond)

    Private Sub graphicsForm_Paint(ByVal sender As Object, _
        ByVal e As System.Windows.Forms.PaintEventArgs) _
        Handles MyBase.Paint
            ' Generate dots (snowflakes) in random locations.
            ' Draw a snowman at the bottom center of the screen.
            Dim xInteger As Integer = Convert.ToInt32(Me.Width / 2)
            Dim yInteger As Integer = Convert.ToInt32(Me.Height / 2)
            Dim indexInteger As Integer
            Dim whitePen As New Pen(Color.White, 2)

            With e.Graphics
                ' Draw the snowman.
                .FillEllipse(Brushes.White, xInteger, yInteger, 100, 100)
                ' Top of last circle.
                yInteger -= 80
                ' Offset for smaller circle.
                xInteger += 10
                .FillEllipse(Brushes.White, xInteger, yInteger, 80, 80)
                yInteger -= 60
                xInteger += 8
                .FillEllipse(Brushes.White, xInteger, yInteger, 60, 60)

                ' Add a top hat.
                .DrawLine(Pens.Black, xInteger - 10, yInteger, _
                    xInteger + 80, yInteger)
                .FillRectangle(Brushes.Black, xInteger + 10, yInteger - 40, 40, 40)
```

```
                         ' Make it snow in random locations.
                         For indexInteger = 1 To 40000
                             xInteger = generateRandom.Next(1, Me.Width)
                             yInteger = generateRandom.Next(1, Me.Height)
                             .DrawLine(whitePen, xInteger, yInteger, _
                             xInteger + 1, yInteger + 1)
                         Next
                     End With
                 End Sub
         End Class
```

> ## Feedback 13.1
>
> 1. Write the statements necessary to draw a green vertical line down the center of a form.
> 2. Write the statements to draw one circle inside another one.
> 3. Write the statements to define three points and draw lines between the points.

TIP

Use the time's millisecond property as a seed for the Random class to generate different random numbers for each execution of the program. ■

Simple Animation

There are several ways to create animation on a form. The simplest way is to display an animated .gif file in a PictureBox control. The animation is already built into the graphic. Other simple ways to create animation are to replace one graphic with another, move a picture, or rotate through a series of pictures. You also can create graphics with the various Graphics methods.

If you want to create animation on a Web page, displaying an animated .gif file is the best way. Another way is to write script using a scripting language such as VBScript or JavaScript or to embed a Java applet, which creates the animation on the client side. It doesn't make any sense to create animation using server-side controls, since each movement would require a round-trip to the server.

Displaying an Animated Graphic

You can achieve animation on either a Windows Form or a Web Form by displaying an animated .gif file (Figure 13.4). Use a PictureBox control on a Windows Form and an Image control on a Web Form.

Note: You can find the graphics for the programs in this chapter in the Graphics folder of your text CD.

Controlling Pictures at Run Time

You can add or change a picture at run time. To speed execution, it is usually best to have the pictures loaded into controls that you can make invisible until you are ready to display them. But you also can use the **FromFile method** of the Image object to load a picture at run time.

If you store a picture in an invisible control, you can change the Visible property to True at run time; or you may decide to copy the picture to another control.

```
Me.logoPictureBox.Visible = True
Me.logoPictureBox.Image = invisiblePictureBox.Image
```

You can use the FromFile method to retrieve a file during run time. One problem with this method is that the path must be known. When you are running an application on multiple systems, the path names may vary.

```
Me.logoPictureBox.Image = Image.FromFile("C:\VB\LOGO.BMP")
```

If you store your image file in your project's bin\Debug folder, you can omit the path. The bin\Debug folder is the default folder for the application's executable file.

```
Me.logoPictureBox.Image = Image.FromFile("LOGO.BMP")
```

To remove a picture from the display, either hide it or use the Nothing constant.

```
Me.logoPictureBox.Visible = False
Me.logoPictureBox.Image = Nothing
```

Switching Images

An easy way to show some animation is to replace one picture with another. Many of the icons in the Visual Studio icon library have similar sizes but opposite states, such as a closed file cabinet and an open file cabinet; a mailbox with the flag up and with the flag down; a closed envelope and an open envelope; or a traffic light in red, yellow, or green. (Recall that in Chapter 2 you used the two light bulbs, LightOn and LightOff.)

This sample program demonstrates switching between two phone icons: a phone and a phone being held. The program has three PictureBox controls: one to display the selected image and two, with their Visible property set to false, to hold the two phone images. The two icons are Phone12.ico and Phone13.ico in the Graphics\Icons\Comm folder (or the Graphics\MicrosoftIcons folder on your text CD). When the user clicks the *Change* button, the icon is switched to the opposite one. (See Figure 13.5.)

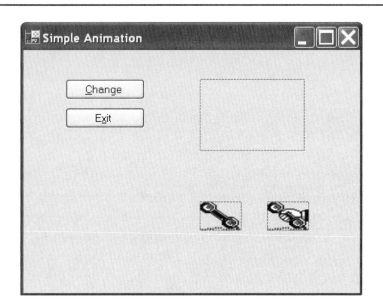

Figure 13.5

Create animation by switching from one icon to another. Each of these graphics is placed into the upper picture box when the user clicks the **Change** *button.*

```
'Program:       Chapter 13 Simple Animation
'Programmer:    Bradley/Millspaugh
'Date:          June 2005
'Description:   Change a picture of a phone to show someone holding it.
'Folder:        Ch13SimpleAnimation

Public Class animationForm

    Private Sub exitButton_Click(ByVal sender As System.Object, _
      ByVal e As System.EventArgs) Handles exitButton.Click
          ' End the program.

          Me.Close()
    End Sub

    Private Sub changeButton_Click(ByVal sender As System.Object, _
      ByVal e As System.EventArgs) Handles changeButton.Click
          ' Toggle the image from one to the other.
          Static switchBoolean As Boolean = True

          With Me
              If switchBoolean Then
                  .displayPictureBox.Image = withHandPictureBox.Image
                  switchBoolean = False
              Else
                  .displayPictureBox.Image = phonePictureBox.Image
                  switchBoolean = True
              End If
          End With
    End Sub
```

```
    Private Sub animationForm_Load(ByVal sender As Object, _
        ByVal e As System.EventArgs) Handles MyBase.Load
        ' Set the initial image.

        With Me
            .displayPictureBox.Image = .phonePictureBox.Image
        End With
    End Sub
End Class
```

Moving a Picture

The best way to move a control is to use the control's **SetBounds method**. The SetBounds method produces a smoother appearing move than the move that is produced by changing the Left and Top properties of controls.

The SetBounds Method—General Form

General Form

```
SetBounds(xInteger, yInteger, widthInteger, heightInteger)
```

You can use a control's SetBounds method to move it to a new location and/or to change its size.

The SetBounds Method—Examples

Examples

```
Me.planePictureBox.SetBounds(xInteger, yInteger, planeWidthInteger, planeHeightInteger)

Me.enginePictureBox.SetBounds(xInteger, yInteger, widthInteger, heightInteger)
```

The program example in the next section uses a timer and the SetBounds method to move a graphic across the screen.

The Timer Component

Generally events occur when the user takes an action. But what if you want to make events occur at some interval, without user action? You can cause events to occur at a set interval using the **Timer component** and its **Tick event**. Timers are very useful for animation; you can move or change an image each time the Tick event occurs.

When you have a Timer component on a form, it "fires" each time an interval elapses. You can place any desired code in the Tick event procedure; the code executes each time the event occurs. You choose the interval for the timer by setting its **Interval property**, which can have a value of 0 to 65,535. This value specifies the number of milliseconds between the calls to the Tick event. One second is equivalent to 1,000 milliseconds. Therefore, for a three-second delay, set the timer's Interval property to 3,000. You can set the value at run time or at design time.

You can keep the Tick event from occurring by setting the Timer's Enabled property to False. The default value is False, so you must set it to True when you want to enable the Timer. You can set the Enabled property at design time or run time.

When you add a timer to your form, it goes into the component tray. The tool for the timer is represented by the little stopwatch in the toolbox (Figure 13.6).

This Timer example program achieves animation in two ways: It moves an animated .gif file for a steam engine across the screen. When the steam engine moves off the left edge of the form, it reappears at the right edge, so it comes around again. Figure 13.7 shows the form. You'll have to use your imagination for the animation.

Figure 13.6

The tool for the Timer component in the toolbox.

Figure 13.7

Each time the Timer fires, the train moves 10 pixels to the left.

```
'Program        Ch13 Timer Animation
'Programmer:    Bradley/Millspaugh
'Date:          June 2005
'Description:   Move a steam engine across the screen.
'               It reappears on the other side after leaving the screen.
'Folder:        Ch13TimerAnimation

Public Class timerForm

    Private Sub trainTimer_Tick(ByVal sender As System.Object, _
        ByVal e As System.EventArgs) Handles trainTimer.Tick
        ' Move the graphic across the form.

        Static xInteger As Integer = enginePictureBox.Left
        Static yInteger As Integer = enginePictureBox.Top
        Static widthInteger As Integer = enginePictureBox.Width
        Static heightInteger As Integer = enginePictureBox.Height
```

```
        With Me
            ' Set new X coordinate.
            xInteger -= 10
            If xInteger <= -.enginePictureBox.Width Then ' Graphic off edge of form.
                xInteger = .Width
            End If
            ' Move image.
            .enginePictureBox.SetBounds(xInteger, yInteger, widthInteger, heightInteger)
        End With
    End Sub
End Class
```

> ## Feedback 13.2

1. Write the statement(s) to move commandButton 10 pixels to the left using the SetBounds method
2. How long is an interval of 450?
3. What fires a Timer's Tick event?

The Scroll Bar Controls

You can add **horizontal scroll bars** and **vertical scroll bars** to your form
(Figure 13.8). These scroll bar controls are similar to the scroll bars in Windows that can be used to scroll through a document or window. Often scroll bars
are used to control sound level, color, size, and other values that can be
changed in small amounts or large increments. The HScrollBar control and
VScrollBar control operate independently of other controls and have their own
methods, events, and properties.

Figure 13.8

*Horizontal scroll bars and
vertical scroll bars can be used
to select a value over a given
range.*

Scroll Bar Properties

Properties for scroll bars are somewhat different from the controls we have
worked with previously. Because the scroll bars represent a range of values,

they have the following properties: **Minimum** for the minimum value, **Maximum** for the maximum value, **SmallChange** for the distance to move when the user clicks on the scroll arrows, and **LargeChange** for the distance to move when the user clicks on the gray area of the scroll bar or presses the Page-Up or Page-Down keys (Figure 13.9). Each of these properties has a default value (Table 13.2).

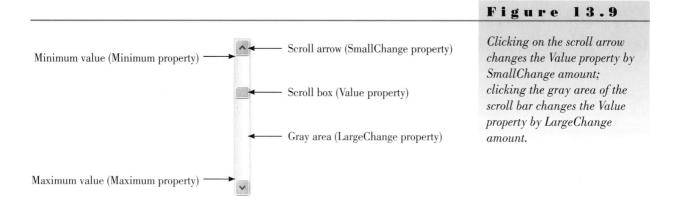

Figure 13.9

Clicking on the scroll arrow changes the Value property by SmallChange amount; clicking the gray area of the scroll bar changes the Value property by LargeChange amount.

Default Values for Scroll Bar Properties

Table 13.2

Property	Default Value
Minimum	0
Maximum	100
SmallChange	1
LargeChange	10
Value	0

The **Value property** indicates the current position of the scroll box (also called the *thumb*) and its corresponding value within the scroll bar. When the user clicks the up arrow of a vertical scroll bar, the Value property decreases by the amount of SmallChange (if the Minimum value has not been reached) and moves the scroll box up. Clicking the down arrow causes the Value property to increase by the amount of SmallChange and moves the thumb down until it reaches the bottom or Maximum value.

Figure 13.10 shows the horizontal scroll bar tool and vertical scroll bar tool from the toolbox.

Figure 13.10

The toolbox tools for horizontal scroll bars and vertical scroll bars.

Scroll Bar Events

The events that occur for scroll bars differ from the ones used for other controls. Although a user might click on the scroll bar, there is no Click event; rather there are two events: a **ValueChanged event** and a **Scroll event**. The ValueChanged event occurs any time that the Value property changes, whether it's changed by the user or by the code.

If the user drags the scroll box, a Scroll event occurs. In fact, multiple scroll events occur, as long as the user continues to drag the scroll box. As soon as the user releases the mouse button, the Scroll events cease and a ValueChanged event occurs. When you write code for a scroll bar, usually you will want to code both a ValueChanged event procedure and a Scroll event procedure.

A Programming Example

This little program uses scroll bars to move an image of cars around inside a container (Figure 13.11). The image is in a PictureBox and a GroupBox is the container. By placing the image inside a container, you use the container's coordinates rather than those of the form.

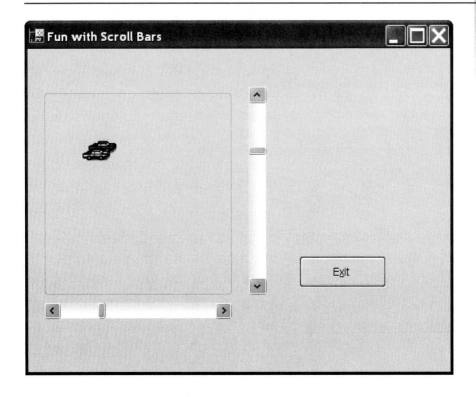

Figure 13.11

The form for the scroll bar programming example. Move the cars around inside the container using the scroll bars.

A horizontal scroll bar will make the image move sideways in the container, and the vertical scroll bar will make it move up and down. Although you want the Maximum properties of the scroll bars to reflect the height and width of the container, due to the shape of the image, you may need to set the properties using trial and error. For example, the width of the GroupBox is 247 pixels but the Maximum property of the horizontal scroll bar is set to 210; that's the point at which a car's bumper touches the edge of the container.

```
'Program:       Ch13ScrollBars
'Programmer:    Bradley/Millspaugh
'Date:          June 2005
'Description:   Use scroll bars to move an image
'               horizontally and vertically within the
'               limits of a group box.
'Folder:        Ch13ScrollBars

Public Class scrollForm

    Private Sub exitButton_Click(ByVal eventSender As System.Object, _
      ByVal eventArgs As System.EventArgs) Handles exitButton.Click
        ' Terminate the project.

        Me.Close()
    End Sub

    Private Sub moveCarHorizontalScrollBar_Scroll(ByVal eventSender As System.Object, _
      ByVal eventArgs As System.Windows.Forms.ScrollEventArgs) _
      Handles moveCarHorizontalScrollBar.Scroll
        ' Control the side-to-side movement.
        ' Used when scroll box is moved.

        With Me
            .carPictureBox.Left = .moveCarHorizontalScrollBar.Value
        End With
    End Sub

    Private Sub moveCarVerticalScrollBar_Scroll(ByVal eventSender As System.Object, _
      ByVal eventArgs As System.Windows.Forms.ScrollEventArgs) _
      Handles moveCarVerticalScrollBar.Scroll
        ' Position the up and down movement.
        ' Used when scroll box is moved.

        With Me
            .carPictureBox.Top = .moveCarVerticalScrollBar.Value
        End With
    End Sub

    Private Sub moveCarVerticalScrollBar_ValueChanged(ByVal sender As Object, _
      ByVal e As System.EventArgs) Handles moveCarVerticalScrollBar.ValueChanged
        ' Position the up and down movement.
        ' Used for arrow clicks.

        With Me
            .carPictureBox.Top = .moveCarVerticalScrollBar.Value
        End With
    End Sub

    Private Sub moveCarHorizontalScrollBar_ValueChanged(ByVal sender As Object, _
      ByVal e As System.EventArgs) Handles moveCarHorizontalScrollBar.ValueChanged
        ' Control the side-to-side movement.
        ' Used for arrow clicks.

        With Me
            .carPictureBox.Left = .moveCarHorizontalScrollBar.Value
        End With
    End Sub
End Class
```

Playing Sounds

It's fun to add sound to an application. Your computer plays sounds as you turn it on or off. There's also likely a sound when you receive e-mail. You can make your program play sound files, called wave files (.wav), by using the new `My.Computer.Audio.Play`.

Adding Sound Files to the Resources for a Project

When you plan to use sounds in a project, the best plan is to add the files to the project's resources. Open the Project Designer (*Project / ProjectName Properties*) and click on the *Resources* tab (Figure 13.12). Drop down the *Add* list and choose *Existing File* to add an existing file to your project. You can browse to find the file wherever it is; the file will be copied into a Resources folder in the project.

When you want to refer to the filename in code, use this form: `"My.Resources.Filename"`.

Example

```
My.Computer.Audio.Play(My.Resources.chimes, AudioPlayMode.WaitToComplete)
```

Figure 13.12

Add sound files to the project resources in the **Resources** tab of the Project Designer.

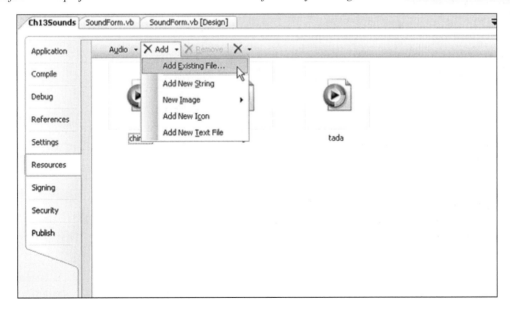

A Sound-Playing Program

The following program (Figure 13.13) plays three different sounds found in the Windows\Media folder or allows the user to select a file using the OpenFileDialog component. The filter property for the OpenFileDialog is set to wave files (WAV Files (*.wav)|*.wav).

Figure 1 3 . 1 3

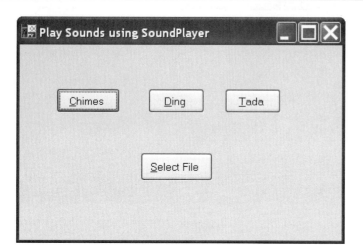

*The user can choose to play
one of three preselected sounds
or select a .wav file to play.*

```
'Program:        Chapter 13 SoundPlayer
'Programmer:     Bradley/Millspaugh
'Date:           June 2005
'Description:     Play sounds.
'Folder:         Ch13SoundPlayer

Public Class SoundForm

    Private Sub chimesButton_Click(ByVal sender As System.Object, _
     ByVal e As System.EventArgs) Handles chimesButton.Click
        ' Play the chimes sound.

        My.Computer.Audio.Play(My.Resources.chimes, _
          AudioPlayMode.WaitToComplete)
    End Sub

    Private Sub dingButton_Click(ByVal sender As System.Object, _
     ByVal e As System.EventArgs) Handles dingButton.Click
        ' Play the ding sound.

        My.Computer.Audio.Play(My.Resources.ding, _
          AudioPlayMode.WaitToComplete)
    End Sub

    Private Sub tadaButton_Click(ByVal sender As Object, _
     ByVal e As System.EventArgs) Handles tadaButton.Click
        ' Play the tada sound.

        My.Computer.Audio.Play(My.Resources.tada, _
          AudioPlayMode.WaitToComplete)
    End Sub

    Private Sub selectButton_Click(ByVal sender As System.Object, _
     ByVal e As System.EventArgs) Handles selectButton.Click
        ' Allow user to select the sound file.
```

```
        If OpenFileDialog1.ShowDialog() = DialogResult.OK Then
            My.Computer.Audio.Play(OpenFileDialog1.FileName)
        End If
    End Sub
End Class
```

If you want to have a sound play as the application opens, you can play the sound in the Form_Load or Form Activate event procedure.

Drag-and-Drop Programming

Often Windows users use drag-and-drop events rather than selecting a menu item or pressing a button. For example, you can copy or move files in My Computer by dragging the file and dropping it on the new location icon.

Drag-and-drop programming requires you to begin the drag-drop with a **MouseDown event** and determine the effect of the drop with a **DragEnter event**. The event that holds the code for the drop is the **DragDrop event**. Figure 13.14 shows the objects and events for a drag-and-drop operation.

Figure 13.14

The Source object is dragged to the Target object in a drag-and-drop operation.

Source → Target	
In MouseDown event: DoDragDrop method.	AllowDrop property must be set to True.

In MouseEnter event (Optional):
    Set cursor to give feedback
    that a drag will occur.
	In DragEnter event:
	    Set DragDrop effect (Move or Copy).

	In DragDrop event: Code to add dragged object to target.

The Source Object

The item that you wish to drag is commonly referred to as the source object. With .NET programming you begin a drag-drop operation by setting the source object using a control's **DoDragDrop method**.

The DoDragDrop Method—General Form

```
ObjectName.DoDragDrop(DataToDrag, DesiredDragDropEffect)
```

The DragDrop effect specifies the requested action for the operation. Choices include `DragDropEffects.Copy`, `DragDropEffects.Move`, and `DragDropEffects.None`.

The DoDragDrop Method—Example

```
With Me.nameTextBox
     .DoDragDrop(.SelectedText, DragDropEffects.Move)
End With
```

Look at the following MouseDown event procedure. First, an `If` statement checks to see if the user pressed the left mouse button. If so, the contents of the text box are selected and the effect of the drag is set to a move operation.

```
Private Sub nameTextBox_MouseDown(ByVal sender As Object, _
  ByVal e As System.Windows.Forms.MouseEventArgs) _
  Handles nameTextBox.MouseDown
      ' Select contents of the text box and invoke the drag/drop.

    If e.Button = Windows.Forms.MouseButtons.Left Then
        With Me.nameTextBox
           .SelectAll()
           .DoDragDrop(.SelectedText, DragDropEffects.Move)
        End With
    End If
End Sub
```

The Target Object

The location at which a user releases the mouse, a drop, is the target. A form may have multiple targets. To set a control to be a target, set its **AllowDrop property** to True. The target control needs a DragEnter event procedure that sets the effect and a DragDrop event procedure that executes the action to take when the drop takes place.

In the following example program (Figure 13.15), the value in a text box can be transferred to one of two list boxes. Each list box would be a potential target and must have its AllowDrop property set to True. And each target object needs a DragEnter event procedure and a DragDrop event procedure.

The DragEnter Event

When the user drags a source object over the target, the target control's DragEnter event fires. Notice in the DragEnter's procedure header that the `e` argument is defined as `DragEventArgs`, which has some special properties for the drag operation. You assign the desired effect to the `e` argument.

```
Private Sub teamAListBox_DragEnter(ByVal sender As Object, _
  ByVal e As System.Windows.Forms.DragEventArgs) _
  Handles teamAListBox.DragEnter
      ' Set the desired DragDrop effect.

    e.Effect = DragDropEffects.Move
End Sub
```

F i g u r e   13.15

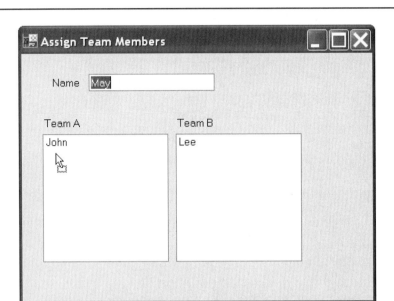

The user types a name in the top text box and then drags the name to one of two list boxes.

The DragDrop Event

Assume that when the user drops the text value on a list box that we want to add the value to the items collection for the list and clear the original text box. The statements to perform these actions are entered into the DragDrop event for the list box.

The data that are being dragged are contained in the Data property of the e argument of the DragDrop event procedure. You can retrieve the dragged data using the GetData method of the Data object. You also can format the data yourself or use a predefined clipboard data format. The predefined format for text is DataFormats.Text.

```
Private Sub teamAListBox_DragDrop(ByVal sender As Object, _
  ByVal e As System.Windows.Forms.DragEventArgs) _
  Handles teamAListBox.DragDrop
      ' Add the item to the list box.

     With Me
        .teamAListBox.Items.Add(e.Data.GetData(DataFormats.Text).ToString())
        .nameTextBox.Clear()
     End With
End Sub
```

Note: .NET actually allows the target to be outside the current application, but that topic is beyond the scope of this text.

The Drag-and-Drop Program

Following is the completed program that is illustrated in Figure 13.15.

```
'Program         Chapter 13 Drag and Drop
'Programmer:     Bradley/Millspaugh
'Date:           June 2005
'Description:    Drag a name from the text box and drop on a list.
'Folder:         Ch13DragDropListBoxes

Public Class TeamAssignmentForm

    Private Sub nameTextBox_MouseDown(ByVal sender As Object, _
        ByVal e As System.Windows.Forms.MouseEventArgs) _
        Handles nameTextBox.MouseDown
            ' Select contents of the text box and invoke the drag/drop.

            If e.Button = Windows.Forms.MouseButtons.Left Then
                With Me.nameTextBox
                    .SelectAll()
                    .DoDragDrop(.SelectedText, DragDropEffects.Move)
                End With
            End If
    End Sub

    Private Sub teamAListBox_DragDrop(ByVal sender As Object, _
        ByVal e As System.Windows.Forms.DragEventArgs) _
        Handles teamAListBox.DragDrop
            ' Add the item to the list box.

            With Me
                .teamAListBox.Items.Add(e.Data.GetData(DataFormats.Text).ToString()
                .nameTextBox.Clear()
            End With
    End Sub

    Private Sub teamAListBox_DragEnter(ByVal sender As Object, _
        ByVal e As System.Windows.Forms.DragEventArgs) _
        Handles teamAListBox.DragEnter
            ' Set the desired DragDrop effect.

            e.Effect = DragDropEffects.Move
    End Sub

    Private Sub teamBListBox_DragDrop(ByVal sender As Object, _
        ByVal e As System.Windows.Forms.DragEventArgs) _
        Handles teamBListBox.DragDrop
            ' Add the item to the list box.

            With Me
                .teamBListBox.Items.Add(e.Data.GetData(DataFormats.Text).ToString()
                .nameTextBox.Clear()
            End With
    End Sub

    Private Sub teamBListBox_DragEnter(ByVal sender As Object, _
        ByVal e As System.Windows.Forms.DragEventArgs) _
        Handles teamBListBox.DragEnter
            ' Set the desired DragDrop effect.

            e.Effect = DragDropEffects.Move
    End Sub
```

```
      Private Sub nameTextBox_MouseEnter(ByVal sender As Object, _
        ByVal e As System.EventArgs) Handles nameTextBox.MouseEnter
              ' Set the mouse pointer to give feedback that a drag is legal.
              ' (Optional extra.)

          With Me.nameTextBox
              If .Text <> "" Then
                  .SelectAll()
                  .Cursor = Cursors.Arrow
              Else
                  .Cursor = Cursors.IBeam
              End If
          End With
      End Sub
  Enn Class
```

▶ Feedback 13.3

1. Code the DragEnter event for taskListBox that will copy the value received in a drag operation.
2. Write the statement for the DragDrop method to add the value to the list box.

Your Hands-On Programming Example

Create a project that will draw a pie chart showing the relative amount of sales for Books, Periodicals, and Food for R 'n R—For Reading and Refreshment.

Include text boxes for the user to enter the sales amount for Books, Periodicals, and Food. Include buttons for *Display Chart*, *Clear*, and *Exit*.

Calculate the values for the pie chart in the *Display Chart* button's Click event procedure and use a `Refresh` method to force the form's Paint event to occur. In the form's Paint event procedure, use the `CreateGraphics.FillPie` method to draw each of the pie segments.

```
Me.CreateGraphics.FillPie(Brush, xInteger, yInteger, widthInteger, heightInteger, _
  beginAngleInteger, lengthInteger)
```

Planning the Project

Sketch a form (Figure 13.16) that your users sign off as meeting their needs.

Figure 13.16

A planning sketch of the hands-on programming example.

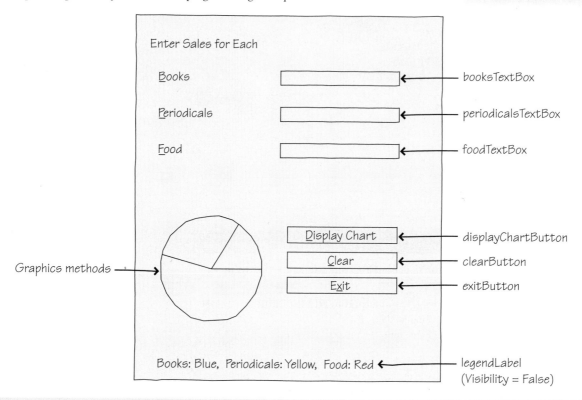

Plan the Objects and Properties
Plan the property settings for the form and each control.

Object	Property	Setting
Form	Name	pieChartForm
	Text	R 'n R Sales Pie Chart
	AcceptButton	displayChartButton
	CancelButton	clearButton
Label1	Name	Label1
	Text	Enter Sales for Each
Label2	Name	Label2
	Text	&Books
booksTextBox	Name	booksTextBox
	Text	(blank)
Label3	Name	Label3
	Text	&Periodicals
periodicalsTextBox	Name	periodicalsTextBox
	Text	(blank)
Label4	Name	Label4
	Text	&Food

Object	Property	Setting
foodTextBox	Name	foodTextBox
	Text	(blank)
legendLabel	Name	legendLabel
	Text	Books: Blue, Periodicals: Yellow, Food: Red
	Visible	False
displayChartButton	Name	displayChartButton
	Text	&Display Chart
clearButton	Name	clearButton
	Text	&Clear Sale
exitButton	Name	exitButton
	Text	E&xit

Plan the Event Procedures

Event Procedure	Actions—Pseudocode

displayChartButton_Click	If text fields are numeric
	    Find each category sales.
	    Find total sales.
	    Force form to repaint (Refresh).

Form_Paint	If drawChartBoolean
	    If total sales <> 0
	        Make legend visible.
	        Calculate ratio of each department to total sales.
	        Draw portions of the pie for each department.
	Else
	    Clear chart.

clearButton_Click	Set each text box and label to blanks. Set the focus in the first text box. Set drawChartBoolean = False. Force form to repaint (Refresh).
exitButton_Click	Exit the project.

Write the Project
Following the sketch in Figure 13.16, create the form. Figure 13.17 shows the completed form.

- Set the properties of each of the objects, as you have planned.

- Write the code. Working from the pseudocode, write each event procedure.

- When you complete the code, use a variety of test data to thoroughly test the project.

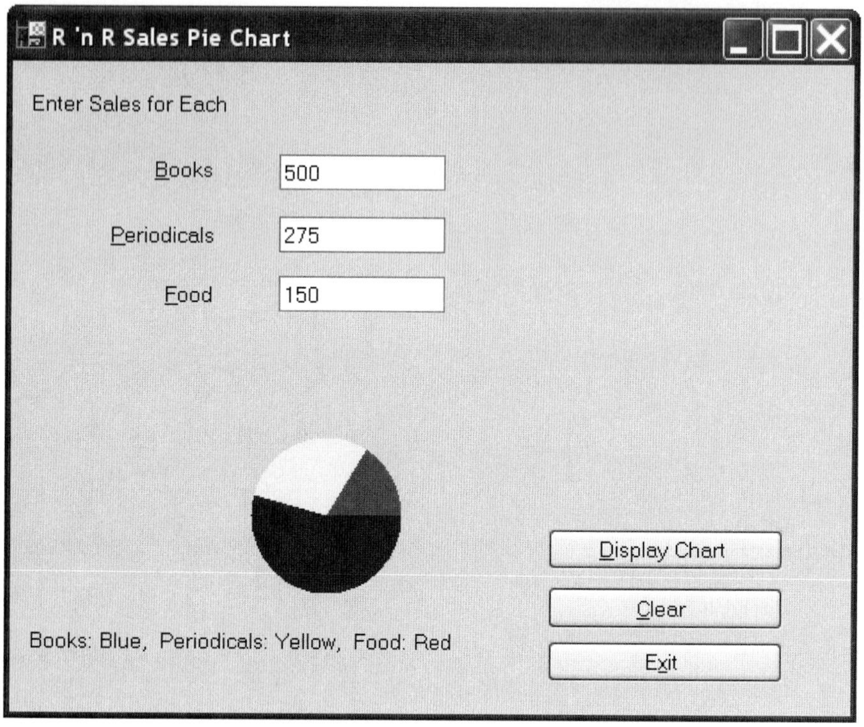

Figure 13.17

The form for the hands-on programming example.

R 'n R Sales Pie Chart

Enter Sales for Each

<u>B</u>ooks	500
<u>P</u>eriodicals	275
<u>F</u>ood	150

Books: Blue, Periodicals: Yellow, Food: Red

<u>D</u>isplay Chart

<u>C</u>lear

E<u>x</u>it

The Project Coding Solution

```
'Program:       Chapter 13 Pie Chart Hands On
'Programmer:    Bradley/Millspaugh
'Date:          June 2005
'Description:   Draw a chart for relative sales amounts.
'Folder:        Ch13PieChart

Public Class pieChartForm

  Private totalSalesDecimal, bookSalesDecimal, periodicalSalesDecimal, _
    foodSalesDecimal As Decimal
  Private drawChartBoolean As Boolean = False

  Private Sub displayChartButton_Click(ByVal sender As System.Object, _
    ByVal e As System.EventArgs) Handles displayChartButton.Click
      ' Display a pie chart showing relative sales by department.
```

```
            ' Need total sales amount.
        With Me
          Try
            bookSalesDecimal = Decimal.Parse(.booksTextBox.Text)
            Try
              periodicalSalesDecimal = Decimal.Parse(.periodicalsTextBox.Text)
              Try
                foodSalesDecimal = Decimal.Parse(.foodTextBox.Text)
                totalSalesDecimal = bookSalesDecimal + periodicalSalesDecimal _
                  + foodSalesDecimal
                drawChartBoolean = True
              Catch
                MessageBox.Show("Invalid Food Sales")
                .foodTextBox.Focus()
              End Try
            Catch
              MessageBox.Show("Invalid Periodical Sales")
              .periodicalsTextBox.Focus()
            End Try
          Catch
            MessageBox.Show("Invalid Book Sales")
            .booksTextBox.Focus()
          End Try

          ' Force a Paint of the form.
          .Refresh()
        End With
    End Sub

    Private Sub exitButton_Click(ByVal sender As System.Object, _
      ByVal e As System.EventArgs) Handles exitButton.Click
        ' End the project.

        Me.Close()
    End Sub

    Private Sub clearButton_Click(ByVal sender As System.Object, _
      ByVal e As System.EventArgs) Handles clearButton.Click
        ' Clear the screen controls.

        With Me
          .foodTextBox.Clear()
          .periodicalsTextBox.Clear()
          With .booksTextBox
            .Clear()
            .Focus()
          End With
          .legendLabel.Visible = False
          drawChartBoolean = False
          .Refresh()
        End With
    End Sub

    Private Sub pieChartForm_Paint(ByVal sender As Object, _
      ByVal e As System.Windows.Forms.PaintEventArgs) Handles Me.Paint
        Dim xCenterInteger As Integer = 140
        Dim yCenterInteger As Integer = 180
        Dim clearBrush As New SolidBrush(pieChartForm.DefaultBackColor)
```

```
      With Me
          If drawChartBoolean Then
            ' Create the pie chart.
            ' Amounts are a portion of the total circle of 360 degrees.
            ' The pie graphic includes a start angle and end angle.
            If totalSalesDecimal <> 0 Then
              .legendLabel.Visible = True
              ' Find the end of the book portion of 360 degrees.
              Dim endBooksInteger As Integer = _
                Convert.ToInt32(bookSalesDecimal / totalSalesDecimal * 360)
              .CreateGraphics.FillPie(Brushes.Blue, xCenterInteger, yCenterInteger, _
                100, 100, 0, endBooksInteger)
              ' Find the end of the Periodicals portion.
              Dim endPeriodicalsInteger As Integer = _
                Convert.ToInt32(periodicalSalesDecimal / totalSalesDecimal * 360)
              .CreateGraphics.FillPie(Brushes.Yellow, xCenterInteger, yCenterInteger, _
                100, 100, endBooksInteger, endPeriodicalsInteger)
              Dim endFoodInteger As Integer = _
                Convert.ToInt32(foodSalesDecimal / totalSalesDecimal * 360)
              .CreateGraphics.FillPie(Brushes.Red, xCenterInteger, yCenterInteger, _
                100, 100, endPeriodicalsInteger + endBooksInteger, endFoodInteger)
            End If
          Else
            .CreateGraphics.FillEllipse(clearBrush, xCenterInteger, yCenterInteger, 100, 100)
          End If
      End With
    End Sub
End Class
```

Summary

1. A drawing surface is created with a Graphics object.
2. The Graphics methods should appear in the form's Paint event procedure so that the graphics are redrawn every time the form is repainted.
3. Pen objects are used for lines and the outline of shapes; brushes are used for filled shapes.
4. Measurements in drawings are in pixels.
5. The coordinate system begins with (0, 0) at the upper-left corner of the container object.
6. You can declare a Point structure, a Size structure, or a Rectangle structure to use as arguments in the Graphics methods.
7. You can generate random numbers using the Random class. Seed the random number generator when instantiating a variable of the class; use the Next method to generate a series of numbers.
8. An animated .gif file can be displayed in a PictureBox control to display animation on a Windows Form or a Web Form.
9. Animation effects can be created by using similar pictures and by controlling the location and visibility of controls.
10. Pictures can be loaded, moved, and resized at run time.
11. The Timer component can fire a Tick event that occurs at specified intervals, represented in milliseconds.

12. Scroll bar controls are available for both horizontal and vertical directions. Properties include Minimum, Maximum, SmallChange, LargeChange, and Value. Scroll and ValueChanged events are used to respond to the action.

13. Use `My.Computer.Audio.Play` for wave (.wav) sound files in the Resources folder.

14. Drag-and-drop programming allows a source object to be dropped on a target object. The target control has its AllowDrop property set to True. The source control calls the `DoDragDrop` method in its MouseDown event. The target control sets the effect of the drag in the DragEnter event and the results in the DragDrop event.

Key Terms

AllowDrop property *522*
Brush object *503*
DoDragDrop method *521*
DragDrop event *521*
DragEnter event *521*
DrawLine method *506*
DrawRectangle method *506*
FillEllipse method *506*
FromFile method *510*
graphics *502*
horizontal scroll bar *515*
Interval property *513*
LargeChange property *516*
Maximum property *516*
Minimum property *516*
MouseDown event *521*

Next method *508*
Pen object *503*
pixel *503*
Point structure *505*
Random class *508*
Rectangle structure *506*
Scroll event *517*
SetBounds method *513*
Size structure *505*
SmallChange property *516*
Tick event *513*
Timer component *513*
Value property *516*
ValueChanged event *517*
vertical scroll bar *515*

Review Questions

1. What is a pixel?
2. What class contains the Graphics methods?
3. Describe two ways to add a Graphics object to a form.
4. Name three methods available for drawing graphics.
5. How is a pie-shaped wedge created?
6. Differentiate between using a Brush and a Pen object.
7. Which function loads a picture at run time?
8. How can you remove a picture at run time?
9. What steps are necessary to change an image that contains a turned-off light bulb to a turned-on light bulb?
10. What is the purpose of the Timer component?
11. Explain the purpose of these scroll bar properties: Minimum, Maximum, SmallChange, LargeChange, and Value.

12. What determines the file to be played by a SoundPlayer?
13. Explain the purpose of the following events for a drag-and-drop operation:
    a. MouseDown
    b. DragEnter
    c. DragDrop
14. Explain the parameters of the DoDragDrop method.

Programming Exercises

13.1 Create a project that contains two buttons labeled "Smile" and "Frown". The *Smile* button will display a happy face; *Frown* will display a sad face. Use Graphics methods to draw the two faces.

    Optional: Add sound effects when the faces appear.

13.2 Use Graphics methods to create the background of a form. Draw a picture of a house, including a front door, a window, and a chimney.

13.3 Use a PictureBox control with a .bmp file from Windows. Set the Size-Mode property to StretchImage. Use scroll bars to change the size of the image.

13.4 Use graphics from any clip art collection to create a project that has a button for each month of the year. Have an appropriate image display in a PictureBox for each month.

13.5 Use the bicycle icon and a Timer component to move the bicycle around the screen. Add a *Start* button and a *Stop* button. The *Stop* button will return the bicycle to its original position. (The bicycle icon is stored as Graphics\Icons\Industry\Bicycle.ico or in the Graphics\MicrosoftIcons folder on the text CD.)

13.6 Modify the snowman project (Random Numbers) from earlier in the chapter by adding eyes, a mouth, and buttons. Play an appropriate sound file.

13.7 Modify the chapter hands-on example to add two more categories: Drinks and Gifts. Allow the user to enter the additional values and make the pie chart reflect all five categories. Make sure to set the legend label at the bottom of the form to include the new categories.

13.8 Write a project that has list boxes for a potluck party: appetizers, salad, entrée, dessert. Have a text box for entering attendees' names and then drag them to the appropriate list box.

    Optional extra: Code a save feature to save the contents of each of the list boxes to a separate file. Then add a feature to load the list boxes when the program begins.

Case Studies

VB Mail Order

Create a logo for VB Mail Order using Graphics methods. Place the logo in the startup form for the project from Chapter 12. Add appropriate images and graphics to enhance each form. The graphics may come from .bmp files, .gif files, clip art, or your own creation from Paintbrush.

VB Auto Center

Have the startup screen initially fill with random dots in your choice of colors. Use Graphics methods to draw an Auto Center advertisement that will appear on the screen. Have various appropriate images (icons) appear in different locations, remain momentarily, and then disappear.

Video Bonanza

Use the Timer component and the random number generator to create a promotional game for Video Bonanza customers. Create three image controls that will display an image selected from five possible choices. When the user clicks on the *Start* button, a randomly selected image will display in each of the image controls and continue to change for a few seconds (like a "slot machine") until the user presses the *Stop* button. If all three images are the same, the customer receives a free video rental.

Display a message that says "Congratulations" or "Better Luck Next Visit".

Very Very Boards

Modify your Very Very Boards project from Chapter 8 or 12 to add a moving graphic to the About form. Use the graphic Skateboard.wmf or other graphic of your choice. Include a Timer component to move the graphic across the form. When the graphic reaches the edge of the form, reset it so that the graphic appears at the opposite edge of the form and begins the trip again.

Note: For help in basing a new project on an existing project, see "Copy and Move Projects" in Appendix C.

14

Additional Topics in Visual Basic

at the completion of this chapter, you will be able to . . .

1. Validate user input in the Validating event and display messages using an ErrorProvider component.

2. Use code snippets in the editor.

3. Create a multiple document project with parent and child forms.

4. Arrange the child forms vertically, horizontally, or cascaded.

5. Add toolbars and status bars to your forms using tool strip and status strip controls.

6. Use calendar controls and date functions.

7. Display a Web page on a Windows form using a WebBrowser control.

8. Capture and check an individual keypress from the user.

This chapter introduces some topics that can make your programs a bit more professional. You can use an ErrorProvider control to display error messages to the user and perform field-level validation, rather than validate an entire form. You can improve the operation of multiple-form applications by using a multiple document interface (MDI), which allows you to set up parent and child forms. Most professional applications have toolbars and status bars, which you learn to create in this chapter.

Advanced Validation Techniques

You already know how to validate user input using `Try`/`Catch`, `If` statements, and message boxes. In addition to these techniques, you can use .NET Error-Provider components, which share some characteristics with the Web validation controls. Other useful techniques are to set the MaxLength and/or CharacterCasing properties of text boxes and to perform field-level validation using the Validating event of input controls.

The ErrorProvider Component

In Chapters 3 and 4 you learned to validate user input and display message boxes for invalid data. Now you will learn to display error messages directly on the form using an **ErrorProvider component**, rather than pop up messages in message boxes. Using an ErrorProvider component, you can make an error indication appear next to the field in error, in a manner similar to the validator controls in Web applications.

Although you can add multiple ErrorProvider components to a form, generally you use a single ErrorProvider for all controls on a form. Once you add the ErrorProvider into the component tray, you can validate a control. If the data value is invalid, the ErrorProvider component can display a blinking icon next to the field in error and display a message in a pop-up, similar to a ToolTip (Figure 14.1).

The logic of your program can be unchanged from a MessageBox solution. When you identify an error, you use the ErrorProvider **SetError method**, which pops up the icon.

ErrorProvider SetError Method—General Form

```
ErrorProviderObject.SetError(ControlName, MessageString)
```

ErrorProvider SetError Method—Examples

```
ErrorProvider1.SetError(Me.quantityTextBox, "Quantity must be numeric.")
ErrorProvider1.SetError(Me.creditCardTextBox, "Required field.")
```

The following example is taken from Chapter 3. The message boxes have been removed and replaced with ErrorProvider icons and messages. Notice that all messages are cleared at the top of the calculateButton_Click procedure so that no icons appear for fields that have passed validation. Figure 14.2 shows the form in design view.

Figure 14.1

The ErrorProvider displays a blinking icon next to the field in error. When the user points to the icon, the error message appears in a pop-up.

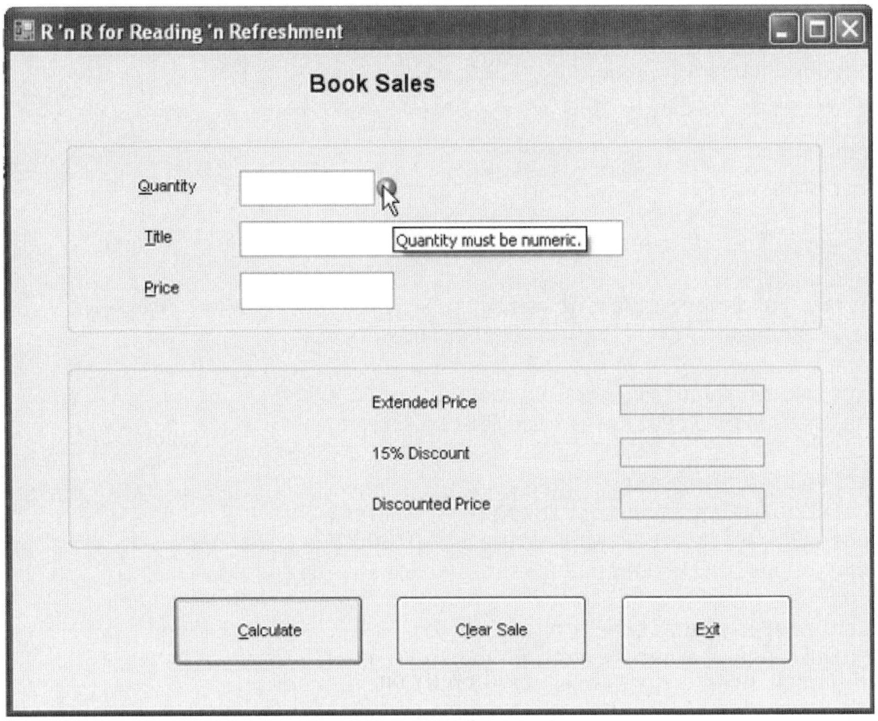

Figure 14.2

The calculation form from Chapter 3 with an ErrorProvider added.

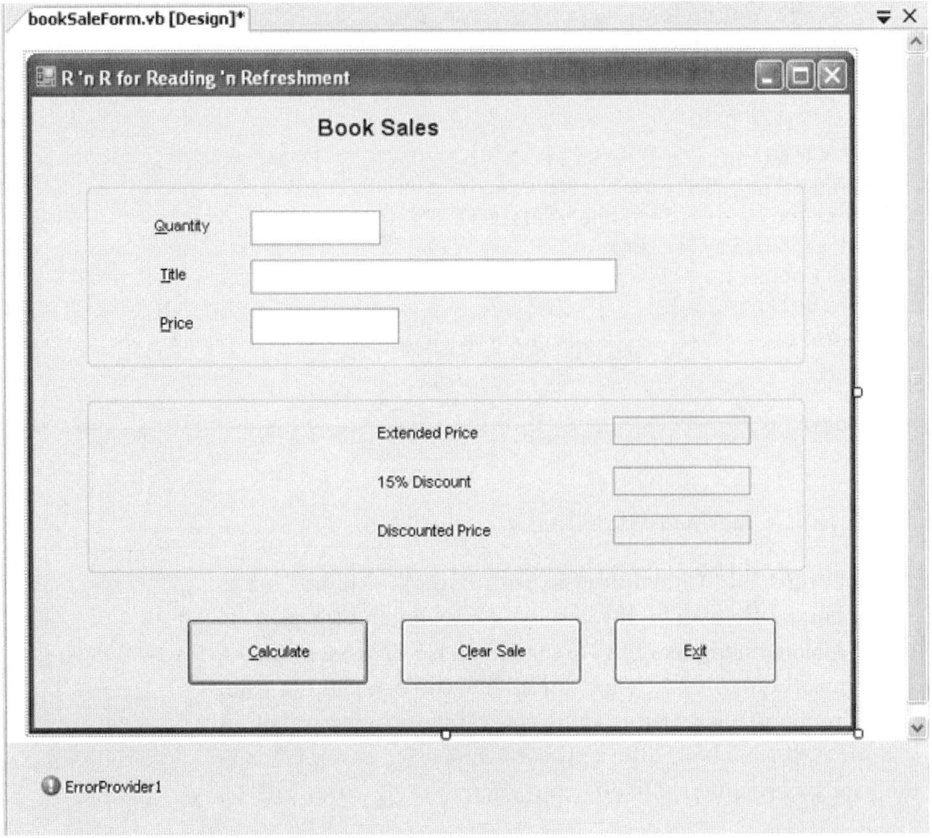

```vb
Private Sub calculateButton_Click(ByVal sender As System.Object, _
    ByVal e As System.EventArgs) Handles calculateButton.Click
    ' Calculate the price and discount.
    Dim quantityInteger As Integer
    Dim priceDecimal, extendedPriceDecimal, discountDecimal, _
        discountedPriceDecimal As Decimal

    With Me
        ' Clear all the error messages.
        .ErrorProvider1.Clear()

        Try
            ' Convert quantity to numeric variables.
            quantityInteger = Integer.Parse(.quantityTextBox.Text)
            Try
                ' Convert price if quantity was successful.
                priceDecimal = Decimal.Parse(.priceTextBox.Text)

                ' Calculate values for sale.
                extendedPriceDecimal = quantityInteger * priceDecimal
                discountDecimal = extendedPriceDecimal * DISCOUNT_RATE_Decimal
                discountedPriceDecimal = extendedPriceDecimal - discountDecimal

                ' Format and display answers for the sale.
                .extendedPriceTextBox.Text = extendedPriceDecimal.ToString("C")
                .discountTextBox.Text = discountDecimal.ToString("N")
                .discountedPriceTextBox.Text = discountedPriceDecimal.ToString("C")

            Catch ex As Exception
                ' Handle a price exception.
                .ErrorProvider1.SetError(priceTextBox, "Price must be numeric.")
                With .priceTextBox
                    .Focus()
                    .SelectAll()
                End With
            End Try

        Catch ex As Exception
            ' Handle a quantity exception.
            .ErrorProvider1.SetError(quantityTextBox, "Quantity must be numeric.")
            With .quantityTextBox
                .Focus()
                .SelectAll()
            End With
        End Try
    End With
End Sub
```

The MaxLength and CharacterCasing Properties

You can use the **MaxLength** and **CharacterCasing properties** of text boxes
to help the user enter correct input data. If you set the MaxLength property, the
user is unable to enter more characters than the maximum. The user interface
beeps and holds the insertion point in place to indicate the error to the user.
The CharacterCasing property has possible values of Normal, Upper, or Lower,
with a default of Normal. If you change the setting to Upper, for example, each
character that the user types is automatically converted to uppercase, with no

Figure   14.3

State   AK

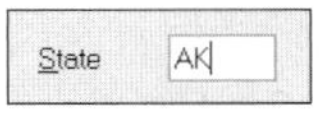

error message or warning. Figure 14.3 shows a State text box on a form. The user can enter only two characters, and any characters entered are converted to uppercase.

Note: Although the MaxLength property limits user input, the program can assign a longer value to the text box in code, if necessary.

Field-Level Validation

So far all of the validation you have coded is for the entire form, after the user clicks a button such as *OK*, *Calculate*, or *Save*. If the form has many input fields, the validation code can be quite long and complex. Also, the user can become confused or annoyed if multiple message boxes appear, one after another. You can take advantage of the Validating event, the CausesValidation property, and the ErrorProvider components to perform **field-level validation**, in which any error message appears as soon as the user attempts to leave a field with invalid data.

Using the Validating Event and CausesValidation Property

As the user enters data into input fields and tabs from one control to another, multiple events occur in the following order:

Enter
GotFocus
Leave
Validating
Validated
LostFocus

Although you could write event procedures for any or all of these events, the Validating event is the best location for validation code. The Validating event procedure's header includes a CancelEventArgs argument, which you can use to cancel the event and return the focus to the control that is being validated.

Each control on the form has a **CausesValidation property** that is set to True by default. When the user finishes an entry and presses Tab or clicks on another control, the Validating event occurs for the control just left. That is, the event occurs if the CausesValidation property of the *new* control (receiving the input focus) is set to True. You can leave the CausesValidation property of most controls set to True, so that validation occurs. Set CausesValidation to False on a control such as Cancel or Exit to give the user a way to bypass the validation if he or she doesn't want to complete the transaction.

In the Validating event procedure, you can perform any error checking and display a message for the user. If the data value does not pass the error checking, set the Cancel property for the e argument of the event to True. This cancels the Validating event and returns the focus to the text box, making the text box "sticky." The user is not allowed to leave the control until the input passes validation.

```
Private Sub firstNameTextBox_Validating(ByVal sender As Object, _
    ByVal e As System.ComponentModel.CancelEventArgs) _
    Handles firstNameTextBox.Validating
        ' Validate for a required entry.

        With Me
            ' Cancel any previous error.
            .ErrorProvider1.SetError(.firstNameTextBox, "")

            ' Check for an empty string.
            If .firstNameTextBox.Text = String.Empty Then
                ' Cancel the event.
                e.Cancel = True
                .ErrorProvider1.SetError(.firstNameTextBox, "Required Field.")
            End If
        End With
End Sub
```

One note of caution: If you use the validating event on the field that receives focus when the form is first displayed and require an entry, the user will be unable to close the form without filling in the text box. You can work around this problem by setting `e.Cancel = False` in the form's FormClosing event procedure.

```
Private Sub validationForm_FormClosing(ByVal sender As Object, _
    ByVal e As System.Windows.Forms.FormClosingEventArgs) _
    Handles Me.FormClosing
        ' Do not allow validation to cancel the form's closing.

        e.Cancel = False
End Sub
```

A Validation Example Program

The following program combines many of the techniques presented in this section. The form (Figure 14.4) has an ErrorProvider component and all controls have their CausesValidation property set to True. The stateTextBox has its MaxLength property set to 2 and its CharacterCasing property set to Upper. Although it seems out of place, the amountTextBox is included strictly to show an example of numeric range validation.

```
'Program:        Ch 14 Validation
'Programmer:     Bradley/Millspaugh
'Date:           June 2005
'Description:    Demonstrate validation using the Validating event
'                and an Error Provider component.
'Folder:         Ch14Validation

Public Class validationForm

    Private Sub firstNameTextBox_Validating(ByVal sender As Object, _
        ByVal e As System.ComponentModel.CancelEventArgs) _
        Handles firstNameTextBox.Validating
            ' Validate for a required entry.
```

Figure 14.4

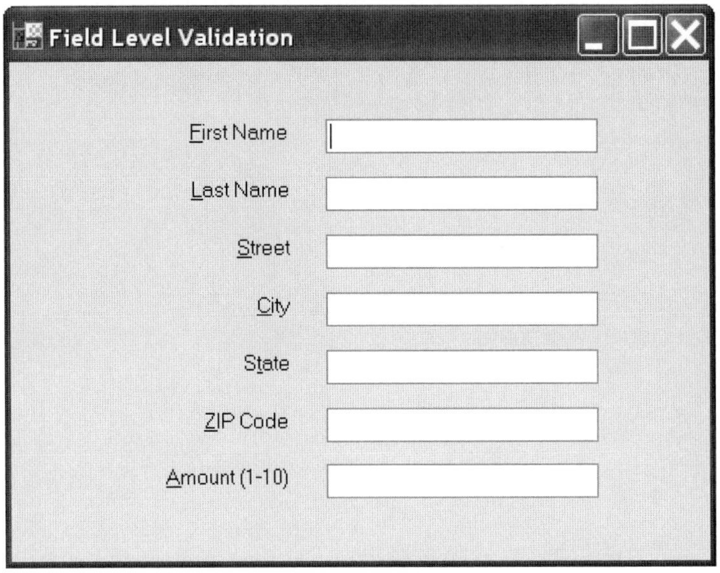

The Validation example form, which provides field-level validation.

```
            ' Cancel any previous error.
            ErrorProvider1.SetError(firstNameTextBox, "")

            With Me.firstNameTextBox
                If .Text = String.Empty Then
                    ' Cancel the event.
                    e.Cancel = True
                    ErrorProvider1.SetError(firstNameTextBox, "Required Field.")
                End If
            End With
    End Sub

    Private Sub lastNameTextBox_Validating(ByVal sender As Object, _
       ByVal e As System.ComponentModel.CancelEventArgs) _
       Handles lastNameTextBox.Validating
            ' Validate for a required entry.

            ' Cancel any previous error.
            ErrorProvider1.SetError(lastNameTextBox, "")

            With Me.lastNameTextBox
                If .Text.Length = 0 Then
                    ' Cancel the event.
                    e.Cancel = True
                    ErrorProvider1.SetError(lastNameTextBox, "Required Field.")
                End If
            End With
    End Sub

    Private Sub stateTextBox_Validating(ByVal sender As Object, _
       ByVal e As System.ComponentModel.CancelEventArgs) _
       Handles stateTextBox.Validating
            ' Make sure the state is two characters.
            ' The control's CharacterCasing property forces uppercase.
            ' The MaxLength property limits input to 2 characters.
```

```vb
            ' Cancel any previous error.
            ErrorProvider1.SetError(stateTextBox, "")

            With Me.stateTextBox
                If .Text.Length <> 2 Then
                    ' Cancel the event and select the text.
                    e.Cancel = True
                    .SelectAll()
                    ErrorProvider1.SetError(stateTextBox, "Must be 2 characters.")
                End If
            End With
        End Sub

    Private Sub amountTextBox_Validating(ByVal sender As Object, _
        ByVal e As System.ComponentModel.CancelEventArgs) _
        Handles amountTextBox.Validating
            ' Validate a numeric amount for a range of values.
            Dim amountInteger As Integer

            ' Reset any previous error.
            ErrorProvider1.SetError(amountTextBox, "")

            With Me.amountTextBox
                Try
                    amountInteger = Integer.Parse(.Text)
                    If amountInteger < 1 Or amountInteger > 10 Then
                        ' Cancel the event.
                        e.Cancel = True
                        .SelectAll()
                        ErrorProvider1.SetError(amountTextBox, _
                            "Amount must be between 1 and 10, inclusive.")
                    End If
                Catch ex As Exception
                    ' Cancel the event.
                    e.Cancel = True
                    .SelectAll()
                    ErrorProvider1.SetError(amountTextBox, _
                        "Enter a numeric amount between 1 and 10, inclusive.")
                End Try
            End With
        End Sub

    Private Sub validationForm_FormClosing(ByVal sender As Object, _
        ByVal e As System.Windows.Forms.FormClosingEventArgs) _
        Handles Me.FormClosing
            ' Do not allow validation to cancel the form's closing.

            e.Cancel = False
        End Sub
End Class
```

Capturing Keystrokes from the User

At times you may want to determine individual keystrokes entered by the
user. You can check for the key that the user entered in a control's KeyDown,
KeyPress, or KeyUp event procedure. These events occur in the order listed
for most keyboard keys. But keystrokes that ordinarily cause an action to
occur, such as the Tab key and the Enter key, generate only a KeyUp event.

The e argument of the KeyPress event procedure is KeyPressEventArgs, which has a KeyChar property that holds the character pressed. Another property of the KeyPressEventArgs is the Handled property, which you can set to True to say "I have already taken care of this keystroke; it doesn't need any further processing." This action effectively "throws away" the keystroke just entered.

In the following code example, the KeyChar property is checked in the KeyPress event procedure. If the character is not a digit or a period, then e.Handled is set to True, which does not pass the keypress on to the text box. This means that *only* digits or a period are allowed through. You can use this technique in a text box for which you want to allow only numeric data to be entered, such as a Quantity or Price text box.

```
Private Sub priceTextBox_KeyPress(ByVal sender As Object, _
  ByVal e As System.Windows.Forms.KeyPressEventArgs) _
  Handles priceTextBox.KeyPress
      ' Accept only a digit or a period.

      If Not Char.IsDigit(e.KeyChar) And e.KeyChar <> "." Then
          e.Handled = True
      End If
End Sub
```

Using the Masked Text Box for Validation

Although you learned about the masked text box in Chapter 2, you may not have thought about using it to aid data validation. You can set the Mask property of a masked text box to any of the predefined masks or write your own. The easiest way to write your own is to modify one of the existing masks, or you can follow the syntax rules of a regular expression (see "Regular Expression Syntax" in MSDN Help).

The predefined masks include date, time, phone number, Social Security number, and ZIP code formats. If the user enters invalid data for the mask, such as a letter for a numeric month in the date mask, the character is not accepted.

Feedback 14.1

1. What is the purpose of the following code:

   ```
   ErrorProvider1.SetError(quantityTextBox, "Quantity must be numeric.")
   ```

2. Name two properties of a TextBox control that help the user enter correct input data. Describe the function of each.
3. What is meant by field-level validation?

Code Snippets and Samples

A great new time saver in Visual Basic 2005 is the ability to add segments of code for a variety of topics directly from the editor. You may wonder why this topic wasn't covered earlier, but it was really necessary for you to understand the code that you add to your program. Now that you understand the basic concepts, you will find that many of your new tools and techniques come from looking at sample projects. Visual Studio includes many sample projects as well as code snippets.

Code Snippets

Code snippets are small samples of code that can show you how to accomplish many programming tasks. The *Insert Snippet* menu option is available on the context menu (right-click) of the Editor window. The Snippet categories include *Collections, Data Types – defined by Visual Basic, Interacting with the Application, Maintaining Collections, File System – Processing Drives, Folders, and Files, Math, Security,* and *Visual Basic Language.* The list varies depending upon the location of the insertion.

You will find the structure for loops, exception handling, and arrays under the *Visual Basic Language* option. The following snippet is from the *Sort an Array* snippet.

```
Dim animals() As String = {"lion", "turtle", "ostrich"}
Array.Sort(animals)
```

You can learn many useful techniques by opening snippets.

Sample Projects

Visual Studio includes many sample projects (all editions except the Express Edition) that you can use to learn new techniques. From the *Help* menu, select *Contents.* Expand the nodes for *Development Tools and Languages/Visual Studio/ Visual Basic* to find the *Samples* node.

The QuickStarts are another avenue for pursuing your study of VB. These tutorials give step-by-step introduction to many techniques and controls.

Multiple Document Interface

All of the projects so far have been **single document interface (SDI)**. Using SDI, each form in the project acts independently from the other forms. However, VB also allows you to create a **multiple document interface (MDI)**. For an example of MDI, consider an application such as Microsoft Word. Word has a **parent form** (the main window) and **child forms** (each document window). You can open multiple child windows, and you can maximize, minimize, restore, or close each child window, which always stays within the boundaries of the parent window. When you close the parent window, all child windows close automatically. Figure 14.5 shows an MDI parent window with two open child windows.

With MDI, a parent and child relationship exists between the main form and the child forms. One of the rules for MDI is that if a parent form closes, all of its children leave with it. Pretty good rule. Another rule is that children cannot wander out of the parent's area; the child form always appears inside the parent's area.

Figure 14.5

The main form is the parent and the smaller forms are the child forms in an MDI application.

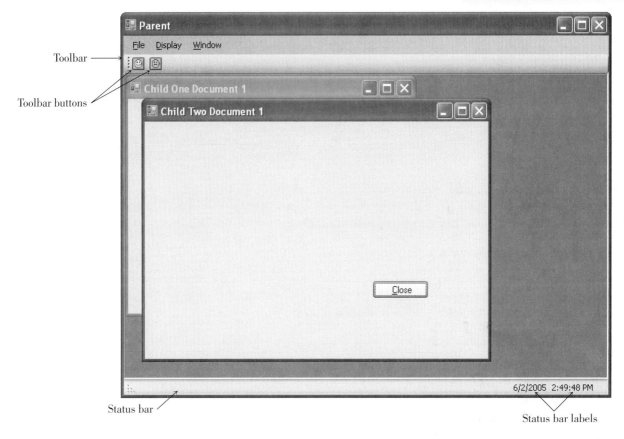

VB allows you to have forms that act independently from each other. You may have a parent form and several child forms *and* some forms that operate independently. For example, a splash form likely should remain SDI.

One feature of MDI is that you can have several documents open at the same time. The menu strip generally contains a *Window* menu that allows you to display a list of open windows and move from one active document to another.

Creating an MDI Project

You can make any form a parent. In fact, a form can be both a parent and a child form (just as a person can be both a parent and a child). To make a form into a parent, simply change its **IsMdiContainer property** to True in the Properties window of the designer. In a .NET project, you can have multiple child forms and multiple parents.

Creating a child is almost as easy. Of course, your project must contain more than one form. You make a form into a child window in code at run time. You must declare a new variable for the form, instantiate it, set the child's MdiParent property to the current (parent) form, and then show it.

```
Private Sub ChildOneMenuItem_Click(ByVal sender As System.Object, _
  ByVal e As System.EventArgs) Handles ChildOneMenuItem.Click
      ' Display Child One form.

      Dim aChildOneForm As New childOneForm
      aChildOneForm.MdiParent = Me
      aChildOneForm.Show()
End Sub
```

Our example application allows the user to display multiple child windows. Therefore, the title bar of each child window should be unique. We can accomplish this by appending a number to the title bar before displaying the form. This is very much like Microsoft Word, with its Document1, Document2, and so forth.

```
' Module-level declarations.
Dim childOneCountInteger As Integer

Private Sub ChildOneMenuItem_Click(ByVal sender As System.Object, _
  ByVal e As System.EventArgs) Handles ChildOneMenuItem.Click
      ' Display Child One form.

      Dim aChildOneForm As New childOneForm
      aChildOneForm.MdiParent = Me
      childOneCountInteger += 1
      aChildOneForm.Text = "Child One Document " _
          & childOneCountInteger.ToString()
      aChildOneForm.Show()
End Sub
```

Adding a Window Menu

A parent form should have a *Window* menu (Figure 14.6). The *Window* menu lists the open child windows and allows the user to switch between windows and arrange multiple child windows. Take a look at the *Window* menu in an application such as Word or Excel. You will see a list of the open documents as well as options for arranging the windows.

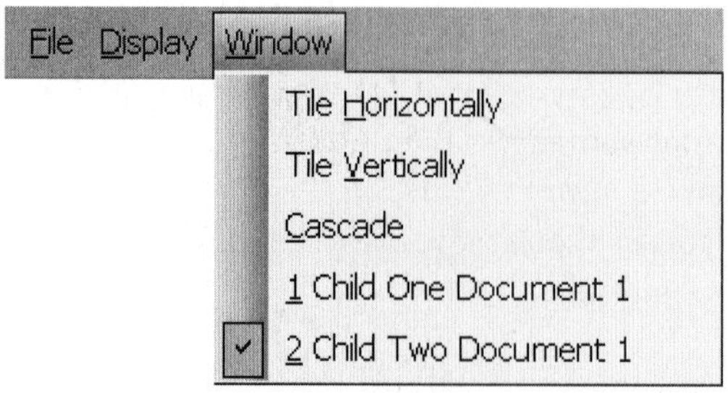

Figure 14.6

The Window menu in an MDI application lists the open child windows and allows the user to select the arrangement of the windows.

After you create the menus for a MenuStrip control, you can make one of the menus display the list of open child windows. Display the properties of the MenuStrip (not a menu item) in the Properties window. Drop down the list for **the MdiWindowListItem property**, which shows all of the menu items that belong to the MenuStrip, and select WindowToolStripMenuItem (Figure 14.7). To actually arrange the windows requires a little code.

Figure 14.7

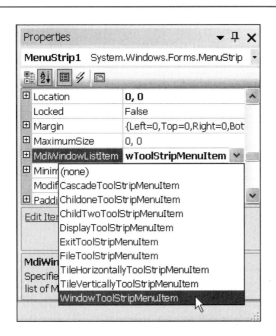

Figure 14.7

Set the MdiWindowListItem property to make the Window menu display the list of open MDI child windows.

Layout Options

When several child windows are open, the windows may be arranged in several different layouts: tiled vertically, tiled horizontally, or cascaded. You set the type of layout in code with an argument of the **LayoutMdi method**.

```
Me.LayoutMdi(MdiLayout.TileHorizontal)
```

You can use one of the three constants: TileHorizontal, TileVertical, and Cascade.

```
Private Sub TileHorizontallyToolStripMenuItem_Click(ByVal sender As System.Object, _
    ByVal e As System.EventArgs) Handles TileHorizontallyToolStripMenuItem.Click
        ' Arrange the child forms horizontally.

    Me.LayoutMdi(MdiLayout.TileHorizontal)
End Sub

Private Sub TileVerticallyToolStripMenuItem_Click(ByVal sender As System.Object, _
    ByVal e As System.EventArgs) Handles TileVerticallyToolStripMenuItem.Click
        ' Arrange the child forms vertically.

    Me.LayoutMdi(MdiLayout.TileVertical)
End Sub

Private Sub CascadeToolStripMenuItem_Click(ByVal sender As System.Object, _
    ByVal e As System.EventArgs) Handles CascadeToolStripMenuItem.Click
        ' Cascade the child forms.

    Me.LayoutMdi(MdiLayout.Cascade)
End Sub
```

Toolbars and Status Bars

You can enhance the usability of your programs by adding features such as a toolbar and/or status bar. You probably find that you use the toolbars in applications as an easy shortcut for menu items. Status bars normally appear at the bottom of the screen to display information for the user.

To create a **toolbar**, you need a **ToolStrip control** and the images in *Resources* to appear on the ToolStrip buttons.

Toolbars

You use the ToolStrip control (Figure 14.8) in the *Menus & Toolbars* tab of the toolbox to create a ToolStrip object for your project. The new ToolStrip is a container that does not yet contain any objects. After you add the ToolStrip, you can add several types of objects. The strip may contain ToolStripButtons, ToolStripLabels, and several other types of objects.

Figure 14.8

The ToolStrip and StatusStrip controls in the toolbox.

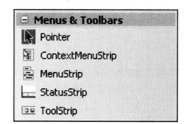

Setting Up the Buttons

The easiest way to set up buttons for a ToolStrip is to click on its Items property in the Properties window, which opens the Items Collection Editor (Figure 14.9).

In the ToolStrip's Items Collection Editor, you can drop down the list of available types of objects (Figure 14.10). For now you will use only the Button. Click on the *Add* button, which adds a new ToolStripButton object to the collection. Then you can set the properties of the new button, such as its Name and ToolTipText properties. Make sure to give it a meaningful name. For example, a button that displays the Summary Window might be called summaryToolStripButton and one that displays the About box might be called aboutToolStripButton.

You also can assign an image to the button's Image property in the Items Collection Editor window. To display only the image and no text, set DisplayStyle to Image.

Note that with the ToolStrip selected, you can click *Insert Standard Items* below the Properties window. You will get New, Open, Save, Print, Cut, Copy, and Paste buttons with pictures added automatically. However, you must write the code for each button yourself.

Coding for the ToolStrip

To code the actions for a ToolStrip button you can create a new event procedure for the button click. However, since most buttons are actually shortcuts for

Set the ToolTipText property of each ToolStrip button to aid the user in case the meaning of each graphic is not perfectly clear. ■

Figure 14.9

Add buttons to a ToolStrip using the Items Collection Editor, which you can open from the ToolStrip's Items property in the Properties window.

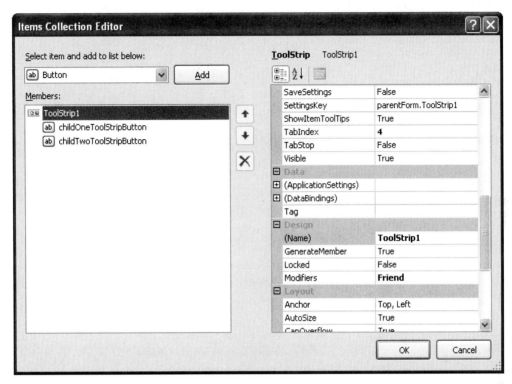

Figure 14.10

Drop down the list of available objects that can be added to the Items collection of a ToolStrip control.

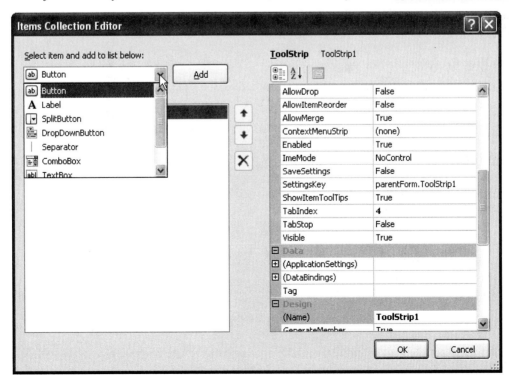

menu items, you normally only need to add your ToolStripButton.Click event to the Handles clause for the menu event procedure.

```
Private Sub displayChildOneMenuItem_Click(ByVal sender As System.Object, _
    ByVal e As System.EventArgs) _
    Handles displayChildOneMenuItem.Click, childOneToolStripButton.Click
    ' Display Child One form.

    Dim aChildOneForm As New childOneForm
    aChildOneForm.MdiParent = Me
    childOneCountInteger += 1
    aChildOneForm.Text = "Child One Document " _
        & childOneCountInteger.ToString()
    aChildOneForm.Show()
End Sub
```

Status Bars

A **status bar** is usually located at the bottom of a form (refer to Figure 14.5). A status bar displays information such as date, time, status of the Caps Lock or Num Lock key, or error or informational messages. If you want a status bar on your form, you need to take two steps: add a **StatusStrip control** (refer to Figure 14.8) to your form and add **ToolStripStatusLabel objects** to the StatusStrip.

Just as with ToolStrips, the easiest way to add items to the StatusStrip object is to select its Items property in the Properties window to open the Items Collection Editor. Click on the *Add* button to add a new ToolStripStatusLabel object. Then set the properties of the ToolStripStatusLabel, including the object's Name and ToolTipText properties.

You can make the labels appear at the right end of the status bar, as in Figure 14.5, by setting the StatusStrip's RightToLeft property to True. The default is False. When you set RightToLeft to True, the labels will appear in the opposite order that you define them.

Assigning Values to ToolStripStatusLabels

A ToolStripStatusLabel can hold text, such as the current date, the time, or error messages. You assign values to the Text property of labels at run time:

```
Me.dateToolStripStatusLabel.Text = Now.ToShortDateString()
Me.timeToolStripStatusLabel.Text = Now.ToLongTimeString()
Me.informationToolStripLabel.Text = "It's very late."
```

Displaying the Date and Time

You use the properties and methods of the **DateTime structure** to retrieve and format the current date and time. The **Now property** holds the system date and time in a numeric format that can be used for calculations. You can format the date and/or time for display using one of the following methods: ToShortDateString, ToLongDateString, ToShortTimeString, or ToLongTimeString. The actual display format of each method depends on the local system settings.

You can set the display value of status strip labels in any procedure; however, the display does not update automatically. Generally you will set initial values in the Form_Load event procedure and use a Timer component to update the time. Or you can skip the Form_Load event, figuring that in just one second the timer will fire and the clock will update.

```
Private Sub clockTimer_Tick(ByVal sender As System.Object, _
  ByVal e As System.EventArgs) Handles clockTimer.Tick
    ' Update the date and time on the status strip.
    ' Interval = 1000 milliseconds (one second).

    With Me
        .dateToolStripStatusLabel.Text = Now.ToShortDateString()
        .timeToolStripStatusLabel.Text = Now.ToLongTimeString()
    End With
End Sub

Private Sub parentForm_Load(ByVal sender As Object, _
  ByVal e As System.EventArgs) Handles MyBase.Load
    ' Display the date and time in the status strip.

    clockTimer_Tick(sender, e)
End Sub
```

Don't forget to set the Enabled and Interval properties of your timer.

▶ **Feedback 14.2**

1. Write the statements to display aboutForm as a child form.
2. Assume that you have a ToolStrip called ToolStrip1 that has buttons for *Exit* and *About*. How are the buttons coded?
3. What steps are necessary to display the current time in a status strip label called currentTimeToolStripStatusLabel?

Some Helpful Date Controls

There are many other controls in the toolbox. You may want to experiment with some of them to see how they work. This section demonstrates two more controls: the DateTimePicker and MonthCalendar controls.

The Calendar Controls

The DateTimePicker and the MonthCalendar controls (Figure 14.11) provide the ability to display calendars on your form. One advantage of the DateTimePicker is that it takes less screen space; it displays only the day and date unless the user drops down the calendar. You can use either control to allow the user to select a date, display the current date, or set a date in code and display the calendar with that date showing.

The DateTimePicker control contains a Value property for the date. When the control initially displays, the Value is set to the current date. You can let the user select a date and then use the Value property or you can assign a Date value to the property.

Figure 14.11

The calendar controls: The DateTimePicker drops down a calendar when selected and shows the selected day and date when not dropped down; the MonthCalendar control displays the calendar.

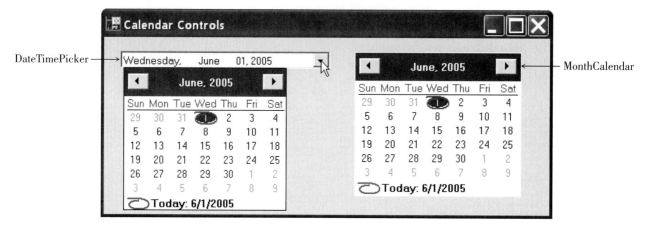

The following example allows the user to enter a birthdate in a text box. It converts the text box entry in a `Try/Catch` in order to trap for illegal date formats.

```
Me.birthdateDateTimePicker.Value = Convert.ToDateTime(Me.birthdateTextBox.Text)
```

This example program demonstrates the use of the calendar, date functions, and some interesting features of Visual Basic. Figure 14.12 shows the form for the project.

Figure 14.12

The birthday form with the calendar for the DateTimePicker dropped down.

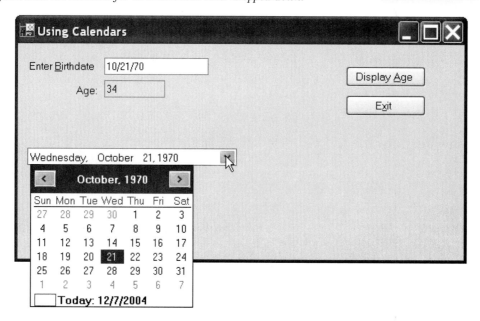

```
'Program:        Chapter 14 Calendar control
'Programmer:     Bradley/Millspaugh
'Date:           June 2005
'Description:     Enters and tests a date, displays a calendar and uses
'                 Date functions.
'Folder:         Ch14Calendar

Public Class calendarForm

    Private Sub displayButton_Click(ByVal sender As System.Object, _
        ByVal e As System.EventArgs) Handles displayButton.Click
            ' If the date is valid set the calendar and display.

        Try
            With Me.birthdateDateTimePicker
                .Value = Convert.ToDateTime(Me.birthdateTextBox.Text)
                .Visible = True
            End With
        Catch err As Exception
            MessageBox.Show("Invalid Date")
            Me.birthdateTextBox.Focus()
        End Try
    End Sub

    Private Sub birthdateDateTimePicker_ValueChanged(ByVal sender As System.Object, _
        ByVal e As System.EventArgs) Handles birthdateDateTimePicker.ValueChanged
            ' Calculate the age when the calendar value changes.
        Dim yearsInteger As Integer

        With Me.birthdateDateTimePicker.Value
            ' If birthday already passed this year.
            If .DayOfYear <= Now.DayOfYear Then
                yearsInteger = Now.Year - .Year
            Else
                ' Birthday yet to come this year.
                yearsInteger = Now.Year - .Year - 1
            End If
        End With

        If yearsInteger > 0 Then
            Me.ageTextBox.Text = yearsInteger.ToString()
        End If
    End Sub

    Private Sub exitButton_Click(ByVal sender As System.Object, _
        ByVal e As System.EventArgs) Handles exitButton.Click
            ' Terminate the project.

        Me.Close()
    End Sub
End Class
```

Notice the statements in the ValueChanged event procedure for the Date-TimePicker. You can use all of the properties of the system time on the Value property of the control.

```
yearsInteger = Now.Year - Me.birthdateDateTimePicker.Value.Year
```

You can see all of the methods and properties using Visual Studio's IntelliSense feature.

Feedback 14.3

1. Write the code to assign the date from appointmentDateTimePicker to the variable appointmentDateTime.
2. Use the IntelliSense feature or Help to list five properties of the Value property for a DateTimePicker control.
3. Which of the five properties listed in question 2 are also available for the Now property?

Displaying Web Pages on a Windows Form

You can add a **WebBrowser control** to a Windows form and display Web pages on the form. The toolbox for VB 2005 Windows Forms includes a WebBrowser control (Figure 14.13). The WebBrowser control can make your form resemble a browser window in Internet Explorer, or you can use the control to display any HTML page, online or offline. Note that you must have a live Internet connection to display Web pages in the WebBrowser control.

Figure 14.13

The Windows WebBrowser control in the toolbox.

The WebBrowser Control

When you add a WebBrowser control to an empty Windows form, by default the control is set to fill the entire form (`Dock = Fill`). You can add a ToolStrip control to provide navigation. Some useful properties, methods, and events of the WebBrowser control follow:

Url property	Set this property to a URL at design time or run time to navigate to the entered page.
	`WebBrowser1.Url = New Uri("http://www.microsoft.com")`
Navigate method	Execute this method at run time to navigate to the desired page.
	`WebBrowser1.Navigate(New Uri("http://www.microsoft.com"))`
DocumentCompleted event	A page has finished loading. You can use this event to add the page to the Items property of the combo box.
	`With Me`
	`    .ToolStripComboBox1.Items.Add(.WebBrowser1.Url)`
	`End With`

DocumentTitleChanged event	A page with a new title finished loading. Use this event to change the form's title bar to the Web page's title.

```
With Me
    .Text = .WebBrowser1.DocumentTitle
End With
```

DocumentTitle property	Retrieves the title of the current Web page.

Notice the use of "Uri" in the preceding table. A Uniform Resource Identifier (URI) is a Web address that is more generic than "URL". The latest version of the WebBrowser control requires that all URL's be instances of the Uri class.

A WebBrowser Program

The following Windows program displays a Web page in a WebBrowser control. The form has a ToolStrip control with a ToolStripComboBox and a ToolStrip-Button to aid navigation. When the user enters a new URL in the text portion of the combo box, he or she can either press Enter or click the *Go* button on the toolbar. The ToolStripComboBox_KeyUp event procedure checks for the Enter key, and the ToolStripButton_Click event procedure checks for a click on the button. Figure 14.14 shows the completed Windows form with a Web page displayed.

Figure   14.14

This Windows form displays a Web page in a WebBrowser control. A ToolStrip control contains a ToolStripComboBox item and a ToolStripButton item.

The Program Code

```
'Program:        Ch14WebBrowser
'Date:           June 2005
'Description:     Add Web browsing to a Windows Form using the WebBrowser control.
'Note:           The computer must have an established link to the Internet for this program
'                to work.

Public Class webBrowserForm
    Private Sub WebBrowser1_DocumentCompleted(ByVal sender As Object, _
        ByVal e As System.Windows.Forms.WebBrowserDocumentCompletedEventArgs) _
        Handles WebBrowser1.DocumentCompleted
            ' New document loaded. Add the URL to the combo box.

            With Me
                .ToolStripComboBox1.Text = .WebBrowser1.Url
                .ToolStripComboBox1.Items.Add(.ToolStripComboBox1.Text)
            End With
    End Sub

    Private Sub WebBrowser1_DocumentTitleChanged(ByVal sender As Object, _
        ByVal e As System.EventArgs) Handles WebBrowser1.DocumentTitleChanged
            ' Change the form's title bar when the document changes.

            Me.Text = Me.WebBrowser1.DocumentTitle
    End Sub

    Private Sub ToolStripButton1_Click(ByVal sender As System.Object, _
        ByVal e As System.EventArgs) Handles ToolStripButton1.Click
            ' Go button clicked; navigate to requested page.

            With Me
                Try
                    If Not .ToolStripComboBox1.Text.StartsWith(("HTTP://").ToUpper) Then
                        .ToolStripComboBox1.Text = "HTTP://" & .ToolStripComboBox1.Text
                    End If
                    '.WebBrowser1.Navigate(New Uri(.ToolStripComboBox1.Text))
                    .WebBrowser1.Url = New Uri(.ToolStripComboBox1.Text)
                Catch
                    MessageBox.Show("Unable to locate the requested page.")
                End Try
            End With
    End Sub

    Private Sub ToolStripComboBox1_KeyUp(ByVal sender As Object, _
        ByVal e As System.Windows.Forms.KeyEventArgs) _
        Handles ToolStripComboBox1.KeyUp
            ' Check for Enter key and navigate to entered URL.

            If e.KeyCode = Keys.Enter Then
                ToolStripButton1_Click(sender, e)
            End If
    End Sub
End Class
```

Checking for the Enter Key

You may have noticed a strange statement in the previous section:

```
If e.KeyCode = Keys.Enter Then
```

This statement checks to see if the key pressed is the Enter key.

As you learned earlier in this chapter, you can check for the key that the user entered in a control's KeyDown, KeyPress, or KeyUp event procedure. But keystrokes that ordinarily cause an action to occur, such as the Tab key and the Enter key, generate only a KeyUp event.

The e argument of the KeyUp event procedure is KeyEventArgs, which has a KeyCode and a KeyData property. These properties hold a numeric representation of the key pressed, but you can use the constants in the Keys enumeration to call the keys by name. For example, the Enter key has a KeyCode of 13. You can check for the Enter key with either of these statements:

```
If e.KeyCode = 13 Then
```

or

```
If e.KeyCode = Keys.Enter Then
```

In the program in the previous section, the user is expected to type a URL into the combo box and press Enter or click a button. To check for the Enter key, you need to code the combo box's KeyUp event procedure. Notice that the line of code compares the event argument e with the desired Keys constant.

```
Private Sub ToolStripComboBox1_KeyUp(ByVal sender As Object, _
    ByVal e As System.Windows.Forms.KeyEventArgs) _
    Handles ToolStripComboBox1.KeyUp
        ' Check for Enter key and navigate to entered URL.

        If e.KeyCode = Keys.Enter Then
            ToolStripButton1_Click(sender, e)
        End If
End Sub
```

Summary

1. An ErrorProvider component can provide an icon and pop-up error message next to the field that does not pass validation. Specify the text box and the message in the ErrorProvider SetError method.

2. A text box MaxLength property limits the number of characters the user is allowed to enter into the control.

3. The CharacterCasing property of a text box can automatically convert user input to uppercase or lowercase.

4. You can validate individual fields in the Validating event procedure for the controls. The Validating event occurs when the user attempts to move the focus to another control that has its CausesValidation property set to True.

5. VB code snippets are small samples of code that illustrate coding techniques. You can add code snippets in the editor.

6. Visual Studio includes many sample programs and quick-start tutorials.

7. A multiple document interface (MDI) contains parent and child forms. Closing the parent also closes all child forms. The child forms stay within the bounds of the parent form.

8. To create an MDI parent form, set a form's IsMdiContainer property to True. To create a child form, instantiate a new form object and set its MdiParent property to the parent form in code.

9. MDI applications generally have a *Window* menu, which displays a list of open child windows and provides choices for arranging the child windows.

10. To create a toolbar, add a ToolStrip control and add buttons to the Items collection.

11. A toolbar provides shortcuts to menu options.

12. A status bar contains information for the user along the bottom of a form. After adding a StatusStrip control to a form, add labels to its Items collection.

13. The date can be assigned to the Text property of a ToolStripStatusLabel during the Form_Load event procedure, but the time display requires an update routine using a Timer component.

14. The DateTimePicker and MonthCalendar controls have accurate calendars for displaying and inputting dates.

15. The WebBrowser control provides the ability to display Web pages from a Windows Form.

16. You can check the e (KeyEventArgs) argument of a control's KeyUp event procedure to determine which key was pressed. The e.KeyCode and e.KeyData properties hold a numeric code for the key, which you can check using the constants in the Keys enumeration.

Key Terms

Review Questions

1. Explain how to use an ErrorProvider component when validating the value in a text box.
2. What properties of a text box determine the number of characters a user can enter and the case (upper or lower) of the input?
3. What are code snippets? How might they be used?
4. What is meant by *MDI*?
5. What are the advantages of having parent and child forms?
6. What are the layouts available for arranging child windows?
7. How can a child form be created? A parent form?
8. What steps are necessary to create a toolbar and have its buttons execute menu procedures?
9. What must be done to create a status bar? To display the current time on the status bar? To keep the time display current?
10. Describe two controls that you can use for displaying dates on a form.
11. What property is used to navigate to a Web page at design time using the WebBrowser control? How is this task accomplished at run time?

Programming Exercises

14.1 Convert any of your earlier programs that use message boxes for error messages to use an ErrorProvider component. Remove all message boxes from the program and display meaningful messages in the pop-up Error Text.

14.2 Write an MDI project that is a simple text editor. Allow the user to open multiple documents, each in a separate child form. For the text editor, use one big TextBox control with its Multiline property set to True or a RichTextBox control. Set the control's Anchor property to all four edges so the control fills its form.

    Each form should have its own Load File and Save File functions. Use the FileStreams that you learned about in Chapter 11.

14.3 Add a toolbar and a status bar to a previous project to provide shortcuts to the menu items.

14.4 Add a toolbar and a status bar to the calendar program from this chapter.

14.5 Create an application for displaying local movie listings. Add a Web-Browser control that navigates to a page showing the movies in your local area.

Case Studies

Note: For help in basing a new project on an existing project, see "Basing a New Project on an Existing Project" in Chapter 5 or "Copy and Move Projects" in Appendix C.

VB Mail Order

Convert any of your earlier VB Mail Order programs that use message boxes for error messages to use an ErrorProvider component. Remove all message boxes from the program and display meaningful messages in the pop-up Error Text.

Add a toolbar and a status bar to the project to provide shortcuts to the menu items.

VB Auto Center

Convert any of your earlier VB Auto Center programs that use message boxes for error messages to use an ErrorProvider component. Remove all message boxes from the program and display meaningful messages in the pop-up Error Text.

Add a toolbar and a status bar to the project to provide shortcuts to the menu items.

Video Bonanza

Convert any of your earlier Video Bonanza programs that use message boxes for error messages to use an ErrorProvider component. Remove all message boxes from the program and display meaningful messages in the pop-up Error Text.

Add a toolbar and a status bar to the project to provide shortcuts to the menu items.

Very Very Boards

Convert any of your earlier Very Very Boards programs that use message boxes for error messages to use an ErrorProvider component. Remove all message boxes from the program and display meaningful messages in the pop-up Error Text.

Add a toolbar and a status bar to the project to provide shortcuts to the menu items.

A

Answers to Feedback Questions

► Feedback 1.1

These exercises are designed to become familiar with the Help system. There are no "correct" answers.

► Feedback 2.1

Property	Setting
Name	iconPictureBox
BorderStyle	Fixed3D
SizeMode	StretchImage
Visible	True

► Feedback 2.2

1.
```
With Me.companyTextBox
    .Clear()
    .Focus()
End with
```
2.
```
Me.customerLabel.Clear()
Me.orderTextBox.Focus()
```
3. (a) Places a check in the check box.
   (b) Radio button is selected.
   (c) Makes the picture invisible.
   (d) Makes the label appear sunken.
   (e) Assigns the text value in cityTextBox.Text to the text value of cityLabel.Text.

► Feedback 3.1

1. Does not specify a data type.
2. Identifiers cannot contain special characters such as "#".
3. An identifier cannot contain blank spaces.
4. Periods are used to separate items such as Object.Property.
5. Identifiers cannot contain embedded special characters such as "$".
6. *Sub* is a reserved word.
7. The name is valid; however, it does not indicate anything about what the variable is used for.
8. *Text* is a property name and should not be used as a variable name. Also, it does not specify a data type.
9. The name is valid, however, the data type should be specified.
10. Valid.
11. Valid.
12. Valid.

► Feedback 3.2

Note: Answers may vary; make sure that the data type is included in each name.

1. (a) hoursDecimal
   (b) employeeNameString
   (c) departmentNumberString
2. (a) quantityInteger
   (b) descriptionString
   (c) partNumberString
   (d) costDecimal
   (e) sellingPriceDecimal

► Feedback 3.3

Note: Answers may vary; make sure the data type is included in each name.

1. `Private totalPayrollDecimal As Decimal`
   Declared at the module level.
2. `Const SALES_TAX_Decimal As Decimal = .08D`
   Declared at the module level.
3. `Private participantCountInteger As Integer`
   Declared at the module level.

► Feedback 3.4

1. 18
2. 1
3. 6
4. 5
5. 22
6. 2048
7. 22
8. 38

► Feedback 3.5

1. (a) `countInteger = countInteger + 5`
   (b) `countInteger += 5`
2. (a) `balanceDecimal = balanceDecimal – withdrawalDecimal`
   (b) `balanceDecimal –= withdrawalDecimal`
3. (a) `priceDecimal = priceDecimal * countInteger`
   (b) `priceDecimal *= countInteger`

▶ Feedback 3.6

1. `Me.averagePayTextBox.Text = averagePayDecimal.ToString("C")`
   $123.46
2. `Me.quantityTextBox.Text = quantityInteger.ToString()`
   176123
3. `Me.totalTextBox.Text = totalCollectedDecimal.ToString("N")`

▶ Feedback 4.1

1. True
2. True
3. True
4. False
5. False
6. True
7. True
8. False
9. True
10. True

▶ Feedback 4.2

1. frogsRadioButton will be checked.   toadsRadioButton will be unchecked.
2. "It's the toads and the polliwogs"
3. "It's true"
4.
```
With Me
   If Integer.Parse(.orangesTextBox.Text) _
     > Integer.Parse(.applesTextBox.Text) Then
     .mostTextBox.Text = "Oranges"
   ElseIf Integer.Parse(.applesTextBox.Text) _
     > Integer.Parse(.orangesTextBox.Text) Then
     .mostTextBox.Text = "Apples"
   Else
     .mostTextBox.Text = "They're equal"
   End If
End With
```
5.
```
If balanceDecimal > 0 Then
   Me.fundsCheckBox.Checked = True
   balanceDecimal = 0
   countInteger += 1
Else
   Me.fundsCheckBox.Checked = False
End If
```

► Feedback 4.3

```
1. With Me
     Select Case tempInteger
       Case Is <= 32
         .commentTextBox.Text = "Freezing"
       Case Is > 80
         .commentTextBox.Text = "Hot"
       Case Else
         .commentTextBox.Text = "Moderate"
     End Select
   End With
2. Select Case countInteger
     Case 0
       MessageBox.Show("No items entered.")
     Case 1 To 10
       MessageBox.Show("1 — 10 items entered.")
     Case 11 To 20
       MessageBox.Show("11 — 20 items entered.")
     Case Else
       MessageBox.Show("More than 20 items were entered.")
   End Select
```

► Feedback 5.1

1. Function procedure; a value will be returned.
2. ```
   Private Function Average(ByVal valueOneInteger As Integer, _
     ByVal valueTwoInteger As Integer, _
     ByVal valueThreeInteger As Integer) As Integer
   ```
   Note: ByVal is optional; the editor will add it for you.
3. `Return (valueOneInteger + valueTwoInteger + valueThreeInteger) / 3`
4. The answer appears on a `Return` statement or is assigned to the variable with the same name as the function.

► Feedback 6.1

1. `Const FAT_CALORIES_Integer As Integer = 9`
   Declared at the module level.
2. `Friend highestNameString As String`
   Declared at the module level.
3. `Friend Const COMPANY_NAME_String As String = "Bab's Bowling Service"`
   Declared at the module level.
4. `Friend totalAmountDecimal As Decimal`
   Declared at the module level.
   ```

5. `Friend personCountInteger As Integer`
   Declared at the module level.
6. `Dim totalString As String`
   Declared at the local level.

▶ Feedback 7.1

1. Alphabetizes the items in a list box or combo box.
2. Stores the index number of the currently selected (highlighted) item; has a value of −1 if nothing is selected.
3. Is a collection that holds the objects, usually text, of all list elements in a list box or combo box.
4. Determines whether or not a combo box will also have a text box for user input. It also determines whether or not the list will drop down.
5. Stores the number of elements in a list box or combo box.
6. Adds an element to a list at run time.
7. Adds an element to a list and inserts the element in the chosen position (index).
8. Clears all elements from a list box or combo box.
9. Removes an element from the list by referring to its index.
10. Removes an element from a list by looking for a given string.

▶ Feedback 7.2

```
itemFoundBoolean = False  ' Set the initial value of the found switch to False.
itemIndexInteger = 0  ' Initialize the counter for the item index.
With Me  ' Easier access to form controls.
   ' Loop through the items until the requested item is found
   ' or the end of the list is reached.
  Do Until itemFoundBoolean Or itemIndexInteger = .itemsListBox.Items.Count
     ' Check if the text box entry matches the item in the list.
    If .newItemTextBox.Text = _
       .itemsListBox.Items(itemIndexInteger).ToString() Then
       itemFoundBoolean = True  ' Set the found switch to True.
    Else   'Otherwise...
       itemIndexInteger += 1  ' Increment the counter for the item index.
    End If
  Loop
End With
```

▶ Feedback 7.3

1. (a) There should not be a comma after the test value.
   (b) The variable named on the `Next` statement must match the one on the `For` statement, indexInteger in this case.

(c) The item following the word For must be a variable and the same variable must be used on the Next statement. 4 is not a proper variable name and For is a reserved word.

(d) Valid.

(e) Valid.

(f) This loop will never be executed; it needs to have a negative Step argument.

2. (a) Will be executed 3 times; countInteger will have an ending value of 4.

(b) Will be executed 4 times; countInteger will have an ending value of 14.

(c) Will be executed 10 times; countInteger will have an ending value of 0.

(d) Will be executed 7 times; counterDecimal will have an ending value of 6.5.

(e) Will never be executed because the starting value is already greater than the test value; countInteger will have an ending value of 5.

▶ Feedback 7.4

1. A component used to set up output for the printer. Add the component to the form's component tray at design time. Begin the printing process by executing the Print method of the component; the component's PrintPage event occurs.

2. Starts the printing process. Belongs in the Click event procedure for the Print button or menu item.

3. The PrintPage event is a callback that occurs once for each page to print. The PrintPage event procedure contains all the logic for printing the page.

4. Sends a line of text to the graphics object. The DrawString method is used in the PrintPage event procedure.

5. An argument passed to the PrintPage event procedure. Holds items of information such as the page margins.

6. MarginBounds.Left is one of the properties of the PrintPageEventArgs argument passed to the PrintPage event procedure. The property holds the left margin and can be used to set the x coordinate to the left margin.

7. A component that allows the user to view the document in Print Preview. The component is added to the component tray at design time. In the event procedure where the user selects Print Preview, the print document is assigned to this component.

▶ Feedback 8.1

1. Valid.

2. Valid.

3. Valid.

4. Invalid; beyond the range of the array.

5. Valid.

6. Invalid; negative number.

7. Gives a decimal number, but Visual Basic will round the fraction and use that integer.

8. Valid.

▶ Feedback 8.2

1.
```
Structure Student
    Dim lastNameString As String
    Dim firstNameString As String
    Dim studentNumberString As String
    Dim unitsCompletedDecimal As Decimal
    Dim gpaDecimal As Decimal
End Structure
```
2.
```
Dim infoStudent(99) As Student
```
3.
```
Structure Project
    Dim projectNameString As String
    Dim formNameString As String
    Dim folderNameString As String
End Structure
```
4.
```
Dim myProject As Project
```
5.
```
Dim ourProjects(99) As Project
```

▶ Feedback 8.3

1.
```
Dim temperatureDecimal(2, 4) As Decimal
```
2.
```
For columnInteger = 0 To 4
    temperatureDecimal(0, columnInteger) = 0
Next columnInteger
```
3.
```
For columnInteger = 0 To 4
    temperatureDecimal(1, columnInteger) = 75
Next columnInteger
```
4.
```
For columnInteger = 0 To 4
    temperatureDecimal(2, columnInteger) = temperatureDecimal(0, columnInteger) _
        + temperatureDecimal(1, columnInteger)
Next columnInteger
```
5.
```
For rowIndexInteger = 0 To 2
  For columnIndexInteger = 0 To 4
    e.Graphics.DrawString(temperatureDecimal(rowIndexInteger, _
      columnIndexInteger).ToString(), printFont, Brushes.Black, _
      printXSingle, printYSingle)
    printXSingle += 200
  Next columnIndexInteger

  ' Begin a new line.
  printXSingle = e.MarginBounds.Left
  printYSingle += lineHeightSingle
Next rowIndexInteger
```

▶ Feedback 9.1

1. The .aspx file holds the specifications for the user interface that are used by the server to render the page. The .aspx.vb file holds the Visual Basic code that you write to respond to events.
2. Right-click on the .aspx file or on the page in the Document window and select View in Browser.
3. Web server controls do not directly correspond to HTML controls but are rendered differently for different browsers in order to achieve the desired look and feel. You cannot write any server-side programming logic for HTML controls. As you submit forms to the server, any HTML controls pass to the server and back as static text. You might want to use HTML controls if you have existing HTML pages that are working and you want to convert to ASP.NET for additional capabilities.

▶ Feedback 9.2

1. Manually move to the bottom of the page using the Enter key or create a table and add the button to a cell.
2. An HTML control doesn't need any server-side programming. The Web server Table control is generally used when you want to write code to add rows, columns, or controls at run time.
3. Store images in the Web site folder.

▶ Feedback 9.3

1. The NavigateUrl property.
2. Add a HyperLink control to both pages. Set the NavigateUrl of each to point to the other page.

▶ Feedback 9.4

Attach a RequiredFieldValidator control so that the field cannot be left blank. Attach a RangeValidator to check if the input falls within the specified range by setting the MinimumValue = 0 and the MaximumValue = 1000. Set the RangeValidator Type property to Integer, to validate that the entry can be converted to a numeric integer.

▶ Feedback 9.5

The Page_Load event occurs and the page is redisplayed for every round-trip to the server. If you have initialization code in the Page_Load event procedure, you don't want to perform the initialization each time the procedure executes.

▶ Feedback 10.1

1. The *file* is the database.
    The *table* contains the *rows* and *columns,* which hold the information about your friends.
    Each *row/record* contains information about an individual friend.
    A *column* or *field* contains an element of data, such as the name or phone number.
    The *key field* is the field used to organize the file; it contains a unique value that identifies a particular record, for example, the telephone number field.
2. XML is stored as text, which can pass through Internet firewalls and can be edited using any text editor.

▶ Feedback 10.2

The binding source object creates a link between the original data source and the program. The table adapter passes information back and forth between the data source and the dataset. The dataset holds a copy of the data retrieved from the data source and is used in your program to access the data, either field by field (for labels and text boxes) or by connecting it to a grid.

▶ Feedback 10.3

1. The smart tag in the Data Sources window allows you to select DataGrid-View or Details view.
2. In the Data Sources window, select **Details** on the smart tag and drag the table to the form. To change to a label, open the smart tag on the text box and select **Label**.
3. Set the DataSource property of the combo box to the binding source used by the other controls. Set the DisplayMember property to the data field to display in the combo box.
4. To sort the list, modify the SQL SELECT statement used by the table adapter.

▶ Feedback 11.1

1. ```
Dim inventoryStreamWriter As New StreamWriter("Inventory.txt")
```
2. ```
inventoryStreamWriter.WriteLine(Me.descriptionTextBox.Text)
```
3. The declaration for the StreamReader object needs to be in a Try/Catch block in case the file does not exist. The declaration for the StreamWriter object does not need to be in a Try/Catch block because, in this case, the program is generating a file, not trying to locate one; however, if you are using a full qualifying pathname, then you should put the StreamWriter declaration in a Try/Catch block.
4. ```
If inventoryStreamReader.Peek <> –1 Then
   Me.descriptionLabel.Text = inventoryStreamReader.ReadLine()
   Me.productNumberLabel.Text = inventoryStreamReader.ReadLine()
End If
```

## ▶ Feedback 11.2

1. ```
Text Files (*.txt)|*.txt
```
2. ```
OpenFileDialog1.InitialDirectory = Application.StartupPath
```
3. ```
If phoneStreamWriter IsNot Nothing Then
   phoneStreamWriter.Close()
End If
```

▶ Feedback 11.3

1. ```
With Me.namesListBox
   For indexInteger As Integer = 0 To .Items.Count – 1
     namesStreamWriter.WriteLine(.Items(indexInteger))
   Next indexInteger
End With
```
2. The above code should be placed in a Save procedure that should be called from the form's FormClosing event procedure.
3. ```
Try
   Dim namesStreamReader As New StreamReader("Names.txt")
   Do Until namesStreamReader.Peek = –1
     Me.namesListBox.Items.Add(namesStreamReader.ReadLine())
   Loop
   namesStreamReader.Close()
Catch
```

► Feedback 12.1

1. An object is an instance of a class. A class defines an item type (like the cookie cutter defines the shape), whereas the object is an actual instance of the class (as the cookie made from the cookie cutter).
2. aProduct is an object, an instance of the Product class.
3. The numeric value of quantityTextBox is assigned to the Quantity property of aProduct.
4.
```
Private lastNameString As String
Private firstNameString As String
Private studentIDNumberString As String
Private gpaDecimal As Decimal
```
These statements appear at the module level.
5.
```
Property LastName() As String
   Get
      Return lastNameString
   End Get
   Set(ByVal value As String)
      lastNameString = value
   End Set
End Property
```
6.
```
ReadOnly Property GPA() As Decimal
   Get
      Return gpaDecimal
   End Get
End Property
```

► Feedback 13.1

1.
```
Dim xInteger As Integer
Dim yInteger As Integer
yInteger = Convert.ToInt32(Me.Height)
xInteger = Convert.ToInt32(Me.Width / 2)
e.Graphics.DrawLine(Pens.green, xInteger, 0, xInteger, yInteger)
```
2.
```
e.Graphics.DrawEllipse(Pens.green, xInteger, yInteger, 100F, 100F)
e.Graphics.DrawEllipse(Pens.blue, xInteger + 25, yInteger + 25, 50F, 50F)
```
3.
```
Dim firstPoint As New Point(20, 20)
Dim secondPoint As New Point(100, 100)
Dim thirdPoint As New Point(200, 50)
e.Graphics.DrawLine(Pens.green, firstPoint, secondPoint)
e.Graphics.DrawLine(Pens.green, secondPoint, thirdPoint)
e.Graphics.DrawLine(Pens.green, thirdPoint, firstPoint)
```

▶ Feedback 13.2

1.
```
Static xInteger As Integer = Me.commandButton.Left - 10
Static yInteger As Integer = Me.commandButton.Top
Static widthInteger As Integer = Me.commandButton.Width
Static heightInteger As Integer = Me.commandButton.Height
Me.commandButton.SetBounds(xInteger, yInteger, widthInteger, heightInteger)
```
or
```
With Me.commandButton
   .SetBounds(.Left - 10, .Top, .Width, .Height)
End With
```
2. A little less than half a second.
3. The Tick event fires each time the specified interval has elapsed.

▶ Feedback 13.3

1.
```
Private Sub taskListBox_DragEnter(ByVal sender As Object, _
  ByVal e As System.Windows.Forms.DragEventArgs) _
  Handles taskListBox.DragEnter
     ' Set the desired DragDrop effect.
     e.Effect = DragDropEffects.Copy
End Sub
```
2.
```
Private Sub taskListBox_DragDrop(ByVal sender As Object, _
  ByVal e As System.Windows.Forms.DragEventArgs) _
  Handles taskListBox.DragDrop
   ' Add the item to the list box.

   With Me
      .taskListBox.Items.Add(e.Data.GetData(DataFormats.Text).ToString()
      .taskTextBox.Clear()
   End With
End Sub
```

▶ Feedback 14.1

1. When the code is placed inside a Catch block, it will place an icon next to the quantityTextBox control when the user inputs invalid data. The message appears as a ToolTip when the user places the pointer over the icon.
2. The MaxLength and CharacterCasing properties.
   - MaxLength: Sets a maximum number of characters that may be entered into a text box. A beep occurs if the user attempts to exceed the maximum.
   - CharacterCasing: Automatically converts data entry to uppercase, lowercase, or normal.
3. With field-level validation the user is notified of an error as the focus leaves a field, rather than waiting until a button's Click event occurs.

▶ Feedback 14.2

1.
```
Dim aboutChildForm As New aboutForm()
aboutChildForm.MdiParent = Me
aboutChildForm.Show()
```
2. Add an event to the Handles clause for the **Exit** and **About** menu items.
3. Add a timer component; set the Interval property and include the following statement in the timer's Tick event procedure and the Form_Load event procedure.

```
currentTimeToolStripStatusLabel.Text = Now.ToLongTimeString()
```

▶ Feedback 14.3

1.
```
appointmentDateTime = appointmentDateTimePicker.Value
```
2. Hour; Millisecond; Minute; Second; Month; Day; Year; Now
3. All of the above properties are available for the Now property.

B

Methods and Functions for Working with Dates, Financial Calculations, Mathematics, and String Operations

Visual Basic and the .NET Framework include many functions and methods that you can use in your projects. This appendix introduces some functions and methods for handling dates, for performing financial calculations and mathematical operations, for converting between data types, and for performing string operations.

Working with Dates

Chapter 14 has a section introducing dates and the Calendar control. You can use the date functions and the methods of the DateTime structure to retrieve the system date, break down a date into component parts, test whether the contents of a field are compatible with the Date data type, and convert other data types to a Date.

The DateTime Structure

When you declare a variable of Date data type in VB, the .NET Common Language Runtime uses the DateTime structure, which has an extensive list of properties and methods. You can use the shared members of the DateTime structure (identified by a yellow *S* in the MSDN Help lists) without declaring an instance of Date or DateTime. For example, to use the Now property:

```
todayDateTime = Now
```

Following is a partial list of some useful properties and methods of the DateTime structure:

Property or Method	Purpose
Add	Add the specified number to an instance of a date/time. Variations include `AddDays`, `AddHours`, `AddMilliseconds`, `AddMinutes`, `AddMonths`, `AddSeconds`, `AddTicks`, and `AddYears`.
Date	Date component.
Day	Integer day of month; 1-31
DayOfWeek	Integer day; Enum expression for each day in the form of DayOfWeek.Sunday.
DayOfYear	Integer day; 1-366
Hour	Integer hour; 0-23
Minute	Integer minutes; 0-59
Second	Integer seconds; 0-59
Month	Integer month; 1 = January.
Now	Retrieve system date and time.

Property or Method	Purpose
Subtract	Finds the difference between date/time values; returns a TimeSpan object.
Today	Retrieve system date.
Year	Year component.
ToLongDateString	Date formatted as long date. (U.S. default: Wednesday, May 04, 2005)
ToLongTimeString	Date formatted as long time. (U.S. default: 12:00:00 AM)
ToShortDateString	Date formatted as short date. (U.S. default: 5/4/2005)
ToShortTimeString	Date formatted as short time. (U.S. default: 12:00 AM)

Retrieving the System Date and Time

You can retrieve the system date and time from your computer's clock using the Now property or the Today property. Now retrieves both the date and time; Today retrieves only the date.

Examples

```
Dim dateAndTimeDate As Date
dateAndTimeDate = Now

Dim todaysDate As Date = Today
```

To display the values formatted:

```
Me.dateAndTimeTextBox.Text = dateAndTimeDate.ToLongDateString()
Me.dateTextBox.Text = todaysDate.ToShortDateString()
Me.nowTextBox.Text = Now.ToShortDateString()
```

In addition to the date formatting methods, you also can format dates and times with the ToString method by using an appropriate format specifier. The table below lists some of the format specifiers. See "Date and Time Format Strings" in MSDN for a complete list. The actual format depends on the local format for the system.

Format Specifier	Description	Example for U.S. Default Setting
d	Short date pattern	5/5/2005
D	Long date pattern	Thursday, May 5, 2005
t	Short time pattern	12:00 AM
T	Long time pattern	12:00:00 AM
f	Full date/time (short)	Thursday, May 05, 2005 12:00 AM
F	Full date/time (long)	Thursday, May 05, 2005 12:00:00 AM

Examples of formatting using `ToString`:

```
Me.dateAndTimeTextBox.Text = dateAndTimeDate.ToString("D")
Me.todayTextBox.Text = Today.ToString("d")
```

User-Defined Date Formatting

VB .NET provides format characters that you can use to create custom formatting for dates. Note that the format characters are case sensitive.

Character	Purpose
/	Separator; the actual character to print is determined by the date separator specified for your locale.
d	Day; displays without a leading zero.
dd	Day; displays with a leading zero.
ddd	Day; uses a three letter abbreviation for the day, such as Mon for Monday.
dddd	Day; spelled out, such as Monday.
M	Month; displays without a leading zero.
MM	Month; displays with a leading zero.
MMM	Month; uses a three letter abbreviation for the month name, such as Jan for January.
MMMM	Month; spelled out, such as January.
y	Year; displays as two characters without a leading zero.
yy	Year; displays as two characters with a leading zero.
yyy *or* yyyy	Year; displays as four characters.

Examples using January 1, 2005:

Format	Result
M/d/yy	1/1/05
MM/dd/yy	01/01/05
MMMM d, yyyy	January 1, 2005

Date Variables

The Date data type may hold values of many forms that represent a date. Examples could be May 25, 2005, 5/25/05, or 5-25-2005. When you assign a literal value to a Date variable, enclose it in # signs:

```
Dim aDate As Date
aDate = #5/25/2005#
```

Converting Values to a Date Format

If you want to store values in a Date data type, you need to convert the value to a Date type. The `Date.Parse` method and the `Convert.ToDateTime` method convert a value to Date type but throw an exception if they are unable to create a valid date from the argument. Use a `Try` block to make sure you have a valid date value and catch the exception.

```
Try
  aDate = Date.Parse(Me.dateTextBox.Text)
Catch
  MessageBox.Show("Invalid date.")
End Try
```

Finding the Difference Between Dates

You can use the `Subtract` method to find the difference between two Date objects. The result is in the format of days, hours, minutes, and seconds. Perhaps you only want the number of days between two dates. The .NET Framework includes the TimeSpan class that stores the time differences with the properties that you need.

```
Dim enteredDate As Date

With Me
  enteredDate = Date.Parse(.dateTextBox.Text)
  Dim daysTimeSpan As TimeSpan = enteredDate.Subtract(Today)
  .dateDifferenceTextBox.Text = daysTimeSpan.Days.ToString()
End With
```

The user enters a date into a text box. That Date object uses its `Subtract` method to compare to today's date.

A similar `Add` method allows you to set a date at a specified time in the future.

```
Dim nextWeekDate As Date

' Add methods require Double arguments.
nextWeekDate = Today.AddDays(7D)
Me.nextWeekTextBox.Text = "Next week is: " & nextWeekDate.ToString("D")
```

Checking for the Day of the Week

Sometimes a program may need to check for the day of the week. Maybe you have a set day for a meeting or perhaps the rates differ on weekends compared to weekdays.

```
If enteredDate.DayOfWeek = DayOfWeek.Saturday Or _
  enteredDate.DayOfWeek = DayOfWeek.Sunday Then
  weekendCheckBox.Checked = True
Else
  weekendCheckBox.Checked = False
End If
```

Financial Functions

Visual Basic provides functions for many types of financial and accounting calculations, such as payment amount, depreciation, future value, and present value. When you use these functions, you eliminate the need to know and code the actual formulas yourself. Each financial function returns a value that you can assign to a variable, or to a property of a control. The functions belong to the Microsoft.VisualBasic the Financial module of namespace.

Category	Purpose	Function
Depreciation	Double-declining balance.	DDB
	Straight line.	SLN
	Sum-of-the-years' digits.	SYD
Payments	Payment.	Pmt
	Interest payment.	IPmt
	Principal payment.	PPmt
Return	Internal rate of return.	IRR
	Rate of return when payments and receipts are at different rates.	MIRR
Rate	Interest rate.	Rate
Future value	Future value of an annuity.	FV
Present value	Present value.	PV
	Present value when values are not constant.	NPV
Number of periods	Number of periods for an annuity. (Number of payments)	NPer

You must supply each function with the necessary arguments. You specify the name of the function, followed by parentheses that enclose the arguments.

IntelliSense helps you type the arguments of functions. When you type the parentheses, the arguments appear in order. The one to be entered next is in bold. The order of the arguments is important because the function uses the values in the formula based on their position in the argument list. For example, the following Pmt function has three arguments: the interest rate, the number of periods, and the amount of the loan. If you supply the values in a different order, the Pmt function will calculate with the wrong numbers.

The Pmt Function

You can use the Pmt function to find the amount of each payment on a loan if the interest rate, the number of periods, and the amount borrowed are known.

The Pmt Function—General Form

```
Pmt(InterestRatePerPeriod, NumberOfPeriods, AmountOfLoan)
```

The interest rate must be specified as Double and adjusted to the interest rate per period. For example, if the loan is made with an annual rate of 12 percent and monthly payments, the interest rate must be converted to the monthly rate of 1 percent. Convert the annual rate to the monthly rate by dividing by the number of months in a year (AnnualPercentageRate / 12).

The number of periods for the loan is the total number of payments. If you want to know the monthly payment for a five-year loan, you must convert the number of years to the number of months. Multiply the number of years by 12 months per year (NumberOfYears * 12).

The Pmt function requires Double arguments and returns a Double value.

The Pmt Function—Example

```
With Me
   Try
      monthlyRateDouble = Double.Parse(.rateTextBox.Text) / 12
      monthsDouble = Double.Parse(.yearsTextBox.Text) * 12
      amountDouble = Double.Parse(.amountTextBox.Text)
      monthlyPaymentDouble = -Pmt(monthlyRateDouble, monthsDouble, amountDouble)
      .monthlyPaymentTextBox.Text = monthlyPaymentDouble.ToString()
   Catch
      MessageBox.Show("Invalid data.")
   End Try
End With
```

Notice in the example that the fields used in the payment function are from text boxes that the user can enter, and the answer is displayed formatted in a text box.

Also notice the minus sign when using the Pmt function. When an amount is borrowed or payments made, that is considered a negative amount. You need the minus sign to reverse the sign and make a positive answer.

The Rate Function

You can use the Rate function to determine the interest rate per period when the number of periods, the payment per period, and the original amount of the loan are known.

The Rate Function—General Form

```
Rate(NumberOfPeriods, PaymentPerPeriod, LoanAmount)
```

The Rate function requires Double arguments and returns a Double value.

The Rate Function—Example

```
With Me
   Try
      monthsDouble = Double.Parse(.yearsTextBox.Text) * 12
      paymentDouble = Double.Parse(.paymentTextBox.Text)
      amountDouble = Double.Parse(.loanAmountTextBox.Text)
      periodicRateDouble = Rate(monthsDouble, -paymentDouble, amountDouble)
      annualRateDouble = periodicRateDouble * 12
      .yearlyRateTextBox.Text = annualRateDouble.ToString("P")
   Catch
      MessageBox.Show("Invalid data.")
   End Try
End With
```

Notice that the `Rate` function, like the `Pmt` function, needs a minus sign for the payment amount to produce a positive result.

Functions to Calculate Depreciation

If you need to calculate the depreciation of an asset in a business, Visual Basic provides three functions: the double-declining-balance method (DDB), the straight-line method (SLN), and the sum-of-the-years' digits (SYD) method.

The `DDB` function calculates the depreciation for a specific period within the life of the asset, using the double-declining-balance method formula. Once again, you do not need to know the formula but only in what order to enter the arguments. Incidentally, the salvage value is the value of the item when it is worn out.

The DDB (Double-Declining-Balance) Function—General Form

```
DDB(OriginalCost, SalvageValue, LifeOfTheAsset, Period)
```

The `DDB` function returns a Double value and requires Double arguments.

The DDB Function—Example

```
costDouble = Double.Parse(Me.costTextBox.Text)
salvageDouble = Double.Parse(Me.salvageTextBox.Text)
yearsDouble = Double.Parse(Me.yearsTextBox.Text)
periodDouble = Double.Parse(Me.periodTextBox.Text)
Me.depreciationTextBox.Text = DDB(costDouble, salvageDouble, yearsDouble, _
   periodDouble).ToString("C")
```

The other financial functions work in a similar manner. You can use Help to find the argument list, an explanation, and an example.

Mathematical Functions

In Visual Studio .NET, the mathematical functions are included as methods in the System.Math class. To use the methods, you must either import System.Math or refer to each method with the Math namespace.

For example, to use the `Abs` (absolute value) method, you can use either of these techniques:

```
answerDouble = Math.Abs(argumentDouble)
```

or

```
' At the top of the file.
Imports System.Math

' In a procedure.
answerDouble = Abs(argumentDouble)
```

A few functions are not methods of the Math class but are Visual Basic functions. These functions, such as `Fix` and `Int`, cannot specify the Math namespace.

A good way to see the list of math functions is to type "Math." in the Editor; IntelliSense will pop up with the complete list. The following table presents a partial list of the Math methods:

Method	Returns	Argument Data Type	Return Data Type
`Abs(x)`	The absolute value of x. $\|x\| = x$ if $x \geq 0$ $\|x\| = -x$ if $x \leq 0$	Overloaded: All numeric types allowed.	Return matches argument type.
`Atan(x)`	The angle in radians whose tangent is x.	Double	Double
`Cos(x)`	The cosine of x where x is in radians.	Double	Double
`Exp(x)`	The value of e raised to the power of x.	Double	Double
`Log(x)`	The natural logarithm of x, where $x \geq 0$.	Double	Double
`Max(x1, x2)`	The larger of the two arguments.	Overloaded: All types allowed. Both arguments must be the same type.	Return matches argument type.
`Min(x1, x2)`	The smaller of the two arguments.	Overloaded: All types allowed. Both arguments must be the same type.	Return matches argument type.
`Pow(x1, x2)`	The value of $x1$ raised to the power of $x2$.	Double	Double
`Round(x)` `Round(x, DecimalPlaces)`	The rounded value of x, rounded to the specified number of decimal positions. *Note*: .5 rounds to the nearest even number.	Overloaded: Double or Decimal; Integer DecimalPlaces	Return matches argument type.
`Sign(x)`	The sign of x. -1 if $x < 0$ 0 if $x = 0$ 1 if $x > 0$	Overloaded: All numeric types allowed	Return matches argument type.
`Sin(x)`	The sine of x where x is in radians.	Double	Double
`Sqrt(x)`	The square root of x where x must be ≥ 0.	Double	Double
`Tan(x)`	The tangent of x where x is in radians.	Double	Double

Here are some useful VB mathematical functions:

Function	Returns	Argument Data Type	Return Data Type
Fix(x)	The integer portion of *x* (truncated).	Any numeric expression.	Integer
Int(x)	The largest integer ≤ *x*.	Any numeric expression.	Integer
Rnd()	A random number in the range 0-1 (exclusive).		Single

Working with Strings

Visual Basic provides many methods for working with text strings. Although several of the methods are covered in this text, many more are available.

Strings in Visual Studio are **immutable**, which means that once a string is created, it cannot be changed. Although many programs in this text seem to modify a string, actually a new string is created and the old string is discarded.

For string handling, you can use any of the many methods of the String class. You also can use the StringBuilder class, which is more efficient if you are building or extensively modifying strings, since the string *can* be changed in memory. In other words, a StringBuilder is *mutable* (changeable) and a String is *immutable*.

Following is a partial list of the properties and methods in the String class. For shared methods, you don't need to specify a String instance; for nonshared methods, you must attach the method to the String instance. Examples of shared methods and nonshared methods follow:

Shared Method

```
If Compare(aString, bString) > 0 Then
      ' Code to execute if true.
```

Nonshared Method

```
If aString.EndsWith("ed") Then
      ' Code to execute if true.
```

Method	Returns

Compare(*aString*, *bString*)
(Shared)
	Integer:
	    Negative if *aString* < *bString*
	    Zero if *aString* = *bString*
	    Positive if *aString* > *bString*

Method	Returns

Compare(*aString*, *bString*, *ignoreCaseBoolean*) (Shared)	Case insensitive if *ignoreCaseBoolean* is True. Integer:
	    Negative if *aString* < *bString*
	    Zero if *aString* = *bString*
	    Positive if *aString* > *bString*

Compare(*aString*, *startAString*, *bString*, *startBString*, *lengthInteger*) (Shared)	Compare substrings; start position indicates beginning character to compare for a length of *lengthInteger*. Integer:
	    Negative if *aString* < *bString*
	    Zero if *aString* = *bString*
	    Positive if *aString* > *bString*

Compare(*aString*, *startAString*, *bString*, *startBString*, *lengthInteger*, *ignoreCaseBoolean*) (Shared)	Case insensitive if *ignoreCaseBoolean* is True. Compare substrings; start position indicates beginning character to compare for a length of *lengthInteger*. Integer:
	    Negative if *aString* < *bString*
	    Zero if *aString* = *bString*
	    Positive if *aString* > *bString*

EndsWith(*anyString*)	Boolean. True if the String instance ends with anyString. Case sensitive.
Equals(*anyString*)	Boolean. True if the String instance has the same value as *anyString*. Case sensitive.

IndexOf(*anyString*)	Integer. Index position in String instance that *anyString* is found.
	    Positive: String found at this position.
	    Negative: String not found.

IndexOf(*anyString*, *startPositionInteger*)	Integer. Index position in String instance that *anyString* is found, starting at *startPositionInteger*.
	    Positive: String found at this position.
	    Negative: String not found.

IndexOf(*anyString*, *startPositionInteger*, *numberCharactersInteger*)	Integer. Index position in String instance that *anyString* is found, starting at *startPositionInteger*, for a length of *numberCharactersInteger*.
	    Positive: String found at this position.
	    Negative: String not found.

Insert(*startIndexInteger*, *anyString*)	New string with *anyString* inserted in the String instance, beginning at *startIndexInteger*.
LastIndexOf(*anyString*)	Integer. Index position of *anyString* within String instance, searching from the right end.
LastIndexOf(*anyString*, *startPositionInteger*)	Integer. Index position of *anyString* within String instance, searching leftward, beginning at *startPositionInteger*.
LastIndexOf(*aString*, *startPositionInteger*, *numberCharactersInteger*)	Integer. Index position of *aString* within String instance, searching leftward, beginning at *startPositionInteger*, for a length of *numberCharactersInteger*.
PadLeft(*totalLengthInteger*)	New String with String instance right justified; padded on left with spaces for a total length of *totalLengthInteger*.

Method	Returns
PadLeft(*totalLengthInteger, padCharacter*)	New String with String instance right justified; padded on left with the specified character for a total length of *totalLengthInteger*.
PadRight(*totalLengthInteger*)	New String with String instance left justified; padded on right with spaces for a total length of *totalLengthInteger*.
PadRight(*totalLengthInteger, padCharacter*)	New String with String instance left justified; padded on right with the specified character for a total length of *totalLengthInteger*.
Remove(*startPositionInteger, numberCharactersInteger*)	New String with characters removed from String instance, beginning with *startPositionInteger* for a length of *numberCharactersInteger*.
Replace(*oldValueString, newValueString*)	New String with all occurrences of the old value replaced by the new value.
StartsWith(*anyString*)	Boolean. True if the String instance starts with *anyString*. Case sensitive.
Substring(*startPositionInteger*)	New String that is a substring of String instance; beginning at *startPositionInteger*, including all characters to the right.
Substring(*startPositionInteger, numberCharactersInteger*)	New String; a substring of String instance, beginning at *startPositionInteger* for the specified length.
anyString.ToLower()	New String; the String instance converted to lowercase.
anyString.ToUpper()	New String; the String instance converted to uppercase.
anyString.Trim()	New String; the String instance with all white-space characters removed from the left and right ends.
anyString.TrimEnd()	New String; the String instance with all white-space characters removed from the right end.
anyString.TrimStart()	New String; the String instance with all white-space characters removed from the left end.

Methods for Conversion between Data Types

Each of the following methods converts an expression to the named data type.

Function	Return Type
Convert.ToBoolean(*Expression*)	Boolean
Convert.ToDateTime(*Expression*)	Date
Convert.ToDecimal(*Expression*)	Decimal
Convert.ToDouble(*Expression*)	Double

Function	Return Type
`Convert.ToInt16(`*`Expression`*`)`	Short
`Convert.ToInt32(`*`Expression`*`)`	Integer
`Convert.ToInt64(`*`Expression`*`)`	Long
`Convert.ToSingle(`*`Expression`*`)`	Single
`Convert.ToString(`*`Expression`*`)`	String
`Convert.ToUInt16(`*`Expression`*`)`	Unsigned Short
`Convert.ToUInt32(`*`Expression`*`)`	Unsigned Integer
`Convert.ToUInt64(`*`Expression`*`)`	Unsigned Long

You also can use functions from the Visual Basic namespace for conversion. Note that the `Convert` methods shown above are used in all .NET languages; the following functions are for Visual Basic only.

Function	Return Type
`CBool(`*`Expression`*`)`	Boolean
`CDate(`*`Expression`*`)`	Date
`CDbl(`*`Expression`*`)`	Double
`CDec(`*`Expression`*`)`	Decimal
`CInt(`*`Expression`*`)`	Integer
`CLng(`*`Expression`*`)`	Long
`CObj(`*`Expression`*`)`	Object
`CShort(`*`Expression`*`)`	Short
`CSng(`*`Expression`*`)`	Single
`CStr(`*`Expression`*`)`	String
`CType(`*`Expression`*`, `*`NewType`*`)`	Specified type

Functions for Checking Validity

The Visual Basic namespace also contains functions that you can use to check for validity or type. These functions were used extensively in earlier versions of VB, but the preferred technique is to use the methods in the .NET Framework.

Function	Returns
IsNumeric(*Expression*)	Boolean: True if the expression evaluates as a valid numeric value.
IsDate(*Expression*)	Boolean: True if the expression evaluates as a valid date value.
IsNothing(*ObjectExpression*)	Boolean: True if the object expression currently does not have an instance assigned to it.

Functions for Formatting Output

In Chapter 3 you learned to format data using specifier codes with the ToString method. Visual Basic also has some formatting functions, which are included in the Visual Basic namespace. Using the ToString method, rather than the Visual Basic functions, is the preferred technique for compatibility among .NET languages.

Function	Effect
FormatCurrency(*ExpressionToFormat* [, *NumberOfDecimalPositions* [, *LeadingDigit* [, *UseParenthesesForNegative* [, *GroupingForDigits*]]]])	Format currency for output.
FormatDateTime(*ExpressionToFormat*[, *NamedFormat*])	Format dates and time for output.
FormatNumber(*ExpressionToFormat* [, *NumberOfDecimalPositions* [, *LeadingDigit* [, *UseParenthesesForNegative* [, *GroupingForDigits*]]]])	Format numbers with decimals, rounding as needed.
FormatPercent(*ExpressionToFormat* [, *NumberOfDecimalPositions* [, *LeadingDigit* [, *UseParenthesesForNegative* [, *GroupingForDigits*]]]])	Format percents for output.

C

Tips and Shortcuts for Mastering the Environment

Set Up the Screen for Your Convenience

As you work in the Visual Studio integrated development environment (IDE), you will find many ways to save time. Here are some tips and shortcuts that you can use to become more proficient in using the IDE to design, code, and run your projects.

Close or Hide Extra Windows

Arrange your screen for best advantage. While you are entering and editing code in the Editor window, you don't need the toolbox, the Solution Explorer window, the Properties window, or any other extra windows. You can hide or close the extra windows and quickly and easily redisplay each window when you need it.

Hiding and Displaying Windows

You can use AutoHide on each of the windows in the IDE. Each window except the Document window in the center of the screen has a pushpin icon that you can use to AutoHide the window or "tack" it into place.

You can AutoHide each window separately, or select *Window / Auto Hide All*. In this screen, all extra windows are hidden.

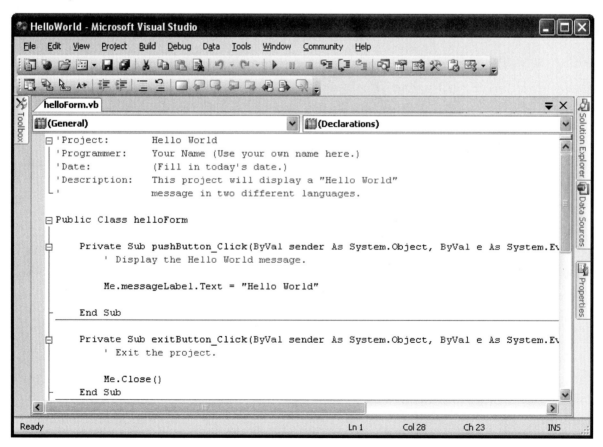

Point to the icon for one of the hidden windows to display it. In the next example, notice the mouse pointer on the *Solution Explorer* icon, which opens the Solution Explorer window temporarily. When you move the mouse pointer out of the window, it hides again.

Mouse pointer

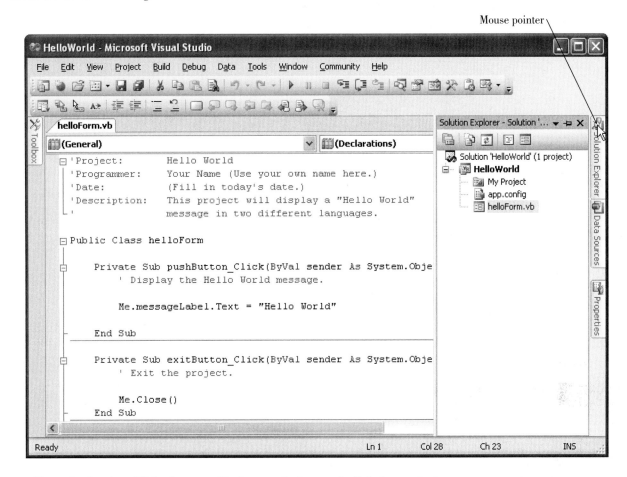

To undo the AutoHide feature, display a window and click its pushpin icon.

Each of the IDE windows that has an AutoHide feature also has a drop-down menu from which you can choose to float, dock, AutoHide, hide, or make into a tabbed window. The tabbed window option is interesting: It makes the window tabbed in the center Document window.

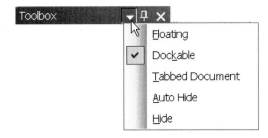

Closing Windows

You can close any window by clicking its Close button. You also can close any extra tabs in the Document window; click on the Close button to the right of the tabs to close the active document.

Displaying Windows

You can quickly and easily open each window when you need it. Each window is listed on the *View* menu, or use the buttons on the Standard toolbar.

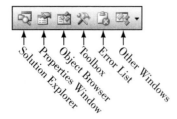

Display Windows Using Keyboard Shortcuts

Solution Explorer window	Ctrl + Alt + L
Properties window	F4
Toolbox	Ctrl + Alt + X

Switch between Documents

When you have several tabs open in the Document window, you can switch by clicking on their tabs or use keyboard shortcuts.

To switch from a form's Editor window to a form's Design View and back again	F7
Cycle through open document tabs	Ctrl + F6
Cycle through all open windows	Ctrl + Tab

Visual Studio displays only as many tabs as fit in the current size of the document window. If you have more documents open than displayed tabs, you can use the new drop-down list of open documents.

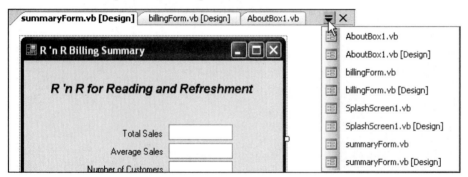

Use the Full Screen

When you are designing a form or editing code, you can work in full-screen mode. This gives you maximum screen space by getting rid of all extra windows. Unfortunately, it also hides all toolbars (the Text Editor toolbar can be a great timesaver while editing code). Select *View / Full Screen* to display in full-screen mode. A small *Full Screen* button appears, which you can use to switch back to regular display. You also can press Shift + Alt + Enter or select *View / Full Screen* a second time to toggle back. If you want to display the Text Editor toolbar while in full-screen mode, select *View / Toolbars / Text Editor*.

Modify the Screen Layout

For most operations, the Visual Studio Tabbed Document window layout works very well and is an improvement over the older VB 6 environment. However, if you prefer, you can switch to MDI (multiple document interface), which is similar to the style used in VB 6. Set this option in the *Tools / Options / Environment / General / Window layout.*

Each of the windows in the IDE is considered either a Tool window or a Document window. The Document windows generally display in the center of the screen with tabs. The rest of the windows—Solution Explorer, Properties window, Task List, Output, Server Explorer, and others—are Tool windows and share many characteristics. You can float each of the Tool windows, tab-dock them in groups, and move and resize individual windows or groups of windows.

Dock Windows Using the Guide Diamonds

Guide diamonds are a new improvement added to VS 2005. When you start dragging a dockable tool window, the diamonds appear to give you visual cues to help dock to the desired location. As you drag toward one of the edges or over the arrow, the corresponding area darkens. To tab-dock a window, you need to make the center of the diamond darken. Experiment!

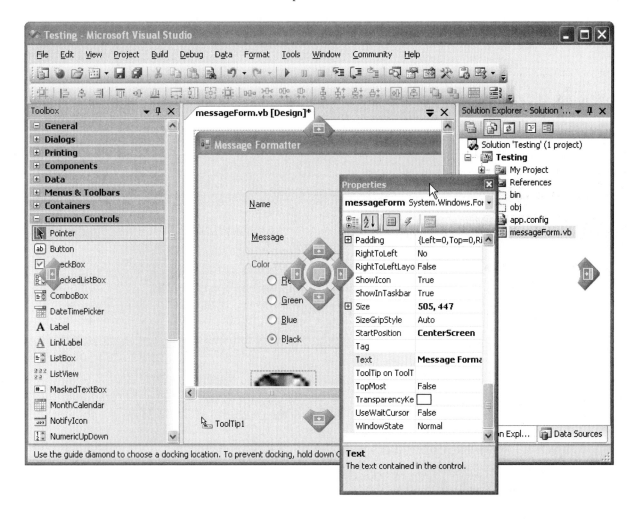

Split the Screen Vertically

You can view the Editor window and the form design at the same time. With at
least two tabs open, select *Window / New Vertical Tab Group*. You may want to
close the extra windows to allow more room for the two large windows.

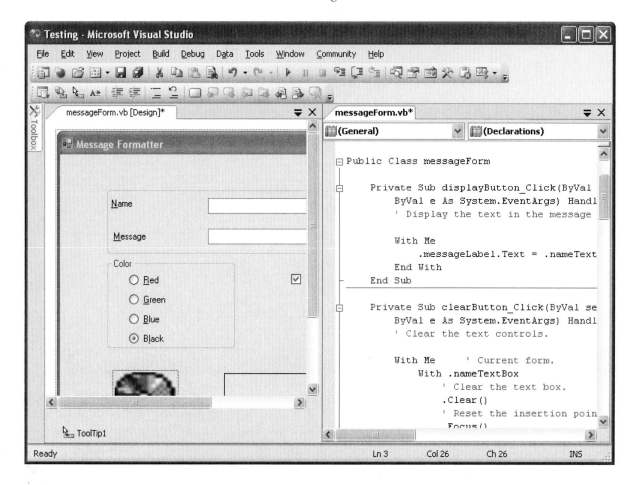

Reset the IDE Layout

To reset the IDE windows to their default locations, select *Window / Reset
Window Layout*.

Set Options for Your Work

You can change many options in the VS IDE. Choose *Tools / Options* to display
the *Options* dialog box. To see all the options that may be changed, make sure
Show all settings is checked. You may want to click on each of the categories to
see the options that you can select.

   Note: If you are working in a shared lab, check with the instructor or lab
technician before changing options.

Projects and Solutions. Set the default folder for your projects. It's best to leave
   the *Build* and *Run* options to automatically save changes but you may prefer
   to have a prompt or save them yourself.

Text Editor. You can set options for all languages or for Basic, which is Visual Basic. The following presume that you first select and expand the entry for *Basic*.

- *General.* Make sure that *Auto list members* is selected and *Hide advanced members* is deselected. You may want to turn on *Word wrap* so that long lines wrap to the next line instead of extending beyond the right edge of the screen.

- *Tabs.* Choose *Smart* indenting; *Tab size* and *Indent size* should both be set to 4.

- *VB Specific.* All options should be selected.

Use Shortcuts in the Form Designer

You can save time while creating the user interface in the Form Designer by using shortcuts.

Use the Layout Toolbar

The Layout toolbar is great for working with multiple controls. You must have more than one control selected to enable many of the buttons. The same options are available from the *Format* menu.

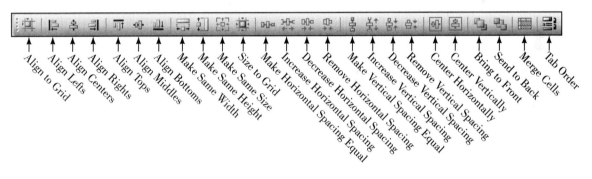

Nudge Controls into Place

Sometimes it is difficult to place controls exactly where you want them. Of course, you can use the alignment options of the *Format* menu or the Layout toolbar. You also can nudge controls in any direction by selecting them and pressing one of the arrow keys. Nudging moves a control one pixel in the direction you specify. For example, the right arrow key moves a selected control one pixel to the right. You can also use Ctrl + an arrow key to align a control to the snap line of a nearby control.

Use Snap Lines to Help Align Controls

As you create or move controls on a form, snap lines pop up to help you align the controls. This new-to-2005 feature is a great help in creating professional-looking forms. Blue snap lines appear to align tops, bottoms, lefts, or rights of controls.

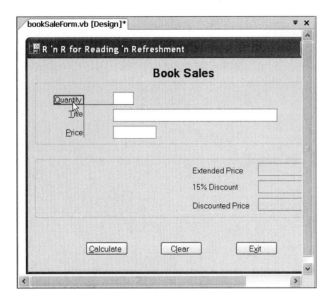

When you see a red line toward the lower edge of controls, that means that the baselines of the text within the controls are aligned.

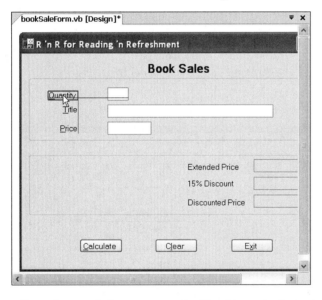

The snap lines also can help you to standardize the vertical spacing between controls. As you drag a control up or down near another control, a small dotted line appears to indicate that the controls are the recommended distance apart.

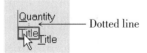

Use Shortcuts in the Editor

Several features of the Editor can save you time while editing code. These are summarized in the following sections.

Use the Text Editor Toolbar

By default the Text Editor toolbar displays when the Editor window is open.

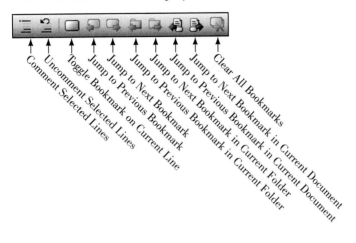

You can save yourself considerable time and trouble if you become familiar with and use some of these shortcuts.

- *Comment Selected Lines.* Use this command when you want to convert some code to comments, especially while you are testing and debugging projects. You can remove some lines from execution to test the effect without actually removing them. Select the lines and click the *Comment Selected Lines* button (or type Ctrl + K, Ctrl + C); each line will have an apostrophe appended at the left end.

- *Uncomment Selected Lines.* This command undoes the *Comment Selected Lines* command. Select some comment lines and click the button (or press Ctrl + K, Ctrl + U); the apostrophes at the beginning of the lines are deleted.

- *Toggle Bookmark on Current Line.* This button sets and unsets individual bookmarks. Bookmarks are useful when you are jumping around in the Editor window. Set a bookmark on any line by clicking in the line and clicking the *Toggle Bookmark* button (or type Ctrl + K, T); you will see a mark in the gray margin area to the left of the marked line. You may want to set bookmarks in several procedures where you are editing and testing code.

- *Jump to Next Bookmark* (Ctrl + K, N) and *Jump to Previous Bookmark* (Ctrl + K, P). Use these buttons to quickly jump to the next or previous bookmark in the code.

- *Clear All Bookmarks.* You can clear individual bookmarks with the *Toggle Bookmark* button or clear all bookmarks (Ctrl + K, Ctrl + L) using this button.

Use Keyboard Shortcuts When Editing Code

While you are editing code, save yourself time by using keyboard shortcuts. Note that these shortcuts are based on the default Visual Basic keyboard mapping. See *Tools / Options* and select *Show all settings*. Then select *Environment / Keyboard / Keyboard mapping scheme*. Drop down the list and select *(Default)*.

Task	Shortcut
Delete from the insertion point left to the beginning of the word.	Ctrl + Backspace
Delete from the insertion point right to the end of the word.	Ctrl + Delete
Complete the word.	Ctrl + Spacebar *or* Alt + right arrow
Jump to a procedure (insertion point on procedure name). Use this shortcut while working on the sub procedures and functions that you write. For example, when writing a call to a function, you might want to check the coding in the function. Point to the procedure name in the `Call` and press F12. If you want to return to the original position, set a bookmark before the jump.	F12
Jump to the top of the current code file.	Ctrl + Home
Jump to the bottom of the current file.	Ctrl + End
View the form's Designer window / Return to the Editor window.	F7

You will find that most of the editing and selecting keyboard shortcuts for Microsoft Word also work in the Editor window.

Split the Editor Window

You can view more than one section of code at a time by splitting the Editor window. Point to the Split bar at the top of the vertical scroll bar and drag the bar down to the desired location. To remove the split, you can either drag the split bar back to the top or double-click the split bar.

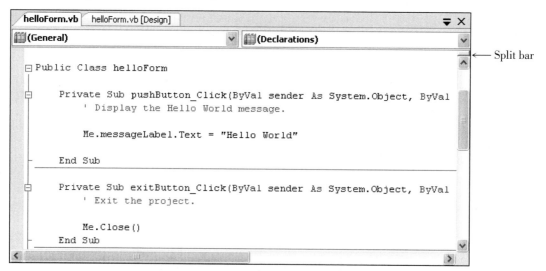

Use Drag-and-Drop Editing

You can use drag-and-drop to move or copy text to another location in the Editor window or to another project. To move code, select the text, point to the selection, and drag it to a new location. You can copy text (rather than move it) by holding down the Ctrl key as you drag.

Drag Commonly Used Code to the Toolbox

When you have some lines of code that you use frequently, you can select the text and drag it to the toolbox. Then when you need to insert the code, drag it from the toolbox to the Editor window. The text appears in the toolbox when the Editor window is open but not when a form is in design mode.

Caution: This shortcut should not be used on shared computers in a classroom or lab, as the text remains in the toolbox. Use it only on your own computer. You can delete previously stored text from the toolbox by right-clicking and selecting *Delete* from the context menu.

Rename Variables and Objects

Automatic renaming is a new feature of VB .NET 2005. In the editor window, right-click on a variable name or an object name and select *Rename*. In the *Rename* dialog box, you can enter the new name and the item is renamed everywhere in that form. For a multiform project, the *Rename* dialog box offers the choice of renaming in only the current form or all forms. This feature, called *Symbol Rename*, is part of a more robust feature called **refactoring**, which is available in some of the .NET languages. Refactoring allows the programmer to modify the name and class of variables and objects.

Use Context-Sensitive Help

The quickest way to get Help is to use context-sensitive Help. Click on a control or a line of code and press F1; Help displays the closest matching item it can locate. You also can get help on the IDE elements: Click in any area of the IDE and press Shift + F1; the Help explanation will be about using the current window or IDE element, rather than about the objects and language.

Copy and Move Projects

In a programming class, you often must move projects from one computer to another and must base one project on another one. To create a new project based on a previous one, you should copy the project folder. Then you can move and rename it as necessary.

Copy and Move a Project

You can copy an entire project folder from one location to another using My Computer. Make sure that the project is not open in Visual Studio and copy the entire folder.

To base one project on a previous project, take the following steps:

- Make sure the project is not open. *Note*: This is *extremely* important.

- Copy the folder to a new location using My Computer.

- Rename the new folder for the new project name, still using My Computer.

- Open the new project (the copy) in the Visual Studio IDE.

- In the IDE's Solution Explorer, rename the solution and the project. The best way to do this is to right-click on the name and choose the *Rename* command from the shortcut menu.

- Rename the forms, if desired. If you rename the startup form, you must open the Project Designer (*Project / ProjectName Properties* or double-click on *My Project* in the Solution Explorer) and set the Startup Object.

- Open the Project Designer and change the root namespace and the assembly name to match your new project name.

Warning: Do not try to copy a project that is open using the *Save As* command, attempting to place a copy in a new location. The original solution and project files are modified and you won't be able to open the original project.

Deploy Applications

When you are ready to distribute your programs to other computers, you use a process called **deployment**. Although VS contains full features for deploying application, VS 2005 introduces a new way to publish a project called **click-once deployment**.

On the *Build* menu you can find an item titled *Publish SolutionName*. Selecting the Publish option launches the Publish Wizard, which gives you the option of specifying a file path, a Web site, or an FTP server. Media options for distribution are CD-ROM or DVD, file share (network), or the Web. You also can have the program check for updates online.

If you deploy to a folder on your system, you will find a Setup.exe application inside of the folder. Try copying the folder to a CD and then install your program on another machine.

.NET Security

As a programmer, you must be aware of many aspects of security. You must not allow any unauthorized access to programs or data, but you must be able to access all needed resources while you are developing applications. For both sides of the security issue you need a basic understanding of security topics.

The .NET Framework includes many features for implementing security. And as time passes and hackers and virus writers discover ways to circumvent the security, Microsoft is forced to tighten security. Because of this fact, you may sometimes find that programs or procedures that worked previously no longer work after you apply updates to Windows, which include updates to the .NET Framework and CLR.

For programmers security means **information assurance**. The .NET Framework provides many object-oriented features to assist in the process. The topic of security can fill multiple books and courses; this appendix is intended as an overview for introductory programmers.

Authentication and Authorization

The two topics of authentication and authorization are frequently lumped together because they are so closely related. **Authentication** determines who the user is and **authorization** decides if the user has the proper authority to access information.

Authentication is based on credentials. When you are working with a Windows application, you only need to be concerned with Windows authentication. However, if your application is Web Forms–based (ASP.NET), authentication might be IIS Authentication, Forms-based (not recommended; it is an HTML request for credentials) or it might use Microsoft Passport, which is a centralized profile service for member sites. It is also possible to create a custom authentication method or use none at all. The settings in the Web.Config file determine the method of authentication.

The following is an excerpt from the automatically generated Web.Config file for an ASP.NET application:

```
<!-
  The <authentication> section enables configuration of the security authentication
  mode used by ASP.NET to identify an incoming user.
  ->
  <authentication mode="Windows" />
```

For no authentication, you can change the last line in the Web.Config file above to

```
<authentication mode = "None" />
```

IIS Authentication

Chapter 9 introduces database access from a Web page. A Web Form can be run using the new Visual Studio Web server or IIS (Internet Information Server). The Visual Studio Web server is designed to simplify development, but most production jobs will use IIS.

When IIS is installed, the Setup creates a user account for anonymous access. The username is IUSR_*computername*. For example, if the machine is called SteveL, the username is IUSR_SteveL. This same anonymous-logon user is then used for all IIS services installed on the computer. The password for the account is randomly generated. The following dialog can be displayed by going to the *Control Panel / Administrative Tools / Computer Management* and then expanding the Local Users and Groups and double-clicking the user name.

The *Authentication Methods* dialog is accessed through IIS. From a project's properties dialog, select the *Directory Security* tab and then click on the *Edit* button under *Anonymous access and authentication control*.

Anonymous access uses the anonymous user account. If you remove the check mark for anonymous access, you allow Windows to perform the authentication.

Another authentication method is Basic authentication. This requires a Windows username and password. As you can see in the *Authentication Methods* dialog, this technique sends the password in clear text.

The Digest authentication, available on Windows domain servers, encrypts the password before it is sent across a network.

The final check box is the Windows integrated authentication, which requires users to run Internet Explorer 3.1 or later.

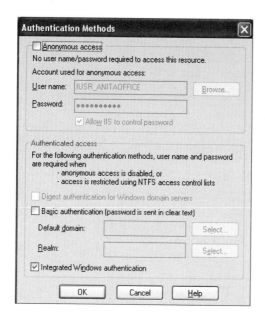

For more information, see Microsoft Knowledge Base at http://support.microsoft.com.

Authorization and Impersonation

After the user is authenticated, another step checks for authorization. If ASP.NET does not use impersonation, the ASP.NET user, which is created when the Framework is installed, runs without any privileges. If impersonation is turned on, ASP.NET takes on the identity from IIS. If anonymous access is turned off, ASP.NET takes on the credentials of the authenticated user; otherwise it impersonates the account that IIS uses.

This is where the following code applies:

```
<identity impersonate = "true"/>
```

For a specific user you can use

```
<identity impersonate = "true" name = "Domain/username" password = "password"/>
```

This is default authorization section in the Web.Config file:

```
<!—
   The <authentication> section enables configuration of the security authentication
   mode used by ASP.NET to identify an incoming user.
   —>
   <authentication mode="Windows" />
```

Writing Secure Code

Programmers need to be aware of how hackers are able to gain access to a database or a network through code. Two primary areas of importance are string injections and error messages that may give away important information about a data source.

SQL Injection

Proper validation of the code is extremely important. A system vulnerability occurs when code is "injected" into a string. A text box or a combo box control allows the user to type in information. It is the responsibility of the programmer to make sure that the code typed does not contain any scripting code or disruptive characters. When a program is working with a database, there must be no way for the user to inject code into that database.

It is wise to validate the keystrokes to be sure that the input text contains only valid characters.

Error Messages

Another technique that hackers use to find information about a database is to input wrong data hoping that the error message will give significant information. The default error messages indicate the name of the field containing an error. Plan your error messages so that you don't allow someone to determine valid field names or values.

Code Access Security

Basically, code access security determines what code is allowed to do on a computer, specifically what resources, such as hardware or files, the code can access. The settings of the computer ultimately determine if the code can execute or if a resource can be used by the code.

Code access security is based on several Permission classes. The Permission classes are organized into three types: code access, identity, and role-based. Examples of the code access type include the PrintingPermission class and the RegistryPermission class; the SiteIdentityPermission and the URLIdentityPermission classes fall into the identity permission type. The PrincipalPermission class is the role-based type for user credentials.

If your program has an OpenFileDialog component, it may be necessary to request permission to access the files from a given system. The following code would appear at the top of the file:

```
Imports System.Security.Permissions
<Assembly: FileDialogPermissionAttribute(SecurityAction.RequestMinimum, Unrestricted: = True)>
```

Glossary

A

About box   A window that displays information about the program; usually displayed from the *Help/About* menu item.

abstract class   A class that cannot be instantiated but instead is used for inheritance.

abstract method   An empty method declared with the `MustOverride` keyword; must be overriden in the derived class.

AcceptButton property   Form property that sets the default button, which is activated with the Enter key.

access key   Underlined character that allows the user to select using the keyboard rather than the mouse; also called a *hot key*.

access level   Specification of the permission required to access an element. Examples: `Private`, `Public`, `Friend`, and `Protected`.

accessor method   The `Get` and `Set` methods written to allow external objects to access the private properties of a class.

AllowDrop property   A property of a form or control used for a drag-and-drop operation.

ANSI code   A coding method used to represent characters on a microcomputer (American National Standards Institute).

Application.StartupPath   The folder from which the application begins execution. In a VB program running from the VS IDE, the project's bin\Debug folder.

argument   The expression to operate upon in a function or method. A value being passed to or from a procedure.

array   A series of variables; each individual element can be referenced by its index position. Also called a *list*.

assignment operator   An equal sign (=); assigns a value to the variable or property named on the left side of the sign.

assignment statement   Assigns a value to a variable or property using an assignment operator.

authentication   The policies used to determine who the user is; may be Windows-based, forms-based, Passport-based, or none (no authentication performed).

authorization   Determination of the rights allowed for a particular user. For ASP.NET applications, can allow access from any user by turning on impersonation.

AutoCorrect   Pop-up suggestions for corrections of misspelled words in the Editor.

Autos window   Window that opens in IDE during execution; automatically displays all variables and control contents that are referenced in the current statement and three statements on either side of the current one.

B

base class   Class that is inherited from; also called a *super class* or *parent class*.

BindingSource   Object that establishes a link to a data source.

block-level variable   A variable declared inside a block of code; only accessible within that block.

BorderStyle property   Property of a control that allows the control to appear flat or three-dimensional.

bound control   A control that automatically displays the contents of database fields.

breakpoint   Indicated point in project code where execution should break; used for debugging.

browser   An application used to render and display HTML code; used to display Web pages; in VB used to execute Web Forms.

Brush object   Graphical object for drawing filled shapes.

Button   Control used to activate a procedure.

ByRef   Declares that an argument passed to a procedure should be passed as the address of the data so that both calling and called procedures have access to the same memory location.

ByVal   Declares that an argument passed to a procedure should be passed as a copy of the data. The calling and called procedures do not have access to each other's variables.

C

Call (procedure call)   Execute a procedure.

callback   An object notifies the program that it needs to do something

607

or that a situation exists that the program needs to handle. The object notifies the program of the situation by firing an event.

camel casing   The naming convention that specifies mixed-case names; the first character must be lowercase and the first character of each word within the name must be uppercase; the rest of the characters must be lowercase.

CancelButton property   Form property that sets the Cancel button, which is activated with the Esc key.

Case structure   Selection structure; can be used in place of an `If` statement.

casting   Converting from one data type to another.

CausesValidation property   Property of a control that forces validation to occur on the control that just lost focus when this control receives the focus.

CharacterCasing property   Property of text boxes that specifies whether input should be left as entered or converted to uppercase or lowercase.

check box   A control used to indicate a value that may be True or False. In any group of check boxes, any number may be selected.

checked   A check mark next to a menu item indicates that the option is currently selected.

Checked property   Determines if a check box is checked or not.

child class   A class inherited from another class, called the *parent*. Also called a *derived class* or *subclass*.

child form   Multiple Document Interface. A child form belongs to a parent form, is displayed inside the parent, and closes when the parent does.

class   A prototype or blueprint for an object; includes specifications for the properties and methods.

clean compile   Code compiles to Common Language Runtime without errors.

click-once deployment   New simplified method of deploying VB applications to another computer. Provides for installation and automatic updates via the Web.

Close method   Closes forms or files; releases resources used by the object.

code   Programming statements in the Basic language.

code separation model   A style of Web Form in which the VB code is in a separate file from the HTML code.

code snippet   Small sample of code that illustrates coding techniques; can be added to a program in the editor.

collection   A series of objects or an object that can contain a series of objects; has properties and methods.

color constant   Values assigned in the Color class. Examples: Color.Red and Color.Blue.

column   A vertical section of a grid control.

ComboBox control   A control that is a combination of a list box and a text box.

common dialog   A set of Windows dialog boxes available to Visual Basic programmers for Open, Save, Fonts, Print, and Color.

comparison operator   See *relational operator*.

component tray   Area across the lower edge of a form designer window; used to store components that are not visible on the form.

compound condition   Multiple conditions combined with the use of the logical operators `And` or `Or`.

concatenation   Joining string (text) fields. The ampersand (&) is used to concatenate text.

condition   An expression that will evaluate True or False. May be a comparison of two values (variables, properties, constants) using relational operators.

constant   A value that cannot change during program execution.

constructor   A procedure that runs automatically when an object is instantiated from that class. In VB, a constructor is coded with `Sub New`.

context menu   A popup menu, sometimes referred to as a *shortcut menu* or a *right-mouse menu*.

context-sensitive Help   Use of the F1 function key to directly access the Help topic related to the code or object containing the cursor.

ContextMenuStrip component   A container control used to create context menus.

control   An object used on a graphical interface, such as a radio button, text box, button, or label.

CType function   Converts from one object type to another; used with a shared event procedure to access the Sender object.

D

data binding   Connecting a control or property to one or more data elements.

data-bound controls   Controls that can be set up to display the data from a database.

Data Designer   A window of the VS IDE that shows a visual representation of the schema of a database; allows modification of the schema.

data file   A file used to store small amounts of information such as the contents of a list box.

data source   The original source of database data; may be a file, a server, or an array or other object.

data type Specifies the type of data a variable or constant can hold, such as Integer, Decimal, or String.

DataGridView control A control used to display database data in a grid format.

dataset A temporary set of data stored in the memory of the computer.

DateTime structure Used to retrieve and format the current date and time.

debug time Temporary break in program execution; used for debugging.

Debug.WriteLine method Statement to write a line in the Debug window; used to write a message for debugging.

debugging Finding and eliminating computer program errors.

declaration Statements to establish a project's variables and constants, give them names, and specify the type of data they will hold.

Declarations section Code outside of a procedure, used to declare module-level variables.

deployment Distribution of a compiled application to another computer; normally done through a setup.exe file. See *click-once deployment*.

derived class A subclass inherited from a base class.

design time The status of the Visual Studio environment while a project is being developed, as opposed to run time or break time.

destructor A method that is called as an object goes out of scope.

DialogResult object Used to check to determine which button the user clicked on a message box.

direct reference Accessing an element of an array by a subscript when the value of the subscript is known.

disabled Enabled property set to False; user can see the control but cannot access it.

Do and Loop statements Statements to indicate the beginning and ending of a loop. A condition can appear on the `Do` or on the `Loop`.

Do/Loop A loop constructed with the `Do` and `Loop` statements.

Document window IDE window that displays the Form Designer, the Code Editor, and the Object Browser.

DoDragDrop method A method to begin a drag-drop operation for a source object.

DragDrop event The event that occurs when the user drags an object and drops it on a form or control that has its AllowDrop property set to True.

DragEnter event The event that occurs when the user drags an object over a form or control that has its AllowDrop property set to True; occurs before the DragDrop event.

DrawLine method Method of the Graphics object.

DrawRectangle method Method of the Graphics object; used to draw squares and rectangles.

DrawString method Method of the Graphics object; sends a line of text to the graphics page

drop-down combo box A combo box control with a down-pointing arrow that allows the user to drop down the list. Allows efficient use of space on a form.

drop-down list A list box with a down-pointing arrow that allows the user to drop down the list. Allows efficient use of space on a form.

E

element Single item within a table, array, list, or grid.

empty string A string that contains no characters; also called a *null string* or *zero-length string*.

Enabled property Determines if the control is available to the user.

encapsulation OOP feature that specifies that all methods and properties of a class be coded within the class. The class can hide or expose the methods and properties, as needed.

End If Terminates a block `If` statement.

entry test A loop that has its test condition at the top. See *pretest*.

ErrorProvider component A component that can display an error icon and message when a validation rule is violated for the specified text box.

event An action that may be caused by the user, such as a click, drag, key press, or scroll. Events also can be triggered by an internal action, such as repainting the form or validating user input.

event procedure A procedure written to execute when an event occurs.

exception An error that occurs at run time.

exit test A loop that has its test condition at the bottom. See *posttest*.

explicit conversion Writing the code to convert from one data type to another; as opposed to *implicit conversion*.

Express Edition A "light" version of Visual Basic. Available for download at msdn.microsoft.com/express.

F

field A group of related characters used to represent one characteristic or attribute of an entity in a data file or database.

field-level validation Checking the validity of input data in each control as it is entered, rather than waiting until the user clicks a button.

file A collection of related records.

FillEllipse method   Method of the Graphics object; used to draw circles and ovals.

focus   The currently selected control on the user interface. For controls such as buttons, the focus appears as a light dotted line. For text boxes, the insertion point (also called the *cursor*) appears inside the box.

Focus method   Sets the focus to a control, which makes it the active control.

For and Next statements   A loop structure; usually used when the number of iterations is known.

For/Next loop   A loop structure; usually used when the number of iterations is known.

For Each and Next   A looping construct for stepping through an array; each element of the array is accessed without the necessity of manipulating subscripts.

ForeColor property   Property that determines the color of the text.

form   An object that acts as a container for the controls in a graphical interface.

Form Designer   The IDE window for creating the user interface.

format   A specification for the way information will be displayed, including dollar signs, percent signs, and the number of decimal positions.

format specifiers   Codes used as arguments for the ToString method; used to make the output easier to read. Can specify dollar signs, commas, decimal positions, percents, and date formats.

FormClosing event   Occurs before a form unloads. A good location to place the code to prompt the users if they wish to save any changes.

Friend   The access level specifier that limits access to the forms in the current project.

FromFile method   Retrieves an image from a file.

function   Performs an action and returns a value.

function procedure   A procedure that returns a value.

G

garbage collection   Automatic deletion of objects from memory after they are out of scope.

general procedure   A procedure not attached to an event; may be a sub procedure or a function procedure.

graphical user interface (GUI)   Program application containing icons, buttons, and menu bars.

graphics   Lines, shapes, and images. An image file assigned to a PictureBox control; methods of the Graphics class, such as DrawString, DrawLine, and DrawEllipse.

group box   A control used as a container for other controls, such as a group of radio buttons.

H

handle   A small square on a selected control at design time; used to resize a control. Also called a *resizing handle*.

Help   The collection of reference pages about programming in VB and using the Visual Studio IDE.

Hide method   Method of a form or a control that makes it invisible but does not unload it from memory.

horizontal scroll bar   A Windows control that provides a scroll bar that appears horizontally on the form.

I

IDE   Integrated development environment. See *Visual Studio environment*.

identifier   A name for a variable, procedure, and named constant; supplied by the programmer.

If...Then...Else   Statement block for testing a condition and taking alternate actions based on the outcome of the test.

Image property   A graphic file with an extension of .bmp, .gif, .jpg, .png, .ico, .emf, or .wmf.

immutable   The inability of a string to be modified once it is created. A new string must be created for any modifications.

implicit conversion   A conversion from one data type to another that occurs automatically or by default according to specified rules.

index   Position within a list or array.

information assurance   Secure programming measure to provide accurate and timely transfer of information.

inheritance   Ability to create a new class based on an existing class.

instance   An object created from a class.

instance property   See *instance variable*.

instance variable   Each object created from the class has a separate occurrence of the variable.

instantiate   Create an object using the New keyword.

integrated development environment (IDE)   Tool for writing projects and solutions; includes an editor, tools, debugger, and other features for faster development.

Interval property   Determines the amount of time until a Timer component fires a Tick event; measured in milliseconds.

intranet   Network within a company.

intrinsic constant   Constant supplied with a language or application such as Color.Blue.

IsMdiContainer property   Used to create a parent form for MDI.

Items property   Collection of elements for a list box or combo box control.

Items.Add method Adds elements to the Items collection of a list box.

Items.Clear method Clears all elements from a list box.

Items.Count property Property that holds the number of elements in a list box.

Items.Insert method Inserts an element in a list for a list box.

Items.Remove method Removes the currently selected item from a list.

Items.RemoveAt method Removes the specified item from a list.

iteration A single pass through the statements in a loop.

K

key field The field (or fields) on which a data file is organized; used to search for a record.

L

Label A control that displays text; cannot be altered by the user.

LargeChange property A property of a scroll bar that determines how far to scroll for a click in the gray area of the scroll bar.

late binding Program elements cannot be determined at compile time, but must be determined at run time. Should be avoided, if possible, for performance reasons.

LayoutMdi method Arranges MDI child windows vertically, horizontally, or cascaded.

lifetime The period of time that a variable exists.

line-continuation character A space and underscore; used in program code to indicate that a Basic statement continues on the next line.

ListBox control A control that holds a list of values; the user cannot add new values at run time.

local The scope of a variable or constant that limits its visibility to the current procedure.

local variable A variable that is declared within a procedure and may be used only in that procedure.

Locals window Window that opens in IDE during execution; displays all objects and variables that are within scope at break time.

logic error An error in a project that does not halt execution but causes erroneous results in the output.

logical operator The operators And, Or, Not, and IsNot; used to construct compound conditions and to reverse the truth of a condition.

loop A control structure that provides for the repetition of statements.

loop index A counter variable used in a For/Next loop.

M

Maximum property Scroll bar property for highest possible value.

MaxLength property Property of text boxes that limits the number of characters the user can enter as input.

MdiWindowListItem property Determines whether the menu will display a list of open MDI child windows; used on the Window menu.

Me A reference to the current object. In a form's code, reference to the current form.

menu A list of choices; the available commands displayed in a menu bar.

Menu Designer Feature of the development environment for creating menus; accessed by adding a Main Menu component to the component tray.

MenuStrip component A control used to create menus for forms.

MessageBox A dialog box that displays a message to the user.

method Predefined actions (procedures) provided with objects.

Minimum property Scroll bar property for lowest possible value.

modal A dialog box that requires a user response before continuing program execution.

modeless A dialog box that does not require a user response before continuing program execution.

module-level variable A variable that can be used in any procedure within the current code module.

MouseDown event The event of a form or control that occurs when the user presses the mouse button.

multiple document interface (MDI) Multiple form project that has parent and child forms.

multitier application A program designed in components or services, where each segment performs part of the necessary actions. Each of the functions of a multitier application can be coded in a separate component and the components may be stored and run on different machines.

MustInherit Modifier on a class definition. The class cannot be instantiated, but instead must be used for inheritance.

MustOverride Modifier on a procedure definition; requires that the procedure be overridden in an inherited class.

N

Name property The property of an object that is used to reference the object in code.

named constant Constant created and named by the developer.

namespace Used to organize a group of classes in the language library; the hierarchy used to locate the class. No two classes may have the same name within a namespace.

namespace-level variable A variable that can be used in any procedure within the current namespace, which is generally the current project.

nested `If` An `If` statement completely contained within another `If` statement.

Nested `Try/Catch` block A `Try/Catch` block completely contained within another `Try/Catch` block.

`New` keyword Used to instantiate an object; creates an object and assigns memory for property values.

NewLine character The Visual Studio constant `ControlChars.NewLine` used to determine line endings.

`Next` method Returns the next in a series of random numbers for an object of the Random class.

`Nothing` An object variable that does not have an instance of an object assigned. Formerly used to destroy an object.

`Now` property Current date and time from the DateTime structure.

O

object An occurrence of a class type that has properties and methods; a specific instance of a control type, form, or other class.

object-oriented programming (OOP) An approach to programming that uses classes to define the properties and methods for objects. Classes may inherit from other classes.

OpenFileDialog Common dialog component used to display the Windows *Open File* dialog box; allows the user to view files and select the file to open.

Option Explicit Setting this option On forces variables and objects to be declared before they can be used.

Option Strict Setting this option On enforces strong data typing.

order of precedence Hierarchy of mathematical operations; the order in which operations are performed.

overloading Allows a method to act differently for different arguments. Multiple procedures in the same class with the same name but with different argument lists.

overriding A method in a derived (inherited) class with the same name and argument list as a method in the parent (base) class. The method in the derived class overrides (supersedes) the one in the parent class for objects of the derived class.

P

parameterized constructor A constructor (`Sub New`) that contains an argument list; as opposed to an empty constructor.

parameterized query A database query that allows a value to be supplied at run time.

parent class The base class for inheritance, also called a *super class*.

parent form MDI container for child forms.

pascal casing The naming convention that specifies mixed-case names; the first character must be uppercase and the first character of each word within the name must be uppercase; the rest of the characters must be lowercase.

Peek method Used to look ahead to determine if records remain in a file stream.

Pen object Graphical object for drawing lines and shapes.

PictureBox control A control used to display an image.

pixel Picture element; a single dot on the screen; a unit of measurement for displaying graphics.

Point structure Holds X and Y coordinates as a single unit.

polymorphism OOP feature that allows methods to take different actions depending on the situation. Methods may have the same name but different argument lists. Also refers to the naming convention of naming methods with similar actions the same in each class.

postback A round-trip to the Web server.

posttest A loop that has its test condition after the body of the loop; the statements within the loop will always be executed at least once; also called an *exit test*.

pretest A loop that has its test condition at the top; the statements inside the loop may never be executed; also called an *entry test*.

Print method A method of the PrintDocument class to begin executing code for printing.

print preview View the printer's output on the screen and then choose to print or cancel.

PrintDocument component Contains methods and events to set up output for the printer.

PrintPage event procedure Contains the logic for printing.

PrintPreviewDialog component Used to allow print previews for an application.

Private Variable or procedure declared with the `Private` keyword; available only inside the current class.

procedure A unit of code; may be a sub procedure, function procedure, or property procedure.

Professional Edition A version of Visual Basic that includes fewer features than the Team System edition but more features than the Standard and Express editions.

Project Designer A window of the IDE used to view and set the project's properties.

project file A text file that contains information about the current project. Displays in the Solution Explorer and can be viewed and edited in a text editor.

Properties window   A window in the IDE used to set values for properties at design time.

property   Characteristic or attribute of an object; control properties may be set at design time or run time depending on the specific property.

property procedure   Procedure written with `Set` and `Get` keywords to pass values to and from private variables in a class.

Protected   Access modifier for a variable or procedure; behaves as private but allows inheritance.

pseudocode   Planning tool for code using an English expression or comment that describes the action.

Public   The access level specifier that allows access from all classes.

R

radio button   A control used to indicate a value that may be True or False (selected or not selected). In any group of radio buttons, only one button may be selected.

Random class   Used to create Random numbers.

ReadLine method   Reads one record from a file; reads to the end of the line.

ReadOnly   A property that can be retrieved but not set by external classes; indicates that only a `Get` method exists for the property.

record   A group of related fields; relates to data files and database tables.

Rectangle structure   Defines a rectangular region, specified by its upper-left corner and its size.

refactoring   Feature of some .NET languages that can automatically change the name and class of variables and objects. VB provides only for renaming variables.

relational operator   Used to compare two fields for greater than >, less than <, or equal to =.

remark   A Basic statement used for documentation; not interpreted by the compiler; also called a *comment*.

resizing handle   See *handle*.

return value   Value returned from a function.

reusability   Code modules that can be used in multiple projects.

row   A horizontal section of a grid control.

run time   During the time a project is executing.

run-time error   An error that occurs as a program executes; causes execution to break.

S

scope   The extent of visibility of a variable or constant. The scope may be namespace, module-level, block, or local.

Scroll event   Scroll bar event that occurs as the user moves the scroll box.

Select Case   Selection structure; can be used in place of an `If` statement.

Select Resource dialog box   A dialog box in which the image and sound files of a project can be added and selected.

SelectedIndex property   Index of the item currently selected in a list box or combo box.

separator bar   A horizontal line used to separate groups of menu commands.

SetBounds method   Set the location of a control; used to move a control.

SetError method   Define the message and turn on the error message for an ErrorProvider control; used for validating input data.

shared property   A property that can be used by all objects of the class; generally used for totals and counts. Only one copy exists for all objects of the class.

shared variable   One variable that can be used by all objects of the class; generally used for totals and counts.

short circuit   Skipping the evaluation of parts of a compound condition that are not required to determine the result.

shortcut menu   The menu that pops up when the right mouse button is clicked. Also called a *popup menu*, *context menu*, or *right-mouse menu*.

Show method   Displays a form or message box. A form displayed with the `Show` method is modeless.

ShowDialog method   Displays a common dialog box or a form; the form is displayed modally.

signature   The argument list of a method or procedure.

simple combo box   Fixed-size combo box.

simple list box   Fixed-size list box.

single document interface (SDI)   Forms act independently in a multiple-form project.

single-file mode   A style of Web Form in which the VB code and HTML are contained in the same file.

Size structure   A size specified by width and height; measured in pixels.

SizeMode property   Allows the size of an image in a picture box to stretch.

SmallChange property   Scroll bar property for amount of move by a click on an arrow.

snap lines   Guidelines that pop up on a form during design time to help align the controls.

snippet   See *code snippet*.

solution   A Visual Basic application; can consist of one or more projects.

Solution Explorer window   An IDE window that holds the filenames for the files included in your project and a list of the classes it references.

solution file   A text file that holds information about the solution and the projects it contains.

Sorted property   Property of a list box and combo box that specifies that the list items should be sorted.

SoundLocation property   The path of the sound file played by the SoundPlayer component.

SoundPlayer component   A component that allows the user to play a sound file.

splash screen   A window that appears before the main application window; generally displays program information and gives the appearance of quicker application loading.

Standard Edition   A version of Visual Basic with fewer features than the Professional and Team System versions.

StartPosition property   Determines the screen location of the first form in a project when execution begins.

startup form   The main form; the first form to display after the splash screen.

stateless   Does not store any information about its contents from one invocation to the next.

Static   A local variable with a lifetime that matches the module. The variable retains its value as long as the form is loaded.

status bar   An area along the lower edge of a window used to display information for the user.

StatusStrip control   A container control that creates a status bar across the lower edge of a form.

Step Into   Debugging command; executes each statement, including those in called procedures.

Step Out   Debugging command; continues rapid execution until the called procedure completes, and then returns to break mode at the statement following the `Call`.

Step Over   Debugging command; executes each statement in the main procedure but does not show statements in called procedures.

stream   An object used to transfer a series of bytes from one location to another.

StreamReader   Object used to input small amounts of information stored in a disk file.

StreamWriter   Object used to write small amounts of information to disk.

StretchImage   Setting for the value of the SizeMode property of a PictureBox control.

string literal   A constant enclosed in quotation marks.

strongly typed   A feature of VB that requires the programmer to always be aware of the data type. If you assign data to a wider type, VB can implicitly (automatically) convert for you; if you are assigning data to a narrower type, where precision or accuracy might be lost, VB will generate a compiler error.

structure   A grouping that combines multiple fields of related data.

sub procedure   A procedure that performs actions but does not return a value.

subclass   A derived class; also called a *child class*.

submenu   A menu within a menu.

subscript   The position of an element within an array; also called an *index*.

subscripted variable   An element of an array.

superclass   A base class for inheritance, also called a *parent class*.

syntax error   An error caused by failure to follow the syntax rules of the language; often caused by typographical errors. The Editor informs you of syntax errors.

System.IO namespace   Holds the stream objects for reading and writing data files.

T

TabIndex property   Determines the order the focus moves as the Tab key is pressed.

table   A two-dimensional array.

table adapter   An object that handles retrieving and updating of the data in a dataset.

table lookup   Logic to find an element within an array.

TabStop property   Determines if a control can receive focus.

Team System   The version of Visual Studio with the most features.

text box   A control for data entry; its value can be entered and changed by the user.

Text property   The value that displays on a control such as the words in a text box or label.

TextAlign property   Used to change the alignment of text within the control.

Tick event   One firing of a Timer component; each time the interval passes, another Tick event occurs.

Timer component   Fires Tick events at a specified time interval.

ToLower method   Converts text to lowercase letters.

toolbar   The bar beneath the menu bar that holds buttons; used as shortcuts for menu commands.

toolbox   A window that holds icons for tools; used to create controls and components on a form.

ToolStrip control A container control that creates a toolbar on a form.

ToolStripStatusLabel object Individual item on a StatusStrip control.

ToolTip Small label that pops up when the mouse pointer pauses over a toolbar button or control.

ToolTip component Placed on a form to allow the individual controls to display ToolTips. A ToolTip property is added to each control.

ToolTip on ToolTip1 property The new property added to each control when a ToolTip component is added to the form.

ToUpper method Converts text to all uppercase.

Try/Catch block Traps user errors or program errors.

U

user interface The display and commands seen by a user; how the user interacts with an application. In Windows, the graphical display of an application containing controls and menus.

Using block A group of statements bounded by Using and End Using; any variables declared inside the block are not available outside the block.

V

validation Checking to verify that appropriate values have been entered.

validator controls Controls that can automatically validate input data; used on Web Forms.

value keyword Incoming value for a Set clause in a property procedure.

Value property Holds the current setting of a scroll bar control.

ValueChanged event Event that occurs when a scroll bar control is scrolled.

variable Memory location that holds data that can be changed during project execution.

vertical scroll bar A Windows control that provides a scroll bar that appears vertically on the form.

Visible property Determines if a control can be seen or not.

visual inheritance Inheritance of the visual elements of a form.

Visual Studio environment The development environment including tools for designing the interface, editing program code, and running and debugging applications; also called the *IDE*.

W

Web Form Form in Visual Studio for creating pages that display in a browser.

Web page A static page consisting of HTML elements; displayed in a browser application.

WebBrowser control Displays Web pages on a Windows form.

With and End With statements A block of code that refers to the same object. The object name appears in the With statement; all subsequent statements until the End With relate to that object.

Write method Writes one record to a stream object; does not include a carriage return.

WriteLine method Writes one record to a stream object; includes a carriage return character at the end.

X

XML Extensible markup language. A format for data; popular for data storage and transfer on the Internet.

Index

Nickanderson57104@yahoo.con

Nickanderson57104@yahoo.con